Analysing English Sentences, 2nd E

Andrew Radford has acquired an unrivalled reputation ove N T ⟨10⟩ for writing syntax textbooks in which difficult concepts are clearly explained without the excessive use of technical jargon. *Analysing English Sentences* continues in this tradition, offering a well-structured introduction to English syntax and contemporary syntactic theory which is supported throughout with learning aids such as summaries, lists of key hypotheses and principles, extensive references, handy hints and exercises. Instructors will also benefit from the book's free online resources, which include PowerPoint slides of each chapter's key points and analyses of exercise material, as well as an answer key for all the in-book exercises.

This second edition has been thoroughly revised and updated throughout, and includes additional exercises, as well as an entirely new chapter on exclamative and relative clauses. Assuming no prior knowledge of grammar, this is an approachable introduction to the subject for undergraduate and graduate students.

ANDREW RADFORD is an emeritus professor at the University of Essex. He has written a number of popular textbooks, including *Transformational Syntax* (1981) and *Minimalist Syntax* (2004), and has co-authored two introductions to linguistics.

CAMBRIDGE TEXTBOOKS IN LINGUISTICS

General editors: P. AUSTIN, J. BRESNAN, B. COMRIE, S. CRAIN, W. DRESSLER, C. EWEN, R. LASS, D. LIGHTFOOT, K. RICE, I. ROBERTS, S. ROMAINE, N. V. SMITH.

Analysing English Sentences

2nd edition

Analysing English Sentences

Second edition
ANDREW RADFORD

University of Essex

CAMBRIDGE
UNIVERSITY PRESS

CAMBRIDGE
UNIVERSITY PRESS

University Printing House, Cambridge CB2 8BS, United Kingdom

Cambridge University Press is part of the University of Cambridge.

It furthers the University's mission by disseminating knowledge in the pursuit of education, learning and research at the highest international levels of excellence.

www.cambridge.org
Information on this title: www.cambridge.org/9780521669702

© Andrew Radford 2016

First published 2016

Printed in the United Kingdom by TJ International Ltd. Padstow Cornwall

A catalogue record for this publication is available from the British Library

Library of Congress Cataloguing in Publication data
Radford, Andrew.
Analysing English sentences / Andrew Radford. – Second Edition.
   pages   cm. – (Cambridge Textbooks in Linguistics)
ISBN 978-0-521-66008-2 (hardback)
1. English language – Syntax.   2. English language – Sentences.   3. Minimalist theory (Linguistics)   4. Grammar, Comparative and general – Syntax.   I. Title.
PE1361.R327   2016
425–dc23

                                                                           2015026792

ISBN 978-0-521-66008-2 Hardback
ISBN 978-0-521-66970-2 Paperback

Contents

Preface

Overview

This book has grown out of a substantial reworking of my *Analysing English Sentences* book published by Cambridge University Press in 2009, which itself was a reworking of my *Minimalist Syntax* book published in 2004. Feedback from teachers, students and reviewers led me to make substantial changes to numerous parts of the text and exercises, and to add new chapters, exercises and references: details of the most substantial revisions are given below. This new book has three main aims. The first is to provide an intensive introduction to key background assumptions in syntactic theory, to how the *syntactic component* of a grammar works, and to the argumentation and critical evaluation skills which underlie contemporary work in syntax. The second is to provide a description of a range of phenomena in English syntax, making use of the theoretical concepts and constructs introduced in the book. The third is (through the extensive exercise material in the book) to enable readers to gain experience in devising analyses of specific phenomena, and in critically evaluating the theoretical and descriptive strengths and weaknesses of competing analyses.

Key features

The book is intended to be suitable for people with little (if any) grammatical knowledge and/or experience of linguistics; it is aimed at intermediate undergraduates, or graduates in the first year of a Masters programme. It is not historicist or comparative in orientation and does not presuppose knowledge of earlier or alternative models of grammar. It is written in an approachable style, avoiding unnecessary complexity and unexplained jargon. Each chapter contains

- a core text (divided up into ten sections or so) focusing on a specific topic
- a summary recapitulating the main points in the chapter
- a list of key concepts/principles introduced in the chapter
- a bibliographical section providing extensive references to original source material
- a workbook section containing two (or more) different kinds of exercise

- a set of model answers accompanying the exercises, together with extensive helpful hints designed to eliminate common errors students make and to help students whose native language is not English
- an extensive glossary and integral list of abbreviations.

The bibliographical background section often contains references to primary research works which are highly technical in nature, and so it would not be appropriate for students to tackle them until they have read the whole book: they are intended to provide a useful source of bibliographical information for extended essays or research projects in particular areas, rather than being essential back-up reading: indeed, the exercises in the book are designed in such a way that they can be tackled on the basis of the coursebook material alone. The Glossary at the end of the book provides guidance on how key technical terms are used (both theory-specific terms like **EPP** and traditional terms like **subject**): technical terms are written in **bold** print when they are mentioned for the first time in any given chapter (*italics* and <u>underlining</u> being used for highlighting particular expressions – e.g. a key word appearing in an example sentence). The Glossary also contains an integrated list of abbreviations.

The book is intensive and progressive in nature, which means that it starts at an elementary level but gets progressively harder as you delve further into the book. Successive chapters become cumulatively more complex, in that each chapter presupposes material covered in previous chapters as well as introducing new material: hence, it is helpful to go back and read material from earlier chapters every so often. In some cases, analyses presented in earlier chapters are subsequently refined or revised in the light of new assumptions made in later chapters.

Differences from *Analysing English Sentences* (2009) and *Minimalist Syntax* (2004)

There are five main differences between the new book and its 2009 and/or 2004 predecessors. One is that the new book has restored and updated the chapter (= Ch. 2) on grammatical categories and features that appeared in the 2004 book but was omitted in the 2009 one, because teachers felt this is useful for students with little or no previous background in linguistics. A second difference is that the present book includes substantial new (text and exercise) material which compares, contrasts and evaluates alternative analyses of specific phenomena (e.g. a range of different analyses of relative clauses in the text and exercise material in Chapter 7): this is in response to a criticism that there wasn't enough evaluation of alternative analyses in the earlier books. A third difference is that there is more explicit formulation of the key hypotheses and principles which guide the discussion throughout the book, and this is designed to give a greater continuity and cohesion between chapters. A fourth difference is that the material from the 2004 and 2009 books is being divided into two separate volumes (*intermediate* and *advanced*): the first (= this one) is intended as an intermediate introduction to syntax, and the second (= to be published at a later date) is intended as a follow-up book covering more advanced topics. This is in response to comments from teachers and students that there simply wasn't enough time in a one-term or one-semester course to cover anything like all the material in my 2009 book. (I will never forget one student telling me that she had studied my book in three different universities in three different countries, but in none of them had the course ever got past Chapter 6.) Specific details of the changes made to individual chapters are given below. The fifth difference is that (in response to widespread requests from teachers) I have produced an *Answer Key* which provides a detailed answer to every one of the exercise examples included in the book: this will be available for free for teachers who adopt the book to download from a password-protected website.

CHAPTER 1 In this chapter on *grammar*, a new section has been added on approaches to grammar (§1.2) comparing prescriptive and descriptive approaches to grammar, and discussing the pros and cons of different methods of collecting data. New sections have also been added on universals (§1.4) and the nature of universals (§1.5), and the discussion of the Minimalist approach has been updated. Additional material has been added to the sections on parameters (§1.7) and on parameter setting (§1.8).

CHAPTER 2 I have restored the chapter on *words* which appeared in the 2004 book (but was omitted in the 2009 one). This chapter includes a discussion of categories and features (in response to remarks from teachers that students with little or no previous knowledge of grammar need more grounding in this). An entirely new section has been included on items difficult to categorise, containing discussion on the nature of *whether, how come* and (factive) *how* in present-day English.

CHAPTER 3 This is a chapter on *structure* which includes new material in §3.5 comparing the NP and DP approaches to nominals, and new material on syntactic structure in §3.6. In addition, a new section on word order has been added in §3.8.

CHAPTER 4 In this chapter on *null constituents*, additional material has been added on small clauses in §4.6, on clause typing in §4.7, on default case in §4.9, on adnominal adjectives in §4.11 and on null prepositions in §4.11.

CHAPTER 5 This chapter deals with *Head Movement*. The analysis of Auxiliary Inversion presented in §5.2 and §5.3 has been completely rewritten, in order to make it more consistent with Chapter 6. New sections have been added on CP recursion (§5.4) and null operators (§5.5). The sections on DO-support (§5.10) and Head Movement in nominals (§5.11) have been completely rewritten. Additional exercise material on DO-support and on nominals in Chaucer has been added to exercise §5.2.

CHAPTER 6 This whole chapter on *Wh-Movement* has been completely rewritten and reorganised (and restricted to wh-questions), with some important changes to details of the analysis. A new section has been added covering constraints on movement (§6.9). Extensive new exercise material has been introduced.

CHAPTER 7 This is an entirely new chapter on *A-bar Movement*. It begins with a section on wh-exclamatives (§7.2), and then goes on (in §7.3) to discuss various types of relative clause. §7.4 provides a Wh-Movement account of restrictive relative clauses, and §7.5 outlines problems with it. §7.6 sketches an alternative Antecedent Raising account, §7.7 refines this and §7.8 outlines potential problems. §7.9 argues that restrictive relatives have two distinct sources, one involving Wh-Movement, and the other Antecedent Raising. §7.10 argues that Wh-Movement in interrogatives, exclamatives and relatives is a specific instance of a more general type of A-bar Movement operation which also subsumes other operations like Neg-Movement, Deg-Movement, Foc-Movement and Top-Movement. A substantial raft of new exercises are included at the end of the chapter, one on exclamatives in contemporary and Elizabethan English, a second on WH+COMP structures, a third on free relatives, a fourth on resumptive relatives and a fifth on restrictive relatives: the aim in all but the first of these exercises is to get students to use the data they are given to evaluate two or more competing analyses of the relevant types of structure.

Teaching materials

I have prepared an accompanying Answer Key providing detailed answers to all the exercise examples in the book. I have additionally prepared some accompanying PowerPoint materials which (for each chapter) provide a brief summary of the key points in the chapter as well as providing answers to some of the exercise examples in the chapter. This is available only to teachers adopting the book as a coursebook (and is provided for free) and can be accessed from a password-protected website.

Acknowledgments

I am grovelingly grateful to Neil Smith for his perennially pertinent and perceptive comments on an earlier draughty draft of the whole manuscript: he has helped to eliminate black holes in argumentation and hopefully make the whole more wholesome. I am also grateful to Martin Atkinson for fertile feedback on an early draft of Chapter 1, and to Bob Borsley, Memo Cinque, Chris Collins and Annabel Cormack for guiding my earlier misguided attempts at producing a draft of Chapter 7. I'm also grateful to the editor Andrew Winnard and his production team for putting up with periodic procrastination, and wimpish wolf-crying and whingeing, and particularly to the copy editor Jacqueline French for teaching me that the Uniformity Principle applies to manuscripts as well as syntactic structures, and that the Economy Principle requires minimising (and in the best-case Minimalist scenario, *eliminating*) the use of *viz*.

Dedication

This book is dedicated to my beloved but beleaguered wife Khadija (with heartfelt thanks for the love, friendship, care and concern she has shown for me over the past four decades – in spite of having to put up with authorial autism, temperamental tantrums, man maladies, etc.) and to her two sons Karim and Mourad, with whom I have shared many memorable moments and a passion for football. *Allez l'OM!*

1 Grammar

1.1 Overview

In broad terms, this book is concerned with **syntax** in general, and with the syntax of English in particular. Syntax is one of the two key areas of what is traditionally called 'grammar' – the other being **morphology**. Morphology is the study of how words are formed out of smaller units (called **morphemes**) and so addresses questions such as 'What are the component morphemes of a word like *antidisestablishmentarianism*, and what is the nature of the operations by which they are combined together to form the overall word?' Syntax is the study of the way in which phrases and sentences are structured out of words, and so addresses questions like 'What is the structure of a sentence like *Where's the president going?* and what is the nature of the grammatical operations by which its component words are combined together to form the overall sentence structure?' This chapter begins (in §1.2) by looking at a range of approaches to the study of grammar, before going on (in §1.3) to look at how syntax was studied in **traditional grammar**: this also provides an opportunity to introduce some useful grammatical terminology. In the remainder of the chapter, we look at the approach to syntax adopted within the theory of **Universal Grammar/UG** developed by Chomsky over the past six decades. (Note that a convention used throughout the book is that key technical terms are in bold print when first introduced in a given chapter; such terms are generally given an entry in the Glossary at the end of the book if they are used in several different sections of the book, though not if they occur in only one section of the book and are glossed there.)

1.2 Approaches to grammar

A fundamental question that needs to be resolved at the outset concerns what kind of approach to adopt in studying grammar. There are two diametrically opposed answers to this question found in work on grammar. One sees the role of grammar as being essentially **prescriptive** (i.e. prescribing norms for grammatical correctness, linguistic purity and literary excellence); the other sees the role of grammar as being inherently **descriptive** (i.e describing the way people speak or write their native language). We can illustrate the differences between these two approaches in relation to the following dialogue between the fictional Oxford detective Morse and his assistant Lewis, as they are looking at a dead body (where capital letters in the dialogue mark emphatic stress, and italics mark items of grammatical interest):

(1)   MORSE: I think he was murdered, Lewis
        LEWIS: *Who by*, sir?
        MORSE: *By whom*, Lewis, *by whom*. Didn't they teach grammar at that COMPRE-
        HENSIVE school of yours?

Morse was educated at a *grammar* school – i.e. an elitist school which sought to give pupils a 'proper education' and taught them grammar, so that they could learn to speak and write 'properly' (i.e. in a prestigious form of Standard English). Lewis, by contrast, was educated at a *comprehensive* school – i.e. a more socially inclusive type of school which admitted pupils from a much broader social spectrum and didn't force-feed them with grammar. The linguistic skirmish between Lewis and Morse in (1) revolves round the grammar of an italicised phrase which comprises the preposition *by* and the pronoun *who(m)*. The differences between what the two men say relates to (i) the form of the pronoun (*who* or *whom*?), and (ii) the position of the pronoun (before or after the preposition *by*?). Lewis uses the pronoun form *who*, and positions the pronoun <u>before</u> the preposition when he asks 'Who by?' Morse corrects Lewis and instead uses the pronoun form *whom* and positions the pronoun <u>after</u> the preposition when he says 'By whom?' But why does Morse correct Lewis? The answer is that Morse was taught traditional prescriptive grammatical rules at his grammar school, including two which can be outlined informally as follows:

(2) (i)   The form *who* is used as a subject of a finite verb, and *whom* as the object of a verb or preposition.
    (ii)   Never end a phrase, clause or sentence with a preposition.

When Lewis asks 'Who by?' he violates both rules. This is because the pronoun *who(m)* is the object of the preposition *by* and rule (2i) stipulates that *whom* must therefore be used, and rule (2ii) specifies that the preposition should not be positioned at the end of a phrase. The corrected form 'By whom?' produced by Morse obeys both rules, in that *whom* is used in conformity with rule (2i), and *by* is positioned in front of its object *whom* in conformity with rule (2ii).

The more general question raised by the dialogue in (1) is the following. When studying grammar, should we adopt a descriptive approach and *describe* what ordinary people like Lewis actually say, or should we adopt a prescriptive approach and *prescribe* what people like Morse think they ought to say? There are several reasons for rejecting the prescriptive approach. For one thing, it is elitist and socially divisive, in that a privileged elite attempts to lay down grammatical norms and impose them on everyone else in society. Secondly, the grammatical norms which prescriptivists seek to impose are often derived from structures found in 'dead' languages like Latin, which is somehow regarded as a model of grammatical precision and linguistic purity: and so, because Latin made a distinction between subject and object forms of pronouns, English must do so as well; and because Latin (generally) positioned prepositions before their objects, English must do so as well. Such an approach fails to recognise typological diversity in languages – i.e. that there are many different types of structure found in the world's 8,000 or so known languages. Thirdly, the prescriptive approach fails to recognise sociolinguistic variation – i.e. that different types of structure are found in different styles and varieties of English (e.g. *Who by?* is used in colloquial English, and *By whom?* in formal styles of English). And fourthly, the prescriptive approach also fails to recognise linguistic change – i.e. that languages are constantly evolving, and that structures used centuries ago may no longer be in use today (e.g. *whom* is an archaic form which has largely dropped out of use and is no longer part of the grammar of teenagers today). For reasons such as these, the approach taken to grammar in work over the past seventy years or so has been descriptive.

What this means is that in attempting to devise a grammar of (e.g.) English, we aim to describe the range of grammatical structures found in present-day English. But how do we determine what is or isn't grammatical in present-day English? One approach is to study **usage** (i.e. the range of structures used by people when they speak or write). Linguists who adopt this kind of approach rely on data from a **corpus** (e.g. a computerised database such as the British National Corpus) containing authentic examples of spoken or written English. Such corpora offer the advantage that they contain millions of sentences, and the sentences have usually been codified/tagged by a team of researchers, so simplifying the task of searching for examples of a particular construction. Some linguists treat the Web as a form of corpus, and use a search engine to find examples from the Internet of the kinds of structures they are interested in.

The usefulness of corpora can be illustrated as follows. One of the ways I collect data on spoken English is by listening to live, unscripted radio and TV broadcasts, and noting down unusual structures (often using them as exercise material in my syntax books). An interesting sentence which I heard one day (reported in Radford 2004: 429; 8a) is the following:

(3)   What is thought has happened to him? (Interviewer, BBC Radio 5 Live)

When I first heard the sentence in (3), I wasn't sure what to make of it. One possibility that occurred to me is that it might be an accidental speech error (perhaps induced by the pressure of live broadcasting), representing a **blend** of the two different structures in (4), formed by combining the italicised part of (4a) with the italicised part of (4b):

(4) (a)   *What is thought* to have happened to him?
    (b)   What is it thought *has happened to him?*

However, an alternative possibility is that the kind of structure in (3) is not a speech error but rather a productive structure – albeit not one described in standard grammars of English. To check on whether (3) is a productive structure or not, I searched for similar structures on the Internet, and found hundreds of them. For example, I came across 116 examples of sentences containing the string (i.e. sequence of words) *is/are thought may*, like those below:

(5) (a)   The toxicology issue is thought may have arisen because of a pre-existing health issue in the animals

   (b)   Police are investigating the cause of the blazes, which is thought may be arson

   (c)   Curiously, about one-third of adults 60 and over are thought may have antibodies that may help protect against the virus

   (d)   The user enters one or more search words which are thought may exist in the definition of the word sought

The fact that I was able to locate thousands of similar examples of the structure in (3) makes it more likely that (3) is a (hitherto unreported) grammatical structure in English, and not a one-off 'slip of the tongue'.

   What the discussion here illustrates is that usage data (from corpora or from the Web) provide a very useful source of information about the productivity of a given type of structure (i.e. how often it is used). However, there are also downsides to the usage-based approach. For one thing, a corpus may contain relatively few examples of low-frequency structures. Secondly, it is generally not possible to ask the speakers who produced them questions about the sentences in the corpus (e.g. 'How would you negate this sentence?'). Thirdly, a corpus may contain examples of production errors (slips of the tongue, or pen, or keyboard) which would probably be judged as unacceptable even by the people who produced them. And (in the case of internet examples), it is sometimes unclear whether someone producing a given sentence (who may use an identity-concealing pseudonym like *CutiePie* or *MasterBlaster* as their name) is a native speaker of English or not, and if so what variety/dialect of English they speak.

   A very different approach to studying grammar has been adopted by Noam Chomsky and his followers in work over the past sixty years. For Chomsky, the goal of studying the grammar of a language is to determine what it is that native speakers *know* about the grammar of their native language which enables them to speak and understand the language: hence, in studying language, we are studying a specific kind of cognition (i.e. human knowledge). In a fairly obvious sense, any native speaker of a language can be said to *know* the grammar of his or her native language. For example, any native speaker of English can tell you that the negative counterpart of *I like syntax* is *I don't like syntax*, and not, e.g., **I no like syntax*. (Note that a prefixed star/asterisk in front of a phrase or sentence indicates that it is ungrammatical.) In other words, native speakers know how to form phrases and sentences in their native language. Likewise, any native speaker of English can tell you that a sentence like *She loves me more than you* is ambiguous and has two **interpretations** which can be paraphrased as 'She loves me more than she loves you' and 'She loves me more than you love me': in other words, native speakers also know how to **interpret** (i.e. assign meaning to) expressions in their language. However, it is important to emphasise that this grammatical knowledge of how to form and interpret expressions in your native language is **tacit** (i.e. subconscious) rather than **explicit** (i.e. conscious): so, it's no good asking a native speaker of English a question such as 'How do you form negative sentences in English?' since human beings have no conscious awareness of the processes involved in speaking and understanding their native language. To introduce a technical term devised by Chomsky, we can say that native speakers have grammatical **competence** in their native language: by this, we mean that they have tacit knowledge of the grammar of their language – i.e. of how to form and interpret words, phrases and sentences in the language.

In work in the 1960s, Chomsky drew a distinction between competence (the native speaker's tacit knowledge of his or her language) and **performance** (what people actually say or understand by what someone else says on a given occasion). Competence is 'the speaker-hearer's knowledge of his language', while performance is 'the actual use of language in concrete situations' (Chomsky 1965: 4). Very often, performance is an imperfect reflection of competence: we all make occasional slips of the tongue, or occasionally misinterpret something which someone else says to us. However, this doesn't mean that we don't know our native language or that we don't have *competence* in it. Misproductions and misinterpretations are **performance errors**, attributable to a variety of performance factors like tiredness, boredom, drunkenness, drugs, external distractions and so forth. A grammar of a language tells you what you need to know in order to have native-like competence in the language (i.e. to be able to speak the language like a fluent native speaker): hence, it is clear that grammar is concerned with competence rather than performance. This is not to deny the interest of performance as a field of study, but merely to assert that performance is more properly studied within the different – though related – discipline of psycholinguistics, which studies the psychological processes underlying speech production and comprehension. (It should, however, be acknowledged that performance errors can provide us with clues about the nature of competence, and we will see some examples of this in later chapters.)

When we study grammatical competence, we're studying a cognitive system internalised within the brain/mind of native speakers which is the product of a 'cognitive organ' which is 'shared among humans and in crucial respects unique to them' (Chomsky 2007: 1). In the terminology adopted by Chomsky (1986a: 19–56), our ultimate goal in studying competence is to characterise the nature of this 'internal language' or **I-language** (to use a term employed by Chomsky) which makes native speakers proficient in their native language.

Although native speakers only have tacit knowledge of the grammar of their language, they do have **intuitions** about grammaticality (i.e. 'gut feelings' about whether a particular sentence is or isn't grammatical in their native language) – e.g. as noted above, any native speaker of English would readily accept *I don't like syntax* as a grammatical sentence of English, but not **I no like syntax*. Consequently, an approach widely used by linguists over the past sixty years has been to devise grammars on the basis of native-speaker intuitions about grammaticality. Where linguists are describing aspects of their own native language, they often rely primarily on their own intuitions/introspective grammaticality judgments.

However, although extensively used, this approach of relying on introspective judgments about the grammaticality of sentences has been criticised by some as being unscientific (hence yielding potentially unreliable results), particularly in relation to judgments about **marginal** sentences – i.e. sentences of uncertain grammaticality. This is for a number of reasons. Firstly, different individuals may disagree in their judgments of particular sentences (and may have different tolerance thresholds): this means that relying on the intuitions of one person alone may give misleading results. Secondly, the same individual may sometimes give conflicting judgments about the same sentence on different occasions. Thirdly, it can sometimes be very difficult to judge the grammaticality of a sentence in isolation (without an appropriate context). Fourthly (as we will see below), grammaticality is often a matter of degree rather than an absolute property (e.g. a given sentence may be more acceptable than some sentences but less acceptable than others). Fifthly, native speakers who are non-linguists very often have no clear idea what it means for a sentence to be 'grammatical' or not (since **grammaticality** is a technical term which non-linguists have little conception of). Rather, all that non-experts can do is say how acceptable they find a sentence, and this may depend on a range of factors which have little to do with grammaticality, including how frequent a given structure is, whether it contains taboo language or concepts and so on. And sixthly, linguists who rely on their own grammaticality judgments tend to give more extreme judgments than non-linguists and are vulnerable to the accusation that (however unwittingly) they may tailor their grammaticality judgments to fit their analysis (e.g. they may judge a given sentence to be grammatical because their analysis predicts that it should be): indeed, Chomsky (1957: 14) even suggested that (as a matter of principle) we should 'let the grammar itself decide' about the status of marginal sentences.

Because of the potential unreliability of informal intuitions, some linguists prefer to elicit native-speaker judgments experimentally, particularly when dealing with 'marginal' structures whose grammaticality status is not clear-cut. Such experimental studies sometimes produce judgments which are at variance with the intuitions of linguists. By way of illustration, consider the claim made by Chomsky (2008) that an (italicised) constituent can be **extracted** out of a passive subject like that bracketed in (6a) below (i.e. moved from the gap position marked by - - - to the italicised position), but not out of the corresponding active subject in (6b):

(6) (a)   *Of which car* was [the driver - - -] awarded a prize?
    (b)   **Of which car* did [the driver - - -] cause a scandal?

In traditional terms, a sentence like that in (6a) is said to be in the **passive voice**, while that in (6b) is in the **active voice**. An assumption made by Chomsky is that the italicised phrase in (6a,b) originates in the gap (---) position within the bracketed subject and is subsequently extracted out of the bracketed subject and moved to the front of the overall sentence. Chomsky develops an elaborate account of why extraction is possible out of a passive subject in sentences like (6a) but not out of an active subject in sentences like (6b). However, the robustness of Chomsky's syntactic analysis ultimately depends on the robustness of his judgment that (6a) is grammatical and (6b) is ungrammatical. But is this judgment shared by others?

To test this, Jurka (2010) ran an online experiment in which thirty-seven native speakers of English were asked to judge the acceptability of a number of sentences, including those in (7) below, where (7a) involves **extraction** of an italicised phrase out of a bracketed passive subject, and (7b) out of a bracketed active subject:

(7) (a)   John wondered *which man* [a book about ---] was released last year
    (b)   John wondered *which man* [a book about ---] caused a scandal last year

Participants were asked to rate the tested sentences on a 7-point scale, and to give a score of 6 or 7 to sentences they found perfectly acceptable, 3–5 to sentences they found not totally unacceptable but also not completely perfect, and 1 or 2 to sentences they found completely unacceptable. Jurka found that extraction from a passive subject in sentences like (7a) yielded a mean score of 2.68, and that this was not significantly different statistically from the score of 2.55 for extraction out of the corresponding active subject in sentences like (7b). The moral of the story would seem to be that the grammaticality judgments of individual linguists need to be treated with caution in cases which are not clear-cut.

At the same time, however, it should be acknowledged that there are a number of drawbacks to experimental studies. For one thing, they require considerable time and money to set up: it can take months to design an experiment, collect the data, and process the results; and a design flaw (or problematic results) may require the whole experiment to be re-designed and re-run subsequently. Moreover, it is in the nature of experiments that (in order to meet stringent methodological requirements on experimental design) they can only be used to collect data relating to a specific (and narrow) set of phenomena. Furthermore, experiments can sometimes produce results which are skewed by the design of the experiment. In addition, how acceptable (or otherwise) people perceive a sentence to be may depend on a whole range of extraneous factors other than its grammaticality: these extraneous factors include, for example, how interesting it is, how long it is, how plausible it is, how frequent the relevant type of structure is, how easy it is to imagine a context where it could be used, whether or not the sentence expresses ideas which offend cultural or religious sensibilities or contains taboo words, etc. Furthermore, the results which experiments yield can be far from straightforward to interpret: for example, they sometimes produce results which represent acceptability in terms of many different shades of grey, rather than as a black-and-white issue. Moreover, in order to achieve statistical significance in results, it may be necessary to discard outliers (i.e. atypical results).

As a case in point, consider the following data reported in Radford and Iwasaki (2015), in a study of the syntax of structures like *Who by?* in sentences like (1). This type of structure is traditionally considered to be grammatical in colloquial English only if the object of the preposition is interrogative (e.g. if it is a question word like *who?*). In order to check whether it is indeed the case that this kind of structure is only acceptable when the object of the preposition is interrogative, we asked Philip Hofmeister to run an online experiment to test the acceptability of the sentences below, each containing a bracketed structure in which the italicised object of a bold-printed preposition is positioned in front of the preposition:

(8) (a)   I wonder where she bought that awful tie, and [*who* **for**]

   (b)   Whenever we argue and [*whatever* **about**], we always make up afterwards

   (c)   I'm amazed at how much he bought on eBay and [*how little* **for**]!

   (d)   I'm going away, but [*not long* **for**]

   (e)   The fewer presents we send and [*the fewer people* **to**], the happier Scrooge will be

   (f)   So hard has he trained and [*so long* **for**] that he is sure to win the race

The italicised object of the preposition is interrogative in (8a), unconditional (in the terminology of Rawlins 2008) in (8b), exclamative in (8c), negative in (8d), comparative in (8e) and consecutive in (8f). Sixty-four native speakers of American English were asked to rate the acceptability of a set of sentences including those in (8) using a 7-point numerical scale on which 7 denotes 'extremely natural' and 1 denotes 'extremely unnatural'. The mean scores for each sentence were as follows: 5.13 for the interrogative (8a); 4.95 for the unconditional (8b); 4.50 for the exclamative (8c); 4.27 for the negative (8d); 3.92 for the comparative (8e) and 2.69 for the consecutive (8f). The results are problematic for the traditional black-and-white view that 'inverted' structures of the form OBJECT+PREPOSITION are grammatical if the object is interrogative, and ungrammatical if it is not. They suggest that we have to recognise different degrees of grammaticality.

The general conclusions to be drawn from our discussion in this section are the following. Contemporary work in grammar is descriptive in orientation rather than prescriptive, so that (e.g.) a grammar of contemporary English seeks to describe the structures found in present-day (spoken and written) English. A grammar is said to be **descriptively adequate** (or achieve **descriptive adequacy**) if it provides a comprehensive description of the full range of structures found in a given language. Three main sources of data are used to devise grammars: (i) usage-based data derived from corpora or the Web; (ii) introspective grammaticality judgments given by individual native speakers; and (iii) experimental studies eliciting accept-ability judgments from groups of speakers. There are heated (but ultimately inconclusive) debates in the research literature about what is the 'best' way of collecting data. For the most part, the judgments presented in this book will be based on my own intuitions about grammaticality (as a native speaker and experienced linguist): I will highlight cases that I am aware of where my intuitions differ markedly from those of other native speakers.

Although the distinction between descriptive and prescriptive approaches to grammar might seem to be clear-cut, it should be noted that even descriptive grammars can sometimes be implicitly prescriptive. This is because descriptive grammars generally try and characterise so-called standard languages. This can involve making judgments about whether a given type of structure is found in standard or non-standard varieties; and this in turn can be regarded as tantamount to *prescribing* what can and can't be said in the standard language.

1.3   Traditional grammar

Contemporary syntactic theory makes use of a wide range of concepts and constructs which are rooted in centuries of earlier grammatical tradition, as well as introducing new techniques, terminology and perspectives of its own. For this reason, a useful starting point for any book about syntax is to look at key ideas from traditional grammar (as reflected, for example, in reference grammars, and in pedagogical grammars for second language learners).

Within traditional grammar, the syntax of a language is described in terms of a taxonomy (i.e. classificatory list) of the range of different types of syntactic structure found in the language. The central assumption underpinning syntactic analysis in traditional grammar is that phrases and sentences are built up of a series of **constituents** (i.e. syntactic units), each of which belongs to a specific **grammatical category** and serves a specific **grammatical function**. Given this assumption, the task of the linguist in analysing the syntactic structure of any given type of sentence is to identify each of the constituents in the sentence, and (for each constituent) to say what category it belongs to and what function it serves. For example, in relation to the syntax of a simple sentence like:

(9)   Students protested

it would traditionally be said that the sentence consists of two constituents (the word *students* and the word *protested*), that each of these constituents belongs to a specific grammatical category (*students* being a plural **noun** and *protested* a past tense **verb**) and that each serves a specific grammatical function (*students* being the **subject** of the sentence, and *protested* being the **predicate**). The overall sentence *Students protested* has the status of a **clause** which is **finite** in nature (by virtue of denoting an event taking place at a specific time) and has the semantic function of expressing a **proposition** which is **declarative** in type (in that it is used to make a statement rather than, e.g., ask a question or issue an order). Accordingly, a traditional grammar of English would tell us that the simplest type of finite declarative clause found in English is a sentence like (9) in which a nominal subject is followed by a verbal predicate. Let's briefly look at some of the terminology used here.

In traditional grammar, words are assigned to grammatical **categories** (called **parts of speech**) on the basis of their **semantic** properties (i.e. meaning), **morphological** properties (i.e. the range of different forms they have) and **syntactic** properties (i.e. word-order properties relating to the positions they can occupy within sentences): a set of words which belong to the same category thus have a number of semantic, morphological and syntactic properties in common. To illustrate this, let's begin by looking at what are sometimes called the **major** categories of English – i.e. those categories which have dozens, hundred or thousands of members. Let's start by looking at the category of **noun** (conventionally abbreviated to N).

Nouns are traditionally said to have the semantic property that they denote entities: so, *bottle* is a noun (since it denotes a type of object used to contain liquids), *water* is a noun (since it denotes a type of liquid) and *John* is a noun (since it denotes a specific person). There are a number of distinct subtypes of noun: for example a noun like *chair* is a **count noun** in that it can be counted (cf. *one chair, two chairs . . .*), whereas a noun like *furniture* is a **non-count** (or **mass**) **noun** in that it denotes an uncountable mass (hence the ungrammaticality of **one furniture, *two furnitures*: recall that a prefixed star/asterisk is used to indicate that an expression is ungrammatical). Likewise, a distinction is traditionally drawn between a **common noun** like *boy* (which can be modified by a **determiner** like *the*, as in '*The boy* is lying') and a **proper noun** like *Andrew* (which can't be used in the same way in English, as we see from the ungrammaticality of *'*The Andrew* is lying'). Typical count nouns exhibit the morphological property of having two different forms: a **singular** form (like *horse* in *one horse*) used to denote a single entity, and a **plural** form (like *horses* in *two horses*) used to denote more than one entity. Common nouns have the syntactic property that only (an appropriate kind of) common noun can be used to end a sentence such as *They have no . . .* In place of the dots here we could insert a singular count noun like *car*, or a plural count noun like *friends*, or a mass noun like *money*, but not other types of word (e.g. not *see* or *slowly* or *up*, as these are not nouns).

A second major category is that of **verb** (= V). Verbs are traditionally said to have the semantic property that they denote actions or events: so *eat, sing, pull, resign* and *die* are all verbs. From a syntactic point of view, verbs have the property that only an appropriate kind of verb (in its uninflected **infinitive** form) can be used to complete a sentence such as *They/It can . . .* So words like *stay, leave, hide, die, starve* and *cry* are all verbs and hence can be used in place of the dots here (but words like *apple, under, pink* and *if* aren't). From a morphological point of view, regular verbs like *cry* in English have the property that they have four distinct forms: e.g. alongside the **bare** (i.e. uninflected) **form** *cry* we find the **present tense** form *cries*, the **past tense+perfect participle+passive participle** form *cried* and the **progressive participle+gerund** form *crying*. (See the Glossary at the end of this book if you are not familiar with such terms: terms which are in bold print generally have an entry in the Glossary.)

A third major category found in English is that of **adjective** (=A). Adjectives are traditionally said to have the semantic property of denoting states or attributes (cf. *ill, happy, tired, conscientious, red, cruel, old*, etc.). Many (but not all) adjectives have the morphological property that they have **comparative** forms ending in *-er* and **superlative** forms ending in *-est* (cf. *big/bigger/biggest*). From a syntactic point of view, adjectives have the property that they can occur after *be* to complete a sentence like *They may be . . .* (as with 'They may be *tired/ill/happy*, etc.'), and the further syntactic property that (if they denote a **gradable** property which can exist in varying degrees), they can be modified by a **degree adverb** like *very/rather/somewhat* (as in 'She is *very happy*').

A fourth major category is that of **adverb** (= ADV). These often have the semantic property that they denote the manner in which an action is performed (as with *badly* in *She performed badly*). Regular adverbs have the morphological property that they are formed from adjectives by the addition of the suffix *-ly* (so that corresponding to the adjective *bad* we have the adverb *badly*). A syntactic property of adverbs is that an adverb (like *badly*) is the only kind of word which could be used to end sentences like *She behaved - - -, He treats her - - -*, or *He worded the statement - - -*. (It should be noted, however, that there are numerous irregular adverbs which don't end in *-ly* – e.g. *well* in 'She behaved *well*')

A fifth major category is that of **preposition** (= P). Many prepositions have the semantic property of marking location (e.g. *in/on/off/inside/outside/under/above/below*). They have the syntactic property that a preposition (with the appropriate kind of meaning) can be modified by *right* in the sense of 'completely', or by *straight* in the sense of 'directly' (as with the preposition *down* in 'He fell *right* **down** the stairs' and the preposition *to* in 'He went *straight* **to** bed'). Prepositions have the morphological property that they are invariable forms which don't allow **inflectional** or **derivational affixes** attached to them: for example, the preposition *off* has no past tense form **offed*, no superlative derivative **offest* and so on.

In addition to the five major categories identified above, English has half a dozen or so **minor** categories with a highly restricted membership (generally comprising no more than a dozen or so items per category). One such minor category is that of **determiner** (= DET/D) – a category whose members are traditionally said to include the **definite article** *the* and the **demonstratives** *this/that/these/those*. They are called determiners because they have the semantic property that they determine specific semantic properties of the noun expression that they introduce, like definiteness/specificity: for example, using the determiner *the* to modify the noun *car* in a sentence such as *Shall we take the car?* makes the expression *the car* into a referring expression which refers to a definite (specific) car which is assumed to be familiar to the hearer/addressee. A related class of words are those which belong to the category **quantifier** (= Q), denoting expressions of quantity, such as *some/any/each/every/all/much/many/most*.

A further type of minor category found in English is that of **pronoun** (= PRN). Pronouns are items which are traditionally said to 'stand in place of' (the meaning of the prefix *pro-*) noun expressions. In this connection, consider the following dialogue:

(10)   SPEAKER A: What did *the president of the Students' Union* say?
         SPEAKER B: **He** said that courses should place more emphasis on employability skills

In order to avoid repeating the noun expression *the president of the Students' Union* used by speaker A in the dialogue above, speaker B can replace it by the pronoun *he*, so shortening the sentence considerably.

Another minor category found in English is that of **auxiliary (verb)**. Words belonging to this category have the semantic property of marking grammatical properties such as **tense**, **aspect**, **voice** or **mood**. One of the defining syntactic properties of auxiliaries is that (unlike lexical/main/non-auxiliary verbs) they can be inverted with their subject in questions, as illustrated below (where the auxiliary is italicised):

(11) (a)   **He** *had* finished by 9 o'clock
     (b)   *Had* **he** finished by 9 o'clock?

In a statement like (11a), the italicised auxiliary *had* is positioned after the bold-printed subject *he*; but in the corresponding question (11b), the auxiliary *had* is **inverted** with respect to its subject *he* (i.e. *had* is moved in front of *he*), and so comes to precede the subject. The auxiliary *had* in (11) serves to mark grammatical properties including **past tense**, **perfect aspect** and **indicative mood**.

Another minor category posited in traditional grammar is a kind of word (like each of the words italicised in the examples below) which is traditionally termed a **conjunction** (= CONJ):

(12) (a)   I went out with her *before* she got married
     (b)   We met *when* we were teenagers
     (c)   The doctors think *that* he will make a full recovery
     (d)   Did he apologise to her *and* did she accept his apology?

In (12a,b,c) the words *before/when/that* serve to connect a main clause (the *went/met/think* clause) to a subordinate clause (the *got/were/make*) clause, and for this reason they are termed **subordinating conjunctions**. In (12d), the word *and* serves to coordinate/conjoin (i.e. 'join together') two clauses of the same type (two interrogative main clauses) and so is termed a **coordinating conjunction**. Because it generally serves to introduce a clause which serves as the **complement** of a verb/adjective/noun, the subordinating conjunction *that* in sentences like (12c) is categorised in more recent work as a **complementiser** (abbreviated to COMP or C): consequently, *that* in (12c) is a complementiser/COMP/C because it introduces a clause which serves as the complement of the verb *think*.

The final type of minor category which we will look at here is that of **particle** (= PRT). This is something of a catch-all or 'dustbin' category, in the sense that a word (particularly a short, monosyllabic word) which can't be straightforwardly categorised as belonging to any other category tends to be termed a *particle*. In this connection, consider the following sentence:

(13)   Maria turned *out not to* be able *to* pick Spanish *up* any quicker *than* me

Here, the words *out* and *up* are traditionally categorised as (adverbial) particles, *not* as a negative particle, *to* as an infinitive particle, and *than* as a comparative particle.

Using a set of syntactic categories like those outlined above, we can employ a traditional technique known as **labelled bracketing** to *categorise* words (i.e. assign them labels which mark the grammatical category they belong to) in a way which describes how they are being used in a particular sentence. Employing this technique, the words in sentence (14a) below can be categorised as in (14b):

(14) (a)   The president is clearly not feeling happy that Congress has refused to negotiate with him

(b)   [D the] [N president] [AUX is] [ADV clearly] [PRT not] [V feeling] [A happy] [C that] [N Congress] [AUX has] [V refused] [PRT to] [V negotiate] [P with] [PRN him]

The labelled bracketing in (14b) tells us that *the* is a D/determiner, *president* a N/noun, *is* an AUX/auxiliary, *clearly* an ADV/adverb, *not* is a (negative) PRT/particle, *feeling* a V/verb, *happy* an A/adjective, *that* a C (a complementiser/subordinating conjunction that here serves to introduce a clause which is the complement of the adjective *happy*), *Congress* a N/noun, *has* an AUX/auxilary, *refused* a V/verb, *to* an (infinitival) PRT/particle, *negotiate* a V/verb, *with* a P/preposition, and *him* a PRN/pronoun.

We see from (14) that a traditional grammatical analysis of a sentence involves assigning each of the words in the sentence to a category which provides a broad characterisation of its grammatical properties. (Since the whole of Chapter 2 will be devoted to the grammatical properties of words, I will say no more about such categories for now.) However, traditional grammar also recognises that sentences are structured out of **phrases** as well as words. By way of illustration, consider the sentence below:

(15)   Desire for success leads to fear of failure

Such a sentence/S is formed by combining the **noun phrase/NP** *desire for success* with the **verb phrase/VP** *leads to fear of failure*, with the NP functioning as the subject of the VP. The NP *desire for success* comprises the noun/N *desire* and its prepositional phrase/PP complement *for success*. The PP *for success* comprises the preposition/P *to* and its noun/N complement *success*. The VP *leads to fear of failure* comprises the verb/V *leads* and its prepositional phrase/ PP complement *to fear of failure*. The PP *to fear of failure* comprises the preposition/P *to* and its noun phrase/NP complement *fear of failure*. The NP *fear of failure* comprises the noun/N *fear* and its prepositional phrase/PP complement *of failure*. The PP *of failure* comprises the preposition/P *of* and its noun/

N complement *failure*. Using the labelled bracketing technique, we can show how the sentence/S in (15) is structured out of words and phrases as follows:

(16)   [s [NP [N desire] [PP [P for] [N success]]] [VP [V leads] [PP [P to] [NP [N fear] [PP [P of] [N failure]]]]]]

However, the proliferation of labelled brackets in (16) makes such representations difficult to read: identifying the unlabelled right-hand brackets is particularly difficult – as you can see for yourself if you try and work out the label of each of the right-hand brackets after the word *failure*. For this reason, an alternative technique is to represent structure in terms of a tree diagram similar to that used to represent relationships between members of a family. Using this alternative technique, we can represent the structure of (15) in terms of the tree in (17) below (where you have to imagine that the tree has been uprooted in a storm and so is upside down):

(17)

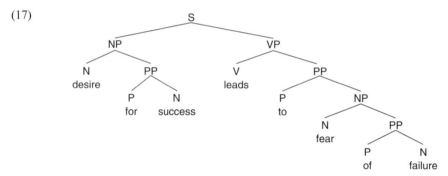

A tacit assumption embodied in traditional trees like (17) is that words belonging to major categories can be used to form phrases (so we find noun phrases like *supporters of the president*, verb phrases like *close the door*, adjectival phrases like *fond of chocolate*, adverbial phrases like *independently of me* and prepositional phrases like *in Portugal*), but words belonging to minor categories cannot (so that we find no auxiliary phrases, pronoun phrases or particle phrases, for example). Since the whole of Chapter 3 is devoted to phrase structure (i.e. how sentences are structured out of phrases), I will say no more about it for the time being.

As noted at the beginning of this section, traditional grammarians are also concerned to describe the grammatical functions which words and phrases fulfil within the sentences containing them. We can illustrate this point in terms of the following set of sentences:

(18) (a)   *John* smokes
    (b)   *The president* smokes
    (c)   *The president of Utopia* smokes
    (d)   *The former president of the island paradise of Utopia* smokes

Sentence (18a) comprises the noun *John* which serves the function of being the subject of the sentence (and denotes the person performing the act of smoking), and the verb *smokes* which serves the function of being the predicate of the sentence (and describes the act being performed). In (18a), the subject is the single noun *John*; but as the examples in (18b,c,d) show, the subject of a sentence can also be an (italicised) phrase like *the president*, or *the president of Utopia* or *the former president of the island paradise of Utopia*.

Now consider the following set of sentences:

(19) (a) John smokes *cigars*
     (b) John smokes *Cuban cigars*
     (c) John smokes *Cuban cigars imported from Havana*
     (d) John smokes *a specific brand of Cuban cigars imported by a friend of his from Havana*

Sentence (19a) comprises the subject *John*, the predicate *smokes* and the complement (or **direct object**) *cigars*. (The complement *cigars* describes the entity on which the act of smoking is being performed; as this example illustrates, subjects normally precede the verb with which they are associated in English, whereas complements typically follow the verb.) The complement in (19a) is the single noun *cigars*; but a complement can also be a phrase: in (19b), the complement of *smokes* is the phrase *Cuban cigars*; in (19c) the complement is the phrase *Cuban cigars imported from Havana*; and in (19d) the complement is the phrase *a specific brand of Cuban cigars imported by a friend of his from Havana*. A verb which has a noun or pronoun expression as its direct object complement is traditionally said to be **transitive**.

From a semantic perspective, subjects and complements have in common the property that they generally represent entities directly involved in the particular action or event described by the predicate: to use the relevant semantic terminology, we can say that subjects and complements are **arguments** of the predicate with which they are associated. Predicates may have one or more arguments, as we see from sentences such as (20) below, where each of the bracketed nouns is a different argument of the italicised predicate:

(20) (a) [John] *resigned*
     (b) [John] *felt* [remorse]
     (c) [John] *sent* [Mary] [flowers]

A predicate like *resign* in (20a) which has a single argument is said to function as a **one-place predicate** (in the relevant use); one like *feel* in (20b), which has two arguments, is a **two-place predicate**; and one like *send* in (20c), which has three arguments, is a **three-place predicate**.

In addition to predicates and arguments, sentences can also contain **adjuncts**, as we can illustrate in relation to (21) below:

(21) (a) The president smokes a cigar *after dinner*
     (b) The president smokes a cigar *in his office*

In both sentences in (21), *smokes* functions as a two-place predicate whose two arguments are its subject *the president* and its complement *a cigar*. But what is the function of the phrase *after dinner* which also occurs in (21a)? Since *after dinner* isn't one of the entities directly involved in the act of smoking (i.e. it isn't consuming or being consumed), it isn't an argument of the predicate *smoke*. On the contrary, *after dinner* simply serves to provide additional information about the time when the smoking activity takes place. In much the same way, the italicised expression *in his office* in (21b) provides additional information about the location of the smoking activity. An expression which serves to provide (optional) additional information about the time or place (or manner, or purpose etc.) of an activity or event is said to function as an adjunct. So, *after dinner* and *in his office* in (21a,b) are both adjuncts.

So far, the sentences we have looked at in (18–21) have been **simple sentences** which contain a single clause. However, alongside these we also find **complex sentences** which contain more than one clause, like (22) below:

(22)   Mary knows John smokes

If we take the traditional definition of a clause as a predication structure (more precisely, a structure containing a predicate which has a subject, and which may or may not also contain one or more complements and adjuncts), it follows that since there are two predicates (*knows* and *smokes*) in (22), there are correspondingly two clauses – the *smokes* clause on the one hand, and the *knows* clause on the other. The *smokes* clause comprises the subject *John* and the predicate *smokes*; the *knows* clause comprises the subject *Mary*, the predicate *knows* and the complement *John smokes*. So, the complement of *knows* here is itself a clause – namely the clause *John smokes*. More precisely, the *smokes* clause is a **complement clause** (because it serves as the complement of *knows*), while the *knows* clause is the **main clause** (or **principal clause** or **independent clause** or **root clause**). The overall sentence (22) *Mary knows John smokes* is a complex sentence because it contains more than one clause.

In much the same way, (23) below is also a complex sentence:

(23)   The press clearly think the president deliberately lied to Congress

Once again, it comprises two clauses – one containing the predicate *think*, the other containing the predicate *lie(d)*. The main clause comprises the subject *the press*, the adjunct *clearly*, the predicate *think* and the complement clause *the president deliberately lied to Congress*. The complement clause in turn comprises the subject *the president*, the adjunct *deliberately*, the predicate *lie(d)*, and the complement *to Congress*.

As was implicit in our earlier classification of (9) *Students protested* as a **finite** clause, traditional grammars draw a distinction between **finite** and **non-finite** clauses. In this connection, consider the contrast between the italicised clauses below (all of which function as the complement of the word immediately preceding them):

(24) (a)   Mary was glad *that he apologised*
   (b)   Mary demanded *that he apologise*
   (c)   I can't imagine *him apologizing*
   (d)   It would be sensible *for him to apologise*
   (e)   It's important to know *when to apologise*

The italicised clauses in (24a,b) are finite, and one characteristic of finite clauses in English is that they contain a verb marked for tense/mood: in (24a) the verb *apologised* is finite by virtue of marking **past tense** and **indicative mood**; and in (24b), the verb *apologise* is finite by virtue of marking **subjunctive mood**. A clause containing a verb in the indicative mood (like that italicised in 24a) can be used to denote a real (or **realis**, to use the relevant grammatical term) event or state occurring at a specific point in time; by contrast, a subjunctive clause (like that italicised in 24b) denotes a hypothetical or unreal (= **irrealis**) event or state which has not yet occurred and which may never occur. In contrast to the italicised clauses in (24a,b), the clauses italicised in (24c–e) are non-finite, in that they contain no verb marked for tense or mood. For example, the verb *apologising* in (24c) is non-finite because it is a tenseless and moodless **gerund** form. Likewise, the verb *apologise* in (24d,e) is a tenseless and moodless **infinitive** form (as we see from the fact that it follows the infinitive particle *to*).

A second property of finite clauses which differentiates them from non-finite clauses is that only finite clauses permit subjects with **nominative case**. Pronouns in English have up to three distinct case forms: for example, the **third person** masculine singular personal pronoun in English has the nominative form *he*, the **accusative** form *him* and the genitive form *his*. Finite clauses permit a nominative subject (like *I, we, he, she* or *they*), whereas non-finite clauses permit either an accusative subject (like *me, us, him*, or *them*) or a silent (i.e. unpronounced) subject. On the basis of the case properties of their subjects, we can therefore categorise the italicised clauses in (24a,b) as finite, since they have a nominative subject (*he*). By contrast, the italicised clauses in (24c,d) are non-finite, since they have an accusative subject (*him*). Similarly, the italicised clause in (24e) is also non-finite, because it has a silent subject – i.e. an 'understood' but 'unpronounced' subject which is a silent counterpart of the overt subject pronoun *you* in 'It's important to know when *you* have to apologise.' (Excluded from our discussion here are gerund structures with genitive subjects like that italicised in 'I can't stand *his perpetual whining about money*', since these are more nominal than clausal in nature.)

As the examples in (24) illustrate, whether or not a clause is finite in turn determines the kind of subject it can have, in that finite clauses can only have a nominative subject, whereas non-finite clauses can only have an accusative or silent subject. Accordingly, one way of telling whether a particular clause is finite or non-finite is to look at the kind of subject it can have. In this connection, consider whether the italicised clauses in the dialogues in (25a, b) below are finite or non-finite:

(25) (a)   SPEAKER A: I know you cheat on me
            SPEAKER B: OK, I admit it. *I cheat on you*. But not with any of your friends.
     (b)   SPEAKER A: I know you cheat on me
            SPEAKER B: *Me cheat on you*! No way! I never would!

The fact that the italicised clause in speaker B's reply in (25a) has the nominative subject *I* suggests that it is finite, and hence that the verb *cheat* (as used in the italicised sentence in 25a) is a first person singular present indicative form. By contrast, the fact that the italicised clause in speaker B's reply (25b) has the accusative subject *me* suggests that it is non-finite, and that the verb *cheat* (as used in the italicised sentence in 25b) is an infinitive form (and indeed this is clear from sentences like *Me be a cheat? No way!* where we find the infinitive form *be*).

In addition to being finite or non-finite, clauses can be of different types (i.e. can serve different semantic or pragmatic functions). In this connection, consider the following simple (single-clause) sentences:

(26) (a)   He went home
     (b)   Are you feeling OK?
     (c)   You be quiet!
     (d)   What a great idea that is!

A sentence like (26a) is traditionally said to be **declarative** in type (or **force**), in that it is used to make a statement. (26b) is **interrogative** in type in that it is used to ask a question. (26c) is **imperative** in type, by virtue of being used to issue an order or command. (26d) is **exclamative** in type, in that it is used to exclaim surprise or delight. In complex sentences, the different clauses may be of different types, as illustrated below:

(27) (a)   He asked where she had gone
     (b)   Did you know that he has retired?
     (c)   Tell her what a great time we had!

In (27a), the main (*asked*) clause is declarative, whereas the complement (*gone*) clause is interrogative; in (27b) the main (*know*) clause is interrogative, whereas the complement (*retired*) clause is declarative; and in (27c), the main (*tell*) clause is imperative, whereas the complement (*had*) clause is exclamative.

We can summarise this section as follows. From the perspective of traditional grammar, the syntax of a sentence in a given language is characterised by describing the grammatical category and grammatical function of each of the words and phrases in the sentence. The grammar of a language is described in terms of a taxonomy (i.e. a classificatory list) of the range of different phrase-, clause- and sentence-types found in the language. So, for example, a typical traditional grammar of (say) English will include chapters on the syntax of negatives, interrogatives, exclamatives, imperatives and so on.

1.4   Universals

Using data collected by one or more of the methods outlined in §1.2, a linguist analysing a particular language attempts to devise a grammar of the language. However, if we are to attain a deeper understanding of the nature of language, we need to investigate the extent to which the properties of the grammar of a given language reflect universal properties (i.e. properties shared by the grammars of all natural/human languages). This means that the ultimate goal of the study of grammar is to develop a theory of **Universal Grammar/UG** which identifies the defining properties of all natural (i.e. human) languages. UG is a theory about the nature of possible grammars of human languages: hence, a theory of UG answers the question: 'What are the defining characteristics of the grammars of natural/human languages which differentiate them from, for example, artificial languages like those used in mathematics and computing (e.g. Java, Prolog, C, etc.), or from animal communication systems (e.g. the tail-wagging dance performed by bees to communicate the location of a food source to other bees)?' A theory of UG must provide us with the tools needed to describe the grammar of any and every human language. After all, a theory of UG would be of little interest if it enabled us to describe the grammar of English and French, but not that of Swahili or Chinese. In this section, we take a brief look at aspects of syntax which are potentially universal.

However, at the outset, it is useful to reflect on the meaning of the word *universal*. Let us suppose that there is a universal set of grammatical categories found across the languages of the world. Does this imply that all languages make use of all of these categories? Not necessarily. It may be that a given language will make use of only a specific subset of these universal categories. If so, a potentially universal category may occur in a wide range of languages, but not necessarily all. In this respect, it is interesting to note that some categories seem to occur in all languages, whereas others occur in only a subset of languages. For example, all languages have nouns, but not all languages have determiners (e.g. English has definite and indefinite articles, but Japanese does not). Thus, the term *universal* can be taken to denote an entity or property that is found in a wide range of languages, though not necessarily all.

As is implicit in the discussion in the preceding paragraph, grammatical categories are one potential type of universal. In addition, the grammars of languages appear to make use of a universal set of **grammatical operations**. Below, I briefly outline four such types of operation.

One of these is known in recent work as **Merge** and is a process by which words are combined together to form phrases and sentences (as we will see in more detail in Chapter 3). For example, by merging the preposition *to* with the pronoun *us*, we form the prepositional phrase *to us*. By merging the verb *lied* with this prepositional phrase, we form the verb phrase *lied to us*. And by merging the resulting verb phrase with the pronoun *he*, we form the sentence *He lied to us*.

Although this is a (simplified) example from English, it is clear that all languages allow more complex grammatical structures to be built up out of simpler ones by Merge. When we merge two constituents together, the new constituent thereby formed is assigned a **label** characterising the grammatical properties of the new constituent: for example, when we merge the preposition *to* with the pronoun *us*, we form a new constituent *to us* which carries the label PP telling us that it is a Prepositional Phrase. An important property of Merge is that it is **recursive**, in the sense that it allows us to build up structures containing multiple occurrences of particular types of constituent. For example, we can build up more and more complex sentences by recursively embedding one clause inside another (cf. *John did it; He said that John did it; She thinks that he said that John did it; I know that she thinks that he said that John did it*, etc.).

A second type of universal syntactic operation found in the grammars of all natural languages is **Movement**. Under a variety of conditions and for a variety of reasons, words or phrases can be moved from one position in a sentence into another in order to highlight them in some way, usually moving into a position closer to the front of the overall sentence. In this connection, consider the difference between a statement such as (28a) below and the corresponding yes–no question in (28b):

(28) (a)   He *was* lying to you
   (b)   *Was* he lying to you?

How can we convert the statement in (28a) into the question in (28b)? A traditional answer is that we do this by moving the auxiliary *was* from its position after the subject *he* in (28a) into a new position in front of *he*, so resulting in the question (28b) *Was he lying to you?* The movement operation by which an auxiliary is moved in front of its subject in a question is traditionally referred to as **(Subject-)Auxiliary Inversion**.

But now suppose that we want to make a further change in our sentence and that we want to ask for the identity of the person that he was lying to. In this case, we would replace *you* in (28b) by the corresponding question word *who*, and move *who* to the front of the overall sentence, so forming:

(29)   *Who* was he lying to?

The operation responsible for moving a word like *who* to the front of the overall sentence is known as **Wh-Movement** (because it moves words which begin with *wh-*, such as *who/what/where/when/why*, etc. to the front of the sentence): questions like (29) are known as **wh-questions** for the same reason. The more general conclusion that we draw from our discussion here is that a wh-question like (29) involves two different movement operations, Auxiliary Inversion and Wh-Movement.

A third type of potentially universal syntactic operation is **Agreement**. This can be illustrated by the examples in (30) below (with a star/asterisk in front of a word used to indicate that the sentence becomes ungrammatical if the word in question is used):

(30) (a)   I/*we/*you/*he/*she/*they *am* working
   (b)   He/she/*I/*we/*you/*they *is* working
   (c)   We/they/you/*I/*he/*she *are* working

What the sentences in (30) illustrate is that the form of the auxiliary verb BE is determined by the choice of subject. To be more precise, we require the first person singular form *am* if the subject is a first person singular pronoun like *I*; we need the third person singular form *is* if the subject is a third person singular expression like *he/she*; and we must use the **second person**/plural form *are* if the subject is a second person expression like *you* or a plural expression like *we/they*. In other words, the grammars of languages like English incorporate an agreement operation by which an auxiliary is made to agree in person and **number** with its subject. (In auxiliariless sentences like *She likes you*, it is the main verb that agrees with the subject: here, the subject *she* is a third person singular pronoun, so the verb LIKE has to be used in its third person singular form *likes*.)

Another form of agreement (traditionally called **Concord**) is found between nouns and certain types of words used to modify them. In this connection, compare the English noun expression in (31a) with its Italian counterpart in (31b), where [F.Pl] denotes 'feminine gender, plural number':

(31) (a)   these beautiful cars
   (b)   queste$_{these[F.Pl]}$ belle$_{beautiful[F.Pl]}$ macchine$_{cars[F.Pl]}$

In both examples, we have a noun *cars/macchine* modified by two other types of word. The first type of word *these/queste* is a determiner (since it determines which particular cars we are talking about), and the second type of word *beautiful/belle* is an adjective. If we use the plural noun *cars* in (31a), we also have to use the plural determiner form *these* to modify it, not the singular form *this*. What this illustrates is that determiners must agree in number with nouns they modify in English; however, adjectives like *beautiful* are invariable in English, and so there is no number concord/agreement between the adjective *beautiful* and the noun *cars* in English. By contrast, in Italian, nouns and all their modifiers inflect for both number and gender: the *-e* suffix on the end of each of the three words in (31b) is a feminine plural marker. Because the noun *macchine*$_{cars}$ is feminine plural, both the adjective *belle*$_{beautiful}$ and the determiner *queste*$_{these}$ must also be used in their feminine plural form (so that use of the masculine singular forms *questo bel*, or the masculine plural forms *questi bei* or the feminine singular forms *questa bella* would be ungrammatical in 31b).

What the discussion in the two preceding paragraphs illustrates is that Agreement is a pervasive operation found (in various types of structure) in a wide variety of languages, even though the precise details of a particular type of agreement operation may vary from one language to another (e.g. nouns agree in number but not gender with determiners but not adjectives in English, whereas nouns agree in both number and gender with both determiners and adjectives in Italian).

A fourth type of potentially universal operation is **Ellipsis** (i.e. deletion). This is a type of operation by which a string of one or more words can be deleted if it is redundant (e.g. if it has already been mentioned earlier in the discourse). For example, in the sentences below the material marked by strikethrough can be deleted:

(32) (a)   I know I should *go to the dentist's*, but I just don't want to ~~go to the dentist's~~
   (b)   I'm pretty sure *he has gone*, but I have no idea where ~~he has gone~~
   (c)   John *ate* an apple, and Mary ~~ate~~ a pear

In (32a), the deleted material *go to the dentist's* is (as we will see in Chapter 3) a verb phrase (abbreviated to VP), and so this type of deletion is referred to as **VP Ellipsis**. In (32b), ellipsis affects the clause *where he has gone* and deletes all the material following *where*: this type of ellipsis is known as **Sluicing**. In (32c), the verb *ate* is deleted, and thereby leaves a gap in the middle of the clause: hence, this type of ellipsis is referred to as **Gapping**. In cases such as these, the material marked by strikethrough can be deleted because it has already been mentioned (the earlier mention being italicised): the italicised string is said to serve as the **antecedent** of the deleted string. Ellipsis operations serve to maximise economy and efficiency, by shortening sentences and ensuring that redundant material is not pronounced. On one view of ellipsis, the deleted material is present in the syntax, but is not pronounced in the phonology.

In addition to there being a universal set of operations (like Merge, Movement, Agreement and Ellipsis) found in natural language grammars, there is also a set of universal **principles** that govern how grammatical operations work. To illustrate one such principle, let's take a closer look at how wh-questions are formed in English. In this connection, consider the following dialogue:

(33)   SPEAKER A: He had said someone would do something
        SPEAKER B: He had said who would do what?

In (33), speaker B largely echoes what speaker A says, except for replacing *someone* by *who* and *something* by *what*. For obvious reasons, the type of question produced by speaker B in (33) is called an **echo question**. However, speaker B could alternatively have replied with a **non-echo question** like that below:

(34)   Who had he said would do what?

If we compare the echo question *He had said who would do what?* in (33B) with the corresponding non-echo question *Who had he said would do what?* in (34), we find that (34) involves two movement operations (familiar from our earlier discussion) that are not found in (33B). One is Auxiliary Inversion, moving the auxiliary *had* in front of its subject *he*; the other is Wh-Movement, moving the wh-word *who* to the front of the overall sentence, and positioning it in front of *had*.

A closer look at questions like (34) provides evidence that there are universal principles which constrain the way in which movement operations may apply. An interesting property of the questions in (33B) and (34) is that they contain two auxiliaries (*had* and *would*) and two wh-words (*who* and *what*). If we compare (34) with the echo question in (33B), we find that the first of the two auxiliaries (*had*) and the first of the wh-words (*who*) is moved to the front of the sentence in (34). If we try inverting the second auxiliary (*would*) and fronting the second wh-word (*what*), we end up with ungrammatical sentences, as we see from (35c–e) below. (Key items are bold-printed/italicised, and the corresponding echo question is given in parentheses; 35a is repeated from the echo question in 33B, and 35b from 34. Recall that a star/asterisk in front of a sentence indicates that it is ungrammatical.)

(35) (a)   He **had** said *who* **would** do *what*? (= echo question)
     (b)   *Who* **had** he said would do what? (cf. He **had** said *who* would do what?)
     (c)   **Who** **would** he had said do what? (cf. He had said *who* **would** do what?)
     (d)   **What** **had** he said who would do? (cf. He **had** said who would do *what*?)
     (e)   **What** **would** he had said who do? (cf. He had said who **would** do *what*?)

If we compare (35b) with its echo-question counterpart (35a) *He had said who would do what?* we see that (35b) involves preposing/fronting the <u>first</u> wh-word *who* and the <u>first</u> auxiliary *had*, and that this results in a grammatical sentence. By contrast, (35c) involves preposing the <u>first</u> wh-word *who* and the <u>second</u> auxiliary *would*; (35d) involves preposing the <u>second</u> wh-word *what* and the <u>first</u> auxiliary *had*; and (35e) involves preposing the <u>second</u> wh-word *what* and the <u>second</u> auxiliary *would*. The generalisation which emerges from the data in (35) is that in order to yield a grammatical outcome, Auxiliary Inversion must prepose the *closest* auxiliary *had* (i.e. the one nearest the beginning of the sentence in 35a above) and Wh-Movement must likewise prepose the *closest* wh-word *who*. The fact that two different movement operations (Auxiliary Inversion and Wh-Movement) are subject to the same condition (which requires preposing of the closest word of the relevant type) suggests that grammatical operations are governed by a universal principle which can be outlined informally as:

(36)   **Economy Principle**
        Structures and the operations used to form them should be as economical as possible.

In consequence of the Economy Principle, Auxiliary Inversion preposes the first auxiliary *had* (i.e. the one closest to the beginning of the sentence), because this will involve a shorter/more economical movement (with the auxiliary *had* crossing only one other word, namely *he*) than if we were to move the second auxiliary *would* (which would then have to be moved across four words *he had said who*). Likewise, in consequence of the Economy Principle, Wh-Movement preposes the first wh-word *who* because this will involve a shorter/more economical movement (with the wh-word *who* moving across the three words *he had said*) than if we were to move the second wh-word *what* (which would have to be moved across the six words *he had said who would do*).

While the Economy Principle (36) has been posited here on the basis of evidence from one type of structure in one language (wh-questions in English), there have been hundreds of published studies presenting evidence that the same principle constrains the operation of numerous different types of movement operation in a wide range of other languages. Moreover, there is evidence that the Economy Principle applies to other types of grammatical operation as well. So, for example, agreement typically involves a verb agreeing with the closest expression of the relevant kind (typically, its own subject). Likewise, the function of pronouns could be seen as that of making sentences more economical in structure (hence shorter): e.g. we can shorten a sentence like *My new book on syntax has been so unsuccessful that nobody has bought my new book on syntax* by replacing the second occurrence of the repeated phrase *my new book on syntax* with the pronoun *it* (as in *My new book on syntax has been so unsuccessful that nobody has bought it*).

1.5   The nature of universals

Our discussion in the previous section leads to the conclusion that there is a universal set of grammatical categories found throughout the various languages of the world, together with a universal set of grammatical operations (including Merge, Movement, Agreement and Ellipsis), and a universal set of principles (like the Economy Principle) governing how these operations apply. However, the assumption that there is a universal set of categories, operations and principles found in natural language grammars raises fundamental questions about the nature of these universals. Do universals reflect special properties unique to human language? Or do they reflect more general properties of cognitive systems in the human mind/brain? Or do they reflect even more general properties of natural systems (e.g. fundamental principles of the natural world such as laws of physics)?

To make our discussion more concrete, consider the status of the Economy Principle (36). Although implicitly formulated in (36) as a condition specific to the grammars of natural languages, it can be argued to be a reflection of 'principles of computational efficiency that may well be reducible to laws of nature' (Chomsky 2013: 5), and hence of principles which govern natural systems in general rather than being specific to language. In this context, it is interesting to note that Cherniak (2005, 2009) has sought to explain properties of nervous systems in terms of a related principle of minimisation of 'wire length' (a principle which also guides microchip design).

A more difficult case is the issue of whether Merge is a language-specific property or a more general property of combinatorial systems. In essence, Merge is an operation which combines two elements into a set containing these two elements, and thus is in essence simply a set-formation operation. As we will see in Chapter 3, Merge has been argued to operate only on *pairs* of element (in the sense that only two elements can be combined by any given merge operation, not three or four: for example, a prepositional phrase like *in Paris* is formed by merging one and not more than one preposition (= *in*) with one and not more than one object (= *Paris*). It has been argued that the binarity property of Merge is a reflection of principles that play a role in the description of the natural world, e.g. Fibonacci sequences (Carnie and Medeiros 2005). This point is underlined by Smith and Allott (forthcoming) in the following terms:

> As Hauser put it speculatively (in Cherniak 2009: 118) 'Could the fact that trees, lightning, neurons and capillaries all show binary branching indicate that this is an optimal solution across the board, including the way in which the mind computes tree structures in language?'

However, one difference with other set-formation operations is that Merge gives rise to the formation of *labelled* sets: for example, merging the preposition *in* with the noun *Paris* gives rise to a string (i.e. set of words) *in Paris* which is labelled as (i.e. analysed as having the grammatical properties of) a *prepositional phrase*. This raises the possibility that *labels* (which are in effect grammatical categories) may be a uniquely defining feature of natural language.

Now consider the nature of the *Movement* operations found in natural language grammars. What is the nature of movement operations? In order to understand Chomsky's answer to this question, it's important to have an overview of his conception of the internal organisation of grammars. So let's look at this.

One component of a grammar is a **lexicon** (= dictionary = list of all the **lexical items**/words in the language and their linguistic properties), and in forming a given sentence out of a set of words, we first have to take the relevant words out of the lexicon. Our chosen words are then combined together by a series of syntactic computations in the **syntax** (i.e. in the **syntactic/computational component** of the grammar), thereby forming a **syntactic structure**. This syntactic structure serves as input into two other components of the grammar. One is the **semantic component** which **maps** (i.e. 'converts') the syntactic structure into a corresponding **semantic representation** (i.e. into a representation of linguistic aspects of its meaning): since semantic representations specify the logical relations between constituents (and so provide a representation of their **Logical Form/ LF**), they are widely referred to as **LF representations**, and the semantic component is likewise referred to as the **LF component**. The second component that syntactic structures are inputted into is the **PF component** (or **phonological component**), so called because it maps the syntactic structure into a **PF representation** (i.e. a representation of its **Phonetic Form**, giving us a phonetic **spellout** for each word, telling us how it is pronounced). The LF/semantic representation interfaces (i.e. connects) with systems of thought, and the PF representation with systems of speech – as shown in diagrammatic form below (where ≈ means 'interfaces with'):

(37)

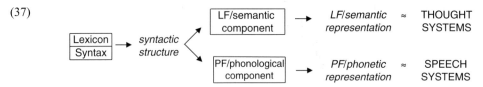

The interface with thought systems links with 'the conceptual/intentional (semantic-pragmatic) systems that make use of generated linguistic expressions for thought, interpretation, and organizing action' (Chomsky 2010: 45); while the interface with speech systems links with 'the sensorimotor systems that externalize expressions in production and assign them to sensory data in perception' (ibid.). On this view, a grammar is 'a computational system generating syntactic structures along with mappings to the two interfaces' (ibid., fn.3).

In the light of the model in (37), let's return to the question of why the grammars of natural languages contain syntactic movement operations. Chomsky's answer is that movement serves to satisfy **interface conditions** (i.e. requirements of the semantics interface with thought systems, and/or of the phonetics interface with speech systems). In this connection, consider why the italicised words are fronted (i.e. moved to the front of the clause containing them) in the sentences below:

(38)   SPEAKER A: What are the subjects you enjoy most and least?
        SPEAKER B: *Syntax* I enjoy most. *Phonetics* I enjoy least

In these sentences, speaker B provides the new information that speaker A asks for. To use a technical term, fronting the two italicised words serves to mark them as **focused** (i.e. as providing information which is new in the relevant discourse context). Movement (in such cases) thus plays an important role at the semantics interface in signalling **focus**. Now compare (38) above with (39) below:

(39)   He has witnessed acts of horrific violence, mutilation and torture. *Such brutality*, he prayed that he would never again encounter as long as he lived

Here, the fronted phrase *such brutality* refers back to the acts of violence, mutilation and torture referred to in the first sentence. To use the relevant terminology, fronting *such brutality* in (39) serves to mark it as a **topic** – i.e. as old information previously mentioned in the discourse. Generalising, we can say that the types of movement illustrated in (38) and (39) serve to mark whether the fronted expression represents information which is old or new in the relevant discourse setting. Thus, one function of movement is to provide the semantics interface with discourse information about whether a constituent is focused (and so represents new information) or topicalised (and so represents old information).

However, this is not the only function that movement serves at the semantic interface, as we can see by comparing the two sentences below:

(40) (a)   He didn't fail *one of the students*
   (b)   *One of the students*, he didn't fail

(40a) is ambiguous and has two interpretations. One is paraphraseable as 'There is **not** *one* student that he failed' (i.e. he passed all the students): in this case, the negative adverb *not* is said to have **scope** over the quantifier *one* (denoted informally as *not > one*, where > means 'has scope over'). However, (40a) can also have a second interpretation, paraphraseable as 'There is **one** student that he did *not* fail' (i.e. he passed only one of the students): in this case, the quantifier *one* is said to have scope over the negative adverb *not* (denoted informally as *one > not*). By contrast, (40b) only has the *one > not* interpretation paraphraseable as 'There is **one** student that he did *not* fail.' What this illustrates is that the movement operation by which *one of the students* is fronted (i.e. moved to the front of the sentence) serves to disambiguate the scope relations in the sentence by unambiguously signalling that *one* has scope over *not*. This illustrates a different kind of semantic function for movement operations, namely to mark **scope relations**.

The upshot of our discussion here is that certain types of movement operation serve to provide information which is important at the semantics interface (e.g. information about discourse or scope properties). However, other types of movement operation are motivated by requirements of the phonetics interface. In this connection, compare the French sentences below:

(41) (a)   Il   a   vu   *Paul*
             He   has   seen   Paul
   (b)   Il   *l'a*   vu
             He   him's   seen   ('He has seen him')

In (41a), the object/complement of the verb *vu*$_{seen}$ is *Paul*, and this occupies the normal position for objects in a language like French, which is (as in English) after the verb. However in (41b), *Paul* has been replaced by the corresponding **clitic pronoun** *l(e)*$_{him}$, and this occupies a very different position in front of the auxiliary *a*$_{has}$. The traditional way of describing this is to say that the pronoun *l(e)*$_{him}$ in (41b) undergoes a movement operation termed **Clitic Movement** which results in it being moved in front of the auxiliary *a*$_{has}$ and cliticising (i.e. attaching) to it. What drives this kind of movement operation? The answer is: PF interface requirements. Clitics have the phonological/prosodic property that they are too weak to survive as independent words and must attach to an appropriate **host** at PF. A perfect participle like *vu*$_{seen}$ is not an appropriate host for a clitic in French, but an auxiliary like *a*$_{has}$ is. Thus, Clitic Movement is motivated by PF interface requirements.

The overall conclusion to be drawn from our discussion here is that movement serves to satisfy interface conditions which hold at the semantics or phonetic interface – in simpler terms, movement is designed to satisfy semantic or phonetic requirements. Our discussion of movement can be put into a broader context in the following terms. In the previous section, we saw that there is a universal set of categories, operations and principles which are found in the languages of the world (though any given language may utilise only a subset of these). The question which then arises is whether these are properties which are idiosyncratic to natural language, or whether they can be explained in other terms. Chomsky has argued that most (perhaps all) universal properties of languages are reducible either to interface conditions, or to more general properties of cognitive or natural systems (e.g. general principles of biology, or fundamental principles of the natural world such as computational efficiency). His aim in work since the 1990s has been to **minimise** the set of properties which are idiosyncratic to language (i.e. not found in other biological or natural systems). This methodological standpoint is the defining characteristic of the *Minimalist Program for Linguistic Theory* which he has been developing over the past three decades. The strongest version of the Minimalist Program (known as the **Strong Minimalist Thesis/SMT**) is that all properties of natural language grammars reflect **conceptual necessity**, in the sense that they are 'properties of language that are logically or conceptually necessary, properties such that if a system failed to have them we would simply not call it a language' (Chomsky 1980: 28–9). The SMT hypothesis is minimalist in the sense that it attempts to minimise (and in the best-case scenario eliminate) recourse to constructs or principles which are not conceptually necessary (i.e. which are not imposed by interface requirements, or by biological or natural principles).

But why should Chomsky want to minimise what is special and unique about language? The answer lies in his desire to account for the evolution of language. If there was a single evolutionary step which took place at some point in human evolution which gave rise to language, it is unlikely to have been a step in which a whole range of different properties idiosyncratic to language were acquired at the same time. Rather, it seems more likely that some genetic development gave rise to one new type of operation which enabled humans to acquire language. But what is the nature of the relevant operation? For Hauser, Chomsky and Fitch (2002) and Fitch, Hauser and Chomsky (2005), it is the property of **recursion** – that is, the ability to form structures which contain more than one instance of a given category (e.g. the ability to form complex sentences containing more than one clause). A related suggestion made by Chomsky is that it is the unbounded nature of Merge (i.e. the fact that words can be merged together to form an unbounded number of different sentences): cf. his (2007: 5) comment that 'unbounded Merge is not only a genetically determined property of language, but also unique to it'. By contrast, for Hornstein and Pietroski (2009) it is the operation *Label* by which constituents are assigned category labels characterising their grammatical properties. The search for some aspect of language which is genetically determined has given rise to a field of enquiry known as **biolinguistics** (which is sometimes represented somewhat inaccurately in the popular press as the search for a so-called grammar gene).

1.6   Language acquisition

A central fact about language is that children acquire the fundamentals of the grammar of their native language/s within a relatively short period (around 5% of their total life span), and that all normally developing children go through similar stages of acquisition. Children generally produce their first recognisable word (e.g. *Mama* or *Dada*) by around the age of 12 months (with considerable variation between individual children, however). For the next 6 months or so, there is little apparent evidence of grammatical development in their speech production, although the child's productive vocabulary typically increases by about five words a month until it reaches around thirty words at age 18 months. Throughout this single-word stage, children's utterances comprise single words spoken in isolation: e.g. a child may say *apple* when reaching for an apple, or *up* when wanting to climb up onto someone's knee. During the single-word stage, it is difficult to find any immediately visible evidence of the acquisition of grammar, in that children do not make productive use of inflections (e.g. they don't productively add the plural *-s* ending to nouns, or the past tense *-d* ending to verbs) and don't productively combine words together to form two- and three-word utterances. (However, it should be noted that perception experiments have suggested that infants may acquire some syntactic knowledge even before 1 year of age.)

At around the age of 18 months (though with considerable variation from one child to another), we find the first visible signs of the acquisition of grammar: children start to make productive use of inflections (e.g. using plural nouns like *doggies* alongside the singular form *doggy*, and inflected verb forms like *going/gone* alongside the uninflected verb form *go*) and similarly start to produce elementary two- and three-word utterances such as *Want Teddy, Eating cookie, Daddy gone office*, etc. From this point on, there is a rapid expansion in their grammatical development, until by the age of around 30 months they have typically acquired a wide variety of inflections and grammatical structures, and are able to produce adult-like sentences such as *Where's Mummy gone? What's Daddy doing? Can we go to the zoo, Daddy?* etc. (though occasional morphological and syntactic errors persist until the age of 4 years or so – e.g. *We goed there with Daddy, What we can do?* etc.).

So, the central phenomenon which any theory of language acquisition must seek to explain is this: how is it that after a long-drawn-out period of many months in which there is no obvious sign of grammatical development, at around the age of 18 months there is a sudden spurt as multiword speech starts to emerge, and a phenomenal growth in grammatical development then takes place over the next 12 months? This *uniformity* and (once the spurt has started) *rapidity* in the pattern of children's linguistic development are the central phenomena which a theory of language acquisition must seek to explain. But how?

In work dating back more than half a century, Chomsky has argued that the most plausible explanation for the uniformity and rapidity of first language acquisition is to posit that the course of acquisition is determined by a biologically endowed innate **Faculty of Language/FL** which provides children with a genetically transmitted programme for acquiring a grammar, on the basis of their linguistic **experience** (i.e. on the basis of the speech input they perceive). The way in which Chomsky visualises the acquisition process can be represented schematically as in (42) below (where L is the language being acquired):

(42)

Children acquiring a language will observe people around them using the language, and the set of expressions in the language which a child hears (and the contexts in which they are used) in the course of acquiring the language constitute the child's linguistic experience of the language. This experience serves as input to the child's Language Faculty, which incorporates a (universal) programme which enables the child to use the experience to devise a grammar of the language being acquired. Thus, the input to the Language Faculty is the child's experience, and the output of the Language Faculty is a grammar of the language being acquired.

The claim that the course of language acquisition is determined by an innate Language Faculty unique to human beings is known popularly as the **Innateness Hypothesis**. There are a range of arguments that Chomsky has put forward in defence of innateness over the past half-century. For one thing, he maintains that the ability to speak and acquire languages is unique to human beings and that natural languages incorporate principles which are also unique to humans and which reflect the nature of the human mind:

> Whatever evidence we do have seems to me to support the view that the ability to acquire and use language is a species-specific human capacity, that there are very deep and restrictive principles that determine the nature of human language and are rooted in the specific character of the human mind.   (Chomsky 1972: 102)

Moreover, he notes, language acquisition is an ability which all humans possess, entirely independently of their general intelligence:

> Even at low levels of intelligence, at pathological levels, we find a command of language that is totally unattainable by an ape that may, in other respects, surpass a human imbecile in problem-solving activity and other adaptive behavior.   (Chomsky 1972: 10)

In addition, the apparent uniformity in the types of grammars developed by different speakers of the same language suggests that children have genetic guidance in the task of constructing a grammar of their native language:

> We know that the grammars that are in fact constructed vary only slightly among speakers of the same language, despite wide variations not only in intelligence but also in the conditions under which language is acquired.   (Chomsky 1972: 79)

Furthermore, the rapidity of acquisition (once the grammar spurt has started) also points to genetic guidance in grammar construction:

> Otherwise it is impossible to explain how children come to construct grammars … under the given conditions of time and access to data.   (Chomsky 1972: 113)

(The sequence 'under … data' means simply 'in so short a time, and on the basis of such limited linguistic experience'.) What makes the uniformity and rapidity of acquisition even more remarkable is the fact that the child's linguistic experience is often degenerate (i.e. imperfect), since it is based on the linguistic performance of adult speakers, and this may be a poor reflection of their competence:

> A good deal of normal speech consists of false starts, disconnected phrases, and other deviations from idealised competence.   (Chomsky 1972: 158)

If much of the speech input which children receive is ungrammatical (because of performance errors), how is it that they can use this degenerate experience to develop a (competence) grammar which specifies how to form grammatical sentences? Chomsky's answer is to draw the following analogy:

> Descartes asks: how is it when we see a sort of irregular figure drawn in front of us we see it as a triangle? He observes, quite correctly, that there's a disparity between the data presented to us and the precept that we construct. And he argues, I think quite plausibly, that we see the figure as a triangle because there's something about the nature of our minds which makes the image of a triangle easily constructible by the mind.   (Chomsky 1968: 687)

The obvious implication is that in much the same way as we are genetically predisposed to analyse shapes (however irregular) as having specific geometric properties, so too we are genetically predisposed to analyse sentences (however ungrammatical) as having specific grammatical properties.

A further argument Chomsky uses in support of the Innateness Hypothesis is that language acquisition is an entirely subconscious and involuntary activity (in the sense that you can't consciously choose whether or not to acquire your native language – though you can choose whether or not you wish to learn chess); it is also an activity which is largely unguided (in the sense that parents don't teach children to talk):

> Children acquire … languages quite successfully even though no special care is taken to teach them and no special attention is given to their progress.   (Chomsky 1965: 200–1)

The implication is that we don't learn to have a native language, any more than we learn to have arms or legs; the ability to acquire a native language is part of our genetic endowment – just like the ability to learn to walk.

Studies of language acquisition lend empirical support to the Innateness Hypothesis. Research has suggested that there is a critical period for the acquisition of syntax, in the sense that children who learn a given language before puberty generally achieve native competence in it, whereas those who acquire a (first or second) language after the age of 9 years or so rarely manage to achieve native-like syntactic competence. A particularly poignant example of this is a child called Genie, who was deprived of speech input and kept locked up on her own in a room until age 13. When eventually taken into care and exposed to intensive language input, her vocabulary grew enormously, but her syntax never developed. This suggests that the acquisition of syntax is determined by an innate *language acquisition programme* which is in effect switched off (or gradually atrophies) around the onset of puberty.

Further support for the key claim in the Innateness Hypothesis that the human Language Faculty is (in certain respects) autonomous of non-linguistic cognitive systems such as vision, hearing, reasoning or memory comes from the study of language disorders. Some disorders (such as Specific Language Impairment) involve impairment of linguistic abilities without concomitant impairment of other cognitive systems. By contrast, other types of disorder (such as Williams Syndrome) involve impairment of cognitive abilities in the absence of any major impairment of linguistic abilities. This double dissociation between linguistic and cognitive abilities lends additional plausibility to the claim that linguistic competence is the product of an autonomous Language Faculty.

Given the assumption that human beings are endowed with an innate Language Faculty, the overall goal of linguistic theory is to attempt to uncover

> the properties that are specific to human language, that is, to the 'faculty of language' FL. To borrow Jespersen's formulation eighty years ago, the goal is to unearth 'the great principles underlying the grammars of all languages' with the goal of 'gaining a deeper insight into the innermost nature of human language and of human thought.' The biolinguistic perspective views FL as an 'organ of the body,' one of many subcomponents of an organism that interact in its normal life.   (Chomsky 2008: 133)

But what kind of knowledge does the innate Language Faculty endow children with? Chomsky's view is that it incorporates a theory of Universal Grammar which gives the child innate knowledge of the range of grammatical structures, operations and principles found in natural language grammars. If whatever is universal in language forms part of the innate knowledge which children are genetically endowed with by the Language Faculty, then it follows that children do not have to learn (e.g.) what Agreement is, since this is part of their innate linguistic knowledge. By contrast, they do have to learn (e.g.) whether verbs in the language they are acquiring inflect for gender (yes in Arabic, no in

English), and likewise whether adjectives in the language they are acquiring inflect for gender (yes in Spanish, no in English), and they clearly have to learn the different forms of the various inflections.

In this section, we have examined Chomsky's claim in much work at the end of the last century that the rapidity and uniformity of first language acquisition seems to entail the need for massive innate structure. However, as Neil Smith (p.c.) points out, this conclusion is seemingly at variance with Chomsky's claim in more recent times that the rapidity of the evolution of language seems to argue equally persuasively for minimal innate structure (see the end of §1.5).

1.7   Parameters

In the previous section, we looked at Chomsky's claim that children are genetically endowed with a Language Faculty which provides them with innate knowledge of universal aspects of grammar. However, it clearly cannot be the case that all aspects of the grammar of languages are universal; if this were so, all natural languages would have the same grammar and there would be no **grammatical learning** involved in language acquisition (i.e. no need for children to learn anything about the grammar of the language they are acquiring), only **lexical learning** (learning the lexical items/words in the language and their idiosyncratic linguistic properties, e.g. whether a given item has an irregular plural or past tense form). But although there are universal grammatical properties which all natural languages have in common, there are also particular aspects of grammar which vary from one language to another along a number of **parameters** (i.e. dimensions). And while children don't have to learn universal aspects of grammar (if the Language Faculty equips them with knowledge of these), they do have to learn those aspects of grammar which vary in a parametric fashion from one language to another (as was implicit in the suggestion in §1.4 that although Agreement is a universal operation, the precise details of what agrees with what in a given language vary somewhat from one language to another). Thus, language acquisition involves not only lexical learning but also some grammatical learning. Let's take a closer look at the kind of grammatical learning that is involved.

If children have innate knowledge of universal properties of language, it is clear that grammatical learning is not going to involve learning those aspects of grammar which are universal. Rather, grammatical learning will be limited to **parametrised** aspects of grammar (i.e. those aspects of grammar which vary in a parametric fashion from one language to another). The obvious way to determine just what aspects of the grammar of their native language children have to learn is thus to examine the range of parametric variation found in the grammars of different languages.

We can illustrate one type of parametric variation across languages in terms of the following contrast between the English example in (43a) below and its Italian counterpart in (43b):

(43) (a)   Maria thinks that *(they) speak French
   (b)   Maria   pensa   che   parlano   francese
             Maria   thinks   that   speak   French

(The notation *(*they*) in 43a means that the sentence is ungrammatical if *they* is omitted – i.e. that the sentence *Maria thinks that speak French* is ungrammatical.) The English verbs *thinks/speak* in (43a) and their Italian counterparts *pensa*$_{thinks}$/*parlano*$_{speak}$ are finite verb forms in that they are inflected for indicative mood, tense and agreement (and can have a nominative subject). In English, all finite verbs require an overt subject, so that the finite (third person singular present tense) verb *thinks* in (43a) has the overt subject *Maria* and the finite (third person plural present tense) verb *speak* has the overt subject *they*. By contrast, finite verbs don't require overt subjects in Italian, so although the (third person singular present tense indicative) verb *pensa*$_{thinks}$ has the overt subject *Maria*, the (third person plural present tense indicative) verb *parlano*$_{speak}$ by contrast does not have an overt subject. However, there are two pieces of evidence suggesting that the Italian verb *parlano*$_{speak}$ must have a 'silent' subject of some kind. One is semantic in nature, in that the verb *parlano*$_{speak}$ is understood as having a third person plural subject, and this understood subject is translated into English as *they*. The second piece of evidence is grammatical in nature. Finite verbs agree with their subjects in person and number in Italian: hence, in order to account for the fact that the verb *parlano*$_{speak}$ is in the third person plural form in (43b), we need to posit that it has a third person plural subject to agree with. Since the Italian verb *parlano*$_{speak}$ has no overt subject, it must have a **null subject** that can be thought of as a silent or 'unpronounced' counterpart of the pronoun *they* which appears in the corresponding English sentence (43a). This silent subject pronoun is conventionally designated as **pro**, so that (43b) has the fuller structure:

(44)   Maria   pensa$_{thinks}$ che$_{that}$ *pro*   parlano$_{speak}$ francese$_{French}$

where *pro* is a null subject pronoun which (as used in 44) has much the same grammatical properties as its overt English counterpart *they*.

The more general conclusion to be drawn from our discussion here is that in languages like Italian, any finite verb can have either an overt subject like *Maria* or a null *pro* subject. This is true of verbs both in main clauses (like the *pensa*$_{thinks}$ clause in 43b) and in subordinate clauses (like the *parlano*$_{speak}$ clause in 43b), so that we could replace the overt main-clause subject *Maria* in (43b) by a null *pro* subject and say simply *Pensa*$_{thinks}$ *che*$_{that}$ *parlano*$_{speak}$ *francese*$_{French}$ 'She thinks that they speak French.'

However, things are very different in English. Although finite verbs can have an overt subject like *Maria* in English, they cannot have a null *pro* subject – hence the ungrammaticality of **Maria thinks that speak French* (where the verb *speak* has a null subject). So, a finite verb in a language like Italian (whether in main or subordinate clauses) can have either an overt or a null *pro* subject, but in a language like English, a finite verb can have only an overt subject, not a null *pro* subject. We can describe the differences between the two types of language by saying that Italian is a **null subject language**, whereas English is a **non-null subject language**. More generally, there appears to be parametric variation between languages as to whether or not they allow all finite verbs to have null subjects. The relevant parameter is conventionally termed the **Null Subject Parameter/NSP** (though in earlier work it was termed the **Pro Drop Parameter** because null subject languages appear to allow a subject pronoun to be 'dropped'). The NSP would appear to be a binary parameter, with only two possible settings for any given language L: *L either does or doesn't allow every finite verb to have a null subject*. There appears to be no language which allows the subjects of some finite verbs to be null, but not others – e.g. no language in which it is OK to say *Drinks wine* (meaning 'He/she drinks wine') but not OK to say *Eats pasta* (meaning 'He/she eats pasta'). The range of grammatical variation found across languages appears to be strictly limited to just two possibilities – languages either do or don't systematically allow finite verbs to have null subjects (but see the cautionary note in §1.10).

A more familiar aspect of grammar which is also parametrised relates to word order, in that different types of language have different word orders in specific types of structure. One type of word order variation can be illustrated in relation to the following contrast between English and Chinese questions:

(45) (a)   *What* do you think he will say?

   (b)   Ni   xiang   ta   hui   shuo   *shenme*
           You   think   he   will   say   *what*?

In wh-questions like (45a) in English, an (italicised) interrogative wh-word is moved to the beginning of the sentence. By contrast, in the Chinese sentence in (45b), the interrogative wh-word *shenme*$_{what}$ does not move to the front of the sentence, but rather remains **in situ** (i.e. in the same place as would be occupied by a corresponding non-interrogative word), so that *shenme*$_{what}$ is positioned after the verb *shuo*$_{say}$ because it is the (direct object) complement of the verb, and complements of the relevant type are normally positioned after their verbs in Chinese. Thus, another parameter of variation between languages is the **Wh-Parameter** – a parameter which determines whether wh-words are fronted (i.e. moved to the front of the relevant clause) or not. Significantly, this parameter again appears to be one which is binary in nature, in that it allows for only two possibilities: a language is either a **Wh-Movement** language like English, or a **wh-in-situ** language like Chinese. Many other possibilities for Wh-Movement just don't seem to occur in natural languages: for example, there is no language in which the counterpart of *who* undergoes wh-fronting but not the counterpart of *what* (e.g. no language in which it is OK to say *Who did you see?* but not *What did you see?*). Likewise, there is no language in which wh-complements of some verbs can undergo fronting, but not wh-complements of other verbs (e.g. no language in which it is OK to say *What did he drink?* but not *What did he eat?*). It would seem that the range of parametric variation found with respect to wh-fronting is limited to just two possibilities: a language either does or doesn't allow wh-words to be systematically fronted (but see the caveats noted in §1.10).

Let's now turn to look at a rather different type of word-order variation, concerning the relative position of **heads** and **complements** within phrases. It is a property of phrases that every phrase has a head word which determines the nature of the overall phrase. For example, an expression such as *students of philosophy* is a plural noun phrase because its head word (i.e. the key word in the phrase whose nature determines the properties of the overall phrase) is the plural noun *students*: the noun *students* (and not the noun *philosophy*) is the head word because the phrase *students of philosophy* denotes kinds of student, not kinds of philosophy. The following expression *of philosophy* (which combines with the head noun *students* to form the noun phrase *students of philosophy*) functions as the complement of the noun *students*. In much the same way, an expression such as *in Portugal* is a prepositional phrase which comprises the head preposition *in* and its complement *Portugal*. Likewise, an expression such as *stay with me* is a verb phrase which comprises the head verb *stay* and its complement *with me*. And similarly, an expression such as *fond of fast food* is an adjectival phrase formed by merging the head adjective *fond* with its complement *of fast food*.

In English all heads (nouns, verbs, prepositions, adjectives, etc.) immediately precede their complements; however, there are also languages like Korean in which all heads immediately follow their complements. In informal terms, we can say that English is a **head-first** (i.e. head-before-complement) language, whereas Korean is a **head-last** (i.e. head-after-complement) language. This difference between the two languages can be illustrated by comparing the English examples in (46a,b) below with their Korean counterparts in (46c,d):

(46) (a)   Eat kimchi!
    (b)   love for kimchi
    (c)   Kimchi   meokeola!
           Kimchi   eat
    (d)   kimchi-edaehan   sarang
           kimchi-for   love

(Thanks to Sun-Ho Hong for examples 46c,d; *kimchi* is the Korean national dish of pickled vegetables left to ferment underground in jars for several months.) In the English verb phrase *eat kimchi* in (46a), the head verb *eat* immediately precedes its complement *kimchi*. Likewise, in the English noun phrase *love for kimchi* in (46b), the head noun *love* immediately precedes its complement *for kimchi*; and the complement *for kimchi* is in turn a prepositional phrase in which the head preposition *for* likewise immediately precedes its complement *kimchi*. Since English consistently positions heads before complements, it is a head-first language. By contrast, we find precisely the opposite ordering in Korean. In the verb phrase *kimchi meokeola* (literally 'kimchi eat') in (46c), the head imperative verb *meokeola* 'eat' immediately follows its complement *kimchi*; likewise, in the noun phrase *kimchi-edaehan sarang* (literally 'kimchi-for love') in (46d) the head noun *sarang* 'love' immediately follows its complement *kimchi-edaehan* 'kimchi-for'; the expression *kimchi-edaehan* 'kimchi-for' is in turn a prepositional phrase whose head preposition *edaehan* 'for' immediately follows its complement *kimchi* (so that *edaehan* might more appropriately be called a **postposition**; prepositions and postpositions are differents kinds of **adposition**). Since Korean consistently positions heads immediately after their complements, it is a head-last language. Given that English is head-first and Korean head-last, it is clear that the relative positioning of heads with respect to their complements is one word-order parameter along which languages differ; the relevant parameter can be termed the **Head Position Parameter/HPP**.

However, there are two complications which should be noted in relation to the Head Position Parameter. One is that while there are languages (like English and Korean) which have a uniform setting for the parameter (in the sense that all heads occupy the same position with respect to their complements in all types of structure), there are also languages (like German) in which some types of structure are head-first and others are head-last. This can be illustrated by the German sentence below (kindly provided by Claudia Felser), which could be used in an appropriate context to reply to a question like Was_{what} $denkst_{think}$ du_{you}? 'What do you think?'

(47) Dass   Hans   an   dem   Wettbewerb   teilnehmen   sollte
      that   Hans   at   the   competition   participate   should
      'That Hans should take part in the competition'

If we look at the structure of the sentence in (47), we see that the conjunction $dass_{that}$, the preposition an_{at} and the determiner dem_{the} precede their complements, but the verb $teilnehmen_{participate}$ and the auxiliary $sollte_{should}$ follow their complements. This shows us that German is a language in which some types of structure are head-first and others are head-last. This in turn suggests that the Head Position Parameter should be revised so as to say that languages vary parametrically with respect to whether *a given type of structure* shows head-first (i.e. head-before-complement) or head-last (i.e. head-after-complement) order: we can then say (e.g.) that prepositional phrases are head-first in German, but verb phrases are head-last.

However, the situation turns out to be more complex than this. For example, while almost all prepositions precede their complements in German, there are a handful of irregular prepositions which follow their complements. Thus, the German preposition in_{in} is regular in respect of occupying head-first position in prepositional phrases like in_{in} den_{the} $Fluß_{river}$ 'in the river', whereas its irregular counterpart $entlang_{along}$ occupies head-last position in prepositional phrases like den_{the} $Fluß_{river}$ $entlang_{along}$ 'along the river'. What this suggests is that the Head Position Parameter specifies the canonical (i.e. normal) position occupied by particular kinds of head in a given language and that exceptional heads which occupy non-canonical positions will have to be specified as exceptions to HPP in their lexical/dictionary entry (e.g. exceptional German prepositions like *entlang* 'along' will be listed in the lexicon/dictionary as showing head-last order and hence being positioned after their complements). To use appropriate technical terminology, the Head Position Parameter specifies the **default** ordering of particular kinds of heads with respect to their complements – i.e. the ordering which we use by default (i.e. which we fall back on) for a head which is not marked as exceptional in its lexical entry.

A second complicating factor to note with respect to the Head Position Parameter is that the way it is set in a given language determines the canonical (i.e. 'normal', 'basic' or 'unmarked') word order in the language. However, this canonical order can be disrupted by movement operations, as is illustrated by the contrast below:

(48) (a)   I can't **stand** *cabbage*
     (b)   *Cabbage*, I can't **stand**

In (48a), the verb *stand* precedes its complement *cabbage*, in conformity with the head-first setting of the Head Position Parameter in English. However, in (48b), the complement *cabbage* has been moved to the front of the sentence in order to highlight it, with the result that the bold-printed verb no longer precedes its italicised complement. This shows us that the setting of the Head Position Parameter can be masked by movement.

Setting aside this complication, it remains true that word-order variation in respect of the relative positioning of heads and complements falls within narrowly circumscribed limits. There are many logically possible types of word-order variation which just don't seem to occur in natural languages. For example, we might imagine that in a given language some verbs would precede and others follow their complements, so that (e.g.) if two new hypothetical verbs like *scrunge* and *plurg* were coined in English, then *scrunge* might take a following complement, and *plurg* a preceding complement. And yet, this doesn't ever seem to happen: rather all verbs typically occupy the same position in a given language with respect to a given type of complement.

Our discussion in this section suggests that there are universal **constraints** (i.e. principles imposing restrictions) on the range of parametric variation found across languages in respect of the relative ordering of heads and complements. It would seem that there are only two different possibilities which Universal Grammar allows for: a given type of structure in a given language must be either head-first (with the relevant heads positioned immediately before their complements) or head-last (with the relevant heads positioned immediately after their complements). Many other logically possible orderings of heads with respect to complements appear not to be found in natural language grammars. The obvious question to ask is why this should be. The answer given by the theory of parameters is that the Language Faculty imposes constraints on the range of parametric variation permitted in natural language grammars. In the case of the Head Position Parameter (i.e. the parameter which determines the relative positioning of heads with respect to their complements), the Language Faculty allows only a binary set of possibilities – namely that a given kind of structure in a given language is either consistently head-first or consistently head-last.

We can generalise the discussion in this section in the following terms. If the Head Position Parameter reduces to a simple binary choice, and if the Wh-Parameter and the Null Subject Parameter also involve binary choices, it seems implausible that **binarity** could be an accidental property of these particular parameters. Rather, it seems much more likely that it is an inherent property of parameters that they constrain the range of structural variation between languages and limit it to a simple binary choice. Generalising still further, it seems possible that all grammatical variation between languages can be characterised in terms of a set of parameters and that for each parameter, the Language Faculty specifies a binary choice of possible values for the parameter.

1.8   Parameter setting

The account of parameters outlined in the previous section has important implications for a theory of language acquisition. If all syntactic variation can be characterised in terms of a series of parameters with binary settings, it follows that the only learning which children have to undertake in relation to the syntactic properties of the relevant class of constructions is to determine (on the basis of their linguistic experience) which of the two alternative settings for each parameter is the appropriate one for the language being acquired. So, for example, children have to learn whether the native language they are acquiring is a null subject language or not, whether it is a Wh-Movement language or not and whether it is a head-first language or not . . . and so on for all the other parameters along which languages vary. Of course, children also face the formidable task of lexical learning – i.e. building up their vocabulary in the relevant language, learning what words mean and what range of forms they have (e.g. whether they are regular or irregular in respect of their morphology), what kinds of structures they can be used in and so on. On this view, the acquisition of grammar involves the twin tasks of lexical learning and grammatical learning (with the latter involving **parameter setting**).

This leads us to the following view of the language acquisition process. The central task which the child faces in acquiring a language is to construct a grammar of the language. The innate Language Faculty incorporates (i) a set of grammatical categories, operations and principles, and (ii) a set of grammatical parameters that impose severe constraints on the range of grammatical variation permitted in natural languages (perhaps limiting variation to binary choices). Since universal aspects of grammar don't have to be learned, the child's syntactic learning task is limited to that of parameter setting (i.e. determining an appropriate setting for each of the relevant grammatical parameters). For obvious reasons, the theory outlined here (developed by Chomsky at the beginning of the 1980s) is known as **Principles-and-Parameters Theory** (abbreviated to **PPT**).

The PPT model clearly has important implications for the nature of the language acquisition process, since it vastly reduces the complexity of the acquisition task which children face. PPT hypothesises that grammatical properties which are universal will not have to be learned by the child, since they are wired into the Language Faculty and hence part of the child's genetic endowment: on the contrary, all the child has to learn are those grammatical properties which are subject to parametric variation across languages. Moreover, the child's learning task will be further simplified if the values which a parameter can have fall within a narrowly specified range, perhaps characterisable in terms of a series of binary choices. This simplified **parameter-setting model** of the acquisition of grammar has given rise to a metaphorical acquisition model in which the child is visualised as having to set a series of switches in one of two positions (*up/down*) – each such switch representing a different parameter. In the case of the Head Position Parameter, we can imagine that if the switch is set in the *up* position (for particular types of head), the language will show head-first word order in relevant kinds of structure, whereas if it is set in the *down* position, the order will be head-last. Of course, an obvious implication of the switch metaphor is that the switch must be set in either one position or the other and cannot be set in both positions. (This would preclude, for example, the possibility of a language having both head-first and head-last word order in a given type of structure.)

The assumption that acquiring the syntax of a language involves the relatively simple task of setting a number of grammatical parameters provides a plausible account of why the acquisition of specific parameters is a remarkably rapid and error-free process in young children. For example, children acquiring English as their native language seem to set the Head Position Parameter at its appropriate head-first setting from the very earliest multi-word utterances they produce (at around age 1;6 – i.e. 1 year; 6 months) and seem to know (tacitly, not explicitly, of course) that English is a head-first language. Accordingly, the earliest verb phrases and prepositional phrases produced by young children acquiring English consistently show verbs and prepositions positioned before their complements, as structures such as the following illustrate (produced by a young boy called Jem/James at age 20 months; head verbs are italicised in (49a) and head prepositions in (49b), and their complements are in non-italic print):

(49) (a)   *Touch* heads. *Cuddle* book. *Want* crayons. *Want* malteser. *Open* door. *Want* biscuit. *Bang* bottom. *See* cats. *Sit* down

   (b)   *On* Mummy. *To* lady. *Without* shoe. *With* potty. *In* keyhole. *In* school. *On* carpet. *On* box. *With* crayons. *To* mummy

A plausible conclusion to draw from structures like (49) is that English children consistently position head words before their complements from the very earliest multiword utterances they produce. They do not use different orders for different words of the same type (e.g. they don't position the verb *see* after its complement but the verb *want* before its complement), or for different types of word (e.g. they don't position verbs before and prepositions after their complements).

Just as children acquiring English seem to know from the outset that English is the type of language which positions heads before complements, so too they also seem to know that English is the type of language that has Wh-Movement and so positions wh-words at the front of a sentence. Some evidence that this is so comes from the examples in (50) below, which illustrate typical wh-questions produced by a girl called Claire at age 2;0–2;1 (the data below being taken from the Appendix to Hill 1983):

(50) (a)   *Where* girl go? *Where* pencil go? *Where* cow go? *Where* the horse go?
     (b)   *What* kitty doing? *What* squirrel doing? *What* lizard doing? *What* the dog doing? *What* the cow say?

Although Claire omits various words which would be obligatory in the corresponding adult questions (e.g. *Where girl go?* shows omission of the auxiliary *did* and the determiner *the*), all the sentences in (50) show correct positioning of the italicised wh-words *where/what* at the beginning of the sentence.

A natural question to ask at this point is why it should be that from the very onset of multiword speech we find English children correctly preposing wh-words, and correctly positioning heads before their complements. The parameter-setting model of acquisition enables us to provide a principled answer to this question, by supposing that learning these aspects of word order involves the comparatively simple task of setting each of two binary parameters (the Wh-Parameter, and the Head Position Parameter) at its appropriate value. This task will be a relatively straightforward one if each parameter involves a simple binary choice (e.g. a language either does or doesn't position heads before their complements, and either does or doesn't front/prepose wh-words). Given such an assumption, the child could set the parameter correctly on the basis of minimal linguistic experience. For example, once the child is able to analyse the structure of an adult sentence such as *Help Daddy!* and knows that it contains a verb phrase comprising the head verb *help* and its complement *Daddy*, then (on the assumption that the Language Faculty specifies that all heads of a given type behave uniformly with regard to whether they are positioned before or after their complements), the child will automatically know that all verbs in English are normally positioned before their complements, and so the child will be able to set the Head Position Parameter at the head-first setting appropriate for verb phrases (and indeed for all other types of phrase) in English. Similarly, once a child is able to analyse the structure of an adult sentence like *Where's Daddy going?* and knows that *where* is the complement of the verb *going* (as in the echo question *Daddy is going where?*) and has been moved to the front of the sentence, the child can immediately infer that English is a Wh-Movement language, and set the Wh-Parameter at the appropriate value.

So, child utterances like (49) and (50) are consistent with the parameter-setting model of acquisition outlined in this section. However, influential research by Nina Hyams in the 1980s uncovered what appeared to be some puzzling counter-evidence to the claim that children set parameters at their appropriate setting as soon as they start learning how to combine words together to form phrases and sentences. Hyams observed that in the very earliest sentences which they produce (until around two-and-a-quarter years of age), English children frequently omit subjects and produce seemingly subjectless sentences such as those below:

> (51)   Play it. Eating cereal. Shake hands. See window. Want more apple. No go in

Hyams argued that child sentences like (51) are not actually subjectless, but rather have an implicit/understood 'silent' subject. One piece of evidence she adduced in support of this claim comes from the observation that when children produce a seemingly subjectless sentence, they sometimes produce an expanded version of the same sentence immediately afterwards in which the implicit subject is made explicit – as the following examples (from Braine 1971) produced by Stevie at ages 2;1–2;2 illustrate:

(52) (a)   Go nursery . . . Lucy go nursery.
  (b)   Push Stevie . . . Betty push Stevie
  (c)   No touch . . . This no touch
  (d)   Want that . . . Andrew want that
  (e)   Plug in . . . Andrew plug in

Hyams concluded from this that seemingly subjectless child sentences such as (51) have an understood 'silent' subject, and argued that this is the same kind of null pronoun subject (= *pro*) as is found in adult Italian sentences such as (44). This would mean that a child sentence like *Want more apple* would have the fuller structure shown informally below:

> (53)   *pro* want more apple

So, according to Hyams, the child uses the null pronoun *pro* in sentences like (53) where an adult would use the overt subject pronoun *I*. The more general conclusion which Hyams drew was that Child English (at the very earliest stage of development) is a null subject language and so allows verbs to have null subjects. If so, this would provide an obvious challenge to the claim that children correctly set parameters from the outset, since adult English is a not a null subject language.

What this would imply is that children sometimes initially adopt the wrong setting for a parameter, and so have to **reset** the parameter at the right setting subsequently. So, for example, an English child who initially sets the Null Subject Parameter at the wrong [+NS] (i.e. 'allows null subjects') value would subsequently have to reset the parameter at the right [−NS] (i.e. 'doesn't allow null subjects') value. This raises two questions: (i) How does the child arrive at the wrong setting for the parameter in the first place? and (ii) How does the child subsequently come to reset the parameter at the right setting subsequently?

Since adult English speakers typically don't use null subjects (unlike adult Italian speakers, who use null subjects with around two-thirds of their finite verbs), Hyams concluded that the speech input children receive can't mislead them into thinking that English is a null subject language. So why do children wrongly start out by assuming that English allows null subjects? The answer suggested by Hyams was that the Language Faculty provides children with an initial setting for each parameter (i.e. a setting for children to adopt as an initial hypothesis, to be modified if and when they encounter evidence that the initial setting provided by the Language Faculty is not right for the particular language they are acquiring). The initial setting for the Null Subject Parameter, Hyams hypothesised, is [+NS] 'allow null subjects'. This would mean that the Language Faculty in effect tells children 'Assume that any language you are acquiring allows null subjects unless and until you find evidence to the contrary.' Once children come across evidence that English does not allow null subjects, the Language Faculty will then automatically reset the Null Subject Parameter at the [−NS] 'doesn't allow null subjects' value appropriate for English.

But what kind of evidence could English children come across that would make them reset the Null Subject Parameter in this way? Hyams' answer was the following. She noted that a general property of non-null subject languages like English is that they have so-called **expletive pronouns** – that is, pronouns which have no reference (i.e. don't refer to anything) but simply serve the function of filling the subject position in a sentence when it would otherwise be empty, in order to satisfy the requirement for every finite verb to have an overt subject in a non-null-subject language like English. English has two such expletive pronouns, namely *it* and *there* which function as expletive subject pronouns in the kind of uses illustrated in (54) below:

(54) (a)   *It* is obvious that Maria lied
     (b)   *There* have been three students arrested

Because (when used as expletive pronouns) they have no reference, such pronouns cannot be questioned by a question word like *what?/where?* (cf. **What is obvious that Maria lied?/*Where have been three students arrested?*). Hyams hypothesised that null subject languages don't have expletive subject pronouns – a claim seemingly borne out by the observation that the Italian counterparts of (54) given in (55) below do not contain expletive pronouns:

(55) (a)   È   evidente   che   Maria   ha   mentito
            Is   obvious   that   Maria   has   lied
     (b)   Sono   stati   arrestati   tre   studenti
            Are   been   arrested   three   students

She therefore conjectured that the acquisition of expletive subject pronouns by English children serves as a **trigger** for the Language Faculty to reset the Null

Subject Parameter from its initial value [+NS] 'allows null subjects' to the [−NS] 'doesn't allow null subjects' value appropriate for English. And she maintained that English children acquire expletive pronouns at around age 2;3 (i.e. 2 years; 3 months), thus accounting for why they cease to use null subjects from that point on.

Hyams' findings were potentially extremely important because they appeared to provide evidence that children sometimes initially mis-set parameters and subsequently have to reset them, taking us towards a **parameter-resetting** model of acquisition in which the Language Faculty gives the child an initial setting for each parameter, and the child then has to decide whether to reset the parameter or not (English children subsequently resetting the initial [+NS] value of the Null Subject Parameter, but Italian children not doing so). However, since her work was first published, a number of researchers have cast doubt on Hyams' claim that children sometimes mis-set parameters. For example, nobody has ever found any convincing evidence of children mis-setting other parameters like the Wh-Parameter or the Head Position Parameter. Furthermore, her claim that English children go through an initial stage when they mis-set the Null Subject Parameter and use Italian-style null *pro* subjects turns out to be questionable.

Particularly damning evidence against Hyams' analysis came from a contrastive study of American and Italian children reported in Valian (1991). While the Italian children in her study (like Italian adults) used null subjects in all types of finite clause (both main clauses and subordinate clauses), the American children by contrast used null subjects only in *main* clauses, never in *subordinate* clauses (not one of the 132 subordinate clauses produced by the American children in her study had a null subject). So, while American children might omit the main-clause subject *I* in a sentence like *I think he likes chocolate* (and say *Think he likes chocolate*), they never omitted the subordinate clause subject *he* (hence never said **I think likes chocolate*); by contrast, Italian children would freely omit either or both subjects. Since it is a defining characteristic of a null subject language like Italian that *any* (finite) verb in *any* type of clause can have a null subject, Valian's finding undermined Hyams' claim that English children go through an initial stage in which they use Italian-style null *pro* subjects.

Furthermore, research by other scholars called into question her claim that the acquisition of expletive subject pronouns triggers automatic resetting of the Null Subject Parameter. If this were so, we should expect to find that immediately English children acquire expletive pronouns, they stop using null subjects. However, Valian's (1991) study reported that the American children she studied continued to use null subjects long *after* they had acquired expletives. Conversely, a study by Ingham (1992) reported that a girl called Sophie stopped using null subjects several months *before* she acquired expletive pronouns. Studies like these provided evidence that (contrary to what Hyams claimed), there is no correlation between the point at which children acquire expletive pronouns and the point at which they stop using null subjects. This means that Hyams' account of how the Language Faculty triggers the resetting of the Null Subject Parameter is problematic.

But if English children who omit subjects in sentences like (53) aren't using an Italian-style null *pro* subject, how do their sentences seemingly come to have missing subjects? An intriguing answer to this question was suggested by Rizzi (2000), who argued that missing subjects in Child English are the result of a phenomenon of **Truncation** which is also found in colloquial adult English. In adult English, we often leave unpronounced a sequence of one or more 'weak' (i.e. short, unstressed) words at the beginning of a sentence, perhaps for phonological reasons (e.g. the desire to start a sentence with a stressed syllable). This results in truncated sentences such as those below (in which the italicised words marked by strikethrough in parentheses are 'silent' - i.e. unpronounced):

(56) (a)   Can't find it (= ~~I~~ can't find it, with truncation of *I*)
   (b)   Know anything about it? (= ~~Do you~~ know anything about it? with truncation of *do you*)
   (c)   Time is it? (= ~~What~~ time is it? with truncation of *what*)
   (d)   Nice day, isn't it? (= ~~It's a~~ nice day, isn't it? with truncation of *It's a*)

An interesting property of truncation is that it can only affect words at the beginning of a sentence, and not, e.g., words in the middle of a sentence. So, for example, it is not possible to truncate *can* and/or *we* in the middle of sentences like those below:

(57) (a)   What can we do?
   (b)   *What ~~can~~ we do?
   (c)   *What can ~~we~~ do?
   (d)   *What ~~can we~~ do?

Rizzi argues that subjectless sentences like those in (51) produced by English children can come about as a result of them truncating a weak subject pronoun when it is the first word in a sentence. Some evidence that truncation operates in Child English comes from sentences like those below, produced by a girl called Claire at age 2;1 (in which the words in parentheses marked by strikethrough have been truncated; the data are from the Appendix to Hill 1983):

(58) (a)   Bunnies doing? (~~What are the~~ bunnies doing?)
   (b)   Mummy gone? (~~Where has~~ Mummy gone?)
   (c)   This go? (~~Where does~~ this go?)

So, according to Rizzi, missing subjects in Child English are not the result of children mis-setting the Null Subject Parameter, but rather are the result of them behaving like adult English speakers in truncating a sequence of one or more weak words at the beginning of a sentence. Given that very young children have problems in producing long sentences, it is not surprising that children initially tend to make more frequent use of truncation than adults.

The assumption that missing subjects in Child English are the result of Truncation rather than of parameter-mis-setting accounts for the finding reported by Valian (1991) that English children only omit subjects in *main* clauses, not in *subordinate* clauses. This is because truncation only affects one or more words *at the beginning of* a sentence/main clause, and the subject of a main clause is typically the first word in a sentence (whereas the subject of a subordinate clause is not). It follows from this that whereas (in a sentence like *I think he likes chocolate*) English children could truncate the main-clause subject *I* (and say *Think he likes chocolate*) because *I* is the first word in the sentence, they would not truncate the subordinate-clause subject *he* (and say **I think likes chocolate*) because *he* is not positioned at the beginning of the overall sentence, and only words at the very beginning of a sentence can be truncated.

Rizzi's truncation analysis also accounts for an important research finding reported in a study by Roeper and Rohrbacher (2000). They noted that while English children often omit subjects in statements like *I don't like cabbage* (truncating the subject and saying instead *Don't like cabbage*), they never omit subjects in wh-questions like *What don't you like?* and hence never say **What don't like?* Why should this be? Rizzi's truncation analysis provides a straightforward answer. In a statement such as *I don't like cabbage*, the subject *I* is the first word in the sentence, and so can be truncated. But in a wh-question such as *What don't you like?* the subject *you* is the third word in the sentence and so cannot be truncated (because truncation can only affect a continuous sequence of one or more 'weak' words at the very beginning of a sentence).

To summarise: there is a wide range of research suggesting that the 'missing' subjects found in the earliest sentences produced by English-speaking children are the result of Truncation (a process by which a sequence of one or more weak words at the beginning of a sentence are 'silent' and so unpronounced), and not the result of the children initially misanalysing English as a null subject language. On the contrary, the fact that English-speaking children (unlike Italian children) never omit subjects in the middle of sentences provides clear-cut evidence that they correctly identify English as a non-null subject language from the outset. And this finding is in turn compatible with the more general conclusion that children set parameters correctly from the very earliest stage in the acquisition of syntax.

However, this conclusion raises the question of how children come to arrive at the appropriate setting for a given parameter, and what kind(s) of evidence they make use of in setting parameters. There are two types of evidence which we might expect to be available to the language learner in principle, namely **positive evidence** and **negative evidence**. Positive evidence comprises a set of observed expressions illustrating a particular phenomenon: for example, if the speech input of children acquiring English as their native language is made up of structures in which heads precede their complements, this provides children with positive evidence that enables them to set the Head Position Parameter at the head-first (head-before-complement) setting appropriate to English. Negative evidence might be of two kinds – **direct** or **indirect**. Direct negative evidence could come from the correction of children's errors by other speakers of the language. However, (contrary to what is often imagined) correction plays a fairly insignificant role in language acquisition, for two reasons. Firstly, correction is relatively infrequent: adults simply don't correct all the errors children make (if they did, children would soon become inhibited and discouraged from speaking). Secondly, children are notoriously unresponsive to correction, as the following dialogue (from McNeill 1966: 69) illustrates:

(59)   CHILD: Nobody don't like me
            ADULT: No, say: 'Nobody likes me'
            CHILD: Nobody don't like me
                (*8 repetitions of this dialogue*)
            ADULT: No, now listen carefully. Say 'Nobody likes me'
            CHILD: Oh, nobody don't likes me

As Hyams (1986: 91) notes: 'Negative evidence in the form of parental disapproval or overt corrections has no discernible effect on the child's developing syntactic ability.'

Direct negative evidence might also take the form of self-correction by other speakers. Such self-corrections tend to have a characteristic intonation and rhythm of their own, and may either involve simply replacing the incorrect (italicised) word or phrase by the correct (bold-printed) one as in (60a–c) below, or be signalled explicitly by material like that underlined in (60d–e):

(60) (a)   You can't put a price on the way that the Olympics will *inspirate* . . . **inspire** future generations (Ray Stubbs, Talk Sport Radio)

    (b)   I *don't still* . . . **still don't** think we're good enough to win the under-21 championship (John Barnes, Talk Sport Radio)

    (c)   *He just not gets* . . . **He just doesn't get** his feet ready in time (Michael Owen, BT Sport TV)

    (d)   He was *at tune* . . . <u>sorry</u> **in tune** <u>I should say</u> . . . with the car (David Coulthard, BBC2 TV)

    (e)   He's coming *onto form* . . . <u>or</u> **into form** at the right time (Stuart Storey, BBC3 TV)

However, self-correction is arguably too infrequent a phenomenon to play a major role in the acquisition process.

Rather than say that children rely on direct negative evidence, we might instead imagine that they learn from **indirect negative evidence** (i.e. evidence relating to the non-occurrence of certain types of structure). Suppose that a child's experience includes no examples of structures in which heads follow their complements (e.g. no prepositional phrases like **dinner after* in which the head preposition *after* follows its complement *dinner*, and no verb phrases such as **cake eat* in which the head verb *eat* follows its complement *cake*). On the basis of such indirect negative evidence (i.e. observing that such structures never occur in English), the child might infer that English is not a head-last language.

Although it might seem natural to suppose that indirect negative evidence plays some role in the acquisition process, there are potential **learnability** problems posed by any such claim. After all, the fact that a given construction does not occur in a given chunk of the child's experience does not provide conclusive evidence that the structure is ungrammatical, since it may well be that the non-occurrence of the relevant structure in the relevant chunk of experience is an accidental (rather than a systematic) gap. Thus, the child would need to process a massive chunk of experience in order to be sure that non-occurrence reflects ungrammaticality. It is implausible that young children process massive chunks of experience in this way and search through it for negative evidence about the non-occurrence of certain types of structure, since this would impose an unrealistic memory load on them. In any case, given the assumption that parameters are binary and single-valued, negative evidence becomes entirely unnecessary: after all, once the child hears a prepositional phrase like *with Daddy* and is able to parse it and so knows that the head preposition *with* precedes its complement *Daddy*, the child will have positive evidence that English allows head-first order in prepositional phrases; and given the assumption that the Head Position Parameter is a binary one and the further assumption that each parameter allows only a single setting, then it follows (as a matter of logical necessity) that if English allows head-first prepositional phrases, it will not allow head-last prepositional phrases. Thus, in order for the child to know that English doesn't allow head-last prepositional phrases, the child does not need negative evidence from the non-occurrence of such structures, but rather can rely on positive evidence from the occurrence of the converse order in head-first structures (on the assumption that if a given structure is head-first, the Language Faculty specifies that it cannot be head-last). And, as already noted, a minimal amount of positive evidence is required in order to identify English as a uniformly head-first language (i.e. a language in which *all* heads precede their complements). Learnability considerations such as these led Chomsky (1986a: 55) to conclude that 'There is good reason to believe that children learn language from positive evidence only.' The claim that children do not make use of negative evidence in setting parameters is known as the **No-Negative-Evidence Hypothesis**; it is a hypothesis which has been widely adopted in acquisition research for several decades.

1.9   Summary

We began this chapter in §1.2 by noting that contemporary work in syntax is descriptive rather than prescriptive, and by comparing three different methods of collecting data: using a corpus, or relying on the intuitions of a native speaker, or conducting experiments on groups of subjects. In §1.3, we took a brief look at traditional grammar, noting that this is a taxonomic (i.e. classificatory) system in which the syntax of a given sentence is described by assigning each of the constituents in the sentence a label representing its grammatical category, and saying what grammatical function it has. In §1.4, we looked at the question of what aspects of grammar can plausibly be taken to be universal, and saw that these include categories, operations (such as Merge, Movement, Agreement and Ellipsis) and principles such as the following:

(61)   **Economy Principle** (= 38)
         Structures and the operations used to form them should be as economical as possible.

In §1.5, we explored the nature of universals and examined the Strong Minimalist Thesis put forward by Chomsky under which universals are a reflection either of interface conditions, or of more general biological principles or physical principles of natural law (e.g. the Economy Principle (61) is a reflection of principles of efficient computation); the theory is *minimalist* in the sense that it attempts to minimise (and, in the best-case scenario, eliminate) recourse to other types of constructs or principles. In §1.6, we went on to look at the nature of language acquisition and saw that the most fundamental questions for a theory of language acquisition to answer are how children come to acquire most of the grammar of their native language/s in as little as 5 per cent of their life span, and why acquisition is uniform across children (in the sense that different children acquiring different languages appear to go through much the same stages of acquisition). We saw that Chomsky's answer to such questions is that the course of language acquisition is genetically guided by an innate Language Faculty. In §1.7, we saw that the grammars of natural languages vary along a number of parameters. We looked at three such parameters, which can be summarised as follows:

(62)   **Wh-Parameter**
         Some languages (like English) allow movement of a wh-constituent to the front of a clause, whereas others (like Chinese) leave wh-constituents in situ.

(63)   **Null Subject Parameter/NSP**
         Some languages (like Italian) allow a null pronoun (= *pro*) to be used as the subject of any finite (auxiliary or main) verb in any clause, whereas other languages (like English) do not.

(64)   **Head Position Parameter/HPP**
         Languages vary with respect to whether or not they position the head words of particular types of phrase before or after their complements.

I hypothesised that each such parameter has a binary choice of settings. In §1.8, I argued that the syntactic learning task which children face involves parameter setting – i.e. determining which of two possible settings is the appropriate one for each parameter in the language being acquired. I conjectured that if parameters have binary settings (e.g. so that a given kind of structure in a given language is either head-first or head-last), we should expect to find evidence that children correctly set parameters from the very onset of multiword speech, and I presented evidence that this is so. I concluded that the acquisition of grammar involves the twin tasks of lexical learning (i.e. acquiring a lexicon/vocabulary) and parameter setting. I went on to ask what kind of evidence children use in setting parameters and concluded that they use positive evidence from their experience of the occurrence of specific types of structure (e.g. head-first structures, or null subject structures, or Wh-Movement structures).

1.10   Bibliographical background

For discussion of the issue touched on in §1.2 of the relative merits and reliability of different methods of collecting linguistic data, see Schütze (1996), Cowart (1997), Weskott and Fanselow (2011) and Schütze and Sprouse (2012). For discussion of the drawbacks of collecting linguistic data from a corpus (or from the Web), see Schütze (2009). For a defence of the use of introspective judgment data rather than other sources of data, see Newmeyer (2003, 2005a, 2006a, 2006b) in relation to usage-based data, and Sprouse (2011), Sprouse, Schütze and Almeida (2011) and Sprouse and Almeida (2011, 2012a,b) in relation to experimental data. On the syntax of sentences like (5) in the main text, see Danckaert and Haegeman (2014). For a fuller account of the nature of grammatical categories discussed in §1.3, see Chapter 2 and the references given there. On the (illocutionary) force of sentences, see Huddleston (1994); on clause types, see Cheng (1997). For more extensive discussion of the notion of I-language, see Smith (2004). For a defence of the idea outlined in §1.4 that there is a universal set of categories in language, see Greenberg (1963) and Newmeyer (2007); for a dissenting view, see Haspelmath (2007, 2010). For a survey of various types of ellipsis, see van Craenenbroek and Merchant (2013). The idea that grammars incorporate a set of universal principles is developed in Chomsky (1981); the Economy Principle derives from Chomsky (1989: 69). The Strong Minimalist Thesis discussed in §1.5 is developed in Chomsky (1993, 1995, 1998, 1999, 2001, 2002, 2005, 2007, 2008, 2010, 2013, 2014): for a critical evaluation, see Al-Mutairi (2011, 2014) and Atkinson and Al-Mutairi (2012). The idea that recursion might be the defining characteristic of natural language is called into question by research by Everett (2005a,b, 2006, 2009) arguing that there is at least one language (Pirahã) which does not have recursive structures (but see Nevins, Pesetsky and Rodriguez 2009ba,b for a reply). For a critique of the idea that Merge is conceptually necessary, see Postal (2003). For discussion of the idea of an innate Language Faculty discussed in §1.6, see Lightfoot (1999), Anderson and Lightfoot (2002), Antony and Hornstein (2003), Givón (2002), Hauser, Chomsky and Fitch (2002), Fitch, Hauser and Chomsky (2005), Berwick et al. (2011) and Chomsky (2010, 2013, 2014); for a more critical view, see Everett (2005a,b, 2006, 2009) and Sampson (2005), and for a reply to such criticism, see Chomsky's contributions to Antony and Hornstein (2003). For evaluation of the idea that children learn languages in spite of receiving *degenerate input*, see

Pullum and Scholz (2002), Thomas (2002), Sampson (2002), Fodor and Crowther (2002), Lasnik and Uriagereka (2002), Legate and Yang (2002), Crain and Pietroski (2002), Scholz and Pullum (2002), Lewis and Elman (2002), Gualmini and Crain (2005) and Berwick et al. (2011). For discussion of the critical period in language acquisition, see Lenneberg (1967), Hurford (1991) and Smith (1998, 2004); on Genie, see Curtiss (1977) and Rymer (1993). On evidence of a double dissociation between linguistic and cognitive abilities, see Clahsen (2008). The hypothesis put forward in §1.7 that grammatical differences between languages can be reduced to a small number of parameters was developed in Chomsky (1981). A complication glossed over in the text discussion of the Null Subject Parameter is posed by languages in which only some finite verb forms can have null subjects: see Vainikka and Levy (1999) and the collection of papers in Jaeggli and Safir (1989) for illustration and discussion. The discussion of the Wh-Parameter is simplified by ignoring the complication that some languages allow more than one wh-word to be fronted in wh-questions (see Bošković 2002a; Grohmann 2006; and Surányi 2006), and the additional complication that Wh-Movement appears to be optional in some languages, either in main clauses or in main and complement clauses alike (see Denham 2000, and Cheng and Rooryck 2000); on wh-in-situ structures, see Pesetsky (1987), Cheng (1997), Cole and Hermon (1998), Reinhart (1998) and Bruening (2007). On non-uniform settings for the Head Position Parameter in German, see Koster (1975), Biberauer, Holmberg and Roberts (2007) and Jurka (2010). Although it is claimed in the main text that parameters have binary settings, it should be noted that some researchers have assumed that parameters can have more than two alternative settings (e.g. Manzini and Wexler 1987). For discussion of a wide-range parametric variation between languages, see Cinque and Kayne (2005). For a critique of the idea that cross-linguistic variation is reducible to a small number of structural *parameters*, see Culicover and Nowak (2003), Newmeyer (2004, 2006c), Abeillé and Borsley (2006) and Boeckx (2010); for a defence of parameters, see Roberts and Holmberg (2006). For a defence of the claim made in §1.8 that parameters are correctly set by children at a very early stage in their development, see Wexler (1998). On the acquisition of the Null Subject Parameter by English-speaking children, see Hyams (1986), Valian (1991), Ingham (1992), Rizzi (2000) and Roeper and Rohrbacher (2000). On truncated null subjects in spoken English (and in diary styles of written English), see Thrasher (1977), Haegeman (1990, 1997, 2000a, 2000b, 2008), Rizzi (1994, 2000), Haegeman and Ihsane (1999, 2002), Franks (2005, fn. 5) and Weir (2008, 2012). The claim that no negative evidence is used in setting parameters is made in Chomsky (1981: 8–9); supporting evidence can be found in McNeill (1966), Brown, Cazden and Bellugi (1968), Brown and Hanlon (1970), Braine (1971), Bowerman (1988), Morgan and Travis (1989) and Marcus (1993) – but for potential counter-evidence, see Lappin and Shieber (2007). On how children set parameters, see Fodor (2001) and Fodor and Sakas (2005). For technical accounts of language acquisition within the framework used here, see Guasti (2002) and Lust (2006).

Exercise 1.1

This exercise is about parameter settings. Sentences 1–10 below are designed to show how movement operations can mask parameter settings, while sentences 11–19 aim to show that this is also true of other languages, and that some languages don't always have uniform settings for any given parameter. Sentences 1–10 are taken from various plays written by Shakespeare, representing a variety of English sometimes referred to as *Elizabethan English* (because it was spoken during the reign of Queen Elizabeth I): Elizabethan English (like present-day English) was a uniformly head-first language in which all heads were canonically (i.e. normally) positioned in front of their complements. In relation to the sentences below, show how movement operations which front various types of expression could mask the head-first setting of the Head Position Parameter in Elizabethan English.

1. Seawater shalt thou drink (Prospero, *The Tempest*, I.ii)
2. That letter hath she delivered (Speed, *Two Gentlemen of Verona*, II.i)
3. Friend hast thou none (Duke, *Measure for Measure*, III.i)
4. True is it that we have seen better days (Duke Senior, *As You Like It*, II.vii)
5. She may more suitors have (Tranio, *The Taming of the Shrew*, I.ii)
6. Run you to the citadel! (Iago, *Othello*, V.i)
7. Came you from the church? (Tranio, *Taming of the Shrew*, III.ii)
8. What think you he hath confessed? (First Lord, *All's Well That Ends Well*, IV.iii)
9. What will this come to? (Flavius, *Timon of Athens*, I.ii)
10. What visions have I seen! (Titania, *Midsummer Night's Dream*, V.i)

In §1.7 in the main text, it was noted that there are some languages which don't have a uniform setting for the Head Position Parameter, in the sense that some types of head precede their complements, and other types of head follow their complements. German is a language of this type, in which some heads (e.g. prepositions, determiners and complementisers) canonically precede their complements, but others (e.g. auxiliary and main verbs) canonically follow their complements. However, as noted in §1.7, the picture is complicated by the existence of a handful of exceptional prepositions which follow their complements. Discuss the extent to which German sentences like those in 11–15 below (kindly provided for me by Harald Clahsen) bear out this claim, and say which examples prove problematic and why.

11. Hans   muss   stolz   auf   seine   Mutter   sein
    Hans   must   proud   of   his   mother   be
    'Hans must be proud of his mother'

12. Hans   muss   auf   seine   Mutter   stolz   sein
    Hans   must   of   his   mother   proud   be
    'Hans must be proud of his mother'

13. Hans geht den   Fluss entlang
    Hans goes the   river along
    'Hans goes along the river'

14. Hans muss die Aufgaben lösen
    Hans must the exercises do
    'Hans must do the exercises'

15. Ich glaube dass Hans die Aufgaben lösen muss
    I   think   that Hans the exercises do   must
    'I think that Hans must do the exercises'

Likewise, in the text it was claimed that the Wh-Parameter has a uniform setting in each language, so that a given language either does or doesn't systematically prepose wh-expressions. Discuss the potential problems posed for this claim by colloquial French interrogative structures such as those below:

16. Où   tu   vas?
    Where you   go?
    'Where are you going?'

17. Tu   vas   où?
    You   go   where?
    'Where are you going?'

18. Dis-moi où   tu   vas
    Tell-me where you   go
    'Tell me where you are going'

19. *Dis-moi tu   vas   où
    Tell-me   you   go   where
    (intended as synonymous with 18)

Helpful hints

In relation to the sentences in 1–10, take *none* in 3, *more* in 5 and *what* in 10 to be quantifiers with a noun as their complement (and assume that the negative quantifier is spelled out as *no* if immediately followed by a nominal complement, but as *none* otherwise). Note that 1–5 are declarative sentences (used to make a statement), 6 is an imperative sentence (used to issue an order), 7–9 are interrogative sentences (used to ask a question) and 10 is an exclamative sentence (used to exclaim amazement). In relation to the German sentences in 11–15, make the following assumptions about their structure. In 11 and 12 *muss* is a finite (modal) verb, *Hans* is its subject and *stolz*proud *auf*of *seine*his *Mutter*mother *sein*be is its complement; *sein*be is an infinitive verb form and *stolz*proud *auf*of *seine*his *Mutter*mother is its complement; *stolz*proud is an adjective, and *auf*of *seine*his *Mutter*mother is its complement; *auf*of is a preposition and *seine*his *Mutter*mother is its complement. In 13 *geht*goes is a verb, *Hans* is its subject and *den*the *Fluss*river *entlang*along is its complement; *entlang*along is a preposition (or, more precisely, a postposition) and *den*the *Fluss*river is its complement; *den*the is a determiner and *Fluss*river is its complement. In 14 *muss*must is a finite verb, *Hans* is its subject and *die*the *Aufgaben*exercises *lösen*do is its complement; *lösen*do is a non-finite verb in the infinitive form, and *die*the *Aufgaben*exercises is its complement; *die*the is a determiner and *Aufgaben*exercises is its complement. In 15 *glaube*think is a finite verb, *ich*I is its subject and *dass*that *Hans die*the *Aufgaben*exercises *lösen*do *muss*must is its complement; *dass*that is a complementiser, and *Hans die*the *Aufgaben*exercises *lösen*do *muss*must is its complement; *muss*must is a finite verb, *Hans* is its subject and *die*the *Aufgaben*exercises *lösen*do is its complement; *lösen*do is a non-finite verb in the infinitive form and *die*the *Aufgaben*exercises is its complement; *die*the is a determiner and *Aufgaben*exercises is its complement.

In relation to the examples in 11–15, identify all the prepositions, complementisers and determiners you can find in the sentences, and say whether (as claimed above) these precede their complements. Likewise, identify all the (auxiliary and main) verbs found in the sentences, and say whether they do (or do not) follow their complements, as claimed above. Pay particular attention to any head which is an exception to the relevant generalisations about head position. Assume that exceptional word order can be accounted for either in lexical terms (e.g. that the dictionary entry for a particular preposition may say that it is an exceptional item which does not occupy the canonical head-first position found in typical prepositional phrases) or in structural terms (in that a particular kind of head may undergo a movement operation which moves it out of its canonical position). In relation to possible structural factors that mask the underlying word order in German, bear in mind that German is traditionally claimed to be a *verb-second/V2* language – i.e. a language in which a finite verb (= V) in a main clause is moved out of its canonical clause-final position into second position in the clause – e.g. into a position where it immediately follows some other constituent (e.g. a subject like *Hans* or *ich*I). In addition, comment on the problems posed by determining the canonical setting of the Head Position Parameter for adjectival phrases in German (i.e. in determining whether adjectives canonically precede or follow their complements).

In relation to the French sentences in 16–19, bear in mind that *Où*where *tu*you *vas*go and *Tu*you *vas*go *où*where are main clauses in 16/17 and complement clauses in 18/19 (in that they serve as the complement of the imperative verb *dis*tell in 18/19). Is there an asymmetry between how Wh-Movement works in main clauses and in complement clauses? Does this suggest that it may be too simplistic to posit a Wh-Parameter under which wh-expressions either are or aren't systematically preposed? Why?

Model answer for 1

The auxiliary verb *shalt* 'shall' has the subject *thou* 'you'singular' and the complement *drink seawater*. The main verb *drink* has the complement *seawater*. If no movement operations took place in the relevant sentence, we should expect to find the word order *Thou shalt drink seawater*, with the auxiliary *shalt* immediately preceding its complement *drink seawater*, and the verb *drink* immediately preceding its complement *seawater*, in keeping with the assumption that Elizabethan English has a head-first setting for the Head Position Parameter. However, the noun *seawater* undergoes a fronting/preposing operation in order to highlight it, and this means that instead of occupying its canonical position immediately after the verb *drink*, it is instead moved to a new position at the front of the overall sentence. Likewise, the auxiliary *shalt* undergoes a separate (Subject-Auxiliary) Inversion operation which means that instead of occupying its canonical position immediately preceding its complement *drink seawater*, it is instead moved to a new position immediately preceding its subject *thou*. The effect of these two movement operations is shown schematically below:

UNDERLYING ORDER: Thou <u>shalt</u> drink *seawater*   SUPERFICIAL ORDER: *Seawater* <u>shalt</u> thou drink

In the underlying order, the auxiliary *shalt* immediately precedes its complement *drink seawater*, and the verb *drink* immediately precedes its complement *seawater*. But preposing *seawater* and inverting *shalt* means that the verb *drink* no longer immediately precedes its complement *seawater*, and likewise that the auxiliary *shalt* no longer immediately precedes its complement *drink seawater*. The main theoretical point which our discussion here illustrates is that word-order parameters like the Head Position Parameter determine the canonical (i.e. 'normal') order of constituents rather than their actual order (which can be disrupted by movement operations). A point of incidental interest to note in relation to sentence 1 is that Inversion was not just restricted to interrogative sentences in Elizabethan English but could also take place in declaratives and other types of sentence. Moreover (as you will see from other examples in this exercise), it could affect main verbs as well as auxiliary verbs.

Model answer for 11

In 11, the preposition *auf*$_{of}$ precedes its complement *seine*$_{his}$ *Mutter*$_{mother}$, the adjective *stolz*$_{proud}$ precedes its complement *auf*$_{of}$ *seine*$_{his}$ *Mutter*$_{mother}$, but the verb *sein*$_{be}$ follows its complement *stolz*$_{proud}$ *auf*$_{of}$ *seine*$_{his}$ *Mutter*$_{mother}$. This suggests the following generalisation about the setting of the Head Parameter in German:

(i)   In German, (auxiliary and main) verbs immediately *follow* their complements, but other heads immediately *precede* their complements.

However, an apparent exception to the claim made in (i) is posed by the fact that the finite modal verb *muss*$_{must}$ in the main clause precedes its own complement *stolz*$_{proud}$ *auf*$_{of}$ *seine*$_{his}$ *Mutter*$_{mother}$ *sein*$_{be}$. This apparently exceptional word order is arguably attributable to the status of German as a so-called *verb-second* language – i.e. a language that has a Verb Fronting operation which moves a finite verb in a main clause out of the canonical clause-final position occupied by verbs (including by the modal verb *muss*$_{must}$ in 15) into second position within the clause: as a result of this movement operation, the verb *muss*$_{must}$ comes to follow the main-clause subject *Hans* – in the manner shown by the arrow below:

UNDERLYING ORDER: Hans stolz$_{proud}$ auf$_{of}$ seine$_{his}$ Mutter$_{mother}$ sein$_{be}$ *muss*$_{must}$

SUPERFICIAL ORDER: Hans *muss*$_{must}$ auf$_{of}$ seine$_{his}$ Mutter$_{mother}$ stolz$_{proud}$ sein$_{be}$

Since present-day English is not a V2 language, it could be argued that English and German differ in respect of a **Verb-Second Parameter** – i.e. in respect of whether or not all finite verbs move into second position in main clauses. (For a discussion of the structure of verb-second clauses in German, see Radford et al. 2009: 321–5 – though some of the material there may not be clear to you until you have read the first six chapters in this book.)

Exercise 1.2

This exercise is about how children set parameters. Below are examples of utterances produced by a girl called Lucy at age 24 months. Comment on whether Lucy has correctly set the Head Position Parameter, the Wh-Parameter and the Null Subject Parameter. Discuss the implications of the relevant data for the parameter-setting model of acquisition.

CHILD SENTENCE	ADULT COUNTERPART
1. What doing?	'What are you doing?'
2. Want bye-byes	'I want to go to sleep'
3. Daddy play with me	'Daddy played with me'; this was in reply to 'What did Daddy do in the park yesterday?'
4. Mummy go shops	'Mummy went to the shops'; this was in reply to 'Where did Mummy go?'
5. Where Daddy gone?	'Where's Daddy gone?'
6. Gone office	'He's gone to the office'
7. Me have yoghurt?	'Can I have a yoghurt?'
8. Daddy doing?	'What's Daddy doing?'
9. Cry	'(I) cry'; this was in reply to 'What do you do when Daddy gets cross with you?'
10. I play	'I play'; this was in reply to 'What do you do in the park?'
11. What me having?	'What am I having?'; this followed her mother saying 'Mummy's having fish for dinner'
12. No me have fish	'I'm not going to have fish'
13. Want bickies	'She wants some biscuits'; this was her reply to 'What does Dolly want?'
14. What Teddy have?	'What can Teddy have?'
15. Where going?	'Where are you going?'
16. What Nana eating?	'What's Grandma eating?'
17. Dolly gone?	'Where's Dolly gone?'
18. Watch te'vision	'I'm going to watch television'
19. Me have more	'I want to have some more'
20. Open door	'Open the door!'

Helpful hints

If Lucy has correctly set the Wh-Parameter, we should expect to find that she systematically preposes wh-expressions and positions them sentence-initially. If she has correctly set the Head Position Parameter, we should expect to find (e.g.) that she correctly positions the complement of a verb after the verb, and the complement of a preposition after the preposition; however, where the complement is a wh-expression, we expect to find that the complement is moved into sentence-initial position in order to satisfy the requirements of the Wh-Parameter (if the Wh-Parameter in some sense over-rides the Head Position Parameter). If Lucy has correctly set the Null Subject Parameter, we should expect to find that she does not use null subjects in finite clauses: however, it seems clear that many of the sentences produced by 2-year-old English children like Lucy do indeed have null subjects – and (as we saw in §1.7) this led Nina Hyams in influential research (1986, 1992) to conclude that English children go through a *null subject stage* in which they use Italian-style null (*pro*) subjects in finite clauses. If Hyams is right, this implies that children may sometimes start out with incorrect settings for a given parameter, and then later have to *re-set* the parameter – a conclusion which (if true) would provide an obvious challenge to the simple parameter-setting model of acquisition outlined in the main text.

However, the picture relating to the use of null subjects is complicated by the fact that although English does not have **finite null subjects** (i.e. the kind of null *pro* subject found in finite clauses in languages like Italian), it has three other types of null subject. One is the kind of **imperative null subject** found in imperatives such as *Shut up!* and *Don't say anything!* (Imperatives are sentences used to issue orders; they are the kind of sentences you can add *please* to – as in *Please don't say anything!*) Another is the kind of **non-finite null subject** found in a range of non-finite clauses in English (i.e. clauses containing a verb which is not marked for tense and agreement), including main clauses like *Why worry?* and complement clauses like those bracketed in *I want* [*to go home*] and *I like* [*playing tennis*]: the kind of null subject found in non-finite clauses in English is usually designated as *PRO* and called 'big PRO' (whereas the kind of null subject found in a finite clause in a null subject language like Italian is designated as *pro* and called 'little pro'. The terms *big* and *little* here simply reflect the fact that, in order to distinguish between these two different kinds of silent pronoun, PRO is written in 'big' capital letters, and *pro* in 'small' lower case letters). A third type of null subject found in English can be called a **truncated null subject**, because (as noted in §1.8) English has a process of Truncation that allows one or more weak words at the beginning of a sentence to be truncated (i.e. omitted) in certain types of style (e.g. diary styles of written English and informal styles of spoken English). Hence in colloquial English, a question like *Are you doing anything tonight?* can be reduced (by truncation) to *You doing anything tonight?* and further reduced (again by truncation) to *Doing anything tonight?* Truncation is also found in abbreviated written styles of English: for example, a diary entry might read *Went to a party. Had a great time. Got totally smashed* (with the subject *I* being truncated in each of the three sentences). An important constraint on truncation is that it can only affect words at the beginning of a sentence, not, for example, words in the middle of a sentence: hence, although we can truncate *are* and *you* in *Are you doing anything tonight?*, we can't truncate them in *What are you doing tonight?* (as we see from the ungrammaticality of **What doing tonight?*) since here *are* and *you* are preceded by *what* and hence occur in the middle of the sentence.

What all of this means is that in determining whether Lucy has mis-set the Null Subject Parameter and misanalysed English as a null subject language (i.e. a language which allows the kind of finite null 'little *pro*' subject found in Italian), you have to bear in mind the alternative possibility that the null subjects used by Lucy may represent one or more of the three kinds of null subject used in adult English (imperative null subjects, truncated null subjects and non-finite null subjects).

Since truncation occurs only sentence-initially (at the beginning of a sentence), but finite null (little *pro*) subjects in a genuine null subject language like Italian can occur in any subject position in a sentence, one way of telling the difference between a finite null subject and a truncated null subject is to see whether children omit subjects only when they are the first word in a sentence (which could be the result of Truncation), or whether they also omit subjects when they occur in the middle of sentences (as is the case in a genuine null subject language like Italian). Another way of differentiating the two is that in null subject languages like Italian with null finite *pro* subjects, we find that overt pronoun subjects are only used for emphasis, so that in an Italian sentence like *Lo faccio io* (literally 'It do I') the subject pronoun *io* 'I' has a contrastive interpretation, and the relevant sentence is paraphraseable in English as '*I* am the one who will do it' (where italics indicate contrastive stress): by contrast, in a non-null subject language like English, subject pronouns are not intrinsically emphatic – e.g. *he* doesn't necessarily have a contrastive interpretation in an English diary-style sentence such as *Went to see Jim. Thought he might help*). A third way of telling whether truncation is operative in Lucy's grammar is to see whether expressions other than subjects can be truncated, as can happen in adult English (e.g. *What time is it?* can be reduced to *Time is it?* via truncation in rapid spoken English).

At first sight, it might seem unlikely that (some of) Lucy's null subjects could be non-finite ('big PRO') null subjects, since all the clauses she produces in the data given above occur in finite contexts (i.e. in contexts where adults would use a finite clause). Note, however, that 2-year-old children typically go through a stage which Wexler (1994) calls the 'Optional Infinitives/OI' stage during which (in finite contexts) they sometimes produce finite clauses, and sometimes non-finite clauses (the relevant non-finite clauses typically containing an infinitive form like *go* or a participle like *going/gone*). Hence, an additional possibility to bear in mind is that some of Lucy's clauses may be non-finite and have non-finite ('big PRO') null subjects.

In relation to the sentences in 1–20, make the following assumptions. In 1 *doing* is a verb which has a null subject and the complement *what*. In 2 *want* is a verb which has a null subject and the complement *bye-byes*. In 3 *play* is a verb which has the subject *Daddy* and the complement *with me* (and in turn *me* is the complement of the preposition *with*). In 4 *go* is a verb which has the subject *Mummy* and the complement *shops*. In 5 *gone* is a verb which has the subject *Daddy* and the complement *where*. In 6 *gone* is a verb which has a null subject and the complement *office*. In 7 *have* is a verb which has the subject *me* and the complement *yoghurt*. In 8 *doing* is a verb which has the subject *Daddy*, and its complement is a null counterpart of *what*. In 9 *cry* is a verb with a null subject. In 10, *play* is a verb and *I* is its subject. In 11, *having* is a verb which has the subject *me* and the complement *what*. In 12 *no* is a negative particle which has the complement *me have fish* (assume that *no* is the kind of word which doesn't have a subject), and *have* is a verb which has the subject *me* and the complement *fish*. In 13 *want* is a verb which has a null subject and the complement *bickies*. In 14 *have* is a verb which has the subject *Teddy* and the complement *what*. In 15 *going* is a verb which has a null subject and the complement *where*. In 16 *eating* is a verb which has the subject *Nana* and the complement *what*. In 17 *gone* is a verb which has the subject *Dolly* and its complement is a null counterpart of *where*. In 18 *watch* is a verb which has a null subject and the complement *te'vision*. In 19 *have* is a verb which has the subject *me* and the complement *more*. In 20 *open* is a verb whose subject is null and whose complement is *door*.

Model answer for 1

In *What doing?* the verb *doing* has an overt complement *what* and a null subject of some kind. Since the complement *what* does not occupy the normal postverbal position associated with complements in English (cf. the position of the complement *something* in *Do something!*), *what* has clearly undergone Wh-Movement: this suggests that Lucy has correctly set the Wh-Parameter at the 'requires Wh-Movement' value appropriate for English. Because the complement *what* has undergone Wh-Movement, we cannot tell (from this sentence) whether Lucy generally positions (unmoved) complements after their heads: in other words, this particular sentence provides us with no evidence of whether Lucy has correctly set the Head Position Parameter or not (though other examples in the exercise do).

Much more difficult to answer is the question of whether Lucy has correctly set the Null Subject Parameter at the value appropriate to English, and hence (tacitly) 'knows' that finite clauses do not allow a null finite *pro* subject in English. At first sight, it might seem as if Lucy has wrongly analysed English as a null subject language (and hence mis-set the Null Subject Parameter), since *What doing?* has a null subject of some kind. But the crucial question here is: what kind of null subject does the verb *doing* have? It clearly cannot have an imperative null subject, since the sentence is interrogative in force, not imperative (i.e. it is a question, not an order). Nor can it have a truncated null subject, since truncated subjects occur only in sentence-initial position (i.e. as the first word in a sentence), and *what* is the first word in the sentence in *What doing?* (since preposed wh-words occupy sentence-initial position in questions). This leaves two other possibilities. One is that the null subject in *What doing?* is the 'little *pro*' subject found in finite clauses in genuine null subject languages like Italian: since the verb *doing* is non-finite, this would entail positing that the sentence *What doing?* contains a null counterpart of the finite auxiliary *are* (raising questions about why the auxiliary is null rather than overt); this in turn would mean that Lucy has indeed mis-set the Null Subject Parameter (raising questions about how she comes to do so, and why she doesn't mis-set the other two parameters we are concerned with here). However, an alternative possibility is that the structure *What doing?* is a non-finite clause (like adult questions such as *Why worry?*) and has the kind of non-finite ('big PRO') null subject found in non-finite clauses in many languages (English included). If so (i.e. if *What doing?* is a non-finite clause which has the structure *What PRO doing?*), there would be no evidence that Lucy has mis-set the Null Subject Parameter – i.e. no evidence that she ever produces finite clauses with a 'little *pro*' subject. This in turn would mean that we can maintain the hypothesis put forward in the main text that children correctly set parameters at their appropriate value from the very earliest stages of the acquisition of syntax. The error Lucy makes in producing sentences like *What doing?* lies in not yet having learned that main clauses generally have to be finite in English, and that main-clause questions generally have to contain a finite auxiliary.

2   Words

2.1   Overview

This chapter provides a more in-depth look at the grammatical properties of words than was possible in the brief sketch provided in §1.3. It begins by recapitulating (and exploring in more detail) what was said about the categorial properties of words in §1.3, and goes on to explore how we determine what grammatical category a given word belongs to in a given use. In the course of the discussion, some new categories will be introduced which are not familiar from traditional grammar. We will see that categorial information alone is not sufficient to describe the grammatical properties of words and that a more fine-grained analysis requires the use of **grammatical features**.

2.2   Grammatical categories

In §1.3, we saw that words are assigned to grammatical categories in traditional grammar on the basis of their shared semantic, morphological and syntactic properties. The kind of semantic criteria (sometimes called 'notional' criteria) used to categorise words in traditional grammar are illustrated in much simplified form below:

(1) (i)   Verbs denote actions (*go, destroy, buy, eat*, etc.)
   (ii)   Nouns denote entities (*car, cat, hill, John*, etc.)
   (iii)   Adjectives denote states (*ill, happy, rich*, etc.)
   (iv)   Adverbs denote manner (*badly, slowly, painfully, cynically* etc.)
   (v)   Prepositions denote location (*under, over, outside, in, on* etc.)

However, semantically based criteria for identifying categories must be used with care: for example, *assassination* denotes an action but is a noun, not a verb; *illness* denotes a state but is a noun, not an adjective; in *fast food*, the word *fast* denotes the manner in which the food is prepared but is an adjective, not an adverb; and *Cambridge* denotes a location but is a noun, not a preposition. Because semantic criteria can give misleading results if not applied carefully, it is generally more reliable to use morphosyntactic (i.e. morphological and syntactic) criteria to categorise words.

The **morphological** criteria for categorising words concern their **inflectional** and **derivational** properties. Inflectional properties relate to different forms of the same word (e.g. the plural form of a noun like *cat* is formed by adding the plural inflection *-s* to give the form *cats*); derivational properties relate to the processes by which a word can be used to form a different kind of word by the addition of an **affix** of some kind (e.g. by adding *-ness* to the adjective *ill* we can form the noun *illness*). Although English has a highly impoverished system of inflectional morphology, there are nonetheless two major categories of word which have distinctive inflectional properties – namely **nouns** and **verbs**. We can identify the class of nouns in terms of the fact that (countable) nouns generally inflect for **number**, and thus have distinct **singular** and **plural** forms, as we see from pairs like *dog/dogs, man/men, ox/oxen*, etc. Accordingly, we can differentiate a noun like *fool* from an adjective like *foolish* in that only (regular, countable) nouns like *fool* – not adjectives like *foolish* – can carry the noun plural inflection *-s*: cf.

(2)   They are *fools* [noun]/**foolishes* [adjective]

There are several complications which should be pointed out, however. One is the existence of irregular nouns like *sheep* which are invariable and hence have a common singular/plural form (cf. *one sheep, two sheep*). A second is that some nouns are intrinsically singular (and so have no plural form) by virtue of their meaning: only those nouns (called **count/countable nouns**) that denote entities which can be counted have a plural form (e.g. *chair* – cf. *one chair, two chairs*); some nouns denote an uncountable mass and for this reason are called **mass/uncountable/non-count nouns** and so cannot be pluralised (e.g. *furniture* – hence the ungrammaticality of **one furniture*, **two furnitures*). A third is that some nouns (like *scissors* and *trousers*) have a plural form but no countable singular form. A fourth complication is posed by compound noun expressions which contain more than one noun; only the **head** noun in such expressions can be pluralised, not any preceding noun used as a **modifier** of the head noun: thus, in expressions such as *car doors, policy decisions, skate boards, horse boxes, trouser presses, coat hangers*, etc. the second noun is the head and can be pluralised, whereas the first noun is a modifier and so cannot be pluralised. (In a compound like *car doors*, the word *doors* is the head in the sense that the expression *car doors* describes kinds of door, not kinds of car.)

In much the same way, we can identify verbs by their inflectional morphology in English. Verbs can appear in a range of different forms in different contexts – as illustrated below for the verb SHOW:

(3) (a)   Would you like me to *show* you the library?
    (b)   *Show* me your passport, please!
    (c)   Students generally *show* little interest in syntax
    (d)   They demanded that he *show* greater application and determination

(4) (a)   He has *shown* considerable courage
    (b)   He was *shown* a red card by the referee

(5)   He *showed* her his credentials

(6)   He rarely *shows* his feelings

(7) (a)   The patient is *showing* signs of improvement
   (b)   I can't stand him *showing* off

The form *show* is the uninflected **base form** (or **stem form**) of the verb SHOW – i.e. the form from which other inflected forms are derived by the addition of a range of inflectional affixes, and the citation form under which the verb is listed in dictionaries. In (3a), the base form *show* functions as an **infinitive** form (i.e. the form used after the infinitive particle *to*); in (3b), *show* functions as an **imperative** form (i.e. the form used to issue an order); in (3c), it functions as a **present tense** form which also marks **indicative mood** (when used with a subject which is not third person singular); and in (3d) it functions as a form used to mark **subjunctive mood** (see the Glossary at the end of the book for any terms which are unfamiliar to you). In (4a), the form *shown* (carrying the suffix *-n*) functions as a **participle**, marking **perfect aspect** in (4a) and **passive voice** in (4b); consequently, *shown* is a **perfect participle** in (4a), and a **passive participle** in (4b). In (5), the form *showed* carrying the suffix *-(e)d* is a **past tense** form. In (6), *shows* is a form which is **third person singular** (i.e. is only used with a third person singular subject like *he*), **present tense** and **indicative mood**. In (7), the form *showing* (carrying the suffix *-ing*) is a participle marking **progressive aspect** (hence it is a **progressive participle**); by contrast in (6b) *showing* functions as a **gerund** form. The examples in (3–7) above illustrate that (in addition to their base form), verbs typically have up to four different inflected forms, formed by adding one of four inflections (*-n*/*-d*/*-s*/*-ing*) to the base/stem form of the verb.

Like most morphological criteria, however, this one is complicated by the irregular and impoverished nature of English inflectional morphology; for example, many verbs have irregular past or perfect forms, and in some cases either or both of these forms may not in fact be distinct from the (uninflected) base form, so a single form may serve two or three functions (thereby **neutralising** or **syncretising** the relevant distinctions – i.e. masking them). This is illustrated by the Table in (8) below, where 3.SG PRESENT denotes a verb form which is third person, singular number, present tense, indicative mood:

(8)   **TABLE OF VERB FORMS**

BASE	PERFECT	PAST	3.SG PRESENT	PROGRESSIVE
show	shown	showed	shows	showing
go	gone	went	goes	going
speak	spoken	spoke	speaks	speaking
see	seen	saw	sees	seeing
come		came	comes	coming
wait	waited		waits	waiting
meet	met		meets	meeting
cut			cuts	cutting

The largest class of verbs in English are regular verbs which have the morphological characteristics of *wait*, and so have past, perfect and passive forms ending in the suffix *-(e)d*. However, the picture becomes more complicated for the irregular verb BE, which has eight distinct forms (the base form *be*, the perfect form *been*, the progressive form *being*, the past forms *was/were*, and the present forms *am/are/is*). The most regular verb suffix in English is *-ing*, which can be attached to the base form of almost any verb (though a handful of defective verbs like *beware* are exceptions).

The obvious implication of our discussion of nouns and verbs here is that it would not be possible to provide a systematic account of English inflectional morphology unless we were to posit that words belong to grammatical categories, and that a specific type of inflection attaches only to a specific category of word. The same is also true if we wish to provide an adequate account of **derivational morphology** in English (i.e. the processes by which one type of word is derived from another type of word): this is because particular derivational affixes can only be attached to words belonging to particular categories. For example, the negative prefixes *un-* and *in-* can be attached to adjectives to form a corresponding negative adjective (cf. pairs such as *happy/unhappy* and *flexible/inflexible*) but not to nouns (so a noun like *fear* has no negative counterpart **unfear*), nor to prepositions (so a preposition like *inside* has no negative antonym **uninside*). Similarly, the adverbialising (i.e. adverb-forming) suffix *-ly* in English can be attached only to adjectives (giving rise to adjective/adverb pairs such as *sad/sadly*) and cannot be attached to a noun like *computer*, or to a verb like *accept*, or to a preposition like *with*. Likewise, the nominalising (i.e. noun-forming) suffix *-ness* can be attached only to adjective stems (so giving rise to adjective/noun pairs such as *coarse/coarseness*), not to nouns, verbs or prepositions (Hence we don't find *-ness* derivatives for a noun like *boy*, or a verb like *resemble* or a preposition like *from*). In much the same way, the comparative suffix *-er* can be attached to adjectives (cf. *tall/taller*) and some adverbs (cf. *soon/sooner*), but not e.g. to nouns (cf. *woman/ *womanner*); and the superlative suffix *-est* can attach to adjectives (cf. *tall/ tallest*) but not other types of word – e.g. not to a preposition like *from* (cf. **fromest*), nor to a noun like *donkey* (cf. **donkiest*), nor to a verb like *enjoy* (cf. **enjoyest*). There is no point in multiplying examples here: it is clear that derivational affixes have categorial properties, and any account of derivational morphology will clearly have to recognise this.

As noted in §1.3, there is also syntactic evidence for assigning words to categories: this essentially relates to different categories of word having different **distributions** (i.e. occupying a different range of positions within phrases or sentences). For example, if we want to complete the sentence in (9) below by inserting a single word at the end of the sentence in the position marked by the gap (- - -):

(9)   They have no - - -

we can use an (appropriate kind of) noun, but not a verb, preposition, adjective or adverb, as we see from:

(10) (a)   They have no *car/conscience/friends/ideas* [nouns]
     (b)   *They have no *went* [verb]/*for* [preposition]/*older* [adjective]/*conscientiously* [adverb]

So, using the relevant syntactic criterion, we can define the class of nouns as the set of words which can occupy the gap position in a sentence like (9).

Using the same type of syntactic evidence, we can argue that only a verb (in its infinitive/base form) can occur in the gap position in (11) below to form a complete (non-elliptical) sentence:

(11)   They/it can - - -

Support for this claim comes from the contrasts in (12) below:

(12) (a)   They can *stay/leave/hide/die/starve/cry* [verb]
     (b)   *They can *gorgeous* [adjective]/*happily* [adverb]/*with* [preposition]/*door* [noun]

And the only category of word which can occur after *very* (in the sense of *extremely*) is an adjective or adverb, as we see from (13) below:

(13) (a)   He is *very* **slow** [*very*+**adjective**]
     (b)   He walks *very* **slowly** [*very*+**adverb**]
     (c)   **Very* **fools** waste time [*very*+**noun**]
     (d)   *He *very* **adores** her [*very*+**verb**]
     (e)   *It happened *very* **after** the party [*very*+**preposition**]

(But note that *very* can only be used to modify adjectives/adverbs which by virtue of their meaning are **gradable** and so can be qualified by words like *very/rather/somewhat*, etc; adjectives/adverbs which denote an absolute state are **ungradable** by virtue of their meaning and so cannot be qualified in the same way – hence the oddity of *!Fifteen students were very present, and five were very absent*, where ! marks semantic anomaly.)

Moreover, we can differentiate adjectives from adverbs in syntactic terms. For example, if we want to complete sentences such as *He treats her - - -, She behaved - - -, He worded the statement - - -* by inserting a single word in the gap position at the end of the sentence, we can only use an adverb, as the examples below illustrate:

(14) (a)   He treats her *badly* [adverb]/*kind* [adjective]/*shame* [noun]/ *under* [preposition]
     (b)   She behaved *abominably* [adverb]/*appalling* [adjective]/ *disgrace* [noun]/ *with* [preposition]
     (c)   He worded the statement *carefully* [adverb]/*good* [adjective]/ *tact* [noun]/ *in* [preposition]

(A complication which I will set aside here is that some non-standard varieties of English use adjectives in some contexts where standard varieties use adverbs.)

And since adjectives (but not adverbs) can serve as the complement of the verb BE (i.e. can be used after BE), we can delimit the class of (gradable) adjectives uniquely by saying that only adjectives can be used to complete a four-word sentence of the form *They are very - - -*:

(15) (a)   They are very *tall/pretty/kind/nice* [adjective]
     (b)   *They are very *slowly* [adverb]/*gentlemen* [noun]/*astonish* [verb]/*outside* [preposition]

Another way of differentiating between an adjective like *real* and an adverb like *really* is that adjectives are used to modify nouns, whereas adverbs are used to modify other types of expression:

(16) (a)   There is a *real* **crisis** [*real*+**noun**]
     (b)   He is *really* **nice** [*really*+**adjective**]
     (c)   He walks *really* **slowly** [*really*+**adverb**]
     (d)   He is *really* **down** [*really*+**preposition**]
     (e)   He must *really* **squirm** [*really*+**verb**]

Adjectives used to modify a following noun in English (like *real* in *There is a real crisis*) are traditionally said to be **attributive** in function, whereas those which do not modify a following noun (like *real* in *The crisis is real*) are said to be **predicative** in function.

As for the syntactic properties of prepositions, they alone can be intensified by *right* in the sense of 'completely', or by *straight* in the sense of 'directly':

(17) (a)   Go *right* **up** the ladder
     (b)   He went *right* **inside** the building
     (c)   He walked *straight* **into** a wall
     (d)   He fell *straight* **down** the stairs

By contrast, other categories cannot be intensified by *right/straight* (in Standard English): cf.

(18) (a)   *He *right/straight* **despaired** [*right/straight*+**verb**]
     (b)   *She is *right/straight* **pretty** [*right/straight*+**adjective**]
     (c)   *She looked at him *right/straight* **strangely** [*right/straight*+**adverb**]
     (d)   *They are *right/straight* **fools** [*right/straight*+**noun**]

It should be noted, however, that since *right/straight* serve to intensify the meaning of a preposition, they can only be combined with those (uses of) prepositions which express the kind of meaning which can be intensified in the appropriate way (so 'He made *right/straight* **for** the exit' is OK, but *'He bought a present *right/straight* **for** Mary' is not). It should also be noted that there are varieties of English which allow *right* to modify other types of word: e.g. in some varieties of Northern British English, *right* can modify adjectives (as in 'She were *right pretty*', corresponding to Standard English 'She was very pretty').

A further syntactic property of some prepositions (namely those that take a following noun or pronoun expression as their complement – traditionally called

transitive prepositions) which they share in common with (transitive) verbs is the fact that they permit an immediately following **accusative** pronoun as their complement (i.e. a pronoun which is accusative in **case**, like *me/us/him/them*): cf.

(19) (a)   She was *against* **him** [*transitive preposition*+**accusative pronoun**]
   (b)   She was *watching* **him** [*transitive verb*+**accusative pronoun**]
   (c)   *She is *fond* **him** [*adjective*+**accusative pronoun**]
   (d)   *She works *independently* **him** [*adverb*+**accusative pronoun**]
   (e)   *She showed me a *photo* **him** [*noun*+**accusative pronoun**]

Even though a preposition like *with* does not express the kind of meaning which allows it to be intensified by *right* or *straight*, we know it is a (transitive) preposition because it is invariable (so not, e.g., a verb) and permits an accusative pronoun as its complement, for example in *He argued with me/us/him/them*.

An interesting property of prepositions is that in addition to being used with a following (italicised) complement as in the (a) examples in (20–24) below, some of them can also be used without any complement at all, as in the corresponding (b) examples:

(20) (a)   The boy fell **off** *the bike*
   (b)   The boy fell **off**

(21) (a)   She came **down** *the stairs*
   (b)   She came **down**

(22) (a)   He jumped **over** the fence
   (b)   He jumped **over**

(23) (a)   The bouncer wouldn't let her **in** *the club*
   (b)   The bouncer wouldn't let her **in**

(24) (a)   I haven't seen her **since** *the party*
   (b)   I haven't seen her **since**

As we saw in §1.3, the bold-printed items in the (b) examples in (20–24) are categorised in traditional grammar as (adverbial) particles. However, since their homonyms in the (a) examples are prepositions, it seems preferable to treat the bold-printed items in the (b) examples as prepositions used without a complement. One reason for this is that prepositions which can be modified by *straight/right* when used with an italicised complement in examples like (25a,26a) below can also be modified in the same way when used without a complement in examples like (25b,26b):

(25) (a)   He drove <u>straight</u> **past** *the roadblock*
   (b)   He drove <u>straight</u> **past**

(26) (a)   The bullet went <u>right</u> **through** *the door*
   (b)   The bullet went <u>right</u> **through**

We can then draw a parallel with verbs like *steal*, which can be used both with a complement (as in 'It's a crime to **steal** *things*') and without a complement (as in 'It's a crime to **steal**').

Indeed, the parallel between prepositions and verbs goes even further. Some verbs (e.g. *see*) allow both a nominal (i.e. noun-containing) complement like that italicised in (27a) below, and a clausal complement like that italicised in (27b):

(27) (a)   I could **see** *the car*
     (b)   I could **see** *the car had broken down*

In the same way, some prepositions (like those bold-printed below) allow both a nominal complement (like that italicised in 28a,29a,30a,31a below) and a clausal complement (like that italicised in 28b,29b,30b,31b):

(28) (a)   I haven't seen her **since** *the party*
     (b)   I haven't seen her **since** *I met her at the party*

(29) (a)   Don't hand it in **until** *this afternoon*
     (b)   Don't hand it in **until** *you have checked it*

(30) (a)   He resigned **after** *the scandal*
     (b)   He resigned **after** *the newspapers exposed him*

(31) (a)   Try and get it done **before** *sunset*
     (b)   Try and get it done **before** *the sun sets*

In the use illustrated in the (a) examples in (28–31), the bold-printed items are traditionally categorised as prepositions taking an italicised nominal complement. By contrast, in the (b) examples, the bold-printed items have an italicised finite clause as their complement, and in this second use they are categorised in traditional grammar as belonging to an entirely different category of subordinating conjunction. However, an alternative (more unitary) analysis is to suppose that the bold-printed items function as prepositions in both uses, the only difference being that in the (a) examples they have a nominal complement, whereas in the (b) examples they have a clausal complement. Such a unitary analysis would enable us to account for syntactic similarities between the related pairs of items in the (a) and (b) sentences. For example, just as *since* can be preceded by *ever* when it has a nominal complement in a sentence like (32a) below, so too it can be preceded by *ever* when it has a clausal complement in a sentence like (32b), and also when it has no complement in a sentence like (32c):

(32) (a)   I haven't seen her <u>ever</u> **since** *the party*
     (b)   I haven't seen her <u>ever</u> **since** *I met her at the party*
     (c)   I haven't seen her <u>ever</u> **since**

Thus, syntactic evidence favours treating such items as prepositions in all three uses.

Interestingly, some prepositions can even have a prepositional complement. In this connection, consider the use of *out* in the lyrics of the following song by John Lennon:

(33)   Love isn't certain, it comes <u>right</u> **out** *the blue*

It seems clear that *out* is a preposition in (33), since it has an italicised nominal complement and is preceded by the adverb *right*. However, an alternative way of expressing the same sentiment is:

(34)   Love isn't certain, it comes <u>right</u> **out** *of the blue*

In (34) the complement of the preposition *out* is a prepositional phrase headed by the preposition *of.* This opens up the possibility that some prepositions may allow a prepositional complement. And this in turn opens up the possibility of treating *because* as a preposition in structures such as:

(35) (a)   I did it **because** *of you*
   (b)   I did it because *I love you*

We could then say that *because* is a preposition which can take either a prepositional (*of*-phrase) complement as in (35a) or a clausal complement as in (35b).

The broader conclusion which our discussion here leads us to is that all the items bold-printed in (20–26) and (28–35) above are prepositions, but that it is a lexical (i.e. word-specific) property of individual prepositions whether or not they can be used with a particular type of complement (e.g. a nominal complement, and/or a clausal complement, and/or no complement at all).

2.3   Categorising words

Given that different categories have different morphological and syntactic properties, it follows that we can use the morphosyntactic properties of a word to determine its categorisation (i.e. what category it belongs to). The morphological properties of a given word provide an initial rough guide to its categorial status: in order to determine the categorial status of an individual word, we can ask whether it has the inflectional and derivational properties of a particular category of word. For example, we can tell that *happy* is an adjective because it has the derivational properties of typical adjectives: it can take the negative prefix *un-* (forming the negative adjective *unhappy*), the comparative/superlative suffixes *-er/-est* (giving rise to the forms *happier/happiest*), the adverbialising suffix *-ly* (deriving the adverb *happily*) and the nominalising suffix *-ness* (giving rise to the noun *happiness*).

However, we cannot always rely entirely on morphological clues: this is because morphology is sometimes irregular, sometimes subject to idiosyncratic restrictions and sometimes of limited productivity. For example, although regular adverbs (like *quickly* in *He walks quickly*) generally end in the derivational suffix *-ly*, this is not true of irregular adverbs like *fast* (e.g. in *He walks fast*); this seems to correlate with a syntactic difference between the two types of adverb: for example, we can use either *quickly* or *fast* in a sentence like *He walked home quickly/fast*, but can only use *quickly* in *He quickly/*fast walked home*. Moreover, when they have the comparative suffix *-er* added to them, regular adverbs lose their *-ly* suffix because English is a monosuffixal language (in the sense that words can have only one suffix attached to them in English), so that the comparative form of the adverb *quickly* is *quicker* not *quicklier. What all of this means is that a word belonging to a given class may have only *some* of the relevant morphological properties, or even (in the case of a completely irregular item) *none* of them. For example, although the adjective *fat* has comparative/superlative forms in *-er/-est* (cf. *fat/fatter/fattest*), it has no negative *un-* counterpart (cf. *unfat), and no adverb counterpart in *-ly* (cf. *fatly). Even more exceptional is the adjective *little*, which has no negative *un-* derivative (cf. *unlittle), no adverb *-ly* derivative (cf. *littlely/*littly), no noun derivative in *-ness* (at least in my variety of English – though *littleness* does appear in the *Oxford English Dictionary*) and no *-er/-est* derivatives (the forms *littler/*littlest are likewise not grammatical in my variety).

What makes morphological evidence even more problematic is the fact that many affixes/inflections may have more than one use. For example, the participial inflections *-n/-d* and *-ing* attach to verbs to give perfect or progressive participle forms. However, some of these *-n/-d* and *-ing* forms seem to function as adjectives, suggesting that *-n/-d* and *-ing* can also serve as adjectivalising (i.e. adjective-forming) suffixes. So, although a word like *interesting* can function as a verb (in sentences like *Her charismatic teacher was gradually interesting her in syntax*), it can also function as an adjective (used attributively in structures like *This is an interesting book*, and predicatively in structures like *This book is very interesting*). In its use as an adjective, the word *interesting* has the negative derivative *uninteresting* (cf. *It was a rather uninteresting play*) and the *-ly* adverb derivative *interestingly* (though, like many other adjectives, it has no noun derivative in *-ness*, and no comparative or superlative derivatives in *-er/-est*). Similarly, although *-n/-d* can serve as a perfect participle inflection (in structures like *We hadn't known/expected that he would quit*), it should be noted that many words ending in *-n/-d* can also function as adjectives. For example, the word *known* in an expression such as *a known criminal* seems to function as an (attributive) adjective, and in this adjectival use it has a negative *un-* counterpart (as in *the tomb of the unknown warrior*). Similarly, the form *expected* functions as a perfect participle verb form in structures like *We hadn't expected him to complain*, but seems to function as an (attributive) adjective in structures such as *He gave the expected reply*; in its adjectival (though not in its verbal) use, it has a negative *un-* derivative, and the resultant negative adjective *unexpected* in turn has the noun derivative *unexpectedness*.

So, given the potential problems which arise with morphological criteria, it is unwise to rely solely on morphological evidence in determining categorial status: rather, we should use morphological criteria in conjunction with syntactic criteria (i.e. distributional criteria relating to the range of positions that words can occupy within phrases and sentences). One syntactic test which can be used to determine the category that a particular word belongs to is that of **substitution** – i.e. seeing whether (in a given sentence) the word in question can be substituted by a regular noun, verb, preposition, adjective, or adverb etc. We can use the substitution technique to differentiate between comparative adjectives and adverbs ending in -*er*, since they have identical forms. For example, in the case of sentences like the following we find that *better* can be replaced by a *more+adjective* expression like *more fluent* in (36a) but not (36b):

(36) (a)   He is *better* at French than you
     (b)   He speaks French *better* than you

Conversely, *better* can be replaced by a *more+adverb* expression like *more fluently* in (36b) but not in (36a): cf.

(37) (a)   He is *more fluent/*more fluently* at French than you
     (b)   He speaks French *more fluently/*more fluent* than you

Thus, the substitution test provides us with syntactic evidence that *better* is an adjective in (36a), but an adverb in (36b).

The overall conclusion to be drawn from our discussion in this section is that morphological evidence may sometimes be inconclusive and has to be checked against syntactic evidence. A useful syntactic test which can be employed is that of substitution: e.g. if a morphologically indeterminate word can be substituted by a regular noun wherever it occurs, the relevant word has the same categorial status as the substitute word which can replace it, and so is a noun.

2.4   Functional categories

Thus far, we have looked at five different types of grammatical category of English (**noun**, **verb**, **preposition**, **adjective** and **adverb**). As we saw in §1.3, for typographical convenience it is standard practice to use capital-letter abbreviations for categories, and so to use N for noun, V for verb, P for preposition, A for adjective and ADV for adverb. Nouns, verbs, adjectives and adverbs are traditionally said to be **contentives** (or **content words**), in that they have substantive descriptive/lexical semantic content. However, in addition to content words, languages also contain **functors** (or **function words**) – i.e. words which serve primarily to carry information about the grammatical function of particular types of expression within the sentence (e.g. information about grammatical properties such as **person**, **number**, **gender**, **case**, **tense**, **mood**, **aspect**, etc.). The differences between contentives and functors can be illustrated by comparing a (contentive) noun like *car* with a (functional) pronoun like *they*. A noun like *car* has obvious descriptive content in that it denotes an object which typically has four wheels and an engine, and it would be easy enough to draw a picture of a typical *car*; by contrast, a pronoun such as *they* has no descriptive content (e.g. you can't draw a picture of *they*), but rather is a functor which (as we shall see shortly) simply encodes a set of grammatical (more specifically, person, number and case) properties in that it is a third person plural nominative pronoun.

One test of whether words have descriptive content is to see whether they have **antonyms** (i.e. opposites): if a word has an antonym, it is a contentive (though if it has no antonym, you can't be sure whether it is a functor or a contentive). For example, a noun/N such as *loss* has the antonym *gain*; a verb/V such as *rise* has the antonym *fall*; an adjective/A such as *tall* has the antonym *short*; and an adverb/ADV such as *early* (as in *He arrived early*) has the antonym *late*. This reflects the fact that nouns, verbs, adjectives, adverbs and prepositions typically have substantive descriptive content, and so are contentives. By contrast, a particle like infinitival *to*, or an auxiliary like *do*, or a determiner like *the*, or a pronoun like *they* (as in '*Do they* want *to* sell *the* house?') have no obvious antonyms, and thus can be said to lack descriptive content, and so to be functors. Using rather different (but equivalent) terminology, we can say that contentives have substantive lexical content (i.e. idiosyncratic semantic content which varies from one lexical item/word to another), whereas functors have functional content. We can then conclude that nouns, verbs, adjectives and adverbs are **lexical** or **substantive categories** (because the words belonging to these categories have substantive lexical/descriptive content) whereas particles, auxiliaries, determiners, and pronouns are **functional categories** (because words belonging to these categories have an essentially grammatical function).

A second property of lexical categories which differentiates them from functional categories is that lexical categories are potentially **open** classes, whereas functional categories are **closed** classes. To see what this means, consider the difference between *verbs* (a lexical category) and *auxiliaries* (a functional category). There are thousands of lexical (i.e. main/non-auxiliary) verbs in English, but only a handful of auxiliaries (*can/could, may/might, shall/should, will/would, must, ought* and some uses of *be, have, do, need* and *dare*). Moreover, we can readily create new verbs (like the italicised verb in 'I'm going to *nurgle* you') because verbs are an open class, but we cannot create new auxiliaries because auxiliaries are a closed class.

Thus, at first sight, the distinction between lexical and functional categories seems straightforward: lexical categories have descriptive content, can have antonyms and form an open set with a very large membership, whereas functional categories lack descriptive content, have no antonyms and form a closed set with a very small membership. However, closer inspection suggests that the distinction between lexical and functional categories is not always clear-cut. Take the category P/preposition by way of illustration. Are prepositions contentives or functors? Some prepositions have antonyms (giving rise to pairs like *in/out, inside/outside, up/down, on/off*, etc.) suggesting that they have lexical meaning and so are contentives. Moreover, some prepositions can have derivational affixes attached to them (e.g. comparative *-er*, giving rise to forms like *inner, outer, upper*), and this is generally a property of contentives. On the other hand, prepositions comprise a closed class and this is more consistent with them being functors: thus, there are only a few dozen prepositions in English (compared to thousands of nouns, verbs and adjectives), and we cannot freely coin new prepositions in English (although we can readily coin new nouns, verbs and adjectives). This means that the question of whether prepositions are contentives or functors is not a straightforward one to answer.

One possible way of resolving the conundrum over the status of prepositions is to suppose that some prepositions are contentives (including those with antonyms), whereas others (those with little if any semantic content) are functors. In this connection, it is interesting to note that some prepositions (in some uses) have been said to function as **case particles**. By way of illustration, consider the use of the preposition *of* in (38a) below:

(38) (a)   the assassination *of* Kennedy
     (b)   They assassinated Kennedy

In (38a), the preposition serves to mark *Kennedy* as the complement of the noun *assassination* (and victim of the relevant act). However, *of* seems to have little intrinsic semantic content in this use, as we see from the fact that it is not used to introduce the complement of the verb *assassinated* in (38b). Since many languages (e.g. Latin) would not use a preposition like *of* in a structure like (38a) but rather would use a genitive case form of the noun, some linguists have suggested that *of* in the kind of use found in (38a) is **a genitive case particle** and assign it to the functional category K (denoting 'case particle'). Much the same could be said about the phrase *out (of) the blue* discussed in (33,34) above. Since *of* is optional here, it seems to have little or no semantic content of its own, and hence can plausibly be taken to be a genitive case particle. However, the picture is complicated by the fact that *of* has uses where it can be substituted by a lexical preposition (e.g. by *with* in *A lot of men die of/with prostate cancer*). This raises the possibility that *of* may be a genitive case particle in some uses, but a lexical preposition in other uses.

A similar line of reasoning could lead us to conclude that the preposition *to* in a sentence like (39a) below is a **dative** case particle (used to mark the recipient of the flowers):

(39) (a)   He sent some flowers *to* Mary
     (b)   He sent Mary some flowers

Since *to* does not appear in the so-called **double object construction** in (39b) and the phrase *to Mary* in English would be translated by using a dative case-form of the noun *Mary* in a language like Latin, *to* could be argued to have little or no independent semantic content in (39a). If so, *to* in this kind of use would be classified as belonging to the functional category K of 'case particle' rather than to the lexical category P of preposition. Given that there is by no means universal agreement among linguists as to whether some prepositions (in some uses) should be categorised as belonging to the category K of case particle, I shall simplify discussion throughout the rest of the book by categorising all prepositions (in all uses) as belonging to the category P of 'preposition'. (You might be wondering at this point why the category of 'case particle' is abbreviated to K rather than C. The answer is that C is the abbreviation conventionally used to denote the category of **complementiser** introduced in 2.9, so K is used for 'case particle' in order to avoid confusion.)

Having briefly looked at one category (= preposition) which proves problematic to classify as a lexical or functional category, in sections §§2.5–2.9 below, we take a closer look at more clear-cut instances of functional categories found in English.

2.5   Determiners and quantifiers

The first type of functional category which we shall look at here is the category of determiner (here abbreviated to D, but in some other works abbreviated to DET). Items such as those bold-printed in (40) below (as used there) are traditionally said to be determiners:

(40) (a)   Shall we take **the** *car*?
    (b)   **This** *appalling behaviour* has got to stop/**These** *woollen sweaters* are a bargain
    (c)   **That** *dog of yours* is crazy/**Those** *papers* are for shredding

They are called determiners because they have the semantic property that they determine specific semantic properties of the noun expression that they introduce. For example, the phrase *the car* in (40a) *Shall we take the car?* is a definite referring expression in the sense that it refers to a definite (specific) car which is assumed to be familiar to the hearer/addressee.

A related class of words are those which belong to the functional category **quantifier** (= Q), denoting expressions of quantity like those bold-printed below:

(41) (a)   **Most** *good comedians* tell **some** *bad jokes*
    (b)   **Many** *students* have **no** *money*
    (c)   **Every** *true Scotsman* hates **all** *Englishmen*
    (d)   **Each** *exercise* contains **several** *examples*

Such items are termed quantifiers because they serve to quantify the italicised noun expression which follows them. (I shall also take numerals like *one/two/three/four*, etc. and the indefinite article *a* to be quantifiers, even though a more fine-grained analysis might suggest that a case could be made for treating numerals as belonging to a separate category **NUM**, and articles as belonging to a further category **ART**).

Since determiners and quantifiers are positioned in front of nouns (cf. *the boys* and *many boys*), and adjectives can similarly be positioned in front of nouns (cf. *tall boys*), an obvious question to ask at this point is why we couldn't just say that the determiners/quantifiers in (40,41) have the categorial status of adjectives. The answer is that any attempt to analyse determiners or quantifiers as adjectives in English runs up against a number of descriptive problems. Let's see why.

One reason for not subsuming determiners/quantifiers within the category of adjectives is that they are semantically, syntactically and morphologically distinct from adjectives. From a semantic perspective, one important difference is that adjectives (e.g. *thoughtful*) have descriptive semantic content but determiners and quantifiers do not – as we can illustrate in terms of the following contrast (where *?* and *!* are used to denote increasing degrees of semantic/pragmatic anomaly):

(42) (a)   a **thoughtful** *friend/?cat/??fish/?!pan/!problem*
    (b)   **a/another/every/the/this** *friend/cat/fish/pan/problem*

As (42a) illustrates, an adjective like *thoughtful* can only be used to modify certain types of noun; this is because its descriptive content is such that it is only compatible with (e.g.) an expression denoting a rational (mind-possessing) entity. By contrast, determiners/quantifiers like those bold-printed in (42b) lack specific descriptive content, and hence can be used to modify any semantic class of noun. Thus, it seems appropriate to conclude on semantic grounds that determiners and quantifiers are functional categories, and adjectives a lexical category.

There are also morphological differences between them. In general, quantifiers and determiners differ from adjectives in not allowing derivational affixes to be attached to them: for example, a quantifier like *some* has no negative *un-* derivative (**unsome*), no comparative or superlative form (**sommer/sommest*), no adverb derivative in *-ly* (**somely*), and no noun derivative in *-ness* (**someness*). It should be noted, however, that the quantifier *few* has the comparative/superlative derivatives *fewer/fewest* (and, incidentally, also has the potential antonym *many*).

A further morphological property which differentiates determiners/quantifiers from adjectives is that determiners/quantifiers generally have specific number (or countability) properties. For example (as illustrated in 40b,c above), demonstrative determiners have separate singular/plural forms (*this-these/that-those*). Similarly, other determiners and quantifiers have inherent number or countability properties. For example, *a* modifies a singular count noun, *much* modifies a (singular) mass noun, *several* modifies a plural count noun, *more* modifies either a plural count or a (singular) mass noun:

(43) (a)   Can you pass me **a** *chair/****a** *chairs/****a** *furniture*?
    (b)   He doesn't have **much** *furniture/****much** *chair/****much** *chairs* of his own
    (c)   He bought **several** *chairs/****several** *chair/****several** *furniture* in the sale
    (d)   Do we need **more** *furniture/***more** *chairs/****more** *chair*?

By contrast, typical adjectives like *nice, simple, comfortable, modern*, etc. can generally be used to modify all three types of noun: cf.

(44) (a)   We need a **nice, simple, comfortable, modern** *chair*
    (b)   We need some **nice, simple, comfortable, modern** *chairs*
    (c)   We need some **nice, simple, comfortable, modern** *furniture*

It should be noted, however, that a determiner like *the* can also be used to modify singular/plural count and non-count nouns alike.

There are also syntactic/distributional differences between determiners/quantifiers and adjectives. For example, adjectives can be iteratively (i.e. repeatedly)

stacked in front of a noun they modify, in the sense that you can go on putting more and more adjectives in front of a given noun (like those italicised in the expressions '*handsome* strangers', '*dark handsome* strangers', '*tall dark handsome* strangers', '*sensitive tall handsome* strangers', etc.). By contrast, neither determiners nor quantifiers can be stacked in this way (so although we can have a quantifier+determiner+noun expression like *both the twins*, we cannot have a multiple determiner expression like *the these books or a multiple quantifier expression such as *all both twins). Moreover, determiners, quantifiers and adjectives can be used together to modify a noun, but when they do so, any determiner or quantifier modifying the noun has to precede any adjective(s) modifying the noun: cf. e.g.

(45) (a)   **the** *same old* excuses [**determiner**+*adjective*+*adjective*+noun]

(b)   *same **the** *old* excuses [*adjective*+**determiner**+*adjective*+noun]

(c)   *same old **the** excuses [*adjective*+*adjective*+**determiner**+noun]

Thus, determiners and quantifiers seem to have a different syntactic distribution (and hence to be categorially distinct) from adjectives.

A further syntactic difference between determiners/quantifiers and adjectives can be illustrated in relation to what speaker B can – and cannot – reply in the following dialogue:

(46)   SPEAKER A: What are you looking for?

SPEAKER B: *Chair/*Comfortable chair/*A* chair/*Another* chair/*The* chair/*That* chair

As noted earlier, nouns like *chair* have the property that they are countable (in the sense that we can say *one chair, two chairs*, etc.), and in this respect they differ from mass nouns like *furniture* which are uncountable (hence we can't say *one furniture, *two furnitures, etc). We see from (46) that a singular count noun like *chair* cannot stand on its own as a complete noun expression, nor indeed can it function as such even if modified by an adjective like *comfortable*; rather, a singular count noun requires a modifying determiner or quantifier like *a*/*another*/*the*/*that*, etc. This provides us with clear evidence that determiners and quantifiers in English are syntactically distinct from adjectives.

Some linguists treat quantifiers as a subtype of determiner and hence assign quantifiers to the category D: one possibility along these lines is to suppose that items like *the*/*this*/*that* are **definite** determiners, and those like *many*/*some*/*a* are **indefinite** determiners (and such a categorisation could be said to be implicit in the traditional claim that *the* is a 'definite article' and *a* an 'indefinite article'). However, the fact that a determiner like *the* can combine with a quantifier like *all*/*every* in a sentence like:

(47)   *All* **the** servile courtiers pandered to **the** *every* witless whim of King Kostas of Kostalotte

provides some syntactic evidence that the two have different distributions and hence belong to different categories (since one determiner generally cannot be combined with another). Moreover, quantifiers and determiners exhibit different syntactic behaviour in respect of questions such as:

(48) (a)   **Who** didn't he want [*any* pictures of - - -]?
     (b)   *****Who** didn't he want [*the* pictures of - - -]?

In both cases, *who* is the complement of the word *of* and is moved to the front of the sentence from its original position in the gap (- - -) after *of*. But whereas fronting *who* when it is the complement of the quantifier expression *any pictures of* results in a grammatical sentence, fronting *who* when it is the complement of a determiner expression like *the pictures of* generally leads to considerable degradation because it violates a **Definiteness Constraint** barring movement out of a definite nominal. Consequently, sentences like (47) and (48) could be said to provide evidence that quantifiers and determiners are syntactically distinct and so belong to different categories (though there is far from being general agreement on this – and indeed some speakers do not detect a clear difference in acceptability between examples like 48a and 48b).

2.6   Pronouns

Traditional grammars posit a category of **pronoun** (here abbreviated to **PRN**) to denote a class of words which are said to 'stand in place of' or 'refer to' noun expressions. Pronouns are functors in the sense that they constitute a closed class (with a very restricted membership) and have no lexical semantic content but rather (as we shall see below) simply mark grammatical properties like number, gender, case, etc.

Although in our brief discussion of pronouns in §1.3 it was tacitly assumed that pronouns form a unitary category, closer reflection suggests that there are a number of different types of pronoun found in English and other languages. One such type is represented by the word *one* in the use illustrated below:

(49) (a)   John has a red **car** and Jim has a blue *one*
     (b)   I'll take the green **apples** if you haven't got any red *ones*

From a grammatical perspective, *one* behaves like a regular count noun here in that it has the *s*-plural form *ones* and occurs in a position (after an adjective like *blue/red*) in which a count noun could occur. However, it is a *pronoun* in the sense that it has no descriptive content of its own, but rather takes its descriptive content from its **antecedent** (i.e. the expression it refers to): for instance, *one* in (49a) refers back to the noun *car* and so *one* is interpreted as meaning 'car'. Let's refer to this kind of pronoun as an **N-pronoun** (or pronominal noun).

By contrast, in the examples in (50) below, the bold-printed pronoun seems to serve as a pronominal quantifier. In the first (italicised) occurrence in each pair of examples, it is a **prenominal** (i.e. noun-preceding) quantifier which modifies a following noun expression (*guests/miners/protesters/son/cigarettes/bananas*); in the second (bold-printed) occurrence, it has no noun expression following it and so functions as a **pronominal** quantifier:

(50) (a)   *All guests* are welcome/**All** are welcome
    (b)   *Many miners* died in the accident/**Many** died in the accident
    (c)   *Several protesters* were arrested/**Several** were arrested
    (d)   *Each son* was envious of the other/**Each** was envious of the other
    (e)   I don't have *any cigarettes*/I don't have **any**
    (f)   We have *no bananas*/We have **none**

We can therefore refer to pronouns like those bold-printed in (50) as **Q-pronouns** (or pronominal quantifiers). In much the same way, we can categorise *what/which* as interrogative quantifiers when (as in the first use italicised in 51 below) serving to modify a following (underlined) noun expression like *kind of uniform/photo*, but as interrogative pronouns when standing on their own without modifying a following noun, as in the second (bold-printed) use below:

(51) (a)   *What* <u>kind of uniform</u> was he wearing?/**What** was he wearing?
    (b)   *Which* <u>photo</u> do you like best?/**Which** do you like best?

As we see from (52) below, the question word *who* behaves differently from *what/which*:

(52) (a)   **Who** were you talking to?
    (b)   **Who* <u>teenage pop idol</u> was arrested for throwing eggs at his neighbour's house?

More specifically, *who* can function as an interrogative pronoun in sentences like (52a), but cannot serve as an interrogative quantifier modifying a following noun expression like that underlined in (52b).

A third type of pronoun is that bold-printed in the examples below:

(53) (a)   I prefer *this* <u>tie</u>/I prefer **this**
    (b)   I haven't read *that* <u>book</u>/I haven't read **that**
    (c)   I don't particularly like *these* <u>pictures</u>/I don't particularly like **these**
    (d)   Have you already paid for *those* <u>items</u>/Have you already paid for **those**?

Since the relevant words can also serve (in the italicised use) as prenominal determiners which modify a following noun, we can say that they function as **D-pronouns** (i.e. as pronominal determiners) in their bold-printed use. Interestingly, the definite article *the* differs from demonstrative determiners like *this/that/these/those* in that it can be used as a prenominal determiner modifying a following noun in a sentence like 'Close *the* <u>door</u>', but cannot be used as a pronoun (cf. *'Close *the*'). This suggests that it is a lexical (i.e. word-specific) property of individual determiners whether they can be used prenominally and/or pronominally.

A fourth type of pronoun are **personal pronouns** like *I/me/we/us/you/he/him/she/her/it/they/them*. These are called personal pronouns not because they denote people (the pronoun *it* is not normally used to denote a person), but rather because they encode the grammatical property of **person**. In the relevant technical sense, *I/me/my/we/us/our* are said to be **first person** prounouns, in that they are expressions whose reference includes the person/s speaking; *you/your* are **second person** pronouns, in that their reference includes the addressee/s (i.e. the person/s being spoken to), but excludes the speaker/s; *he/him/his/she/her/it/its/they/them/their* are **third person** prounouns, in the sense that they refer to entities other than the speaker/s and addressee/s. Personal pronouns differ morphologically from nouns and other pronouns in modern English in that they generally have (partially) distinct **nominative**, **accusative** and **genitive** case forms, whereas nouns have a common nominative/accusative form and a distinct genitive form ending in *'s* – as we see from the contrasts below:

(54) (a)   *John* snores/**He** snores

(b)   Find *John*!/Find **him**!

(c)   Look at *John's* trousers!/Look at **his** trousers!

Personal pronouns like *he/him/his* and nouns like *John/John's* change their morphological form according to the position which they occupy within the sentence, so the nominative forms *he/John* are required as the subject of a finite verb like *snores*, whereas the accusative forms *him/John* are required when used as the complement of a transitive verb like *find* (or when used as the complement of a transitive preposition like *to* in 'I spoke *to* **him** yesterday'), and the genitive forms *his/John's* are required (*inter alia*) when used to express possession: these variations reflect different **case forms** of the relevant items.

Personal pronouns are functors by virtue of lacking descriptive content: whereas a noun like *dogs* denotes a specific type of animal, a personal pronoun like *they* denotes no specific type of entity but rather has to have its reference determined from the linguistic or non-linguistic context. Personal pronouns encode the grammatical properties of (first, second or third) person, (singular or plural) number, (**masculine**, **feminine** or **neuter**) gender and (nominative, accusative or genitive) case, as shown in the table in (55) below:

(55)   **Table of personal pronoun forms**

PERSON	NUMBER	GENDER	NOMINATIVE	ACCUSATIVE	GENITIVE
1	SG	M/F	*I*	*me*	*my/mine*
1	PL	M/F	*we*	*us*	*our/ours*
2	SG/PL	M/F	*you*	*you*	*your/yours*
3	SG	M	*he*	*him*	*his*
3	SG	F	*she*	*her*	*her/hers*
3	SG	N	*it*	*it*	*its*
3	PL	M/F/N	*they*	*them*	*their/theirs*

(SG = singular; PL = plural; M = masculine; F = feminine; N = neuter. So-called *neuter* pronouns are typically used to refer to inanimate or non-human entities. Note that some genitive pronouns have separate weak/short and strong/long forms, the weak form being used prenominally to modify a following noun expression – as in 'Take *my car*' – and the strong form being used pronominally – as in 'Take *mine*'.)

But what grammatical category do personal pronouns belong to? Many researchers (in work dating back sixty years) have suggested that they are pronominal determiners and hence D-pronouns. This assumption would provide us with a unitary analysis of the syntax of the bold-printed items in the bracketed expressions in sentences such as (56a,b) below:

(56) (a)   [**We** *republicans*] don't trust [**you** *democrats*]
     (b)   [**We**] don't trust [**you**]

Since *we* and *you* in (56a) modify the nouns *republicans*/*democrats* and since determiners like *the* are typically used to modify nouns, it seems reasonable to suppose that *we*/*you* function as prenominal determiners in (56a). But if this is so, it is plausible to suppose that *we* and *you* also have the categorial status of determiners (i.e. D-pronouns) in sentences like (56b). It would then follow that *we*/*you* have the categorial status of determiners in both (56a) and (56b) but differ in that they are used *pre*nominally (i.e. with a following noun expression) in (56a), but *pro*nominally (i.e. without any following noun expression) in (56b). Note, however, that third person pronouns like *he*/*she*/*it*/*they* are typically used only pronominally – hence the ungrammaticality of expressions such as *they boys in standard varieties of English (though there are non-standard varieties of English spoken around Bristol and Exeter in the South West of England where expressions like *they boys* are found; and I heard the Scottish football manager Gordon Strachan say '*They three* have made a mark on the manager' when commenting on a televised football match). Whether or not such items are used prenominally, pronominally or in both ways is a lexical property (i.e. an idiosyncratic property of individual words).

Although the discussion in this section might suggest that it is easy enough to identify different types of pronoun, it should be acknowledged that there are cases which are not entirely straightforward to deal with. For example, a typical D-pronoun like *these*/*those* can be premodified by the universal quantifier *all*, but a personal pronoun like *they* cannot: cf.

(57) (a)   *All* **these** are broken
     (b)   *All* **those** are broken
     (c)   *All **they** are broken

Such a contrast is unexpected if personal pronouns like *they* are D-pronouns like *those*/*these* and clearly raises questions about the true status of personal pronouns (an issue which I will leave open here).

Also potentially problematic to classify are items such as *when*/*where*/*why*/*how* (and related items such as *then*/*there*). These are widely classified in grammars and dictionaries as adverbs. However, if *who?* (with a meaning paraphraseable as 'what person?') is categorised as a pronoun, it would seem equally plausible to take *when* to be a pronoun meaning 'what time?', *where* to be a pronoun meaning 'what place', *why* to be a pronoun meaning 'what reason?' and *how* to be pronoun meaning 'what way?'. These two seemingly contradictory categorisations can be resolved if such items are taken to function as adverbial pronouns. (We will take another look at the status of such items in §4.11.)

A second issue which arises in relation to pronouns is that it is important to draw a distinction between the type of position that a pronoun can occupy (a syntactic property) and the type of constituent it can refer to (a semantic property). The two can sometimes be quite distinct, as the following dialogue illustrates:

(58)   SPEAKER A: Are you sure *he's innocent?*
         SPEAKER B: Yes, I'm certain of **it**

The pronoun *it* in (58B) occupies a nominal position (as the object of the preposition *of*) – i.e. the kind of position that could equally be occupied by a noun expression like *the fact*. However, its antecedent (i.e. the expression that it refers back to) is the clause *he's innocent*. What this underlines is that in classifying pronouns into types, we need to bear in mind not only the syntactic property of the kind of position that the pronoun can occupy but also the semantic property of the kind of constituent which the pronoun can have as its antecedent (i.e. which it can refer to).

Our discussion in this section has shown that there are a number of different types of pronoun (including N-pronouns, Q-pronouns and D-pronouns). Because the word *pronoun* could be taken to imply (wrongly) that all pronouns are pronominal *nouns*, some linguists prefer to use the alternative term **proform**: using this terminology, an item like *many* (when used pronominally) would be categorised as a Q-proform. However, given that a number of aspects of the syntax of pronouns are poorly understood and the category pronoun is familiar from centuries of grammatical tradition, the label PRN/pronoun will be used throughout the rest of this book to designate pronouns of all kinds.

2.7   Auxiliaries

A second type of functional category found in English is that of **auxiliary**. Traditional grammarians use this term to denote a class of items which once functioned simply as verbs, but in the course of the evolution of the English language have become sufficiently distinct from main verbs that they are now regarded as belonging to a different category of auxiliary (abbreviated to **AUX**).

Auxiliaries differ from main verbs in a number of ways. Whereas a typical main verb like *want* may take a range of different types of complement (e.g. an infinitival *to*-complement as in 'I **want** (*you*) *to go home*', or a noun expression as in 'I want *lots of money*'), by contrast auxiliaries typically allow only a verb expression as their complement, and have the semantic function of marking grammatical properties associated with the relevant verb, such as tense, aspect, voice or mood. The items italicised in (59) below (in the use illustrated there) are traditionally categorised as auxiliaries taking a [bracketed] complement containing a bold-printed non-finite verb:

(59) (a)   He *has/had* [**gone**]
    (b)   She *is/was* [**staying** at home]
    (c)   They *are/were* [**taken** away for questioning]
    (d)   He really *does/did* [**say** a lot]
    (e)   You *can/could* [**help** us]
    (f)   They *may/might* [**come** back]
    (g)   He *will/would* [**get** upset]
    (h)   I *shall/should* [**return**]
    (i)   You *must* [**finish** your assignment]
    (j)   You *ought* [to **apologise**]

In the uses illustrated here, *have/be* in (59a,b) are (perfect/progressive) aspect auxiliaries, *be* in (59c) is a (passive) voice auxiliary, *do* in (59d) a (present/past) tense auxiliary, and *can/could/may/might/will/would/shall/should/must/ought* in (59e–j) **modal** auxiliaries. As will be apparent, *ought* differs from other modal auxiliaries like *should* which take an infinitive complement in requiring use of infinitival *to*.

There are clear syntactic differences between auxiliaries and verbs. For example (as we saw in §1.3), auxiliaries can undergo **Inversion** (and thereby be moved into pre-subject position) in questions such as (60) below, where the inverted auxiliary is italicised and the subject is bold-printed:

(60) (a)   *Can* **you** speak Japanese?
    (b)   *Does* **he** smoke?
    (c)   *Is* **it** raining?

By contrast, typical verbs do not themselves permit Inversion, but rather require what is traditionally called **DO-support** (i.e. they have inverted forms which require the use of the auxiliary DO):

(61) (a)   **Intends* **he** to come?
    (b)   *Does* **he** intend to come?
    (c)   **Saw* **you** the mayor?
    (d)   *Did* **you** see the mayor?
    (e)   **Plays* **he** the piano?
    (f)   *Does* **he** play the piano?

A second difference between auxiliaries and verbs is that auxiliaries can generally be directly negated by a following *not* (which can usually attach to the auxiliary in the guise of its contracted form *n't*):

(62) (a)   John *could not/couldn't* come to the party
    (b)   I *do not/don't* like her much

(c)   He *is not/isn't* working very hard
(d)   They *have not/haven't* finished

By contrast, verbs cannot themselves be directly negated by *not/n't*, but require indirect negation using DO-support:

(63) (a)   *They *like not/liken't* me
   (b)   They *do not/don't* like me
   (c)   *I *see not/seen't* the point
   (d)   I *do not/don't* see the point
   (e)   *You *came not/camen't*
   (f)   You *did not/didn't* come

(Note that in structures such as *John decided not to stay*, the negative particle *not* negates the infinitive complement *to stay* rather than the verb *decided*, as is clear from the position of *not* in a sentence like 'What John decided was *not to stay*'.)

A third difference between auxiliaries and verbs is that auxiliaries can appear in a position like that illustrated below, where the part of the sentence following the comma is traditionally referred to as a **tag**:

(64) (a)   You don't like her, *do* you?
   (b)   He won't win, *will* he?
   (c)   She isn't working, *is* she?
   (d)   He can't drive, *can* he?

In contrast, verbs can't themselves be used in tags, but rather require the use of *do*-tags: cf.

(65) (a)   You like her, *do/*like* you?
   (b)   They want one, *do/*want* they?

So, on the basis of these (and other) syntactic properties, we can conclude that auxiliaries constitute a different category from verbs.

2.8   Infinitival *to*

A fourth type of functor found in English is the infinitive particle *to* – so called because the only kind of complement it allows is one containing a verb in the **infinitive** form. (The infinitive form of the verb is its uninflected base form, i.e. the citation form found in dictionary entries.) Typical uses of infinitival *to* are illustrated in (66) below:

(66) (a)   I wonder whether *to* [**go** home]
   (b)   Many people want the government *to* [**change** course]
   (c)   We don't intend *to* [**surrender**]

In each example in (66), the [bracketed] complement of *to* is an expression containing a (bold-printed) verb in the infinitive form. But what is the categorial status of infinitival *to*?

We are already familiar with an alternative use of *to* as a preposition, e.g. in sentences such as:

(67) (a)   He stayed *to* [the end of the film]
     (b)   He went *to* [the police]

In (67), *to* behaves like a typical (transitive) preposition in taking a [bracketed] nominal (i.e. noun-containing expression) as its complement (*the end of the film*, and *the police*). It might therefore seem as if *to* is a preposition in both uses – one which takes a following nominal complement in (67) and a following verbal complement in (66).

However, infinitival *to* is very different in its behaviour from prepositional *to* in English: whereas prepositional *to* is a contentive with intrinsic lexical semantic content (e.g. it means something like 'as far as'), infinitival *to* seems to be a functor with no lexical semantic content. Because of its intrinsic lexical content, the preposition *to* can often be modified by intensifiers like *right/straight* (a characteristic property of prepositions) – cf.

(68) (a)   He stayed *right* **to** the end of the film
     (b)   He went *straight* **to** the police

By contrast, infinitival *to* (because of its lack of lexical content) cannot be intensified by *right/straight*: cf.

(69) (a)   *I wonder whether *right/straight* **to** go home
     (b)   *Many people want the government *right/straight* **to** change course
     (c)   *We don't intend *right/straight* **to** surrender

Moreover, what makes the prepositional analysis of infinitival *to* even more problematic is that infinitival *to* takes a different range of complements from prepositional *to* (and indeed different from the range of complements found with other prepositions). For example, prepositional *to* (like other prepositions) can have a nominal complement, whereas infinitival *to* requires a verbal complement:

(70) (a)   I intend **to** *resign* [= **to**+*verb*]/*I intend **to** *resignation* [= **to**+*noun*]
     (b)   She waited for John **to** *arrive* [= **to**+*verb*]/She waited for John ***to** *arrival* [= **to**+*noun*]
     (c)   Try **to** *decide* [= **to**+*verb*]/*Try **to** *decision* [= **to**+*noun*]

Significantly, genuine prepositions in English (such as those bold-printed in the examples below) only permit a following verbal complement when the verb is in the *-ing* form (known as the gerund form in this particular use), not when the verb is in the uninflected base/infinitive form: cf.

(71) (a)   I am **against** *capitulating/*capitulate*
     (b)   Try and do it **without** *complaining/*complain*
     (c)   Think carefully **before** *deciding/*decide*

By contrast, infinitival *to* can only take a verbal complement whose verb is in the infinitive form, never one whose verb is in the gerund form: cf.

(72) (a)   I want **to** *go/*going* there

(b)   You must try **to** *work/*working* harder

(c)   You managed **to** *upset/*upsetting* them

A further difference between infinitival and prepositional *to* (illustrated in 73 below) is that infinitival *to* permits **ellipsis** (i.e. omission/deletion) of its complement, whereas prepositional *to* does not. This is illustrated below, where strikethrough marks material which undergoes ellipsis and hence is unpronounced:

(73)   SPEAKER A: Do you want to go to the cinema?

SPEAKER B: No, I don't really want **to** ~~go to the cinema~~

*No, I don't really want to go *to* ~~the cinema~~

In (73A) the deleted material is the complement of the infinitive particle *to*, whereas in (73B) it is the complement of the preposition *to*. The fact that infinitival *to* allows ellipsis of its complement but prepositional *to* does not provides further evidence that infinitival *to* is a different **lexical item** (i.e. a different word) belonging to a different category from prepositional *to*. But what category does infinitival *to* belong to?

In traditional grammar, infinitival *to* was categorised as a 'particle': however, as we saw in §1.3, this term was something of a 'dustbin category' used to designate a wide variety of disparate items (e.g. *not* was characterised as a negative particle, and *off* as an adverbial particle, and neither seems to have anything in common with infinitival *to*). However, if we abandon the traditional analysis of infinitival *to* as an infinitive particle, how are we to categorise it?

In the late 1970s, Chomsky suggested that there are significant similarities between infinitival *to* and a typical auxiliary like *should*. For example, they occupy a similar position within the clause: cf.

(74) (a)   It's vital [that John *should* show an interest]

(b)   It's vital [for John *to*   show an interest]

We see from (74) that *to* and *should* are both positioned between the subject *John* and the verb *show*. Moreover, just as *should* requires after it a verb in the infinitive form (cf. 'You should *show/*showing/*shown* more interest in syntax'), so too does infinitival *to* (cf 'Try to *show/*showing/*shown* more interest in syntax'). Furthermore, infinitival *to* behaves like typical auxiliaries (e.g. *should*) but unlike typical non-auxiliary verbs (e.g. *want*) in allowing ellipsis/deletion of its complement (marked by strikethrough below): cf.

(75) (a)   I don't really want to go to the dentist's, but I know I *should* ~~go to the dentist's~~

(b)   I know I should go to the dentist's, but I just don't want *to* ~~go to the dentist's~~

(c)   *I know I should go to the dentist's, but I just don't *want* ~~to go to the dentist's~~

The fact that *to* patterns like the auxiliary *should* in several respects strengthens the case for regarding infinitival *to* and auxiliaries as belonging to the same category. But what category?

Chomsky (1981: 18) suggested that the resulting category (comprising finite auxiliaries and infinitival *to*) be labelled **INFL** or **Inflection**: however (in accordance with the standard practice of using single-letter symbols to designate word categories), in later work (1986b: 3) he replaced INFL by the single-letter symbol **I**. Under the INFL analysis, an auxiliary like *should* is a finite I/INFL constituent, whereas the particle *to* is an infinitival I/INFL.

In work since the mid 1990s, a somewhat different categorisation of auxiliaries and infinitival *to* has been adopted. As illustrated by our earlier examples in (59a–h) above, finite auxiliaries typically have two distinct forms – a present tense form, and a corresponding past tense form (cf. pairs such as *does/did, is/was, has/had, can/could*, etc.). Thus, a common property shared by all finite auxiliaries is that they mark (present/past) **Tense**. In much the same way, it might be argued that infinitival *to* has tense properties, as we can see from the contrast below:

(76) (a)   We believe [the President *may* have been lying]
     (b)   We believe [the President *to*   have been lying]

In (76a), the bracketed complement clause has a present tense interpretation (paraphraseable as 'We believe it *is* possible that the president has been lying'): this is because it contains the present tense auxiliary *may*. However, the bracketed infinitive complement clause in (76b) can also have a present tense interpretation, paraphraseable as 'We believe the President *has* been lying.' Why should this be? A plausible answer is that infinitival *to* carries tense in much the same way as an auxiliary like *may* does. In a sentence like (76b), *to* is most likely to be assigned a present tense interpretation. However, in a sentence such as (77) below:

(77)   The Feds believed [the junkies *to* have already stashed the hash in the trash-
            can before they were caught]

infinitival *to* seems to have a past tense interpretation, so that (77) is paraphraseable as 'The Federal Agents believed that the junkies *had* already stashed the hash in the trash-can before they were caught.' In much the same way, infinitival *to* in a sentence like (78a) below seems to have much the same future time reference as the auxiliary *will* in (78b):

(78) (a)   She is hoping for you *to* invite her out tomorrow
     (b)   She is hoping that you *will* invite her out tomorrow

What sentences like (76–78) suggests is that infinitival *to* has abstract (i.e. invisible) tense properties. If finite auxiliaries and infinitival *to* both have (visible or invisible) tense properties, we can assign the two of them to the same category of **T/tense marker** – as is done in much contemporary work. The difference between them is that auxiliaries carry **finite** tense (i.e. they are overtly specified for tense, in the sense that, for example, *does* is overtly marked as a present tense form and *did* as a past tense form), whereas infinitival *to* carries **non-finite** tense (i.e. it has an unspecified tense value which has to be determined from the context).

2.9   Complementisers

The last type of functional category which we shall look at in this chapter is that of **complementiser** (abbreviated to **C** in recent work, but to **COMP** in earlier work). This is a term used to describe the kind of word (italicised in the examples in 79) which is used to introduce complement clauses such as those bracketed below:

(79) (a)   I **think** [*that* you may be right]
    (b)   I **wonder** [*if* you can help me]
    (c)   I'm **anxious** [*for* you to receive the best treatment possible]

Each of the bracketed clauses in (79) is a complement clause, in that it functions as the complement of the bold-printed word immediately preceding it (e.g. the *that*-clause is the complement of the verb *think* in 79a). The italicised word which introduces each clause is known in work since 1970 as a complementiser (i.e. complement-clause-introducing particle), but was known in more traditional work as a particular type of subordinating conjunction.

Complementisers are functors in the sense that they encode particular sets of grammatical properties. For example, complementisers encode (non)finiteness by virtue of the fact that they are intrinsically finite or non-finite. More specifically, the complementisers *that* and *if* are inherently finite in the sense that they can only be used to introduce a finite clause (i.e. a clause containing a present or past tense auxiliary or verb), and not, for example, an infinitival *to*-clause; by contrast, *for* is an inherently infinitival complementiser, and so can be used to introduce a clause containing infinitival *to*, but not a finite clause containing a tensed auxiliary like (past tense) *should*. To see this, compare the examples in (79) above with those in (80) below:

(80) (a)   *I think [*that* you **to** be right]
    (b)   *I wonder [*if* you **to** help me]
    (c)   *I'm anxious [*for* you **should** receive the best treatment possible]

(80a,b) are ungrammatical because *that*/*if* are finite complementisers and so cannot introduce an infinitival *to*-clause; (80c) is ungrammatical because *for* is an infinitival complementiser and so cannot introduce a finite clause containing a past tense auxiliary like *should*. (A point to note in passing is that our discussion of *if* in this section relates solely to its use as an interrogative complementiser which can be substituted by *whether*, not to its conditional use in clauses like *If he confesses, you should report him* where *if* can be substituted by *unless*).

Complementisers in structures like (79) serve three grammatical functions. Firstly, they mark the fact that the clause they introduce is an **embedded clause** (i.e. a clause which is embedded/contained within another expression – in this case, within a main clause containing *think*/*wonder*/*anxious*). Secondly, they serve to indicate whether the clause they introduce is finite or non-finite (i.e. denotes an event taking place at a specified or unspecified time): *that* and *if* serve to introduce finite clauses, while *for* introduces non-finite (more specifically, infinitival) clauses. Thirdly, complementisers mark **clause type** – i.e. the type of clause that they introduce: typically, *if* introduces an **interrogative** (i.e. question-asking) clause, *that* introduces a **declarative** (statement-making) clause and *for* introduces an **irrealis** clause (i.e. a clause denoting an 'unreal' or hypothetical event which hasn't yet happened and may never happen).

However, an important question to ask is whether we really need to assign words such as *for/that/if* (in the relevant function) to a new category of C/complementiser, or whether we couldn't simply treat (e.g.) *for* as a preposition, *that* as a determiner and *if* as an adverb. The answer is 'No', because there are significant differences between complementisers and other apparently similar words. For example, one difference between the complementiser *for* and the preposition *for* is that the preposition *for* has substantive lexical semantic content and so (in some but not all of its uses) can be intensified by *straight/right*, whereas the complementiser *for* is a functor and can never be so intensified: cf.

(81) (a)   He headed *straight/right* **for** the pub [*for* = preposition]
    (b)   The dog went *straight/right* **for** her throat [*for* = preposition]
    (c)   *He was anxious *straight/right* **for** nobody to leave [*for* = complementiser]
    (d)   *It is vital *straight/right* **for** the hostages to be released [*for* = complementiser]

Moreover, the preposition *for* and the complementiser *for* also differ in their syntactic behaviour. For example, a clause introduced by the complementiser *for* can be the subject of an expression like *would cause chaos*, whereas a phrase introduced by the preposition *for* cannot: cf.

(82) (a)   *For him to resign* would cause chaos [= *for*-clause]
    (b)   **For him* would cause chaos [= *for*-phrase]

What makes it even more implausible to analyse infinitival *for* as a preposition is the fact that (bold-printed) prepositions in English aren't generally followed by a [bracketed] infinitive complement, as we see from the ungrammaticality of:

(83) (a)   *She was surprised **at** [*there to be nobody to meet her*]
    (b)   *I'm not sure **about** [*you to be there*]
    (c)   *I have decided **against** [*us to go there*]

On the contrary, as examples such as (71) above illustrate, the only verbal complements which can be used after prepositions are gerund structures containing a verb in the *-ing* form.

A further difference between the complementiser *for* and the preposition *for* is that a noun expression or pronoun following the preposition *for* (or a substitute interrogative expression like *who?/what?/which one?*) can be preposed to the front of the sentence (with or without *for*) if *for* is a preposition, but not if *for* is a complementiser. For example, in (84) below, *for* functions as a preposition and the nominal *Senator Megabucks* functions as its complement, so that if we replace *Senator Megabucks* by *which senator?* the wh-expression can be preposed either on its own (in informal styles of English) or together with the preposition *for* (in formal styles): cf.

(84) (a)   I will vote **for** *Senator Megabucks* in the primaries
   (b)   *Which senator* will you vote **for** in the primaries? [= informal style]
   (c)   **For** *which senator* will you vote in the primaries? [= formal style]

To use the relevant technical term, the preposition *for* can be **pied-piped** (i.e. dragged along) together with its complement when its complement is fronted/preposed. (The colourful pied-piping metaphor was coined by Ross 1967, based on a traditional fairy story in which the Pied Piper in the village of Hamelin enticed a group of children to follow him out of a rat-infested village by playing his pipe.) However, in (85a) below, the italicised expression is not the complement of the complementiser *for* (the complement of *for* in (85a) is the infinitival clause *Senator Megabucks to keep his cool*) but rather is the subject of the expression *to keep his cool*. Hence, even if we replace *Senator Megabucks* by the interrogative wh-phrase *which senator*, the wh-expression can't be preposed (irrespective or whether *for* is pied-piped along with it, or whether *for* remains **in situ**/in place):

(85) (a)   They were anxious **for** *Senator Megabucks* to keep his cool
   (c)   **Which senator* were they anxious **for** to keep his cool?
   (b)   ****For** *which senator* were they anxious to keep his cool?

Furthermore, when *for* functions as a complementiser, the whole *for*-clause which it introduces can often (though not always) be substituted by a clause introduced by another complementiser. For example, the italicised *for*-clause in (86a) below can be replaced by the italicised *that*-clause in (86b):

(86) (a)   Is it really necessary *for there to be a showdown*?
   (b)   Is it really necessary *that there (should) be a showdown*?

By contrast, the italicised *for*-phrase in (87a) below cannot be replaced by a *that*-clause, as we see from the ungrammaticality of (87b):

(87) (a)   We are heading *for a general strike*
   (b)   **We are heading *that there (will) be a general strike*

So, there is considerable evidence in favour of drawing a categorial distinction between the preposition *for* and the complementiser *for*: they are different lexical items (i.e. words) belonging to different categories.

   Consider now the question of whether the complementiser *that* could be analysed as a determiner. At first sight, it might seem as if such an analysis would provide a straightforward way of capturing the apparent parallelism between the two uses of *that* in sentences such as the following:

(88) (a)   I refuse to believe **that** [*rumour*]
   (b)   I refuse to believe **that** [*Randy Rabbit frequents Benny's Bunny Bar*]

Given that the word *that* has the status of a prenominal determiner in sentences such as (88a), we might suppose that it has the function of a preclausal determiner (i.e. a determiner introducing the following italicised clause *Randy Rabbit frequents Benny's Bunny Bar*) in sentences such as (88b).

However, there is evidence against a determiner analysis of the complementiser *that*. Part of this is phonological in nature. In its use as a complementiser (in sentences such as 88b above), *that* typically has a **reduced** vowel and is pronounced /ðət/, whereas in its use as a determiner (e.g. in sentences such as 88a above), *that* invariably has an **unreduced** vowel and is pronounced /ðæt/: the phonological differences between the two suggest that we are dealing with two different lexical items here (i.e. two different words), one of which functions as a complementiser and typically has a reduced vowel, the other of which functions as a determiner and always has an unreduced vowel.

Moreover, *that* in its use as a determiner (though not in its use as a complementiser) can be substituted by another determiner (such as *this/the*):

(89) (a)   Nobody else knows about *that* incident/**this** incident/**the** incident (= determiner *that*)

(b)   I'm sure *that* it's true/**this* it's true/**the* it's true (= complementiser *that*)

Similarly, the determiner *that* can be used pronominally (without any complement), whereas the complementiser *that* cannot: cf.

(90) (a)   Nobody can blame you for *that* mistake (prenominal determiner)
(b)   Nobody can blame you for *that* (pronominal determiner)

(91) (a)   I'm sure *that* you are right (preclausal complementiser)
(b)   *I'm sure *that* (pronominal complementiser)

The clear phonological and syntactic differences between the two argue that the word *that* which serves to introduce complement clauses is a different item (belonging to the category complementiser/C) from the determiner/D *that* which modifies noun expressions.

The third item which was claimed earlier to function as a complementiser in English is interrogative *if*. However, at first sight, it might seem as if there is a potential parallelism between *if* and interrogative adverbs like *when/where/why*, since they appear to occupy the same position (at the beginning of a bracketed embedded clause) in sentences like:

(92)   I don't know [*where/when/why/if* he wants to go]

Hence it might seem tempting to analyse *if* as an interrogative adverb.

However, there are a number of reasons for rejecting this possibility. For one thing, *if* differs from interrogative adverbs like *where/when/why* in its phonological form, in that it doesn't begin with *wh*. A more cogent reason for treating *if* as a complementiser rather than an interrogative adverb is that there are distributional differences between the two – i.e. *if* differs from interrogative adverbs in the range of syntactic positions it can occupy. For example, whereas typical wh-adverbs can occur in finite and infinitive clauses alike, the complementiser *if* is restricted to introducing finite clauses – cf.

(93) (a)   I wonder [*when*/*where*/*if* I should go] [= finite clause]
     (b)   I wonder [*when*/*where*/*if to go] [= infinitive clause]

Moreover, *if* is different from interrogative wh-adverbs (but similar to other complementisers like finite *that* and infinitival *for*) in that it cannot be used to introduce a (bracketed) clause which is used as the complement of a (bold-printed) preposition: cf.

(94) (a)   I'm not certain **about** [*when*/*where*/*why* he wants to go]
     (b)   *I'm concerned **over** [*if* taxes are going to be increased]
     (c)   *I'm puzzled **at** [*that* he should have resigned]
     (d)   *I'm not very keen **on** [*for* you to go there]

A further piece of evidence for treating *if* as an interrogative complementiser rather than an interrogative adverb comes from contrasts such as the following:

(95) (a)   I wonder [*when*/*where*/*why* he is going]
     (b)   *When/Where/Why* is he going?

(96) (a)   I wonder [*if* he is going]
     (b)   *If is he going?

As (95) illustrates, typical interrogative adverbs like *when*/*where*/*why* can be used to introduce either an embedded/subordinate clause like that bracketed in (95a) or a main/principal/independent clause like that in (95b). By contrast, interrogative *if* can introduce an embedded clause like that bracketed in (96a), but not a main clause like that in (96b). Since it is characteristic of complementisers that they can introduce embedded clauses but not main clauses, the contrast between (95) and (96) provides strong evidence for categorising *if* (in the relevant use) as an interrogative complementiser.

   Yet another reason for treating interrogative *if* as a complementiser rather than a wh-adverb relates to a type of ellipsis termed **Sluicing** (mentioned in §1.4). This is found in interrogative clauses and involves deletion of all the material following an interrogative expression in a clause like that bracketed below (where strikethrough marks deleted material):

(97)   I know she is going to Paris, but I'm not sure [*when*/*how*/*why* ~~she is going to Paris~~]

Although (as we see in 97) interrogative adverbs like *when*/*how*/*why* permit material following them to be sluiced/deleted, interrogative *if* does not – as we see from the ungrammaticality of (98):

(98)   *The prosecution claimed she was defrauding the company, but the jury was unable to decide [*if* ~~she was defrauding the company~~]

We can account for the contrast between (97) and (98) if we suppose that complementisers don't allow Sluicing, and that interrogative *if* is a complementiser.

A final piece of evidence for treating interrogative *if* as a complementiser comes from the observation that (unlike wh-adverbs) it is incompatible with Auxiliary Inversion. Embedded/subordinate interrogative clauses generally don't allow Auxiliary Inversion, but one exception to this is found in clauses which are instances of what is known as **free indirect speech**. By way of introduction, consider the difference between the two clauses italicised below:

(99) (a)   He asked Mary: '*When are you leaving?*'
   (b)   He asked Mary *when she was leaving*

A direct quotation (like that enclosed in inverted commas in 99a) is traditionally said to be an instance of **direct speech** (or **free speech**). By contrast, an embedded clause like that italicised in (99b) is said to be an instance of indirect speech (or **reported speech**). As we can see by comparing (99a) with (99b), when direct speech is transposed into indirect speech, various changes take place. These include tense transposition (the present tense auxiliary *are* in 99a is transposed into the past tense form *was* in 99b to match the past tense of the verb *asked*), person transposition (the second person pronoun *you* in 99a is transposed into the third person pronoun *she* in 99b), and absence of Auxiliary Inversion. However, alongside indirect speech structures like (99b), we also find free indirect speech structures like the clause italicised in (100a) below (though this type of structure cannot be used in a sentence like 100b):

(100) (a)   John asked Mary *when was she leaving*
   (b)   *John discovered *when was she leaving*

Embedded clauses like that italicised in (100a) resemble indirect speech in that they show tense and person transposition, but resemble direct speech in that they show Auxiliary Inversion. However, there are interesting restrictions on the use of free indirect speech, as we see from the ungrammaticality of (100b).

Embedded interrogative clauses with Auxiliary Inversion seem to be permitted only where the issue raised by the question is unresolved: hence, Inversion is possible in (100a) because John doesn't know the answer to the question asked, but not in (101b) where he does know the answer.

Now compare the wh-question examples in (99,100a) above with the corresponding yes–no question examples in (101) below (where the status of the italicised material is indicated in square brackets):

(101) (a)   He asked: '*Are you leaving?*'   [direct speech]
   (b)   He asked *if she was leaving*   [indirect speech]
   (c)   He asked *was she leaving*   [free indirect speech]
   (d)   *He asked *if was she leaving*   [free indirect speech]

In the direct speech italicised in (101a) we find Auxiliary Inversion. However, in the indirect speech italicised in (101b), there is no Inversion. By contrast, in the free indirect speech italicised in (101c), we again find Auxiliary Inversion. Nevertheless, there is no Inversion if the italicised clause is introduced by the complementiser *if*, as we see from (101d), even though Inversion would be possible if the clause were introduced by a wh-adverb like *when* (as in *He asked when was she leaving*). The fact that interrogative *if* blocks Auxiliary Inversion (but wh-adverbs do not) provides us with further evidence that *if* is a complementiser. (In chapter 5 we will see that the reason why complementisers block Auxiliary Inversion is that inverted auxiliaries occupy the same position within clauses as complementisers, and hence Inversion is barred when the position which would otherwise be occupied by an inverted auxiliary is already filled by a complementiser.)

The conclusion that our discussion in this section leads to is that there is extensive evidence for positing a category C of complementiser, and for supposing that complementisers have a set of unique properties which differentiate them from other types of word, e.g. in typing clauses as declarative or interrogative, and as finite or non-finite.

Our discussion in §§2.2–2.9 may have given the impression that it is relatively straightforward to determine what category a given word belongs to. However, in the next section I'll show that this is not always as straightforward as we might like, and that categorisation problems sometimes arise with specific items which makes it difficult to determine what category to assign them to.

2.10   Categorisation problems

In this section, we take a look at three individual cases which illustrate the kind of categorisation problems that can arise when we try and categorise words, and the conflicting considerations which can sometimes lead different linguists to arrive at different categorisations for the same word. All three cases will involve items which may or may not be complementisers. Let's begin by looking at the case of interrogative *whether*.

The issue which arises with interrogative *whether* is that it is unclear whether we should treat it as an interrogative complementiser (like *if*), or as an interrogative adverb (like *when/why/where/how*). At first sight, *whether* might appear to be a clear-cut case of an interrogative complementiser (like *if*), because it behaves like *if* (and other complementisers) in several key respects. For one thing, like the complementiser *if* (and unlike interrogative adverbs such as *when/ why/how*), *whether* is restricted to introducing an embedded clause like that bracketed in (102a) below and cannot introduce a main clause like that in (102b):

(102) (a)   I wonder [*when/why/how/whether/if* he is going to London]
　　　(b)   *When/Why/How/*Whether/*If* is he going to London?

Moreover, although a (bold-printed) auxiliary can undergo Inversion in a [bracketed] subordinate clause introduced by a wh-adverb in cases of free indirect speech (as in 100 above), no such Inversion is possible in an embedded clause introduced by the complementiser *if*, or by *whether*:

(103)   He wondered [*where/when/why/*whether/*if* **had** she gone]

A third reason for treating *whether* as a complementiser is that like *if* (but unlike wh-adverbs) it doesn't allow Sluicing of the material following it, as illustrated below:

(104)   I think she is going to Paris, but I'm not sure [*when/how/why/*if/*whether* ~~she is going to Paris~~]

A fourth reason is that *whether* differs from wh-adverbs in respect of the type of modifiers it allows. For example, wh-adverbs (like *where/when/why*) can be modified by *the hell* (as can wh-pronouns like *who* and *what*), but *whether* (like *if*) cannot be modified in the same way:

(105) (a)   I want to know [*why the hell* you told her]
    (b)   *Where the hell* have you been?
    (c)   I've no idea [*when the hell* he is coming back]
    (d)   *I wonder [*whether the hell/if the hell* he will resign]

A fifth reason is that wh-adverbs (and indeed wh-pronouns) can be modified by *exactly*, but *whether* (like *if*) cannot:

(106) (a)   I'm not sure [*when exactly* she'll be back]
    (b)   I don't know [*why exactly* he was rude to her]
    (c)   *Where exactly* are you going?
    (d)   *I have no idea [*whether exactly/if exactly* he attended the lecture]

A sixth reason concerns so-called **cleft sentences** – i.e. sentences like 'It was *money* that he wanted', where the italicised item is said to be **focused**. As we see from examples like those in (107) below, wh-adverbs like *when/where/why* can be focused in a cleft structure, but not a complementiser like *whether/if*.

(107)   I'm not sure *when/why/where/*whether/*if* it was that the accident occurred

The differences illustrated in (102–107) above are consistent with *whether* being a complementiser like *if* rather than a wh-adverb like *when/where/why*.

However, in certain other respects, *whether* behaves more like a wh-adverb than a complementiser. For one thing, it begins with *wh-* (just like wh-adverbs such as *when/where/why*). Still, this may tell us simply that just as there is a contrast between interrogative adverbs (like *when/where/why*) that begin with *wh-* and others (like *how*) that do not, so too there is a contrast between an interrogative complementiser like *whether* that begins with *wh-* and one like *if* that does not. Consequently, this may not be a decisive consideration.

A rather more persuasive argument for treating *whether* as a wh-adverb is that (like other wh-adverbs) it can occur both in finite clauses like that bracketed in (108a) below and in infinitive clauses like that bracketed in (108b):

(108) (a) I wonder [how/when/where/whether I *should* do it]
     (b) I wonder [how/when/where/whether *to* do it]

At first sight, this would seem to provide a compelling argument in favour of treating *whether* as a wh-adverb. However, closer reflection suggests that this may not be so. An alternative way of looking at things is the following. Whereas the complementiser *if* is specified as both interrogative and finite, its counterpart *whether* (by contrast) is specified simply as interrogative. This means that whereas *if* is restricted to occurring in interrogative clauses which are finite, by contrast *whether* can occur in any type of interrogative clause – hence both in a finite interrogative clause like that bracketed in (108a) and in an infinitival interrogative clause like that bracketed in (108b).

Added plausibility is lent to this way of viewing things by the observation that for some speakers, even the interrogative complementiser *if* is not restricted to use in finite clauses – as illustrated by the following headings/examples from online articles/postings:

(109) (a) FA to review reports before deciding *if to* take action against Blades for pitch invasion *(MailOnline)*
     (b) Advice on *if to* go to hosp(ital) *(Multiple Sclerosis Society)*
     (c) Wondering *if to* offer same day dispatch? *(Ebay)*
     (d) Funds are pending so not sure *if to* send item *(Ebay)*
     (e) Not sure *if to* max 401k *(Reddit)*

Since interrogative *if* is a complementiser which (for some speakers, albeit not for me) can introduce both finite and non-finite clauses, there is no reason not to treat *whether* as an interrogative complementiser which is able to occur in finite and non-finite clauses alike.

A further potential argument for treating *whether* as a wh-adverb rather than a complementiser comes from the observation that it can be used to introduce a clause used as the complement of a preposition, e.g. in sentences like those in (110) below:

(110) (a) They were arguing **about** *whether they should go to the party*
     (b) They were arguing **about** *whether to go to the party*

Since we saw in (94) that clauses introduced by wh-adverbs like *when/where/why* can serve as the complement of a preposition but clauses introduced by complementisers like *if/that* cannot, this surely provides an argument in favour of categorising *whether* as a wh-adverb, doesn't it?

Not necessarily. One way of dealing with this is to suppose that in the same way as the infinitival complementiser *for* is prepositional in nature, so too the complementiser *whether* can be nominal in nature. If we further suppose that only nominal constituents can occur as the complement of a preposition, it follows that a *whether*-clause can be used in this way, but not a *that*-clause or an *if*-clause (if *that* and *if* are non-nominal complementisers).

Support for this assumption comes from the observation that some speakers (though not me) seemingly treat the complementisers *if* and *that* as nominal. Such speakers allow *if*-clauses and *that*-clauses to serve as the complement of a preposition, as illustrated by sentences like those in (111) below, which I recorded from live radio and TV broadcasts:

(111) (a)   It depends **on** *if Laudrup stays* (Nat Coombs, Talk Sport Radio)
    (b)   It's not **about** *if I bowl a bad ball* (Shane Warne, Sky Sports TV)
    (c)   Moyes seemed to be completely in the dark **about** *that this could happen* (Tony Evans, Talk Sport Radio)
    (d)   We got wind **of** *that there was gonna be a big announcement tomorrow* (Dwight Yorke, Talk Sport Radio)

Overall, then, it is doubtful that sentences like (110) seriously undermine the case for treating *whether* as an interrogative complementiser. At any rate, from this point on I will treat *whether* as an interrogative complementiser in present-day English.

Another item which has proved problematic to categorise is *how come?* In colloquial English, this is often written as the single word *howcome* – as in the following conversation (from the online *Urban Dictionary*):

(112)   DAVE: yo, u hungry?
          TODD: no, u?
          DAVE: howcome?

There are two good reasons for taking *how come* to function as a single word in present-day English. Firstly, *how come* is invariable, in the sense that *how* cannot be replaced by other wh-words (as we see in 113a below), and *come* cannot be replaced by other forms of the same verb (as we see in 113b):

(113) (a)   *How/*However/*When/*Where* come he resigned?
    (b)   How *come/*comes/*came/*coming* he resigned?

And secondly, the string *how come* is indivisible, in the sense that no other word/s (like those italicised in 114 below) can intrude between the two items:

(114) (a)   How (**else*/*the devil*/*exactly*) come he resigned?
    (b)   How, (**in your view,*) (**Charles,*) come he resigned?

Moreover, *come* cannot be deleted via an ellipsis operation like Sluicing (leaving *how* on its own), e.g. in (115):

(115)   You're always grinning about something. *How *(come)*? (Kim and Kim 2011: 4, 13a)

The fact that the string *how come* is invariable and indivisible is consistent with it having become a single word in present-day English – hence, I'll write it as *howcome* from now on. (An important caveat to note, however, is that the observations made about *how come* above and below hold for speakers like me, but not for all speakers: there is a great deal of variation between speakers in how they use *how come*, as discussed in Radford 2015.)

Having established that *howcome* functions as a single word in colloquial English, let's ask what category it belongs to. One possibility is to treat it as an adverbial pronoun like *why* (meaning 'for what reason'); however, another possibility (argued for by Collins 1991) is to treat it as a complementiser like *if/whether*. So which is it? Adverb or complementiser?

There are a number of ways in which *howcome* appears to behave like a complementiser rather than an adverb such as *why*. For one thing, unlike *why* it does not allow Auxiliary Inversion: cf.

(116) (a)   **Why**/**Howcome* did he lie to congress?

(b)   *Howcome*/***Why** he lied to Congress?

In blocking Inversion, *howcome* behaves in the same way as the complementisers *if/whether* in (102) above. Moreover, *howcome* resembles the complementisers *whether/if* (but differs from wh-adverbs like *why/where/when*) in not being able to appear in focus position in a cleft sentence like that below:

(117)   I'm not sure *when/why/where/*whether/*if/*howcome* it was that the accident occurred

Furthermore, like the complementiser *if* (but unlike wh-adverbs), *howcome* is restricted to use in finite clauses and cannot occur in infinitival clauses like that bracketed below:

(118) (a)   It can be hard to decide [*when, where, how* and *why* to forgive someone]

(b)   *It can be hard to decide [**howcome/if** to forgive someone]

Thus, it would seem that a strong case can be made for treating *howcome* as an interrogative complementiser.

And yet, categorising *howcome* as a complementiser proves problematic in other respects. For one thing, *howcome* differs from typical complementisers like *that/if/whether* in being able to occur in main/root/principal/independent clauses like the following:

(119)   **Howcome**/**That/*If/*Whether* he has resigned?

Moreover, unlike typical complementisers (but like typical wh-words), *how come* allows Sluicing of its complement in sentences such as (120):

(120)   I suspected he had left, but I wasn't sure **why/howcome**/**whether/*if* ~~he had left~~

Furthermore, like the adverb *why* (but unlike the complementisers *whether/if*), *howcome* can be modified by the adverb *exactly*, e.g. in (121):

(121)   I have no idea *howcome exactly/why exactly/*whether exactly/*if exactly* the server is working

In addition, *howcome* can be coordinated with other wh-adverbs, as we see from the internet-sourced examples below:

(122) (a)   I don't know *why, or where, or how come*, but about 6 years ago my dad decided we didn't need 'The Weasley's' in our life (fanfiction.net)

(b)   I spend many hours on the computer assessing *why, when and how come* – Jose did not care (books.google.co.uk)

And in some varieties of English (though not mine), *howcome* behaves like *why* in allowing Auxiliary Inversion after it – as in the following example which I sourced from the Internet:

(123)   How come *is it* that even ugly women my age can get a boyfriend but I am still single?

Indeed, as shown by the % sign below, there are some varieties of English which allow *how come* (and *why*) to be followed by the complementiser *that*, but do not allow *whether/if* to be followed by *that*:

(124)   He wanted to know %*howcome* **that**/%*why* **that**/*whether* **that**/*if* **that** I had apologised

Thus, there are numerous respects in which *howcome* behaves more like the adverb *why* than the complementisers *whether/if*.

What emerges from the above discussion is that in some respects *howcome* behaves like a complementiser, but in others it behaves like an adverb. Choosing between these two analyses is thus extremely difficult. For what it's worth, my own inclination is to treat it as an adverb (an analysis defended in Radford 2015).

Let's now move on to consider a third item which is problematic to categorise – namely *how*. This can serve as an interrogative pronoun meaning 'in what manner?' in sentences like (124a) below, and as a **free** (i.e. antecedentless) **relative pronoun** meaning 'the manner in which' in sentences like (124b):

(125) (a)   *How* did you behave and *how* did people treat you?

(b)   [*How* you behave] determines [*how* people treat you]

But now consider the use of *how* in a sentence such as the following:

(126)   They were shocked at [**how** the tooth fairy doesn't really exist] (Legate 2010: 122)

Here, *how* doesn't seem to have a manner interpretation paraphraseable as 'the way in which', but rather a **factive** interpretation paraphraseable as 'the fact that' – and indeed, *how* in (126) can be substituted by the string *the fact that*, as we see from:

(127)   They were shocked at [*the fact that* the tooth fairy doesn't really exist]

This raises the possibility that *how* may function as a factive complementiser in the use illustrated in (126).

Evidence in support of taking factive *how* to be a complementiser comes from the observation by Nye (2013: 192) that it behaves like the complementisers *if/whether* (see 104 above) in not allowing Sluicing in sentences such as the following:

(128)   *I know he's a very successful author, but there's really no need for him to keep repeating [**how** ~~he's a very successful author~~]

It would seem, therefore, that a plausible case can be made for treating factive *how* as a complementiser.

But if complementisers can be of different types (e.g. infinitival *for* is prepositional in type), what kind of complementiser is factive *how*? There is some *prima facie* evidence suggesting that it might be nominal in nature. One reason for thinking this is that a factive *how*-clause can be co-ordinated with a nominal (i.e. a noun-containing expression), as, for example, in (129):

(129)   He complained about **the dirty windows** and *how nobody had been to clean them*

Another reason is that (according to Legate 2010) factive *how*-clauses (like pronouns) are restricted to occurring in **case positions** (i.e. in positions where they can be assigned case by an appropriate case assigner). This point can be illustrated by comparing the behaviour of the pronoun *this* in (130a) below with that of the italicised factive *how*-clause in (130b):

(130) (a)   *I'm really sorry *(about) *this*
      (b)   I'm really sorry *(**about**) *how the tooth fairy doesn't really exist*

Pronouns have the property that they must be assigned case by an appropriate case assigner (as we will see in §4.9). Because the adjective *sorry* is not a case assigner (i.e. in traditional terms it is **intransitive**), it cannot have a pronoun like *this* as its complement in (130a), as we see from the ungrammaticality of **I'm really sorry this*. By contrast, if we use the transitive (i.e. accusative-case-assigning) preposition *about* after *sorry* in (130a), the resulting sentence *I'm really sorry about this* is fine because *this* can be assigned accusative case by *about* (albeit the pronoun *this* does not overtly inflect for case). We can offer a similar account of the contrast in (130b) if we suppose that *how* is a nominal complementiser, and hence (like nouns and pronouns) must occur in a case position (i.e. in a position where it can be assigned case). In *I'm really sorry about how the tooth fairy doesn't really exist*, the nominal complementiser *how* can be assigned accusative case by the transitive preposition *about*, and the resulting sentence is grammatical. By contrast, in **I'm really sorry how the tooth fairy doesn't really exist*, the complementiser *how* is in a **caseless** position (i.e. in a position where it cannot be assigned case, because *sorry* is intransitive and not a case assigner), and consequently the resulting sentence is ungrammatical.

However, Legate's claim that factive *how* is restricted to occurring in case positions is disputed by Nye (2013), who argues that factive *how* can occur in caseless positions, e.g. in sentences such as the following:

(131) (a)   It's **funny** [*how* the tooth fairy doesn't exist]
      (b)   It's **strange** [*how* good can come out of tragedy]

Since adjectives like *funny/strange* are not case assigners, it is difficult to defend the view that *how* occurs in a case position in sentences like (130). Legate concludes that factive *how* can occur in both case positions and caseless positions – and this weakens the argument for taking it to always be nominal in nature.

Our discussion of *whether, howcome* and *how* in this section has served to underline that it can sometimes be quite difficult to categorise particular uses of particular items. In the next section, we will see that the reason for this is that categories are in effect complex bundles of grammatical features, rather than primitive, atomic elements.

2.11   Grammatical features

In this chapter, we have seen that we can assign words in sentences to grammatical categories on the basis of their grammatical properties (albeit this is not always straightforward). However, while categories provide a rough classification of words into types (on the basis of their morphological, syntactic and semantic properties), a finer-grained analysis of words shows that they have subcategorial properties which cannot adequately be characterised in terms of grammatical categories alone. This can be illustrated in relation to the following sentence:

(132)   He is working

The word *he* is generally categorised as a pronoun (perhaps as a D-pronoun, as we saw in §2.6). However, it has a number of grammatical properties which mark it out as different in nature from other pronoun forms. For example, *he* differs in person from *I* and *you*, in that *I* is a first person pronoun denoting the person speaking, *you* is a second person pronoun denoting the person/s being spoken to, and *he* is a third person pronoun denoting someone who is neither speaking nor being spoken to. *He* also differs in number from *they* in that (although both are third person pronouns), *he* is a pronoun with **singular number** (and so refers to only one person), whereas *they* is a pronoun with plural number (and so refers to more than one person). *He* also differs in gender from *she* and *it*, in that *he* has **masculine gender** by virtue of denoting a male being, *she* has **feminine gender** by virtue of denoting a female being, and *it* has **neuter gender** by virtue of denoting an inanimate entity. *He* also differs in case from *him* and *his*, in that *he* has nominative case, *him* has accusative case and *his* has genitive case. Different case forms of pronouns are used in different positions within sentences, as the following example illustrates:

(133)   *He* was told that the police would charge *him* with driving *his* car without due
            care and attention

When used as the subject of a finite auxiliary like *wasn't*, a pronoun has to be in the nominative form – hence the use of *he* as the subject of *wasn't* in (133). When used as the complement/object of a transitive verb, a pronoun has to be in the accusative form – hence the use of *him* as the object of the verb *accuse* (denoting the person that the accusation is levelled at). When used to mark possession, a pronoun is used in the genitive form – hence the use of *his* to mark the possessor of the car in (133).

Thus, simply categorising items like *I/you/them/his*, etc. as pronouns provides no way of characterising important (subcategorial) grammatical differences between various pronoun forms. There is a great deal of additional grammatical information about words which is not represented by simply attaching a category label to the word – information which provides a finer level of detail than relatively coarse categorial descriptions. This additional information is generally described in terms of sets of grammatical features; by convention, features are enclosed in square brackets and often abbreviated (to save space). Using grammatical features, we can describe the subcategorial properties of the pronoun *he* in (132) in terms of the set of features shown below:

(134)   [3-Pers, Sg-Num, Masc-Gen, Nom-Case]

(i.e. Third-Person, Singular-Number, Masculine-Gender, Nominative-Case). Each of these features comprises an **attribute** (i.e. a property like person, number, gender or case) and a **value** (which can be first/second/third for person, singular/plural for number, masculine/feminine/neuter for gender, and nominative/accusative/genitive for case).

A similar point can be made in relation to the grammatical properties of the word *is* as it is used in (132). In categorial terms, *is* belongs to the category of AUX/T, by virtue of being a tense-marking auxiliary. However, simply categorising it as a T auxiliary doesn't tell us in what ways it is different from other auxiliary forms. For example, *is* differs from *are* (as in 'They *are* working') in that *is* marks singular number and so is used with a singular subject like *he*, whereas *are* marks plural number and so is used with a plural subject like *they*. Similarly, *is* differs from *am* (as in 'I *am* working') in that *is* serves as a third person form used with a third person subject like *he*, whereas *am* is a first person form used with the first person subject *I*. Moreover, *is* differs from *was* (as in 'I *was* working') in that *is* marks present tense whereas *was* marks past tense. In addition, *is* differs from the auxiliary *be* (in a sentence like 'The army demands that every soldier *be* prepared to lay down their life for their country') in that *is* marks indicative mood, whereas *be* marks subjunctive mood. Overall, then, we can characterise the subcategorial properties of the auxiliary *is* in (132) in terms of the features in (135) below:

(135)   [3-Pers, Sg-Num, Pres-Tns, Ind-Mood]

– i.e. 'Third-Person, Singular-Number, Present-Tense, Indicative-Mood'.

The same point can also be made about the grammatical properties of the word *working* in (131). This belongs to the grammatical category of verb. However, it carries an -*ing* suffix which (in this use) marks the property of aspect. Aspect is a term used to denote the duration of the activity described by the main verb in the sentence (e.g. whether the activity is ongoing or completed). In sentence (131) *He is working*, the action of working is still ongoing/in progress at the time of speaking, and for this reason, the form *working* is said to carry a grammatical feature marking [Progressive-Aspect]. By contrast, in a sentence such as *He has learned French*, the learning activity is now completed/perfected, and the traditional grammatical term for describing this is to say that the verb *left* marks [Perfect-Aspect] in this kind of use. A non-finite verb form which marks aspect is traditionally called a particle, so that *working* in *He is working* is a progressive participle, and *learned* in *he has learned French* is a perfect participle.

The overall conclusion which the preceding discussion leads us to is the following. Grammatical categories provide a broad categorisation of words into types (on the basis of their morphological, syntactic and semantic properties); but a finer-grained analysis requires that the grammatical properties of words should further be characterised in terms of sets of subcategorial features.

However, it should be noted that the relation between features and categories is far from straightforward. Consider, for example, how to handle similarities and differences between the auxiliaries *may, have* and *be* in a sentence like the following:

(136)   They *may have been* lying

Assigning them all to the category AUX accounts for similarities between them (e.g. all three can undergo Auxiliary Inversion when finite), but fails to account for differences between them – e.g. *may* is a modal auxiliary, whereas *have* and *be* are aspectual auxiliaries. One way of differentiating between aspectual and non-aspectual auxiliaries would be in terms of a binary/two-valued subcategorial feature like [±ASP] (i.e. does/doesn't mark aspect), with *have/be* being [+ASP] and *may* being [−ASP]. However, this solution wouldn't account for differences between the two aspectual auxiliaries *have* and *be*, including the fact that *have* marks perfect aspect and *be* marks progressive aspect. We could account for this aspectual difference by positing that any auxiliary specified as [+ASP] carries a further binary feature like [±PERF] (i.e. does/doesn't mark perfect aspect). We could then say that *may, have* and *be* (in their use as auxiliaries) all belong to the category AUX, but that the modal auxiliary *may* carries the subcategorial feature [−ASP], whereas the perfect aspect auxiliary *have* carries the subcategorial features [+ASP, +PERF], and the progressive aspect auxiliary *be* carries the subcategorial features [+ASP, −PERF]. (An interesting point to note in passing here is that some binary features are taken to be privative in nature, in the sense that an item either does or doesn't have some feature F, and is thus valued as either [+F] or [−F].)

However, an alternative approach would be to handle the differences between the auxiliaries *may, have* and *be* in categorial terms, and suppose that they belong to entirely separate categories, with *may* belonging to the category M (of modal marker), *have* belonging to the category PERF (of perfect aspect marker) and *been* belonging to the category PROG (of progressive aspect marker). The problem with this solution is that it would fail to capture the observation that *may/have/be* are all auxiliaries and hence (e.g.) they can all undergo Auxiliary Inversion in appropriate contexts. One way of accounting for this would be to posit that *may/have/be* carry a subcategorial feature [+AUX] which serves (*inter alia*) to trigger Auxiliary Inversion in finite clauses in appropriate contexts – and this in turn illustrates an important use of features (which we will encounter throughout the book) as devices used to trigger grammatical operations.

What this brief discussion demonstrates is that a mixed (categories-and-features) system raises important (and difficult-to-answer) theoretical questions about which grammatical properties should be described in terms of categories, and which in terms of features.

This dilemma was recognised by Chomsky in work in the 1960s and 1970s. He suggested that all the grammatical properties of a word (including its categorial properties) should be described in terms of a set of grammatical features. For example, he argued that the categorial distinction between nouns, verbs, adjectives and prepositions should be handled in terms of two sets of binary features, namely [±V] 'verbal/non-verbal' and [±N] 'nominal/non-nominal'. More specifically, he suggested that the categorial properties of nouns, verbs, adjectives and prepositions could be described in terms of the sets of features in (137) below:

(137)   verb = [+V, –N]   adjective = [+V, +N]   noun = [–V, +N]   preposition = [–V, –N]

What (137) claims is that verbs have verbal but not nominal properties, adjectives have both nominal and verbal properties, nouns have nominal but not verbal properties, and prepositions have neither nominal nor verbal properties. This analysis was designed to capture the observation that some grammatical properties extend across more than one category and so can be said to be cross-categorial. By way of illustrating one such cross-categorial property, consider the use of the prefix *un-* in English. Verbs and adjectives in English share the morphological property that they alone permit *un-*prefixation (hence we find verbs like *undo* and adjectives like *unkind*, but not nouns like **unfriend* or prepositions like **uninside*): in terms of the set of grammatical features in (137), we can account for this by positing that *un-* can only be prefixed to words which have the feature [+V]. Likewise, as the following example kindly provided for me by Andrew Spencer shows, nouns and adjectives inflect for case in Russian, but not verbs or prepositions: cf.

(138)   Krasiva*ya*   dyevushk*a*   vsunula   chornu*yu*   koshk*u*   v   pustu*yu*   korobk*u*
         Beautiful   girl   put   black   cat   in   empty   box
         'The beautiful girl put the black cat in the empty box'

The nouns and adjectives in (138) carry (italicised) case endings (*-a* is a nominative suffix and *-u* an accusative suffix), but not the verb or preposition. In terms of the set of categorial features in (138), we can account for this by positing that case is a property of items which carry the categorial feature [+N].

An obvious drawback to the system of categorial features in (137) above is that it describes the categorial properties of a number of substantive/lexical categories, but not those of functional categories. Each functional category seems to be closely related to a corresponding lexical category: for example, auxiliaries appear to be related to verbs, determiners to adjectives, and the complementiser *for* to the preposition *for*. One way of handling both the similarities and differences between substantive categories and their functional counterparts is in terms of a binary functionality feature [±F], with functional categories carrying the feature [+F], and substantive categories carrying the feature [−F]. On this view, main verbs would have the feature specification [−N, +V, −F] whereas auxiliary verbs would have the feature specification [−N, +V, +F]; likewise, the complementiser *for* would have the feature specification [−N, −V, +F], and the preposition *for* would be specified as [−N, −V, −F].

Although many details remain to be worked out, it seems clear that in principle, all grammatical properties of words (including their categorial properties) can be described in terms of sets of grammatical features. However, in order to simplify exposition, I shall continue to make use of category labels throughout the rest of the book, only making use of grammatical features where some descriptive purpose is served by doing so.

2.12   Summary

In this chapter, we have looked at the role played by categories in characterising the grammatical properties of words. In §2.2, we looked at the criteria used for categorising words, noting that semantic criteria have to be used with care, and that morphological criteria (relating to the inflectional and derivational properties of words) and syntactic criteria (relating to the range of positions which words can occupy within phrases and sentences) tend to be more reliable. In §2.3 we saw that we can determine the categorial status of a word from its morphological and syntactic properties, with substitution being used as a test in problematic cases. In §2.4 a distinction was drawn between substantive/lexical categories (whose members have substantive lexical content) and functional categories (whose members have no substantive lexical content and serve only to mark grammatical properties such as number, person, case, tense, aspect, mood, etc.). We then looked at a number of different types of functional category found in English. We began in §2.5 with determiners (= D) and quantifiers (= Q), and I argued that they are categorially distinct from adjectives since they precede (but don't follow) adjectives, they can't be stacked and they impose grammatical restrictions on the types of expression they can modify (e.g. *a* can only modify a singular count noun expression). In §2.6, we looked at pronouns and saw that English has at least three distinct types of pronoun, namely N-pronouns (like *one*), Q-pronouns (like *several*) and D-pronouns (like *this*). I noted that recent research has suggested that personal pronouns like *he* are also D-pronouns, but that this categorisation is not entirely unproblematic. In §2.7 we looked at the functional counterparts of verbs, namely auxiliaries: I argued that these are functors in that (unlike lexical verbs) they describe no specific action or event, but rather encode verb-related grammatical properties such as tense, mood, voice and aspect; we saw that auxiliaries are syntactically distinct from verbs in that (*inter alia*) they undergo (Subject-Auxiliary) Inversion. In §2.8 we examined the nature of infinitival *to*: I showed that it is distinct from the preposition *to* and shares a number of properties in common with finite auxiliaries (e.g. auxiliaries and infinitival *to* allow ellipsis of their complements, but prepositional *to* does not). I noted the assumption made in much research over the past three decades that finite auxiliaries and infinitival *to* are different exponents of the same category (labelled I/INFL/ Inflection in earlier work and T/tense marker in more recent work), with an auxiliary like *will* marking finite tense, and infinitival *to* marking non-finite tense. In §2.9 I argued that complementizers (= C or COMP) like *that/for/if* are a further category of functors and that they mark clause type (in that they indicate whether the clause they introduce is finite or non-finite, interrogative or non-interrogative, etc.). In §2.10, I went on to argue that it is sometimes difficult to categorise a particular use of a particular item and, by way of illustration, considered the *pros* and *cons* of treating *whether* and *how come* as interrogative complementisers and *how* as a factive complementiser. Finally, in §2.11 I noted that assigning words to grammatical categories provides a description of only some of their grammatical properties, and that a fuller description requires the use of grammatical features to describe their subcategorial properties. I went on to note Chomsky's claim that the categorial properties of words can also be described in terms of a set of grammatical features – bringing us to the conclusion that all grammatical properties of words can be characterised in terms of sets of features.

2.13   Bibliographical background

For accounts of English morphology, see Carstairs-McCarthy (2002), Plag (2003), Spencer (2004), Harley (2006), and Bauer, Lieber and Plag (2013). On the monosuffixal nature of words in English, see Aronoff and Fuhrhop (2002). On the nature of determiners (discussed in §2.5), see Giusti (1997), Spinillo (2004) and Isac (2006). On the possibility of categorising quantifiers as a subtype of determiner discussed in §2.5, see Lyons (1999) and Adger (2003). On the nature of various types of pronoun (discussed in §2.6), see Cardinaletti and Starke (1999), Wiltschko (2001) and Déchaine and Wiltschko (2002). On the claim that personal pronouns in English belong to the category D, see Postal (1966), Abney (1987), Longobardi (1994) and Lyons (1999). On the nature of gender features in English, see Namai (2000). The claim made in §2.7 that modals have (present/past) tense properties is disputed by some linguists who analyse them as tenseless, on the grounds (*inter alia*) that they never carry the regular present tense *-s* ending (cf. **He mays/wills resign*): for discussion of modals, see Chomsky (1957), Jackendoff (1972, 1977a), Fiengo (1974), Akmajian, Steele and Wasow (1979), Palmer (1983, 1986, 1990, 2001),

Bobaljik (1995), Bobaljik and Thráinsson (1998), Aelbrecht (2009, 2010). For a technical discussion of tense, see Julien (2001) and Ishii (2006). On the claim made in §2.8 that infinitival *to* is a tense particle, see Stowell (1982) and Freidin (2004: 117, fn.32). The term *complementiser* introduced in §2.9 dates back to Rosenbaum (1965, 1967) and Bresnan (1970). On free indirect speech, see Banfield (1982), Ginzburg and Sag (2000) and McCloskey (2006b). The claim that *how come* is a complementiser was made by Collins (1991); for a range of alternative treatments of it (e.g. as an adverb), see Zwicky and Zwicky (1971), Ochi (2004), Conroy (2006), Fitzpatrick (2005), Kim and Kim (2011), Shlonsky and Soare (2011) and Radford (2015). On the use of *how* as a factive complementiser, see Legate (2010) and Nye (2013). The observation in §2.11 that categories can be decomposed into sets of features is due to Chomsky (1965, 1970). The claim that verbs and adjectives share the property of permitting *un*-prefixation is due to Stowell (1981: 57, fn.17). For an attempt to motivate a feature-based analysis of functional categories, see Radford (1997b: 65–8, 84). On the relation between categories and features, see Ramat (2014).

Workbook section

Exercise 2.1

Discuss the grammatical properties and categorial status of the highlighted words in each of the following examples, giving arguments in support of your analysis:

1 a. Nobody *need/dare* say anything
   b. Nobody *needs/dares* to ask questions
   c. John *is* working hard
   d. John *may* stay at home
   e. John *has* done it
   f. John *has* to go there
   g. John *used* to go there quite often
   h. John *ought* to apologise

2 a. Executives like *to* drive *to* work
   b. I look forward *to* learning *to* drive
   c. It's difficult *to* get him *to* work
   d. I've never felt tempted *to* turn *to* taking drugs
   e. Better *to* yield *to* temptation than *to* submit *to* deprivation!
   f. Failure *to* achieve sometimes drives people *to* drink
   g. Try *to* go *to* sleep

3 a. It is important *for* parents to spend time with their children
   b. It would be disastrous *for* me *for* my driving license to be withdrawn
   c. He was arrested *for* being drunk
   d. We are hoping *for* a peace agreement to be signed
   e. Ships head *for* the nearest port in a storm

    f.   Congress voted *for* the treaty to be ratified

    g.   It was disappointing *for* the students to fail their exams

4 a.   *If* you wouldn't mind passing the salt

    b.   I was struck (by) *how* the winter was so much colder in New York than London

    c.   As the heir to the throne, one has to learn *how* to conduct oneself in a manner befitting one's status

    d.   One little boy told me *how* that he had 'done three months at Maidstone' (victorianlondon.org)

    e.   I reckon *as* he's still carryin' a torch for you, I do (from *The Bad Apple* by Rosie Goodwin, 2010)

    f.   Reckon *as how* I love you (title of a song by Slim Williams)

    g.   *How in the world come* you treat me this-a-way? (lyrics to *Lorenzo Blues* by Skip James)

Helpful hints

The key issue of interest in the examples in 1 is whether each of the italicised items (as used in each of the relevant sentences) has the categorial status of a verb or an auxiliary (or indeed can have dual status and function as either). The key issue in 2 is whether each use of *to* is a preposition/P or infinitival tense marker/T. In 3, the key issue is whether each use *for* is a complementiser/C or a preposition/P. A particular problem which arises in the case of some of the examples in 3 is that some words allow a prepositional phrase complement (comprising a preposition and a noun or pronoun expression) in one use, and a *for*-infinitive clause in another – as with *arrange* in the examples below

(i) (a)   I can arrange **for** *immediate closure of the account*

    (b)   I can arrange **for** *the account to be closed immediately*

In (i.a) *for* is used with the noun expression *immediate closure of the account* as its complement and is clearly a preposition/P – as we can see from the observation that (like the complement of a typical preposition) the relevant noun expression can be moved to the front of the sentence to highlight it:

(ii)   *Immediate closure of the account*, I can certainly arrange **for**

By contrast, *for* in (i.b) seems to be a complementiser/C rather than a preposition. For one thing, prepositions don't allow an infinitival complement, as we see from examples like (71) in the main text. Moreover, the complement of *for* in (i.b) cannot be preposed – as we see from the ungrammaticality of (iii):

(iii)   **The account to be closed immediately*, I can certainly arrange **for**

What we might have expected to find is two occurrences of *for*, one serving as an (italicised) preposition introducing the complement of *arrange*, and the other serving as a (bold-printed) complementiser introducing the infinitive complement – much as we find in (iv):

(iv)   What I can certainly arrange *for* is **for** the account to be closed immediately

But the expected *for for* sequence isn't grammatical in sentences like the following:

(v)   *I can certainly arrange *for* **for** the account to be closed immediately

The reason seems to be that a word which takes a prepositional complement generally drops the (italicised) preposition when it has a complement introduced by a (bold-printed) complementiser – but only if the complement immediately follows the preposition: cf.

(vi) (a)   What you can't be entirely sure *of* is **that** he is telling the truth
   (b)   **That** he is telling the truth, you can't be entirely sure *of*
   (c)   *You can't be entirely sure *of* **that** he is telling the truth
   (d)   You can't be entirely sure **that** he is telling the truth

Thus, the preposition *of* is retained in (vi.a) and (vi.b) because in neither case is it immediately followed by *that*. By contrast, keeping the preposition in a structure like (vi.c) where it is immediately followed by *that* leads to ungrammaticality: but if the preposition is dropped as in (vi.d), the outcome is grammatical. The upshot of all of this is that although we might in principle expect to find a P+C (i.e. preposition+complementiser) structure in (v), what seems to happen in practice is that the preposition is dropped in such cases – hence in (i.b) the *for* which we find is the complementiser *for* rather than the (dropped) preposition *for*.

In (4a), the problem is whether *if* can plausibly be treated as an interrogative complementiser. In (4b–d) and (4f), the issue is whether *how* (in any given use) functions as a (free relative) pronoun meaning 'the manner in which', or as a factive complementiser meaning 'the fact that', and whether (when used as a complementiser), it is nominal or not. In 4f–g, the issue concerns the status of *as* in non-standard varieties of English which use such structures: I leave you to speculate on this yourself. And in (4h), the question that arises is whether *how come* can plausibly be treated as a complementiser in the relevant use.

Model answer for 1a, 2a, 3a and 4a

The main problem raised by the examples in 1 is whether the highlighted items have the categorial status of verbs or auxiliaries as they are used in each example – or indeed whether some of the items in some of their uses have a dual verb/auxiliary status (and so have one use in which they function as auxiliaries, and another use in which they function as verbs). The words *need/dare* in (1a) resemble modal auxiliaries like *will/shall/can/may/must* in that they lack the third person singular -*s* inflection and take a bare infinitive complement (i.e. a complement containing the infinitive verb form *say* but lacking the infinitive particle *to*). They behave like auxiliaries (in Standard English) in that they undergo Inversion in questions, can appear in tags and can be negated by *not/n't*:

(i) (a)   *Need/Dare* anyone say anything?
   (b)   He *needn't/daren't* say anything, *need/dare* he?

Conversely, they are not used with DO-support in any of these three constructions in Standard English:

(ii) (a)   *Does* anyone need/dare say anything?
   (b)   *He *doesn't* need/dare say anything, does he?

Thus, *need/dare* when followed by a bare infinitive complement seem to have the status of (modal) auxiliaries. In 1a, *need/dare* are finite auxiliary forms, as we see from the fact that the subject of *need* is the nominative pronoun *they* in (iii) below:

(iii)   Nobody need say anything, need *they*?

(Recall that finite verbs and auxiliaries require nominative subjects.)

In 2a, the first *to* is an infinitive particle, and the second *to* is a preposition. Thus, the second *to* (but not the first) can be modified by the adverb *straight* (cf. *Executives like to drive straight to work*, but not **Executives like straight to drive to work*). Moreover, the second *to* is a contentive preposition which has the antonym *from* (cf. *Executives like to drive from work*), whereas the first has no obvious antonym since it is an infinitive particle (cf. **Executives like from drive/driving to work*). In addition, like a typical transitive preposition, the second *to* (but not the first) can be followed by an accusative pronoun complement like *them* – cf. *Executives think the only way of getting to their offices is to drive to them*). Conversely, the first (infinitival) *to* allows ellipsis of its complement (cf. *Executives like to*), whereas the second (prepositional) *to* does not (cf. **Executives like to drive to*). Thus, in all relevant respects the first *to* behaves like an infinitive particle, whereas the second *to* behaves like a preposition.

In 3a, *for* could be either a complementiser (introducing the infinitival clause *parents to spend time with their children*) or a preposition (whose complement is the noun *parents*). The possibility that *for* might be used here as a preposition is suggested by the fact that the string *for parents* (or an interrogative counterpart like *for how many parents?*) could be preposed to the front of its containing sentence, as in:

(iv) (a) *For parents*, it is important to spend time with their children
    (b) *For how many parents* is it important to spend time with their children?

Moreover, *for* in this use can be substituted by the preposition *to* (as in 'It is important *to* parents to spend time with their children').

The alternative possibility that *for* might be used as a complementiser (with the infinitival clause *parents to spend time with their children* serving as its complement) is suggested by the observation that the *for*-clause here could be substituted by a *that*-clause, as in:

(v) It is important that parents should spend time with their children

Thus, 3a is ambiguous between one analysis on which *for* functions as a transitive preposition, and a second on which *for* functions as an infinitival complementiser which marks the clause as irrealis in type.

In 4a, the issue which arises is whether the sentence is a root/main clause introduced by the interrogative complementiser *if*. If so, we can account for the ungrammaticality of Auxiliary Inversion in:

(vi) **If wouldn't you* mind passing the salt

Sentences like (vi) would be ruled out because the presence of a complementiser blocks Inversion from applying (as we see from 101 in the main text).

However, treating *if* as an interrogative complementiser in sentences like 4a is problematic in certain respects. One such problem is that it is not obvious why *if* cannot be replaced by the interrogative complementiser *whether* here – as we see from the ungrammaticality of the following:

(vii) **Whether* you wouldn't mind passing the salt

Another problem is that main-clause questions always end in a question mark in the written language, and yet there is no question mark in 4a. Moreover, we see from sentences like (119) in the main text that complementisers are not generally used in main clauses. But if 4a is not a root interrogative clause (i.e. a main-clause question), what is it?

One possibility is that it is a truncated conditional sentence – it is a sentence which has the fuller structure in (viii) below, with the main-clause material marked by strikethrough ultimately being given a silent pronunciation (i.e. in effect deleted), leaving only the subordinate conditional clause intact:

(viii) ~~I'd be grateful~~ if you wouldn't mind passing the salt

Three properties of this type of sentence would follow from such a *conditional* analysis. Firstly, conditional *if* must be used, not interrogative *whether*. Secondly, there is no question mark: this is because question marks are only used in interrogative main clauses, and the *if*-clause in (viii) is neither an interrogative clause nor a main clause. Thirdly, there is no violation of the constraint against using complementisers in a main clause in (viii), since *if* introduces a subordinate clause. Overall, then, it seems preferable to analyse 4a as a truncated conditional structure.

Exercise 2.2

Use the labelled bracketing technique to assign each word in each of the sentences below to a grammatical category which represents how it is being used in the position in which it occurs in the sentence concerned. Give reasons in support of your proposed categorisation, highlight any analytic problems which arise and comment on any interesting properties of the relevant words.

1. He was feeling disappointed at only obtaining average grades in the morphology exercises
2. Student counsellors know that money troubles can cause considerable stress
3. Opposition politicians are pressing for election debates to receive better television coverage
4. Seasoned press commentators doubt if the workers will ever fully accept that substantial pay rises lead to runaway inflation
5. Students often complain to their high school teachers that the state education system promotes universal mediocrity
6. Most scientists believe that climatic changes result from ozone depletion due to excessive carbon dioxide emission
7. Linguists have long suspected that peer group pressure shapes linguistic behaviour patterns in very young children
8. You don't seem to be too worried about the possibility that many of the shareholders may now vote against your revised takeover bid

For the purposes of this exercise, use the system of categories summarised in the table below:

Category	Examples of words belonging to the category
N/noun	*dog, bread, science, glasses, syntax, thing*
V/verb	*go, disappear, like, eat, think, say*
A/adjective	*tall, pretty, gentle, intelligent, sad, hungry*
ADV/adverb	*slowly, suddenly, fortunately, badly*
P/preposition	*in, on, by, with, from, to, for, at, despite*
D/determiner	*the, this, that, these, those*
Q/quantifier	*much, many, most, some, any, no, several, each, every, both, all, three*
PRN/pronoun	*I, me, he, him, she, her, we, us, you, they, them, nobody, everything, none*
C/complementiser	*that, if, whether, for*
T/tense marker	Finite auxiliaries like *will, would, can, could, am, is, was* and the non-finite infinitival tense particle *to*

Model answer for 1

(i) $[_{PRN}$ he] $[_T$ was] $[_V$ feeling] $[_A$ disappointed] $[_P$ at] $[_{ADV}$ only] $[_V$ obtaining] $[_A$ average] $[_N$ grades] $[_P$ in] $[_D$ the] $[_N$ morphology] $[_N$ exercises]

An issue of particular interest which arises in (i) relates to the status of the words *average* and *morphology*. Are these nouns or adjectives – and how can we tell? Since nouns used to modify other nouns are invariable in English (e.g. we say *skate boards*, not **skates boards*), we can't rely on morphological clues here. However, we can use syntactic evidence. If (as assumed here), the word *average* functions as an adjective in 1, we should expect to find that it can be modified by the kind of adverb like *relatively* which can be used to modify adjectives (cf. *relatively good*); by contrast, if *morphology* serves as a noun in 1, we should expect to find that it can be modified by the kind of adjective (e.g. *inflectional*) which can be used to modify such a noun. In the event, both predictions are correct:

(ii)   He was feeling disappointed at only obtaining **relatively** *average* grades in the **inflectional** *morphology* exercises

Some additional evidence that *average* can function as an adjective comes from the fact that it has the *-ly* adverb derivative *averagely*, and (for some speakers at least) the noun derivative *averageness* – cf. *The very averageness of his intellect made him the CIA's choice for president.* Moreover (like most adjectives), it can be used predicatively in sentences like *His performance was average.* (Note, however, that in structures such as *morphology exercises*, you will not always find it easy to determine whether the first word is a noun or adjective. Unless there is evidence to the contrary – as with *average* in (ii) above – assume that the relevant item is a noun if it clearly functions as a noun in other uses and does not exhibit the characteristic properties of any other type of word.)

3 Structure

3.1 Overview

This chapter provides an introduction to **syntactic structure**, and to how words are combined together to form phrases and sentences. We shall see that phrases and sentences are built up by a series of **Merge** operations, each of which combines a pair of constituents together to form a larger constituent. We look at how the resulting structure can be represented in terms of a **tree diagram**. We also examine some of the principles which underlie sentence formation and explore ways of testing the structure of phrases and sentences.

3.2 Phrases

To put our discussion on a concrete footing, let's consider how an elementary two-word phrase such as the italicised response produced by speaker B in the following mini-dialogue is formed:

(1)   SPEAKER A: What are you trying to do?
        SPEAKER B: *Help you*

As speaker B's utterance illustrates, the simplest way of forming a phrase is by **merging** (a technical term meaning 'combining') two words together: for example, by merging the word *help* with the pronoun *you* in (1), we form the phrase *help you*. The resulting phrase *help you* has verb-like rather than pronoun-like properties, as we see from the observation that it can occupy the same range of positions as the simple verb *help*, and hence, for example, occur after the infinitive particle *to*: cf.

(2) (a)   We are trying to *help*
    (b)   We are trying to *help you*

By contrast, the phrase *help you* cannot occupy the same kind of position as a pronoun such as *you*, as we see from (3) below:

(3) (a)   *You* are very difficult
    (b)   **Help you* are very difficult

So it seems clear that the grammatical properties of a phrase like *help you* are determined by the verb *help*, and not by the pronoun *you*. Much the same can be said about the semantic properties of the expression, since the phrase *help you* describes an act of help, not a kind of person. Using the appropriate technical terminology, we can say that the verb *help* is the **head** of the phrase *help you*, and hence that *help you* is a verb phrase: and in the same way as we abbreviate category labels like verb to V, so too we can abbreviate the category label verb phrase to VP. If we use the traditional labelled bracketing technique to represent the category of the overall verb phrase *help you* and of its constituent words (the verb *help* and the pronoun *you*), we can represent the structure of the resulting phrase as in (4) below:

(4)   [$_{VP}$ [$_V$ help] [$_{PRN}$ you]]

As we saw in §1.3, an alternative (equivalent) way of representing the structure of phrases like *help you* is via a labelled tree diagram such as (5) below (which resembles a family tree diagram showing the relation between a mother and her two daughters):

(5)

What the tree diagram in (5) tells us is that the overall phrase *help you* is a verb phrase (VP), and that its two **constituents** are the verb (V) *help* and the pronoun (PRN) *you*. The verb *help* is the head of the overall phrase (and so is the key word which determines the grammatical and semantic properties of the phrase *help you*). Introducing another technical term at this point, we can say that conversely, the VP *help you* is a **projection** of the verb *help*, in the sense that the verb *help* is projected into a larger structure by merging it with another constituent of an appropriate kind: in this case, the constituent which is merged with the verb *help* is the pronoun *you*, which has the grammatical function of being the (**direct object**) **complement** of the verb *help*. The head of a projection/phrase determines grammatical properties of its complement: in this case, since *help* is a **transitive** verb, it requires a complement with accusative case (e.g. a pronoun like *me/us/him/them*), and this requirement is satisfied here since *you* can function as an accusative form (as you can see from the table of pronouns in §2.6, repeated under the entry for **case** in the Glossary at the end of the book). The tree diagram in (5) is entirely equivalent to the labelled bracketing in (4), in the sense that the two provide us with precisely the same information about the structure of the phrase *help you*. The differences between a labelled bracketing like (4) and a tree diagram like (5) are purely notational: each category is represented by a single labelled **node** in a tree diagram (i.e. by a point in the tree which carries a category label like VP, V or PRN), but by a pair of labelled brackets in a labelled bracketing (with the left-hand member of each pair of brackets carrying a label representing the category of the bracketed expression).

Since our goal in developing a theory of **Universal Grammar/UG** is to uncover general structural principles governing the formation of phrases and sentences, let's generalise our discussion of (5) at this point and hypothesise that all phrases are formed in essentially the same way as the phrase in (5), namely by a **binary** (i.e. pairwise) Merge operation which combines two constituents together to form a larger constituent. In the case of (5), the resulting phrase *help you* is formed by merging two words. However, not all phrases contain only two words – as we see if we look at the structure of the italicised phrase produced by speaker B in (6) below:

(6)   SPEAKER A: What was your intention?
           SPEAKER B: *To help you*

The phrase in (6B) is formed by merging the infinitive particle *to* with the verb phrase *help you*. What's the head of the resulting phrase *to help you?* A reasonable guess would be that the head is the infinitival tense particle/T *to*, so that the resulting expression *to help you* is an infinitival **TP** (= infinitival tense projection = infinitival tense phrase). This being so, we'd expect to find that TPs containing infinitival *to* have different syntactic properties (and hence occur in a different range of positions) from VPs/verb phrases – and this is indeed the case, as we see from the contrast below:

(7) (a)   They **ought** *to help you* (= **ought** + TP *to help you*)
    (b)   *They **ought** *help you* (= **ought** + VP *help you*)

(8) (a)   They **should** *help you* (= **should** + VP *help you*)
    (b)   *They **should** *to help you* (= **should** + TP *to help you*)

If we assume that *help you* is a VP whereas *to help you* is a TP, we can account for the contrasts in (7) and (8) by saying that *ought* is the kind of word which **selects** (i.e. 'takes') an infinitival TP as its complement, whereas *should* is the kind of word which selects an infinitival VP as its complement. Implicit in this claim is the assumption that different words like *ought* and *should* have different **selectional** properties which determine the range of complements which they can take.

The infinitive phrase *to help you* is formed by merging the infinitive particle *to* with the verb phrase *help you*. If (as argued in the previous chapter) infinitival *to* is an **infinitival tense particle** (belonging to the category T) and if *to* is the head of the phrase *to help you*, the structure formed by merging *to* with the verb phrase/ VP *help you* in (5) will be the TP in (9) below:

(9)

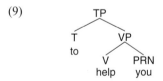

The head of the resulting infinitival tense projection *to help you* is the infinitive particle *to*, and the verb phrase *help you* is the complement of *to*; conversely, *to help you* is a projection of *to*. In keeping with our earlier observation that 'The head of a projection/phrase determines grammatical properties of its complement', the infinitival tense particle *to* requires an infinitival verb phrase as its complement: more specifically, *to* requires the head V of its VP complement to be a verb in the infinitive form so that we require the (bare/uninflected) infinitive form *help* after infinitival *to* (and not an inflected form like *helping/helped/helps*). Refining our earlier observation somewhat, we can therefore say that 'The head of a projection/phrase determines grammatical properties of the *head word of* its complement.' In (9), *to* is the head of the TP *to help you*, and the complement of *to* is the VP *help you*; the head of this VP is the V *help* so that *to* determines the form of the V *help* (requiring it to be in the infinitive form *help*).

More generally, our discussion here suggests that we can build up more and more complex phrases by a series of binary Merge operations which combine successive pairs of constituents to form ever larger structures. For example, by merging the infinitive phrase *to help you* with the verb *trying*, we can form the even larger italicised phrase *trying to help you* produced by speaker B in (10) below:

(10)   SPEAKER A: What are you doing?
         SPEAKER B: *Trying to help you*

The resulting phrase *trying to help you* is headed by the verb *trying*, as we see from the fact that it can be used after words like *be, start* or *keep* which select a complement headed by a verb in the *-ing* form (cf. 'They **were/started/kept** *trying to help you*'). This being so, the italicised phrase produced by speaker B in (10) is a VP (= verb phrase) with the structure (11) below:

(11)

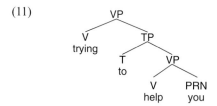

(11) tells us (amongst other things) that the overall expression *trying to help you* is a verb phrase/VP; its head is the verb/V *trying*, and the complement of *trying* is the TP/infinitival tense phrase *to help you*: conversely, the VP *trying to help you* is a projection of the V *trying*. An interesting property of syntactic structures which is illustrated in (11) is that of **recursion** (briefly mentioned at the end of §1.5) – that is, the property of being able to contain more than one instance of a given category (in this case, more than one verb phrase/VP, one headed by the verb *help* and another headed by the verb *trying*).

Since one of the goals which a theory of Universal Grammar/UG seeks to attain is to establish universal principles governing the nature of linguistic structure, an important question to ask is whether there are any general principles of **constituent structure** which we can abstract from a structure like (11). If we look closely at (11), we can see that it obeys the following two (putatively universal) constituent structure principles:

(12) (i)   **Headedness Principle**
             Every non-terminal node in a syntactic structure is a projection of a head
             lexical item.

(ii)   **Binarity Principle**
        Every non-terminal node in a syntactic structure is binary-branching.

Before illustrating how these principles work, let's first clarify the terminology used in (12). A **terminal** node is one at the foot/bottom of a tree (i.e. one which does not branch down into any other node): consequently, the V-*trying*, T-*to*, V-*help* and PRN-*you* are the terminal nodes in the tree in (11). By contrast, a **non-terminal** node is one which is not at the foot of a tree and so branches down into other nodes beneath it: consequently, the TP node and both VP nodes in (11) are non-terminal because each of them branches down into other nodes. A **lexical item** is an item listed in the lexicon/dictionary, and for present purposes can be thought of as corresponding to a word. A node is **binary-branching** if it has two **immediate constituents** (i.e. if it has two constituents branching down immediately beneath it) – or, to use more familiar kinship terminology, if it is the mother of two daughters.

Having clarified this distinction, let's now look at whether the structure in (11) obeys each of the two principles in (12). The tree in (11) obeys the Headedness Principle (12i) because each of the non-terminal VP and TP nodes is a projection of a corresponding lexical item/word: thus, the VP *help you* is headed by the V *help*; the TP *to help you* is headed by the non-finite/infinitival T-constituent *to*; and the VP *trying to help you* is headed by the V *trying* (and each of these heads is a lexical item/word). Likewise, (11) obeys the Binarity Principle (12ii) in that each of the three non-terminal nodes has two daughters: in the case of the VP *trying to help you*, one of its daughters is the V *trying*, and the other is the TP *to help you*; in the case of the TP *to help you*, one of its daughters is the T *to*, and the other is the VP *help you*; in the case of the VP *help you*, one if its daughters is the V *help* and the other is the pronoun/PRN *you*.

Our discussion in the two preceding paragraphs shows us that one of the goals of linguistic theory is to develop a principled account of constituent structure – i.e. one based on a set of principles of Universal Grammar. There are several reasons for trying to uncover constituent structure principles like those in (12). One relates to learnability: if we suppose that children have innate knowledge of such principles, this reduces the range of alternatives which they have to choose between when trying to determine the structure of a given kind of expression, and thus facilitates acquisition. Moreover, additional support for the Binarity Principle (12ii) comes from evidence that binarity is a defining characteristic of other types of linguistic structure. For example, research in phonology has shown that a syllable like *bat* has a binary structure, consisting of the onset |b| and the rhyme |at|, and the rhyme in turn has a binary structure, consisting of the nucleus |a| and the coda |t|. Likewise, there is evidence that morphological structure is also binary, and hence (e.g.) that the noun *indecipherability* is formed by adding the prefix *de-* to the noun *cipher* to form the verb *decipher*; then adding the suffix *-able* to this verb to form the adjective *decipherable*; then adding the prefix *in-* to this adjective to form the adjective *indecipherable*; and then adding the suffix *-ity* to the resulting adjective to form the noun *indecipherability*. It would thus seem that binarity is an inherent characteristic of the phonological, morphological and syntactic structure of natural languages: as our discussion develops below, we will uncover empirical evidence in support of the claim that syntactic structure is indeed binary. As noted in §1.5, the binarity property of Merge may well be a reflection of principles that play a role in the natural world, e.g. in relation to the structure of trees, lightning, neurons and capillaries, and in Fibonacci sequences.

3.3   Clauses

Having considered how phrases are formed, let's now turn to look at how **clauses** and **sentences** are formed. By way of illustration, suppose that speaker B had used the simple (single-clause) sentence italicised in (13B) below to reply to speaker A, rather than the phrase used by speaker B in (10):

(13)   SPEAKER A: What are you doing?
          SPEAKER B: *We are trying to help you*

What's the structure of the italicised clause produced by speaker B in (13)?

In work in the 1960s, clauses were generally taken to belong to the category **S** (*Sentence/Clause*), and the sentence produced by B in (13) would have been taken to have a structure along the following lines (simplified by not showing the internal structure of the VP/verb phrase *trying to help you*):

(14)

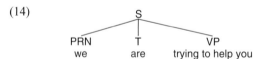

However, the S analysis of clauses in (14) violates both of the constituent structure principles posited in (12) above. More particularly, it violates the Headedness Principle (12i) in that the S *we are trying to help you* is a structure which has no head of any kind. Likewise, it also violates the Binarity Principle (12ii) in that the S constituent *We are trying to help you* is not binary-branching but rather **ternary**-branching, because it branches into three immediate constituents/daughters, namely the PRN *we*, the T *are* and the VP *trying to help you*. If our theory of Universal Grammar requires every syntactic structure to be a binary-branching projection of a head word, it is clear that we have to reject the S-analysis of clause structure in (14) as one which is not in keeping with UG principles.

Let's therefore explore an alternative analysis of the structure of clauses which is consistent with the headedness requirement in (12i) and the binarity requirement in (12ii). More specifically, let's make the unifying assumption that clauses are formed by the same binary Merge operation as phrases. This in turn will mean that the italicised clause in (13B) is formed by merging the (present) tense auxiliary *are* with the verb phrase *trying to help you*, and then subsequently merging the resulting expression *are trying to help you* with the pronoun *we*. Since *are* belongs to the category T of tense auxiliary, it might at first sight seem as if merging *are* with the verb phrase *trying to help you* will derive (i.e. form) the **TP**/tense projection/tense phrase *are trying to help you*. But this can't be right, since it would provide us with no obvious account of why speaker B's reply in (15) below is ungrammatical:

(15)   SPEAKER A: What are you doing?

            SPEAKER B: **Are trying to help you*

If *are trying to help you* is a complete TP, how come it can't be used to answer A's question in (15), since we see from sentences like (6B) that TP constituents like *to help you* can be used to answer questions?

    An informal answer we can give is to say that the expression *are trying to help you* is somehow 'incomplete', and that only 'complete' expressions can be used to answer questions. In what sense is *are trying to help you* incomplete? The answer is that finite (e.g. present/past tense) T constituents require a subject, and the finite auxiliary *are* doesn't have a subject in (15B). More specifically, let's assume that when we merge a tense auxiliary (= T) with a verb phrase (= VP), we form an **intermediate projection** which we shall here denote as T' (pronounced 'tee-bar'); and that only when we merge the relevant T-bar constituent with a subject like *we* do we form a **maximal projection** – or, more informally a 'complete projection/complete phrase'. Given these assumptions, the italicised clause in (13B) will have the structure below (simplified by not showing the internal structure of the VP *trying to help you*, because this is shown in 11 above):

(16)

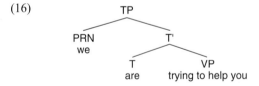

What this means is that a tense auxiliary like *are* has two projections: a smaller intermediate projection (T') formed by merging *are* with its complement *trying to help you* to form the T-bar (intermediate tense projection) *are trying to help you*; and a larger maximal projection (TP) formed by merging the resulting T' *are trying to help you* with its subject *we* to form the TP *We are trying to help you*. Saying that TP is the maximal projection of *are* in (16) means it is the largest constituent headed by the auxiliary *are*.

    Given these assumptions, there are three kinds of T constituent in (16): T-*are* is a head (or, equivalently a **minimal projection**); the T-bar *are trying to help you* is an intermediate projection; and the TP *we are trying to help you* is a maximal projection. We can define these terms informally as below:

(17)   **Projection types**
A constituent C is
(a) a *maximal projection* if C does not have a mother with the same head as C
(b) an *intermediate projection* if C has a mother and a daughter with the same head as C
(c) a *minimal projection/head* if C has no daughter.

Consider what these definitions tell us about the status of various constituents in (16). The TP *we are trying to help you* is a maximal projection because it doesn't have a mother with the same head (by virtue of not having any mother at all). The T-bar *are trying to help you* is an intermediate projection because it has a mother (namely the TP *we are trying to help you*) and a daughter (= T-*are*) which are both headed by the T auxiliary *are*. The T auxiliary *are* is a minimal projection because it has no daughter.

But now consider the status of PRN-*we*. Under the definition in (18a), PRN-*we* is a maximal projection because it has a mother with a different head: the mother of PRN-*we* is TP *we are trying to help you*, and this TP is headed by T-*are*, not by PRN-*we*. However, under the definition in (18c), PRN-*we* is also a head/minimal projection, because it has no daughter. Thus, PRN-*we* has dual status as both a minimal and a maximal projection. This accounts for why it behaves in some respects like a phrase (e.g. it can be co-ordinated with a phrase such as *right-minded people like us* – cf. '*We* and *right-minded people like us* always vote for the Green Party'), but in other respects behaves like a simple word (e.g. in allowing another word like *have* to cliticise to it in structures like *We've won*).

Having clarified the difference between maximal, intermediate and minimal projections, let's now address the question of why tense auxiliaries require *two* different projections, one in which they merge with a following complement to form an intermediate projection (T-bar), and another in which the resulting T-bar merges with a preceding subject to form a maximal projection (TP). The requirement for auxiliaries to have two projections (in a structure like 16 above) was taken by Chomsky in earlier work to be a consequence of a principle of Universal Grammar known as the **Extended Projection Principle** (conventionally abbreviated to **EPP**), which specified that a tense constituent T must be extended into a TP projection containing a subject.

However, comparative evidence suggests that there are other languages in which a tense auxiliary does not require a preceding subject of its own – as illustrated by the Italian sentence below:

(18)   È   stata   arrestata   una   vecchia   signora
         Is   been   arrested   an   old   lady   (=‘An old lady has been arrested’)

The absence of any subject preceding the present tense auxiliary *è* ‘is’ in (18) suggests that it cannot be a principle of Universal Grammar that every tense auxiliary in every language has a subject. Rather, it seems more likely that this is a property of tense auxiliaries in particular languages like English, but not of their counterparts in some other languages. Recall that we noted in §2.10 that the grammatical properties of words can be described in terms of sets of **features**, and by convention these are enclosed in square brackets. Consequently, in order to describe the grammatical properties of the auxiliary *are* (in a sentence like *They are lying*) as a third person plural present indicative progressive auxiliary, we could say that it carries the features [Third-Person, Plural-Number, Present-Tense, Indicative-Mood, Progressive-Aspect]. Using this convention, Chomsky suggested in later work that English tense auxiliaries like *are* carry an **EPP feature** which requires them to have an extended projection into a TP containing a subject. If all finite auxiliaries in English carry an EPP feature, it follows that any English clause (like that produced by speaker B in 16 above) containing a tense auxiliary which does not have a subject will be ungrammatical.

The EPP requirement (for a finite auxiliary to have a subject in a language like English) would seem to be essentially syntactic (rather than semantic) in nature, as we can see from sentences such as those below:

(19) (a)   *It* was alleged that he lied under oath
   (b)   *There* has been no trouble

In structures like (19), the italicised subject pronouns *it/there* seem to have no semantic content (in particular, no referential properties) of their own, as we see from the fact that neither can be questioned by the corresponding interrogative words *what?/where?* (cf. the ungrammaticality of **What was alleged that he lied under oath?* and **Where has been no trouble?*), and neither can receive contrastive focus (hence *it/there* cannot receive contrastive/emphatic stress in sentences like 19 above). Rather, they function as **expletive** pronouns – i.e. pronouns with no intrinsic meaning which are used to satisfy the syntactic requirement for a finite auxiliary like *was/has* to have a subject.

A question which we have not so far asked about the structure of clauses concerns what role is played by complementisers like *that, for, if* and *whether*. For instance, what role is played by the complementiser *that* in speaker B's reply below?

(20)   SPEAKER A: What are you saying?
           SPEAKER B: *That we are trying to help you*

Where does the C/complementiser *that* fit into the structure of the sentence? The answer suggested in work in the 1970s was that a complementiser merges with an S constituent like that in (14) above to form an **S'/S-bar** (pronounced 'ess-bar') constituent like that shown below, simplified by not showing the internal structure of the VP *trying to help you*):

(21)

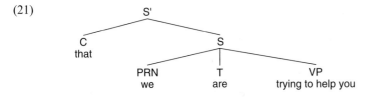

However, the claim that a clause introduced by a complementiser has the status of an S-bar constituent falls foul of the Headedness Principle (12i), which requires every non-terminal node in a tree to be a projection of a head lexical item/word. The principle is violated because S-bar in (21) is analysed as a projection of the S constituent *we are trying to help you*, and S is not a word (but rather a string of words).

We can solve the headedness problem by supposing that the head of a clausal structure introduced by a complementiser is the complementiser itself: since this is a single word, there would then be no violation of the Headedness Principle (12i) requiring every syntactic structure to be a projection of a head word. Let's therefore assume that merging the complementiser *that* with the TP *we are trying to help you* forms the **CP/complementiser projection/complementiser phrase** in (22) below (where the structure of the VP *trying to help you* is not shown because it was shown earlier in 11 above):

(22)

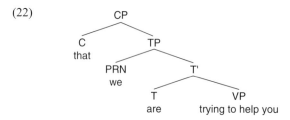

(22) tells us that the complementiser *that* is the head of the overall clause *that we are trying to help you* (and conversely, the overall clause is a projection of the complementiser *that*) – and indeed this is implicit in the traditional description of such structures as *that*-clauses. (22) also tells us that the complement of *that* is the TP/tense phrase *we are trying to help you*. Clauses introduced by complementisers have been taken to have the status of CP/complementiser phrase constituents since the early 1980s.

An interesting aspect of the analyses in (17) and (22) above is that clauses and sentences are analysed as **headed** structures – i.e. as projections of head words (in conformity with the Headedness Principle 12i). In other words, just as phrases are projections of a head word (e.g. a verb phrase like *help you* is a projection of the verb *help*), so too a sentence like *We will help you* is a projection of the auxiliary *will*, and a complement clause like the bracketed *that*-clause in *I can't promise* [*that we will help you*] is a projection of the complementiser *that*. This assumption enables us to arrive at a unitary analysis of the structure of phrases, clauses and sentences, in that clauses and sentences (like phrases) are projections of head words. More generally, it leads us to the conclusion that clauses/sentences are simply particular kinds of phrase (e.g. a *that*-clause is a complementiser phrase).

An assumption implicit in the analyses presented here is that phrases and sentences are **derived** (i.e. formed) in a **bottom-up** fashion (i.e. they are built up from bottom to top). For example, the clause in (22) involves the following sequence of Merge operations: (i) the verb *help* is merged with the pronoun *you* to form the VP *help you*; (ii) the resulting VP is merged with the non-finite T/tense particle *to* to form the infinitival TP *to help you*; (iii) this TP is in turn merged with the verb *trying* to form the VP *trying to help you*; (iv) the resulting VP is merged with the T/tense auxiliary *are* to form the T-bar *are trying to help you*; (v) this T-bar is merged with its subject *we* to form the TP *we are trying to help you*; and (vi) the resulting TP is in turn merged with the C/complementiser *that* to form the CP structure (22) *that we are trying to help you*. By saying that the structure (22) is derived in a bottom-up fashion, we mean that lower parts of the structure nearer the bottom of the tree are formed before higher parts of the structure nearer the top of the tree.

3.4 Specifiers

A question which arises from the analysis of tense auxiliaries in (17) and (22) above as having an intermediate projection into T-bar and an extended projection into TP is whether there are other constituents which can have both an intermediate and an extended projection. The answer is 'Yes', as we can see by comparing the alternative answers (23i/ii) given by speaker B below:

(23)   SPEAKER A: Where did she hit him?
         SPEAKER B: (i) *On the nose*   (ii) *Right on the nose*

Let's first look at the structure of reply (i) *On the nose* in (23B), before turning to consider the structure of reply (ii) *Right on the nose*. *On the nose* in (23Bi) is a prepositional phrase/PP derived in the following fashion. The determiner *the* is merged with the noun *nose* to form the DP/determiner phrase *the nose* in (24) below:

(24)
```
        DP
       /  \
      D    N
     the  nose
```

The preposition *on* is then merged with the resulting DP *the nose* to form the prepositional phrase/PP *on the nose*, which has the structure (25) below:

(25)
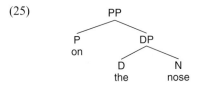

The overall expression *on the nose* is a projection of the preposition *on* and so has the status of a prepositional phrase: the head of the PP *on the nose* is the preposition *on* and the complement of the preposition *on* is the DP *the nose*. Given the traditional assumption that a verb or preposition which takes a noun or pronoun expression as its complement is transitive, *on* is a transitive preposition in this use, and *the nose* is its complement.

Now consider the structure of reply (ii) *right on the nose* in (23B). This differs from the PP *on the nose* in that it also contains the adverb *right*. It seems implausible to suppose that the adverb *right* is the head of the overall expression, since this would mean that *right on the nose* was an **adverbial phrase/ADVP**: on the contrary, it seems more plausible to suppose that *right on the nose* is a prepositional phrase/PP in which the adverb *right* is a **modifier** of some kind which serves to extend the prepositional expression *on the nose* into the even larger prepositional expression *right on the nose* (so that the head of the structure is once again the preposition *on*). Some evidence that *right on the nose* is indeed a PP (and not an ADVP) comes from **cleft sentences** (i.e. structures of the form 'It was *a car* that John bought', where the italicised constituent *a car* is said to be **focused**, and hence to occupy **focus** position in the cleft sentence structure). Consider (26) below:

(26) (a)   It was *with great sadness* that he announced the resignation of the chairman
     (b)   *It was *very sadly* that he announced the resignation of the chairman

Such sentences provide evidence that a prepositional phrase/PP like *with great sadness* can be focused in a cleft sentence, but not an adverbial phrase/ADVP like *very sadly*. In the light of this observation, consider the sentences below:

(27) (a)   It was *on the nose* that she hit him
     (b)   It was *right on the nose* that she hit him

The fact that both *on the nose* and *right on the nose* can occupy focus position in the cleft sentence in (27) suggests that both are PP/prepositional phrase constituents: *right on the nose* cannot be an ADVP/adverbial phrase since we see from (26b) above that adverbial expressions cannot be focused in cleft sentences.

The conclusion we reach from the data in (26–27) above is that the adverb *right* in *right on the nose* serves to extend the prepositional expression *on the nose* into the even larger prepositional expression *right on the nose*. Using the **bar notation** introduced in (16) above, we can analyse *right on the nose* in the following terms. The preposition *on* merges with its DP complement *the nose* to form the intermediate prepositional projection *on the nose* which has the categorial status of **P'** (or **P-bar**, pronounced 'pee-bar'); the resulting P-bar *on the nose* is then merged with the adverb *right* to form the PP below:

(28)

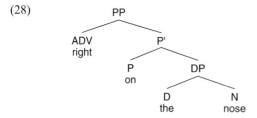

In other words, just as a tense auxiliary like *are* can be projected into a T' like *are trying to help you* by Merge with a following VP complement and then further projected into TP by Merge with a preceding pronoun subject such as *we*, so too a preposition like *on* can be projected into a P′ like *on the nose* by Merge with a following DP complement and then further projected into a PP like *right on the nose* by Merge with a preceding adverbial modifier such as *right*.

Although *we* in (16) serves a different grammatical function from *right* in (28) (in that *we* is the **subject** of *are trying to help you*, whereas *right* is a modifier of *on the nose*), there is a sense in which the two occupy parallel positions within the overall structure containing them: just as *we* merges with a T′ to form a TP, so too *right* merges with a P′ to form a PP. Introducing a new technical term at this point, let's say that *we* serves as the **specifier** of the T *are* and of the TP *we are trying to help you* in (16) – and we can abbreviate this by saying that *we* occupies the **spec-T** 'specifier-of-T' position (or equivalently the **spec-TP** 'specifier-of-TP') position within TP. Likewise, *right* serves as the specifier of the P *on* and of the PP *right on the nose* in (28), and so can be said to occupy the **spec-P** (or **spec-PP**) position. More generally, we can say that a specifier is an expression which merges with an intermediate projection H-bar (where H-bar is a projection of some head word H) to project it into a maximal projection HP in the manner shown in (29) below:

(29)

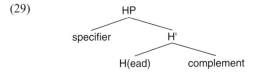

Our conclusion that prepositions and tense auxiliaries alike can merge with both a complement and a specifier raises the question of whether this is a more general property of all types of head. The answer is 'Yes', as we can see by looking at the italicised expressions below:

(30) (a)   *Government increases in taxation* have slowed the economy
    (b)   She arrived at the solution *quite independently of me*
    (c)   I have never known a patient make *quite so rapid a recovery*
    (d)   Shall we invite *Peter and Paul*?

In (30a) the noun/N *increases* merges with its complement *in taxation* to form the intermediate projection (N-bar) *increases in taxation*, and the resulting N-bar in turn merges with the noun *government* to form the maximal projection (NP) *government increases in taxation*. In (30b) the adverb *independently* merges with its complement *of me* to form the intermediate projection (ADV-bar) *independently of me*, and this in turn merges with the adverb *quite* to form the maximal projection (ADVP) *quite independently of me*. In (30c) the indefinite article *a* (which, following the assumption made in §2.5, we can take to be a Q/quantifier) merges with its complement *recovery* to form the Q-bar *a recovery*, and the resulting Q-bar is in turn merged with its specifier *quite so rapid* to form the QP *quite so rapid a recovery*. If we suppose that the expression *quite so rapid* is a **degree phrase/DEGP** constituent (by virtue of containing the degree adverb *so*), the relevant QP will have the structure shown below (simplified by not showing the internal structure of DEGP):

(31)

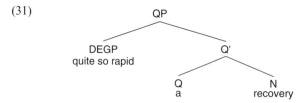

An analysis like (31) would mean that there is symmetry between the structure of quantifier phrases and other types of phrase, in that (like other phrases), QPs allow a specifier of an appropriate kind.

Other types of structure which could be argued to have a SPECIFIER+HEAD+ COMPLEMENT structure are **coordinate** structures such as *Peter and Mary* in (30d) (where two nouns have been coordinated – i.e. joined together by use of the coordinating conjunction *and*), or *tired but happy* (where two adjectives have been co-ordinated), or *the president and the prime minister* (where two determiner phrases have been coordinated), or *in Spring or at the beginning of Summer* (where two prepositional phrases have been coordinated). One way of analysing such structures is to take them to be headed by a coordinating conjunction like *and/but/or* (which we will designate as belong to the category of & - i.e. coordinator). On this view, a coordinate phrase such as *Peter and Mary* will have the structure shown below:

(32)

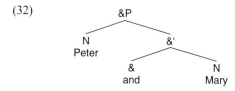

It would seem that such coordinate structures allow multiple specifiers (unlike – say – T in English, which allows only one subject). For example, one way of analysing a structure such as *Peter, Paul and Mary* is as shown below:

(33)

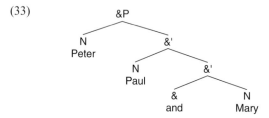

Under the analysis in (33), the &-constituent (coordinator) *and* is merged with its complement *Mary* to form the intermediate &-bar projection *and Mary*; this &-bar constituent is then merged with N-*Paul* to form the even larger intermediate &-bar projection *Paul and Mary*; and this larger &-bar projection is in turn merged with N-*Peter* to form the maximal &P projection *Peter, Paul and Mary*. On this view, *Paul* is the **inner specifier** and *Peter* the **outer specifier** of the &P (i.e. coordinate phrase). Numerous questions of detail obviously arise (including how to distinguish, e.g., a co-ordinate nominal structure like *Peter, Paul and Mary* from a co-ordinate adjectival structure like *tall, dark and handsome*), but I will not delve into them here.

As those of you familiar with earlier work will have noticed, the kind of structures proposed here are very different from those assumed in traditional grammar and in work in linguistics in the 1960s and 1970s. Earlier work implicitly assumed that only items belonging to **substantive/lexical** categories could project into phrases, not words belonging to **functional** categories. More specifically, earlier work assumed that there were noun phrases headed by nouns, verb phrases headed by verbs, adjectival phrases headed by adjectives, adverbial phrases headed by adverbs and prepositional phrases headed by prepositions. However, more recent work has argued that not only content words but also function words can project into phrases, so that we have tense phrases headed by a tense-marker, complementiser phrases headed by a complementiser, determiner phrases headed by a determiner, quantifier phrases headed by a quantifier – and so on. More generally, the assumption made in work over the last three decades is that in principle *all* types of word can project into phrases. This means that some of the structures made use of here may seem (at best) rather strange to those of you with a more traditional background, or (at worst) just plain *wrong*. However, the structure of a given phrase or sentence cannot be determined on the basis of personal prejudice or pedagogical precepts inculcated into you at secondary school, but rather has to be determined on the basis of syntactic evidence of the kind discussed in §3.6 below. I would therefore ask traditionalists to be prepared to be open to new ideas and new analyses (a prerequisite for achieving understanding in any discipline).

3.5   Intermediate and maximal projections

One aspect of the analysis of prepositional phrases in §3.4 which might at first sight seem puzzling is that the same expression *on the nose* is analysed as a PP in (23Bi/25), but as a P-bar in (23Bii/28). Why should this be? The answer is that the label PP denotes the maximal projection of (i.e. the largest constituent headed by) the relevant preposition in a given structure. In (23Bi), speaker B replies *On the nose*: since the largest constituent headed by *on* in (23Bi) is *On the nose*, it follows that *On the nose* has the status of a PP here. By contrast, in (23Bii) speaker B replies *Right on the nose*: here, *on the nose* is not the largest constituent headed by *on*, and hence is not a PP but rather a P-bar; on the contrary, the largest constituent headed by *on* in (23Bii) is *Right on the nose*, so it is this largest prepositional constituent which has the status of PP.

Interestingly, there is some evidence in support of the claim that *on the nose* is not a PP in (23Bii/28). As we see from examples like (34) below, a PP (like that italicised below) can generally be **preposed/fronted** (i.e. moved to the front of the sentence) in order to highlight it:

(34) (a)   They found a safe *under the floorboards*
     (b)   *Under the floorboards*, they found a safe

In the light of this observation, consider the following examples (where *right* in each case is to be interpreted as a modifier of *on the nose*):

(35) (a)   She hit him *right on the nose*
     (b)   *Right on the nose*, she hit him
     (c)   **On the nose*, she hit him *right*

The fact that *right on the nose* can be preposed in (35b) but not *on the nose* in (35c) provides evidence in support of the claim in (28) that *right on the nose* is a PP in (35a) but *on the nose* is not. If we assume that the only kinds of phrase which can be preposed in this type of structure are maximal projections, it follows that *right on the nose* can be preposed in (35) because it is the maximal projection of the preposition *on* (hence a PP), whereas *on the nose* cannot because it is an intermediate projection of the preposition *on* (hence a P-bar).

   Although there are similarities between the structure of a PP like that in (28) and the structure of a TP like that in (16), there is also a very important difference between the two. As we saw earlier from the grammaticality of *We are trying to help you* and the ungrammaticality of **Are trying to help you* as replies to the question *What are you doing?* tense auxiliaries like *are* obligatorily require an appropriate specifier (e.g. a subject pronoun like *we*). By contrast, the fact that we can reply either *On the nose* or *Right on the nose* to a question like *Where did she hit him?* tells us that prepositions can be used either with or without an appropriate kind of specifier (e.g. an adverbial modifier like *right*). So, a significant difference between auxiliaries and prepositions is that it is *obligatory* for a T auxiliary to have a specifier in English but *optional* for a preposition to have a specifier. As we saw in §3.3, this is because T-auxiliaries in English have an EPP feature requiring them to project a specifier. This in turn may be because T-auxiliaries require a subject/specifier to agree with, but prepositions (being agreementless) do not.

   Just as prepositional phrases can have an (optional) adverbial modifier as their specifier, so too can adjectival phrases – as we see from the alternative replies given by speaker B in (36) below:

(36)   SPEAKER A: How does your mother feel about your brother's success?
        SPEAKER B: (i) *Proud of him* (ii) *Very proud of him*

Reply (i) *proud of him* in (36B) is an adjectival phrase/**AP** formed as follows. The preposition *of* merges with the pronoun *him* to form the PP/prepositional phrase *of him*. This is then merged with the adjective *proud* to form the AP/adjectival phrase *proud of him*, which has the structure (37) below:

(37)

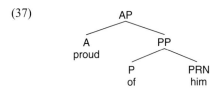

But what is the structure of reply (ii) *Very proud of him* in (36ʙ)? This differs from *Proud of him* in that it contains the adverb *very*. It seems implausible that the adverb *very* could be the head of the overall expression *Very proud of him* since this would mean that *very proud of him* was an ADVP (adverbial phrase); but an ADVP analysis would be problematic because a question like *How does she feel?* can have an adjectival expression like *Happy* as an appropriate reply but not an adverbial expression like *Happily*. Since *very proud of him* can be used to reply to the *how*-question asked by speaker A in (36), *very proud of him* must be an adjectival expression headed by the adjective *proud*. Using the bar notation introduced earlier, we can say that the A/adjective *proud* merges with its PP/prepositional phrase complement *of him* to form the A-bar (intermediate adjectival projection) *proud of him*, and that the resulting A-bar in turn merges with the adverbial specifier *very* to form the full AP/adjectival phrase in (38) below:

(38)

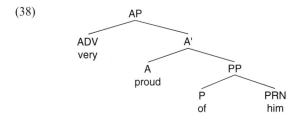

Evidence in support of the analysis in (38) comes from data relating to the preposing of (italicised) adjectival expressions in sentences such as (39) below:

(39) (a)   She certainly seems to be *very proud of him*
     (b)   *Very proud of him*, she certainly seems to be
     (c)   **Proud of him*, she certainly seems to be *very*

If we assume (as we did in our earlier discussion of 35 above) that only maximal projections can be preposed in this way (not intermediate projections), we can provide a straightforward account of the data in (39) in terms of the analysis in (38). The structure in (38) tells us that *very proud of him* is the maximal projection of the adjective *proud*, and so is an AP/adjectival phrase constituent; hence it can be preposed in (39a) by virtue of its status as a maximal projection. By contrast, (38) tells us that *proud of him* is an intermediate projection of the adjective *proud* and hence an A-bar constituent: because only maximal projections like AP can be preposed, and because *proud of him* is only an intermediate A-bar projection, it cannot be preposed – hence the ungrammaticality of (39c).

A variety of other types of expression can also have extended projections via Merge with an optional specifier of an appropriate kind. As we saw earlier in (30b), one such are adverbial expressions like those italicised in (40) below:

(40) (a)   She made up her mind *independently of me*
    (b)   She made up her mind *quite independently of me*

The adverb *independently* can be merged with a PP/prepositional phrase complement like *of me* to form the adverbial expression *independently of me*: this can either serve as an ADVP/adverbial phrase on its own – as in (40a) – or can serve as an intermediate ADV-bar projection which can be extended into an ADVP by Merge with an appropriate specifier (like the adverb *quite*) as in (40b).

Much the same might be said about the italicised noun phrases in (41) below (cf. 30a):

(41) (a)   The opposition will oppose *the/any ban on imports*
    (b)   The opposition will oppose *the/any government ban on imports*

The noun *ban* can be merged with a following prepositional phrase complement like *on imports* to form the nominal expression *ban on imports*: this can either serve as a complete noun phrase/NP on its own, or can serve as an intermediate N-bar projection which is subsequently merged with an appropriate specifier (like the noun *government*) to form the larger noun phrase/NP *government ban on imports*. Because a noun expression headed by a singular count noun (like *ban*) must be modified by a determiner or quantifier, the resulting NP in either case must subsequently be merged with a determiner like *the* or a quantifier like *any*, so deriving a DP/determiner phrase like *the (government) ban on imports* or a QP/quantifier phrase like *any (government) ban on imports*.

Before continuing, let us briefly pause to reflect on the syntax of structures like *the/any ban on imports* in sentences like (41). In earlier work before the mid 1980s, these were taken to have the status of noun phrases/NPs, and the determiner/quantifier *a/an* was taken to serve as the specifier of the NP. On this (earlier) view, the phrase *the ban on imports* would have been analysed as an NP with the structure shown in (42) below (simplified by not showing the internal structure of the PP *on imports*):

(42)

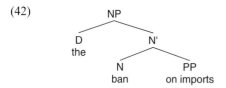

The structure in (42) claims that merging the noun *ban* with its PP complement *on imports* forms the N-bar *ban on imports*, and merging this N-bar with the determiner *the* forms the NP *the ban on imports*, with *the* serving as the specifier of the N-bar *ban on imports*. However, an analysis like (42) proves problematic in certain respects.

For one thing, it raises the question of where the noun *government* is positioned in a larger phrase like that in (41b) *the government ban on imports*. In (41b), the noun *government* plays much the same semantic role as that of *the government* in *The government has banned imports*, in that in both cases *(the) government* is the agent performing the action of banning imports. Since *the government* is the specifier of the T-bar *has banned imports* in the clause *The government has banned imports*, we can capture this parallelism of roles by supposing that *government* functions as the specifier of the N-bar *ban on imports* in (41b). However, if we suppose that no constituent can have two (or more) specifiers of different types, it follows that *the* cannot be in spec-NP if the noun *government* is in spec-NP. Consequently, it is reasonable to take *the* to be the head of a separate DP projection, and to posit that the italicised nominals in (41a,b) have the respective structures in (43a,b) below:

(43)

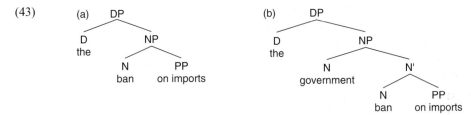

This means that the resulting structures are DPs rather than (as in earlier work) NPs.

Moreover, there are theoretical reasons for supposing that nominals modified by a determiner (or quantifier) are DPs (or QPs) rather than NPs. In this respect, consider the structure of a simple nominal like *the ban* in a sentence such as (44):

(44)   They have lifted *the ban*

Under the earlier NP analysis, *the ban* would be an NP, and *the* would serve as its specifier. But since a specifier is the sister of an intermediate (single-bar) projection, this would mean analysing *the ban* as having the structure below:

(45)

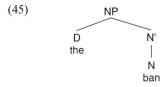

However, the problem with the structure in (45) is that it violates the Binarity Principle (12i), which specifies that 'Every non-terminal node in a syntactic structure is binary-branching.' The reason is that the N-bar node in (45) is a non-terminal node but is unary-branching (because it has only one daughter – namely the N-node *ban*), in violation of the binarity requirement. Note that we can't get round this problem by reanalysing (45) as an NP with the following structure:

(46)

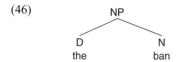

This is because (46) treats *the* as the sister of the noun *ban*, and since the sister of a head is its complement, this would wrongly claim that *the* is the complement of the noun *ban*, and the Head Position Parameter would then wrongly specify that *the* should be positioned after *ban*, because English is a head-first language which positions heads before complements. By contrast, if instead we analyse a phrase like *the ban* as a DP with the structure shown below:

(47)

there is no longer any violation of the Binarity Principle (12ii), since the only non-terminal node in (47) is the DP node, and this has two daughters (the D-node *the* and the N-node *ban*).

An interesting property of the noun *ban* in (47) is that it has a dual status as both a minimal projection and a maximal projection. To see this, let's return to the definition of projection types given in (17) above, repeated below:

(17)   **Projection types**
        A constituent C is
        (a) a *maximal projection* if C does not have a mother with the same head as C
        (b) an *intermediate projection* if C has a mother and a daughter with the same head as C
        (c) a *minimal projection/head* if C has no daughter.

The N constituent *ban* in (47) is a minimal projection in terms of the definition in (17c), by virtue of having no daughter. However, in terms of (17a), it is a maximal projection, because its mother has a different head: i.e. the mother of N-*ban* is the DP constituent *the ban*, and this DP is not headed by N-*ban* but rather by D-*the*. Since the label XP is used to represent the maximal projection of a head X, one way of recognising that N-*ban* is a maximal projection in (47) is to label the relevant node as an NP – as in (48) below:

(48)

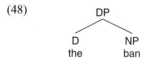

Labelling the word *ban* as an NP in (48) means it is the largest constituent headed by the noun *ban*. The NP label for *ban* also tells us that the noun *ban* occupies a position which could alternatively be occupied by a full noun phrase like *government ban on imports* in (43b). And this is indeed the case, as we see from the observation that the noun *ban* in (44) above (repeated as 49a below) can be replaced by the noun phrase *government ban on imports* in (49b):

(49) (a)   They have lifted the *ban* (= 44)
    (b)   They have lifted the *government ban on imports*

Given that (as we have seen) the noun *ban* in a sentence like (44/49a) has a dual status as a minimal and maximal projection, it should come as no surprise to find that two different conventions are used in the relevant literature for labelling such dual-status constituents: in some works they are labelled as N (as in 47), while in others they are labelled as NP (as in 48). A similar labelling dilemma arises in relation to other dual-status constituents, as I shall point out at appropriate points in the exposition below. Throughout the rest of this book, I will generally use the N-notation in (47), but occasionally use the alternative NP notation in (48) when it is important to stress the maximal projection status of a given constituent.

In all of the structures that we have looked at so far which contain a specifier (i.e. in 16, 22, 28, 31, 32, 33, 38, 40b, 41b and 43b above), the specifier has been a single word. However, this is by no means always the case, as we can see by comparing the two clauses in (50) below:

(50) (a)   *He* has resigned
    (b)   *The chairman* has resigned

(50a) is derived by merging the T/tense auxiliary *has* with its verb complement *resigned* to form the intermediate T-bar projection *has resigned*, and then merging the resulting T-bar with the pronoun *he* which serves as its specifier/subject to derive the extended TP projection in (51) below:

(51)

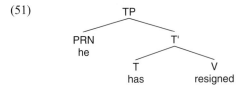

(An incidental point to note in passing is that *resigned* has a dual status as a minimal/maximal projection, and thus could alternatively be labelled as a VP here.) Now consider how we derive (50b) *The chairman has resigned*. As before, the tense auxiliary *has* merges with its verb complement *resigned* to form the T-bar *has resigned*; and as before, the resulting T-bar then merges with its subject/specifier. However, this time the subject is not the single word *he* but rather a determiner phrase/DP *the chairman* which has itself been formed by merging the determiner *the* with the noun *chairman*. Thus, the T-bar *has resigned* and the DP *the chairman* have to be formed independently of each other (either sequentially/one after the other or simultaneously/both at the same time) before the two are eventually merged together to derive the TP (52) below (where *resigned* has dual status as a minimal and maximal projection, and so could alternatively be labelled as VP rather than V):

(52)

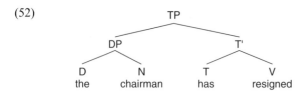

Evidence that *the chairman* is indeed the subject (and specifier) of *has* in (52) comes from Auxiliary Inversion in sentences such as:

(53) (a)   *Has* **he** resigned?
     (b)   *Has* **the chairman** resigned?

If we compare the statement (50a) *He has resigned* with the corresponding question (53a) *Has he resigned?* we can see that a question like (53a) is formed by moving a finite auxiliary (*has*) in front of its subject (*he*). Hence, the fact that the auxiliary *has* in (50b) moves in front of *the chairman* in (53b) *Has the chairman resigned?* suggests that *the chairman* is indeed the subject of *has* in (50b) *The chairman has resigned* – precisely as is claimed in (52).

   If we compare (48) with (49), we see that a specifier can be either a single word like *we* in (48) or a phrase like the DP *the chairman* in (49). In much the same way, a complement can be either a single word or a phrase. For example, in (52), the complement of *has* is the verb *resigned*; since V-*resigned* has dual status as a minimal and maximal projection in (52), it can be replaced by a maximal projection like the VP *resigned from the board*, as in (54) below:

(54)

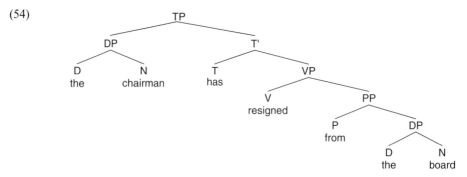

Here, the complement of *has* is the VP/verb phrase *resigned from the board*, which is formed by merging the verb *resigned* with its PP/prepositional phrase complement *from the board*.

3.6   Testing structure

Thus far, we have seen that phrases and sentences are built up by merging successive pairs of constituents to form larger and larger structures, and that the resulting structure can be represented in terms of a labelled tree diagram. The tree diagrams which we use to represent syntactic structure make specific claims about how sentences are built up out of various different kinds of constituent (i.e. syntactic unit): hence, trees can be said to represent the constituent structure of sentences. But this raises the question of how we know (and how we can test) whether the claims made about syntactic structure in tree diagrams are correct. So far, we have relied mainly on intuition in analysing the structure of sentences – we have in effect guessed at the structure. However, it is unwise to rely on intuition in attempting to determine the structure of a given expression in a given language. For, while experienced linguists over a period of years tend to acquire fairly strong intuitions about structure, novices by contrast tend to have relatively weak, uncertain and unreliable intuitions; moreover, even the intuitions of supposed experts may ultimately turn out to be based on little more than personal preference.

For this reason, it is more satisfactory (and more accurate) to regard constituent structure as having the status of a theoretical construct. That is to say, it is part of the theoretical apparatus which linguists find they need to make use of in order to explain certain observations about language (just as molecules, atoms and subatomic particles are constructs which physicists find they need to make use of in order to explain the nature of matter in the universe). It is no more reasonable to rely wholly on intuition to determine syntactic structure than it would be to rely on intuition to determine molecular structure. Inevitably, then, much of the evidence for syntactic structure is of an essentially empirical character, based on the observed grammatical properties of particular types of expression. The evidence typically takes the form 'If we posit that such-and-such an expression has such-and-such a structure, we can provide a principled account of the observed grammatical properties of the expression.' Thus, structural representations ultimately have to be justified in empirical terms, i.e. in terms of whether or not they provide a principled account of the observed grammatical properties of phrases and sentences.

So, a tree diagram like (51) has the status of a hypothesis (i.e. untested and unproven assumption) about the structure of the corresponding sentence *The chairman has resigned from the board*. How can we test our hypothesis and determine whether (51) is or isn't an appropriate representation of the structure of the sentence? The answer is that there are a number of heuristics (i.e. 'tests') which we can use to determine structure. One such test relates to the phenomenon of **coordination** briefly touched on in §2.4. As we saw there, English and other languages have a variety of coordinating conjunctions like *and/but/or* which can be used to coordinate expressions such as those bracketed below:

(55) (a)   [fond of cats] *and* [afraid of dogs]
    (b)   [slowly] *but* [surely]
    (c)   [to go] *or* [to stay]

In each of the expressions in (55), an italicised coordinating conjunction has been used to conjoin the bracketed pairs of expressions. Clearly, any adequate grammar of English will have to provide a principled answer to the question: 'What kinds of strings (i.e. sequences of words) can and cannot be coordinated?'

Now, it turns out that we can't just coordinate any random set of strings, as we see by comparing the grammatical reply produced by speaker B in (56) below:

(56)   SPEAKER A: What does he do to keep fit?
         SPEAKER B: Run *up the hill* and *up the mountain*

with the ungrammatical reply produced by speaker B in (57) below:

(57)   SPEAKER A: What did he do about his bills?
         SPEAKER B: *Ring *up the phone company* and *up the electricity company*

Why should it be possible to coordinate the string *up the hill* with the string *up the mountain* in (56), but not possible to coordinate the string *up the phone company* with the string *up the electricity company* in (57)? We can provide a principled answer to this question in terms of constituent structure: the italicised string *up the hill* in (56) is a constituent of the phrase *run up the hill* (*up the hill* is a prepositional phrase, in fact), and so can be coordinated with another similar type of prepositional phrase (e.g. a PP such as *up the mountain*, or *down the hill* or *along the path*, etc.). Conversely, however, the string *up the phone company* in (57) is not a constituent of the phrase *ring up the phone company* and so cannot be coordinated with another similar string like *up the electricity company*. (Traditional grammarians say that *up* is associated with *ring* in expressions like *ring up someone*, and that the expression *ring up* forms a kind of complex/phrasal verb which carries the sense of 'telephone'.) On the basis of contrasts such as these, we can formulate the following generalisation:

(58)   **Coordination Condition**
         Only constituents of the same type can be coordinated.

A **constraint** (i.e. principle imposing restrictions on grammatical operations) along the lines of (58) is assumed in much work in traditional grammar.

Having established the condition (58), we can now make use of it as a way of testing the tree diagram in (54) above. In this connection, consider the data in (59) below (in which the bracketed strings have been coordinated by *and*):

(59) (a)   The chairman has resigned from [*the board*] and [*the company*]
     (b)   The chairman has resigned [*from the board*] and [*from the company*]
     (c)   The chairman has [*resigned from the board*] and [*gone abroad*]
     (d)   The chairman [*has resigned from the board*] and [*is living in Ruritania*]
     (e)   *The [*chairman has resigned from the board*] and [*company has replaced him*]
     (f)   [*The chairman has resigned from the board*] and [*the company has replaced him*]

(59a) provides us with evidence in support of the claim in (54) that *the board* is a determiner phrase constituent, since it can be coordinated with another DP like *the company*; similarly, (59b) provides us with evidence that *from the board* is a prepositional phrase constituent, since it can be coordinated with another PP like *from the company*; likewise, (59c) provides evidence that *resigned from the board* is a verb phrase constituent, since it can be coordinated with another VP like *gone abroad*; in much the same way, (59d) provides evidence that *has resigned from the board* is a T-bar constituent, since it can be coordinated with another T' like *is living in Utopia* (thereby providing interesting evidence in support of the binary-branching structure assumed in the TP analysis of clauses, and against the ternary-branching analysis assumed in the S analysis of clauses); and in addition, (59f) provides evidence that *the chairman has resigned from the board* is a TP constituent, since it can be coordinated with another TP like *the company have replaced him*. Conversely, however, the fact that (59e) is ungrammatical suggests that (precisely as (54) claims) the string *chairman has resigned from the board* is not a constituent, since it cannot be coordinated with a parallel string like *company have replaced him* (and the constraint in 58 tells us that two strings of words can only be coordinated if both are constituents – and more precisely, if both are constituents of the same type). Overall, then, the coordination data in (59) provide empirical evidence in support of the analysis in (54). (It should be noted, however, that the coordination test is not always straightforward to apply: for example, apparent complications arise in relation to sentences like 'He is *cross with her* and *in a filthy mood*', where the AP/adjectival phrase *cross with her* has been coordinated with the PP/prepositional phrase *in a filthy mood*: to say that these seemingly different AP and PP constituents are 'of the same type' requires a more abstract analysis than is implied by category labels like AP and PP, perhaps taking them to share in common some grammatical feature which enables them to be used as predicative expressions. Further complications are posed by the rather different type of coordinate structure found in sentences like *John will – but Mary won't – apologise to Joe*, but these will not be discussed here. The moral of the story is that the coordination test has to be used with care.)

A second way of testing structure is to use the **modification** test. We can illustrate how the test works by considering the types of string (i.e. sequences of words) which can be modified by a **modal adverb** such as *possibly, perhaps, maybe, probably, conceivably, definitely* or *certainly* in examples such as the following, where the bold-printed modal adverb modifies the italicised material following it:

(60) (a) **Perhaps** *the chairman has resigned from the board*
   (b) The chairman **definitely** *has resigned from the board*
   (c) The chairman has **certainly** *resigned from the board*
   (d) *The **probably** chairman has resigned from the board

A key assumption underlying the adverb test is that modifiers are subject to the following condition on their use:

(61)   **Modification Condition**
       Only a string of words which is a constituent can be modified by an appropriate type of modifier.

Given (61), the fact that the string *the chairman has resigned from the board* in (60a) can be modified by *perhaps* is consistent with the claim made in (54) that the relevant string is a TP constituent: likewise, the fact that the string *has resigned from the board* in (60b) can be modified by *definitely* is consistent with the claim in (54) that it is a T-bar constituent; and similarly, the fact that *resigned from the board* can be modified by *certainly* in (60c) provides evidence in support of the claim made in (54) that it is a VP constituent. By contrast, the impossibility of using the adverb *probably* to modify the string *chairman has resigned from the board* in (60d) provides evidence in support of the claim made in (54) that the relevant string is not a constituent of any kind. (The alternative possibility of using *probably* to modify just the noun *chairman* on its own can be ruled out by a constraint barring adverbs from occurring internally within nominals: nominals are instead modified by adjectives, as in *the probable chairman*).

An important point to note about the modification test, however, is that (61) claims that any string of words which can be modified by a given kind of modifier is a constituent, but does not say that *every* string of words which is a constituent can be modified by the relevant type of modifier. This latter claim is clearly untrue, as can be seen from the ungrammaticality of the following:

(62) (a)   *The chairman has resigned **conceivably** *from the board*
     (b)   *The chairman has resigned from **possibly** *the board*
     (c)   *The chairman has resigned from the **maybe** *board*

There is surely little doubt, on the basis of other evidence, that *from the board* is a constituent (more specifically, a PP/prepositional phrase) of the sentence *The chairman has resigned from the board*, that *the board* is likewise a constituent (a DP/determiner phrase) and that the word *board* is also a constituent (an N/noun). Why should it be, then, that none of these three italicised constituents can be modified by the relevant bold-printed adverb in (62)? The answer is that there are additional constraints on the use of adverbial modifiers. For example, modal adverbs in English cannot generally occur internally within VP (between a verb and its complement as in 62a), or internally within PP (between a preposition and its complement as in 62b), or internally within DP (between a determiner and its complement as in 62c). Consequently, we need to interpret the results yielded by the modification test with caution: if a string can be modified by a given type of modifier, it is a constituent; if not, it may or may not be a constituent.

A third way of testing whether a given string of words is a constituent is to use **substitution** – that is, testing whether the relevant string can be substituted by a single word. In this connection, consider:

(63) (a)   *The chairman* has resigned from the board, and **he** is now living in Utopia
     (b)   The press say that the chairman has *resigned from the board*, and **so** he has
     (c)   %If the Managing Director says the chairman has *resigned from the board*, he must have **done**
     (d)   If the chairman has *resigned from the board* (**which** you say he has), how come his car is still in the company car park?

(The percentage sign in front of 63c indicates that this type of structure is only found in certain varieties of English – notably, British English.) In each of the above sentences, the italicised string can be replaced (or referred back to) by a particular kind of **proform**. (Recall that a proform is a function word that can stand 'in place of' some other expression.) The fact that the expression *the chairman* in (63a) can be substituted by a single word (in this case, the pro-form/pronoun *he*) provides evidence in support of the claim in (54) that *the chairman* is a single constituent (a DP/determiner phrase, to be precise). Likewise, the fact that the expression *resigned from the board* in (63b,c,d) can serve as the **antecedent** of the proforms *so/done/which* provides evidence in support of the claim in (54) that *resigned from the board* is a constituent (analysed in 54 as being a VP/verb phrase). Unfortunately, since English has a very limited inventory of proforms, the *proform* test is of limited usefulness.

A fourth kind of constituent structure test is the **fragment** test. The underlying premise of the test is that there are restrictions on the types of expression which can (or can't) be used as **sentence fragments** (i.e. expressions which are not complete sentences but represent fragments of sentences which can be used as free-standing expressions, e.g. in answer to a question). This premise can be justified by the contrast found in dialogues such as the following:

(64)   SPEAKER A: Who were you talking to?
            SPEAKER B: To the electricity company

(65)   SPEAKER A: Who were you ringing up?
            SPEAKER B: *Up the electricity company

Why should it be that *to the electricity company* can serve as a sentence fragment in (64B), but not *up the electricity company* in (65B)? The traditional answer is that only constituents can serve as sentence fragments. Given this assumption, we can account for the contrast between (64B) and (65B) in a straightforward fashion if we maintain that *to the electricity company* is a constituent of the verb phrase *talking to the electricity company*, whereas *up the electricity company* isn't a constituent of the verb phrase *ringing up the electricity company.*

In the light of our assumption that only constituents can serve as sentence fragments, consider the following mini-dialogue, paying particular attention to the kind of (italicised) sentence fragments which speaker B can use to reply to speaker A's question:

(66)   SPEAKER A: What has the chairman resigned from?
            SPEAKER B: *The board/From the board*

Given our premise that only constituents can serve as sentence fragments, the fact that the string *the board* can be used as a sentence fragment in (66) is consistent with the claim made in (54) that it is a DP constituent. Likewise, the fact that speaker B could alternatively use the string *from the board* as a sentence fragment in (66) is consistent with the claim made in (54) that it is a PP constituent. Given the conversational maxim 'Be concise!' postulated by Grice (1975), the shorter response *the board* will generally be preferred to the longer response *from the board* for economy reasons.

Now consider the mini-dialogue below:

(67)   SPEAKER A: What has the chairman done?
            SPEAKER B: *Resigned from the board/*Has resigned from the board*

The string *resigned from the board* can be used as a sentence fragment in (67) because it is a VP/verb phrase, and hence the maximal projection of the V/verb *resigned*. But why should it be that the string **Has resigned from the board* can't be used to reply to speaker A's question in (67)? After all, our tree diagram in (54) claims that it is a constituent – more precisely, a T-bar constituent. So why can't it serve as a sentence fragment in (67)? The answer would seem to lie in a condition such as the following:

(68)   **Fragment Condition**
            Only a maximal projection can serve as a sentence fragment.

We can then say that the reason why the DP *the board*, the PP *from the board* and the VP *resigned from the board* can be used as sentence fragments in (66, 67) is that each of these expressions is a maximal projection (i.e. a constituent which does not project into a larger constituent with the same head). Conversely, the reason why **Has resigned from the board* cannot serve as a sentence fragment in (67) is that it is an intermediate (T-bar) projection of the T-auxiliary *has* – the corresponding maximal projection being the complete TP constituent *He has resigned from the board*.

    A question which arises in the wake of our discussion is why speaker B cannot simply use the noun *board* to reply to speaker A's question in (69) below:

(69)   SPEAKER A: What has the chairman resigned from?
            SPEAKER B: **Board*

In terms of the structure in (54), the word *board* is a maximal projection by virtue of being the largest expression headed by the noun *board*. Thus, the word *board* could alternatively be labelled as an NP rather than as an N, and so could the noun *chairman*. If we did this, the structure in (54) above could alternatively be represented as in (70) below (where the relevant constituents are bold-printed):

(70)

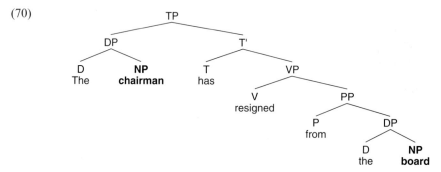

The nouns *board* and *chairman* are maximal projections (hence NPs) because neither has a mother with the same head (the mother of the noun *board* is a DP whose head is the determiner *the*, and the mother of the noun *chairman* is likewise a DP headed by D-*the*). Given that the noun *board* is a maximal projection, we might expect it to be able to occur as a sentence fragment. However, note that (68) says that *only* a maximal projection can serve as a sentence fragment, and not that *every* maximal projection can serve as a sentence fragment. The ungrammaticality of speaker B's reply in (69) would suggest that a singular count noun cannot function as a sentence fragment, and the obvious question to ask is why. One possible answer is that a count noun needs to be assigned a (singular/plural) number feature via **Concord** with a determiner or quantifier used to modify it, with the result that a count noun used without a preceding determiner/quantifier is ungrammatical. Our discussion of (69) illustrates that constituent structure tests sometimes don't yield the expected results, usually because of constraints on grammatical operations or syntactic structures.

   A fifth kind of test we can use for constituent structure involves **Ellipsis** (i.e. deletion of redundant information in a sentence – e.g. information which has been mentioned in the preceding discourse, or which can be inferred from the context). Let's suppose that this is an operation taking place in the phonological component, whereby a given type of constituent is given a silent spellout (i.e. is unpronounced). There are two rather different kinds of ellipsis operation – one involving the omission of heads, the other of maximal projections. We can illustrate the difference in terms of the sentences in (71) below (where the ellipsed material marked by strikethrough is 'silent' and so not pronounced):

(71) (a)   He can speak French better than she can ~~speak~~ German
     (b)   He can speak French better than she can ~~speak French~~

In (71a), the head verb *speak* of the VP/verb phrase *speak German* is given a silent spellout in the PF component, leaving a 'gap' in the middle of the VP where the verb *speak* would otherwise have been: as we saw in §1.4, this type of ellipsis is referred to as **Gapping**. By contrast, in (71b) the whole VP *speak French* is silent – a phenomenon termed **VP Ellipsis**. The data in (71) are consistent with the following condition:

(72)   **Constituency Condition**
          Heads and maximal projections are the only types of constituent which can take part in linguistic operations like movement, agreement or ellipsis.

In the light of (72), consider the following contrast:

(73) (a)   They say the chairman has resigned from the board, but I don't think he has
              ~~resigned from the board~~
     (b)   *They say the chairman has resigned from the board, but I don't think he ~~has resigned from the board~~

In (73a) the second occurrence of the string *resigned from the board* (marked by strikethrough) undergoes ellipsis and so is 'silent'. If only heads and maximal projections (and not intermediate projections) can undergo operations like ellipsis, this observation is consistent with the claim made in (54/70) that *resigned from the board* is a VP, and hence the maximal projection of the verb *resigned*. By contrast, in (73b) we cannot omit the string *has resigned from the board*, and the obvious question to ask is why. The answer given by the structure in (54/70) is that *has resigned from the board* is an intermediate projection and not a maximal projection (because it is a T-bar and not a complete TP), and hence cannot undergo ellipsis. To put things the other way round, sentences like (73) provide empirical evidence in support of the structure assumed in (54/70) – or, to phrase things rather more carefully, sentences like (73) are *consistent* with the structure (54/70).

However, an apparent complication is posed by the ungrammaticality of elliptical sentences such as those in (74):

(74) (a)   *They say the chairman has resigned from the board, but I don't think he has resigned from ~~the board~~

(b)   *They say the chairman has resigned from the board, but I don't think he has resigned from the ~~board~~

Given that our tree in (54/70) tells us that *the board* is the maximal projection of the determiner *the* and that *board* is the maximal projection of the noun *board*, the question arises as to why these two expressions cannot undergo ellipsis in (74). The answer is that there are constraints (of a poorly understood nature) on the kinds of maximal projection which can undergo ellipsis. For instance, the VP complement of *to* marked by strikethrough can be ellipsed in (75a) below, but not the CP complement of *believes* in (75b), or the TP complement of *if* in (75c), or the PP complement of *rely* in (75d):

(75) (a)   Joe knows he should go to the dentist, but he stubbornly refuses to ~~go to the dentist~~

(b)   *Joe claims that he saw a ghost, but nobody else believes ~~that he saw a ghost~~

(c)   *Joe claims he has done his assignment, but I wonder if ~~he has done his assignment~~

(d)   *Joe says I can rely on him, but I don't think I can rely ~~on him~~

In view of the fact that there are poorly understood constraints on ellipsis, it is clear that the ellipsis test has to be used with considerable caution: if a string of words can undergo ellipsis, it is a constituent (and more precisely, a maximal projection); if not, we cannot be sure whether it is a constituent or not.

A sixth type of constituent structure test which we can use to determine the structure of sentences is the focus test. This can be illustrated in relation to the following sentences:

(76) (a)   It was *the front of the house* that Mary didn't like

(b)   What Mary didn't like was *the front of the house*

The type of sentence illustrated in (76a) is termed a cleft sentence, whereas that illustrated in (76b) is known as a **pseudo-cleft sentence**. In both sentences, the highlighted italicised material is said to be focused (or to occupy the **focus position** within the structure). Focusing is used as a way of highlighting new/ unfamiliar information and is subject to the following structural condition:

(77)   **Focus Condition**
        Only a maximal projection can be focused in a cleft or pseudo-cleft sentence.

In the light of the constraint in (77), consider the following sets of sentences:

(78) (a)   It is *the board* that the chairman has resigned from
    (b)   It is *from the board* that the chairman has resigned
    (c)   *It is *resigned from the board* that the chairman has

(79) (a)   What the chairman has resigned from is *the board*
    (b)   *What the chairman has resigned is *from the board*
    (c)   What the chairman has done is *resign(ed) from the board*

The fact that the string *the board* can be focused in both a cleft sentence such as (78a) and a pseudo-cleft such as (79a) is consistent with the claim made in (54/70) that it is a DP, and hence a maximal projection. Likewise, the fact that the string *from the board* can be focused in the cleft sentence (78b) is consistent with the claim made in (54/70) that it is a PP constituent, and hence also a maximal projection. Finally, the fact that the VP *resign(ed) from the board* can be focused in a pseudo-cleft sentence such as (79c) is consistent with the claim made in (54/70) that *resigned from the board* is a VP constituent, and so also a maximal projection.

Although the focus test lends support to relevant parts of the analysis in (54/70), it leaves behind in its wake the question of why sentences like (78c) and (79b) should be ungrammatical. The reason for the ungrammaticality of (78c) would appear to be that only very restricted types of maximal projection can be focused in clefts – more specifically, (pro)nominal or prepositional structures. The reason for the ungrammaticality of (79b) lies not in what is focused, but rather in the fact that the first part of the structure is ungrammatical – as we see from the ungrammaticality of speaker B's reply below:

(80)   SPEAKER A: What was your topic of conversation?
        SPEAKER B: *What the chairman has resigned

This is because the verb *resigned* (in the relevant use) requires a *from*-phrase complement and does not have one in (80B) – nor indeed in the part of the sentence preceding *is* in (79b). The overall conclusion which this leads to is that the focus test (like other tests we have looked at) needs to be used with caution.

The seventh (and final) type of constituent structure test which we will look at here is the movement test (a test made use of in §3.5 above) relating to the possibility of preposing a constituent in order to highlight it in some way (e.g. in order to mark it out as a topic containing familiar/old information, or as a focused constituent containing unfamiliar/new information). It follows from the Constituency Condition (72) that only heads or maximal projections can undergo movement. Structures in which heads undergo movement include questions like '*Has* the chairman resigned?' where the auxiliary *has* moves from its canonical position following the underlined subject (in 'The chairman *has* resigned') to a position immediately preceding the subject. (In Chapter 5, we will see that an inverted auxiliary moves from the head T position of TP into the head C position of CP.) In addition to operations moving heads, we also find operations moving phrases. In our earlier discussion of structures like (34), (35) and (39) above, we concluded that only a string of words which is a maximal projection can be highlighted in this way. This being so, one way we can test whether a given expression is a maximal projection or not is by seeing whether it can be preposed. In this connection, consider the following sentence:

(81)   The press said that the chairman would resign from the board, and *resigned from the board* he has

The fact that the italicised string of words *resigned from the board* can be preposed in (81) indicates that it must be a maximal projection: this is consistent with the analysis in (54/70) which tells us that *resigned from the board* is a verb phrase which is the maximal projection of the verb *resigned*.

However, an important caveat which should be noted in relation to the preposing test is that particular expressions can sometimes be difficult (or even impossible) to prepose, even though they are maximal projections. This is because there are constraints (i.e. restrictions) on such movement operations. One such constraint can be illustrated by the following contrast:

(82) (a)   He resolutely refused to surrender to the enemy
    (b)   %*Surrender to the enemy*, he resolutely refused to
    (c)   ***To surrender to the enemy*, he resolutely refused

Here, for speakers such as me, the VP/verb phrase *surrender to the enemy* can be highlighted by being preposed (though for other speakers it seems that this is not possible – an issue I return to shortly). By contrast, the TP/infinitival tense phrase *to surrender to the enemy* cannot be preposed in (82c) – even though it is a maximal projection (by virtue of being the largest expression headed by infinitival *to*). What is the nature of the restriction on preposing *to+infinitive* expressions illustrated by the ungrammaticality of (82c)? The answer is not clear but may be semantic in nature. When an expression is preposed, this is in order to highlight its semantic content in some way (e.g. for purposes of contrast – as in e.g. '*Syntax*, I don't like but *phonology* I do'). It may be that its lack of intrinsic lexical semantic content makes infinitival *to* an unsuitable candidate for highlighting. If so, this suggests that when preposing material for highlighting purposes, we should prepose *as few words as possible*. This requirement is arguably related to Grice's (1975) *Conciseness* maxim (which amounts to 'Use as few words as possible'). More generally, the conciseness requirement can be argued to be a reflection of the more general Economy Principle posited in §1.4, which in turn can plausibly be taken to be a principle of computational efficiency governing natural systems in general rather than being specific to language. This principle is presented in a slightly reformulated fashion below:

(83)   **Economy Principle**
        Structures and operations should be as economical as possible.

Given that only a maximal projection can be preposed for highlighting purposes, it follows from the Economy Principle that the following (more specific) condition will hold on preposing:

(84)   **Preposing Condition**
          When material is preposed in order to highlight it, what is preposed is the
          smallest possible maximal projection containing the highlighted material.

So, if we want to highlight the semantic content of the VP *surrender to the enemy*,
we prepose the VP *surrender to the enemy* rather than the TP *to surrender to the
enemy* because the VP is smaller than the TP containing it.

However, this is by no means the only constraint on preposing, as we see from
(85) below (where *FBA* is an abbreviation for the Federal Bureau of Assassinations –
a purely fictitious body, of course):

(85) (a)   Nobody had expected that the FBA would assassinate the king of Ruritania
     (b)   *King of Ruritania*, nobody had expected that the FBA would assassinate the
     (c)   *The king of Ruritania*, nobody had expected that the FBA would assassinate
     (d)   *The FBA would assassinate the king of Ruritania*, nobody had expected that
             (NB. *that* = ðət)
     (e)   *That the FBA would assassinate the king of Ruritania*, nobody had expected

The ungrammaticality of (85b) tells us that we can't prepose the NP *king of
Ruritania*.Why should this be? The answer is that there is a constraint on the
structures produced by movement operations to the effect that some types of
function word cannot be **stranded** – i.e. left without their complement immediately following them. Unstrandable function words include the determiners and
quantifiers that introduce nominal constituents, and the complementisers that
introduce clauses.We can therefore characterise this constraint as follows:

(86)   **Stranding Constraint**
          No D/determiner, Q/quantifier or C/complementiser can be stranded without
          its complement.

(It may well be that speakers who reject sentences like 82b extend this constraint to
infinitival *to* as well – but I shall set aside this detail here.) In the light of (86), consider
what will happen if we want to highlight the NP *king of Ruritania* in (85a) by
preposing. (84) tells us to move *the smallest possible maximal projection containing
the highlighted material*, and hence we first try to move the NP *king of Ruritania* on
its own: but the Stranding Constraint (86) tells us that it is not possible to do so,
because this results in the determiner *the* being stranded at the end of the sentence. We
therefore prepose the next smallest maximal projection containing the hightlighted
NP *king of Ruritania* – namely the DP *the king of Ruritania*; and as the grammaticality of (85c) shows, the resulting sentence is grammatical. To use the relevant
technical term introduced in §2.9, a moved constituent sometimes has to **pied-pipe**
(i.e. drag) another constituent along with it when it moves. Using this terminology,
we can say that the NP *king of Ruritania* can't move on its own in (85) because this
would violate the Stranding Constraint (86): instead, the NP has to pied-pipe the
determiner *the* along with it when it moves; this in turn means that the whole DP *the
king of Ruritania* has to be preposed.

Now suppose that we want to highlight the TP *the FBA would assassinate the
king of Ruritania*. (84) tells us to move the smallest maximal projection containing

the highlighted material – but the Stranding Constraint (86) tells us that we cannot prepose the TP on its own because this will leave the complementiser *that* stranded at the end of the sentence – so accounting for the ungrammaticality of (85d).

Hence, we prepose the *next smallest* maximal projection containing the TP which we want to highlight, namely the CP *that the FBA would assassinate the King of Ruritania* – as in (85e). Consequently, the complementiser *that* (in spite of having minimal semantic content) ends up being pied-piped along with the TP that we want to highlight.

The overall conclusion to be drawn from our discussion here is that the preposing test has to be used with care. If an expression can be preposed in order to highlight it, it is a maximal projection; if it cannot, this may be either because it is not a maximal projection, or because (even though it *is* a maximal projection) a syntactic constraint of some kind prevents it from being preposed, or because its head word has insufficient semantic content to make it a suitable candidate for highlighting.

It is interesting to note that alongside sentences like (85c,e) above in which a phrase or clause has been highlighted by being preposed, we also find sentences in which a single word has been highlighted by being preposed. In this connection, consider the following set of examples:

(87) (a)   I feel sure John will resign
   (b)   *John* I feel sure will resign
   (c)   *Resign*, I feel sure John will

In (87b) the noun *John* has been preposed on its own, and in (87c) the verb *resign* has been preposed on its own. Given the claim in (84) that only maximal projections can undergo preposing, this means that both the noun *John* and the verb *resign* must be maximal projections. But how can this be, since nouns are normally the heads of noun phrases (and hence minimal rather than maximal projections), and verbs are normally the heads of verb phrases?

The answer provided to this question in earlier work (dating back to the era of **X-bar Syntax** in the 1970s) was to assume that a single noun standing on its own had essentially the same internal structure as a noun phrase, and likewise that a single verb standing on its own had essentially the same internal structure as a verb phrase. Given this assumption, the complement clause *John will resign* in a sentence such as (87a) above would have been analysed as having the structure shown in (88) below:

(88)

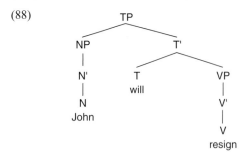

This would mean that *John* has a triple status and functions not only as a minimal projection (by virtue of being an N) but also as an intermediate projection (by virtue of being an N-bar) and as a maximal projection (by virtue of being an NP). Likewise, *resign* would also have a triple status and be not only a minimal projection (by virtue of being a V) but also an intermediate projection (by virtue of being a V-bar) and a maximal projection (by virtue of being a VP).

However, a structure such as (88) is not in keeping with the requirement imposed by the Principle (83) that 'Structures … should be as economical as possible', since *John* is treated as being three separate constituents (an N, an N-bar and an NP), and *resign* is likewise treated as being three separate constituents (a V, a V-bar and a VP). Moreover, a structure such as (88) involves multiple violations of the Binarity Principle (12) requiring that 'Every non-terminal node in a syntactic structure is binary-branching.' The principle is violated by the four unary-branching constituents in (88) – more specifically, by the NP node branching down into a single N-bar constituent, by the N-bar node branching down into a single N constituent, by the VP node branching down into a single V-bar constituent, and by the V-bar node branching down into a single V constituent. Clearly, then, the structure in (88) is untenable within the framework used here. But if we reject the structure in (88), how can we account for the noun *John* and the verb *resign* functioning as maximal projections in (87) and so being able to be preposed?

The answer is that the dual status of these two words can be accounted for straightforwardly if we posit that the complement clause *John will resign* in (87a) has the more economical structure below:

(89)

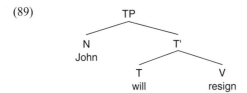

Let us suppose that the terms *maximal projection* and *minimal projection* can be defined as in (17) above, repeated below:

(17)   **Projection types**
        A constituent C is
        (a) a *maximal projection* if C does not have a mother with the same head as C
        (b) an *intermediate projection* if C has a mother and a daughter with the same head as C
        (c) a *minimal projection/head* if C has no daughter.

It follows from the definition in (17a) that the N constituent *John* in (89) is a maximal projection because its mother is the TP node, and TP is not headed by N-*John* but rather by T-*will*. Likewise, it follows from the definition in (17c) that the N-*John* is also a minimal projection by virtue of having no daughter. Similarly, it follows from the definition in (17a) that the V constituent *resign* in (89) is a maximal projection because its mother is the T-bar node, and T-bar is not headed by the verb *resign* (but rather by T-*will*). Likewise, it follows from the definition in (17c) that the V-*resign* is also a minimal projection by virtue of not having a daughter. A more economical structure like (89) can therefore provide a principled account of how a single word which has no complement or specifier of its own can have a dual status as both a minimal and a maximal projection – and this is therefore the type of structure which I will adopt here.

As noted in our earlier discussion of (47/48) and (54/70) above, an alternative labelling system widely used in the relevant literature is to label individual words which have the status of maximal projections as XPs. Using this system, the complement clause *John will resign* in a sentence such as (87a) above would be analysed as having the structure (90) below:

(90)

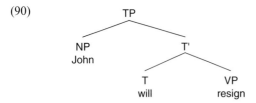

Such a system explicitly marks the status of *John* as a maximal projection by categorising *John* as an NP, and likewise explicitly marks the status of *resign* as a maximal projection by categorising it as a VP. If we suppose that an XP with no daughter is also an X, then it can be inferred from (90) that the NP *John* is also an N (because the relevant NP node has no daughter), and likewise that the VP *resign* is also a V (again, because the relevant VP node has no daughter). Consequently, either of the two labelling systems in (89) or (90) can be used in structural representations/tree diagrams. As noted earlier, I will generally use the labelling convention in (89), but will adopt that in (90) where I want to emphasise that a particular word has the status of a maximal projection in a particular use.

The overall conclusion to be drawn from our discussion in this section is that there are a number of tests which can be used to determine the constituent structure of sentences. However, these tests must be used with caution, because sometimes a constraint of some kind may mean that a test does not yield the expected results when applied to a particular kind of structure.

3.7   Structural relations

In this chapter, we have looked at evidence that phrases and sentences are formed by a series of binary Merge operations, and we have seen that the resulting structures can be represented in the form of tree diagrams. Because they mark the way that words are combined together to form phrases of various types, tree diagrams are referred to in earlier work as **phrase-markers** (abbreviated to **P-markers**). They show us how a phrase or sentence is built up out of constituents of various types: hence, a tree diagram provides a visual representation of the constituent structure of the corresponding expression. Each node in the tree (i.e. each point in the tree which carries a category label like N, V, A', T', PP, CP, etc.) represents a different constituent of the sentence; hence, there are as many different constituents in any given phrase marker as there are nodes carrying category labels. As we saw earlier, nodes at the very bottom of the tree are called terminal nodes, and other nodes are non-terminal nodes.

This distinction can be illustrated by taking another look at the structure in (54) above, repeated as (91) below:

(91)

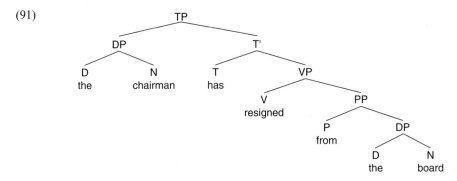

All the D, N, T, V and P nodes in (91) are terminal nodes, and all the DP, PP, VP, T' and TP nodes are non-terminal nodes. The topmost node in any tree structure (i.e. TP in the case of 91 above) is said to be its **root**. Each terminal node in the tree carries a single lexical item (= an item from the lexicon/dictionary, e.g. a word like *dog* or *go* etc.): lexical items are sets of phonological, semantic and grammatical features (with category labels like N, V, T, C, etc. being used as shorthand abbreviations for the set of grammatical features carried by the relevant items).

It is useful to develop some terminology to describe the syntactic relations between constituents, since these relations turn out to be central to syntactic description. Essentially, a P-marker is a graph comprising a set of points (= labelled nodes), connected by branches (= solid lines) which represent **containment** relations (telling us which constituents contain or are contained within which other constituents). We can illustrate what this means in terms of the following abstract tree structure (where A, B, C, D, E, F, G, H and J are different nodes in the tree, representing different constituents):

(92)

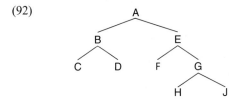

In (92), G **immediately contains** H and J (and conversely H and J are the two constituents immediately contained within G, and hence are the two **immediate constituents** of G): this is shown by the fact that H and J are the two nodes immediately beneath G connected to G by a **branch** (solid line). Likewise, E immediately contains F and G; B immediately contains C and D; and A immediately contains B and E. We can also say that E **contains** F, G, H and J; and that A contains B, C, D, E, F, G, H and J (and likewise that G contains H and J; and B contains C and D). Using equivalent kinship terminology, we can say that A is the **mother** of B and E (and conversely B and E are the two **daughters** of A); B is the mother of C and D; E is the mother of F and G; and G is the mother of H and J). Likewise, B and E are **sisters** (by virtue of both being daughters of A) – as are C and D; F and G; and H and J.

A particularly important syntactic relation is **c-command** (a conventional abbreviation of constituent-command), which provides us with a useful way of determining the relative position of two different constituents within the same tree. We can define this relation informally as follows:

(93)   **C-command**

If X and Y are independent constituents (i.e. if neither contains the other), X c-commands Y iff (i.e. 'if an only if') the mother of X contains Y.

For those of you who find it difficult to conceptualise such abstractions, a more concrete way of visualising this is to think of a tree diagram as representing a network of train stations, with each of the labelled nodes representing the name of a different station in the network, and the branches representing the rail tracks linking the stations. We can then say that one node X c-commands another node Y if you can get from X to Y on the network by taking a northbound train, getting off at the first station and then travelling one or more stops south on a different line.

In the light of the definition of c-command given above, let's consider which constituents each of the nodes in (92) c-commands. A doesn't c-command any of the other nodes, since A has no mother. B c-commands E, F, G, H and J because B's mother is A, and the only constituents independent of B which A contains are E, F, G, H and J. C c-commands only D, because C's mother is B, and the only constituent independent of C that B contains is D; for parallel reasons, D c-commands only C. E c-commands B, C and D because A is the mother of E, and the only constituents independent of E which A contains are B, C and D. F c-commands G, H and J, because the mother of F is E, and the only constituents independent of F which E contains are G, H and J. G c-commands only F, because G's mother is E, and the only constituent independent of G which E contains is F. H c-commands only J because the mother of H is G and the only constituent independent of H which G contains is J; and for parallel reasons, J c-commands only H.

The relation c-command plays a central role in a wide range of syntactic phenomena. One such is the phenomenon of **anaphor binding**. Anaphors are expressions which have the property that they cannot be used to refer directly to an entity in the outside world, but rather must be **bound** by (i.e. take their reference from) an antecedent within the same clause. There are two types of anaphor found in English, namely (i) **reflexives** (i.e. *self/ selves* forms like *myself/yourself/themselves*, etc.), and (ii) **reciprocals** like *each other* and *one another*. Where an anaphor has no (suitable) antecedent to bind it, the resulting structure is ungrammatical – as we see from the examples in (94) below:

(94) (a)   **He** must feel proud of *himself*
     (b)   *__She__ must feel proud of *himself*
     (c)   *For *himself* to work hard is important

In (94a), the third person masculine singular anaphor *himself* is bound by a suitable third person masculine singular antecedent (*he*), with the result that (94a) is grammatical. But in (94b), *himself* has no suitable antecedent (the feminine pronoun *she* not being a suitable antecedent for the masculine anaphor *himself*) and so is **unbound** (with the result that 94b is ill-formed). In (94c), there is no antecedent of any kind for the anaphor *himself*, with the result that the anaphor is again unbound and the sentence ill-formed.

There are structural restrictions on the binding of anaphors by antecedents, as we see from:

(95) (a)   **The president** may blame *himself*
     (b)   *Supporters of **the president** may blame *himself*

(96) (a)   **They** may implicate *each other*
     (b)   *The evidence against **them** may implicate *each other*

As a third person masculine singular anaphor, *himself* must be bound by a third person masculine singular antecedent like *the president* (which is masculine if denoting a male president); similarly, as a plural anaphor, *each other* must be bound by a plural antecedent like *they/them*. However, it would seem from the contrasts above that the antecedent must occupy the right kind of position within the structure in order to bind the anaphor or else the resulting sentence will be ungrammatical. The question of what is the right position for the antecedent can be answered in terms of the structural condition in (97) (where an antecedent is *local* if it is immediately contained in the same TP as the anaphor – i.e. if the closest TP containing the anaphor is also the closest TP containing the antecedent):

(97)   **Anaphor Binding Condition**
         An anaphor must be bound by a local antecedent which c-commands the anaphor.

In (95a), the antecedent of the reflexive anaphor *himself* is the DP *the president*: in (96a), the antecedent of the reciprocal anaphor *each other* is the pronoun *they/ them*. Sentence (95a) has the structure (98) below:

(98)

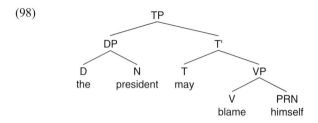

The reflexive pronoun *himself* can be bound by the DP *the president* in (98) because this satisfies the two requirements imposed on anaphor binding in (97): (i) the locality condition is satisfied because the closest TP containing the anaphor *himself* is the TP node at the top/root of the tree, and the same TP node is also the closest TP containing the DP *the president*; and (ii) the c-command condition is satisfied because the DP and the reflexive are independent constituents, and the mother of DP (= TP) contains the reflexive pronoun *himself*. (Or, to use the train metaphor: if you go one stop north of DP you arrive at TP; and if you then travel south of TP on a different line and pass through T-bar and VP, you eventually arrive at PRN-*himself*.)

But now consider why sentence (95b) with the structure (99) below is ungrammatical:

(99)

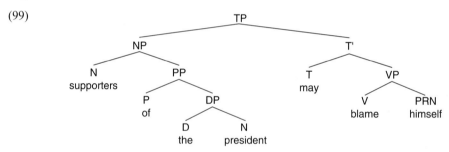

Why can't the DP *the president* serve as the antecedent of the anaphor *himself* in (99)? Even though the locality condition on binding is satisfied (because the TP node at the root/top of the tree is the closest TP containing the anaphor *himself*, and the same TP node is also the closest TP containing its potential antecedent *the president*), the c-command condition is not satisfied. This is because the DP node containing *the president* doesn't c-command the PRN node containing *himself*, because (even though the two are independent constituents) the mother of the DP node is the PP node, and *himself* is not contained within this PP. Since there is no other suitable antecedent for *himself* within the sentence (e.g. although the NP *supporters of the president* c-commands *himself*, it is not a suitable antecedent for *himself* because it is a plural expression, and *himself* requires a singular antecedent), the anaphor *himself* remains unbound – in violation of the Anaphor Binding Condition (97). This is the reason why (95b) **Supporters of the president may blame himself* is ungrammatical.

Our brief discussion of anaphor binding in this section illustrates that the relation c-command plays an important role in syntactic description – e.g. in describing the syntax of anaphors. I note in passing, however, that our discussion of anaphor binding here has been simplified by setting aside what are sometimes called *exempt anaphors* – i.e. anaphors used in ways which make them exempt from the Anaphor Binding Condition in (97). For example, anaphors inside noun phrases seem to be exempt from the binding requirement in (97) – as with *myself* in '[People like *myself*] are a dying breed', where *myself* is contained within the bracketed NP.

A further class of constituents whose syntax seems to be best characterised in terms of the relation c-command are are so-called **polarity expressions**. These are expressions which have an inherent 'polarity' in the sense that they are restricted to occurring in certain types of sentence. In this connection, consider the quantifier *any* in English (and its compounds like *anyone, anything, anywhere*, etc.). The word *any* has two different uses. One is as a **universal** (or **free choice**) **quantifier** with a meaning similar to *every* (as in *You can have* ANY *cake you like*): in this use, the initial *a* of *any* is stressed, and the relevant word is not a polarity item. The second use of *any* is as a **partitive** (or **existential**) **quantifier**: in this use, it has a meaning similar to *some* and can be unstressed (with its initial vowel reduced to schwa or even being truncated in rapid colloquial speech styles – e.g. *He wouldn't do 'nything to hurt me*), and in this second use it is indeed a polarity item. Partitive *any* (and its compounds) must occur in a clause containing an appropriate (bold-printed) **licenser** for the (italicised) polarity item – i.e. an expression which creates the right context for a polarity expression to be used. Licensers for polarity expressions include an interrogative constituent like *how often* in (100a) below, a negative constituent like *no student* in (100b) or a conditional constituent like *if* in (100c). However, where the sentence contains no licenser for the polarity item, the resulting sentence is ungrammatical, as in (100d):

(100) (a) I wonder **how often** we find *any morality* in business
    (b) **No student** will complain about *anything*
    (c) **If** he should say *anything*, let me know at once
    (d) *I'd like *any coffee*, please

Klima (1964: 313) conjectured that negative, interrogative and conditional constituents which license polarity expressions share 'a common grammatico-semantic feature to be referred to as *affective*'. In his terms, expressions like *how often, no student* and *if* are all 'affective' constituents (by which he seems to mean that they are non-assertive – or *nonveridical* to employ the alternative term used by Giannakidou 1997, 1998, 1999). Using Klima's terminology, we can suppose that a polarity item such as (partitive) *any* is restricted to occurring in a structure where it is licensed by an affective constituent. It turns out that numerous other expressions (like those italicised below) are similarly restricted to occurring in a structure containing a (bold-printed) affective licenser:

(101) (a)   I **didn't** think I would *ever* pass the exam
      (b)   *I thought I would *ever* pass the exam

(102) (a)   **Nobody** *dare* contradict him
      (b)   *Everybody *dare* contradict him

(103) (a)   I **don't** think he *need* apologise
      (b)   *I think he *need* apologise

(104) (a)   I doubt **whether** he would *lift a finger* to help you
      (b)   *He would *lift a finger* to help you

(Note that the asterisk on 104b indicates that it is ungrammatical on the intended idiomatic interpretation of 'He would do something to help you.') Curiously, the items *need* and *dare* are polarity items when they function as auxiliaries (and so do not take the third person singular present tense *s*-affix and are not followed by infinitival *to*), but not when they function as main verbs: hence although *need* is a polarity item in its auxiliary use in sentences like (103), it is not a polarity item in its main verb use in sentences like *Professor Knutter needs to see a psychiatrist.*

It might at first sight seem as if we can characterise the relevant restriction on the use of polarity expressions by saying that they can only be used when they *follow* an affective licenser. However, any such word-order-based account proves problematic. The reason is that although the claim that polarity items can be used when they follow an appropriate licenser is consistent with sentences like (105a), it is inconsistent with sentences like (105b):

(105) (a)   The fact that he has resigned **won't** change *anything*
      (b)   *The fact that he **hasn't** resigned will change *anything*

In both (105a) and (105b), the polarity item *anything* follows a bold-printed affective item (the negative auxiliary *won't* in 105a and the negative auxiliary *hasn't* in 105b), and yet only (105a) is grammatical. How come? The answer is that (as originally noted by Klima), polarity items like partitive *any* are subject to a hierarchical (i.e. structural) condition on their use which can be characterised in the following terms:

(106)   **Polarity Licensing Condition**
          A polarity expression must be c-commanded by an appropriate (e.g. negative, interrogative or conditional) licenser.

To see how this works, consider whether the polarity item *anything* satisfies the Polarity Licensing Condition (106) in a sentence like (105a) with the structure in (107) below:

(107)

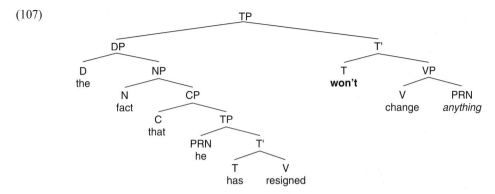

Since a negative auxiliary like *won't* can license a polarity item like *anything* but a positive auxiliary like *have* cannot, the structure will only be grammatical if *won't* occupies a position where it is able to license *anything*. Given the Polarity Licensing Condition (106), this will only be the case if *won't* c-commands the pronoun *anything*. Since the mother of [T *won't*] is the T-bar *won't change anything*, and since *anything* is contained within this T-bar, it follows that [T *won't*] does indeed c-command [PRN *anything*]. This means that *won't* can license the polarity item *anything* in (107), so correctly predicting that the corresponding sentence (105a) *The fact that he has resigned won't change anything* is grammatical.

But now consider why sentence (105b) with the structure in (108) below is ungrammatical: the structure (108) is the same as (107), except for replacing *has* by *hasn't* and *won't* by *will*.

(108)

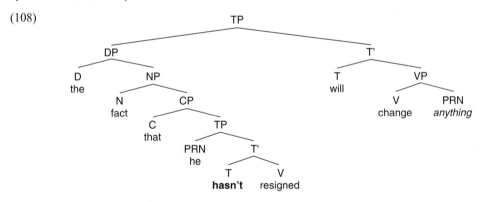

In (108), the only potential licenser for the polarity item *anything* is the negative auxiliary *hasn't*, not the positive auxiliary *will*. But does *hasn't* occupy the kind of structural position where it can license *anything*? Given the Polarity Condition (106), this will only be the case if *hasn't* c-commands the pronoun *anything*. However, this is not the case, because the mother of T-*hasn't* is the T-bar *hasn't resigned*, and *anything* is clearly not contained within this T-bar. Accordingly, *hasn't* does not c-command (and so cannot license) *anything* in (108). The Polarity Licensing Condition (106) thus provides us with a principled account of the ungrammaticality of (105b) *The fact that he hasn't resigned will change anything. More generally, our discussion here shows that the relation *c-command* plays a central role in syntactic description (e.g. in describing the syntax of polarity items).

3.8 Word order

The overall conclusion which our discussion in the previous section leads to is that syntactic phenomena such as anaphor binding and polarity licensing are independent of word order and are best characterised in terms of hierarchical structure alone, utilizing the relation c-command. This can also be argued to be true of other syntactic phenomena (e.g. case-marking and agreement), and also of semantic phenomena (e.g. scope). This leads to the wider conclusion that word order is essentially a phonological phenomenon, in the sense that it determines the linear order in which words are pronounced at PF, in representations of the Phonetic Form of phrases and sentences. This in turn suggests that Merge operations in the syntax generate (i.e. form) hierarchical structures which contain no information about the linear (i.e. left-to-right) order in which constituents are spelled out/pronounced (i.e. they contain no information about what *precedes* what at PF). Instead, word order is added to syntactic structures by linearisation rules in the phonological component, which determine the order in which words are pronounced in PF representations. Thus, the syntactic component of the grammar generates linearly unordered structures, and these are then mapped/converted into linearly ordered structures by linearisation conditions in the PF component.

In order to make our discussion more concrete, let's consider how linearisation works in a sentence like the following:

(109)   They have gone straight to the theatre

A series of Merge operations in the syntactic component will form the structure in (110) below (where the adverb *straight* is the specifier of the P-bar *to the theatre*):

(110)

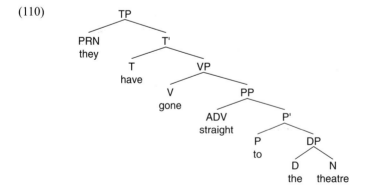

By hypothesis, syntactic structures like (110) are unordered, in the sense that they contain no information about the left-to-right ordering of words. When the structure in (110) is handed over to the PF component, linearisation rules will add information about the relative ordering of the words/terminal nodes in (110).

Let us suppose that the linearisation conditions operating in the PF component in English include the following:

(111)   **Linearisation Conditions**
          (i) *Specifier-Head Linearisation Condition/SHLC*: Specifiers precede their heads.
          (ii) *Head-Complement Linearisation Condition/HCLC*: Heads precede their complements.

Let's also suppose that if a specifier precedes a head, then all the items contained in the specifier precede the head; and likewise that if a head precedes a complement, all the items contained in the complement follow the head.

Consider what the Linearisation Conditions in (111) imply for word order in (110). It follows from HCLC (111ii) that the determiner *the* will precede its complement *theatre* in (110). Likewise, it follows from HCLC that the preposition *to* will precede its DP complement *the theatre*, and hence will precede *the* because *the* is part of the relevant DP. Since *straight* is the specifier of the preposition *to*, it follows from SHLC that *straight* will precede *to*. Likewise, it follows from HCLC that the verb *gone* will precede its PP complement *straight to the theatre*, and therefore will precede *straight* (because this is part of the PP complement). It also follows from HCLC that the T auxiliary *have* will precede its VP complement *gone straight to the theatre* and hence will precede *gone* because this is part of the relevant VP. Finally, it follows from SHLC (110) that the specifier *they* will precede its associated head *have*.

Given the assumptions made above, syntactic structures are linearly unordered, and word order is imposed on the items/words which serve as the terminal nodes in the relevant structures by linearisation rules like SHLC (111i) and HCLC (111ii) which operate in the PF component. An important consequence of assuming that linear order is not a syntactic phenomenon (but rather a PF phenomenon) is that it entails that syntactic operations cannot be sensitive to word order (e.g. we can't handle agreement between an auxiliary and its subject by saying that a finite auxiliary agrees with a *preceding* noun or pronoun expression). Instead, all syntactic operations are sensitive to hierarchical rather than linear structure, in accordance with the following UG principle:

(112)   **Structure Dependence Principle**
          All syntactic operations are structure-dependent (in the sense that they are sensitive only to hierarchical containment relations between constituents, not left-to-right linear ordering).

It follows from (112) that word order is purely a phonological property (in the sense that it determines the order in which words are pronounced at PF), assigned to constituents in the phonological component on the basis of linearisation rules like those in (111) above.

3.9   Summary

In this chapter, we have looked at how words are combined together to form phrases and sentences. In §3.2 we saw how more and more complex phrases can be built up by successive binary Merge operations, each of which combines a pair of constituents to form a larger constituent. In §3.3 I argued that clauses containing a finite tense auxiliary are formed by merging the T auxiliary with a verbal complement to form an intermediate T-bar projection which is then merged with a subject to form an extended TP/tense phrase projection. On this view, a sentence like *It may rain* would be formed by merging the present tense auxiliary (T constituent) *may* with the verb *rain* to form the T-bar constituent *may rain*, and then merging the resulting T-bar with the pronoun *it* to derive the TP *It may rain*. I also noted that the requirement for T-auxiliaries to have a subject can be described by saying that a T auxiliary has an EPP-feature requiring it to have an extended phrasal projection containing a subject/specifier. I went on to suggest that clauses introduced by a complementiser/C are formed by merging C with a TP complement to form a CP/complementiser phrase. In §3.4, I argued that a prepositional phrase like *right on the nose* has a similar internal structure to a TP like *He has resigned* and that in both cases the head P/T *on/has* merges with a following complement to form the intermediate P-bar/T-bar projection *on the nose/has resigned* which in turn is merged with a preceding specifier to form the extended PP/TP projection *right on the nose/he has resigned*. In §3.5, I went on to argue that other types of head (e.g. adjectives, adverbs and nouns) can likewise project both into an intermediate projection via Merge with a following complement, and into an extended projection via Merge with a preceding specifier. I introduced the term maximal projection to denote the largest constituent headed by a particular word in a given structure. In §3.6, we looked at ways of testing constituent structure, using tests relating to coordination, modification, substitution, sentence fragments, ellipsis, focusing and movement. I noted that a variety of factors can sometimes prevent a test from yielding an expected result. For example, the movement test can sometimes yield unexpected negative results because items with little or no substantive lexical semantic content generally cannot be preposed, or because the Stranding Constraint bars the complement of a certain type of functional head (e.g. determiner, quantifier or complementiser) from being moved on its own and leaving D, Q or C stranded. In §3.7, we looked at the syntactic relations between constituents within tree diagrams, noting that the relation c-command plays a central role in syntax, e.g. in relation to accounting for anaphor binding and the licensing of polarity expressions. In §3.8, I argued that the structures generated/formed by a series of Merge operations in the syntactic component of the grammar contain only information about hierarchical containment relations, not about the linear (left-to-right) ordering of constituents, and that linear (left-to-right) order is imposed by linearisation rules operating in the PF component.

For those of you familiar with work in traditional grammar, it will be clear that the assumptions about syntactic structure made here are somewhat different from those made in traditional grammar (or indeed in older/alternative versions of Generative Grammar). Of course, there are some similarities: within both types of framework, it is assumed that lexical categories project into phrases, so that by combining a noun/verb/preposition/adjective/adverb with one or more other constituents we can form a noun phrase/verb phrase/prepositional phrase/adjectival phrase/adverbial phrase. But there are three major differences between the two types of framework. One is that Minimalism (unlike traditional grammar) assumes that function words also project into phrases (so that by merging a determiner/D with a noun expression we form a determiner phrase/DP, by merging a (present or past tense) auxiliary/T with a complement and a subject we form a tense projection/TP, and by merging a complementiser with a TP we form a complementiser projection/CP. This in some cases results in an analysis which is rather different from that found in traditional grammar so that (for example) *the nose* would be considered a noun phrase in traditional grammar, but is taken to be a determiner phrase within the framework adopted here. A second difference between the two frameworks is that Minimalism assumes that all syntactic structure is binary-branching, whereas traditional grammar does not. A third difference is that Minimalism assumes that syntactic structures are linearly unordered, whereas traditional grammar assumes that they contain information about word order.

Key principles/conditions/constructs/definitions introduced in this chapter include the following:

(12i)   **Headedness Principle**
Every non-terminal constituent in a syntactic structure is a projection of a head lexical item.

(12ii)   **Binarity Principle**
Every non-terminal constituent in a syntactic structure is binary-branching.

(17)   **Projection types**
A constituent C is
(a) a *maximal projection* if C does not have a mother with the same head as C
(b) an *intermediate projection* if C has a mother and a daughter with the same head as C
(c) a *minimal projection/head* if C has no daughter.

(58)   **Coordination Condition**
Only constituents of the same type can be coordinated.

(61)   **Modification Condition**
Only a string of words which is a constituent can be modified by an appropriate type of modifier.

(68)   **Fragment Condition**
Only a maximal projection can serve as a sentence fragment.

(72)   **Constituency Condition**
Heads and maximal projections are the only types of constituent which can take part in linguistic operations like Movement, Agreement or Ellipsis.

(77)   **Focus Condition**
Only a maximal projection can be focused in a cleft or pseudo-cleft sentence.

(83)   **Economy Principle**
Structures and operations should be as economical as possible.

(84)   **Preposing Condition**
When material is preposed in order to highlight it, what is preposed is the smallest possible maximal projection containing the highlighted material.

(86)   **Stranding Constraint**
No determiner, quantifier or complementiser can be stranded without its complement.

(97)   **Anaphor Binding Condition**
An anaphor must be bound by a local antecedent which c-commands the anaphor (where an antecedent is local if the closest TP containing the anaphor is also the closest TP containing the antecedent).

(106)   **Polarity Licensing Condition**
A polarity expression must be c-commanded by an appropriate (e.g. negative, interrogative or conditional) licenser.

(111)   **Linearisation Conditions**
(i) *Specifier-Head Linearisation Condition/SHLC*: specifiers precede their heads.
(i) *Head-Complement Linearisation Condition/HCLC*: heads precede their complements.

(112)   **Structure Dependence Principle**
All syntactic operations are structure-dependent (in the sense that they are sensitive only to hierarchical containment relations between constituents, not linear ordering).

An important relation introduced in the chapter is the following:

(93)   **C-command**
If X and Y are independent constituents (i.e. if neither contains the other), X c-commands Y iff (i.e. 'if and only if') the mother of X contains Y.

(More informally, using a train metaphor, we can say that X c-commands Y if you can get from X to Y by taking a northbound train, getting off at the first station, and then travelling one or more stops south *on a different line*.)

3.10   Bibliographical background

The claim made in §3.2 that syntactic structures are headed dates back in spirit to Bloomfield (1935) – but with the difference that Bloomfield assumed that some structures are headless. The idea that all syntactic structure is binary is defended in Kayne (1983). On the claim that syllable structure and morphological structure are binary, see Radford et al. (2009, pp. 81ff. and pp.140ff. respectively). The traditional S-analysis of clauses outlined in §3.3 dates back to Chomsky (1955, 1957, 1975), and the S-bar analysis to Bresnan (1970, 1972, 1979). Chomsky (1981, 1986b) argued for an alternative analysis of S constituents as projections of a head I/INFL/Inflection constituent and hence as IP constituents; when INFL was supplanted by T/tense in later work (e.g. Chomsky 1986b), S was re-analysed as a TP projection; likewise, Chomsky (1981, 1986b) and Stowell (1981) reanalysed S-bar as CP. For a range of views on the nature of the EPP property of T, see Chomsky (1982, 1995, 1998), Rothstein (1983), Alexiadou and Anagnostopoulou (1998), Déprez (2000), Grohmann, Drury and Castillo (2000), Holmberg (2000), Kiss (2001), Bošković (2002b), Roberts and Roussou (2002), Rosengren (2002), Haeberli (2003), van Craenenbroeck and den Dikken (2006), Miyagawa (2005, 2006, 2010), Landau (2007) and Lin (2011). On the notion extended projection, see Grimshaw (2000, 2005). An alternative to Chomsky's bottom-up model of syntax is the top-down model presented in Phillips (2003): but see Chomsky (2007) for arguments that the bottom-up/top-down dichotomy may be a false one. The claim made in §3.4 that phrases are formed by combining heads with complements and specifiers dates back to the model of X-bar Syntax developed in Jackendoff (1974, 1977a, 1977b): for a textbook introduction to X-bar Syntax, see Radford (1981, 1988). In earlier work (e.g. Chomsky 1957, 1965) nominal expressions like *the nose* were taken to have the status of NP/noun phrase; however, in much work since Abney (1987) they have been analysed as having the status of DP/determiner phrase constituents – though it should be pointed out that the DP analysis is not without posing problems (see e.g. Pollard and Sag 1994; Sadler and Arnold 1994; van Langendonck 1994; Escribano 2004 and van Eynde 2006). The DEGP analysis of phrases such as *quite so rapid* also derives from Abney (1987). On the structure of phrases such as *how good a student*, see Kennedy and Merchant (2000) and Borroff (2006). For discussion and alternative analyses of coordinate structures, see Goodall (1987), Munn (1993, 1999), Johannessen (1993, 1996, 1998), Borsley (1994, 2005), Kayne (1994), Zoerner (1995), Bayer (1996), Aoun and Benmamoun (1999), Johnson (2002), Phillips (2003) and Citko (2006). The text analysis of nominal expressions like *the government ban on imports* in §3.5 is taken from Radford (1993). The Stranding Constraint is inspired by observations made in Chomsky (1999). For a more detailed discussion of the coordination criterion used to test structure in §3.6, see Radford (1988: 75–8); for a detailed study of conditions on coordination, see George (1980), Sag et al. (1985) and Goodall (1987). On VP Ellipsis, see Potsdam (1997b), Johnson (2001), Fox and Lasnik (2003), Merchant (2008b), Kim et al. (2011), Rouveret (2012) and Cormack and Smith (2012). For evidence that the sentences like *Someone failed the exam, but I don't know who ~~failed the exam~~* involve a form of TP Ellipsis known as Sluicing, see Ross (1969), Merchant (2001, 2002), Fox and Lasnik (2003), van Craenenbroeck (2004, 2010), Agüero-Bautista (2007), Almeida and Yoshida (2007) and Nakao (2009). The c-command condition on polarity items discussed in §3.6 dates back in spirit to Klima (1964): fuller discussion of the syntactic and semantic conditions governing the licensing of polarity items can be found in Fauconnier (1975, 1978), Ladusaw (1979), Linebarger (1987), Giannakidou (1997, 1998, 1999), Lahiri (1998), von Fintel (1999), Acquaviva (2002), Watanabe (2004), Benmamoun (2006), Borroff (2006), Chierchia (2006) and Herdan and Sharvit (2006). The c-command condition on anaphor binding (and the binding principles discussed in exercise §3.2) date back to Chomsky (1980): more recent technical accounts of binding can be found in Reuland (2001), Reuland and Everaert (2001), Büring (2005), Lasnik (2006) and Giorgi (2007). A technical defence of the primitive nature of c-command can be found in Frank and Vijay-Shanker (2001). Although it was assumed in §3.7 that anaphors/pronouns are generated independently of their antecedents, it should be noted that under the alternative Movement Theory of Anaphora, they are taken to be related by movement (Hornstein 2001; Kayne 2002; Grohmann 2003). On the claim made in §3.8 that syntactic structure contains information about hierarchical structure but not linear structure (i.e. word order), and on the nature of PF linearisation conditions, see Kayne (1994), Yang (1999), Chomsky (1995, 2001), Ko (2005), Kural (2005) and Collins (2014).

Workbook section

Exercise 3.1

Discuss the derivation of the following sentences, showing how their structure is built up in a pairwise fashion by successive binary Merge operations.

1. He has become very fond of Mary
2. He must have been taking bribes
3. She must be quite pleased to see you
4. He will need to ask for help
5. They are expecting to hear from you
6. You should try to talk to the president of Utopia
7. Inflation has undermined some parts of the economy
8. He won't admit that he was defrauding the company
9. Nobody would believe that Sam was working for the government

Specify which of the terminal nodes in your tree are maximal projections (and which are not), and say why. Say how the linear ordering of the words in the structure is determined. Show how evidence from coordination and substitution can be used in support of your analysis. In addition, say which constituents can (and cannot) be preposed – and why.

Helpful hints

Assume that the sentences are derived in a bottom-up fashion by first merging the last two words in the sentence to form a constituent, and then merging the constituent thereby formed with the third-from-last word to form an even larger constituent, then merging this even larger constituent with the fourth-from-last word ... and so on. (It should be noted, however, that while this simple procedure will work for most of the sentences in the two exercises in this chapter, it requires modification to handle structures with complex specifiers – i.e. with specifiers containing more than one word: see the discussion immediately preceding example 52 in the main text.) Take *has/could/must/will/are/should/has/would* to be finite auxiliaries (marking tense) which occupy the head T position of TP (and likewise take *won't* to be an inherently negative auxiliary which also occupies the head T position of TP). In 1 and 3, take *very* and *quite* to be adverbs which function as the specifiers of the adjectival expressions *fond of Mary* and *pleased to see you* respectively. In relation to 2, assume that *have* is a PERF constituent (i.e. an auxiliary marking perfect aspect) and that *have been taking bribes* is a PERFP; similarly, assume that *been* is a PROG constituent (i.e. an auxiliary marking progressive aspect) and that *been taking bribes* is a PROGP. (See §2.10 for discussion of PERF and PROG.)

Model answer for 1

Merging the preposition *of* with the noun *Mary* which serves as its complement derives the PP (prepositional phrase) *of Mary*, with the structure in (i) below:

(i)

Merging the adjective *fond* with the resulting PP (which is the complement of *fond*) forms the intermediate adjectival projection (A-bar) *fond of Mary* in (ii) below:

(ii)
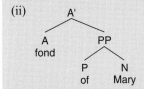

Merging the A-bar in (ii) with the adverb *very* which serves as its specifier (in that it modifies *fond of Mary*) forms the AP/adjectival phrase *very fond of Mary* in (iii) below:

(iii)
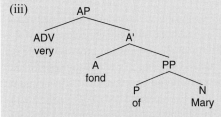

Merging the verb *become* with the AP *very fond of Mary* which serves as the complement of *become* forms the VP/verb phrase in (iv) below:

(iv)

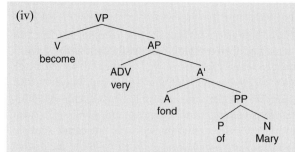

Merging the tense auxiliary (T constituent) *has* with its verb phrase complement *become very fond of Mary* forms the intermediate T-bar projection (v) below:

(v)

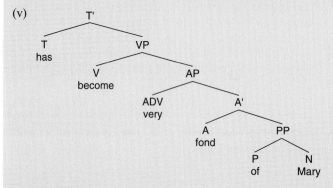

Merging the T-bar in (v) with the pronoun *he* which serves as its subject/specifier will derive the TP:

(vi)

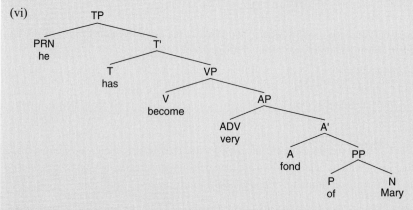

When the (unordered) structure in (vi) is handed over to the PF component, the Linearisation Conditions in (111) determine the relative order of the words in the structure. It follows from the Head-Complement Linearisation Condition/HCLC (111ii) that the preposition *of* will precede its complement *Mary*. Likewise, it follows from HCLC that the adjective *fond* will precede its PP complement *of Mary* and hence will precede *of*. It follows from the Specifier-Head Linearisation Condition/SHLC (111i) that the specifier *very* will precede its associated head *fond*. In addition, it follows from HCLC that the verb *become* will precede its AP complement *very fond of Mary*, and hence will precede *very*. Furthermore, it follows from HCLC that the T auxiliary *has* will precede its

VP complement *become very fond of Mary*, and hence will precede *become*. Finally, it follows from SHLC that the specifier *he* will precede its associated head *has*.

In terms of the definition in (17a), a constituent C is a maximal projection if C does not have a mother with the same head as C. In the light of this definition, consider whether some or all of the terminal nodes in (vi) are maximal projections. PRN-*he* is a maximal projection because its mother (= the TP node) is not a projection of PRN-*he* (but rather of T-*has*). Neither T-*has* nor V-*become* is a maximal projection, because each has a mother (T-bar/VP) with the same head. ADV-*very* is a maximal projection because its AP mother is not a projection of ADV-*very* (but rather of A-*fond*). A-*fond* and P-*of* are not maximal projections because each has a mother (A-bar/PP) with the same head. By contrast, N-*Mary* is a maximal projection because its mother (= the PP node) is not a projection of N-*Mary* (but rather of P-*of*).

Empirical evidence in support of the structure posited in (vi) comes from coordination data in relation to sentences such as:

(vii) (a) He has become very fond [*of Mary*] and [**of her sister**]
    (b) He has become very [*fond of Mary*] and [**proud of her achievements**]
    (c) He has become [*very fond of Mary*] but [**less fond of her sister**]
    (d) He has [*become very fond of Mary*] and [**grown used to her mother**]
    (e) He [*has become very fond of Mary*] and [**is hoping to marry her**]

The fact that each of the italicised strings can be coordinated with another similar (bold-printed) string is consistent with the claim made in (vi) that *of Mary* is a PP, *fond of Mary* is an A-bar, *very fond of Mary* is an AP, *become very fond of Mary* is a VP and *has become very fond of Mary* is a T-bar.

Additional evidence in support of the analysis in (vi) comes from the use of the proforms *so/which* in:

(viii) (a) He is apparently *very fond of Mary*, though nobody expected him to become **so**
     (b) If he has *become very fond of Mary* (**which** he has), why doesn't he ask her out?

The fact that *very fond of Mary* is the antecedent of *so* in (viii.a) is consistent with the claim made in (vi) that *very fond of Mary* is an AP; likewise, the fact that *become very fond of Mary* is the antecedent of *which* in (viii.b) is consistent with the claim made in (vi) that *become very fond of Mary* is a VP.

If we look at the question of which expressions in the sentence can and cannot be preposed in order to highlight them, we find the following picture (where *?* indicates questionable grammaticality):

(ix) (a) *Mary*, he (certainly) has become very fond of
    (b) ?*Of Mary*, he (certainly) has become very fond
    (c) **Fond of Mary*, he (certainly) has become very
    (d) *Very fond of Mary*, he (certainly) has become
    (e) *Become very fond of Mary*, he (certainly) has
    (f) **Has become very fond of Mary*, he (certainly)

(Adding the adverb *certainly* improves the acceptability of some of the relevant sentences, for discourse reasons which need not concern us.) In the main text, it was suggested that highlighting involves preposing the smallest possible maximal projection containing the highlighted material. Suppose that we want to highlight *Mary* via preposing. Since *Mary* is a maximal projection in (vi) by virtue of being the largest expression headed by the word *Mary*, preposing *Mary* in (ix.a) yields a grammatical outcome, as expected. (By virtue of its status as a maximal projection, *Mary* could alternatively be labelled as an NP rather than an N.) By contrast, preposing the prepositional phrase *of Mary* yields a somewhat degraded sentence, as we see from (ix.b): this may be because if we want to highlight *Mary* alone, we prepose the *smallest* maximal projection containing *Mary*, and this is clearly the N/NP *Mary* not the PP *of Mary*. There would only be some point in preposing *of Mary* if we wanted to highlight *of* as well as *Mary*; but since the preposition *of* (rather like infinitival *to*) has little or no semantic content (some linguists suggesting that it is a **genitive case particle** in this kind of use and hence a functor, as we saw in §2.4), an *of*-phrase of this kind is not a good candidate for highlighting. The string *fond of Mary* cannot be preposed in (ix.c) because it is an intermediate (A-bar) projection of the adjective *fond*, not its maximal projection (the maximal projection of the adjective *fond* being the AP *very fond of Mary*), and the Constituency Condition (72) does not allow intermediate constituents to undergo movement. By contrast, the string *very fond of Mary* can be preposed in (ix.d) by virtue of its status as the maximal projection of *fond* (i.e. the largest expression headed by *fond*). In (ix.e) we see that *become very fond of Mary* can also be preposed by virtue of being the maximal projection of the verb *become*. By contrast, the string *has become very fond of Mary* cannot be preposed in (ix.f) because of its status as an intermediate (T-bar) projection of *has* – the corresponding maximal projection of *has* being the TP *He has become very fond of Mary*.

Helpful hints for sentences 2–9

Discuss whether the analysis you propose accounts for the (un)grammaticality of the sentences below (which represent intuitions about grammaticality in my own British English variety). To help you, I have italicised parts of the sentences of particular interest. Note that ? in front of a sentence indicates that it is of somewhat questionable grammaticality, ?* means that it is of highly questionable grammaticality, and * means that it is completely ungrammatical.

Example 2
a. He must have been taking *bribes* and *back-handers*
b. He must have been *taking bribes* and *corrupting officials*
c. He must have *been taking bribes* and *been corrupting officials*
d. He must *have been taking bribes* and *have been corrupting officials*
e. He *must have been taking bribes* and *must have been corrupting officials*
f. If he has been *taking bribes*, (*which* he must have been) he deserves to be punished
g. If he has *been taking bribes* (*which* he must have), he deserves to be punished
h. SPEAKER A: He must *have been taking bribes*
    SPEAKER B: *So* he must
i. *Bribes*, he certainly must have been taking
j. *Taking bribes*, he certainly must have been
j. ?*Been taking bribes*, he certainly must have
k. ?**Have been taking bribes*, he certainly must
l. **Must have been taking bribes*, he certainly

Example 3
a. She must be quite pleased to *see you* and *hear your news*
b. She must be quite pleased *to see you* and *to meet your mother*
c. She must be quite *pleased to see you* and *glad that you are OK*
d. She must be *quite pleased to see you* and *very glad that you are OK*
e. She must *be quite pleased to see you* and *feel relieved that you're OK*
f. She *must be quite pleased to see you* but *will not admit it*

g.   She must be *quite pleased to see you*, even if she doesn't seem *so*.
h.   *You* she must be quite pleased to see (though not your sister)
i.   ?*See you*, she (certainly) must be quite pleased to
j.   **To see you*, she (certainly) must be quite pleased
k.   **Pleased to see you*, she (certainly) must be quite
l.   *Quite pleased to see you*, she (certainly) must be
m.   ?*Be quite pleased to see you*, she (certainly) must
n.   **Must be quite pleased to see you*, she (certainly)

Example 4

a.   He will need to ask *for help* and *for advice*
b.   He will need to *ask for help* and *seek advice*
c.   He will need *to ask for help* and *to accept it*
d.   He will *need to ask for help*, and *expect to get it*
e.   He *will need to ask for help*, but *can't count on it*
f.   A lot of people think he will *need to ask for help*, and *so* he will
g.   If he has to *ask for help* (*as* he will need to), will he get any?
h.   *Help*, he will (certainly) need to ask for (though not money)
i.   ?*For help* he will (certainly) need to ask (though not for money)
j.   *Ask for help*, he will (certainly) need to
k.   **To ask for help*, he will (certainly) need
l.   *Need to ask for help*, he (certainly) will
m.   **Will need to ask for help*, he (certainly)

Example 5

a.   They are expecting to hear *from you* and *from her*
b.   They are expecting to *hear from you* and *meet you*
c.   They are expecting *to hear from you* and *to meet you*
d.   They are *expecting to hear from you* and *longing to meet you*
e.   They *are expecting to hear from you* and *are longing to meet you*
f.   They said they were *expecting to hear from you*, and *so* they are
g.   *You*, they are (certainly) expecting to hear from (though not your sister)
h.   ?*From you*, they (certainly) are expecting to hear (though not from your sister)
i.   *Hear from you*, they (certainly) are expecting to
j.   **To hear from you*, they (certainly) are expecting
k.   *Expecting to hear from you*, they (certainly) are
l.   **Are expecting to hear from you*, they

Example 6

a.   You should try to talk to the president *of Utopia* and *of Ruritania*
b.   You should try to talk to the *president of Utopia* and *head of the government*
c.   You should try to talk to *the president of Utopia* and *the leader of the opposition*
d.   You should try to talk *to the president of Utopia* and *to the leader of the opposition*
e.   You should try to *talk to the president of Utopia* and *convince him*
f.   You should try *to talk to the president of Utopia* and *to convince him*
g.   You should *try to talk to the president of Utopia* and *contact his aides*
h.   You *should try to talk to the president* but *may not succeed*

    i.   He said you should *try to talk to the president of Utopia*, and *so* you should

    j.   ?*Utopia*, you should certainly try to talk to the president of

    k.   *Of Utopia, you should certainly try to talk to the president

    l.   **President of Utopia*, you should (certainly) try to talk to the

   m.   *The president of Utopia*, you should (certainly) try to talk to

   n.   ?*To the president of Utopia*, you should (certainly) try to talk (though not to his aides)

   o.   *Talk to the president of Utopia*, you should (certainly) try to

   p.   **To talk to the president of Utopia*, you should certainly try

   q.   *Try to talk to the president of Utopia*, you (certainly) should

   r.   **Should try to talk to the president of Utopia*, you (certainly)

Example 7

    a.   Inflation has undermined some parts of *the economy* and *the stockmarket*

    b.   Inflation has undermined some parts *of the economy* and *of the stockmarket*

    c.   Inflation has undermined some *parts of the economy* and *sectors of the stockmarket*

    d.   Inflation has undermined *some parts of the economy* and *many sectors of the stockmarket*

    e.   Inflation has *undermined some parts of the economy* and *jeopardised growth*

    f.   Inflation *has undermined some parts of the economy* and *is spiralling out of control*

    g.   If inflation has *undermined some parts of the economy* (*as* it has), why doesn't the government act?

    h.   The president said that inflation has *undermined some parts of the economy*, and *so* it has.

    i.   *Economy, inflation (certainly) has undermined some parts of the

    j.   *The economy*, inflation (certainly) has undermined some parts of

    k.   *Of the economy, inflation (certainly) has undermined some parts

    l.   **Parts of the economy*, inflation (certainly) has undermined some

   m.   *Some parts of the economy*, inflation (certainly) has undermined

   n.   *Undermined some parts of the economy*, inflation (certainly) has

   o.   **Has undermined some parts of the economy*, inflation (certainly)

Example 8

    a.   He won't admit that he was defrauding *the company* and *the workforce*

    b.   He won't admit that he was *defrauding the company* and *bankrupting it*

    c.   He won't admit that he *was defrauding the company* and *had bankrupted it*

    d.   He won't admit that *he was defrauding the company* and *it was being bankrupted*

    e.   He won't admit *that he was defrauding the company* or *that he was bankrupting it*

    f.   He won't *admit that he was defrauding the company* or *concede that he lied*

    g.   He *won't admit that he was defrauding the company* and *doesn't accept that he has bankrupted it*

    h.   If he won't *admit that he was defrauding the company* (*which* he won't), what can we do about it?

    i.   He won't admit *that he was defrauding the company*, even though everybody knows *it*

    j.   *Company, he (certainly) won't admit that he was defrauding the

    k.   *The company*, he (certainly) won't admit that he was defrauding

    l.   *Defrauding the company*, he (certainly) won't admit that he was

   m.   **Was defrauding the company*, he (certainly) won't admit that he

   n.   **He was defrauding the company*, he (certainly) won't admit that (= ðət)

   o.   *That he was defrauding the company*, he (certainly) won't admit

p. *Admit that he was defrauding the company,* he (certainly) won't
q. **Won't admit that he was defrauding the company,* he (certainly)

Example 9
a. Nobody would believe that Sam was working for *the government* and *the opposition*
b. Nobody would believe that Sam was working *for the government* and *for the opposition*
c. Nobody would believe that Sam was *working for the government* and *siding with the opposition*
d. Nobody would believe that Sam *was working for the government* and *was siding with the opposition*
e. Nobody would believe that *Sam was working for the government* and *his wife was working for the opposition*
f. Nobody would believe *that Sam was working for the government* and *that his wife was working for the opposition*
g. Nobody would *believe that Sam was working for the government* or *imagine that his wife was working for the opposition*
h. Nobody *would believe that Sam was working for the government* or *would admit that his wife was working for the opposition*
i. If people wouldn't *believe that Sam was working for the government* (*which* nobody would), why didn't they ask him whether it was true?
j. If nobody would believe that Sam was *working for the government* (*as* he was), why didn't they ask him whether it was true?
k. **Government,* nobody would believe that Sam was working for the
l. *The government,* nobody would believe that Sam was working for
m. ?*For the government,* nobody would believe that Sam was working
n. *Working for the government,* nobody would believe that Sam (really) was
o. **Was working for the government,* nobody would believe that Sam
p. **Sam was working for the government,* nobody would believe that (= ðət)
q. *That Sam was working for the government,* nobody would believe
r. *Believe that Sam was working for the government,* nobody would
s. **Would believe that Sam was working for the government,* nobody

Exercise 3.2

We saw in §2.7 that the relation c-command plays an important role in accounting for the syntax of polarity expressions, since these are restricted to occurring in structures where they are c-commanded by an appropriate (e.g. negative or interrogative) licenser. Show how the c-command condition on the use of polarity items accounts for the (un)grammaticality of the following:

1. You mustn't talk to anyone
2. Nobody need do anything
3. Who dare blame anyone?
4. He is refusing to eat anything
5. She will know whether anyone has seen it
6. I don't think that anyone dare lift a finger
7. He may have no desire to change anything

8.   Nobody will believe that anything has changed
9.   He may feel unable to do anything
10.   No politician dare offend anyone
11.   *Anyone isn't helping me
12.   *The fact that nothing has happened will change anything
13.   John may deny that anything has happened to anyone

In relation to 11 (intended to be synonymous with *There isn't anyone helping me*), show how the traditional ternary-branching analysis of clauses as S-constituents (whereby 11 would be analysed as an S constituent comprising the pronoun/PRN *anyone*, the present-tense auxiliary/T *isn't* and the verb phrase/VP *helping me*) would be unable to provide a principled account of the ungrammaticality of 11 in terms of the c-command condition on the licensing of polarity items.

In addition, show how the Polarity Licensing Condition (106) is unable to provide a principled account of the contrast between (4) above and (14) below, where *anything* is an unstressed partitive pronoun and hence a polarity item (and not a stressed free-choice pronoun with much the same meaning as *everything*):

He is weak after his illness, so we are trying to get him to eat soup and vegetables, but

4.   *he is refusing to eat anything*
14.   **he is refusing anything*

Consider whether the contrast between the italicised clauses (4) and (14) can be accounted for if the Polarity Licensing Condition (106) is revised as follows (where the revision is italicised):

(i)   **Polarity Licensing Condition** (revised)
      A polarity expression must be *asymmetrically* c-commanded by an appropriate (e.g. negative, interrogative or conditional) licenser.

The asymmetric c-command relation can be defined as follows, where X and Y represent different constituents (i.e. different nodes in a tree):

(ii) **Asymmetric c-command**
      X asymmetrically c-commands Y iff ('if and only if') X c-commands Y but Y does not c-command X.

(Using the informal train metaphor, we can say that X asymmetrically c-commands Y if you can get from X to Y by travelling one stop north, and then travelling *more than one stop* south on a different line.)

In §3.7, we saw how the relation c-command plays an important role in accounting for the syntax of reflexive and reciprocal anaphors. The same can be argued to be true of two other types of expression, namely non-anaphoric pronominals like *he/him/her/it/them*, etc. and referential noun expressions like *John* or *the president*. Chomsky (1980, 1981) developed a Theory of Binding which included the three binding principles outlined in a slightly revised form below (where *free* means 'not bound'):

(iii) **Binding Principles**
      Principle A: An anaphor must be bound within its local domain.
      Principle B: A (non-anaphoric) pronominal (expression) must be free within its local domain.

Principle C: An R-expression (i.e. referring noun expression) must be free everywhere (i.e. within all the constituents containing it).

Although there is controversy about how best to define the notion of *local domain* in relation to binding, for present purposes assume that the local domain of an anaphor/pronominal is the closest TP containing it, and that the three binding principles in (iii) thus amount to the following:

(iv)   A: An anaphor (like *himself*) must be bound by (i.e. must refer to) a c-commanding constituent within the closest TP immediately containing the anaphor.
B: A pronominal (like *him*) must not be bound by (i.e. must not refer to) any c-commanding constituent within the closest TP immediately containing the pronominal.
C: An R-expression (i.e. a referring noun expression like *John/the president*) must not be coreferential to (i.e. must not refer to the same entity as) any constituent which c-commands it.

Given the Binding Principles in (iv), discuss the binding properties of the expressions *Fred, John, he/him* and *himself* in sentences 15–20 below, drawing trees to represent the structure of the sentences.

15 a.   John must feel that Fred has disgraced himself
   b.   *John must feel that himself has disgraced Fred

16 a.   He must feel that Fred has disgraced him
   b.   John must feel that he has disgraced Fred

17 a.   John may suspect that Fred has taken some pictures of him
   b.   John may suspect that Fred has taken some pictures of himself

18 a.   The rumours about Fred have upset him
   b.   *The rumours about Fred have upset himself

19 a.   The rumours about him have upset Fred
   b.   *The rumours about himself have upset Fred

20 a.   John may wonder if the rumours about Fred will affect him
   b.   John may wonder if the rumours about him will affect Fred

Helpful hints

Make the following assumptions about examples 1–14. When *need/dare* take a bare (*to*-less) infinitive complement, they are modal auxiliaries which occupy the head T position of TP and take a VP complement, and they are polarity items in this use. Assume that *no* in 7 and 10 is a quantifier (= Q) which heads a quantifier phrase (= QP) constituent and has a noun or noun phrase as its complement: assume that when the head Q of QP is negative, the overall QP is negative as well (because a phrase carries the same features as its head by virtue of being a projection of the relevant head). In addition, assume that *mustn't/don't/isn't* are (inherently negative) T/tense auxiliaries occupying the head T position of TP. Treat *refuse/deny* as negative verbs, and *unable* as a negative adjective; and (in accordance with the analysis in §2.9) treat *whether* as an interrogative complementiser occupying the head C position of CP. Finally, assume that *anyone/anything/nobody/nothing* are pronouns belonging to the category PRN (although more specifically, they are Q-pronouns, i.e. pronominal quantifiers). In addition, assume that in the examples in 1–14 above, *any* and its compounds are partitive in use, and hence polarity items. In relation to examples 15–20, assume (when drawing your trees) that *him* and *himself* belong to the category PRN/pronoun – even though they have different binding properties (*himself* being an anaphoric pronoun, and *him* being a non-anaphoric pronoun).

Model answer for 1

Given the assumptions made in the text, 1 will have the syntactic structure (i) below:

(i)

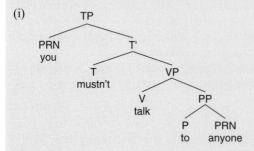

The T node containing the negative auxiliary *mustn't* here c-commands the PRN node containing the polarity item *anyone* because the two are independent constituents (in the sense that neither contains the other), and the mother of T-*mustn't* is the T-bar *mustn't talk to anyone*, and *anyone* is contained within this T-bar. If you prefer to use the alternative train metaphor suggested in §3.7 (under which X c-commands Y if you can get from X to Y on a train by going one stop north, then taking a southbound train on a different line and travelling one or more stops south), you can say that T-*mustn't* c-commands PRN-*anyone* because if you travel one stop north from the T station you arrive at the T-bar station, and if you then change trains at the T-bar station you can get a southbound train on a different line which will take you to the PRN station containing *anyone* (at the end of the line) via the VP and PP stations. Since the polarity item *anyone* is c-commanded by the negative auxiliary *mustn't*, the c-command condition on the licensing of polarity items is satisfied, and sentence 1 is therefore grammatical.

Model answer for 18a

Given the assumptions made in this chapter, 18a will have the structure (ii) below:

(ii)

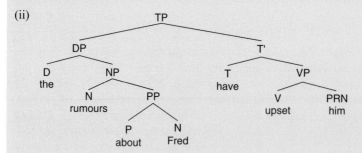

(A point of incidental detail here is that the N constituent *Fred* could alternatively be labelled as an NP here, by virtue of its status as a maximal projection: it is a maximal projection because its mother is the PP *about Fred*, and this PP is not headed by *Fred* but rather by P-*about*.) *Him* is a pronominal (i.e. a non-anaphoric pronoun), and hence subject to Principle B of Binding Theory. This specifies that a pronominal like *him* cannot refer to any expression c-commanding it within the closest TP containing *him*; and from this it follows that such a pronominal can (a) refer to an expression contained in a different TP within the same sentence, or (b) refer to an expression within the same TP as long as that expression does not c-command *him*, or (c) refer to some entity in the domain of discourse (i.e. some person not mentioned in the relevant sentence, but present or previously mentioned in the discourse setting). The second of these possibilities (b) allows for *him* to refer to *Fred* in (ii), since although *him* and *Fred* are contained within the same TP, *Fred* does not c-command *him* (the only constituent which *Fred* c-commands being the preposition *about*) so that principle B is satisfied if *him* refers to *Fred* (or if indeed *him* refers to some other person not mentioned in the sentence).

The noun *Fred* is an R-expression (i.e. a referring noun expression), and so subject to Principle C of Binding Theory, which specifies that an R-expression cannot be coreferential with any expression c-commanding it. This means that *Fred* and *him* cannot refer to the same individual if *Fred* is c-commanded by *him*. However, *him* does not c-command *Fred* because the mother of PRN-*him* is the VP *upset him*, and this VP does not contain *Fred*. Since *Fred* is not c-commanded by *him*, Principle C does not prevent *Fred* from being coreferential with *him*.

Overall, then, neither Principle B nor Principle C will be violated if *Fred* and *him* are interpreted as conferential (though of course the two could equally refer to different individuals – e.g. *him* could refer to someone not mentioned in the sentence).

4 Null constituents

4.1 Overview

So far, our discussion of syntactic structure has tacitly assumed that all constituents in a given structure are overt (in the sense that they have audible phonetic features, as well as carrying grammatical and semantic features). However, in this chapter we will see that syntactic structures may also contain **null** constituents (also known as **empty** categories) – i.e. constituents which have grammatical and semantic features but lack audible phonetic features (and so are 'silent', 'inaudible' or 'unpronounced').

4.2 Null subjects

We are already familiar with one kind of null constituent from the discussion of the **Null Subject Parameter** in §1.7. There, we saw that alongside finite clauses like that produced by SPEAKER A in the dialogue in (1) below with an overt subject like *Maria*, Italian also has finite clauses like that produced by SPEAKER B, with a null subject pronoun conventionally designated as *pro* (and referred to affectionately as 'little *pro*'):

(1)   SPEAKER A: Maria è$_{3.Sg}$ tornata$_{F.Sg}$?
                 Maria is   returned?
                 'Has Maria returned?'
       SPEAKER B: Sì,   *pro* è$_{3.Sg}$ tornata$_{F.Sg}$
                 Yes, *pro* is   returned
                 'Yes, she has returned'

(The subscripts in the glosses mark the following properties: 3 = third person; Sg = singular number; F = feminine gender.) One reason for positing *pro* in (1B) is that it captures the intuition that the sentence has an 'understood' subject (as is clear from the fact that its English translation contains the subject pronoun *she*). A second reason relates to the agreement morphology carried by the auxiliary *è* 'is' and the participle *tornata* 'returned' in (1). Just as the form of the (third person singular) auxiliary *è* 'is' and the (feminine singular) participle *tornata* 'returned' is determined via agreement with the overt (third person feminine singular) subject *Maria* in (1A), so too the auxiliary and participle agree in exactly the same way with the null *pro* subject in (1B), since *pro* (as used here) is third person feminine singular by virtue of referring to *Maria*. If the sentence in (1B) were subjectless, it is not obvious how we could account for the relevant agreement facts. Since *pro* is found in all types of finite clause in Italian (e.g. both indicative and subjunctive clauses), we can refer to it as a **finite null subject**.

Although English is not an Italian-style null subject language (in the sense that it is not a language which allows any and every kind of finite clause to have a null *pro* subject), it does have three different types of null subject (briefly discussed in exercise 1.2). As the examples in (2) below illustrate, an imperative sentence in English can have an overt subject which is either a second person expression like *you*, or a third person expression like *anyone*:

(2) (a)   Don't *you* lose your nerve!
   (b)   Don't *anyone* lose their nerve!

However, English also allows an **imperative null subject** in imperative sentences like (3a) below, and this is intrinsically second person – as the contrast with (3b) illustrates:

(3) (a)   Don't lose your nerve!
   (b)   *Don't lose their nerve!

In other words, imperative null subjects seem to be a silent counterpart of *you*. One way of describing this is to say that the pronoun *you* can have a **null spellout** at PF (and thereby be unpronounced) when it is the subject of an imperative sentence.

English also has a second kind of null subject which I will call a **truncated null subject**. In informal styles of spoken English (and also in diary styles of written English) a sentence can be truncated (i.e. shortened) by giving a subject pronoun (like *I* in the sentences in 4 below) a null spellout if it is the first word in a sentence, and if it is weak (i.e. unstressed/non-contrastive). So, in sentences like:

(4) (a)   *I* can't find my pen
   (b)   *I* think I left it at home
   (c)   Why do I always lose things?

the two italicised occurrences of the subject pronoun *I* can be given a null/silent spellout because in each case *I* is the first word in the sentence, but other occurrences of *I* cannot be given a null spellout – as we see from (5) below:

(5) (a)   Can't find my pen
   (b)   Think I left it at home
   (c)   *I think left it at home
   (d)   *Why do always lose things?

However, not all sentence-initial subjects can be truncated (e.g. we can't readily truncate *He* in a sentence like *He is tired*, giving **Is tired*): the precise nature of the constraints on Truncation are unclear.

A third type of null subject found in English is a **non-finite null subject**, found in non-finite clauses which don't have an overt subject. In this connection, compare the structure of the bracketed infinitive clauses in the (a) and (b) examples below:

(6) (a)   We would like [*you* to stay]
    (b)   We would like [to stay]

(7) (a)   We don't want [*anyone* to upset them]
    (b)   We don't want [to upset them]

The bracketed infinitive complement clauses in (6a) and (7a) each contain an overt (italicised) subject. By contrast, the bracketed complement clauses in (6b) and (7b) appear to be subjectless. However, there are good reasons for supposing that apparently subjectless infinitive clauses contain a **null subject**. The particular kind of null subject found in the bracketed clauses in the (b) examples has the same grammatical and referential properties as a pronoun and hence appears to be a null pronoun. In order to differentiate it from the null ('little *pro*') subject found in finite clauses in null subject languages like Italian, the null subject found in infinitives is conventionally designated as **PRO** and referred to as 'big PRO'. Given this assumption, a sentence such as (6b) will have a parallel structure to (6a), except that the bracketed TP has an overt pronoun *you* as its subject in (6a), but a null pronoun PRO as its subject in (6b) – as shown below:

(8)

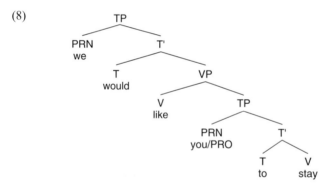

Using the relevant technical terminology, we can say that the null PRO subject in (8) is **controlled** by (i.e. refers back to) the subject *we* of the **matrix** (= containing = next highest) clause – or, equivalently, that *we* is the **controller** or **antecedent** of PRO: hence, a structure like 'We would like PRO to stay' has an interpretation akin to that of 'We would like *ourselves* to stay'. Verbs (such as *like*) which allow an infinitive complement with a PRO subject are said to function (in the relevant use) as **control verbs**; likewise, a complement clause with a null PRO subject is known as a **control clause**.

    An obvious question to ask at this juncture is why we should posit that apparently subjectless infinitive complements like those bracketed in (6b) and (7b) have a null PRO subject. Part of the motivation comes from the intuition that the verb *stay* in (6b) above has an understood subject – and positing a PRO subject for the *stay* clause captures this intuition. The null PRO subject of a control infinitive becomes overt if the infinitive clause is substituted by a finite clause, as we see from the paraphrase for (9a) below given in (9b):

(9) (a) Jim promised [*PRO* to come to my party]
  (b) Jim promised [*he* would come to my party]

The fact that the bracketed clause in (9b) contains an overt (italicised) subject makes it plausible to suppose that the bracketed clause in the synonymous example (9a) has a null PRO subject. (Note, however, that only verbs which can take both an infinitive complement and a finite complement allow a control clause to be paraphrased by a finite clause with an overt subject – hence, not a control verb like *want* in *I want to go home* because *want* does not allow a *that*-clause complement in varieties of English like my own British one in which it is ungrammatical to say **I want that I should leave*.)

Further evidence in support of positing a null PRO subject in such clauses comes from the syntax of **reflexive anaphors** (i.e. *self/selves* forms such as *myself/yourself/himself/themselves* etc.). As we saw in §3.7 (and as examples such as those below illustrate), reflexives generally require a local antecedent (the reflexive being italicised and its antecedent bold-printed):

(10) (a) They want [**John** to help *himself*]
  (b) ****They** want [John to help *themselves*]

In the case of structures like (10), a local antecedent means 'a **clausemate** antecedent' – i.e. an antecedent contained within the same [bracketed] clause/ TP as the reflexive. (10a) is grammatical because it satisfies this clausemate condition: the antecedent of the reflexive *himself* is the noun *John*, and *John* is contained within the same (bracketed) *help*-clause as *himself*. By contrast, (10b) is ungrammatical because the reflexive *themselves* does not have a clausemate antecedent (i.e. it does not have an antecedent within the bracketed clause containing it): its antecedent is the pronoun *they*, and *they* is contained within the *want* clause, not within the [bracketed] *help* clause. In the light of the requirement for reflexives to have a local antecedent, consider now how we account for the grammaticality of the following kind of structure:

(11) John wants [to prove himself]

It follows from the clausemate condition on reflexives that *himself* must have an antecedent within the clause/TP immediately containing it. This clausemate condition is satisfied if we assume that the bracketed clause in (11) has a PRO subject of its own, as shown in simplified form in (12) below:

(12) John wants [$_{TP}$ PRO [$_T$ to] prove himself]

We can then say that PRO serves as a clausemate antecedent for *himself* (i.e. PRO is the antecedent of *himself* and is immediately contained within the same bracketed TP as *himself*). Since PRO in turn is controlled by *John* (i.e. *John* is the antecedent of PRO), this means that *himself* is **coreferential** to (i.e. refers to the same individual as) *John*.

It might be objected that we can account for sentences like (11) without the need for positing a PRO subject for the bracketed *to*-clause if we posit that a reflexive contained within a subjectless clause can have an antecedent in a higher clause. We could then suppose that the bracketed TP in (11) is subjectless, and that the antecedent of *himself* is the main clause subject *John*. However, the assumption that infinitival TPs like that bracketed in (11) don't have a subject of their own but rather the main clause subject serves as the subject of both the main and the complement clause proves problematic in respect of structures such as those below (where 13c–e are acceptable to some speakers – including me – but not to all):

(13) (a)   It's vital [to prepare *myself* properly for the exam]
     (b)   It's important [not to take *oneself* too seriously]
     (c)   %John didn't want [to get *themselves* into trouble]
     (d)   %John proposed [to become *partners*]
     (e)   %John wanted [to work *together*]

If the bracketed infinitive clause were subjectless in (13a,b), the reflexive *myself/ yourself* would have to refer to the main-clause subject *it*, so we would wrongly predict that *itself* has to be used and that sentences like (13a,b) are ungrammatical. Likewise, if the bracketed infinitive clause in (13c) were subjectless, the only possible antecedent for the reflexive *themselves* within the sentence would be the main-clause subject *John* – and yet it is clear that the two don't match (in that *John* is singular and *themselves* plural): so once again, we would wrongly predict that sentences like (13c) are ungrammatical. A similar mismatch would arise if the bracketed infinitive clause in (13d) were subjectless, since there would then be a mismatch between the plural noun *partners* and the singular subject *John* with which it is associated – the same kind of mismatch that we find in **John became partners*. And since the adverb *together* as used in sentences like (13e) must be associated with a plural expression (cf. *They/*John worked together*), it is clear that saying that the bracketed infinitive clause in (13e) is subjectless would wrongly predict that (13e) should be ungrammatical, because of the number mismatch between (singular) *John* and (plural) *together*.

By contrast, we can overcome these problems if we suppose that seemingly subjectless clauses have a null subject, and that sentences like those in (13) have the structure shown in simplified form below:

(14) (a)   It's vital [PRO to prepare *myself* properly for the exam]
     (b)   It's important [PRO not to take *oneself* too seriously]
     (c)   John didn't want [PRO to get *themselves* into trouble]
     (d)   John proposed [PRO to become *partners*]
     (e)   John wanted [PRO to work *together*]

We could then say that PRO in (14a) refers to the speaker who uttered the sentence, so PRO is a first person singular subject (like *I*) and hence can serve as the antecedent of *myself*: when PRO refers to some entity within the domain of discourse which is not directly mentioned in the sentence, we say that PRO has a **discourse controller**. In (14b), PRO has **arbitrary reference** and so denotes 'any arbitrary person you care to mention' and hence has essentially the same interpretation as arbitrary *one* in sentences like '*One* can't be too careful these days': consequently, PRO can serve as the antecedent of *oneself*. In (14c–e), PRO is a third person plural subject (like *they*), and it is **partially controlled** by the main-clause subject *John* (in the sense that the antecedent of PRO is a plural expression which denotes a set of individuals including *John* – i.e. referring to John and one or more other people): since PRO is a plural subject in this use, it is compatible in number with expressions like *themselves/partners/together*.

We can formulate a further argument in support of positing a null PRO subject for the seemingly subjectless infinitive clauses discussed above in the following terms. As the examples in (15) below illustrate, the quantifier *each* can be associated with a plural subject like *they*, and in such cases *each* can either immediately follow the subject, or be positioned after the (underlined) T constituent (i.e. after the finite auxiliary *had*, or after the infinitive particle *to*):

(15) (a)   **They** *each* <u>had</u> wanted to help the other
     (b)   **They** <u>had</u> *each* wanted to help the other
     (c)   I expected [**the twins** *each* <u>to</u> help the other]
     (d)   I expected [**the twins** <u>to</u> *each* help the other]

If (as claimed here) control infinitives have a null PRO subject, we'd expect to find that the quantifier *each* can either be positioned after the PRO subject (as in 16a) below, or after infinitival *to* (as in 16b):

(16) (a)   It would be nice [$_{TP}$ PRO *each* [$_T$ to] help the other]
     (b)   It would be nice [$_{TP}$ PRO [$_T$ to] *each* help the other]

The fact that both types of structure in (16) are grammatical (cf. *It would be nice each to help the other/It would be nice to each help the other*) provides us with further evidence in support of positing that control clauses have a null subject.

A different kind of argument in support of positing that control clauses have a silent PRO subject can be formulated in theoretical terms. In the previous chapter, we saw that T-auxiliaries like *will* have an EPP feature which requires them to project a subject on the edge of TP. However, since we saw in §2.8 that infinitival *to* also belongs to the category T (by virtue of its status as an infinitival tense particle), we can suggest the broader generalisation that all T constituents have an EPP feature requiring them to project a subject on the edge of TP – not only T-auxiliaries like *will* but also the infinitival T constituent *to*. The analysis in (8) above is consistent with this generalisation, since it posits that the *stay*-clause either has an overt *you* subject or a null PRO subject, with either type of subject satisfying the EPP feature of *to*. This leads us to the more general conclusion that just as infinitive complements like *you to stay* in (6a) have an overt subject (*you*), so too seemingly subjectless infinitive complements like *to stay* in (6b) have a null PRO subject – as shown in (8) above.

4.3   Null T in elliptical finite clauses

So far, all the clauses we have looked at in this chapter and the last have contained a TP projection headed by a finite auxiliary or infinitival *to*. A plausible generalisation suggested by this is that all clauses contain a TP constituent. An important question begged by this assumption, however, is how to analyse finite clauses which contain no overt T auxiliary, like that bracketed below:

(17)   He could have helped her, or [she have helped him]

Both clauses here (i.e. the *he* clause and the bracketed *she* clause) appear to be finite, since both have nominative subjects (*he/she*). If all finite clauses contain a TP projection headed by a finite T constituent, it follows that both clauses in (17) must be TPs containing a finite T. This is clearly true of the *he* clause, since this contains the finite modal auxiliary *could*; however, the *she* clause doesn't seem to contain any finite auxiliary constituent, since *have* is an infinitive form in (17) (the corresponding finite form which would be required with a third person subject like *she* being *has*). How can we analyse finite clauses as projections of a finite T constituent when clauses like that bracketed in (17) contain no finite auxiliary?

A plausible answer is to suppose that the string *she have helped him* in (17) is an **elliptical** (i.e. abbreviated) variant of *she could have helped him*, and that the T constituent *could* in the second clause undergoes a particular form of ellipsis called **Gapping** (mentioned in §1.4). Gapping is an operation which allows the head of a phrase to be given a null spellout in the PF component – and so be 'silent' – when the same item occurs elsewhere within the sentence: it is so called because it leaves an apparent 'gap' in the phrase where the head would otherwise have been. If the T auxiliary *could* undergoes Gapping in the bracketed clause in (17), the bracketed clause will have the structure shown below (where *~~could~~* marks an ellipsed counterpart of *could*, and *have* is taken to be a perfect aspect auxiliary which occupies the head PERF position of a PERFP projection when non-finite – as suggested in the *helpful hints* for example 2 in exercise §3.1):

(18)

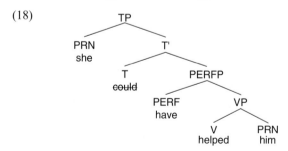

The head T position of TP in a structure like (18) is filled by the ellipsed auxiliary *~~could~~*. Let us suppose that an ellipsed auxiliary is present in the syntactic (and semantic) structure of the sentence, but is given a null/silent spellout in the phonological component (marked by strikethrough). The null T analysis in (18)

provides a principled account of three observations. Firstly, the bracketed clause in (17) is interpreted as an elliptical form of *she could have helped him*: this can be straightforwardly accounted for under the analysis in (18) since T contains a null counterpart of *could* in the syntax and semantics. Secondly, the subject is in the nominative case form *she*: this can be attributed to the fact that the T position in (18) is filled by a 'silent' counterpart of the finite auxiliary *could*, which (like other finite auxiliaries) requires a nominative subject. Thirdly, the perfect auxiliary *have* is in the infinitive form: this is because ~~could~~ (being a silent counterpart of *could*) has the same selectional properties as *could* and selects a complement headed by a word (like *have*) in the infinitive form.

A fourth argument in support of the null T analysis in (18) comes from data relating to **cliticisation** (a process by which one word attaches itself in a leech-like fashion to another). The perfect auxiliary form *have* has a range of variants in the spoken language. When unstressed, it can lose its initial /h/ segment and have its vowel reduced to schwa /ə/, and so be pronounced as /əv/, e.g. in sentences such as *You should have been there*. (Because *of* is also pronounced /əv/ when unstressed, some people write this as *You should of been there* – not you, of course!) However, when *have* is used with a subject ending in a vowel or diphthong (e.g. a pronoun like *I/we/you/they*), it can lose its vowel entirely and be contracted down to /v/; in this weak form, it is phonetically too insubstantial to survive as an independent word and **encliticises** onto (i.e. attaches to the end of) its subject, resulting in structures such as:

(19) (a)   *You've* done your duty
     (b)   *They've* retired General Gaga
     (c)   *I've* forgotten to lock the door
     (d)   *We've* saved you a place

However, note that *have* cannot cliticise onto *she* in (17), as we see from (20) below:

(20)   *He could have helped her or *she've* helped him

(where *she've* is intended to be homophonous with the word *sheave*). Why should cliticisation of *have* onto *she* be blocked here? In order to answer this question, we need to take a closer look at the nature of *have*-cliticisation.

An important property of *have*-cliticisation is that it appears to be a PF operation (i.e. an operation taking place in the PF/phonological component) rather than a syntactic operation. One reason for thinking this is that it is subject to a phonological condition on its application, in that *have* can only encliticise onto a word (like *you/they/I/we* in 19) which ends in a vowel or dipthong. A further reason for treating *have*-cliticisation as a phonological operation comes from the following observations. As we saw in §1.4, English has a syntactic movement operation by which a constituent can be moved to the front of a sentence in order to highlight it. So, for example, if we want to focus *you* (and contrast it with *other witnesses*) in a sentence such as (21a) below, we can move *you* to the front of the sentence as in (21b) (where capitals mark contrastive stress):

(21) (a)   I don't think YOU have been lying, even though other witnesses have
     (b)   YOU I don't think have been lying, even though other witnesses have

In (21a), *have* can encliticise onto *have*, resulting in

(22)   I don't think YOU've been lying, even though other witnesses have.

Now, if *have*-cliticisation were a syntactic operation, we'd expect that *have* can attach to *you* in the syntax, and then the resulting complex constituent *you've* can undergo syntactic movement to the front of the overall sentence, so deriving

(23)   *YOU've I don't think been lying, even though other witnesses have

The fact that *have* cannot be preposed along with YOU when YOU undergoes syntactic movement suggests that *have*-cliticisation is phonological (rather than syntactic) in nature. This means that *you* and *have* remain separate words in the syntax, but are fused together if immediately adjacent in the PF component in a sentence like (22) once the structure **generated** (i.e. formed) by the syntax has been handed over to the PF component for morphological and phonological processing. Since linearisation (i.e. assignment of word order) takes place in the PF component (as we saw in §3.8), this means that PF operations (unlike syntactic operations) can be sensitive to word order. Given this assumption, it would seem plausible to take *have*-cliticisation to be a PF operation whereby *have* can encliticise onto an immediately preceding word ending in a vowel or diphthong.

However, this would appear to be too simplistic, since it fails to account for why *have* can cliticise onto *you* in (24a) below, but not in (24b):

(24) (a)   *You've* been causing quite a stir
     (b)   **Pictures of *you've* been causing quite a stir

Why should encliticisation of *have* onto *you* be possible in (24a), but not in (24b)? In order to try and answer this question, let's look at the structure of the two sentences. (24a) has the structure shown in (25a) below (simplified by not showing the internal structure of the VP *causing quite a stir*), while (24b) has the structure (25b). In both cases, *have* is a present tense auxiliary occupying the head T position of TP, and *been* is a progressive aspect auxiliary occupying the head PROG position of a separate PROGP projection:

(25) (a)

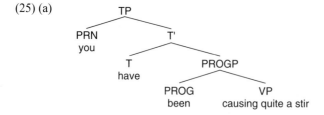

(25) (b)

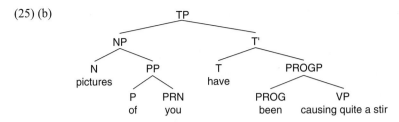

In the light of the structures in (25), consider why *have* can cliticise onto *you* in (25a), but not in (25b).

The answer would seem to lie in the fact that the pronoun *you* **c-commands** the T auxiliary *have* in (25a), but not in (25b). More particularly, PRN-*you* c-commands T-*have* in (25a) because the mother of PRN-*you* is the TP node at the root of the tree, and this TP node contains T-*have* as one of its constituents.

By contrast, PRN-*you* does not c-command T-*have* in (25b) because the mother of PRN-*you* is the PP node, and the only constituent other than *you* contained within this PP node is the preposition *of*: this means that PRN-*you* c-commands P-*of* in (25b), but PRN-*you* does not c-command T-*have*. If *have* can only cliticise onto a word that c-commands it, it follows that cliticisation will be barred in (25b) because *you* does not c-command *have*.

The discussion above suggests that *have*-cliticisation is a PF operation which is subject to the three conditions specified in (26) below:

(26)   ***Have*-cliticisation**
         The word *have* can encliticise to (i.e. attach to the end of) another word W in the phonological component, provided that
         (i)   W ends in a vowel/diphthong
         (ii) W immediately precedes *have*
         (iii) W c-commands *have*

Have-cliticisation is possible in a structure like (25a) because all three conditions in (26) are met. Condition (26i) is met because *you* ends in the vowel |uː|. Condition (26ii) is met because *you* immediately precedes *have* at PF (in the sense that there is no overt or null constituent intervening between the two). And condition (26iii) is met because *you* c-commands *have*. By contrast, *have*-cliticisation is barred in (25b) because although conditions (26i,ii) are met, the c-command condition in (26iii) is not met because (as we saw earlier) *you* does not c-command *have*. (A descriptive detail set aside here is that 26 applies specifically to encliticisation of *have*: encliticisation of other contracted auxiliary forms like the contracted *'d* variant of *did/had/would*, the contracted *'s* variant of *is/has*, the contracted *'re* variant of *are* and the contracted *'ll* variant of *will* is subject to somewhat less restrictive conditions, but this will not be pursued here.)

In the light of our formulation of *have*-cliticisation in (26), let's now return to consider why cliticisation of *have* onto *she* is blocked in sentences like (20) *'He could have helped her or *she've* helped him.' Under the null T analysis outlined above, the second clause in (20) contains a silent variant of *could* and has the structure shown in (18) above, repeated as (27) below:

(27)

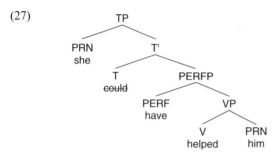

Consider now whether the conditions for *have*-cliticisation set out in (26) are met in the structure (27). The phonological condition (26i) is met in (27) because *she* ends in the vowel [i:]. Likewise the c-command condition (26iii) is met: *she* c-commands *have* because the mother of PRN-*she* is TP, and TP contains *have* as one of its constituents. However, the word-order condition (26ii) is not met: *she* does not immediately precede *have* because the null auxiliary T-*could* intervenes between the two. Thus, the presence of the intervening null auxiliary ~~could~~ blocks cliticisation of *have* onto *she* in (27), thereby accounting for the ungrammaticality of (20) *'He could have helped her or *she've* helped him.' Turning this conclusion on its head, we can say that the ungrammaticality of (20) provides us with empirical evidence that the bracketed clause in (17) contains a null counterpart of *could* intervening between *she* and *have* – precisely as claimed in the analysis in (27) above. An interesting implication of the analysis presented here is that phonological operations like *have*-cliticisation are sensitive to the presence of null constituents.

   Our discussion so far in this section has suggested that some seemingly auxiliariless clauses are TPs headed by a T constituent containing an auxiliary which (via ellipsis) is given a silent spellout. A rather different kind of null auxiliary structure is found in African American English (AAE), in sentences such as the following:

(28)   He just feel like he gettin' cripple up from arthritis (Labov 1969: 717)

In AAE, specific forms of the auxiliary BE have null variants, so we find null forms of *are* and *is* in contexts where Standard Colloquial English (SCE) would require the contracted forms *'s* and *'re*. Hence, in place of SCE *He's getting crippled* and *He's gonna be there* we find AAE *He gettin' cripple* and *He gonna be there* (with a null counterpart of *'s*). Evidence in support of the assumption that AAE sentences like (28) contain a null variant of *is* comes from the observation that a (bold-printed) copy of the missing auxiliary *is* may surface in a sentence like (29a) below, suggesting that the italicised string in (29a) has the structure in (29b):

(29) (a)   *He gonna be there*, I know he **is** (Fasold 1980: 29)
     (b)   [TP He [T ~~is~~] gonna be there]

In a sentence like (29a), the sequence following the comma is known as a **tag**. In tag sentences, the (italicised) auxiliary in the tag is generally a copy of the auxiliary used in the main clause. This being so, it follows that the main *gonna* clause in (29a) must contain a null variant of the progressive auxiliary *is*. In other words, the main clause in (29a) must be a TP with the structure shown in skeletal form in (29b), with strikethrough indicating that the phonetic features of the auxiliary are not pronounced. Interestingly, the form *am* (contracted to *'m*) has no null counterpart in AAE, nor do the past tense forms *was/were*. It would seem, therefore, that the only forms of BE which have a null counterpart in AAE are the specific auxiliary forms *are* and *is*. Wolfram (1971: 149) reports that in non-standard Southern White American English the use of null auxiliaries is even more restricted, and that the only form of BE with a null counterpart is *are*; cf. the parallel observation by Fasold (1980: 30) that 'There are many southern whites who delete only *are*.'

4.4   Null T in indicative clauses

Our analysis of the kind of auxiliariless clauses discussed in §3.3 as TPs headed by a T which has a null phonetic spellout suggests the more general hypothesis in (30) below:

(30)   **TP Hypothesis**
           All clauses contain a TP headed by an (overt or null) T constituent.

We saw in the previous section that the TP Hypothesis has interesting implications for how we analyse elliptical clauses in which a T constituent undergoes Gapping. However, the TP Hypothesis also has important implications for the analysis of non-elliptical finite clauses such as the following, which contain a finite main/non-auxiliary verb in the **indicative mood**, but no auxiliary:

(31) (a)   He enjoys syntax
      (b)   He enjoyed syntax

The TP Hypothesis implies that we should analyse auxiliariless indicative clauses like those in (31a,b) above as TP constituents which have the respective structures shown in (32a,b) below:

(32)

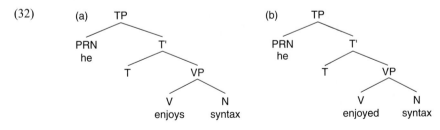

Structures like those in (32) differ from null-auxiliary structures like *He could have helped her or she ~~could~~ have helped him* and *He ~~is~~ gonna be there* in that they don't contain a silent counterpart of a specific auxiliary like *could* or *is*, but rather simply don't contain any auxiliary at all.

However, there's clearly something very odd about a null T analysis like (32) if we say that the relevant clauses are TPs which are headed by a T constituent that contains *absolutely nothing*. For one thing, a category label like T is an abbreviation for a set of features (i.e. grammatical properties) carried by a lexical item – hence, if we posit that structures like (32) are TPs, the head T position of TP has to be occupied by some kind of lexical item. Moreover, the structures which are generated by the syntactic component of the grammar are eventually handed over to the semantic component to be assigned a semantic interpretation – as shown in the diagram below (repeated from §1.5, where ≈ means 'interfaces with'):

(33)

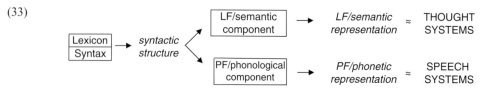

Given the architecture of the grammar in (33), empty categories present in syntax will be handed over to both the PF and LF components to be processed. At PF they receive a null spellout, but can serve to block certain PF processes from applying – as we saw in our discussion of *have*-cliticisation in §4.3. At LF, they will need to be assigned some semantic interpretation, and hence to play a role in determining the meaning of the overall structure. If so, it clearly has to be the case that the head T of TP contains some item which contributes in some way to the meaning of the sentence. But what kind of item could T contain, and what semantic function could it serve?

In order to try and answer this question, it's instructive to contrast auxiliariless structures like those in (32) above with auxiliary-containing structures like those in (34) below:

(34)

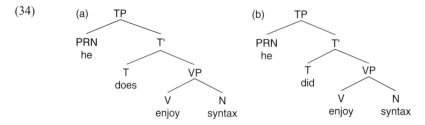

The head T position in TP is occupied by the present tense auxiliary *does* in (34a), and by the past tense auxiliary *did* in (34b). If we examine the internal morphological structure of these two words, we see that *does* contains the present tense affix *-s*, and that *did* contains the past tense affix *-d* (each of these affixes being attached to an irregular stem form of the auxiliary DO). In schematic terms, then, we can say that the head T constituent of TP in structures like (34) is of the form AUXILIARY STEM+TENSE AFFIX.

If we now look back at the auxiliariless structures in (32), we see that the head V position of VP in these structures is occupied by the verbs *enjoys* and *enjoyed*, and that these have a parallel morphological structure, in that they are of the form VERB STEM+TENSE AFFIX. So, what finite clauses like (32) and (34) have in common is that in both cases they contain an (auxiliary or main) verb carrying a tense affix. In structures like (34) which contain an auxiliary like DO, the tense affix is attached to the auxiliary; in structures like (32) which contain no auxiliary, the tense affix attaches instead to the main verb *enjoy*. If we make the reasonable assumption that (as its label suggests) T is the **locus** of the tense properties of a finite clause (in the sense that T is the constituent on which tense features originate), an interesting possibility to consider is that the relevant tense affix (in both types of clause structure) originates in the head T position of TP. Since tensed verbs agree with their subjects in person and number, let us suppose that the tense affix (below abbreviated to *Af*) also carries person and number features. On this view, sentences like *He does enjoy syntax* and *He enjoys syntax* would have the respective syntactic structures indicated in (35a,b) below, where [3SgPr] is an abbreviation for the features [third-person, singular-number, present-tense]:

(35)

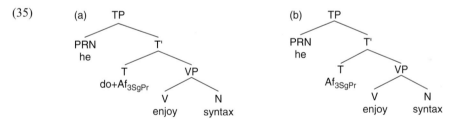

(35a) and (35b) have in common that they both contain a tense affix (*Af*) in T; they differ in that the tense affix is attached to the auxiliary DO in (35a), but is unattached in (35b) because there is no auxiliary in T for the affix to attach to. (An interesting implication of the analysis in 35b is that it entails that we can't assume that all terminal nodes in a tree are *words*, since a tense affix is a **morpheme** rather than a *word*: let's therefore assume that terminal nodes are morphemes – e.g. the V node in 35b contains the verb stem *enjoy*, and the T node in 35b contains a tense affix.)

Under the analysis in (35), it is clear that T in auxiliariless clauses like (35b) would not be empty, but rather would contain a tense/agreement affix whose semantic contribution to the meaning of the overall sentence is that it marks (present) tense and (indicative) mood. But what about the phonetic spellout of the tense affix? In a structure like (35a), it is easy to see why the (third person singular present) tense affix is ultimately spelled out as an *s*-inflection on the end of the auxiliary *does*, because the affix is directly attached to the auxiliary DO in T. But how come the affix ends up spelled out as an *s*-inflection on the main verb *enjoys* in a structure like (35b)? We can answer this question in the following terms. Once the syntax has formed a clause structure like (35b), the relevant syntactic structure is then sent to the **semantic component** to be assigned a semantic interpretation, and to the **PF component** (i.e. phonological component) to be assigned a phonetic form. In the PF component, a number of morphological and phonological operations apply. One such operation is traditionally referred to as **Affix Hopping** (though I shall also refer to it as **Affix Lowering**) and it can be characterised informally as follows:

(36)   **Affix Hopping**
         When a tense affix in T remains unattached at the end of the syntactic derivation, in the PF component the affix is lowered onto the closest V below T (i.e. c-commanded by T).

Via the Affix Hopping operation (36), the unattached affix in T in (35b) will be lowered onto the verb *enjoy* in the PF component, in the manner shown by the arrow in (37) below:

(37)

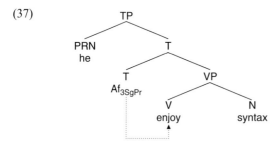

Since inflections in English are **suffixes**, we can assume that the Tense affix will be lowered onto the *end* of the verb *enjoy*, to derive the structure [*enjoy*+Af_{3SgPr}]. Given that *enjoy* is a regular verb, the resulting structure will ultimately be spelled out in the phonology as the form *enjoys*.

What I have done so far in this section is sketch out an analysis of auxiliariless finite clauses as TPs headed by a T constituent containing an abstract tense affix which is subsequently lowered onto the verb by an Affix Hopping operation in the PF component (so resulting in a clause structure which looks as if it contains no T constituent). However, an important question to ask at this juncture is why we should claim that auxiliariless clauses contain an abstract T constituent. From a theoretical point of view, one advantage of the abstract T analysis is that it provides a unitary characterisation of the syntax of clauses, since it allows us to say that all clauses contain a TP projection, that the subject of a clause is always in spec-TP (i.e. always serves as the specifier of TP), that a finite clause always contains an (auxiliary or main) verb carrying a tense affix, and so on. Lending further weight to theory-internal considerations such as these is a substantial body of empirical evidence, as we shall see.

One argument in support of the tense affix analysis comes from coordination data in relation to sentences such as:

(38) (a)   He *enjoys syntax*, and **has learned a lot**
     (b)   He *enjoyed syntax*, and **is taking a follow-up course**

In both sentences, the italicised string *enjoys syntax/enjoyed syntax* has been coordinated with a bold-printed constituent which is clearly a T-bar in that it comprises a present tense auxiliary (*has/is*) with a verb phrase complement (*learned a lot/taking a follow-up course*). On the assumption that only the same kinds of constituent can be conjoined by *and*, it follows that the italicised (seemingly T-less) strings *enjoys syntax/enjoyed syntax* must also be T-bar constituents; and since they contain no overt auxiliary, this means they must contain an abstract T constituent of some kind – precisely as the analysis in (37) claims.

A direct consequence of the tense affix analysis (37) of auxiliariless finite clauses is that finite auxiliaries and finite main verbs occupy different positions within the clause: finite auxiliaries occupy the head T position of TP, whereas finite main verbs occupy the head V position of VP. An interesting way of testing this hypothesis is in relation to the behaviour of items which have the status of auxiliaries in some uses, but of verbs in others. One such word is HAVE. This has a variety of different uses, three of which are illustrated below:

(39) (a)   They *have* seen the ghost
     (b)   They *had* been warned about the ghost
     (c)   The doctor *had* an eye-specialist examine the patient
     (d)   The doctor *had* the patient examined by an eye-specialist
     (e)   The teacher *had* three students walk out on her
     (f)   I've never *had* anyone send me flowers

In the kind of use illustrated in (39a,b) above, HAVE is a **perfect (aspect)** auxiliary and so requires the following verb to be in the perfect participle form *seen/been*. However, in the use illustrated in (39c,d), HAVE is a main verb which is causative in sense (and so has much the same meaning as the verb CAUSE). Likewise, in the use illustrated in (39e,f), HAVE is a main verb which is experiential in sense (and so has much the same meaning as the verb EXPERIENCE). By traditional tests of auxiliarihood, perfect HAVE is an auxiliary, and causative/experiential HAVE is a main verb: e.g. perfect HAVE can undergo Subject-Auxiliary Inversion (*Has she gone to Paris?*) whereas causative/experiential HAVE cannot (**Had the doctor an eye specialist examine the patient? *Had the teacher three students walk out on her?*). In terms of the assumptions we are making here, this means that finite forms of HAVE occupy the head T position of TP in their perfect use, but occupy the head V position of VP in their causative or experiential use.

Evidence in support of this claim comes from cliticisation. We saw earlier in (26) above that the form *have* can cliticise onto an immediately preceding c-commanding pronoun ending in a vowel/diphthong. In the light of this, consider contrasts such as the following:

(40) (a)   *They've* seen a ghost (= perfect *have*)
      (b)   **They've* their car serviced regularly (= causative *have*).
      (c)   **They've* students walk out on them sometimes (= experiential *have*)

How can we account for this contrast? If perfect *have* in (40a) is a finite (present tense) auxiliary which occupies the head T position of TP, but causative *have* in (40b) and experiential *have* in (40c) are main verbs occupying the head V position of a VP complement of a null T, then prior to cliticisation the three clauses will have the respective simplified structures indicated by the partial labeled bracketings in (41a–c) below (where *Af* is a tense affix):

(41) (a)   [TP they [T *have+Af*] [VP [V *seen*] a ghost]]
      (b)   [TP they [T *Af*] [VP [V *have*] their car serviced regularly]]
      (c)   [TP they [T *Af*] [VP [V *have*] students walk out on them sometimes]]

(Here and throughout the rest of the book, *partial* labelled bracketings are used to show those parts of a structure most relevant to the discussion at hand, omitting other parts. In such cases, only relevant heads and the corresponding phrases are shown, not intermediate projections – as in (41) above where, e.g., T and TP are shown but not T-bar.) Since cliticisation of *have* onto a pronoun is blocked by the presence of an intervening constituent (even one which is null, as in 27 above), it should be obvious why *have* can cliticise onto *they* in (41a) but not in (41b,c): after all, there is no intervening constituent separating the pronoun *they* from *have* in (41a), but *they* is separated from the verb *have* in (41b,c) by an intervening T constituent containing a tense affix (*Af*), so blocking contraction. It goes without saying that a crucial premise of this account is the assumption that *have* (in its use as a finite form) is positioned in the head T position of TP when it is a perfect auxiliary, but in the head V position of VP when it is a causative or experiential verb. More generally, *have*-cliticisation data suggest that finite clauses which lack a finite auxiliary are TPs headed by an abstract T constituent containing a Tense affix.

Further evidence for the TP analysis comes from tag questions. As we see from the examples below, sentences containing (a finite form of) perfect HAVE are tagged by an appropriate form of HAVE, whereas sentences containing (a finite form of) causative HAVE are tagged by an appropriate form of DO:

(42) (a)   Mary *has* gone to Paris, *has/*does* she?
      (b)   Jules *has* his hair styled by Quentin Quiff, *does/*has* he?

If we adopt the T analysis of perfect HAVE and the V analysis of causative HAVE, and if we assume (in accordance with the TP Hypothesis) that all finite clauses contain a TP constituent, the main clauses in (42a,b) will have the respective (simplified) structures indicated in (43a,b) below:

(43) (a)   [TP Mary [T *have+Af*] [VP [V *gone*] to Paris]]
      (b)   [TP Jules [T *Af*] [VP [V *have*] his hair styled by Quentin Quiff]]

If we suppose that the T constituent which appears in the tag is generally a copy of the T constituent in the main clause, the contrast in (43) can be accounted for in the following manner. In (43a), the head T position of TP is filled by the T constituent *have+Af* (ultimately spelled out as *has* in the PF component), and so the tag contains a copy of this T constituent and this copy is also spelled out as *has*. In (43b), however, T contains only an abstract tense affix, and so we would expect the tag to contain a copy of this affix. Now, in the main clause, the affix can be lowered from T onto the verb *have* in the head V position of VP, with the resulting verb eventually being spelled out as *has*. But in the tag, there is no verb stem for the affix to be lowered onto, so that if the T constituent in the tag contained only an affix, the relevant structure would crash at PF, because a tense affix can't be stranded without a verbal stem to attach to. In this kind of situation, English resorts to the use of the 'dummy' or 'expletive' (i.e. semantically contentless) auxiliary DO to 'support' the stray affix – a phenomenon traditionally referred to as **DO-support**. This means that T in the main clause in (43b) contains just a tense affix, whereas T in the tag contains both a tense affix and a stem form of the supporting auxiliary DO. This in turn implies that the T constituent in the main clause is not identical to that in the tag, since the T constituent in the main clause contains only an affix, whereas the T constituent in the embedded clause contains an affix attached to the auxiliary DO and is thus of the form DO+*Af*. However, since DO has no intrinsic semantic content, the T constituents in the main clause and the tag have the same semantic properties (in that they serve to mark present tense and indicative mood). This in turn suggests that the key requirement on tag formation is that the T constituent in the tag have the same semantic properties as those of the T constituent in the main clause. It would appear that some speakers impose the weaker requirement that the auxiliary in the tag should have *similar* semantic properties to the T constituent in the main clause, since in spoken English we find sentences like the following (where labelled brackets have been added by me):

(44) (a)   He [$_T$ *ought*] to apologise to her, [$_T$ **shouldn't**] he?
     (b)   The flight [$_T$ *may*] be delayed, [$_T$ **mightn't**] it? (wiktionary.org)
     (c)   We [$_T$ *shall*], [$_T$ **won't**] we Roofus? (cortexrp.com)

Here, the italicised T auxiliary in the main clause is phonetically distinct from (but semantically similar to) the bold-printed negative auxiliary in the tag. The reason for using a different auxiliary in the tag may be that negative forms like *oughtn't/mayn't/shan't* have an archaic or obsolescent feel about them, and so they are avoided.

4.5   Null T in subjunctive clauses

Having seen in the previous section that **indicative** clauses always contain a T constituent, let's now turn to look at **subjunctive** clauses like those bracketed in (45) below, found in formal style:

(45) (a)   She requested [that he *have* a second chance]
  (b)   They demanded [that he *produce* his identity card]
  (c)   The nurse insisted [that he not *get* out of bed]

At first sight, such clauses might appear not to contain any form of auxiliary/T constituent, but rather simply to contain an italicised infinitive verb form – and some linguists have indeed claimed that subjunctive clauses contain no T constituent. However, an alternative analysis of subjunctive clauses (consistent with the TP Hypothesis in 30) is to suppose that such clauses contain a null counterpart of *should* (below symbolised as ~~should~~) which occupies the head T position of TP. If so, a sentence like (45c) will have the partial structure shown below:

(46)   The nurse insisted [CP [C that] [TP he [T ~~should~~] not get out of bed]]

In order to account for the fact that *should* can optionally occur overtly in structures like (46), we can suppose that (when used as a subjunctive modal), *should* can optionally have a silent spellout.

    Given the null T analysis of subjunctive clauses in (46), we can then account for why the italicised verbs in (45) are in the infinitive form, since it is a property of a modal auxiliary like *should* that it selects a complement headed by an (auxiliary or main) verb in the infinitive form. We can also account for why the *he* subject of each of the bracketed subjunctive clauses in (45) has nominative case, since a clause containing a modal like *should* has a nominative subject. The null T analysis also allows us to account for the absence of DO-support in negative subjunctive clauses such as the following:

(47)   The nurse insisted [that he (*do) not get out of bed]

The reason why the head T position of TP cannot be filled by *do* in (47) is that it is already filled by a null counterpart of *should* (as shown in 46 above). In addition, we can also account for why *have*-cliticisation is not possible in (45a) – as we see from the ungrammaticality of the following:

(48)   *She requested that he*'ve* a second chance

Under the null T analysis of subjunctive clauses, (48) will have the partial structure shown below:

(49)   She requested [CP [C that] [TP he [T ~~should~~] [VP [V have] a second chance]]]

Given the structure in (49), *have* will be blocked from cliticising onto the pronoun *he* by the intervening null subjunctive modal ~~should~~ which occupies the head T position of TP – thereby accounting for the ungrammaticality of sentences like (48).

    However, the *should*-deletion analysis of subjunctive clauses outlined above proves potentially problematic in certain respects. For one thing, the null-*should* analysis does not accurately characterise the semantics of subjunctive clauses: for example, the subjunctive clause in (47) *The nurse insisted that he not get out of bed* imposes a stronger prohibition than the corresponding *should* sentence *The nurse insisted that he should not get out of bed*. Moreover, some speakers of

American English are reported not to allow *should* to be used in subjunctive clauses like the *that*-clauses in (50a–c) below; and while the use of *should* is acceptable in my own British English variety in (50a–c) below, I would not use *should* in the subjunctive structure in (50d):

(50) (a)   I demand that you (*should*) do the dishes (Hojo, 1971: 103–4)
     (b)   John ordered that Tom (*should*) leave immediately (Chiba 1987: 146)
     (c)   It is crucial that the war between Iran and Iraq (?*should*) be settled (Matsui 1981: 47)
     (d)   I'd rather that she (*should*) be there with you

The data in (50) seem more compatible with an alternative analysis under which T in subjunctive clauses contains an inherently null subjunctive modal (below symbolised as ø), and not a null counterpart of *should*. If so, a sentence such as (45a) above would have the structure (51) below (where the subscript SUBJ indicates that the null modal in T marks subjunctive mood):

(51)   She requested [$_{CP}$ [$_C$ that] [$_{TP}$ he [$_T$ ø$_{SUBJ}$] [$_{VP}$ [$_V$ have] a second chance]]]

If the null subjunctive modal in (51) has the same selectional properties as *should*, it follows that it will require the verb *have* to be in the infinitive form. However, irrespective of whether we take T in subjunctive clauses to be occupied by a null counterpart of *should* or by an inherently null modal, the fact remains that subjunctive clauses are another type of finite clause containing a null T constituent, thereby reinforcing the claim embodied in the TP Hypothesis that finite clauses (whether indicative or subjunctive) always contain an (overt or null) T constituent.

4.6   Null T in infinitive clauses and small clauses

In the previous two sections, we saw that auxiliariless (indicative and subjunctive) finite clauses are TP constituents headed by an abstract T constituent containing a tense affix. Given that clauses containing a finite auxiliary are also TPs, a plausible conclusion to draw is that all finite clauses are TPs. However, since clauses containing infinitival *to* are also TPs (with *to* serving as a non-finite tense particle), a more general hypothesis is that all clauses (whether finite or infinitival) are TPs – and indeed this claim is implicit in the formulation of the TP Hypothesis given earlier in (30) above, repeated below:

(30)   **TP Hypothesis**
           All clauses contain a TP headed by an (overt or null) T constituent.

An apparent challenge to the TP Hypothesis is posed by **bare** (i.e. *to*-less) infinitive complement clauses such as those bracketed below (where the italicised verb is infinitival in form):

(52) (a)   I have never known [Tom *criticise* anyone]
    (b)   A reporter saw [Senator Sleaze *leave* Benny's Bunny Bar]
    (c)   You mustn't let [the pressure *get* to you]

Nonetheless, clauses like those bracketed in (52) will be compatible with the TP Hypothesis if they are analysed as TPs headed by a null T constituent. Since the relevant null T constituent resembles infinitival *to* in requiring the (italicised) verb in the bracketed complement clause to be in the infinitive form, we can take it to be a null counterpart of infinitival *to* (below symbolised as *to̶*). This in turn will mean that the bracketed infinitive clause in (52a) has the structure (53) below:

(53)

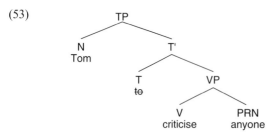

We can then say that verbs like *know, see* and *let* (as used in 52 above) take an infinitival TP complement headed by an infinitive particle with a null spellout, whereas verbs like *expect, judge, report, believe,* etc. take a TP complement headed by an infinitive particle which is overtly spelled out as *to* in structures like those below:

(54) (a)   I expect [him *to* win]
    (b)   I judged [him *to* be lying]
    (c)   They reported [him *to* be missing]
    (d)   I believe [him *to* be innocent]

In other words, all infinitive clauses are TPs headed by an infinitival T which is overtly spelled out as *to* in infinitive clauses like those bracketed in (54), but which has a null spellout in infinitive clauses like those bracketed in (52).

From a historical perspective, the null infinitive particle analysis is far from implausible since bare infinitive clauses in present-day English had *to* infinitive counterparts in earlier varieties of English – as illustrated by the following Shakespearean examples:

(55) (a)   I saw [her coral lips *to* move] (Lucentio, *Taming of the Shrew*, I.i)
    (b)   My lord your son made [me *to* think of this] (Helena, *All's Well That Ends Well*, I.iii)
    (c)   What would you have [me *to* do]? (Lafeu, *All's Well That Ends Well*, V.ii)
    (d)   I had rather hear [you *to* solicit that] (Olivia, *All's Well That Ends Well*, III.i)

Moreover, some bare infinitive clauses have *to* infinitive counterparts in present-day English: cf.

(56) (a)   The generous donations will help [(*to*) pay for repairs to the church steeple]
    (b)   The refugees were helped [(*to*) leave Syria by humanitarian organisations]

(57) (a)   I've never known [Tom (*to*) criticise anyone]

(b)   Tom has never been known [*to* criticise anyone]

(58) (a)   A reporter saw [Senator Sleaze (**to*) leave Benny's Bunny Bar]

(b)   Senator Sleaze was seen [*to* leave Benny's Bunny Bar]

In (56), the infinitive particle *to* can optionally be given an overt or null spellout irrespective of whether the infinitive clause is used as the complement of the active verb form *help* in (56a) or as the complement of the passive participle *helped* in (56b). In (57), the infinitive particle *to* can optionally have an overt or null spellout after the active (perfect participle) form *known* in (57a) but must be spelled out as *to* after the passive participle *known* in (57b). In (58), the infinitival particle must obligatorily receive a null spellout after the active verb form *saw* in (58a) but must obligatorily receive an overt spellout as *to* after the passive participle *seen* in (58b). However, occasional 'slips of the tongue' can result in the infinitive particle sometimes being overt even in active structures like (58a) – as we see from the sentences in (59) below which I recorded from radio and TV programmes:

(59) (a)   The Mayor of New Orleans would like to see parts of the city which were devastated in the hurricane *to* get back to normal (BBC TV newsreader)

(b)   It's great to see a player like that, who's worked hard all his career, *to* get his reward (Roy Keane, ITV)

(c)   Arsenal's back five are making Essien and Frank Lampard *to* work very hard across the pitch (Commentator, Sky Sports TV)

(d)   I think sometimes the fear of failure makes you *to* strive for things (Sir Alex Ferguson, BBC Radio 5)

(e)   You cannot let the ball *to* bounce in that fashion (Alan Smith, Sky Sports TV)

Although data like (55–59) are suggestive rather than conclusive, they make it plausible to suppose that bare infinitive clauses are TPs headed by a null variant of infinitival *to*.

Additional support for the null infinitive particle analysis of bare infinitive clauses comes from cliticisation data in relation to sentences such as the following:

(60) (a)   I can't let [*you have* my password]

(b)   *I can't let [*you've* my password]

If we suppose that the bracketed infinitive complement in (60b) is a TP headed by a null variant of infinitival *to* as in

(61)   I can't let [$_{TP}$ you [$_T$ *to*] have my password]

we can account for the fact that *have* cannot cliticise onto *you* by positing that the presence of the null infinitive particle *to* intervening between *you* and *have* blocks cliticisation of *have* onto *you*.

A further argument leading to the same conclusion comes from structures like the following:

(62) (a)   I consider [*there* to be an economic crisis]
   (b)   I know that [*there* has been opposition to the proposal]
   (c)   Let [*there* be peace]
   (d)   I've never known [*there* be complaints about syntax]

The word *there* in this use is an **expletive** (i.e. meaningless) pronoun – as we see from the observation that (since it does not refer to any specific place) it cannot be questioned by locative *where* (cf. **Where do you consider to be an economic crisis?*). In its use as an expletive pronoun, it typically serves as the specifier/subject of a TP, whether an infinitival TP like that bracketed in (62a) or a finite TP like that bracketed in (62b). If expletive *there* generally occurs in spec-TP, it follows that the bracketed infinitive complement clauses in (62c,d) can plausibly be taken to be TPs headed by a null infinitival T.

Our discussion here leads to the wider conclusion that both *to*+infinitive clauses and bare (*to*-less) infinitive clauses are TP constituents headed by an infinitive particle which has the overt spellout *to* in most types of infinitive clause, but has a null spellout in bare infinitive clauses. Given that I argued in §4.4 and §4.5 that all indicative and subjunctive clauses contain a TP projection (headed by a T which contains a tense affix or tensed auxiliary), this lends support to the claim embodied in the TP Hypothesis in (30) that all clauses (whether finite or infinitival) contain a TP, and that T is overt in clauses containing a finite auxiliary or infinitival *to*, but is null elsewhere (because *to* in bare infinitive clauses has a null spellout, and the tense affix in auxiliariless finite clauses is lowered onto the main verb in the PF component). One advantage of this analysis is that it enables us to attain a uniform characterisation of the syntax of (finite and infinitival) clauses as containing a TP headed by a T constituent.

A further type of clause structure which can be argued to contain a null T constituent are **small clauses** like those bracketed below (so called because they are smaller than other clauses by virtue of not containing a verb):

(63)   I consider
   (a) [**the article** *full of good ideas*]
   (b) [**the remarks** *in poor taste*]
   (c) [**you** *the best candidate*]

Such clauses comprise a (bold-printed) nominal or pronominal subject and an (italicised) adjectival, prepositional or nominal predicate. Although they are verbless, it is interesting to note that they can be paraphrased by infinitive clauses containing the copula (i.e. 'linking verb') *be*. Thus, the bracketed small clauses in (63) are paraphraseable as the infinitival TPs containing the underlined string *to be* in (64):

(64)   I consider
   (a) [**the article** <u>to be</u> *full of good ideas*]
   (b) [**the remarks** <u>to be</u> *in poor taste*]
   (c) [**you** <u>to be</u> *the best candidate*]

This raises the possibility that small clauses like those bracketed in (63) have the same TP structure as infinitival clauses like those bracketed in (64), except that they contain a null T and a null V, with the null T being a silent counterpart of infinitival *to* and the null V being a null counterpart of the verb *be*. If so, then the two types of complement clause bracketed in (63) and (64) have essentially parallel structures (shown in 65a and 65b below), differing only in that the small clause structure (65b) contains a null counterpart of infinitival *to* and a null counterpart of the verb *be*:

(65)

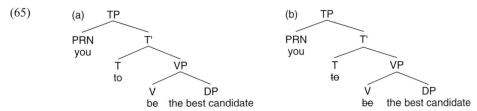

The verb *be* in (65b) can arguably be unpronounced because it has minimal semantic content; and since the overt infinitive particle *to* requires a complement headed by an overt verb in the infinitive form, it is plausible to suppose that if *be* is unpronounced, the infinitive particle *to* must be unpronounced as well.

The null T and null V analysis in (65b) gains plausibility from the observation that there are other types of infinitive clause like those in (66) below which allow a null spellout for the (underlined) copula verb *be* and the infinitive particle *to*:

(66)   He seems
    (a) (to be) *very fond of her*
    (b) (to be) *in a bad mood*
    (c) (to be) *the best candidate*

Moreover, further support for the null T and null V analysis comes from the observation that a small clause like that bracketed in (67a) below can be negated by *not* in precisely the same way as the corresponding *to be* clause in (67b):

(67) (a)   I consider [this *not* the best outcome]
     (b)   I consider [this *not* **to be** the best outcome]

Moreover, just as *to be* clauses like that bracketed in (68a) below allow an expletive *there* subject, so too small clauses like that bracketed in (68b) also allow an expletive subject:

(68) (a)   I consider [*there* **to be** no reason to take the threats seriously]
     (b)   I consider [*there* no reason to take the threats seriously]

Given that (as we see from examples such as 62a and 68a) expletive *there* typically occurs as the subject of a TP with a VP complement headed by the verb *be*, small clauses like that bracketed in (68b) with an expletive *there* subject provide evidence for a null T and null V analysis under which (e.g.) the expletive small clause in (68b) is a TP with the structure shown below:

(69)   I consider [$_{TP}$ there [$_T$ ~~to~~] [$_{VP}$ [$_V$ ~~be~~] no reason to take the threats seriously]]

Such small clauses are thus reduced infinitival TPs containing a null counterpart of T-*to* and a null counterpart of V-*be*.

A further argument in support of positing a null T constituent in small clauses is that this T constituent (like infinitival *to* in the corresponding *to be* clause) can have independent tense properties of its own – as illustrated by the examples below:

(70) (a)   They are now expecting [the president back tomorrow]
     (b)   They are now expecting [the president *to be* back tomorrow]

In (70b), T-*are* in the main clause has present time reference and hence allows the use of *now*, whereas T-*to* in the bracketed complement clause has future time reference and so allows the use of the future adverb *tomorrow*. Since the bracketed small clause in (70b) also allows *tomorrow*, it is plausible to conclude that it is a TP headed by a null counterpart of T-*to* with future time reference.

The overall conclusion to be drawn from this section is that there is evidence for analysing bare (i.e. *to*-less) infinitive clauses and small clauses as TPs headed by a null counterpart of infinitival *to*, and also containing a null counterpart of the verb *be* in the case of small clauses. This reinforces the TP Hypothesis (30), whereby all clauses contain a TP constituent headed by an (overt or silent) T.

4.7   Null C in finite clauses

The overall conclusion to be drawn from our discussion in §§4.3–4.6 is that all finite and infinitive clauses contain an overt or null T constituent which projects into TP (with the subject of the clause occupying the specifier position within TP). However, given that clauses can be introduced by complementisers such as *if/whether/that/for*, a natural question to ask is whether bare (i.e. apparently complementiserless) clauses can likewise be argued to be CPs headed by a null complementiser. In this connection, consider the following:

(71) (a)   We didn't know [*if* he had resigned]
     (b)   We didn't know [*that* he had resigned]
     (c)   We didn't know [he had resigned]

The bracketed complement clause is interpreted as interrogative in type in (71a) and declarative in type in (71b), and it is plausible to suppose that clause type is determined by the nature of the complementiser introducing the clause. If so, the bracketed clause is interrogative in type in (71a) because it is introduced by the interrogative complementiser *if* and is declarative in type in (71b) because it is introduced by the declarative complementiser *that*.

But now consider the bare clause bracketed in (71c): this can only be interpreted as declarative in type (not as interrogative), so (71c) is synonymous with (71b) and not with (71a). Why should this be? One answer is to suppose that the bracketed clause in (71c) is a CP headed by a null complementiser (below symbolised as ø) and that the bracketed complement clauses in (71a,b,c) have the structure (72) below:

(72)

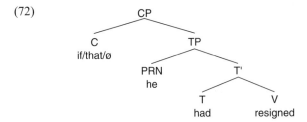

Given the analysis in (72), we can then say that (in structures like those bracketed in 71) clause type is determined by the nature of the head C of the overall CP; in (71a) the bracketed clause is a CP headed by the interrogative complementiser *if* and so is interrogative in type; in (71b) it is a CP headed by the declarative complementiser *that* and so is declarative in type; and in (71c) it is a CP headed by a null complementiser. If we suppose that the null complementiser introducing the finite clause bracketed in (71c) is inherently declarative, this will account for why the bracketed clause in (71c) has the same declarative interpretation as the *that*-clause in (71b). More generally, the **null complementiser** analysis would enable us to arrive at a uniform characterisation of clauses as CPs, in accordance with the CP Hypothesis below (to be modified slightly in §4.10):

(73)   **CP Hypothesis**
            All clauses are CPs.

We can then suppose that in a CP, clause type is signalled by the nature of the (overt or null) complementiser introducing the clause (though this idea will be refined towards the end of this section).

    Empirical evidence in support of positing that bare finite clauses like that bracketed in (71c) are CPs headed by a null complementiser comes from coordination data in relation to sentences such as:

(74)   We didn't know [*he had resigned*] or [**that he had been accused of corruption**]

In (74), the italicised bare clause has been coordinated with a bold-printed clause which is clearly a CP since it is introduced by the overt complementiser *that*. If we make the traditional assumption that only constituents of the same type can be coordinated, it follows that the italicised clause *he had resigned* in (74) must be a CP headed by a null complementiser because it has been coordinated with a bold-printed clause headed by the overt complementiser *that* – as shown in simplified form in (75) below:

(75)   We didn't know [*ø he had resigned*] or [**that he had been accused of corruption**]

Thus, evidence from coordination provides support for the postulation of a null complementiser in seemingly complementiser-less finite clauses. More generally, data like (75) lend empirical support to the CP Hypothesis (73).

Further evidence in support of positing that bare finite clauses are CPs comes from data such as the following:

(76) (a)   We didn't *know* [(**that**) he had resigned]
    (b)   [**That/*ø** he had resigned], we simply didn't *know*
    (c)   What we didn't *know* was [**that/*ø** he had resigned]
    (d)   We didn't *know*, <u>until we read the story in the paper</u>, [**that/*ø** he had resigned]
    (e)   We didn't *know* that he had been accused of corruption, nor [**that/*ø** he had resigned]
    (f)   Mary knew that he had been accused of corruption and Jim ~~knew~~ [**that/*ø** he had resigned]

In (76a), the bracketed complement clause immediately follows its italicised *selector* (i.e. the verb which selects the bracketed clause as its complement), and can either be bare, or introduced by the overt complementiser *that*. However when the same complement clause is fronted (as in 76b), it becomes obligatory to use *that*. Likewise, if the complement clause is focused in a pseudo-cleft sentence like (76c), it is once again obligatory to use *that*. Similarly, if the complement clause is separated from its selecting verb *know* by intervening material like that underlined in (76d), it is again obligatory to use *that*. In addition, if the bracketed complement clause is a non-initial conjunct in a coordinate structure as in (76e), it is again obligatory to use *that*. Furthermore, if the selector undergoes ellipsis (as when Gapping deletes ~~knew~~ in 76f), *that* is again obligatory. What all of this suggests is that the bracketed complement clause in all the examples in (76) is a CP, and that its head C is obligatorily spelled out as *that* in most environments, but can optionally be given a null spellout if it is immediately adjacent to (and c-commanded by) an overt occurrence of its selector – hence only in (76a) where it immediately follows (and is c-commanded by) the overt selector *know*.

An interesting question arising from the analysis outlined above is why the null complementiser in clauses like that bracketed in (71c) should be interpreted as declarative. One plausible answer to this question is to take the null complementiser to be a variant of the declarative complementiser *that*, exhibiting exactly the same behaviour as *that*. One way of implementing this analysis (which dates back more than half a century) is to take *that* to be present in the syntax, and to undergo an optional *that*-deletion operation in the phonological component when *that* is c-commanded by and immediately adjacent to an overt selector: since these conditions are met in (76a) but not in (76b–f), it follows that (76a) is the only sentence in (76) which allows the complementiser to have a null spellout. On this view, *that* and its null counterpart are simply two different spellout forms of the same complementiser.

However, an alternative analysis would be to suppose that the overt complementiser *that* and its null counterpart *ø* are in fact distinct lexical items with distinct properties (rather than a single item with two different spellouts). For example, if the null complementiser (unlike *that*) is a clitic which needs to attach to an immediately adjacent c-commanding overt host of an appropriate kind, and if the host for the null clitic complementiser has to be the selector, we can handle the data in (76) straightforwardly, because only in (76a) *We didn't know [ø he had resigned]* is the null complementiser immediately adjacent to and c-commanded by an overt selector (*know*).

Both analyses outlined in the preceding paragraph (one treating the null complementiser as a variant of *that*, the other treating it as a separate item) seem equally plausible at first sight. However, below I will highlight a number of key differences between *that* and the null complementiser which argue in favour of treating them as two distinct items.

One such difference is the following. Although *that* can freely be replaced by the null complementiser *ø* in an indicative clause like that bracketed in (77a) below, for conservative speakers *that* is obligatory in a subjunctive clause like that bracketed in (77b) and cannot be replaced by a null complementiser:

(77) (a)   She said [CP [C *that/ø*] she was tired]
     (b)   It is imperative [CP [C *that/*ø*] he be here on time]

The contrast in (77) suggests that (for conservative speakers) the overt complementiser *that* marks finiteness (and so can occur either in a finite indicative clause or in a finite subjunctive clause), whereas the null complementiser *ø* marks indicative mood and hence can only occur in an indicative clause. If so, the two would appear to be different items with different properties.

Further evidence for treating *that* and its null counterpart as distinct items comes from contrasts such as the following (found in conservative varieties of English):

(78) (a)   Lord Profumo *denied* [**that/ø** he had been having an affair]
     (b)   Lord Profumo's *denial* [**that/*ø** he had been having an affair] cost him his job

(79) (a)   The President was *confident* [**that/ø** he would be re-elected]
     (b)   The President's *confidence* [**that/*ø** he would be re-elected] proved to be misplaced

Whereas the overt complementiser *that* can head a CP selected as the complement of a verb like *denied*, or an adjective like *confident* or of a noun like *denial/confidence*, by contrast the null complementiser *ø* can only head a CP selected by a verb or adjective, not a CP selected by a noun. These selectional differences again suggest that the complementisers are distinct items.

This conclusion is reinforced by lexical differences in the items which can select a CP headed by the two types of complementiser. As we see from the examples below, it is not the case that all adjectives can select a CP headed by a null complementiser. Although *clear* selects a complement headed by either *that* or a null complementiser, by contrast *undeniable* only selects a complement headed by *that*:

(80) (a)   It is **clear** [*that* he was framed]
   (b)   It is **clear** [ø he was framed]
   (c)   It is **undeniable** [*that* he was framed]
   (d)   *It is **undeniable** [ø he was framed]

If the complementiser *that* is a different lexical item from the null complementiser ø, we can account for this contrast by supposing that the lexical entry for a word like *clear* specifies that it can select a CP complement headed by either *that* or ø, whereas the entry for a word like *undeniable* specifies that it can select a CP complement headed by *that* but not ø. By contrast, if we take the null complementiser to arise from deletion of *that*, it would not be obvious why *that*-deletion should be able to apply in structures like (80b) but not in those like (80d). Sentences like those in (80) provide evidence of selectional differences between the two types of complementiser which suggest that we should treat the null indicative complementiser ø as a separate item from *that*. (I note in passing that liberal speakers allow the use of a null complementiser after certain types of selector in subjunctive clauses and noun complement clauses, and for such speakers the relevant restrictions seem to be lexical: for example, I personally allow a null complementiser after *imperative* but not *command*, and after *confidence* but not *denial*.)

   There are a number of other differences between *that* and the null complementiser which provide additional evidence that the two are distinct items (and not simply variants of each other). For one thing (in standard varieties of English), the head C position in embedded wh-clauses like those bracketed below can contain a null complementiser, but cannot contain the overt complementiser *that*:

(81) (a)   I wonder [$_{CP}$ **where** [$_C$ ø/*that] she has gone]
   (b)   You can't imagine [$_{CP}$ **what a wonderful time** [$_C$ ø/*that] we had]
   (c)   This is something [$_{CP}$ **which** [$_C$ ø/*that] I simply can't accept]

The bracketed clauses in (81) are wh-clauses in the sense that they are clauses which begin with a bold-printed wh-constituent (i.e. a constituent comprising or containing a wh-word like *who/what/which/why/where/when*, etc.): the bracketed CP is an interrogative clause in (81a), an exclamative clause in (81b) and a relative clause in (81c); furthermore, as we will see in Chapters 5 and 6, the wh-constituent occupies the specifier position within CP (i.e. spec-CP) in such clauses. The fact that only the null complementiser ø (and not the overt complementiser *that*) can occupy the head C position in a wh-CP (i.e. in a CP with a wh-constituent as its specifier) provides further distributional evidence that the overt C *that* and the null C ø are different items with different properties: one way of capturing this difference is to suppose that a complementiser must undergo (invisible) wh-agreement with a wh-specifier, and that a null complementiser can undergo this type of agreement, but the overt complementiser *that* is inert and cannot.

An alternative account of the difference between the null complementiser ø and its overt counterpart *that* would be to treat the null complementiser/C as a clitic which attaches to an appropriate kind of selector/S at PF when S immediately precedes and c-commands C (e.g. C-ø cliticises to *clear* in 80b). However, the clitic analysis proves problematic for sentences like those in (81). For example, in (81a), the bracketed complement clause is selected by the verb *wonder*, and yet the null complementiser cannot cliticise onto *wonder* because cliticisation requires immediate adjacency and the intervening wh-word *where* will block cliticisation. This suggests that we need to adopt an alternative approach to null complementisers. In work in the 1980s, the restrictions on the use of null/empty complementisers were taken to be the consequence of a more general constraint on empty categories of all kinds which can be given the highly simplified formulation below:

(82)   **Empty Category Principle/ECP**
          Every empty category must be licensed.

Although (to simplify exposition) I shall not go into further technical details here, it should be noted that empty categories can be licensed in a number of ways. In the case of a sentence like (76a) 'We didn't *know* [ø he had resigned]', the empty complementiser can be lexically licensed by being immediately adjacent to (and c-commanded by) a lexical head (i.e. a head which is not a functional category) like *know*. By contrast, in wh-clauses like those bracketed in (81), the null complementiser can be licensed by invisible wh-agreement with the wh-constituent serving as its specifier.

Another difference between the overt complementiser *that* and the null complementiser ø is illustrated in the following structures:

(83) (a)   I don't think [CP **that/ø** [TP *John* has done the assignment]]
     (b)   *John* I don't think [CP **ø/*that** [TP --- has done the assignment]]

In (83a), the italicised nominal *John* is the subject of the bracketed embedded clause and remains in situ as the specifier of the TP headed by T-*has*; in this kind of structure, the head C position of the embedded CP can be filled either by the overt complementiser *that* or by the null complementiser ø. In (83b), however, *John* is moved to the front of the sentence in order to mark it as focused, and this leaves the subject/spec-TP position in the embedded clause *empty* (the relevant position being marked by the gap --- in 83b): in this kind of structure, the embedded CP can only be introduced by the null complementiser ø, not by the overt complementiser *that*. Chomsky and Lasnik (1977) argued that the ungrammaticality of *that* in a sentence like (83b) is attributable to violation of a PF filter/constraint which can be characterised as follows:

(84)   **COMP-Trace Filter/CTF**
          Any structure in which an overt complementiser is immediately adjacent to
          and c-commands a trace (i.e. a gap left behind by a moved constituent) is
          filtered out as ill-formed at PF.

The fact that the complementiser *that* is subject to CTF but the null complementiser is exempt from it provides further evidence for treating the two as distinct items. (I note in passing that an interesting consequence of the adjacency condition in 84 is that sentences like 83b are acceptable if other material intervenes between the complementiser and trace – like that underlined in '*John*, I don't think that <u>at the present time</u> - - - has done the assignment.')

The overall conclusion which our discussion here leads us to is that the finite complementisers *that* and *ø* are distinct items – *that* introducing indicative or subjunctive clauses and being unable to occur in wh-clauses, and the null complementiser *ø* introducing only indicative clauses and being able to occur in wh-clauses.

So far in this section, I have argued that seemingly complementiserless finite complement clauses are introduced by a null complementiser *ø*. However, the CP Hypothesis in (73) would suggest that not only finite *complement* clauses but also finite *root* clauses (i.e. main/principal/independent finite clauses) like those below should be analysed as CPs:

(85)   SPEAKER A: I am feeling thirsty
         SPEAKER B: Do you feel like a Coke?

The sentence produced by speaker A in (85) is declarative in type (by virtue of being a statement). If clause type is determined by the nature of the head C of CP, this suggests that such declarative main clauses are CPs headed by a null declarative complementiser. And indeed, theoretical considerations require us to assume this, if we suppose that syntactic structures are constrained by a principle of UG/Universal Grammar such as the following:

(86)   **Structural Uniformity Principle**
         All constituents of the same type belong to the same category.

Since declarative *that*-clauses like that bracketed in (71b) *We didn't know* [*that he had resigned*] are clearly CPs, it follows from the Structural Uniformity Principle (86) that all other declarative clauses (including declarative main clauses) must be CPs. This leads to the conclusion that a declarative root clause like that produced by speaker A in (85) is a CP headed by a null declarative complementiser. If so (as I shall assume), (85A) has the following structure:

(87)

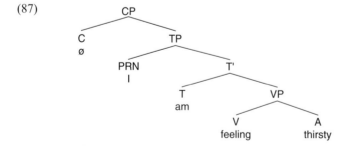

Under the CP analysis of root/main clauses in (87), the declarative force of the overall sentence is attributed to the sentence being a CP headed by a null declarative complementiser. This underlines a further distributional difference between the null C-*ø* and the overt C-*that*: whereas C-*that* is restricted to introducing embedded clauses, the null C-*ø* can introduce both complement clause structures like (72) and root clause structures like (87).

An analysis such as (87) which posits that main clauses are CPs headed by a complementiser marking clause type gains cross-linguistic plausibility from the fact that we find languages like Arabic in which declarative and interrogative main clauses can be introduced by an overt complementiser, as the examples below illustrate:

(88) (a)   *?inna*   l-walada   taraka   l-bayta (adapted from Ross 1970: 245)
            That   the-boy   left   the-house
            'The boy left the house' (declarative)

   (b)   *Hal*   taraka   l-waladu   l-bayta?
            If   left   the-boy   the-house
            'Did the boy leave the house?' (interrogative)

Moreover (as we will see in more detail in §5.2), there is some evidence from sentences like (89) below that inverted auxiliaries in main-clause yes–no questions occupy the head C position of CP in English:

(89)   SPEAKER A: What were you going to ask me?
            SPEAKER B: (a) *If* **you** feel like a Coke
                        (b) *Do* **you** feel like a Coke?
                        (c) **If do* **you** feel like a Coke?

The fact that the inverted auxiliary *do* in (89b) occupies the same pre-subject position (in front of the bold-printed subject **you**) as the complementiser *if* in (89a) and the fact that *if* and *do* are mutually exclusive (as we see from the ungrammaticality of structures like 89c) suggest that inverted auxiliaries (like complementisers) occupy the head C position of CP. This in turn means that main-clause questions are CPs headed by a C constituent containing an inverted auxiliary.

Interestingly, an interrogative main clause can be coordinated with a declarative main clause, as we see from (90) below:

(90)   [I am feeling thirsty], but [*should I save my last Coke till later*]?

In (90) we have two (bracketed) main/root clauses joined together by the coordinating conjunction *but*. The second (italicised) conjunct *should I save my last Coke till later?* is an interrogative CP containing an inverted auxiliary in the head C position of CP. Given the traditional assumption that only constituents which belong to the same category can be coordinated, it follows that the first conjunct *I am feeling thirsty* must also be a CP; and since it contains no overt complementiser, it must be headed by a null complementiser – precisely as assumed in (87) above. And, as noted earlier, clause-typing considerations lead to the same conclusion (i.e. a main clause must contain a CP constituent in order for us to be able to type the clause as declarative, interrogative, exclamative, etc.).

Our discussion in this section has led to the conclusion that English has a null complementiser which can be used to introduce both root and embedded indicative clauses. In structures like (87) above, the null complementiser serves to mark the sentence as declarative in type/force (i.e. to indicate that it is a statement). However, if English has two different declarative complementisers (the overt complementiser *that* and its null counterpart *ø*) and if both can introduce embedded clauses (as we see from sentences like 'He said *that/ø* he was tired'), an obvious question to ask is why only a null complementiser and not an overt one like *that* can introduce a root clause. The relevant restriction against using an overt complementiser to introduce a root clause in English seems to extend from *that* to other complementisers, as we see from the ungrammaticality of root clauses like those below containing an overt (italicised) complementiser:

(91) (a)   *That it is raining again
     (b)   *If you two know each other?
     (c)   *Whether you apologised?

We can account for the ungrammaticality of the relevant structures by supposing that English imposes the following constraint on the use of overt complementisers:

(92)   **Root Complementiser Constraint**
        No overt complementiser can be the head of a root projection in a language like English.

(where a root projection is the highest projection in a structure). A constraint like (92) would then account for why the head C position of the root CP in a structure like (87) can't be filled by *that* but rather has to be occupied by a null complementiser.

Thus far, I have argued that English has a null complementiser which can be used in both root and embedded declarative clauses in English. However, the use of a null complementiser is not restricted to declarative clauses alone (like that bracketed in 93a below) below, but is also found in other types of clause like those bracketed in (93b,c) (repeated from 81a,b above):

(93) (a)   I know [CP [C ø] she is hiding something]
     (b)   I wonder [CP **where** [C ø] she has gone]
     (c)   You can't imagine [CP **what a great time** [C ø] we are having]

Although the bracketed CP in (93a) is indeed declarative in type (as we see from the fact that we can use declarative *that* in place of the null complementiser), this is not true of the bracketed wh-clauses in (93b,c). On the contrary, the bracketed clause in (93b) is interrogative, and the bracketed clause in (93c) is exclamative. How can we account for this?

One way would be to posit that English has three distinct types of null indicative complementiser: a declarative one used in clauses like that bracketed in (93a), an interrogative one used in clauses like that bracketed in (93b), and an exclamative one used in clauses like that bracketed in (93c). However, this would result in increasing the number of null indicative complementisers found in English from one to three, in violation of the Economy Principle in §1.4 which requires us to minimise the number of different types of constituent which we posit. An alternative (more economical) approach would be to posit that English has a single null indicative complementiser, which serves simply to mark the clause containing it as indicative in mood. But how can we then account for the fact that a clause containing a null complementiser is sometimes interpreted as declarative in type, sometimes as interrogative and sometimes as exclamative?

Anticipating the discussion in the next two chapters, let us suppose that the bold-printed wh-constituents in interrogative/exclamative clauses like those bracketed in (93b,c) above occupy the specifier position within CP, but that the CP in the declarative clause bracketed in (93a) contains no specifier. This means that the bracketed complement clauses in (93a–c) will be CPs with the structures shown in (94a–c) below:

(94)

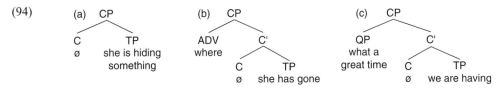

Let us further suppose that clause typing is determined by the following condition:

(95)   **Clause Typing Condition**
A CP is typed as interrogative (i.e. interpreted as interrogative in type in the semantic component) if it has an interrogative specifier, exclamative if it has an exclamative specifier... etc. Otherwise, a CP headed by an indicative complementiser is interpreted as declarative in type by default.

This means that (in accordance with 95) the CP in (93b/94b) will be interpreted as interrogative in type by virtue of having the interrogative specifier *where*. Similarly, the CP in (93c/94c) will be interpreted as exclamative in type, because it has the exclamative specifier *what a great time*. By contrast, the CP in (93a/94a) will be interpreted as declarative by default – i.e. by virtue of not having an interrogative or exclamative specifier.

As we will see in more detail in the next chapter, the Clause Typing Condition (95) has interesting implications for the structure of yes–no questions like (85B) *Do you feel like a Coke?* It implies that such questions contain an (invisible) interrogative constituent in spec-CP which types the relevant CP as a yes–no question. This idea gains plausibility from the observation that yes–no questions in Shakespearean English could be introduced by the interrogative adverb *whether* – as we see from:

(96) (a)   *Whether* **had** you rather lead mine eyes or eye your master's heels? (Mrs
Page, *Merry Wives of Windsor*, III.ii)

   (b)   *Whether* **dost** thou profess thyself a knave or a fool? (Lafeu, *All's Well That
Ends Well*, IV.v)

As we saw in §2.9, *whether* in present-day English functions as an interrogative
complementiser occupying the head C position of CP in embedded clauses and
cannot introduce main clauses like (91c) **Whether you apologised?* because this
would violate the Root Complementiser Constraint (92). However, in Shakespearean
English, *whether* functioned as an interrogative wh-adverb (like *when/why/where*,
etc.) and so could introduce not only embedded clauses but also main clauses like
those in (96). This means that in the same way as the wh-adverb *where* occupies spec-
CP in a root wh-question like *Where has she gone?* so too *whether* occupies the
specifier position in CP in a Shakespearean English root yes–no question like (96b).
Accordingly, the two types of question have essentially parallel structures, as shown
in (97) below:

(97)

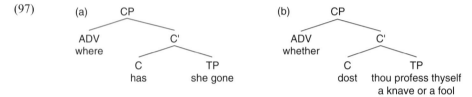

There are clear meaning differences between a wh-question structure like (97a) and a
yes–no question structure like (97b). More specifically, *where* asks for the identity of a
place, and hence an appropriate reply to a *where* question would be a locative
expression like 'Home' or 'To the supermarket'. By contrast, *whether* asks for the
truth value of a proposition (i.e. it asks if a given proposition is true or false), and
hence an appropriate reply would be 'Yes' or 'No'. Using the relevant technical
terminology, we can say that *where* functions as a **wh-question operator** in a
structure like (97a), and *whether* as a **yes–no question operator** in a structure like
(97b).

   The occurrence of the overt question operator *whether* in Shakespearean yes–
no questions like (96) suggests that we can treat yes–no questions in present-day
English as having essentially the same structure as their Shakespearean counterparts, except that present-day English uses a null/silent yes–no question operator
in place of *whether*. If we take this null operator to be adverbial in nature (like
whether), (85B) *Do you feel like a Coke?* will be a CP with the structure (98)
below, where Op_{YNQ} denotes a silent yes–no question operator:

(98)

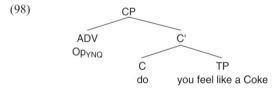

Under this analysis, the present-day CP in (98) and the Shakespearean CP in (97b) will be typed as yes–no questions by the Clause Typing Condition (95) because they both contain an adverbial yes–no question operator in spec-CP: the only difference is that the operator is overtly spelled out as *whether* in (97b) but has a silent spellout in (98). We will return to look at yes–no questions in much more detail in the next chapter, so I will have no more to say about them for the time being. (A point to remember from our discussion in §2.9 is that *whether* in present-day English no long functions as a yes–no question operator in spec-CP, but rather has become a yes–no question complementiser occupying the head C position of CP: we'll return to this in the next chapter.)

The conclusion that our discussion in this section leads to is that all finite clauses have the status of CPs introduced by a complementiser, in accordance with the CP Hypothesis (73). Finite complement clauses are CPs headed either by an overt complementiser like *that/if/whether* or by the null indicative complementiser *ø*. Finite root/main clauses are CPs headed by a C which contains an inverted auxiliary if the clause is interrogative, and a null complementiser otherwise. Clause type is determined by the Clause Typing Condition (92), with any indicative clause which does not have an interrogative or exclamative (etc.) specifier being interpreted as declarative in type by default.

4.8   Null C in infinitive clauses

The overall conclusion to be drawn from our discussion in §4.7 is that all finite clauses (whether main clauses or complement clauses) are CPs headed by an (overt or null) complementiser. But what about non-finite clauses? It seems clear that *for-to* infinitive clauses such as that bracketed in (99a) below are CPs since they are introduced by the infinitival complementiser *for*, but it is far less clear what the status is of the (bracketed) infinitive complement clause found after verbs like *want* in sentences such as (99b):

(99) (a)   I will arrange [*for* them to see a specialist]
     (b)   She wanted [*him* to apologise]

At first sight, it might seem as if the bracketed complement clause in a sentence like (99b) can't be a CP, since it isn't introduced by the infinitival complementiser *for*. However, the type of infinitive complement bracketed in (99b) can be coordinated with a CP introduced by *for* in sentences such as the following:

(100)   I want [Mary to come to Japan] and [for her to meet my parents]

This suggests that the infinitive complement of *want* is always a CP, and that the head C of the relevant CP sometimes has an overt spellout as *for* and sometimes has a null spellout. This in turn would mean that the bracketed complement of *want* in structures like (99b) is a CP headed by a variant of *for* which ultimately receives a silent spellout in the PF component (below symbolised as *for*) so that

(99b) has the skeletal structure (101) below (simplified by showing only those parts of the structure directly relevant to the discussion at hand):

(101)   She wanted [CP [C ~~for~~] [TP him [T to] apologise]]

We can then say that the infinitive subject *him* is assigned accusative case by the complementiser ~~for~~ in structures like (101) in exactly the same way as the accusative subject *them* is assigned accusative case by the complementiser *for* in the bracketed complement clause in (99a). (How case-marking works will be discussed in more detail in §4.9.) One way of accounting for why the complementiser isn't overtly spelled out as *for* in structures like (101) is to suppose that it is given a silent spellout (and thereby has its phonetic features deleted) when introducing the complement of a verb like *want*: this is why verbs like *want* are referred to in earlier work as *for*-deletion verbs. An alternative account is to suppose that *for* has a null counterpart *for*, and that the two are separate items which share many properties in common (e.g. case-marking) but have a somewhat different distribution.

For speakers of varieties of English like my own (British) variety, the null counterpart of *for* must obligatorily be used when the relevant complement clause immediately follows a verb like *want*, but use of the overt variant *for* is required when the complement clause is separated from *want* in some way – e.g. when the two are separated by an (underlined) intervening expression such as *more than anything*, as the examples below illustrate:

(102) (a)   *<u>More than anything</u>, she **wanted** *for him to apologise*
    (b)   <u>More than anything</u>, she **wanted** *him to apologise*
    (c)   She **wanted** <u>more than anything</u> *for him to apologise*
    (d)   *She **wanted** <u>more than anything</u> *him to apologise*

Likewise, when the complement of *want* is in focus position in a pseudo-cleft sentence as in (103) below, it is obligatory for the complementiser to have an overt spellout as *for* (because it does not immediately follow the verb *want*, but rather immediately follows the copula *was*):

(103) (a)   What she **wanted** was *for him to apologise*
    (b)   *What she **wanted** was *him to apologise*

It would seem, therefore, that the use of a null counterpart of *for* is subject to much the same strict adjacency requirement as the use of a null counterpart of indicative *that* in complement clauses (discussed in §4.7): that is, in consequence of the Empty Category Principle (82), a null complementiser must be c-commanded by (and immediately adjacent to) an appropriate licenser (like the verb *want*).

Interestingly, not all *for*-deletion verbs behave exactly like *want*: for example, in my own (British) variety of English, the verb *prefer* optionally (rather than obligatorily) allows deletion of *for* when it immediately follows *prefer* – cf.

(104) (a)   We would very much **prefer** *for you to be there*
    (b)   We would very much **prefer** *you to be there*

The precise set of verbs which optionally allow (or obligatorily require) use of a null counterpart of *for* when it immediately follows the verb seems to vary from one variety of English to another, and perhaps even from one speaker to another.

Having looked at *for*-deletion verbs which select an infinitival complement with an accusative subject, let's now turn to look at **control** infinitive clauses with a null PRO subject like that bracketed below:

(105)   I will arrange [PRO to see a specialist]

What I shall argue here is that control clauses which have a null PRO subject are introduced by a null infinitival complementiser. However, the null complementiser introducing control clauses differs from the null complementiser *ø* found in structures like *want/prefer* [*ø someone to do something*] in that it never surfaces as an overt form like *for*, and hence is inherently null (and this may well be related to the PRO subject of a control clause also being inherently null). There is, however, parallelism between the structure of a *for* infinitive clause like that bracketed in (99a) above, and that of a control infinitive clause like that bracketed in (105), in that they are both CPs and they both have much the same internal structure, as shown in (106a,b) below (simplified by not showing the internal structure of the VP *see a specialist*):

(106)   (a)   CP   (b)   CP

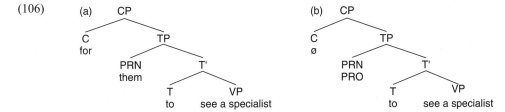

The two types of clause thus have essentially the same CP+TP+VP structure and differ only in that a *for* infinitive clause like (106a) has an overt *for* complementiser and an overt accusative subject like *them*, whereas a control infinitive clause like (106b) has a null *ø* complementiser and a null PRO subject.

Some evidence in support of claiming that a control clause with a null PRO subject is a CP introduced by a null complementiser comes from coordination data in relation to sentences such as the following:

(107)   I will arrange [*to see a specialist*] and [**for my wife to see one at the same time**]

The fact that the italicised control infinitive can be conjoined with the bold-printed CP headed by *for* suggests that control infinitives must be CPs (if only the same types of constituent can be conjoined).

Further evidence in support of the CP status of control infinitives comes from the observation that they can be focused in **pseudo-cleft sentences**. In this connection, consider the contrast below:

(108) (a)   What I'll try and arrange is [*for you to see a specialist*]

    (b)   *What I'll try and arrange for is [*you to see a specialist*]

    (c)   What I'll try and arrange is [*PRO to see a specialist*]

The grammaticality of (108a) suggests that a CP like *for you to see a specialist* can occupy focus position in a pseudo-cleft sentence, whereas conversely the ungrammaticality of (105b) suggests that a TP like *you to see a specialist* cannot. If CP can be focused in pseudo-clefts but TP cannot, then the fact that a control infinitive like *PRO to see a specialist* can be focused in a pseudo-cleft like (105c) suggests that it must have the same CP status as (105a) – precisely as the analysis in (106b) above claims.

Overall, the conclusion which the analysis outlined in this section leads to is that infinitive complements containing the complementiser *for* (or its null counterpart *for*) are CPs, and so are control infinitives (which contain a null complementiser *ø* as well as a null *PRO* subject).

4.9   Null complementisers and case-marking

In this section, we will see that further evidence in support of the postulation of null complementisers comes from the observation that they play a central role in relation to the case-marking of subjects. Noun and pronoun expressions in English must all carry a morphological **case** (nominative like *he*, accusative like *him*, or genitive like *his*) which is assigned to them by a particular **case-assigner** in virtue of the particular position they occupy in the structure containing them (this phenomenon being termed **structural case-marking**). In this section, we take a brief look at case-marking in English. The discussion here will be directly related to the syntax of null constituents (which is the central theme of this chapter), since one of the conclusions reached is that null complementisers can assign case to subjects.

Let's begin by asking how the italicised subject of the bracketed infinitive complement clause in (109) below is assigned accusative case:

(109)   I would much prefer [for/~~for~~ *him* to meet them]

(In such structures, the complementiser *for* can have either an overt spellout as *for* or a null spellout as *for* in varieties of English like mine.) Since *for* is a prepositional complementiser (and the preposition *for* assigns accusative case to its complement – e.g. to its complement *me* in a sentence like 'She bought it **for** *me*'), it seems plausible to suppose that the infinitive subject *him* is assigned accusative case by the prepositional complementiser *for*. items which assign accusative case are traditionally said to be **transitive**. Let us therefore suppose that the infinitive subject *him* is assigned accusative case by the transitive complementiser *for/~~for~~* in (109). But *how?* We've already seen that the relation c-command plays a central role in the description of a wide range of phenomena, including the binding of anaphors, the licensing of polarity items, and cliticisation. So, it seems plausible that c-command is also central to case assignment. Reasoning along these lines, let's suppose that accusative case assignment works along the lines shown below in English:

(110)   **Accusative Case Assignment**
          A transitive head assigns accusative case to a noun or pronoun expression which it c-commands.

In addition, let's suppose that the following UG principle governs the application of grammatical (and other kinds of linguistic) operations:

(111)   **Earliness Principle**
          Operations apply as early in a derivation as possible.

In the light of (110) and (111), let's look at the derivation of the bracketed complement clause in (109). The first step is for the verb *meet* to be merged with its pronoun complement *them* to form the VP below:

(112)

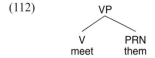

Meet is a transitive verb which c-commands the pronoun *them*. Since (110) specifies that a transitive head assigns accusative case to a pronoun which it c-commands, and since the Earliness Principle (111) specifies that operations like case assignment must apply as early as possible in a derivation, it follows that the pronoun *them* will be assigned accusative case by the transitive verb *meet* at the stage of derivation in (112).

The derivation then continues by merging the infinitive particle *to* with the VP in (112), so forming the T-bar *to meet them*. The resulting T-bar is merged with its subject *him* to form the TP *him to meet them*. This TP in turn is merged with the complementiser *for/for* to form the CP shown in (113) below:

(113)

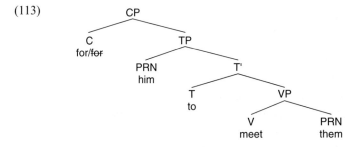

For/for is a transitive (prepositional) complementiser and c-commands the infinitive subject *him*. Since (110) specifies that a transitive head assigns accusative case to a pronoun which it c-commands, and since the Earliness Principle (111) specifies that operations like case assignment must apply as early as possible in a derivation, it follows that the pronoun *him* will be assigned accusative case by the transitive complementiser *for/for* at the stage of derivation shown in (113).

Having looked at how accusative subjects are case-marked, let's now turn to look at the case-marking of nominative subjects. In this connection, consider the case-marking of the subjects italicised below (where *ø* is a null indicative complementiser):

(114)   *He* may suspect [that/*ø she* is lying]

Consider first how the complement clause subject *she* is assigned case. The bracketed complement clause in (114) has the structure (115) below:

(115)

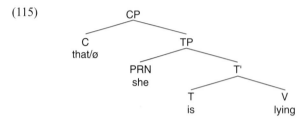

If we are to develop a unitary account of case-marking, it is plausible to suppose that nominative subjects (just like accusative subjects) are assigned case under c-command by an appropriate kind of head. Since the finite complementiser *that/ ø* in (115) c-commands the subject *she*, let's suppose that the pronoun *she* is assigned nominative case by the complementiser *that/ø* (in much the same way as the infinitive subject *him* in (113) is assigned accusative case by the transitive complementiser *for/for*). More specifically, let's posit that nominative case assignment works in the manner described in (116) below:

(116)   **Nominative Case Assignment**
          A finite complementiser assigns nominative case to a noun or pronoun expression which it c-commands.

In (115), the only noun or pronoun expression c-commanded by the finite complementiser *that/ø* is the clause subject *she*, and this is therefore assigned nominative case in accordance with (116).

But how can we account for the main-clause subject *he* in (114) also being assigned nominative case? The answer is that under the CP Hypothesis (73), all finite clauses – including main clauses – are CPs introduced by a complementiser, and if the clause contains no overt complementiser, it is headed by a null complementiser. This being so, the main clause in (114) will have the structure (117) below:

(117)

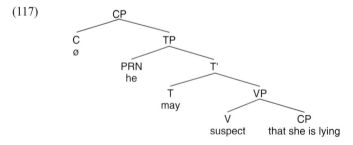

Thus, the overall structure is headed by a null finite indicative complementiser [C ø] in much the same way as the Arabic main clauses in (88) are headed by an overt complementiser, and it is this null finite complementiser which assigns nominative case to the subject *he* in (117) in accordance with (116) above, since the null complementiser c-commands the pronoun *he*. Both CPs in (117) are interpreted as declarative in type (by default) in accordance with the Clause Typing Condition (95).

However, an interesting complication arises in relation to the Arabic data in (88) above. Sentence (88a) is introduced by the transitive finite complementiser *?inna* 'that' and the subject *l-walada* 'the boy' is assigned accusative case in accordance with (110). By contrast, sentence (88b) is introduced by the finite complementiser *hal* 'if': this is intransitive (i.e. non-transitive) and assigns nominative case to the subject *l-waladu* (which therefore carries the nominative ending *-u* rather than the accusative ending *-a*). Such considerations suggest that we need to revise (116) by adding the italicised condition in (118) below:

(118)   **Nominative Case Assignment** (revised)
         An *intransitive* finite complementiser assigns nominative case to a noun or pronoun expression which it c-commands.

Since all English finite complementisers (such as *if, whether, that* and the null indicative complementiser *ø*) are intransitive, all finite clauses in English have nominative subjects.

Having looked at accusative and nominative subjects, let's now turn to consider the null PRO subjects found in control clause structures such as (105) above, repeated as (119a) below, with the bracketed complement clause having the structure shown in (106b) above, repeated as (119b):

(119) (a)   I will arrange [PRO to see a specialist]
      (b)

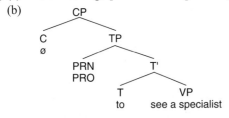

If we suppose that it is a defining characteristic of all pronouns that they carry case, then PRO too must carry case. But what case does PRO carry? The morphological effect of case is to determine how a noun or pronoun expression is spelled out (e.g. as *he, him* or *his*). Since PRO has a null spellout, let us therefore suppose that PRO carries null case. The effect of null case is to ensure that a pronoun is unpronounced – just as the morphological effect of nominative case is to ensure that (e.g.) a third person masculine singular pronoun is pronounced as *he*. But how is PRO assigned null case? If we are to attain a unitary account of case-marking under which a noun or pronoun expression is case-marked by a head which c-commands it, a plausible answer is to suppose that PRO is assigned null case by the complementiser which introduces the clause containing PRO. This means that PRO is assigned null case by the null infinitival complementiser ø in a clause like that bracketed in (120a) below, and by the overt infinitival wh-complementiser *whether* in a clause like that bracketed in (120b):

(120) (a)   I will arrange [CP [C ø] [TP PRO to see a specialist]]
      (b)   I am not sure [CP [C whether] [TP PRO to see a specialist]]

If we suppose that the infinitival complementisers in the bracketed clauses in (120) are intransitive (whereas the infinitival complementiser *for* and its null counterpart *f̶o̶r̶* are transitive), we can posit that null case is assigned in the manner described in (121) below:

(121)   **Null Case Assignment**
         An intransitive non-finite complementiser assigns null case to a noun or pronoun expression which it c-commands.

It follows from (121) that PRO in structures like (119b, 120a, 120b) above will be assigned null case by the (non-finite, intransitive) complementisers ø/*whether* which c-command PRO.

   We can conflate the various claims made about case-marking above into (122) below:

(122)   **Structural Case Assignment Conditions**
         A noun or pronoun expression is assigned
         (i)   accusative case if the closest case assigner c-commanding it is a transitive head (e.g a transitive verb like *meet*, or a transitive preposition like *with*, or a transitive complementiser like *for/f̶o̶r̶*)
         (ii) nominative case if the closest case-assigner c-commanding it is an intransitive finite complementiser (like *that*, or *if*, or *whether* in finite clauses, or the null complementiser introducing bare indicative clauses)
         (iii) null case if the closest case-assigner c-commanding it is an intransitive non-finite complementiser (like ø or *whether* in infinitival control clauses)

If we assume that PRO is the only exponent of null case in English, it follows from (122iii) that control infinitive clauses (which are headed by a null or overt intransitive complementiser under the analysis in 120) will always require a PRO subject.

   What is particularly interesting about our discussion of case-marking here from a theoretical point of view is that it provides yet more evidence for the centrality of the relation c-command in syntax, since a (pro)nominal constituent is case-marked by a c-commanding case-assigner. An important theoretical question to ask at this juncture is why c-command should be such a fundamental relation in syntax. From a Minimalist perspective (since the goal of Minimalism is to utilise only linguistic apparatus which is conceptually necessary), the most principled answer would be one along the following lines. It is clear that the operation Merge (which builds up phrases and sentences out of words) is conceptually necessary, in that (e.g.) to form a prepositional phrase like *to Paris* out of the preposition *to* and the noun *Paris*, we need some operation like Merge which combines the two words together. In order to achieve the Minimalist goal of developing a constrained theory of Universal Grammar/UG which makes use only of constructs which are conceptually necessary, we can suppose that the only kind of syntactic relations which UG permits are those created by the operation Merge. Now, two structural relations created by the operation Merge are **contain(ment)** and c-command: this is because if we merge a head X with a phrase YP to form an XP projection, XP contains X, YP and all the constituents of YP, and X c-commands YP and all the constituents of YP. Minimalist considerations therefore lead us to hypothesise that the containment and c-command relations created by Merge are the only primitive relations in syntax.

Our discussion in this section shows that case-marking phenomena can be accounted for in a principled fashion within a highly constrained Minimalist framework which makes use of the c-command relation which is created by the operation Merge. Note that a number of other grammatical relations which traditional grammars make use of (e.g. relations like subjecthood and objecthood) are not relations which can be used within the Minimalist framework. For example, a typical characterisation of accusative case assignment in traditional grammar is that a transitive verb or preposition assigns accusative case to its object. There are two problems with carrying over such a generalisation into the framework we are using here. The first is that Minimalism is a constrained theory which does not allow us to appeal to the relation objecthood, only to the relations contain and c-command; the second is that the traditional objecthood account of accusative case assignment is empirically inadequate, in that it fails to account for the accusative case-marking of an infinitive subject by a transitive complementiser in structures like (113), because *him* is not the object of the complementiser *for/for* but rather the subject of *to meet them*. As our discussion in later chapters unfolds, it will become clear that there are a number of other syntactic phenomena which can be given a principled description in terms of the relations contain and c-command.

An important detail which remains to be added in relation to our discussion of case in this section is the question of how the italicised constituents in sentences such as those below come to be assigned case:

(123) (a)   *Me*, I'm feeling fine
      (b)   *Him*, everyone knows he's crazy

In such structures, the italicised constituent denotes the **topic** of the sentence (and topics can typically have an *as for* paraphrase, so that (123a) means much the same as 'As for me, I'm feeling fine'). A topic occupies a position above (and to the left of) the TP containing the clause subject, so a reasonable conjecture is that a topic occupies the specifier position within CP. If so, a sentence such as (123a) will have the syntactic structure shown below:

(124)

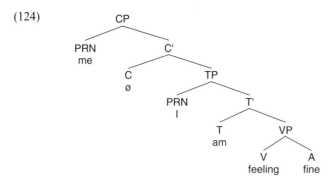

While the subject *I* will be assigned nominative case by the null intransitive finite complementiser *ø* which c-commands it (in accordance with the Case Assignment Condition 122ii), the topic *me* has no constituent c-commanding it and so cannot be assigned case by any of the Case Assignment Conditions in (122). So how does *me* come to be assigned case? Let us suppose that *me* is assigned **default case** by a condition such as the following:

(125)   **Default Case Assignment Condition**
          A noun or pronoun expression which does not fall within the domain of (i.e. which is not c-commanded by) any case-assigner receives default case.

The precise spellout of default case varies from one language to another: it is accusative in English, but nominative in Arabic, for example. So, because there is no case-assigner c-commanding it in (121), the topic *me* is assigned default accusative case by condition (122).

Another type of structure which seems to involve default case assignment arises in root infinitives (i.e. infinitival main clauses), like that italicised below (briefly discussed in §1.3):

(126)   SPEAKER A: I know you cheat on me
          SPEAKER B: *Me cheat on you!* No way! I never would!

While the precise structure of the italicised sentence is unclear (e.g. whether *me* is a topic or a subject),it seems likely that *me* is assigned default accusative case by virtue of not falling within the domain of any case-assigner. Similarly, it may be that the italicised complement of the copular verb *be* is also assigned default accusative case in a sentence such as:

(127)   The teacher asked who wrote the graffiti, and I admitted that it was *me*

While the complementiser *that* assigns structural nominative case to the complement clause subject *it* in (127), it is unlikely that the copula verb *be* assigns structural accusative case to its complement *me*, since *be* is generally agreed to be an intransitive verb in English. The most likely alternative is that the complement of *be* is assigned default case (this being accusative in English).

4.10   Defective clauses

In §4.7, I argued that all finite clauses are CPs, and in §4.8 I went on to argue that *for* infinitive clauses with accusative subjects and control infinitives with null PRO subjects are likewise CPs. In §4.9, we saw that complementisers play an important role in determining the case assigned to subjects. At first sight, this might seem to suggest that we maintain the CP Hypothesis (73) in its strongest form and suppose that all clauses are CPs. However, as we will see in this section, there are certain types of non-finite clause which are **defective clauses** by virtue of lacking CP (although they do contain a TP layer in consequence of the TP Hypothesis, 30).

One class of defective clauses are so-called **exceptional clauses** like the infinitive complement clauses bracketed in (128) below which have (italicised) accusative subjects:

(128) (a)   They believe [*him* to have lied]
      (b)   They expect [*you* to win]

Complement clauses like those bracketed in (128) are exceptional in that their subjects are assigned accusative case by the transitive verb (*believe/expect*) immediately preceding them: what's exceptional about this is that the verb is in a different clause from the subject which it assigns accusative case to. For this reason, such clauses are known as **exceptional case-marking clauses** (or **ECM clauses**); and verbs (like *believe*) when used with an ECM clause as their complement are known as **ECM verbs**.

ECM complement clauses seem to be TPs which lack the CP layer found in complete clauses, and in this respect they are defective clauses. One piece of evidence that ECM infinitive clauses like those bracketed in (128) are TPs rather than CPs is that they can be coordinated with another infinitival TP as in (129a) below, but not with an infinitival CP (e.g. not with a clause introduced by the infinitival complementiser *for*), as we see from the ungrammaticality of (129b):

(129) (a)   They believe [$_{TP}$ HIM [$_T$ to] have lied] and [$_{TP}$ HER [$_T$ to] have told the truth]
      (b)   *They believe [$_{TP}$ HIM] [$_T$ to] have lied] and [$_{CP}$ [$_C$ **for**] [$_{TP}$ HER [$_T$ to] have told the truth]

(The capitalised words in 129 receive contrastive stress.)

A second piece of evidence that ECM infinitive clauses are TPs rather than CPs comes from the observation that they cannot occur in focus position in pseudo-clefts, as we see from the sentences below:

(130) (a)   *What they believe is [*him to have lied*]
      (b)   *What they expect is [*you to apologise*]

If ECM clauses are TPs, the ungrammaticality of sentences like (130) will follow from the restriction noted in (108) that only a CP (not a TP) can occur in focus position in a pseudo-cleft sentence. Moreover, a further property of sentences like (128) which would be difficult to account for if the bracketed complement clause were a CP is the fact that its (italicised) subject can be passivised and thereby made into the subject of the main clause, as in (131) below:

(131) (a)   *He* is believed to have lied
      (b)   *You* are expected to apologise

This is because it is a property of the subject of an infinitival CP complement clause like that bracketed in (132a) below that its subject cannot be passivised – as we see from the ungrammaticality of (132b):

(132) (a)   We didn't intend [for *you* to hurt anyone]
      (b)   **You weren't intended [for to hurt anyone]

Why should the subject of a CP be unable to passivise? The answer lies in a constraint which can be formulated for present purposes as follows:

(133)   **Impenetrability Condition**
         A constituent c-commanded by a complementiser C is impenetrable to (so cannot agree with, or be case-marked by, or be attracted by, etc.) any constituent c-commanding the CP headed by C.

Setting aside details, let's suppose that what happens in a passive structure like (132b) is that the main clause T-constituent *weren't* **attracts** the pronoun *you* to move out of its original position (as the subject of the infinitival T-constituent *to*) into a new position where it becomes the subject of *weren't* – as shown by the arrow below:

(134)   *[CP [C ø] [TP *you* [T weren't] intended [CP [C for] [TP *you* [T to] hurt anyone]]]]

Because the pronoun *you* originates in a position below the complementiser *for*, and the T auxiliary *weren't* occupies a position above the CP headed by the complementiser *for* (where *above/below* can be characterised more accurately in terms of the relation c-command) it follows from the Impenetrability Condition (133) that *you* is impenetrable to the T auxiliary *weren't*, and so *you* cannot be attracted by *weren't* to become its subject via passivisation. For analogous reasons, the subject of the infinitival CP complement of a *for*-deletion verb like *want* cannot be passivised either: cf.

(135) (a)   She wanted [~~for~~ John to apologise]
      (b)   **John was wanted [~~for~~ to apologise]

– and indeed this is precisely what we expect if the Impenetrability Condition prevents the subjects of CPs from passivising, and if the bracketed complement clauses in (135) are CPs headed by a null counterpart of *for*, as claimed in §4.9. However, the fact that the passive sentences in (131) are grammatical suggests that the bracketed complement clauses they contain are TPs rather than CPs, since the Impenetrability Condition allows the subject of an infinitival TP to be passivised, but not the subject of an infinitival CP. Hence, complement clauses like those bracketed in (128) above are defective clauses which have no CP layer, and (128a) *They believe him to have lied* accordingly has the structure (136) below (with *Af* representing a present tense affix, and PERF a perfect aspect auxiliary):

(136)

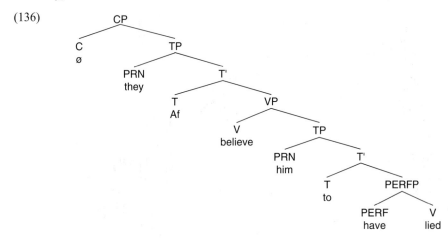

The particular aspect of the analysis in (136) most relevant to our discussion in this section is the claim that the complement clause *him to have lied* is an infinitival TP headed by *to*. Its subject *him* is assigned accusative case by the transitive verb *believe*, in accordance with the Accusative Case Assignment Condition (122i) above.

We can extend the analysis of ECM predicates like *believe* proposed in this section to verbs like those discussed in §4.6 which select a bare infinitive comple-ment. On this view, a sentence like *I have never known him be rude to anyone* (found in varieties of English like my own British one) would be analysed as containing a transitive perfect participle *known* which selects a TP complement headed by a null counterpart of infinitival *to* – as shown in skeletal form below:

(137)   I have never known [TP him [T to] be rude to anyone]

Since the subject of a TP complement can passivise, the analysis in (137) predicts that the subject of the bracketed infinitive complement in (137) can passivise, and this is indeed the case as we see from examples like (138) below:

(138)   *He has never been known to be rude to anyone*

Because (in the relevant variety) infinitival *to* can only have a null spellout when *known* is used as a perfect participle (as in 137) and not when it is a passive participle, it follows that infinitival *to* must be given an overt spellout in passives like (138).

A second type of non-finite clause which is defective comprises small clauses like that bracketed in (139) below:

(139)   They consider [him unsuitable]

A typical small clause has the property that it allows its subject to passivise. Consequently, the small clause subject *him* in (139) can be passivized and become the subject of *is* in:

(140)   *He* is considered unsuitable

Under the TP analysis of small clauses proposed in §4.6, small clauses are TP+VP structures in which TP is headed by a null variant of infinitival *to* and VP is headed by a null counterpart of the verb *be*. If (as claimed here) small clauses are defective clauses, they will contain no CP layer and thus project only as far as TP. On this view, the small clause bracketed in (139) has the structure (141) below:

(141)

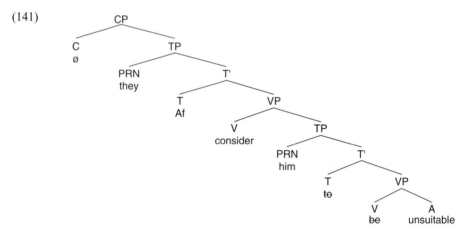

Under the analysis in (141), the small clause subject *him* will be assigned accusative case by the immediately adjacent transitive verb *consider* which c-commands it. Since the small clause is a TP (and not a CP), its subject can passivise (and will then be assigned nominative case if it becomes the subject of a finite T constituent, like *is* in 140).

Not so straightforward to classify is the verb *let*, which allows a bare infinitive complement in active structures like (142a) below but doesn't normally allow the subject of the infinitive to passivise, as we see from the ungrammaticality of sentences like (142b):

(142) (a)   You shouldn't let [him upset you]
      (b)   *He shouldn't be let [(to) upset you]

We can't describe the relevant facts by saying that *let* is a defective verb which has no passive participle form, since *let* is used as a passive participle in sentences like *The prisoners were let out of jail*. An alternative analysis is to suppose that whereas typical ECM predicates select an infinitival TP complement in both active and passive uses, *let* is irregular in that it only selects an infinitival TP complement in active uses, not when used as a passive participle (though I heard one TV sports commentator say 'Several bad tackles have been *let go* in this game', and likewise I heard a Chelsea footballer interviewed about life under a new manager saying 'You are *let know* that you have to perform at the top level'). Similar lexical idiosyncrasies are found with a number of other verbs: for example, *know* (in my British variety of English) only allows a bare infinitival complement with an accusative subject when used as a perfect participle in structures like (137) above. (An alternative way of accounting for the ungrammaticality of passivisation in sentences like 142b would be to take *let* to be a verb selecting a CP complement headed by an inherently null transitive complementiser which in turn selects an infinitival TP complement headed by a null counterpart of infinitival *to*: the ungrammaticality of 142b then follows from the fact that passivising the subject of a CP complement will violate the Impenetrability Condition, 133.)

To summarise: the overall conclusion to be drawn from our discussion in §§4.7–4.10 is that all clauses are CPs, with the exception of defective clauses – i.e. bare clauses with passivisable accusative subjects (where a bare clause is one not introduced by an overt complementiser). The claim that defective clauses lack CP suggests that the CP Hypothesis formulated in (73) above should be given the revised formulation in (143) below:

(143)   **CP Hypothesis** (revised from 73)
        All non-defective clauses are CPs, but defective clauses (e.g. bare non-finite complement clauses with passivisable subjects) lack the CP projection found in non-defective clauses.

Defective clauses have an accusative subject in active structures like (128,137,139), but a nominative subject if the subject is passivized and thereby becomes the subject of a finite clause as in (131,138,140).

It is a moot point whether root infinitive clauses like (126в) *Me cheat on you!* and verbless root clauses like that italicised in '*Me late for work!* Never!' may also be defective clauses lacking a CP layer (with their subjects therefore being assigned default accusative case).

4.11   Null heads in nominals

Thus far, we have seen that empty categories play an important role in the syntax of clauses in that clauses may contain a null subject, a null T constituent and a null C constituent. In this section, we will see that the same is true of the syntax of **nominals** (i.e. noun expressions). I shall begin by arguing that **bare nominals** (i.e. noun expressions which contain no overt determiner or quantifier) are generally headed by a null determiner or null quantifier, and then go on to show that prenominal modifiers are also housed within a projection with a null functional head.

Let's begin by exploring the syntax of the italicised bare nominals in (144) below:

(144)   *John* admires *Mary*

As we see from the Greek example in (145) below (kindly supplied by Georgios Ioannou), the Greek counterparts of the bare nouns in (144) are DPs headed by a (bold-printed) definite determiner:

(145) **O**   *Gianis*   thavmazi   **tin**   *Maria*
    The   John   admires   the   Mary (= 'John admires Mary')

This raises the possibility that bare nouns like those italicised in (144) above are DPs headed by a null definite determiner so that the overall sentence in (144) has the syntactic structure (146) below (where *Af* is a present tense affix):

(146)

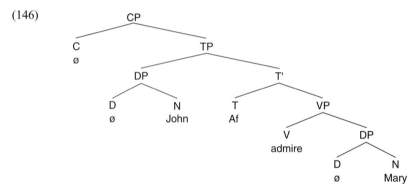

The analysis in (146) is consistent with the view that all definite noun expressions are DPs, including those not containing any overt determiner. A DP analysis of bare definite noun expressions is plausible from a semantic perspective in that a name like *John* is a referring expression which denotes a specific/definite individual in precisely the same way as a DP such as *this/that/the boy* does.

One piece of empirical evidence in support of analysing bare nouns as DPs comes from sentences like:

(147)   *John* and [**the chairman**] are attending a meeting

The fact that a bare noun like *John* can be coordinated with a determiner phrase/ DP like *the chairman* provides us with empirical evidence that such bare nouns must be DPs, given the assumption that expressions can only be coordinated if they belong to the same category.

If (as suggested here) English has a null D constituent, we should expect this not only to have identifiable semantic properties (in marking definiteness/specificity) but also to have identifiable grammatical properties. And indeed there is evidence that (like definite determiners such as *this/these*), the null D constituent carries person properties. In this respect, consider sentences such as the following:

(148) (a)   We linguists take **ourselves/*yourselves/*themselves** too seriously, don't
             *we/*you/*they?*
       (b)   You linguists take **yourselves/*ourselves/*themselves** too seriously, don't
             *you/*we/*they?*
       (c)   John takes **himself/*ourselves/*yourselves** too seriously, doesn't *he/*don't
             *we/*don't *you?*

(148a) shows that a first person expression such as *we linguists* can only bind (i.e.
serve as the antecedent of) a first person reflexive like *ourselves* and can only be
tagged by a first person pronoun like *we*. (148b) shows that a second person
expression like *you linguists* can only bind a second person reflexive like *yourselves* and can only be tagged by a second person pronoun like *you*. (148c) shows
that a bare noun like *John* can only bind a third person reflexive like *himself* and can
only be tagged by a third person pronoun like *he*. One way to account for the
relevant facts is to suppose that the nominals *we linguists/you linguists/John* in
(148a,b,c) are DPs with the respective structures shown in (149a,b,c) below

(149)

and that the person properties of a DP are determined by the person features carried
by its head determiner. If *we* is a first person determiner, *you* is a second person
determiner and *ø* is a third person determiner, the grammaticality judgments in (148a,
b,c) above are precisely as the analysis in (149a,b,c) would lead us to expect. More
generally, we can conclude that all definite referring expressions are D-expressions:
thus, an expression such as *the chairman* is a DP headed by the overt determiner *the*; a
name/proper noun such as *John* is a DP headed by a null determiner; and a definite
pronoun such as *he* is a pronominal D constituent (or a D-pronoun).

   In addition to having a null definite determiner, English can also be argued to have
a null (indefinite) quantifier. In this connection, consider the following sentences:

(150) (a)   *Eggs* and <u>many dairy products</u> cause cholesterol
       (b)   I'd like *toast* and <u>some coffee</u> please

The fact that the bare plural noun *eggs* is coordinated with the QP/quantifier phrase
many dairy products in (150a) suggests that *eggs* is a QP headed by a null quantifier.
Likewise, the fact that the bare singular noun *toast* is coordinated with the QP *some
coffee* in (150b) suggests that *toast* is also a QP headed by a null quantifier, so that the
italicised nominals in (150) are QPs with the structure shown below:

(151)

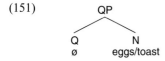

The null quantifier denotes 'an unspecified quantity of' and (depending on the
context) is typically generic or partitive in interpretation: thus, *eggs* in (150a) has

a **generic** interpretation paraphraseable as 'eggs in general', while *toast* in (150b) has a **partitive** interpretation paraphraseable as 'some toast'.

In addition to having its own semantic properties, the null quantifier found in 'bare' indefinite noun expressions in English has its own selectional properties – as illustrated by the following examples:

(152) (a)   I wrote *poems*
      (b)   I wrote *poetry*
      (c)   *I wrote *poem*

If each of the italicised bare nouns in (152) is the complement of a null quantifier ø, the relevant examples show that ø can select as its complement an expression headed by a plural count noun like *poems*, or by a singular mass noun like *poetry* – but not by a singular count noun like *poem*. This means that the complement selection properties of the null quantifier ø mirror those of the overt quantifier *enough*: cf.

(153) (a)   I've read **enough** *poetry*
      (b)   I've read **enough** *poems*
      (c)   *I've read **enough** *poem*

The fact that ø has the same selectional properties as a typical overt quantifier such as *enough* strengthens the case for positing the existence of a null quantifier ø, and for analysing bare indefinite noun expressions as QPs headed by a null quantifier.

The considerations outlined above suggest that bare definite noun expressions (like *John*) are DPs headed by a null determiner which is definite in interpretation, and that bare indefinite noun expressions (like *toast* or *eggs*) are QPs headed by a null quantifier which is generic or partitive in interpretation. The claim that null determiners and quantifiers have specific semantic properties is an important one from a theoretical perspective. In this connection, it is useful to recall the organisation of the grammar presented in diagrammatic form in §1.5, repeated in (154) below (where ≈ means 'interfaces with'):

(154)

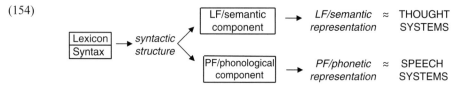

It follows from the architecture of the grammar in (154) that all constituents present in syntax must be assigned an appropriate spellout at PF, and an appropriate semantic interpretation at LF. Null determiners and quantifiers have a null spellout at PF and are assigned an appropriate semantic interpretation at LF (null determiners marking definiteness, and null quantifiers marking partitive or generic quantification). Thus, the postulation of null determiners and quantifiers is justifiable on theoretical grounds.

I have argued in this section that definite/indefinite noun expressions are DPs/QPs with an overt or null head. However, there is evidence that this is true only of nominal expressions used as **arguments** (i.e. nominals used as the subject or complement of a predicate) and that non-argument nominals such as those italicised in (155) below can be simple N-projections lacking a determiner or quantifier:

(155) (a)   Do all syntacticians suffer from asteriskitis, *doctor*?
      (b)   Dr Dolittle is *head of department*
      (c)   *Poor fool*! He thought he'd passed the syntax exam

The italicised nominal expression serves a **vocative** function in (155a) (in that it is used to address someone), a **predicative** function in (155b) (in that the property of being head of department is predicated of the unfortunate Dr Dolittle) and an **exclamative** function in (155c). Each of the italicised nominals in (155) is headed by a singular count noun (*doctor/head/fool*): in spite of the fact that such nouns require an overt quantifier or determiner when used as arguments, here they function as non-arguments and are used without any determiner. This suggests that non-argument nominals can be simple N-expressions, whereas argument nominals are always D-expressions (if definite referring expressions) or Q-expressions (if indefinite or quantified expressions). This assumption has interesting implications for the analysis of sentences such as the following:

(156)   The chairman wanted *a biscuit* with his coffee

It suggests that the definite expression *the chairman* is a DP headed by the definite determiner *the*, whereas the indefinite expression *a biscuit* is a QP headed by the indefinite quantifier *a*. Some evidence in support of this assumption comes from contrasts such as the following (discussed in §2.5):

(157) (a)   *Who* didn't he want [a/any picture of]?
      (b)   **Who* didn't he want [the/this picture of]?

In each of these sentences, the italicised wh-pronoun originates as the complement of the preposition *of* (as we can see from echo questions like *He didn't want a/any/the/this picture of who?*), and is then **extracted** out of the bracketed noun expression and moved to the front of the overall sentence. Why should extraction of *who* be possible out of the bracketed noun expression in (157a), but not out of that in (157b)? One answer is to suppose that *a/any picture of who* is a QP but *the/this picture of who* is a DP, and that QPs allow constituents to be extracted out of them, but DPs do not. If so, the fact that extraction is also possible out of a bare noun expression like that bracketed below in (158) is consistent with the assumption that the bracketed nominal in (158) is a QP headed by a null quantifier.

(158)   Who didn't he want [pictures of]?

The considerations outlined above lead to the following hypotheses:

(159) (i)   **DP hypothesis**
            Definite nominal arguments are DPs (headed by an overt or null D).
      (ii) **QP hypothesis**
            Indefinite nominal arguments are QPs (headed by an overt or null Q).

I will adopt these hypotheses from now on.

A rather different question which arises in relation to nominals concerns the syntax of adjectives used to modify nouns. Traditional grammars draw a distinction between the two different uses of adjectives italicised below:

(160) (a)   The shirt is *blue*
    (b)   I prefer the *blue* shirt

In the kind of use illustrated in (160a), *blue* is said to function as a **predicative** adjective: in this use, it predicates the property of being blue of the relevant shirt, and the adjective *blue* is positioned outside the DP *the shirt* (in that the DP *the shirt* precedes the copula verb *is*, and the adjective *blue* follows *is*). By contrast, in the kind of use illustrated in (160b), *blue* is said to be an **attributive** adjective: it attributes the property of being blue to the shirt in question, and is positioned internally within the DP *the --- shirt* (occupying the position marked by - - -). This raises the question of what position is occupied by an attributive adjective within the bracketed nominal containing it.

Abney (1987) suggested that an attributive adjective like *proud* in a nominal like *a proud mother* is the head of the expression *proud mother* and that the noun *mother* which follows it serves as the complement of *proud*. If this were so (and if we treat *a* as an indefinite quantifier), the nominal *a proud mother* would have the structure shown below:

(161)

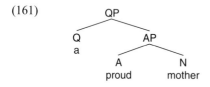

However, the claim made in (161) that the expression *proud mother* is an AP/ adjectival phrase is problematic in numerous respects. For one thing, typical adjectival phrases are expressions like *proud of her son* or *keen on syntax*, and if an indefinite article like *a* can select an AP complement (as is implicitly claimed in 161), we would wrongly expect expressions like those bracketed below to be grammatical (since *a* has an AP complement):

(162) (a)   *She is a [$_{AP}$ proud of her son]
    (b)   *He proved to be a [$_{AP}$ keen on syntax]

Moreover, the analysis in (161) would have difficulty in dealing with adnominal adjectival expressions like those italicised in the nominals bracketed below:

(163) (a)   [a *better than average* student] (Radford 1993: 84)
    (b)   [a *difficult to please* child] (Sadler and Arnold 1994: 190)
    (c)   [a *hard to pronounce* name] (Sadler and Arnold 1994: 190)
    (d)   The Incredible Hunk is [an *easy on the eye* kind of guy]

In (163a), the complement of the comparative adjective *better* is the phrase *than average*, not the underlined noun *student*. Likewise in (163b,c) the complement of the adjective *difficult/hard* is the infinitival clause *to please/to pronounce* and not the underlined noun *child/name*. Similarly in (163d) the complement of *easy* is the phrase *on the eye* and not the underlined NP *kind of guy*.

For reasons such as these, it is unlikely that attributive adjectives are the heads of the expressions containing them; rather, they serve as **modifiers** to the noun expression following them. But if attributive adjectives are not heads, what are they? A plausible alternative is that they are specifiers. One possibility along these lines is to suppose that a prenominal adjective serves as the specifier of a modifier phrase (**MODP**) which has a null **MOD** (= Modifier) head which requires an adjective or adjectival phrase as its specifier. The semantic function of the MOD head is to indicate that the adjectival expression which serves as the specifier of MOD is a modifier of the noun expression which serves as the complement of MOD. On this view, nominals like *a proud mother* and *a hard to pronounce name* would have the respective structures shown in (164a) and (164b) below:

(164)

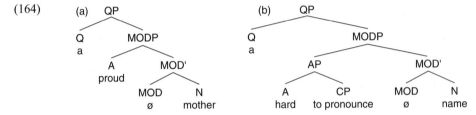

As is implicit in the discussion above, sometimes the modifying adjectival expression in spec-MODP is just a simple adjective like *proud* in (164a), and sometimes it is an adjectival phrase like *hard to pronounce* in (164b). (A point of detail to note in passing is that the adjective *proud* in 164a is a maximal projection, and so could alternatively be labelled as an AP – and for the same reason, the nouns *mother/name* could likewise be labelled as NPs. A further point of detail to note is that the subjectless infinitive *to pronounce* is taken to be a CP headed by a null complementiser in 164b, in line with the analysis in §4.9).

If each attributive adjective modifying a noun serves as the specifier of a separate functional head, structures containing more than one adnominal adjective will involve **recursion** (i.e. multiple occurrences) of MODP. On this view, a phrase like *a big yellow parrot* will have a structure such as that shown below:

(165)

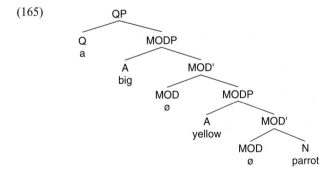

However, a question posed by the MODP recursion analysis in (165) is how to account for the relative ordering of the adjectives in (165) – e.g. why *yellow* can't precede *big* in **a yellow big parrot*. One way of accounting for constraints on the ordering of attributive adjectives (e.g. why size adjectives like *big* generally precede colour adjectives like *yellow*) is to suppose that each different type of adjective serves as the specifier of a dedicated functional head (i.e. a functional head which is dedicated to allowing a particular type of adjective as its specifier). We can then say, for example, that the subtype of MOD head which has a size adjective as its specifier (Let's call it MOD$_{SIZE}$) can select as its complement a MODP with a MOD head which allows a colour adjective as its specifier (Let's call the relevant head MOD$_{COLOUR}$), but not conversely.

An interesting question raised by the analysis in (165) is how come MODP constituents seem to have essentially the same properties as NPs: for example, in the same way as an NP such as *loss of income* can serve as the complement of the indefinite article *a* (as in *a loss of income*), so too can a MODP like *big loss of income* (as in *a big loss of income*). How can we account for this? Let us suppose that a MOD head which modifies a (noun phrase headed by a) noun is nominal in nature, so that a MODP like *big loss of income* is simply an adjectivally modified NP. One way of capturing this would be to treat MOD as a null N (perhaps a 'light noun' – i.e. a noun with little or no lexical content of its own) which takes an NP complement and an AP specifier. However, I will not pursue this issue further here.

A technical point to note in relation to the structure in (165) is that A-node *big*, the A-node *yellow* and the N-node *parrot* are all maximal projections, since each of the relevant nodes is the largest constituent headed by the word it carries. This means that (in accordance with the labelling convention discussed in relation to 47/48 in §3.5), the nodes in question could alternatively be labelled as AP-*big*, AP-*yellow* and NP-*parrot*. Adopting this convention would mean that in place of (165) above we have (166) below (where the nodes concerned are bold-printed):

(166)

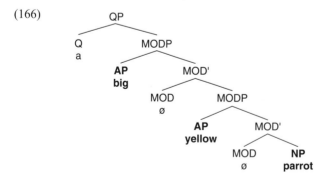

By saying (e.g.) that *big* occupies an AP position in (166), we mean that it occupies a position which could in principle be filled not just by an adjective like *big* but alternatively by an adjectival phrase like *bigger than expected*. Likewise, by saying that *parrot* occupies an NP position, we mean that it occupies a position which can be filled not only by a noun like *parrot* but alternatively by a noun phrase like *flock of parrots*.

The brief discussion here of the syntax of adnominal adjectives (i.e. nominal structures containing an adjective modifying an NP) has been deliberately simplified by setting aside a number of important issues which I will not attempt to delve into here. One is how to deal with postnominal APs (i.e. APs positioned after the NPs they modify), like those italicised below:

(167) (a)   We must choose the best person [*available*] [*suitable for the post*]
      (b)   He is the one person [*present*] [*capable of doing it*]

Postnominal APs appear to be predicative in nature, in the sense that they are the kind of APs which can serve as predicates in sentences like 'He is *available/ suitable for the post/present/capable of doing it*.'

The restriction that only predicative adjectives can be used postnominally means that adjectives like *mere* and *utter* which can only be used prenominally/attributively as in (168a) cannot be used predicatively as in (168b) or postnominally as in (168c):

(168) (a)   They are *mere excuses*/There was *utter chaos*
      (b)   *His excuses were *mere*/*The chaos was *utter*
      (c)   *I have never come across *excuses so mere*/*chaos so utter*

Conversely, there are adjectives like *afraid* which can be used postnominally as in (169a) and predicatively as in (169b), but not prenominally/attributively as in (169c):

(169) (a)   There are *people afraid of the dark*
      (b)   They were *afraid*
      (c)   *They are *afraid people*

A further detail is that some adjectives carry one meaning when used prenominally/attributively, but another when used postnominally or predicatively: cf.

(170) (a)   *present* students (antonym = *past*)
      (b)   students *present* (antonym = *absent*)
      (c)   Most of them are *present* (antonym = *absent*)

These and other issues relating to the syntax of adnominal adjectives, I will set aside here.

Instead, let's move on to consider another kind of nominal modifier found in English – namely **possessives** such as that italicised below:

(171)   I love [*my* red dress]

At first sight, it might seem tempting to take the possessive pronoun *my* to be the head POSS (possessive) constituent of a POSSP (possessive phrase) projection. If that were so, the bracketed nominal in (171) would have the structure shown below (if *red* is analysed as an AP rather than just an A, and if *dress* is analysed as an NP rather than just an N, for reasons analogous to those discussed in relation to *big, yellow* and *parrot* in 166):

(172)

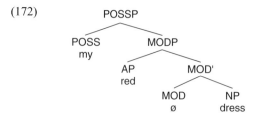

However, there are two problems which arise from treating possessives as the heads of the projections containing them as in (172). One relates to their case properties. Possessives like *my* have **genitive** case and yet the bracketed nominal *my red dress* in (171) is the direct object complement of the transitive verb *love*, and so the nominal and its head must carry **accusative** case (since a phrase projects the properties of its head). The second problem posed by treating possessives as heads is that only individual words (and not phrases) can be heads, and yet possessives can be phrasal in nature – e.g. the possessor below is the genitive DP *the former president's*:

(173)   [*The former president's* main attributes] were incompetence, incoherence and incontinence

Since specifiers can be phrasal, this suggests that genitive expressions are specifiers. But what kind of head are they specifiers of?

In answering this question, we should bear in mind that an interesting property of a possessive nominal such as *my red dress* is that it has a definite interpretation paraphraseable as '*the* red dress belonging to me' and does not have an indefinite interpretation paraphaseable as '*a* red dress belonging to me'. How can we account for this? If we accept the conclusion embodied in the DP Hypothesis that all definite nominal arguments are DPs headed by an overt or null D, we are driven towards an analysis in which the possessor *my* serves as the specifier of a null definite determiner. This means that the string *my red dress* is a definite DP with the fuller structure shown below (see the discussion of 165–166 above on why *red* and *dress* can be categorised as AP and NP constituents respectively):

(174)

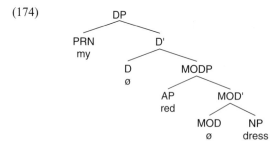

The null D heading the resulting DP serves not only to mark definiteness but also to mark possession (i.e. to indicate that its complement *red ø dress* denotes the **possessum** (i.e. the object possessed) and that its specifier *my* denotes the **possessor** (i.e. the person possessing the object). The analysis in (174) gains cross-linguistic plausibility from languages like Hungarian which have possessive structures like *Marinak*_{Mary's} *a*_{the} *kalapja*_{hat} loosely paraphraseable in English as *Mary's the hat*. If we make the reasonable assumption that no nominal can contain more than one DP constituent, treating *my* as the specifier of a DP headed by a null determiner will also account for why possessives like *my* can't co-occur with a definite determiner like *the* or *this* – as we see from the ungrammaticality of strings like **the my dress/*my this dress*, etc.

One final remark to make briefly about the syntax of (pro)nominals is the following. Certain types of (pro)nominal are traditionally said to have an *adverbial* function, in that (like adverbs) they function as adjuncts which provide optional information about the time, place or manner of an action or event. For example, the nominals italicised below have an adverbial function:

(175) (a)   I'll see you *Sunday*
    (b)   I'll do it *my own way*
    (c)   I'm staying *home* today

An interesting property of such (pro)nominals is that they can serve as the complement of a (bold-printed) preposition, as we see from:

(176) (a)   I'll see you **on** *Sunday*
    (b)   I'll do it **in** *my own way*
    (c)   I'm staying **at** home today

It is therefore plausible to take adverbial nominals like those italicised in (175) to be PPs headed by a null preposition.

Much the same can also be claimed for words like *here/there/where/then/when/why*, which are traditionally analysed as adverbs. However, they can plausibly be taken to be pronouns functioning as the object of a null preposition, with *here* meaning 'at/to/in this place', *there* meaning 'at/to/in that place', *where* meaning 'at/to/in what place', *then* meaning 'at that time', *when* meaning 'at what time' and *why* meaning 'for what reason'. Some support for a PP analysis of such adverbs comes from the observation that the relevant preposition can sometimes be spelled out overtly – as we see from sentences such as the following:

(177) (a)   *Where* is he going **to**?
    (b)   *Where* is he staying **at**?
    (c)   I've had a change of heart in the last week and I'll tell you **for** *why* (www.trollishdelver.com)
    (d)   I can remember getting back to the White House, and Laura said '*Why* did you do that **for**?' (George Bush, www.cnn.com/2005/ALLPOLITICS/01/14/bush.regrets)

Such considerations suggest the following hypothesis:

(178)   **PP Hypothesis**
          Adverbial (pro)nominals are PPs headed by a null preposition.

Given (178), an adverb like *there* in a sentence like *He went there* will have the structure shown below (where *there* is a pronoun meaning 'that place'):

(179)

In a sentence like *He went there*, the preposition heading the PP in (179) can be taken to be a null counterpart of *to*; in a sentence like *He stayed there*, the preposition would be a silent counterpart of *at*.

A piece of empirical evidence in support of the null preposition analysis of adverbial nominals is the following. As we saw in §1.3, certain prepositions (in certain uses) can be modified by the adverb *straight* – e.g. *to* in *He went straight to bed*. Significantly, appropriate types of adverbial (pro)noun can also be modified by *straight*, as we see from:

(180) (a)   I sent him *straight* **home**
      (b)   I'll go *straight* **there**

This can be accounted for straightforwardly if we suppose that the phrases italicised in (180) are PPs headed by a null preposition, with the respective structures indicated below:

(181) (a)   [PP straight [P ø] home]
      (b)   [PP straight [P ø] there]

In the case of the sentences in (180), the preposition in (181) would be a null counterpart of *to*.

A further piece of evidence in support of analysing adverbial nominals as PPs headed by a null preposition comes from the syntax of cleft sentences. As we saw in §3.4, a prepositional phrase (like *with great sadness* in 182a below) can appear in the (italicised) focus position in a cleft sentence, but not an adverbial phrase like *very sadly* in (182b):

(182) (a)   It was *with great sadness* that he announced the resignation of the chairman
      (b)   *It was *very sadly* that he announced the resignation of the chairman

Significantly, however, adverbial (pro)nominals like those italicised below can appear in focus position in cleft sentences:

(183) (a)   It was *then* that I apologised
      (b)   It was *last February* that the incident took place
      (c)   It's *here* that you get the best pizza in town
      (d)   It was *someplace else* that he hid the gun

This is consistent with the view that the focused adverbial nominals are prepositional phrases headed by a null preposition (e.g. *someplace else* in 183d contains a null counterpart of *in*).

Considerations such as those outlined above make it plausible to suppose that adverbial nominals are PPs headed by a null P of some kind. A question which I will not attempt to go into here, however, is the complex issue of which prepositions in which uses can, can't or must have a null spellout.

4.12   Summary

In this chapter, we have seen that null constituents (i.e. constituents which have no overt phonetic form but have specific grammatical and semantic properties) play a central role in syntax. We began by looking at null (finite, imperative, truncated and non-finite) subjects in §4.2, and I argued that control infinitive clauses have a null PRO subject which can refer to some constituent within a higher clause, or refer to some entity in the domain of discourse, or have arbitrary reference. In §4.3 we saw that elliptical clauses like that bracketed in *He could have helped her or* [*she have helped him*] are TPs headed by a null (ellipsed) tense auxiliary. In §4.4 the *null T* analysis was extended to auxiliariless indicative clauses like *He enjoys syntax*, which were argued to contain a TP headed by an abstract tense affix which is lowered onto the main verb by the morphological operation of Affix Hopping in the PF component. In §4.5, I argued that subjunctive clauses contain a null T constituent which may be a null counterpart of the modal auxiliary *should*, or alternatively may be an inherently null subjunctive auxiliary. In §4.6 I claimed that bare (*to*-less) infinitive clauses like that bracketed in *I can't let* [*you have my password*] are TPs headed by a null variant of infinitival *to*. I also argued that small clauses like that bracketed in *I consider* [*Mary the best candidate*] are TPs containing a null counterpart of infinitival *to* and a null variant of the verb *be*. I concluded that all clauses contain a TP headed by an overt or null T constituent (= the TP Hypothesis). In §4.7, I presented evidence that all finite clauses are CPs and that those which are not introduced by an overt complementiser are CPs headed by a null complementiser. We saw that indicative clauses which contain no interrogative/exclamative, etc. constituent in the specifier position of CP are interpreted as declarative in type by default. In §4.8 I argued that *for* infinitives, the infinitive complements of *want*-class verbs and control infinitives are also CPs, and I concluded that all (non-defective) clauses are CPs (= the CP Hypothesis). In §4.9, we looked at structural case-marking, and in particular the role that null complementisers play in this. I argued that a transitive head assigns accusative case to a noun or pronoun expression which it c-commands, an intransitive finite complementiser assigns nominative case to a noun or pronoun expression which it c-commands and an intransitive non-finite complementiser assigns null case to a pronoun which it c-commands. I also noted that in consequence of the Earliness

Principle, noun and pronoun expressions are case-marked as early as possible in the derivation, by the closest case-assigner which c-commands them. In §4.10 I argued that there are a class of defective clauses which lack the CP layer found in other clauses. More particularly, I argued that ECM (exceptional case-marking) clauses like that bracketed in *I believe* [*him to be innocent*] are defective clauses which have the status of TPs rather than CPs, and that their subjects are assigned accusative case by a transitive verb like *believe* in the higher clause. We saw that in consequence of their defective status, ECM clauses allow their subjects to be passivised (unlike the subjects of non-defective clauses). I went on to argue that small clauses are also defective clauses and thus behave like ECM clauses in respect of case-marking and passivisation. In §4.11, we looked at the syntax of nominals, and I argued that bare definite nominal arguments are DPs headed by a null determiner, and bare indefinite nominal arguments are QPs headed by a null quantifier; consequently, in a sentence such as *John wanted eggs*, the bare noun *John* is a DP headed by a null definite determiner, whereas the bare noun *eggs* is a QP headed by a null indefinite quantifier. However, I noted that there is a class of defective (vocative, exclamative and predicate) nominals which can have the status of simple N or NP constituents (lacking a D or Q constituent). I further argued that attributive/prenominal adjectives serve as specifiers of a functional projection MODP with a null head and that possessives serve as specifiers of a DP projection headed by a null definite D. Finally, I noted that adverbial nominals (like *Sunday* in 'See you Sunday') can plausibly be analysed as PPs headed by a null preposition.

Key operations/principles/hypotheses made use of in this chapter are as follows:

(26)   **Have-cliticisation**
         The word *have* can encliticise to (i.e. attach to the end of) another word W in the phonological component, provided that
           (i) W ends in a vowel/diphthong
          (ii) W immediately precedes *have*
         (iii) W c-commands *have*.

(30)   **TP Hypothesis**
         All clauses contain a TP headed by an (overt or null) T constituent.

(36)   **Affix Hopping**
         When a tense affix in T remains unattached at the end of the syntactic derivation, in the PF component the affix is lowered onto the closest V below T (i.e. c-commanded by T).

(82)   **Empty Category Principle/ECP**
         Every empty category must be licensed.

(84)   **COMP-Trace Filter/CTF**
         Any structure in which an overt complementiser is immediately adjacent to and c-commands a trace (i.e. a gap left behind by a moved constituent) is filtered out as ill-formed at PF.

(86)   **Structural Uniformity Principle**
            All constituents of the same type belong to the same category.

(92)   **Root Complementiser Constraint**
            No overt complementiser can be the head of a root projection in a language
            like English.

(95)   **Clause Typing Condition**
            A CP is typed as interrogative (i.e. interpreted as interrogative in type in
            the semantic component) if it has an interrogative specifier, exclamative
            if it has an exclamative specifier, etc. Otherwise, a CP headed by an
            indicative complementiser is interpreted as declarative in type by
            default.

(111)   **Earliness Principle**
            Operations apply as early in a derivation as possible.

(122)   **Case Assignment Conditions**
            A noun or pronoun expression is assigned
            (i) accusative case if the closest case-assigner c-commanding it is a transi-
            tive head (e.g a transitive verb like *meet*, or a transitive preposition like
            with, or a transitive complementiser like *for*/~~for~~)
            (ii) nominative case if the closest case-assigner c-commanding it is an
            intransitive finite complementiser (like *that*, or *if*, or *whether* in finite
            clauses, or the null complementiser *ø* introducing bare indicative
            clauses)
            (iii) null case if the closest case-assigner c-commanding it is an intransitive
            non-finite complementiser (like *ø* in control clauses, or *whether* in
            infinitival clauses).

(125)   **Default Case Assignment Condition**
            A noun or pronoun expression which does not fall within the domain of
            (i.e. which is not c-commanded by) any case assigner receives default
            case.

(133)   **Impenetrability Condition**
            A constituent c-commanded by a complementiser C is impenetrable to (so
            cannot agree with, or be case-marked by, or be attracted by, etc.) any
            constituent c-commanding the CP headed by C.

(143)   **CP Hypothesis**
            All non-defective clauses are CPs, but defective clauses (i.e. bare non-finite
            complement clauses with passivisable subjects) lack the CP projection found
            in non-defective clauses.

(159) (i)   **DP Hypothesis**
            Definite nominal arguments are DPs (headed by an overt or null D).

      (ii) **QP Hypothesis**
            Indefinite nominal arguments are QPs (headed by an overt or null Q).

(178)   **PP Hypothesis**
            Adverbial (pro)nominals are PPs headed by a null preposition.

4.13   Bibliographical background

For a range of accounts of the null *pro* subjects discussed in §4.2, see Chomsky (1981), Rizzi (1982, 1986, 1997), Jaeggli (1982, 1984), Huang (1984), Montalbetti (1984), Safir (1984), Suñer (1984), Hyams (1986), Jaeggli and Safir (1989), Roberts (1993), Barbosa (1995, 2000, 2007), Barbosa, Duarte and Kato (2005), Kato (1999, 2000), Alexiadou and Anagnostopoulou (1998), Holmberg (2005), Neeleman and Szendrői (2005) and Tamburelli (2006, 2007). On truncated null subjects in English, see Thrasher (1977), Haegeman (1990, 1997, 2000a, 2000b, 2008), Haegeman and Ihsane (1999, 2002), Rizzi (1994, 2000), Franks (2005, fn.5) and Weir (2008). On imperatives in English, see Potsdam (1998) and Rupp (2003). The idea that control infinitives have a null PRO subject dates back to Chomsky (1977): for more recent discussion of control infinitives, see Landau (1999, 2001, 2003, 2004, 2006a); it should aso be noted that Xu (2003) claims that all control clauses in Mandarin Chinese allow an overt subject pronoun in place of PRO. Although the discussion in §4.2 focuses on null subjects, it should be noted that some languages (though not English) productively allow null objects (see Rizzi 1986; Raposo 1986; Authier 1989; Farrell 1990 Huang 1991; Groefsema 1995; Cummins and Roberge 2004, 2005). The idea in §4.3 that null constituents can arise via Gapping and other forms of ellipsis has a long history, dating back to Hankamer (1971), Hankamer and Sag (1976), Sag (1980), Kuno (1981), Pesetsky (1982a), Hardt (1993), McCawley (1993), Lobeck (1995), Schwarz (1999, 2000), Johnson (2000), Merchant (1999, 2001, 2002, 2004, 2006, 2008a, 2008b, 2013a, 2013b), Coppock (2002), Kennedy (2002, 2003), Carlson, Dickey and Kennedy (2005) and Frazier and Clifton (2005). The Affix Hopping account of verb morphology outlined in §4.4 dates back in spirit to Chomsky (1955, 1957) and is revised in Lasnik (1981). The idea in §4.5 that subjunctive clauses contain a null counterpart of *should* dates back to Visser (1966: 788–9), Kiparsky and Kiparsky (1970: 171) and Traugott (1972: 180): the alternative possibility that they contain an inherently null subjunctive modal is argued for by Roberts (1985), Haegeman (1986), Chiba (1987), Rizzi (1990), Potsdam (1997a, 1998) and Nomura (2006); by contrast, Zanuttini (1991) and Sawada (1995) claim that subjunctive clauses contain no T constituent of any kind. For alternative analyses of the type of infinitive clause structures discussed in §4.6, see Felser (1999a,b) and Basilico (2003); and for a range of analyses of small clauses, see Stowell (1981, 1983, 1991), Safir (1983), Kitagawa (1985), Contreras (1987), Kaplan (1988), Radford (1988), Aarts (1992), Napoli (1993), Cardinaletti and Guasti (1995), Moro (1997), Jiménez (2000a,b), Bowers (2001), Basilico (2003), Lundin (2003), Progovac (2004), Hartmann (2005), Alhorais (2007), Chomsky (2013) – and, for a repudiation of their existence, see Williams (1983). On the historical development of *to*-infinitives, see Los (2005). The claim that expletive *there* is restricted to occurring in spec-TP is made by Safir (1993). The claim in §4.7 that apparently complementiserless clauses contain a null complementiser dates back in spirit more than four decades (see, e.g., Stockwell, Schachter and Partee 1973: 599): for evidence of null complementisers in Japanese, see Kishimoto (2006). For a counterview that complementiser-less clauses are TPs rather than CPs, see Bošković (1996, 1997), Doherty (1997), Radford (1997a,b) and Franks (2005). For an analysis of null complementisers as clitics, see Ormazabal (1995), Bošković and Lasnik (2003) and Epstein, Pires and Seely (2005). For discussion of further factors governing the use of null complementisers in finite clauses, see Hawkins (2001) and Nomura (2006). The idea that clauses are interpreted as declarative by default is suggested by Roberts and Roussou (2002) and Haegeman (2012). On the Empty Category Principle, see Chomsky (1981) and Rizzi (1990). The Structural Uniformity Principle was devised by Rizzi (2000: 288). The idea in §4.8 that (non-defective) infinitive clauses are introduced by an (overt or null) complementiser dates back to Bresnan (1970); on treating infinitive complements of verbs like *want* as CPs headed by a null counterpart of *for*, see Sawada (1995) and Nomura (2006). The Earliness Principle discussed in relation to case-marking in §4.9 derives from work by Pesetsky (1989, 1995) and Rezac (2003). On finite complementisers being nominative case-assigners, see Chomsky (1999: 35, fn. 17). On dative and quirky-case subjects in languages like Bulgarian, Icelandic and Spanish, see Masullo (1993), Cuervo (1999), Moore and Perlmutter (2000), Sigurðsson (2002) and Rivero (2004). The idea that PRO subjects in English carry null case derives from work by Chomsky and Lasnik (1993), Chomsky (1995) and Martin (1996, 2001). On the claim that null case is assigned to a PRO subject by C, see Rizzi (1997: 304) and Collins (2005: 104). For an alternative proposal that PRO carries 'real' (e.g. nominative, accusative or dative) case, see Cecchetto and Oniga (2004) and Landau (2004, 2006a). On the nature of default case, see Schütze (2001). The idea in §4.10 that ECM clauses are defective in respect of lacking the CP layer found in full clauses is defended in Chomsky (1999). The Impenetrability Condition has its origins in the Phase Impenetrability Condition of Chomsky (1998); its historical antecedents lie in the Subjacency Condition of Chomsky (1973) (amended by Rizzi 1982) and the Barrierhood Condition of Chomsky (1986b). The assumption in §4.11 that bare nominals contain a null determiner/quantifier has a long history, dating back to a suggestion made by Chomsky (1965: 108) which was taken up and extended in later work by Abney (1987), Bernstein (1993, 2001) and Longobardi (1994, 1996, 2001). On the nature of quantified expressions, see Löbel (1989), Giusti (1991) and Shlonsky (1991). On determiners and determiner phrases, see Abney (1987), Bernstein (1993), Giusti (1997), Alexiadou and Wilder (1998), Zamparelli (2000), Grohmann and Haegeman (2002) and Ticio (2003, 2005). There have been a variety of treatments of adjective+noun structures (like *red car*) in the research literature, and these differ in respect of whether the adjective is treated as the head of the structure (Abney 1987), as an adjunct to the noun (Valois 1991a,b, 1996), as compounded with the noun (Sproat and Shih, 1988, 1990; Lamarche 1991) or as the specifier of a functional projection above the noun (Cinque 1994, 2010): see Valois (2011) for a literature review. Moreover, analyses which take adjectives to be specifiers differ in the label they give to the projection housing the adjective; e.g. this is taken to be an AgrP/Agreement phrase projection in Cinque (1994) and Danon (2011). A complication glossed over in the text is that modifiers positioned in front of the nouns they modify in English don't generally allow complements of their own – as we see from the ungrammaticality of *a proud of her son woman, where the modifying adjective *proud* has the complement *of her son*. For attempts to account for this restriction, see Williams (1981, 1982), Giorgi and Longobardi (1991), Escribano (2004) and Biberauer, Holmberg and Roberts (2007). For a range of alternative analyses of the English possessive structures discussed in §4.11, see Abney (1987), Chomsky (1995: 263), Zribi-Hertz (1997) and Bernstein and Tortora (2005). On the relative ordering of attributive adjectives in English, see Cinque (1994, 2010), Feist (2008), and Abels and Neeleman (2012). Although there is evidence that nominals are DPs in languages like English, it has been argued that there are DP-less languages in which nominals are NPs which lack a DP projection (Uriagereka 1988; Corver 1990; Bošković 2005, 2008, 2009; Marelj 2011). The claim that adverbial nominals are PPs headed by a null preposition derives from work by Emonds (1976, 1987), Larson (1985b), McCawley (1988), Collins (2007) and Caponigro and Pearl (2008, 2009).

Workbook section

Exercise 4.1

Draw tree diagrams to represent the structure of the following sentences, presenting arguments in support of your analysis and commenting on any null constituents they contain and the reasons for positing them. Say how each of the noun or pronoun expressions is case-marked in the sentences you analyse.

1. Students enjoy the classes
2. We have fun
3. Voters think politicians lie
4. John promised to behave himself
5. She sees no need for anyone to apologise
6. Me, I would prefer students to do exams
7. Economists expect salaries to rise
8. He might like you to stay
9. They requested that he have a good lawyer
10. John wanted to help him
11. He intended you to win
12. They consider you unsuitable for the job

Also, say how you would account for the grammaticality of sentences such as those below in Belfast English, corresponding to *I wanted (you) to go with them* in standard varieties of English:

13. I wanted [for to go with them]
14. I wanted [you for to go with them]

In addition, say why *have*-cliticisation is or is not permitted in 15b, 16b, 17b and 18b below:

15 a.   They have suffered hardship
   b.   They've suffered hardship

16 a.   The Sioux have suffered hardship
   b.   *The Sioux've suffered hardship

17 a.   Sioux have suffered hardship
   b.   *Sioux've suffered hardship

18.   SPEAKER A: How are students coping with your *Fantasy Syntax* course?
     SPEAKER B: *Two've given up

Helpful hints

Assume that defective clauses (e.g. ECM clauses and small clauses) are TPs, but that other clauses are CPs (= CP Hypothesis). In addition, assume that bare definite nominal arguments are DPs headed by a null definite D (= DP Hypothesis), and bare indefinite nominal arguments are QP constituents headed by a null indefinite Q (= QP Hypothesis). Assume the conditions on *have*-cliticisation given in (26) in the main text/summary. In relation to 3, determine what case *politicians* has (by substituting it by an overtly case-marked pronoun), and how you can use this to decide whether the complement of *know* is a TP or a CP, in the light of the Case Assignment Conditions in (122). In 4, use Binding Principle A to help you account for why the anaphoric pronoun *himself* is coreferential to *John*, and for present purposes, assume that Principle A specifies that 'The closest TP containing an anaphor must also contain an appropriate antecedent that c-commands the anaphor' (cf. exercise 3.2). In 5, assume that *no* is a negative quantifier which has a noun phrase complement. In 6, bear in mind the discussion of Default Case Assignment in §4.9. In relation to 9, take account of the discussion of the syntax of attributive adjectives in §4.11. In 10, use Binding Principle B to help you account for why the pronominal *him* cannot be coreferential to *John*, and assume that Principle B specifies that 'A pronominal cannot refer to any constituent c-commanding it within the closest TP containing the pronominal.' In 11, consider the possibility that some verbs may be able to take either an infinitival CP or an infinitival TP as their complement. In 12, bear in mind the discussion of small clauses in §4.6. In relation to *for-to* infinitives in Belfast English sentences like 13–14 consider the possibility that *for* is not a transitive infinitival complementiser in such sentences but rather that *for-to* functions as a compound T constituent (with properties like those of Standard English infinitival *to*). Compare this to an alternative analysis in which *for* is a clitic which originates in C and cliticises onto T in the PF component, and say why Belfast English data like *I don't know where/*whether for to go* are more compatible with the analysis of *for* as a clitic complementiser. In relation to the (b, B) examples in 15–18, draw trees to represent the structure of the sentences immediately prior to cliticisation, and then show whether or not the account of *have*-cliticisation in (26) predicts that cliticisation is possible; note that the noun *Sioux* is pronounced |su:|. In 17, take *Sioux* to be a QP headed by a null partitive quantifier (so that *Sioux* means 'some Sioux'), and show how the ungrammaticality of 17b can be used to evaluate the hypothesis that a bare noun like *Sioux* in 17 is a QP headed by a null quantifier. In addition, say how sentences like 15b can be used to evaluate the plausibility of analyses (such as that proposed by Freidin and Vergnaud 2001) which take pronouns like *they* to be determiners which have a nominal complement whose phonetic features are given a null spellout in the PF component so that, e.g., if *they* refers to *Sioux*, the pronoun *they* would be a DP with the structure shown below:

19.

Would it be any more or less plausible to suppose that the numeral quantifier (= Q) *two* in sentences like that produced by speaker B in 18 has a null N complement (a null counterpart of the noun *students*)?

Model answer for 1

Given the TP Hypothesis (30), it follows that auxiliariless finite clauses contain a TP headed by a null T constituent containing an Affix which encodes Tense and (Person and Number) agreement features. This in turn means that the sentence *Students enjoy the classes* will contain a TP headed by a tense affix which carries the features [third-person, plural-number, present-tense], which we can abbreviate to Af_{3PLPR}. Likewise, given the CP Hypothesis (143), it follows that all non-defective clauses are CPs headed by an (overt or null) complementiser. This means that the overall sentence will be a CP headed by a null finite complementiser [$_C$ ø], with the relevant CP being interpreted as declarative in type by default, in accordance with the Clause Typing Condition (95). In addition, it follows from the QP Hypothesis (159ii) that the indefinite bare nominal argument *students* will be a QP headed by a null quantifier which (as used here) is generic in interpretation, and so the nominal *students* has a meaning paraphraseable as 'students in general'. Given these assumptions, sentence 1 will have the structure shown below:

(i)

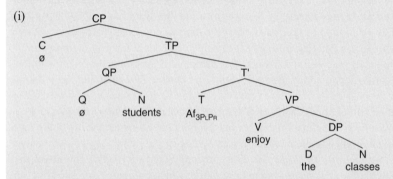

Because there is no auxiliary in T for it to attach to, the tense affix in T is lowered onto the verb *enjoy* by the morphological operation of Affix Hopping in the PF component, forming $enjoy+Af_{3PLPR}$ (which is ultimately spelled out as the third person plural present tense form *enjoy*).

Evidence that the overall clause *Students enjoy the classes* is a CP headed by a null complementiser comes from coordination data in relation to sentences such as:

(ii)   [*Students enjoy the classes*] but [**do they like the lectures**]?

In (ii) the declarative clause *Students enjoy the classes* has been coordinated with the interrogative clause *do they like the lectures?* which contains the inverted auxiliary *do*. If (as claimed in §4.7) root yes–no questions are CPs containing a null yes–no question operator in spec-CP and an inverted auxiliary in C, it follows that the second of the two co-ordinate clauses in (ii) is a CP; and if only

constituents of the same type can be coordinated, it follows that the first clause must also be a CP –
as in (i) above.

Evidence in support of positing a null present tense T constituent in (i) comes from the
observation that the T-bar Af_{3PlPr} *enjoy the classes* can be coordinated with another T-bar like
don't like the lectures, as we see from (iii) below:

(iii)   Students *enjoy the classes*, but *don't like the lectures*

Evidence that the bare nominal *students* is a QP headed by a null quantifier comes from the
possibility of coordinating *students* with a QP such as *many teachers*, as in (iv):

(iv)   *Students* and <u>many teachers</u> enjoy the classes

The DP *the classes* in (i) is assigned accusative case by virtue of being c-commanded by the
transitive verb *enjoy*. Accordingly, the DP *the classes* can be substituted by an accusative pronoun,
as in (v):

(v)   Students enjoy *them*

By contrast, the QP *ø students* is assigned nominative case by virtue of being c-commanded by the
intransitive finite complementiser *ø*. It follows that this QP can be substituted by a nominative
pronoun, as in (vi):

(vi)   *They* enjoy the classes

Additional helpful hints for sentences 2–12

Discuss whether/how your analysis can account for the (un)grammaticality of the sentences below
(the relevant grammaticality judgments holding for my own variety of British English). To help
you, relevant parts of the sentences have been italicised.

2a.   We have *fun* and *some pain*
2b.   **We've* fun
2c.   We *have fun* and *are enjoying syntax*
2d.   *We have fun* but *how long will it last*?

3a.   *Voters* and *most journalists* think politicians lie
3b.   Voters think *politicians* and *many celebrities* lie
3c.   Voters think politicians *lie* and *can't be trusted*
3d.   Voters *think politicians lie* and *don't trust them*
3e.   Voters think *politicians lie* and *that they do so knowingly*
3f.   *Voters think politicians lie*, but *do they care*?

4a.   *John promised to behave himself*, but *how long will he do so*?
4b.   *John* and *the vicar* promised to behave themselves
4c.   John *promised to behave himself* and *has done so*
4d.   What John promised was *to behave himself*
4e.   *John* promised to behave *himself* (How come *himself* refers to *John*?)

5a.   *She sees no need for anyone to apologise*, but *does she think anyone will*?
5b.   She *sees no need for anyone to apologise*, and *would not want anyone to*

6a.   I would prefer very much *for* students to do exams
6b.   I would prefer *students to do exams* and *for their papers to remain confidential*
6c.   What I would prefer is *for students to do exams*
6d.   **Students* would be preferred to do exams

7a. *Salaries* are expected to rise
7b. *They expect *salaries to rise* and *for inflation to fall*
7c. They expect *salaries to rise* and *inflation to fall*
7d. *They expect *fully for* salaries to rise (cf. They *fully* expect salaries to rise)

8a. He might like more than anything *for* you to stay
8b. He might like *you to stay* and *for things to be settled between you*
8c. What he might like is *for you to stay*
8d. *You* might be liked to stay

9a. They requested *(*that*) he have a good lawyer
9b. *They requested that *he 've* a good lawyer

10a. What John wanted was *to help him*
10b. *John* wanted to help *him* (Why can't *him* refer to *John*?)
10c. John wanted very much (**for*) to help *him*

11a. He never intended *you to win* or (%*for*) *her to lose*
11b. You were intended (**for*) to win
11c. What he intended was *(*for*) you to win*
11d. He never intended at any point *(*for*) you to win*

12a. They consider you (*to be*) unsuitable for the job
12b. They consider you *not* (to be) the best candidate
12c. They consider [there (*to be*) little chance of finding the body]
12c. *You* are considered (to be) unsuitable for the job

The notation (%*for*) in 11a means that some speakers accept the sentence with *for* and all accept it without *for*. The notation (**for*) in 11b means that 11b is ungrammatical with *for* and grammatical without *for*. The notation *(*that*) in 9a and *(*for*) in 11c means that 9a/11c is grammatical with *that/ for* and ungrammatical without *that/for*.

Exercise 4.2

Account for the (un)grammaticality of the bracketed infinitive complement clause structures in the following sentences in standard varieties of English:

1 a. They were *planning* [to escape]
  b. *They were *planning* [him to escape]

2 a. We *consider* [him to be unsuitable]
  b. *It is *considered* [him to be unsuitable]

3 a. He would *like* [me to leave]
  b. He would *like* [to leave]

4 a. She seems *keen* [for them to participate]
  b. *She seems *keen* [(**for*) to participate]

5 a. I received a *request* [to resign]
  b. *I received a *request* [him to resign]

6 a. It was *agreed* [to review the policy]
  b. *It was *agreed* [us to review the policy]

7 a. Congress *decided* [to ratify the treaty]
  b. *Congress *decided* [for him to ratify the treaty]

8 a.   She *expected* [to win the nomination]
  b.   She *expected* [him/*he to win the nomination]

9 a.   He should *let* [you have a break]
  b.   *He should *let* [have a break]

10 a.   *He *said* [her to like oysters]
   b.   *He *said* [to like oysters]

Helpful hints

Note that 1b is intended to have an interpretation paraphraseable as 'They were planning for him to escape', 9b to have an interpretation paraphraseable as 'He should let himself have a break', (10a) to have an interpretation paraphraseable as 'He said she liked oysters' and (10b) to have an interpretation paraphrasable as 'He said he liked oysters' (where the two occurrences of *he* refer to the same individual). Assume that each of the italicised words in the above examples has its own idiosyncratic selectional properties and that the selectional properties of any word W are described by saying: 'W selects as its complement an expression headed by . . . ' (where in place of the dots you insert the features characterising the relevant head). So, you might say, for example, that a verb like *arrange* can select a complement headed by an infinitival complementiser (either the transitive infinitival complementiser *for* or the null intransitive infinitival complementiser *ø*), whereas an ECM verb like *believe* selects a complement headed by the infinitival T constituent *to*. By contrast, other verbs (it might turn out) don't select (i.e. don't take/allow) a particular kind of infinitive complement – or indeed *any* kind of infinitive complement. Assume that seemingly subjectless clauses in 1–10 (whether grammatical or not) have a null PRO subject. Pay attention (i) to the selectional properties of the italicised words and (ii) to the case properties of the subjects of the bracketed complement clauses. In the case of the ungrammatical examples, consider whether the ungrammaticality is attributable to a *selectional error* (in that the italicised word is used with a kind of complement which it does not select/take/allow) and/or a *case error* (in that the subject of the bracketed clause has a case which it cannot be assigned in accordance with the case conditions in 122) – or both.

Model answer for 1

Given the CP Hypothesis (143), it follows that each of the clauses in 1a are CPs, so that 1a has the structure (i) below:

(i)

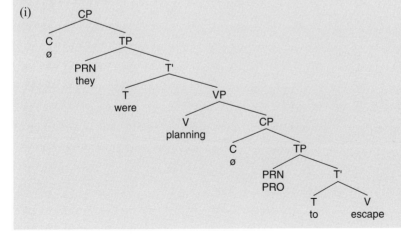

The null complementiser introducing the CP complement of the verb *planning* is intransitive and non-finite, and accordingly assigns null case to the PRO subject which it c-commands in accordance with the Null Case Condition (122iii). Support for the CP analysis of the bracketed complement clause *to escape* in 1a comes from the observation that (like other CPs, but unlike TPs) it can serve as the focused constituent in pseudo-cleft sentences like (ii):

(ii)   What they were planning was *to escape*

The fact that it is also possible to say:

(iii)   They were planning *for him to escape*

suggests that *plan* can also select a complement headed by the transitive infinitival complementiser *for*. This leads to the greater generalisation that *plan* can select a CP complement headed by an infinitival complementiser (either the transitive infinitival complementiser *for* or the null intransitive infinitival complementiser ø). The ungrammaticality of 1b **They were planning him to escape* could be attributable to a case error (if the null complementiser heading the complement clause is intransitive and so assigns null case to the infinitive subject), or to a spellout error (if the complementiser heading the complement clause is the kind of *for* complementiser which can never be given a null spellout – unlike the *for* introducing an infinitival complement of a verb like *want*).

5   Head Movement

5.1   Overview

So far, we have examined a range of syntactic structures which are derived by a series of Merge operations. In the next three chapters, we go on to look at structures whose derivation involves not only Merge but also a range of different types of movement operation. In this chapter, we focus on a specific type of movement operation called **Head Movement** whereby the head of one phrase moves to become the head of the phrase immediately above it. We focus mainly on two specific types of Head Movement operation – one which affects auxiliaries in present-day English, and another which affected main verbs in earlier stages of English. In addition, we also look briefly at how Head Movement can apply to nouns.

5.2   Auxiliary Inversion

English has a number of structures (illustrated below) in which we find a phenomenon which is widely referred to as **Subject-Auxiliary Inversion/SAI**:

(1) (a)   *What time* **will** <u>the guests</u> arrive at the hotel?
     (b)   *Under no circumstances* **would** <u>the president</u> accept a bribe
     (c)   *So quickly* **have** <u>the flames</u> spread that the firefighters are losing control of the fire

In each of these examples, in front of the (underlined) subject we find a (bold-printed) auxiliary, and in front of the auxiliary is an italicised constituent which is an interrogative phrase (*what time*) in (1a), a negative phrase (*under no circumstances*) in (1b), and a degree phrase (*so quickly*) in (1c). What is unusual about this is that subjects are normally positioned in spec-TP and auxiliaries in T (as we saw in Chapter 3), and hence an (underlined) subject would normally precede an associated (bold-printed) auxiliary, as in:

(2) (a)   <u>The guests</u> **will** arrive at the hotel
     (b)   <u>The president</u> **would** not accept a bribe under any circumstances
     (c)   <u>The flames</u> **have** spread so quickly that the firefighters are losing control of the fire

If we make the reasonable assumption that the underlined subjects in (1) are in the same spec-TP position as they occupy in (2), this means that both the bold-printed auxiliary in (1) and the italicised interrogative or negative phrase preceding it must be contained in some projection positioned above TP. Since we saw in Chapters 3 and 4 that CP is positioned above TP, this suggests that in Auxiliary Inversion structures like (1), the auxiliary is in C, and the underlined phrase preceding it is its specifier (and so is in spec-CP). This means that Auxiliary Inversion clauses like those in (1) will have the structure shown in schematic form below (where I adopt the suggestion made at the end of §4.11 that adverbial nominals are PPs headed by a null preposition so that *what time* is a PP headed by a null counterpart of *at*):

(3)

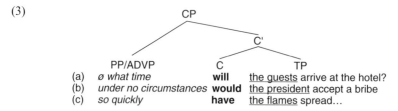

On this assumption, the underlined subject is in spec-CP, the inverted auxiliary is in C and the italicised interrogative/negative/degree phrase is in spec-CP.

However, the assumption made in (3) that the inverted auxiliary is in C raises the question of how it comes to be there, since auxiliaries are normally positioned in T. The answer implicit in the traditional term Auxiliary Inversion is that the auxiliary is 'inverted' with its subject. Within the framework used here, this can be taken to mean that the auxiliary originates in the head T position of TP, and from there moves into the head C position of CP and thereby comes to be positioned between the underlined subject (which is in spec-TP) and the italicised phrase preceding it (which is in spec-CP). If so, Auxiliary Inversion in a sentence like (1a) involves the movement operation arrowed below:

(4)

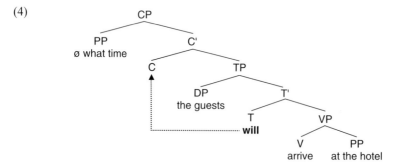

The key assumption made about Auxiliary Inversion in (4) is that the auxiliary *will* originates in T and from there moves to C. This means that Auxiliary Inversion is treated as a case of **T-to-C Movement**. But what exactly is involved in this kind of movement?

To answer this question, let's look in rather more detail at the derivation of (1a) *What time will the guests arrive at the hotel?* The verb *arrive* merges with its PP complement *at the hotel* to form the VP *arrive at the hotel*. This VP is then merged with the T auxiliary *will* to form the T-bar *will arrive at the hotel*, and this T-bar is in turn merged with the DP *the guests* to form the TP *the guests will arrive at the hotel*. The resulting TP is subsequently merged with a null complementiser *ø* to form the C-bar *ø the guests will arrive at the hotel*. This C-bar is merged with the interrogative phrase *what time* (which we can take to be a PP headed by a null counterpart of the preposition *at*), so forming the CP in (5) below:

(5)

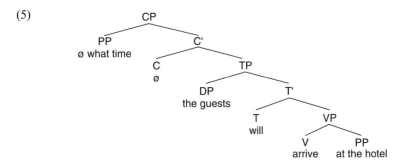

When Auxiliary Inversion (= T-to-C Movement) applies, the null complementiser in C behaves like an affix in attracting the auxiliary *will* in T to adjoin (i.e. attach) to it, resulting in the structure shown in simplified form below (where the + symbol indicates that one constituent has been adjoined to another):

(6)

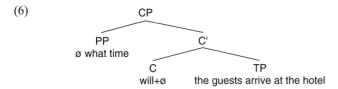

Adjoining the auxiliary *will* to the interrogative affix in C forms what is in effect an interrogative auxiliary.

Such an interrogative affix analysis is far from implausible from a cross-linguistic point of view, since (e.g.) questions in Latin could involve an 'inverted' verb attaching to the affixal interrogative complementiser *-ne*, so forming a *verb+ne* structure like that in (7) below, where Q denotes a question affix:

(7)   **Potes***ne*   dīcere?   (Cicero)
        Can$_{2.Sg}$+Q say
        'Can you say?'

What's interesting about the type of structure in (7) is that Latin is a language which shows **head-last** order in verb phrases, so head verbs normally follow their complements: we would therefore expect the modal verb *potes*$_{can}$ to follow its complement *dīcere*~say~ in such a sentence. The fact that *potes*~can~ ends up at the beginning of the sentence means that something must have attracted it to move out of its underlying clause-final position into its superficial clause-initial position. And since the affix *-ne* is a question particle, and we saw in §4.7 that the edge of CP is the **locus** of the interrogative force of questions, it is reasonable to take *-ne* to be an affixal interrogative complementiser/C, and to suppose that this affixal C attracts the closest finite verb to adjoin to it. Given this assumption, we can then propose a parallel analysis of Interrogative Inversion in English under which an affixal question particle in C attracts an auxiliary in T (like *will* in 4–6 above) to adjoin to it, creating an interrogative auxiliary of the form AUX+AF, comprising an auxiliary with an interrogative affix attached to it. Of course, an important difference between questions in Latin and English is that the interrogative affix is overt in Latin but null in English. However, the idea of a null affix is already familiar from earlier chapters, since under the Affix Hopping analysis of verb morphology outlined in Chapters 3 and 4, a past tense verb like *put* in a sentence like 'I *put* it in the garage yesterday' is analysed as having the structure PUT+AF, where AF is a past tense affix which has a null spellout on a verb like *put*.

An interesting prediction made by the claim that Interrogative Inversion leads to the formation of an interrogative auxiliary form is that there could (in principle) be some auxiliaries in English with distinct interrogative and non-interrogative forms: this is because the relevant auxiliary will have an interrogative affix attached to it in questions but not in other structures, and (even though the affix has no overt phonological form), its presence could affect the spellout of the auxiliary (in much the same way as, under the account of verb morphology given in Chapters 3 and 4, an invisible past tense affix attached to a verb like *sit* causes the string SIT+AF~PAST~ to be spelled out as *sat*). A case of an auxiliary which has a distinct interrogative form arises in relation to the contracted negative counterpart of the (first person singular present tense) auxiliary *am*. This has the negative variant *aren't*, but (in my own variety of English) the form *aren't* (when used with the first person singular subject *I*) is restricted to use in root questions, as we see from the contrast below:

(8) (a)   Why *aren't* I entitled to claim Social Security benefits?

(b)   *I wonder why I *aren't* entitled to claim Social Security benefits (> '... *why I'm not* ...')

In other words, *aren't* is restricted to structures in which it undergoes Interrogative Inversion. This can be accounted for straightforwardly if we suppose that (when used as a first person singular form) *aren't* can only spell out the structure *aren't*+Q (where Q represents an abstract question affix).

An important question raised by the T-to-C Movement analysis of Auxiliary Inversion is what happens to the head T position of TP when an inverted auxiliary moves from T to C. At first sight, it might seem as if the T position vacated by the auxiliary simply disappears once the T auxiliary moves to C. If this were so, (1a) would have the structure shown in simplified form in (9) below:

(9)

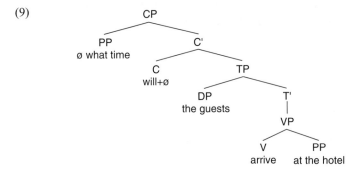

However, a structure like (9) is problematic because the TP constituent it contains violates two constituent structure principles posited in §2.2, namely:

(10) (i)   **Headedness Principle**
            Every non-terminal constituent in a syntactic structure is a projection of a head lexical item.
     (ii)   **Binarity Principle**
            Every non-terminal constituent in a syntactic structure is binary-branching.

(9) violates the headedness requirement (10i) in that TP and T-bar are non-terminal nodes/constituents and yet neither has a head T constituent; (9) also violates the binarity requirement (10ii) in that T-bar is a non-terminal node and yet is not binary-branching (since T-bar does not have two daughters) but rather unary-branching (since T-bar has only one daughter).

For these reasons, it is clear that movement of an auxiliary from T to C cannot result in the loss of the original T constituent which heads TP: consequently, T must remain in place in the form of a **null** constituent of some kind. But what kind of item could the relevant null T constituent contain? The discussion of **Gapping** (i.e. head ellipsis) in §4.4 suggests a possible answer. There, it was proposed that ellipsis of the second (italicised) occurrence of *could* in a sentence such as (11a) below results in a structure such as (11b) containing a null occurrence of *could* (below designated as ~~could~~):

(11) (a)   He **could** have helped her, or she *could* have helped him
     (b)   He **could** have helped her, or she ~~could~~ have helped him

This raises the possibility that T-to-C Movement is a composite operation by which a **copy** of an auxiliary in T is first moved into C, and then the original occurrence of the auxiliary in T is **deleted** (by which is meant that its phonetic features are given a **null spellout** in the PF component and so the auxiliary is unpronounced), leaving a null/silent copy of the auxiliary in T. The assumption that movement is a composite operation involving two suboperations of copying and deletion is the cornerstone of the **Copy Theory of Movement** developed by Chomsky.

To see how the copying analysis of movement works, let's take another look at the derivation of (1a) *What time will the guests arrive at the hotel?* Let us suppose that we have reached a stage in the derivation of the sentence where a series of merge operations have formed the structure in (5) above. At this point, Auxiliary Inversion applies. Under the Copy Theory of Movement, this means that a copy of the T auxiliary *will* is created, and this adjoins to a null interrogative affix in C, forming what is in effect an interrogative auxiliary, because it is an auxiliary with an (invisible) interrogative affix attached to it. There are potential parallels here with the analysis of T-auxiliaries proposed in §4.4, under which the auxiliary *did* in 'He *did* enjoy syntax' was argued to comprise a past tense affix -*d* to which the stem form *do* is adjoined, forming *do+d* (which in turn is spelled out as the irregular past tense form *did* in the PF component).

Given these assumptions and the further assumption that constituents leave a copy behind when they move, this means that Auxiliary Inversion in a sentence like (1a) *What time will the guests arrive?* involves a null affixal question particle in C (below denoted simply as ø) attracting a copy of the auxiliary *will* in T to adjoin to it, so giving rise to the formation of a complex C constituent comprising the auxiliary *will* attached to a null, affixal interrogative complementiser – as shown below:

(12)

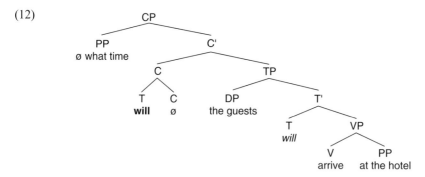

The TP and T-bar constituents in (12) satisfy the Headedness Principle (10i), since both are headed by a T constituent containing the original copy of *will*; TP and T-bar also satisfy the Binarity Principle (10ii), since both have two daughters.

Implicit in (12) is the idea that the auxiliary in T is positioned to the left of the affixal question particle in C at PF: although this is impossible to see directly (because the affix is null), the idea gains support from two observations. Firstly, English is a language in which inflectional affixes are all suffixal in nature (i.e. are positioned after the items they attach to): e.g. the past tense affix -*ed* attaches to the end of the stem *wait* in *waited*. And secondly, in a compound noun like *coffee-maker*, the noun *coffee* adjoins to the left of the head noun *maker* (because English is a language with right-headed compounds – i.e. a language in which the head of a compound word is positioned to the right of other constituents in the compound: the word *maker* is the head of the compound because it carries the suffix -*s* when the compound is pluralised, as in *two coffee-makers*). Thus, the structure in (12) is consistent with the view that English is a suffixal language with right-headed compounds. Let's therefore suppose that the null question particle in (12) is a **suffix**.

Once all the relevant merge and movement operations have taken place in the syntax, the syntactic structure in (12) is handed over to the PF component, which determines how the structure is to be spelled out (i.e. pronounced). Considerations of computational efficiency mean that only one copy of a moved constituent is normally spelled out overtly, since this minimises the amount of material to be pronounced; and considerations of optimal design dictate that the highest copy is normally the one which is overtly spelled out, since otherwise movement would be undetectable. These considerations suggest the following spellout rule (termed the *default* rule because it a fall-back rule which applies to constituents in default of their spellout being determined by some other spellout rule or requirement):

(13)   **Default Spellout Rule**
        For a constituent whose spellout is not determined by some other rule or requirement, the highest copy of the constituent is pronounced at PF, and any lower copies are silent.

It follows from (13) that only the higher (bold-printed) copy of *will* in C is pronounced at PF in (12), and the lower (italicised) copy of *will* in T is silent. Consequently, the structure in (12) will eventually be spelled out at PF as the string/sentence (1a) *What time will the guests arrive at the hotel?*

Empirical evidence in support of a copying analysis of Auxiliary Inversion comes from the phenomenon of *have*-cliticisation discussed in §4.3. In this connection, note that *have* cannot cliticise onto the pronoun *I/we/you/they* in Auxiliary Inversion structures such as the following:

(14) (a)   Why should **they have**/*_they 've_ called the police?
     (b)   When will **you have**/*_you 've_ finished the rehearsal?
     (c)   Never would **I have**/*_I 've_ agreed to such a proposal
     (d)   How could **I have**/*_I 've_ known you were in trouble?

(*'ve* represents the vowel-less clitic form /v/ here.) The sequence *they 've* in (14a) does not rhyme with *grave* in careful speech styles, since it is pronounced /ðeiəv/ not /ðeiv/. Likewise, the sequence *you 've* in (14b) is not homophonous with *groove* in careful speech styles, since *you have* in (14a) can be reduced to /juəv/ but not /ju:v/. Similarly, *I 've* doesn't rhyme with *hive* in (14c,d), since *I have* can be reduced to /aiəv/ not to /aiv/. Why should cliticisation of *have* onto the pronoun be blocked in (14)? We can give a straightforward answer to this question if we posit that when an inverted auxiliary moves from T to C, it leaves behind a silent copy of itself in the T position out of which it moves. Given this assumption, a sentence such as (14a) will have the structure shown below (where *have* belongs to the category PERF of Perfect Aspect Auxiliary and projects into a PERFP/Perfect Phrase constituent, as in §4.3):

(15)

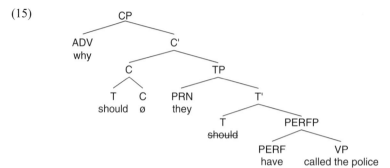

In §4.3, *have*-cliticisation was characterised as follows:

(16)   **Have-cliticisation**
         The word *have* can encliticise to (i.e. attach to the end of) another word W in the phonological component, provided that
         (i)   W ends in a vowel/diphthong
         (ii)   W immediately precedes *have*
         (iii) W c-commands *have*

Although in (15) the pronoun *they* ends in a diphthong and c-commands *have* (because the TP node which is the mother of PRN-*they* contains *have*) the pronoun *they* does not immediately precede the auxiliary *have* at PF because the null auxiliary ~~should~~ which occupies the head T position of TP intervenes between them. This intervening null auxiliary blocks *have*-cliticisation, thereby accounting for the ungrammaticality of (14a) **Why should they've called the police?* Note that a crucial plank in the argumentation here is the assumption that T-to-C Movement leaves behind a silent copy of the moved auxiliary in the head T position of TP, and this silent auxiliary serves to block cliticisation of *have* onto a c-commanding pronoun.

A different source of evidence in support of the copy theory of movement comes from **auxiliary copying/doubling** structures produced by children and adults. Guasti, Thornton and Wexler (1995) note that young children sometimes use auxiliary doubling in negative questions like the following (where the names of the children producing the relevant structures and their ages in YEARS; MONTHS are shown in parentheses):

(17) (a)   Why *could* Snoopy *could***n't** fit in the boat? (Kathy 4;0)
     (b)   What *did* he *did***n't** wanna bring to school? (Darrell 4;1)

Likewise, adults sometimes produce sporadic auxiliary copying errors like the following, which I recorded from live, unscripted radio/TV broadcasts:

(18) (a)   I began by asking him: 'How serious *is* this injury really *is*?' (Adam Hunt, Talk Sport Radio)
     (b)   The manager's uncertain which *is* his best side *is* (Kevin Ratcliffe, ITV4)

(c)   The real question is: 'How much continuity *can* Vidal Pereira (the assistant of Villas Boas, who is now the head coach of Porto) *can* provide?' (Andy Brassell, BBC Radio 5)

The examples in (17–18) all involve an italicised auxiliary moving from T to C, with both the higher copy of the auxiliary in C and the lower copy in T being spelled out overtly. However, while such structures provide empirical support for the claim that Auxiliary Inversion is a copying operation, they raise the following important question of principle. If grammars are governed by 'principles of computational efficiency that may well be reducible to laws of nature' (Chomsky 2013: 5), why don't the children and adults concerned give the lower copy of the auxiliary in T a null spellout in accordance with the Default Spellout Rule (13), rather than (inefficiently, it would seem) pronouncing the auxiliary twice?

Let's first consider the case of the children's auxiliary doubling structures in (17). Let us suppose that the children treat the contracted negative particle *n't* as a PF clitic – i.e. an item which encliticises onto (i.e. attaches to the end of) an immediately preceding overt **host** at PF (the only suitable host for *n't* being a finite auxiliary). If so, the following problem arises. If *could* moves from T to C in (17a), and if the copy of the auxiliary in T is given a null spellout in accordance with the Default Spellout Rule (13), this will result in the string *Why could Snoopy ~~could~~ n't fit in the boat?* But the resulting structure is one in which the clitic *n't* has been illicitly **stranded** without an overt host to attach to. The children circumvent this problem by pronouncing the lower copy of the auxiliary in T (*Why could Snoopy could n't fit in the boat?*), thereby creating an overt host (underlined) for the clitic *n't* to attach to. In this case, an independent requirement (the need for the clitic *n't* to have an overt host) over-rides the normal procedure of giving lower copies a silent pronunciation: and indeed such an eventuality is allowed for in the formulation of the Default Spellout Rule in (13), since this envisages the possibility that 'some other rule or requirement' can sometimes over-rule default spellout. (Although I will not elaborate on this here, I note that adults solve the *n't*-cliticisation problem in a different way, namely by treating *n't* as a syntactic clitic which attaches to an auxiliary in T in the syntax, and then the whole *Aux+n't* string moves to C as single unit, so that in place of 17a, adults say *Why couldn't Snoopy fit in the boat?*)

Now let's turn to consider why auxiliary doubling arises in adult sentences like (18). Here, the cause of the doubling seems to be very different. As we saw in §2.9, English uses Auxiliary Inversion in direct speech (e.g. in the underlined string in *I asked him 'How serious **is** this injury?'*) but not in indirect/reported speech (e.g. in the underlined string in *I asked him how serious this injury **is***). It would seem that adults producing structures like those in (18) start out with the intention of producing direct speech (and so spell out a copy of the inverted auxiliary in C) but forget this halfway through the sentence and instead switch to indirect speech (and so spell out a copy of the auxiliary in T). On this view, sentences like (18) are sporadic production errors which represent a **blend** of direct and indirect speech. (See §1.2 for discussion of blends.)

Our discussion of Auxiliary Inversion in this section has interesting implications for the derivation of sentences. In this connection, consider how we derive a sentence such as:

(19)   Why would you resign?

The first stage is to go to the **lexicon** (= dictionary) and choose a **lexical array** (i.e. a set of lexical items out of which the sentence is going to be built). In the case of (19), the lexical array will consist of the verb *resign*, the pronoun *you*, the auxiliary *would*, a null complementiser *ø* and the interrogative adverb *why*. The next stage is for the auxiliary *would* and the verb *resign* to be taken out of the lexical array and merged, so deriving the T-bar *would resign*. The pronoun *you* is then taken from the lexical array and merged with the T-bar *would resign* to form the TP *you would resign*. The null complementiser *ø* is then taken from the lexical array and merged with the TP *you would resign* to form the C-bar *ø you would resign*. The adverb *why* is then taken from the lexical array and merged with the C-bar *ø you would resign* to form the CP *why ø you would resign*. The null complementiser *ø* in C then attracts a copy of the auxiliary *would* to adjoin to it, forming the syntactic structure *Why would+ø you would resign?* In the PF component, the lower copy of *would* is given a silent spellout via the Default Spellout Rule (13), resulting in the PF structure *Why would+ø you ~~would~~ resign?* and this is ultimately pronounced as the PF string (19) *Why would you resign?*

5.3   Triggering Auxiliary Inversion

A question which we have not so far addressed is 'What triggers Auxiliary Inversion?' Since (as we saw in §2.10) **features** are devices which can trigger grammatical operations, a plausible answer to this question is that C carries a feature of some kind which attracts T to adjoin to C in structures like (12) and (15). Reasoning along these lines, let us suppose that C (in Auxiliary Inversion structures) carries a T-feature which requires C to have a T constituent (more specifically, a tensed auxiliary) adjoined to it. If so, C will carry a T-feature in Auxiliary Inversion structures like (3) above, repeated as (20) below:

(20)

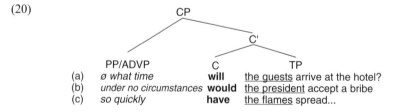

	PP/ADVP	C	TP
(a)	ø what time	will	the guests arrive at the hotel?
(b)	under no circumstances	would	the president accept a bribe
(c)	so quickly	have	the flames spread...

However, we clearly can't simply assume that any C constituent can carry a T-feature triggering Inversion, because seemingly similar Auxiliary Inversion structures like (21) below are ungrammatical in declarative uses (i.e. if used as statements):

(21)

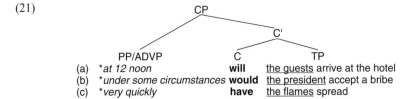

(A complication I set aside here is that such sentences are relatively acceptable as *questions*, especially if there is a pause after the initial constituent, as in 'Under some circumstances, would the president accept a bribe?'. I'll ask you to analyse why this might be in one of the exercises at the end of the chapter.) If we compare structures like (20) where Inversion is permitted with those like (21) where it is not, we see that whether or not Inversion is permitted is correlated with the choice of (italicised) specifier for C. For example, Inversion takes place if C has an interrogative specifier like *ø what time* in (20a), or a negative specifier like *under no circumstances* in (20b), or a degree specifier like *so quickly* in (20c), but not if C has other kinds of specifier like those italicised in (21). If a T-feature on C drives Auxiliary Inversion, we can conclude that certain types of specifier (including interrogative, negative and degree constituents) license/allow C to carry a T-feature triggering Auxiliary Inversion (i.e. adjunction of a present or past tense T auxiliary to C), whereas other types of specifier do not.

However a complication arises when we look at what happens in embedded clauses like those bracketed below, where we find an interesting asymmetry:

(22) (a) *He said [*never* he **had** been so offended in all his life]
     (b) He said [*never* **had** he been so offended in all his life]

(23) (a) *The mayor said [*so quickly* the fire **had** spread that the firefighters lost control of it]
     (b) The mayor said [*so quickly* **had** the fire spread that the firefighters lost control of it]

(24) (a) He found out [*why* she **had** left early]
     (b) *He found out [*why* **had** she left early]

These examples (taken together with those in 1) suggest that Inversion triggered by a negative or degree specifier occurs both in main clauses like (1b,c) and in embedded clauses like those bracketed in (22b, 23b), whereas Inversion triggered by an interrogative specifier is restricted to occurring in main clauses like (1a) and does not occur in embedded clauses like that bracketed in (24b) – in standard varieties of English, at least. (On non-standard varieties, see below.) This suggests the following generalisation about the conditions under which C is licensed to carry an Inversion-triggering T-feature:

(25)   **Inversion Licensing Condition**
              A null C is licensed to carry a T-feature triggering Auxiliary Inversion (i.e.
              adjunction of a T auxiliary to C) if
                  (i) C has a negative or degree specifier
                  or
                  (ii) C has an interrogative specifier in a root clause.

Below, we will see that there are other types of constituent which can license
Auxiliary Inversion. (It should be noted in passing that 25ii may need to be
modified in order to deal with inversion in **free indirect speech** structures like
those discussed in §2.9, e.g. *He asked why had she left early,* but I will set this
issue aside here.)

   A tacit assumption embodied in the Inversion Licensing Condition (25) is
that only a null C can trigger Auxiliary Inversion and attract T to adjoin to C.
An interesting piece of evidence in support of this claim comes from Belfast
English, which is a variety of English that differs from standard varieties in
allowing Auxiliary Inversion in embedded questions as well as main-clause
questions. In Belfast English, we find the following range of structures in
embedded questions like those bracketed below:

(26) (a)   I don't know [*why* he has resigned]
     (b)   I don't know [*why* **that** he has resigned]
     (c)   I don't know [*why* <u>has</u> he resigned]
     (d)   *I don't know [*why* **that** <u>has</u> he resigned]

As these examples show, Belfast English differs from standard varieties of
English in that it allows the complementiser *that* to be used with an
interrogative specifier like *why* in a finite embedded interrogative clause
like that bracketed in (26b): it may be that an overt complementiser like
that has to be the first word in any clause it introduces in standard varieties
(and so is incompatible with an interrogative specifier), but that no such
restriction holds in Belfast English (so allowing *that* to have an interrogative specifier). Belfast English also differs from standard varieties in
permitting Auxiliary Inversion in embedded questions like that bracketed
in (26c). However, Belfast English doesn't allow structures like (26d),
where a finite embedded interrogative clause contains both the complementiser *that* and an inverted auxiliary. Why should this be? If Auxiliary
Inversion involves T-to-C Movement, and if the head position in a phrase
(e.g. the head C position of CP) can only be occupied by one independent
word (not by more than one), we can account for the data in (26) by
supposing that Auxiliary Inversion can apply in embedded as well as
main-clause questions in Belfast English, but that T can only move to C
when C is empty (or more precisely, when C contains a null affixal complementiser), and not when C is filled by a non-affixal complementiser
like *that.*

5.4   CP recursion

The discussion in the previous section suggests that Auxiliary Inversion involves a finite T auxiliary adjoining to a null C which has a T-feature: as we have just seen, this predicts that clauses which contain an overt complementiser like *that* do not allow Auxiliary Inversion. However, the generality of the claim that overt complementisers block Auxiliary Inversion is called into question by sentences such as the following:

(27) (a)   He vowed [**that** *never again* <u>would</u> he take drugs]
     (b)   The mayor reported [**that** *so swiftly* <u>had</u> the fire spread that the firefighters couldn't control it]

Sentences like (27) pose an apparent problem for the claim that inverted auxiliaries move from T to C. This is because the T-to-C Movement analysis of Auxiliary Inversion predicts (as we saw in 26) that a finite clause cannot contain both a complementiser like *that* and an inverted auxiliary. And yet, this claim (and, more generally, the T-to-C Movement analysis of Auxiliary Inversion) is seemingly called into question by sentences like (27), where it is clear that the inverted auxiliary *would* occupies a different position from the complementiser *that*, since *would* follows and *that* precedes the negative adverbial phrase *never again*. How can we deal with such potential exceptions to the T-to-C Movement analysis of Auxiliary Inversion?

A traditional answer is to suppose that clauses like those bracketed in (27) allow **recursion** (i.e. multiple occurrences) of CP. More specifically, let us suppose that they allow one CP to be stacked on top of another, internally within the same clause. On this view, the embedded clause bracketed in (27a) is derived by first forming the CP *never again would he take drugs* and then embedding this CP within a larger CP headed by *that*, forming the CP *that never again would he take drugs*. This means that the bracketed complement clause in (27a) has the derivation shown below (simplified by omitting the internal structure of constituents not directly relevant to the discussion at hand):

(28)

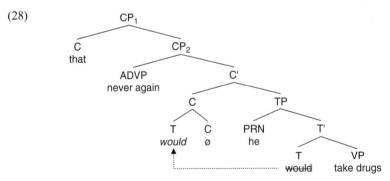

Under this analysis, the relevant clause contains two CP projections, a higher one (= CP$_1$) headed by *that*, and a lower one (= CP$_2$) headed by a null complementiser which attracts T-*would* to adjoin to it, the relevant T-to-C Movement operation being indicated by the dotted arrow. It may be that the need for two CP projections in this kind of structure is forced by the selectional requirements of the verb *vow*, since *vow* selects a CP headed by *that* as its complement, and this selectional requirement will not be met if *vow* has a CP complement headed by a null (Inversion-triggering) C. (Note that the numeral subscripts on the CP nodes in tree 28 are added purely for ease of identification and are not part of the structure.)

At first sight, the claim that there are CP recursion structures in which one CP is embedded within another may seem implausible. However, the idea of CP recursion gains independent motivation from double-*that* structures such as the following (which I recorded from live radio broadcasts):

(29) (a)   I just wanted to say [**that**, despite all these short term problems, **that** they needed to keep in mind the needs of the poor] (Bill Gates, BBC Radio 4)

(b)   My hope is [**that**, by the time we meet, **that** we'll have made some progress] (President Obama, press conference, BBC Radio 5)

(c)   The party opposite said [**that**, if we cut 6 billion from the budget, **that** it would end in catastrophe] (David Cameron, *Prime Minister's Questions*, BBC Radio 5)

Since the bracketed complement clauses in (29) contain two separate occurrences of the complementiser *that*, it is plausible to suppose that they contain two separate CP constituents.

An interesting question to ask about CP recursion structures like those in (27–29) above is whether they involve multiple instances of the same CP category, or whether each CP they contain serves a different function from the others. Pioneering research by Rizzi (1997) has argued that the various CPs involved in CP recursion structures are indeed different in nature. He concludes from this that CPs should be *split* into a number of different types of peripheral projection. Under his **split projection** analysis (whereby CP is split into a number of different types of peripheral projection), the higher CP (= CP_1) in (28) could be taken to be a force projection (**FORCEP**) headed by a **FORCE** constituent which marks the clause as declarative in force/type, and the lower CP projection (= CP_2) could be taken to be a focus projection (**FOCP**) which serves to house the focused negative constituent *never again*. If so, the embedded clause in (27a) would not have the CP recursion analysis in (28), but rather a split projection analysis along the lines presented in a simplified form in (30) below (where the inverted auxiliary *would* adjoins to a null FOC/focus head, below denoted as ø):

(30)

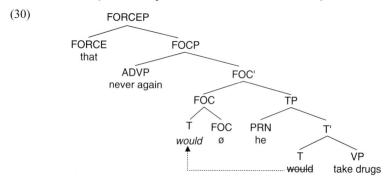

To simplify presentation, however, I'll adopt a CP recursion analysis like that in (28) for clauses like those bracketed in (27, 29).

5.5 Null operators

Thus far, I have argued that Auxiliary Inversion occurs when a C constituent has an interrogative, negative or degree specifier which licenses it to carry a tense feature attracting a T auxiliary to adjoin to C, in conformity with the Inversion Licensing Condition (25). However, an apparent problem for the claim that Inversion is licensed by C having an interrogative/negative/degree specifier is posed by the observation that Auxiliary Inversion can take place in yes–no questions like those below, where there appears to be no specifier to trigger Inversion of the auxiliary:

(31) (a)   **Have** <u>you</u> apologised to her?
   (b)   **Will** <u>the Democrats</u> oppose the reforms?
   (c)   **Have** <u>they</u> withdrawn the advertisement?

How can we reconcile yes–no questions like (31) with the Inversion Licensing Condition in (25)? A traditional answer given in research dating back decades (mentioned in §4.7) is that in yes–no questions, C has a silent yes–no question **operator** as its specifier, and it is this operator which (by virtue of being interrogative) triggers Auxiliary Inversion in main-clause questions, in conformity with the Inversion Licensing Condition (25). It is called a yes–no question operator because it has the semantic function of making a proposition into a yes–no question which questions the truth value of the proposition (e.g. 31a asks whether it is true or false that you have apologised to her).

From a typological perspective, the *null question operator* analysis is by no means implausible, since there are many languages in the world which use an overt yes–no question operator (like those italicised below, glossed as Op_{YNQ}) to introduce yes–no questions:

(32) (a)   *Kas* suitsetate? [Estonian]
      Op_{YNQ} you.smoke
      'Do you smoke?'
   (b)   *Aya* Ali ketab darad? [Persian]
      Op_{YNQ} Ali books has
      'Does Ali have any books?'
   (c)   *Waš* hdarti m^ʕah? [Moroccan Arabic]
      Op_{YNQ} you.spoke with.him
      'Did you speak to him?'
   (d)   *Czy* zamykacie okna? [Polish]
      Op_{YNQ} you.close windows
      'Are you closing the windows?'

(e)   *Walay* sarai khaza khuwakhae? [Pashto]
Op_{YNQ} man woman likes
'Does the man like the woman?'

(f)   *Razve* on ne prixodil? [Russian]
Op_{YNQ} he not came
'Hasn't he come?'
[Comrie 1984: 22]

(g)   *An* bpósfaidh tú mé? [Irish]
Op_{YNQ} will.marry you me
'Will you marry me?'
[McCloskey 1979: 79]

(h)   *Is* idda hmad s tmazirt? [Berber]
Op_{YNQ} went Ahmed to country
'Did Ahmed go to the country?'
[Sadiqi 1986: 9]

Moreover (as noted in §4.7), Shakespearean English had main-clause yes–no questions containing an inverted auxiliary preceded by the adverbial yes–no question operator *whether*, as illustrated below:

(33) (a)   *Whether* **had** you rather lead mine eyes or eye your master's heels? (Mrs Page, *Merry Wives of Windsor*, III.ii)

    (b)   *Whether* **dost** thou profess thyself a knave or a fool? (Lafeu, *All's Well That Ends Well*, IV.v)

If the bold-printed inverted auxiliary adjoins to the head C of CP in (33), this suggests that *whether* in Shakespearean English functioned as a yes–no question operator occupying the specifier position in CP. This being so, a sentence like (33a) would be a CP derived as shown in highly simplified form below:

(34)

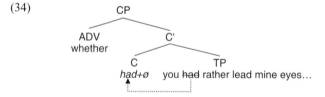

We could then say that the interrogative operator *whether* in spec-CP licenses Auxiliary Inversion in a Shakespearean English structure like (34): more precisely, in conformity with the Inversion Licensing Condition (25), the head C of CP in (34) is licensed to carry a T-feature by virtue of having the interrogative specifier *whether*, and the T-feature on C attracts the T auxiliary *had* to move from T to adjoin to the null complementiser in C.

    By analogy with sentences like (32, 33), let us suppose that present-day English uses a silent question operator in yes–no questions, and (as in §4.7) let's designate this as Op_{YNQ}. Let's also assume that (like *whether*) this silent question operator is an adverb (although nothing hangs on this). On this view, a yes–no question like (31a) *Have you apologised to her?* will be derived as follows. The preposition *to* merges with the pronoun *her* to form the PP *to her*. This PP merges with the verb *apologised* to form the VP *apologised to her*. The resulting VP merges with the T auxiliary *have* to form the T-bar *have apologised* to her, and then this T-bar is merged with the pronoun *you* to form the TP *you have apologised to her*. This TP is in turn merged with a null complementiser to form the C-bar *ø you have apologised to her*. This C-bar is then merged with the null yes–no question operator to form a CP with the structure shown below (simplified by not showing the internal structure of VP):

(35)

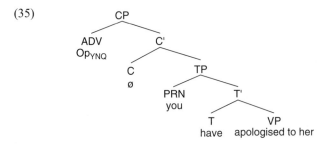

Since C in (35) has an interrogative specifier, C is licensed to carry a tense feature in accordance with the Inversion Licensing Condition (25ii). This tense feature on C attracts the T auxiliary *have* to adjoin to a null affixal complementiser in C, deriving the structure (36) below (with strikethrough indicating that the lower copy of the inverted auxiliary *have* is ultimately given a null spellout in the PF component and so is silent):

(36)

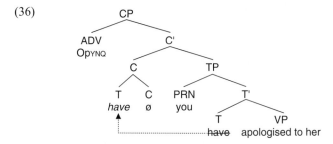

Since the yes–no question operator and complementiser are null/silent, and since the lower copy of *have* is given a silent spellout via the Default Spellout Rule (13), the resulting structure (36) is pronounced at PF as the string (31a) *Have you apologised to her?*

So far, the only justification given for positing a null question operator in yes–no questions like (31) is that, if Auxiliary Inversion is contingent upon the presence of an appropriate (interrogative, negative or degree) specifier, then yes–no questions must have an interrogative specifier in order to account for why they show Auxiliary Inversion. However, if English does have a null yes–no question operator, we should expect it to play an important role at both the PF interface and the LF interface. Its role at the PF interface is to determine that structures like (36) are given the rising intonation characteristic of questions rather than the falling intonation characteristic of statements. The yes–no question operator also plays an important role at the LF/semantic interface, in determining that a structure like (36) is typed as a yes–no question, in accordance with the Clause Typing Condition posited in §4.7, repeated as (37) below:

(37)   **Clause Typing Condition**
         A CP is typed as interrogative (i.e. interpreted as interrogative in type in the semantic component) if it has an interrogative specifier, exclamative if it has an exclamative specifier ... etc. Otherwise, a CP headed by an indicative complementiser is interpreted as declarative in type by default.

An important question to ask is how a sentence like (31a) *Have you apologised to her?* comes to be interpreted as a yes–no question. This cannot be because of the presence of Auxiliary Inversion, since Auxiliary Inversion is also found in non-interrogative clauses (e.g. negative and degree clauses). So what is it that types a sentence like (31a) as a yes–no question? The answer provided by the analysis in (36) is that the presence of a yes–no question operator in spec-CP means that the relevant structure is interpreted as a yes–no question in accordance with the Clause Typing Condition (37).

So, as we see, the yes–no question operator plays an important role at the PF and LF interfaces, in determining intonation and interpretation. Moreover, the operator can also be argued to play an important role in other areas of grammar – for example, in licensing the occurrence of polarity items like those italicised below in a (formal style) yes–no question:

(38)   *Dare anyone say anything?*

We saw in §3.7 that *any*-compounds (in partitive uses) and *need/dare* (in their obsolescent use as modal auxiliaries) are polarity items, and that polarity items are subject to the following licensing condition:

(39)   **Polarity Licensing Condition**
         A polarity expression must be c-commanded by an appropriate (e.g. negative, interrogative or conditional) licenser.

In the light of (39), let's ask what licenses the occurrence of the three italicised polarity items in a yes–no question like *Dare anyone say anything?*

The answer provided by the null operator analysis is that yes–no questions contain a silent yes–no question operator in spec-CP, and this interrogative operator c-commands (and thereby licenses) the relevant polarity items. To see how, consider the superficial structure of sentence (38) above after Auxiliary Inversion has applied (in the manner shown by the arrow below) to move the modal auxiliary *dare* from T to attach to a null affixal complementiser in C, so deriving the structure in (40) below:

(40)

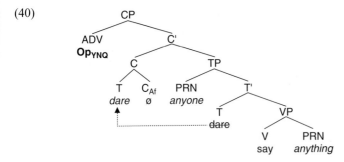

The bold-printed yes–no question operator in (40) c-commands all three italicised polarity items *dare, anyone* and *anything* because the mother of ADV-Op$_{YNQ}$ is CP, and CP contains all three of these polarity items. Thus, all three polarity items are licensed by virtue of being c-commanded by the bold-printed yes–no question operator in (40), in conformity with the Polarity Licensing Condition (39).

An additional piece of evidence in support of positing a null operator in yes–no questions is the following. An interesting property of yes–no questions is that they are incompatible with fronting a negative constituent. Thus, if we replace *anything* by *nothing* in (38) and then move *nothing* to spec-CP, the resulting sentence is ungrammatical as a question (even though it is grammatical as a statement, in formal styles of English):

(41)   *Nothing dare anyone say?

Why should (41) be ungrammatical as a question? The answer suggested by the null operator analysis of yes–no questions is that yes–no questions are CPs which have an abstract yes–no question operator in spec-CP in a structure like (40), and this means that the spec-CP position in the relevant clause is not available for *nothing* to move into (since C cannot have two specifiers which both trigger Auxiliary Inversion, as we see from the ungrammaticality of sentences like *'**Why** *nothing* did he say?').

Overall, then, we see that the postulation of a silent yes–no question operator accounts for four defining properties of yes–no questions, namely (i) why they are interpreted as yes–no questions, (ii) why they show Auxiliary Inversion in main clauses, (iii) why they license the occurrence of polarity items and (iv) why they are incompatible with negative preposing.

Our discussion of yes–no questions has so far been limited to root/main-clause questions. However, unlike these, embedded yes–no questions don't permit Auxiliary Inversion in standard varieties of English and are introduced by *if* or *whether*:

(42) (a)   I'm not sure [*if/whether* he **should** stay]
      (b)   I'm not sure [*if/whether* **should** he stay]

Auxiliary Inversion is barred in embedded questions like those bracketed in (42) because the Inversion Licensing Condition (25) specifies that (in standard varieties of English), C is only licensed to carry a T-feature triggering Auxiliary Inversion *in a main/root clause*. (As noted earlier, the discussion here is simplified by ignoring the phenomenon of free indirect speech discussed in §2.9.)

But what is the structure of an embedded question like that bracketed in (42a)? In §2.9, we saw that the items *if/whether* (as used in 42a) function as yes–no question complementisers occupying the head C position of CP. At the beginning of this section, we also saw that main/root clause yes–no questions contain an abstract yes–no question operator in spec-CP. If we extend this analysis to embedded yes–no questions and assume that *if/ whether* have a null yes–no question operator as their specifier, the embedded yes–no question bracketed in (42a) above will have the structure shown in (43) below:

(43)

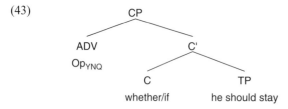

The analysis in (43) gains theoretical support from the Clause Typing Condition (37), since it follows from (37) that the CP in (43) will be typed as a yes–no question by virtue of having a yes–no question operator as its specifier.

In this section, we have seen that there is evidence in favour of positing a null operator in yes–no questions. However, there are also other types of clause in which it is plausible to posit the presence of a null operator. We'll look at just one of these here, namely **conditional** clauses like those bracketed below:

(44) (a)   [**If** anything should happen to me], contact the embassy
    (b)   [*Should* anything happen to me], contact the embassy
    (c)   *[**If** *should* anything happen to me], contact the embassy

As we see from the clauses italicised in (44), a conditional clause can be introduced either by *if* or by an inverted auxiliary, but not by both. This suggests that the head C position of CP in a conditional clause can be occupied either by *if* (as in 44a), or by an inverted auxiliary (as in 44b), but not by both (as in 44c). If Auxiliary Inversion is triggered by an appropriate kind of licenser in spec-CP, this suggests that inverted conditional clauses contain a null conditional operator in spec-CP. This would mean that the conditional clause bracketed in (44b) has the superficial structure shown in simplified form in (45) below (where Op$_{COND}$ denotes a conditional operator):

(45)

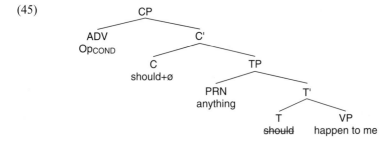

The null conditional operator in spec-CP in (45) will license Auxiliary Inversion if we extend the Inversion Licensing Condition (25i) in such a way as to include conditional operators in the class of inversion licensers. The null operator will also license the polarity item *anything* in conformity with the Polarity Licensing Condition (39), because the conditional operator c-commands *anything* (in that the mother of the ADV node containing the operator is CP, and CP contains *anything*). Positing a null operator will also enable the Clause Typing Condition (37) to type a CP like that in (45) as a conditional clause, since it contains a conditional operator in spec-CP.

A further piece of evidence in support of positing a null operator in conditional clauses comes from the observation that a negative constituent can't be fronted in a conditional clause – as we see from the ungrammaticality of sentences such as (46b) below:

(46) (a)   [Should you *never* feel able to trust me again], I'll understand
     (b)   *[*Never* should you feel able to trust me again], I'll understand

In (46a), the negative adverb *never* is positioned internally within the bracketed conditional clause, between the subject *you* and the verb *feel*. In (46b), *never* is preposed and moved to the front of the bracketed conditional clause, and this results in ungrammaticality. How come? The answer suggested by the null operator analysis is that *never* is prevented from moving to spec-CP in (46b) by the presence of a null conditional operator in spec-CP.

In this section, we have seen that there is evidence that yes–no questions and conditional clauses contain an abstract operator in spec-CP. This operator serves four functions: (i) to type the clause as interrogative/conditional, in accordance with the Clause Typing Condition (37); (ii) to license polarity items, in accordance with the Polarity Licensing Condition (39); (iii) to license Auxiliary Inversion, in accordance with the Inversion Licensing Condition (25) and (iv) to prevent other constituents (e.g. a fronted negative constituent) from moving to spec-CP.

5.6   V-to-T Movement

Our discussion so far has provided evidence that present-day English has an Auxiliary Inversion operation which involves T-to-C

Movement (more specifically, movement of a finite T auxiliary from the head T position of TP into the head C position of CP). In this section, we turn to look at a related kind of movement operation which involves **V-to-T Movement** – more specifically, movement of a finite main verb from the head V position of VP into the head T position of TP. We shall see that this kind of verb movement operation was productive in **Elizabethan English** (i.e. the English used during the reign of Queen Elizabeth I, when Shakespeare was writing around 400 years ago), but is no longer productive in present-day English. Since part of the evidence for V-to-T Movement involves negative sentences, we begin by looking at the syntax of negation.

In Elizabethan English, clauses containing a finite auxiliary are typically negated by positioning *not* between the (italicised) auxiliary and the (bold-printed) verb: cf.

(47) (a)   She *shall* not **see** me (Falstaff, *Merry Wives of Windsor*, III.iii)
   (b)   I *will* not **think** it (Don Pedro, *Much Ado About Nothing*, III.ii)
   (c)   Thou *hast* not **left** the value of a cord (Gratiano, *Merchant of Venice*, IV.i)

Let's suppose (for the time being, pending a reanalysis of negation in §5.9) that *not* in Elizabethan English is an adverb which functions as the specifier of the verbal expression following it (e.g. *not* is the specifier of *see me* in 47a above, and hence modifies *see me*). If so, (47a) will have a structure along the lines of (48) below (where ø is a null indicative complementiser assigning nominative case to the subject *she*):

(48)

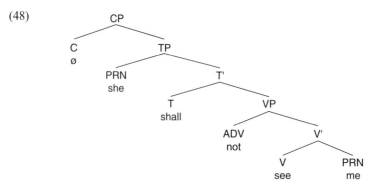

An analysis such as (48) accounts for *not* being positioned in front of the verb *see*. (48) is typed as a declarative clause by the Clause Typing Condition (37).

In negative questions, the auxiliary moves from T to C (as in present-day English), leaving *not* in front of the verb: cf.

(49) (a)   **Have** I *not* heard the sea rage like an angry boar? (Petruchio, *Taming of the Shrew*, I.ii)
   (b)   **Didst** thou *not* hear somebody? (Borachio, *Much Ado About Nothing*, III.iii)
   (c)   **Will** you *not* dance? (King, *Love's Labour's Lost*, V.ii)

If questions involve movement of a finite auxiliary from T to C, then a sentence such as (49a) will involve the T-to-C Movement operation arrowed in (50) below (where the string *the sea rage like an angry boar* is taken to be a TP headed by a null counterpart of the infinitival T constituent *to*, symbolised as *t̶o̶*, and where yes–no questions like 49 are taken to contain a silent interrogative operator in spec-CP):

(50)

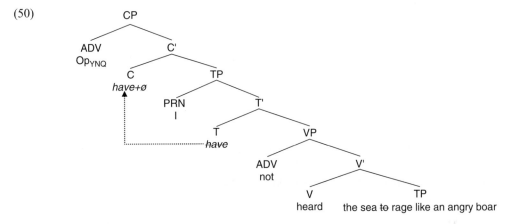

The T auxiliary *have* originates in T and then moves to C (i.e. a copy of the auxiliary is adjoined to the null complementiser in C), leaving behind a copy of *have* in T which is ultimately unpronounced, in accordance with the Default Spellout Rule (13). The assumption that *not* is a VP-specifier provides a straightforward account of the fact that *not* remains positioned in front of the verb *heard* after *have* moves to C.

However, an interesting aspect of negative sentences in Shakespearean English is that in auxiliariless finite clauses like those in (51) below, the (bold-printed) main verb is positioned in front of *not*: cf.

(51) (a)   I **care** *not* for her (Thurio, *Two Gentlemen of Verona*, V.iv)
     (b)   He **heard** *not* that (Julia, *Two Gentlemen of Verona*, IV.ii)
     (c)   My master **seeks** *not* me (Speed, *Two Gentlemen of Verona*, I.i)
     (d)   I **know** *not* where to hide my head (Trinculo, *The Tempest*, II.ii)

If *not* is positioned at the leftmost edge of the verb phrase, how can we account for the fact that the verb (which would otherwise be expected to follow the negative particle *not*) ends up positioned in front of *not* in sentences like (51)? The answer is that when a finite T in Elizabethan English contains no auxiliary, the verb moves out of the head V position of VP into the head T position of TP in order to fill T. Accordingly, a sentence like (51a) *I care not for her* will involve the V-to-T Movement operation arrowed in (52) below:

(52)

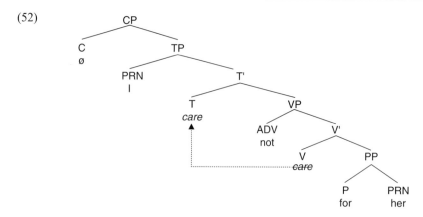

Thus, the verb *care* is first merged in the head V position within VP, and then moves into the head T position in TP, thereby ending up positioned in front of *not* (with the original occurrence of *care* in V being given a null spellout). Because the CP in (52) does not have an interrogative, exclamative or conditional, etc. specifier, it is interpreted as declarative by default, in accordance with the Clause Typing Condition (37).

An important theoretical question to ask at this juncture is why the verb *care* should move from V to T. Using a simple *strength* metaphor, let us suppose that a finite T is **strong** in Elizabethan English and so must be filled by a lexical item/ word of an appropriate kind: this means that in a sentence in which the T position is not filled by an auxiliary, the verb moves from V to T in order to fill the strong T position. One way of characterising what it means for T to be strong is to suppose that T contains a strong tense suffix with a V-feature (which can be thought of informally as an instruction to 'Adjoin a verb to me') which requires T to have an (auxiliary or non-auxiliary) verb adjoined it. Let's suppose that a strong affix is one which can find a host either by Merge with an auxiliary in T or by movement of the head V of VP to adjoin to the affix in T. So, in a structure like (48), the strong (third person singular present) tense affix in T is provided with a host by directly merging the auxiliary verb *shall* with the tense affix in T, as shown in more detail in (53) below:

(53)

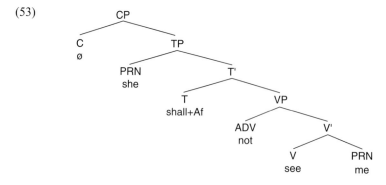

By contrast, in structure like (52) where T does not contain an auxiliary, the V-feature on the strong tense affix in T attracts the closest verb which T c-commands (namely the verb *care*) to move to T and attach to the tense affix so that the affix is provided with a verbal host via movement – as shown in (54) below:

(54)

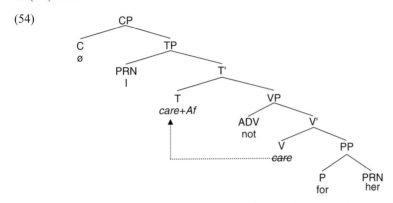

The situation in present-day English is somewhat different, however, since T in present-day English contains a **weak** tense affix, and a weak tense affix cannot attract a verb to move from V to T, but rather can only be attached to a verbal host either by merge of an auxiliary like *shall* directly with the null tense affix in T, or by lowering of the tense affix onto the main verb, e.g. in auxiliariless finite clauses such as *He enjoys the classes*. In such auxiliariless clauses, the weak tense affix in T undergoes the morphological operation of **Affix Hopping** in the PF component (as we saw in §4.4), lowering the affix onto the main verb in the manner shown by the arrow below:

(55)

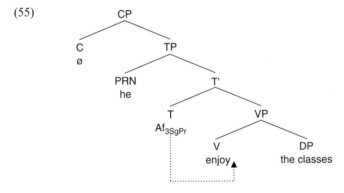

On this view, both strong and weak tense affixes can be directly merged with an auxiliary in T; the two differ in how the affix comes to be attached to a main verb; a strong tense affix (like that found in Elizabethan English) triggers movement of the verb from V to T in structures like (54) above; a weak tense affix (like that found in present-day English) is lowered onto the main verb in the PF component by Affix Hopping in structures like (55) above. (An important point of detail to note is that when an affix is lowered from T onto V, the affix ends up being pronounced only on V, not on T – contrary to what we would be led to expect by the Default Spellout Rule in 13 requiring the highest copy of a moved constituent to be pronounced. There are a variety of ways of dealing with this issue – e.g. supposing that morphological operations like Affix Hopping do not leave a copy behind, or that only the head/last copy in a movement chain is overtly spelled out; however, I will not pursue this issue any further here.)

A potential methodological objection which might be made to using Shakespearean English data to illustrate V-to-T Movement is to question whether it is legitimate to use historical evidence from a 'dead' language variety to illustrate a particular type of syntactic operation permitted by Universal Grammar/UG. There are three types of response which can be given to this kind of objection. One is that if UG involves a set of principles innately programmed into the human Language Faculty, it is highly improbable that this genetic endowment will have changed over a mere 400-year time span. Secondly, we have plenty of evidence from (e.g. negative and interrogative sentences in) Shakespeare's plays that main verbs could raise from V to T, and although this evidence comes from written texts (and may represent a more conservative variety than the spoken language at the time), this is equally true of many descriptive grammars of present-day English. And thirdly, there are plenty of present-day languages which show V-to-T Movement (e.g. French, Italian, Spanish, German, etc.), so it is clear that the phenomenon in question is far from 'dead': I have chosen to illustrate it using data from Elizabethan English rather than (e.g.) French because the central descriptive focus of this book is on English, which means that particular phenomena are illustrated using data from some variety of English wherever possible.

5.7   Head Movement

There seem to be significant parallels between the kind of movement operation involved in T-to-C Movement in (50) on the one hand, and V-to-T Movement in (54) on the other. Both operations involve the head of one phrase adjoining to the head of another phrase. Accordingly, in (50) the auxiliary *have* moves from the head T position of TP to adjoin to a null complementiser in the head C position of CP; and in (54) the verb *care* moves from the head V position of VP to adjoin to a null tense affix in the head T position of TP. This suggests that T-to-C Movement and V-to-T Movement are two different instances of a more general Head Movement operation by which an item occupying the head position in a lower phrase moves to adjoin to the head of a higher phrase.

As we see from (50) above, questions in Elizabethan English involved the same Inversion operation as in present-day English. Given our assumption that Inversion involves movement from T to C, an obvious prediction made by the assumption that verbs move from V to T in Elizabethan English is that they can subsequently move from T to C in questions – and this is indeed the case, as we see from the fact that the (italicised) moved verb ends up positioned in front of its (bold-printed) subject in questions like:

(56) (a) *Saw* **you** my master? (Speed, *Two Gentlemen of Verona*, I.i)
  (b) *Speakest* **thou** in sober meanings? (Orlando, *As you Like It*, V.ii)
  (c) *Know* **you** not the cause? (Tranio, *Taming of the Shrew*, IV.ii)
  (d) *Know'st* **thou** not his looks are my soul's food? (Julia, *Two Gentlemen of Verona*, II.vii)

To see how this comes about, let's take a closer look at the derivation of the negative question in (56d). Prior to any movement applying, the sentence will have the following structure (where yes–no questions are taken to contain a silent operator in spec-CP, and the internal structure of the CP *his looks are my soul's food* is not shown because it is irrelevant to the point at hand):

(57)

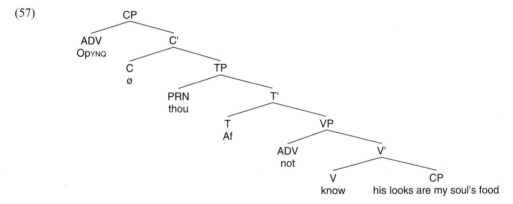

The head V position of VP is occupied by the (uninflected) verb *know*; the head T position of TP is occupied by a strong second person present tense affix *Af* which carries a V-feature requiring a V constituent to adjoin to T; and the head C position of CP is occupied by a strong interrogative affixal complementiser *ø* which carries a T-feature attracting a T constituent to adjoin to it. What then happens is that the strong tense affix in T attracts the verb *know* to move to adjoin to it (by application of Head Movement), as shown by the arrow below:

(58)

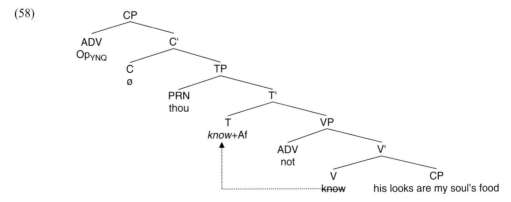

Subsequently, the T-feature carried by the null interrogative complementiser in C attracts the tense affix in T to adjoin to C. Because the verb *know* is adjoined to the tense affix in T, the affix pied-pipes (i.e. drags) the verb *know* along with it when it moves to C, with the result that the whole substructure *know+Af* adjoins to C (by a second application of Head Movement). If (as I assume) the null complementiser in C is suffixal in nature, this will give rise to the movement arrowed below:

(59)

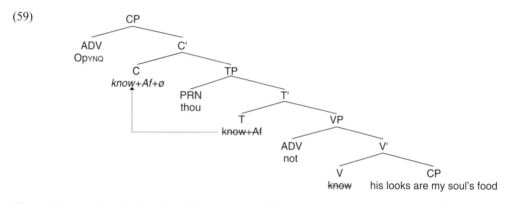

The whole structure is then handed over to the PF component, where the second person singular present tense affix on the verb is spelled out as the suffix *'st*, and the interrogative C has a null spellout, so the *know+Af+ø* string in C is realised as *know'st*. Note in particular that what moves into C is the whole *know+Af* string, not just the verb *know* on its own. This is partly for theoretical reasons (a strong affix being inseparable from any stem it attaches to), and partly for empirical reasons (if the verb *know* moved to on its own from T to C, the affix *'st* would be left stranded on its own in T without a verb stem to attach to, and the verb *know* would in turn be left without any inflectional affix attached to it).

To summarise: the verb *know* is first merged in V, and then moved to T and from there moved to C by two successive applications of Head Movement. In such cases, Head Movement is said to apply in a **successive-cyclic** fashion, moving the verb *know* (in successive **cycles** or steps) first from V to T, and then from T to C. Each time the verb moves, it leaves behind a copy of itself which is eventually deleted in accordance with the Default Spellout Rule (13), deletion being marked by strikethrough in (58) and (59) above.

A key assumption made in (57–59) is that the verb *know* moves to C via the intermediate step of moving to T. This raises the question of why *know* can't move directly from V to C in the manner shown in simplified form in (60) below (where *'st* is a second person singular present tense affix in T):

(60)   [CP OPYNQ [C *know*] [TP thou [T *'st*] [VP not [V *know*] his looks are my soul's food]]]

There are two main reasons why the kind of long-distance movement operation illustrated in (60) is ruled out. One is that if *know* were to move directly from V to C, the present tense affix *'st* would be left stranded in T and the verb stem *know* would be left stranded in C without being attached to each other, and the resulting structure (60) would end up violating the following PF conditions:

(61)   **V-Attachment Conditions**
           (i)   Every verbal affix must be attached to an overt verb stem at PF.
           (ii) Every verb stem must have an appropriate inflectional affix attached to it at PF.

(The constraint in 61 can clearly be generalised to other types of stem and affix in ways that I will not pursue here.) Condition (61i) is violated in (60) because the inflectional suffix *'st* requires an overt verb stem as its host and hasn't got one; and condition (61ii) is violated in (60) because the verb stem *know* requires an inflectional suffix attached to it and hasn't got one. (As should be obvious, 61ii requires us to assume that seemingly uninflected verb forms like *know* have an abstract/null inflectional affix attached to them.)

A second reason why the verb *know* cannot move directly from V to C in (60) is because any such direct movement would violate the following locality condition on Head Movement (i.e. condition on how far a head is allowed to move in any single application of Head Movement):

(62)   **Head Movement Constraint/HMC**
           Head Movement is only possible between a given head H and the head of the sister of H.

If we look at the two movement operations in (58) and (59), we see that both obey HMC: the V-to-T Movement operation in (58) involves movement of the verb *know* into T from the head V position of a VP which is the sister of T; and the T-to-C Movement operation in (59) involves movement of *know* into a C position from the head T position of a TP which is the sister of C. Since both Head Movement operations are strictly **local** (involving the shortest possible movement), there is no violation of HMC. By contrast, direct movement of *know* from V to C in (60) is non-local and violates HMC in that the verb *know* moves from the head V position of VP directly into the head C position of CP, in spite of the fact that VP is not the sister of C.

The analysis sketched above raises the question of why finite verbs should be able to move from V to T in Elizabethan English, but not in present-day English. Using our earlier *strength* metaphor, we can say that the tense affix carried by a finite T was *strong* in Elizabethan English, but is *weak* in present day English. Because the affix was strong in finite clauses in Elizabethan English, it could attract a verb to move from V to T; but because the affix is weak in present-day English, T can only be filled by an auxiliary which is directly merged in T, not by a verb moving from V to T. From this, it follows that present-day English does not allow a lexical/main verb like *know* to undergo Inversion in questions (as we see from the ungrammaticality of **Know you not the answer?*). Indirect (two-step) movement of *know* from V through T and then from T into C is barred because T is too weak in present-day English to be able to attract a lexical verb to move from

V into T, and direct (one-step) movement from V to C is barred by the Head Movement Constraint (62), as we saw earlier in relation to Elizabethan English structures like (60).

A more general conclusion to be drawn from our discussion here is that there is parametric variation with respect to the relative strength of a given type of head so that (e.g.) a finite T was strong in Elizabethan English but is weak in present-day English. Let's term the relevant parameter the **Head Strength Parameter**. Note that the parameter may have different settings for different types of head in a given language: e.g. a finite T is weak in present-day English, but a finite C is strong in clauses where it has an appropriate (e.g. negative) specifier.

But why should a finite tense affix be strong in Elizabethan English and weak in present-day English? An interesting possibility to explore is that the relative strength or weakness of a tense affix in a language may be correlated with the relative richness of the system of subject-agreement inflections which it encodes, in the sense that a tense affix is strong in languages in which finite auxiliaries and verbs carry **rich** subject-agreement inflections (i.e. in which they carry a wide range of different agreement affixes) and weak in languages in which finite auxiliaries and verbs carry **poor** subject-agreement inflections. In this connection, it is interesting to note that whereas third person singular -s is the only regular agreement inflection found on (present tense) verbs in present-day Standard English, in Shakespearean English we find four overt present tense inflections, namely second person singular -st, third person singular -th or -s (the two being dialectal variants), and third person plural -n:

(63) (a)   Thou *sayst* true (Petruchio, *Taming of the Shrew*, IV.iii)
     (b)   The sight of love *feedeth* those in love (Rosalind, *As You Like It*, III.v)
     (c)   It *looks* ill, it *eats* drily (Parolles, *All's Well That Ends Well*, I.i)
     (d)   And then the whole quire hold their lips and laugh, and *waxen* in their mirth (Puck, *Midsummer Night's Dream*, II.i)

If a tense affix is strong in rich agreement languages and weak in poor agreement languages, we can correlate the strength of T in Elizabethan English with the relative richness of its subject-agreement morphology; and conversely, we can correlate the weakness of T in present-day English with the impoverished nature of its subject-agreement morphology.

The relative richness of the agreement features carried by finite verbs in Elizabethan times (as compared to present-day English) is reflected in a further syntactic difference between them. Elizabethan English was a **null subject language**, and hence allowed finite verbs and finite auxiliaries (like those italicised below) to have a null subject (whether in root/main clauses or not, and whether the subject is sentence-initial or not):

(64) (a)   *Sufficeth*, I am come to keep my word (Petruchio, *Taming of the Shrew*, III.ii)
     (b)   *Would* you would bear your fortunes like a man (Iago, *Othello*, IV.i)
     (c)   *Lives*, sir (Iago, *Othello*, IV.i, in reply to 'How does Lieutenant Cassio?')
     (d)   *Hast* any more of this? (Trinculo, *The Tempest*, II.ii)

(e)   After some question with him, *was* converted (Jacques de Boys, *As You Like It*, V.iii)

(f)   Had it stretched so far, *would* have made nature immortal (Countess of Rousillon, *All's Well That Ends Well*, I.i)

(g)   You must be so too, if *heed* me (Antonio, *Tempest*, II.i)

Since the null subject in sentences like (64) occurs in a nominative position (by virtue of being the subject of a finite clause), it has nominative case and so is different from the 'big PRO' subject of infinitives (which has null case), and hence seems to be an instance of the finite 'little pro' subject found in null subject languages like Italian – recall the brief discussion of *pro* subjects in §1.7 and §4.2. By contrast, present-day English is a non-null-subject (i.e. *pro*-less) language, so that the present-day counterparts of (64) require overt subjects (italicised below): cf.

(65) (a)   *It* is enough that I have come to keep my word
(b)   *I* wish you would bear your fortunes like a man
(c)   *He* is alive, sir
(d)   Have *you* (got) any more of this?
(e)   After some discussion with him, *he* was converted
(f)   Had it stretched so far, *it* would have made nature immortal
(g)   You ought to be like that as well, if *you* ask me

It would seem, therefore, that a finite T can have a null nominative *pro* subject in a language like Elizabethan English where finite verbs carry rich agreement morphology (and raise to T), but not in a language like present-day English where finite verbs have impoverished agreement morphology (and remain **in situ** – i.e. in the position in which they were originally merged, hence in the head V position of VP). Why should this be? One possibility is that in a language with a rich system of agreement inflections, the agreement inflections on the verb serve to **identify** the null subject (e.g. the *-st* inflection on *hast* in (64d) is a second person singular inflection and hence allows us to identify the null *pro* subject as a second person singular subject with the same properties as *thou*). But in a weak-agreement language like contemporary English, agreement morphology is too impoverished to allow identification of a null *pro* subject (e.g. if we asked **Can help?* we'd have no way of telling from the agreementless form *can* whether the missing subject is *I, you, he, they* or whatever).

Our discussion here suggests the possibility that there is parametric variation between languages in respect of whether finite verbs carry rich or poor subject-agreement morphology, and that the relative richness of agreement morphology correlates with whether the tense affix in T in finite clauses is strong (and can trigger V-to-T raising) or weak, and with whether a finite T can have a null nominative *pro* subject or not. In rich agreement languages, a finite T contains a strong tense affix and the main verb raises to T if there is no auxiliary to host the affix in T, enabling the verb to identify the null subject via a local specifier-head relationship (in that the verb is in T and the null subject is its specifier). By contrast, in poor agreement languages, T contains a weak tense affix which is lowered onto the main verb by Affix Hopping if there is no auxiliary in T, with the result that the verb and the null subject are not in a local specifier-head relationship, and the verb cannot identify a null subject. (A complication that I will set aside here is that some languages with impoverished agreement have a different kind of null subject: e.g. Japanese and Korean have no agreement morphology except in so-called 'honorific' constructions, but allow subjects and objects to be null if they can be discourse-identified – i.e. if their reference can be determined from the discourse context.)

An interesting possibility raised by the assumption that T was strong in Elizabethan English but is weak in present day English is that historical change can be characterised in terms of **parameter resetting** – i.e. in terms of the settings of individual parameters changing over time (e.g. a T which was strong at some point in time being re-analysed as weak at a later point in time). One way this comes about is by children analysing the speech input they receive and arriving at a different setting for a given parameter from that adopted by their parents. Another is by transfer of parameter settings between one language and another brought about by conquests or colonisation.

5.8   Auxiliary Raising

Although the implicit assumption was made in the previous section that no verbs in present-day English can move from V to T, the picture is complicated by the behaviour of BE in examples like those below:

(66) (a)   She may not *be* enjoying syntax
     (b)   She *is* not enjoying syntax

In (66a), the head T position of TP is occupied by the modal auxiliary *may*, and the head V position of VP is occupied by the verb *enjoying*: the word *be* therefore seems to occupy some intermediate position between the two. Since *be* (in this use) is a Progressive Aspect Auxiliary, let's suppose that *be* in (66a) occupies the head PROG position of a PROGP projection (as we did in §4.3). However, in (66b) progressive *is* precedes *not* and (being marked for present tense) occupies the head T position of TP. One analysis of the relevant data is to suppose that progressive BE originates as the head PROG constituent of PROGP in both sentences in (66) and remains in situ when untensed (i.e. not marked for tense, like the infinitive form *be* in 67a below), but moves from PROG to T when tensed (i.e. marked as present/past tense, like the present tense form *is* in 67b):

(67)   [CP [C ø] [TP she [T may] not [PROGP [PROG *be*] [VP [V enjoying] syntax]]]]

         [CP [C ø] [TP she [T *is*] not [PROGP [PROG i̶s̶] [VP [V enjoying] syntax]]]]

On this view, progressive BE would always originate as the head of a PROGP projection, and present-day English would have an Auxiliary Raising operation moving the progressive auxiliary BE from the head PROG position in PROGP into the head T position in TP when T is tensed/finite.

The different positions occupied by finite and non-finite forms of the progressive auxiliary BE are mirrored by the perfect aspect auxiliary HAVE – as the examples below illustrate:

(68) (a)   He may not *have* done it
     (b)   He *has* not done it

The head T position of TP in (68a) is occupied by *may* and the head V position of VP by *done*; hence the infinitive form *have* must occupy some position intermediate between the two. Under the analysis of perfective HAVE sketched in §4.3, *have* in (68a) will occupy the head PERF position of a PERFP projection, as shown in (69a) below. However, the fact that the present tense form *has* in (68b) is positioned in front of *not* suggests that the perfect auxiliary HAVE raises from PERF to T when tensed, as shown informally in (69b) below:

(69)   (a) [CP [C ø] [TP he [T may] not [PERFP [PERF have] [VP [V done] it]]]]

         (b) [CP [C ø] [TP he [T *has*] not [PERFP [PERF h̶a̶s̶] [VP [V done] it]]]]

The conclusion which our discussion of (66–69) leads us to is that HAVE (in its use as a perfect auxiliary) and BE (in its use as a progressive auxiliary) may originate in a PERF/PROG position below *not* and subsequently raise into the head T position of TP.

There is evidence that certain modal auxiliaries also originate in a position below T and subsequently raise into T. In this connection, consider the interpretation of the following negative sentences:

(70) (a)   You must not do that (= 'It is *necessary* for you <u>not</u> to do that')
     (b)   You need not do that (= 'It is <u>not</u> *necessary* for you to do that')

In (70a) the modal *must* has **wide scope** with respect to negation (i.e. *must* has semantic scope over *not*), whereas in (70b) the modal *need* has **narrow scope** with respect to negation (i.e. *need* falls within the semantic scope of *not*). Although wide-scope modals like *must* are directly generated in T (as in 71a below), there is evidence to suggest that narrow-scope modals like *need* are initially generated in some position below T (e.g. the head M/Modal position of an MP/Modal Projection), and from there move to T (as in 71b below):

(71) (a) [CP [C ø] [TP you [T must] not [VP [V do] that]]]

(b) [CP [C ø] [TP you [T *need*] not [MP [M ~~need~~] [VP [V do] that]]]]

The analysis in (71b) implies that present-day English has an operation by which narrow-scope modal auxiliaries raise from M to T. There are two factors which lend empirical support to the Auxiliary Raising analysis in (71b). Firstly, it enables us to provide a principled account of the relevant scope relations in terms of the relation c-command: since *must* c-commands *not* in (71a), *must* has scope over *not*; but since *not* c-commands the lower copy of *need* in (71b), *not* can have scope over *need*. The second factor which lends support to the Auxiliary Raising analysis is that it allows us to account for how the polarity item *need* can occur in a structure like (71b). Recall from the discussion of the licensing of polarity items in §3.7 and from the Polarity Licensing Condition (39) that a polarity item must be c-commanded by an appropriate kind of (e.g. negative, interrogative or conditional) licenser. The negative adverb *not* is one such kind of licenser, but it does not c-command the polarity item *need* in the superficial syntactic structure (71b). We can solve this seeming puzzle if we suppose that *at least one copy* of a polarity item must be c-commanded by an appropriate licenser (the lower copy of *need* being c-commanded by *not* in 71b). Note that this analysis commits us to adopting the Copy Theory of Movement.

The word *dare* resembles *need* in that (when used as a modal auxiliary which takes a bare *to*-less infinitive complement, does not carry *-s* if used with a third person singular subject, and does not show DO-support in questions and negatives) it is a polarity item which must occur within the scope of an appropriate licenser – hence the ungrammaticality of (72a) below. However, the modal auxiliary *dare* can be used in an (obsolescent) negative structure like (72b):

(72) (a) *[CP [C ø] [TP he [T dare] [VP [V tell] her]]]
     (b)   [CP [C ø] [TP he [T dare] not [VP [V tell] her]]]

There are two things which are puzzling about the grammaticality of (72b). Firstly, *dare* is a polarity item and so must be c-commanded by an appropriate licenser like negative *not*; and secondly, *dare* falls within the semantic scope of (and so must be c-commanded by) *not*, because (72b) has a meaning paraphraseable as 'He does not have the courage to tell her' rather than 'He has the courage not to tell her.' However, since *dare* occupies a position higher than *not* in (72b), it is clear that the requirement that *dare* be c-commanded by *not* isn't met. How can we overcome this problem? One answer is to suppose that *dare* originates as the head modal/M of a modal phrase/MP positioned below *not* and subsequently raises into the head T position of TP, by the Head Movement operation arrowed below:

(73)   [CP [C ø] [TP he [T *dare*] not [MP [M ~~dare~~] [VP [V tell] her]]]]

We can then say that since the lower copy of *dare* in (73) originates below *not*, the requirement for *dare* to be c-commanded by an appropriate licenser like *not* at some stage of derivation is met.

If the progressive auxiliary BE, the perfect auxiliary HAVE, and narrow-scope modal auxiliaries like NEED and DARE all raise to T, it is clear that the suggestion made in the previous section that T in present-day English is a weak head which does not trigger any form of V-raising is untenable. Rather, the appropriate generalisation would appear to be that in present-day English, only auxiliary verbs which originate in a position below T can raise to T. More generally, we can say that the affix in a finite T in present-day English is only strong enough to trigger movement of an *auxiliary* verb to T, not movement of a full lexical verb to T. This means that if the head immediately beneath T is an auxiliary (as in 67b, 69b, 71b, and 73 above), the affix attracts it; but if the head beneath T is a full lexical verb (as in 55 above), the affix is instead lowered onto the main verb in the PF component by Affix Hopping. This assumption raises the question of why an affix in a finite T in present-day English can attract an auxiliary but not a main verb. The answer I shall assume here is that a finite T in present-day English can be filled either by a strong affix carrying an AUX-feature requiring it to have an auxiliary adjoined to it, or by a weak affix carrying a V-feature requiring it to lower onto a non-auxiliary verb in the PF component.

However, the assumption that an affix in T can only attract an auxiliary (not a lexical verb) to move to T in present-day English is seemingly called into question by the behaviour of the verb HAVE in (British English) structures such as:

(74)   Have you any idea where she is?

Here, *have* appears to function as a transitive lexical verb, taking the QP *any idea where she is* as its complement (just as in *They don't seem to have any idea where she is*). If so, *have* originates in the head V position of VP. However, since *have* undergoes Auxiliary Inversion in (74) and thereby moves into the head C position of CP, this means that *have* must move from the head V position of VP into the head T position of TP before moving into the head C position of CP, as shown by the arrows below:

(75)   [CP OPYNQ [C *have*] [TP you [T have] [VP [V have] any idea where she is]]]

But the assumption that *have* moves from V to T before moving to C provides an apparent challenge to the claim that T in present-day English can only attract an *auxiliary* to move into T not a lexical verb.

One way of overcoming this problem (albeit in an ad hoc fashion) is to suppose that verbs like HAVE which raise from V to T carry an auxiliarihood feature of some kind which enables them to raise from V to adjoin to a tensed T. An alternative possibility is to suppose that some verbs (in some uses) have relatively little semantic content and so can be termed **light verbs**. If HAVE (when used to express what might loosely be termed 'possession') is a light verb, we can suppose that a finite T in present-day English is only strong enough to attract a light verb to adjoin to it – e.g. to move from V to T in a structure like (75). In the same way, we might suppose that auxiliaries like *dare* in (73), *need* in (71b), *has* in (69b) and *is* in (67b) are all light verbs. However, the downside to the light verb analysis is that we would then have to suppose that HAVE/NEED/DARE are light verbs when they behave like auxiliaries, but are not light verbs when they behave like main verbs (and trigger DO-support, as in *Do you have any idea where she is?*) – even though there is no obvious meaning difference between the two uses.

An alternative way of dealing with sentences like (74) is suggested by Freidin (2004: 115). He argues that *have* in sentences like (74) is an auxiliary directly generated in T, and that the head V of VP contains a null variant of the verb *got*. This would mean that (74) has the superficial structure shown in simplified form in (76) below, with *have* originating in T and from there moving into C, as shown by the arrow below:

(76)   [CP OPYNQ [C *have*] [TP you [T ~~have~~] [VP [V ~~got~~] any idea where she is]]]

If so, sentences like (76) pose no challenge to the claim that an affix in T can only attract an *auxiliary* to adjoin to it in present-day English, not a main/lexical verb.

Problems analogous to those posed by the verb HAVE arise with the copular verb BE which undergoes Auxiliary Inversion in sentences such as the following:

(77)   *Is* she in the office?

If *is* originates as the head V of VP, it will have to raise into T before raising further into C, in the manner shown by the arrows below:

(78)   [CP OPYNQ [C *is*] [TP she [T ~~is~~] [VP [V ~~is~~] in the office]]]

Such a solution would require us to suppose that BE carries an auxiliarihood feature of some kind which enables it to raise from V to T before raising further into C, or to suppose that BE is a light verb. However, an alternative possibility would be to suppose that *is* originates in T and has the predicative PP *in the office* as its sister. On this alternative view, (77) would have the derivation in (79) below:

(79)   [CP OPYNQ [C *is*] [TP she [T ~~is~~] [PP [P in] in the office]]]

Thus, as we see, there is more than one way of dealing with verbs like HAVE/BE which seemingly raise from V to C. For concreteness, I shall henceforth assume a V-to-T raising analysis in which verbs which carry an auxiliarihood feature can raise from V to T in finite clauses.

In §1.2, I suggested that infinitival *to* resembles auxiliaries in certain respects and occupies the same position (the head T position of TP). However, since we have now seen that auxiliaries can originate in a position below T (and below *not*), this raises the question of whether there are structures in which infinitival *to* can likewise originate in a position below T. One possible structure of this kind occurs in a sentence like (80a) below, if this has the structure in (80b), where INF denotes an infinitive particle:

(80) (a)   John ought not to say anything
      (b)   [CP [C ø] [TP John [T ought] not [INFP [INF to] say anything]]]

Here, *ought* is a modal auxiliary which occupies the head T position of TP; we can see that it is an auxiliary from the fact that like typical auxiliaries, it allows negative cliticisation (giving rise to *oughtn't*) and Auxiliary Inversion (as in *Ought he to apologise?*). However, if sentence (80a) contains a single clause, if no clause can contain more than one T constituent and if *ought* occupies the head T position of TP, it follows that infinitival *to* cannot occupy the head T position of TP but rather must occupy some lower position. One possibility is that *to* originates in the head INF/Infinitive position of an INFP/Infinitive Phrase, as shown in (80b).

However, although *not to* is the normal word order in negative infinitives, the alternative order *to not* is also found, as the examples below illustrate:

(81) (a)   He decided [not to cooperate with the police]
      (b)   He decided [to not cooperate with the police]

It seems reasonable to suppose that the two different word orders in the bracketed complement clauses in (81a/b) reflect two different positions occupied by infinitival *to*, as suggested in (82a/b) below:

(82) (a)   [CP [C ø] [TP PRO [T ø] not [INFP [INF to] cooperate with the police]]]
      (b)   [CP [C ø] [TP PRO [T to] not cooperate with the police]]

It is possible that in a clause like (82b), *to* originates in the head INF position of INFP and can move from there into the head T position of TP, as shown by the arrow below:

(83)   [CP [C ø] [TP PRO [T *to*] not [INFP [INF t̶o̶] [VP [V cooperate] with the police]]]]

Since we see from examples like (18) above that Head Movement can lead to copying errors, this would provide an interesting way of accounting for *to*-doubling errors in sentences like those in (84) below (the first being recorded from the radio by me, and the others being internet-sourced):

(84) (a)   It makes sense **to** not *to* play on a full-size pitch when you're 10 years old (Footballer, Talk Sport Radio)
      (b)   The theme here is **to** not *to* unknowingly sabotage yourself (diycouturier .com)

(c)   I would counsel them **to** not *to* believe everything they read or see (Daily Mail Online)

(d)   Ukraine PM asks West **to** not *to* ease sanctions on Russia (headline, *The Telegraph*)

(e)   11 ways **to** not *to* screw up your first year at university (headline, buzzfeed .com)

If *to* originates in an italicised INF position below *not* and raises to a bold-printed T position above *not*, sentences like (83) will involve a spellout error (spelling out both copies of *to* rather than spelling out only the higher copy).

However, note that there is a subtle meaning difference between sentences in which *to* follows or precedes *not*: for example, (81b) implies a much more deliberate act of defiance than (81a). Given the analysis suggested in (82), this meaning difference can be attributed to a scope difference, with *not* c-commanding and so having scope over *to* in (82a), and *to* c-commanding and having scope over *not* in (82b). A similar scope difference is found between *will* and *not* in sentences like:

(85) (a)   He almost certainly won't co-operate with the police
     (b)   He will almost certainly not co-operate with the police

In (85a), *not* has semantic scope over *will* and the sentence is paraphraseable as 'It is almost certainly *not* the case that he *will* cooperate with the police', whereas in (85b) *will* has scope over *not* and the sentence is paraphraseable as 'It *will* almost certainly be the case that he does *not* co-operate with the police.'

Although there are in principle two distinct positions which auxiliaries and infinitival *to* can occupy within clauses (either T or a PROG/PERF/M/INF head below T), if these two positions correlate directly with scope, it is plausible to assume that a given lexical item L (where L is a finite auxiliary or infinitival *to*) is only projected in a separate PROG/PERF/M/INF position below T if L falls within the scope of an element like *not* which has scope over L but not over T, and that otherwise L is directly projected in the head T position of TP (and the sentence then contains no separate PROG/PERF/M/ INF head). In other words, in negative structures like (80b) and (82a) in which the negative adverb *not* has scope over a narrow-scope auxiliary like *need* or infinitival *to*, the auxiliary *need* and the infinitive particle *to* are generated in a position below T; but in non-negative infinitives like that bracketed in *He may decide* [*to quit his job*], the auxiliary *may* and the infinitival participle *to* are directly generated in the head T position of the TP in the respective clauses containing them, and neither clause contains a projection of a lower M or INF head (if such a head is only projected where required for scope purposes – e.g. in negative clauses). One way of thinking of this is to suppose that PROG/ PERF/M/INF and T are **syncretised** (i.e. collapsed into a single T head) wherever possible (e.g. in structures in which there is no constituent intervening between the two). This assumption has interesting implications for the syntax of an auxiliary like *have* in sentences such as:

(86) (a)   They may *have* gone to the cinema
   (b)   They *have* gone to the cinema

In (86a), it is clear that the perfect aspect auxiliary *have* does not occupy the head T position of TP, since this is occupied by *may*, and moreover *have* is an infinitive form in (86a), as we see from the fact that if we replace the subject *they* by *he*, the auxiliary *have* remains untensed (i.e. uninflected for tense) and is not spelled out as the present tense form *has*. Consequently, it is reasonable to suppose that *have* in (86a) occupies the head PERF position of a PERFP projection as in (87) below:

(87)   [CP [C ø] [TP they [T may] [PERFP [PERF *have*] [VP [V gone] to the cinema]]]]

This opens up the possibility that in a sentence like (86b), *have* may again originate in the head PERF position of PERFP and from there move to T, in the manner shown by the arrow below:

(88)   [CP [C ø] [TP they [T *have*] [PERFP [PERF have] [VP [V gone] to the cinema]]]]

However, given that the Economy Principle of §1.4 requires us to project as little structure as possible, a more economical analysis is to suppose that T and PERF are syncretised (i.e. collapsed into a single head) wherever possible. This means that *have* is directly generated in T in (86b), as in (89) below:

(89)   [CP [C ø] [TP they [T *have*] [VP [V gone] to the cinema]]]

More generally, it follows that when used as a tensed indicative form HAVE is generated in T (as in 89), but in other uses it is generated in PERF (as in 87).

   Similar assumptions can be made about the auxiliary BE in sentences such as:

(90) (a)   He might *be* released from prison
   (b)   He *was* released from prison

In (90a), the head T position of TP is occupied by the tensed auxiliary *might* (which carries the same irregular past tense ending -*t* as verbs like *went*); *be* is an untensed infinitive form, arguably occupying the head VOICE (i.e. passive voice) position of a VOICEP (voice phrase) projection. On this view, (90a) has the structure (91) below:

(91)   [CP [C ø] [TP he [T might] [VOICEP [VOICE *be*] [VP [V released] from prison]]]]

By contrast, in (90b), the passive voice auxiliary *was* is a tensed form (more specifically, a past tense form) and economy considerations therefore suggest that it is directly merged in T (rather than originating in VOICE and from there moving to T). If so, (90b) has the structure (92) below:

(92)   [CP [C ø] [TP he [T *was*] [VP [V released] from prison]]]

In this respect, the auxiliary BE behaves in the same way as the auxiliary HAVE: that is, when finite it originates in T, whereas when non-finite it originates in a position below T.

To summarise: present-day English has a restricted type of Head Movement operation under which a small number of auxiliary verbs/light verbs can raise to T in finite clauses. One way of describing this situation is to posit that T in finite clauses contains a tense affix, and that this can either attach to an auxiliary directly merged in T, or attract a verb with an AUX-feature to raise to T to adjoin to the affix. It may be that English also has a further raising operation by which infinitival *to* can raise from the head INF/infinitive position of an INFP/infinitive phrase projection and adjoin to a null T in an infinitive clause.

5.9   Another look at Negation

In §5.6 and §5.7, the negative particle *not* was treated as a VP-specifier which occupies initial position within VP. However, this assumption is problematic in a number of respects, as will be immediately apparent if you look back at (67a, 69a, 80b, 82a, 83) in §5.8. For example, in a sentence such as (66a) *She may not be enjoying syntax*, it is clear that *not* does not occupy a VP-initial position immediately in front of the verb *enjoying*: on the contrary, *not* appears to occupy some position between the modal auxiliary *may* and the aspectual auxiliary *be* – as shown in (67a), repeated below:

(67) (a)   [CP [C ø] [TP she [T may] *not* [PROGP [PROG be] [VP [V enjoying] syntax]]]]

It is clear, therefore, that our earlier analysis of negation needs to be re-thought. An alternative analysis which I will outline in this section (and which has been widely adopted in work since the end of the 1980s) posits that *not* is contained within a separate **NEGP** (= **negation phrase**) projection. The specific implementation of this analysis which I will adopt here is one which takes the negative particle *not* to be the *specifier* of NEGP (though some linguists adopt an alternative analysis under which *not* is taken to be the head NEG constituent of NEGP).

Empirical evidence in support of positing that *not* is contained within a separate NEGP constituent positioned between TP and VP comes from structures such as the following:

(93) (a)   I most certainly will [NEGP not [NEG ø] [VP [V cooperate] with the police]]
      (b)   [VP [V cooperate] *with the police*], I most certainly will [NEGP not [NEG ø] [VP ---]]
      (c)   [NEGP *not* [NEG ø] [VP [V cooperate] *with the police*]], I most certainly will [NEGP ---]

(I note in passing that sentences like 93c sound odd if you are confronted with them 'out of the blue'; they require an appropriate context: e.g. *If you tell me to deliberately not cooperate with police, then not cooperate with the police, I will.*) Under the NEGP analysis of negation sketched informally in (93a), *not* is housed in a separate NEGP projection positioned between the TP headed by the T auxiliary *will* and the VP headed by the verb *cooperate*. On this view, the string *cooperate with the police* is a maximal projection (= VP), and the string *not cooperate with the police* is likewise a maximal projection (= NEGP). Since we saw in §3.6 that maximal projections can be fronted in order to highlight them, the NEGP analysis predicts that both the VP *cooperate with the police* and the NEGP *not cooperate with the police* can be fronted in order to highlight them – and this claim is borne out by the grammaticality of VP fronting in (93b) and NEGP fronting in (93c).

The NEGP analysis is far from implausible from a historical perspective: in earlier varieties of English, sentences containing *not* also contained the negative particle *ne* (with *ne* arguably serving as the head NEG constituent of NEGP and *not* as its specifier). This can be illustrated by the following Middle English example taken from Chaucer's *Wife of Bath's Tale*:

(94)   A lord in his houshold *ne* hath *nat* every vessel al of gold
              'A lord in his household does not have all his vessels made entirely of gold'

A plausible analysis of a sentence like (94) is to suppose that *ne* originates as the head NEG constituent of NEGP, with *nat* (= 'not') as its specifier: the verb *hath* originates in the head V position of VP and from there moves to the head NEG position of NEGP, attaching to the negative prefix *ne* to form the complex head *ne+hath* as shown in simplified form in (95) below:

(95)   [NEGP nat [NEG ne+*hath*] [VP [V hath] every vessel al of gold]]

The resulting complex head *ne+hath* then moves to T and attaches to a present tense affix (**Af**) in T, as shown in simplified (and abbreviated) form in (96) below:

(96)   [TP a lord... [T *ne+hath+***Af**] [NEGP nat [NEG ne+hath] [VP [V hath] every vessel al of gold]]]

Merging the TP in (96) with a null complementiser will derive the CP structure associated with (94) *A lord in his houshold ne hath nat every vessel al of gold*.

By Shakespeare's time, *ne* had dropped out of use, leaving the head NEG position of NEGP null (just as in *ne* ... *pas* 'n't....not' negatives in present-day French, *ne* has dropped out of use in colloquial styles). Positing that *not* in Elizabethan English is the specifier of a NEGP headed by a null NEG constituent opens up the possibility that V moves through NEG into T, so that (51a) *I care not for her* has the derivation shown (in simplified form) in (97) below:

(97)

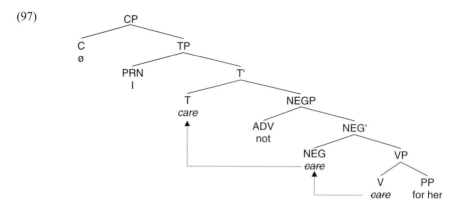

This would mean that Head Movement applies in a successive-cyclic (two-step) fashion. Each of the two Head Movement operations in (97) – movement of *care* from V to NEG, and then from NEG to T – is local in the sense that it satisfies the Head Movement Constraint (62), since in each case movement is from a given head position into the next highest head position in the structure. Let us suppose that both T and NEG contain an affix with a V-feature which triggers movement of a verb to adjoin to T or NEG. This being so, the first step in the movement arrowed in (97) will be for the V-feature on the null affix in NEG to attract the verb *care* to adjoin to the null negative affix (in much the same way as the verb *hath* in 95 moves from V to NEG to attach to the overt negative affix *ne*). The next step will be for the V-feature on the null tense affix in T to attract the verb *care* to adjoin to the affix in T: but since the verb *care* is adjoined to a null negative affix, the verb *care* pied-pipes (i.e. drags) this affix along with it when it moves to T, with the result that all the material in NEG (comprising a verb attached to a null negative affix) moves from NEG to T in order to attach to the strong tense affix in T.

An important question posed by the analysis in (97) is why sentences like (51a) *I care not for her* are ungrammatical in present-day English. The answer is that neither T nor NEG contains a strong affix with a V-feature (so neither can attract a V to adjoin to them) in present day English, and so they are unable to attract a main verb like *care* to move through NEG into T. Still, this assumption in turn raises the question of why we can't simply leave the present tense verb *care* in situ (in the head V position of VP) in present-day English – as in (98) below:

(98)   [CP [C ø] [TP I [T Af] [NEGP not [NEG ø] [VP [V *care*] for her]]]]

One answer is the following. Let's suppose that (just like syntactic operations), morphological and phonological operations in the PF component apply in a **bottom-up** fashion (from bottom to top), and process structures in a **cyclic** fashion (i.e. in a stepwise fashion, one phrase at a time). What this means is that when the syntax hands over the structure in (98) to the PF component, the lowest phrase in the structure (the VP *care for her*) will be processed first, then the next lowest phrase (the NEGP *not ø care for her*), then the next lowest phrase (the TP *I Af not ø care for her*) and finally the overall CP (*ø I Af not ø care for her*). Let's also posit that all operations (whether syntactic, morphological or phonological) are subject to the **Earliness Principle**, which was outlined in §4.9 as follows:

(99)   **Earliness Principle**
        Operations must apply as early as possible in a derivation.

All of this means that **Affix Lowering**/Affix Hopping will apply to the tense affix in (98) on the TP cycle – i.e. at the point where we have already processed VP and NEGP, and are now processing TP. The structure which the PF component can 'see' on the TP cycle is (100) below:

(100)   [TP I [T Af] [NEGP not [NEG ø] [VP [V care] for her]]]

At this point, we might expect Affix Hopping to apply to lower the tense affix in T onto the verb *care*. There are two possible ways in which we could seek to achieve this. One is by lowering the affix directly from T onto V as in (101) below:

(101)   [TP I [T Af] [NEGP not [NEG ø] [VP [V care] for her]]]

However, if we make the reasonable assumption that Affix Lowering is a form of Head Movement (since it moves a higher head to adjoin to a lower one), it follows that a movement operation like (101) which lowers the affix directly from T onto V would violate the Head Movement Constraint (62), since it involves lowering the head T of TP onto the head V of VP; and yet VP is not the sister of T (rather, NEGP is), and HMC only allows a head to be lowered onto the head of its sister (which means that the affix in T can only lower onto the head NEG of NEGP).

Accordingly, we might alternatively suppose that Affix Hopping applies in a successive-cyclic fashion, lowering the affix first from T onto NEG, and then from NEG onto V – as shown by the arrows below:

(102)   [TP I [T Af] [NEGP not [NEG ø] [VP [V care] for her]]]

Each of the two arrowed movements in (102) will then satisfy the Head Movement Constraint. However, the second step of lowering the tense affix from NEG onto V in (102) is problematic, because it is **anticyclic** by virtue of violating the following UG principle:

(103)   **Strict Cyclicity Principle/SCP**
        At a stage of derivation where a given projection HP is being cycled/processed, only operations involving the head H of HP and some other constituent c-commanded by H can apply.

Suppose that the PF component processes the structure in a bottom-up fashion so that VP is processed before NEGP, and NEGP before TP. On the VP cycle (i.e. at the point in the derivation where the PF component is processing VP and determines whether there are any PF operations which can apply to V and some constituent c-commanded by V), there are no operations which can apply. Once the grammar has determined that there are no operations which can apply on the VP cycle, it moves on to process the phrase immediately above VP, namely NEGP. Once again, no operations can apply (e.g. there is no affix in NEG, so no Affix Lowering can take place). Once the grammar has determined that there are no operations which can apply on the NEGP cycle, it moves on to process the phrase immediately above NEGP, namely TP. On the TP cycle, the tense affix in T can lower onto NEG without violating the Strict Cyclicity Principle (103), since T-to-NEG lowering clearly involves T (by moving the tense affix in T) and also involves a NEG constituent which is c-commanded by T (since NEG ends up having a tense affix attached to it). But the subsequent operation of lowering the affix from NEG onto V on the TP cycle is anticyclic, since NEG-to-V lowering does not involve T, in the sense that T is neither the position that the affix moves from (since it is moving from NEG) nor the position that it moves to (since it moves to V): accordingly, there is a violation of SCP, because SCP requires any operation on the TP cycle to involve T and some constituent c-commanded by T. The result is that the tense affix is stranded in T, and this leads to violation of both of the **V-Attachment Conditions** in (61), repeated below:

(61)   **V-Attachment Conditions**
    (i)   Every verbal affix must be attached to an overt verb stem at PF.
    (ii)   Every verb stem must have an appropriate inflectional affix attached to it at PF.

Condition (61i) is violated because the tense affix in T is not attached to a verbal stem; and condition (61ii) is violated because the verb stem *care* has no inflectional affix attached to it. (As noted earlier, I assume here that all verb stems in English must have a suffix attached to them indicating whether the verb is to be spelled out at PF as: an indicative or subjunctive form; a present or past tense form; a singular or plural form; a first, second or third person form; an imperative form; a progressive or perfect participial form; or an infinitive form. The relevant suffix is overt in forms like *cares/cared/caring*, and null in the case of the form *care*.)

A final point to be made here in passing relates to negative interrogatives like *Shouldn't you be at work?* In such sentences the negative particle *n't* has scope over the modal (so that the sentence has a meaning paraphraseable as 'Is it **not** the case that you *should* be at work?') and so must originate in a position above the modal. One way of achieving this would be to suppose that NEGP in such sentences is positioned between CP and TP, and that the auxiliary *should* raises from T through NEG into C, with *n't* cliticising onto the auxiliary. This would allow for the possibility of two types of negation occurring in a sentence such as *Mightn't he not have seen her?* where *not* originates as the specifier of a NEGP immediately above VP, and *n't* as the specifier of a NEGP immediately above TP.

5.10   Do-support

A well-known characteristic of English is that indicative clauses which contain no other auxiliary require the use of the dummy/expletive auxiliary DO in structures like those in (104b–g), but not in a structure like (104a):

(104) (a)   *He won the race*
   (b)   He said he would win the race, and *he did*
   (c)   He said he would win the race, and *win the race he did*
   (d)   *Did he win the race?*
   (e)   Some people don't believe he won the race, but *he* DID *win it*
   (f)   *He did not win the race*
   (g)   *Didn't he win the race?*

The relevant phenomenon is traditionally termed DO-**support**. But how can we account for the use of DO in structures like (104b–g)? Let us suppose that (in accordance with the CP Hypothesis and the TP Hypothesis), all indicative clauses contain both a CP projection and a TP projection. Let us further suppose that the head T position of TP can either be filled by an unattached tense affix, or by a tensed auxiliary (where a tensed auxiliary comprises an auxiliary stem with a tense affix attached to it). In addition, in accordance with the Economy Principle outlined in §1.4, let's assume that 'Structures ... should be as economical as possible.' If we make the reasonable assumption that a structure in which T contains only a tense affix is more economical than one in which T contains both a tense affix and an auxiliary stem (by virtue of containing fewer items), economy considerations would lead us to expect that DO-support will only be used in structures where use of the more economical auxiliariless structure (involving use of a tense affix without a supporting auxiliary) leads to a crash. For obvious reasons, I will call this the *economy* account of DO-support.

In the light of these assumptions, consider how the auxiliariless structure in (104a) is derived. The determiner *the* merges with the noun *race* to form the DP *the race*; the verb *win* merges with this DP to form the VP *win the race*. Suppose that this VP is then merged with a T constituent containing a (past tense) affix *Af* to form the T-bar *Af win the race*. This T-bar then merges with the pronoun *he* to form the TP *he Af win the race*; and the resulting TP in turn is merged with a null indicative complementiser *ø* to form the CP shown in skeletal form in (105) below:

(105) $[_{CP} [_C \ ø] [_{TP} \text{ he } [_T \text{ Af}] [_{VP} [_V \text{ win}] \text{ the race}]]]$

The syntactic structure (105) is then sent to the PF component (and in parallel to the semantic component) to be processed. PF operations apply in a bottom-up, cyclic fashion. On the TP cycle in the PF component, the tense affix in T is lowered onto the verb *win* via Affix Lowering, so deriving the PF structure (106) below (where the original copy of the affix in T receives a null spellout):

(106) $[_{CP} [_C \ ø] [_{TP} \text{ he } [_T \text{ Af}] [_{VP} [_V \text{ win+}Af] \text{ the race}]]]$

The resulting structure (106) satisfies both of the Attachment Conditions in (61). More specifically, condition (61i) is satisfied because the affix *Af* is attached to the overt V-stem *win* in (106), and condition (61ii) is satisfied because the verb stem *win* has an inflectional affix attached to it. Since the lexical entry for the irregular verb *win* specifies that it is spelled out as *won* when it has a past tense affix attached to it, the overall structure in (106) is eventually spelled out as (104a) *He won the race*. Thus, use of an unattached affix in T in a structure like (105) results in a convergent/grammatical outcome. Since use of a tense affix alone results in convergence, it follows from economy considerations that there is no need for (or possibility of) using the less economical DO-support structure in (107) below, whereby the expletive auxiliary DO is attached to the tense affix in T:

(107)   [$_{CP}$ [$_C$ ø] [$_{TP}$ he [$_T$ DO+Af] [$_{VP}$ [$_V$ win] the race]]]

Thus, economy considerations account for the ungrammaticality of **Yesterday, he'd win the race* (where *'d* is an unstressed, contracted form of *did*): the DO-support structure in (107) is not used because the more economical DO-less structure in (105,106) results in convergence/grammaticality. More generally, DO-support is used only as a last resort, where the less economical DO-less structure is ungrammatical. (As we see from 104e, a structure like 107 only leads to a grammatical outcome if the auxiliary receives emphatic stress: see the discussion of 104e below.)

   Now consider what happens in the clause *he did* italicised in (104b) 'He said he would win the race, and *he did*.' We can take *he did* to be an elliptical form of 'he did *win the race*', with the italicised VP subsequently undergoing ellipsis/deletion in the PF component. Suppose that T were filled by an unsupported tense affix (i.e. an affix not attached to an auxiliary). The sentence would then have the syntactic structure (108) below:

(108)   [$_{CP}$ [$_C$ ø] [$_{TP}$ he [$_T$ Af] [$_{VP}$ [$_V$ win] the race]]]

Two operations would then take place in the PF component – Affix Lowering and VP Ellipsis. If VP Ellipsis took place first, this would result in the structure (109) below (where strikethrough shows material that has been deleted):

(109)   [$_{CP}$ [$_C$ ø] [$_{TP}$ he [$_T$ Af] [$_{VP}$ [$_V$ ~~win~~] ~~the race~~]]]

However, lowering the tense affix from T onto the verb *win* in the PF component in (109) would cause the derivation to crash. This is because the resulting structure would violate the Attachment Condition (61i) which requires an inflectional affix to attach to an *overt* verb stem; this condition would be violated because the verb ~~win~~ in (109) is not overt (by virtue of having undergone ellipsis).

   Now consider what would happen if Affix Lowering applied to the structure in (108) *before* VP Ellipsis. Lowering the affix from T onto V-*win* would derive the structure (110) below:

(110)   [$_{CP}$ [$_C$ ø] [$_{TP}$ he [$_T$ Af] [$_{VP}$ [$_V$ win+*Af*] the race]]]]

If VP Ellipsis did not apply to (110), the relevant clause would have the outcome italicised in 'He said that he would win the race and *he won the race.*' However, the VP *won the race* cannot subsequently undergo ellipsis, as we see from the ungrammaticality of *'He said he would win the race and *he*.' What prevents VP Ellipsis from taking place here? The answer lies in a constraint on deletion proposed by Chomsky (1964) which can be formulated as follows:

(111)   **Recoverability Condition**
           Material can only be deleted if its content is recoverable.

The content of a deleted VP will be recoverable if (for instance) there is an identical VP in the same sentence which can serve as an antecedent for the deleted VP. However, the VP *win the race* which appears after *would* in (104b) is not identical to the VP *won the race*, since *win* is an infinitive form and *won* is a past tense form. Because the two VPs are not identical, ellipsis is not possible here. (An alternative way of looking at the situation is to suppose that ellipsis of the VP in 110 would mean that the past tense affix which originated in T would have no audible spellout at PF, with the result that important tense information would not be recoverable, in violation of the Recoverability Condition, 111.)

The overall outcome of our discussion above is that using a tense affix alone in a structure like (108) will lead the derivation to crash. But now consider what would happen if we used DO-support in (104b) so that the affix in T in (108) is supported by the expletive auxiliary DO, as in (112) below:

(112)   [$_{CP}$ [$_C$ ø] [$_{TP}$ he [$_T$ **do**+Af] [$_{VP}$ [$_V$ ~~win~~] ~~the race~~]]]]

Since the tense affix in T is attached to the auxiliary verb *do*, both Attachment Conditions in (61) are satisfied. Since *Af* is a past tense affix, the T constituent *do+Af* is spelled out as the irregular past tense form *did* in the PF component. Thus, under the economy account, use of DO-support in elliptical structures like (104b/112) is forced because the more economical auxiliariless structure (108) crashes.

Next, consider the clause *Win the race he did* in (104c). Let's suppose that the VP *win the race* is preposed in order to highlight it and is thereby moved to the front of the overall clause (to become the specifier of the null complementiser), and that the phonetic features of the original copy of the VP *win the race* are given a null spellout at PF. If T contains only a null affix, this will give rise to the structure shown in simplified form in (113) below:

(113)

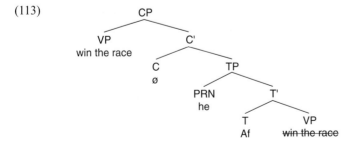

However, the weak tense affix in T cannot be lowered onto the verb ~~win~~ in the PF component because the verb is given a silent spellout through movement, and condition (61i) requires an affix to be attached to an *overt* stem. Thus the affix remains stranded in T, in violation of the Attachment Condition (61i). Note that the possibility of the affix being lowered onto the verb *win* before VP Fronting takes place is ruled out if (as assumed here) VP Fronting is a syntactic operation and affix lowering is a morphological operation, since syntactic operations take place before morphological operations.

By contrast, if we use DO-support in (104c), the affix in T will be supported by the expletive auxiliary DO. Prior to fronting of the VP *win the race*, we will have the structure (114) below:

(114)   [$_{CP}$ [$_C$ ø] [$_{TP}$ he [$_T$ **do**+Af] [$_{VP}$ *win the race*]]]

Fronting the VP *win the race* results in the structure (115) below:

(115)   [$_{CP}$ [$_{VP}$ *win the race*] [$_C$ ø] [$_{TP}$ he [$_T$ **do**+Af] [$_{VP}$ ~~*win the race*~~]]]

There is no violation of the Attachment Conditions in (61), since the verb stem *do* has a verbal affix attached to it, and the affix in turn is attached to the verb stem *do*. The relevant *do+Af* string is ultimately spelled out as *did* in (104c) *Win the race he did*. Thus, use of a less economical DO-support structure (115) is forced because the more economical auxiliariless structure in (113) crashes at PF.

Now consider the derivation of the yes–no question (104d) *Did he win the race?* Suppose that a series of syntactic merge operations apply to form the structure (116) below (containing an abstract yes–no question operator in spec-CP) and that T contains an unsupported past tense affix:

(116)   [$_{CP}$ Op$_{YNQ}$ [$_C$ ø] [$_{TP}$ he [$_T$ Af] [$_{VP}$ [$_V$ win] the race]]]

In accordance with the Inversion Licensing Condition (25), the interrogative C will contain a strong null affix *ø* with a T-feature. However, if this T-feature requires C to attract a T auxiliary to adjoin to C (as is implied in the traditional term Auxiliary Inversion), it follows that C will not be able to attract the tense affix in T in (116) to adjoin to C, because the tense affix in T is not attached to an auxiliary stem. On this view, Auxiliary Inversion cannot apply in (116) because there is no auxiliary in T to undergo Inversion.

But what if we set aside this objection, and instead suppose that the T-feature on C can attract a T constituent containing a tense affix (irrespective of whether the affix is attached to an auxiliary stem) to adjoin to C? Since T in (116) contains a past tense affix, this will allow the affix in T adjoin to the null complementiser in C. The resulting structure is then sent to the PF component, where the lower copy of the affix is deleted, so deriving the structure in (117) below:

(117)   [$_{CP}$ Op$_{YNQ}$ [$_C$ *Af*+ø] [$_{TP}$ he [$_T$ ~~Af~~] [$_{VP}$ [$_V$ win] the race]]]

Since the lower copy of the tense affix in T has been deleted/given a null spellout, nothing else happens to it. But consider what happens to the higher copy of the tense affix (*Af*) in C. It cannot remain where it is, because it is a tense affix which requires an overt verb as its host, and in (117) the affix is instead attached to a null complementiser: consequently, the structure in (117) violates the Attachment Condition (61i), because the affix is not attached to an overt verb stem. But can the affix in C be lowered onto some head below C by Affix Hopping – either onto T or onto V? Let's look at each of these possibilities in turn.

Suppose that the affix lowers onto (and remains) in T. This will derive the structure (118) below:

(118)   [$_{CP}$ Op$_{YNQ}$ [$_C$ A̶f̶+ø] [$_{TP}$ he [$_T$ A̶f̶+*Af*] [$_{VP}$ [$_V$ win] the race]]]

However, any such derivation would violate several constraints. For example, the structure in (118) would violate the Attachment Condition (61i), since the (italicised) affix would then be attached to a null copy of itself, rather than (as 61i requires) being attached to an overt verb stem. A second problem posed by lowering the affix from C onto T is that UG may incorporate a principle barring what Pullum (1976) termed **Duke of York** operations in which a constituent moves into some new position and subsequently moves back into its old position. Let's formulate this condition as follows:

(119)   **Duke of York Condition**
           No constituent can move back into a position it has moved out of.

(The condition is named after the Duke of York, who was made famous in a nursery rhyme which goes as follows: *The grand old Duke of York, He had ten thousand men, He marched them up to the top of the hill, And he marched them down again.* These days, such an up-and-down operation would be barred by regulations forbidding troop-abuse.) Lowering the affix from C onto T would violate the Duke of York Constraint because the affix would first move from T to C in the syntax, and then move back into T in the PF component. (The constraint could alternatively be formulated as barring self-attachment – i.e. barring a constituent from attaching to a copy of itself.)

Furthermore, if the affix in C were to move on its own to T (leaving behind the null complementiser which it is adjoined to, as in 118), the resulting movement would violate a further condition on movement operations embodied in the assumption made by Chomsky (1999: 10) that 'Excorporation is disallowed.' Let's formulate this condition in terms of the following constraint:

(120)   **Excorporation Constraint**
           No head can excorporate (i.e. move) out of another head which it is adjoined to.

This is because when the tense affix in T moves to C in the syntax, it adjoins to C, and hence the constraint (120) prevents T from subsequently being moved out of C on its own.

Thus far, we have seen that leaving the affix in situ in C in (117) causes a crash at PF, and so does lowering the affix onto T in (118). So let's consider what happens if we try lowering the affix from C onto the verb *win* in the head V position of VP. There are two ways in which this might happen in principle. One is by directly lowering the affix from C onto V in a single step, as shown by the arrow in (121) below:

(121)   [$_{CP}$ Op$_{YNQ}$ [$_C$ *Af+ø*] [$_{TP}$ he [$_T$ Af] [$_{VP}$ [$_V$ **win**] the race]]]

However, any such C-to-V lowering operation would violate the Head Movement Constraint (62), because HMC only allows a head to lower onto the head of its sister (and the sister of C is TP, not VP).

But what if the affix were to lower in two steps, first from C onto T and then from T onto V, as shown by the arrows below?

(122)   [$_{CP}$ Op$_{YNQ}$ [$_C$ *Af+ø*] [$_{TP}$ he [$_T$ Af] [$_{VP}$ [$_V$ **win**] the race]]]

The answer is that each of the two steps in this movement would be problematic. The first step of lowering the affix from C onto T would violate the Duke of York Condition (119) (because the affix is being moved back into a T position that it previously moved out of); it would also violate the Excorporation Constraint (120) if the affix moves out of C on its own, and thus excorporates out of the C-head it is adjoined to. Moreover, the second stage of this two-step movement (lowering the affix from T onto V) would also violate the Excorporation Constraint (120), if the lowered affix excorporates out of the null T-affix it is attached to. Furthermore, T-to-V lowering would be anticyclic (and hence would violate the Strict Cyclicity Principle, 103) because on the C-cycle only operations involving C and some constituent below it can apply, and an operation lowering an affix from T onto V does not involve C at all, because C is neither the position that the affix moves out of nor the position that it moves into.

The overall conclusion we reach is that using an unsupported affix in a root question structure like (116) will cause the derivation to crash. Let's therefore consider what happens if we use DO-support so that rather than containing an unsupported affix, T contains a supported affix attached to the verb stem *do*, as in (123) below:

(123)   [$_{CP}$ Op$_{YNQ}$ [$_C$ ø] [$_{TP}$ he [$_T$ **do**+Af] [$_{VP}$ [$_V$ *win*] *the race*]]]

The T-feature on C will then attract all the material in T (= *do+Af*) to adjoin to the null complementiser in C, so deriving the structure below:

(124)   [$_{CP}$ Op$_{YNQ}$ [$_C$ **do**+*Af*+ø] [$_{TP}$ he [$_T$ *do*+*Af*] [$_{VP}$ [$_V$ *win*] *the race*]]]

Since the verbal affix in C is attached to the overt verb stem *do*, and since conversely the verb stem *do* has a verbal affix attached to it, there is no violation of either of the Attachment Conditions in (61). The resulting *do+Af+ø* string is ultimately spelled out as *did*. More generally, DO-support is required in root questions because use of the more economical unsupported affix structure (116) causes the derivation to crash.

Next, let's consider the clause *He* DID *win it* in (104e), where capitals mark emphatic stress (and the sentence is used to deny any implicit or explicit suggestion that he didn't win the race). As we see from sentences like (125) below, such sentences typically involve emphatic stress being placed on a finite T constituent containing an overt auxiliary:

(125) (a)   The opposition say he won't win the election, but he is confident that he WILL win it

(b)   She wants me to revise the budget, but I already HAVE revised it

(c)   He denied that he was claiming benefits, but I am certain that he WAS doing so

If T contains only a past tense affix in (104e), the sentence will have the syntactic structure in (126) below:

(126)   [cp [c ø] [TP he [T Af] [VP [V win] it]]]

However, once the affix lowers onto V-*win* in the PF component, T will be left empty and hence will not be able to carry the emphatic stress which it receives in sentences like (125). By contrast, if DO-support is employed and the auxiliary DO is merged with the affix in T, (104e) will have the structure in (127) below:

(127)   [cp [c ø] [TP he [T **do**+Af] [VP [V win] it]]]

If the affix in T carries a past tense feature, the resulting *do+Af* string in (127) will be spelled out as *did* at PF, and (like other auxiliaries) can be assigned the emphatic stress that it carries in (104e) *He* DID *win it*. Thus, sentences like (104e) provide us with another case where DO-support is required because the more economical *do*-less structure does not yield a convergent outcome at PF.

Now consider why DO-support is required in a negative sentence like (104f) *He did not win the race*. If an unsupported affix were generated in T, (104f) would have the syntactic structure (128) below:

(128)   [cp [c ø] [TP he [T Af] [NEGP not [NEG ø] [VP [V win] the race]]]]

The past tense affix could not remain in T at PF, because this would violate both the Attachment Conditions in (61): condition (61i) would be violated because the affix stranded in T is not attached to a verb stem; and condition (61ii) would be violated because the verb stem *win* would have no inflectional affix attached to it. But could the affix in T be lowered onto the verb *win* in the PF component? One possibility along these lines would be to lower the affix directly from T onto V in a single step, as shown by the arrow below:

(129)   [cp [c ø] [TP he [T *Af*] [NEGP not [NEG ø] [VP [V **win**] the race]]]]

However, any such single-step lowering of the affix directly from T onto V would violate the Head Movement Constraint/HMC (62), because HMC only allows a head to be lowered onto the head of its sister, and the sister of the T constituent containing the affix is not VP but rather NEGP. Accordingly, HMC bars the non-local lowering operation arrowed in (129).

But what if the affix in T were to lower onto V in two steps, first from T onto NEG, and then from NEG onto V, in the manner shown by the arrows below?

(130)   [$_{CP}$ [$_C$ ø] [$_{TP}$ he [$_T$ *Af*] [$_{NEGP}$ not [$_{NEG}$ ø] [$_{VP}$ [$_V$ **win**] the race]]]]

Neither movement would violate HMC (62), since both involve local movements (whereby a head lowers onto the head of its sister). However, the second move-ment (whereby the affix lowers from NEG onto V) is anticyclic (i.e. it violates the Strict Cyclicity Principle, 103), because on the T-cycle in the PF component, only operations affecting T and some constituent that it c-commands can apply, and while an operation lowering an affix from T to NEG involves T, one which lowers an affix from NEG onto V clearly does not involve T. Moreover, if the affix which adjoins to the head null NEG constituent of NEGP lowers onto V *win* on its own (without taking NEG ø with it), there will also be violation of the Excorporation Constraint (120). In short, there is no way of avoiding a derivational crash in auxiliariless negative structures like (128).

But now consider what happens if we use DO-support and the tense affix in T is attached to the stem of the auxiliary *do*, as in (131) below:

(131)   [$_{CP}$ [$_C$ ø] [$_{TP}$ he [$_T$ **do**+Af] [$_{NEGP}$ not [$_{NEG}$ ø] [$_{VP}$ [$_V$ win] the race]]]]

Since the affix is attached to the (auxiliary) verb stem *do* and conversely the verb stem *do* has an affix attached to it, there is no violation of either of the Attachment Conditions in (61) at PF. If the affix in (131) marks past tense, the *do*+*Af* string will be spelled out as *did* – precisely as in (104f) He did not win the race.

Finally, consider the negative question (104g) *Didn't he win the race?* Let us suppose that the contracted negative *n't* has essentially the same syntax as *not* (and so originates in spec-NEGP), except that *n't* is a clitic which must encliticise to (i.e. attach to the end of) an immediately adjacent finite T constituent which c-commands it (like *should* in 132 below) and cannot encliticise to a non-finite T (like *to* in 133):

(132) (a)   He *should not* have interfered
      (b)   He *shouldn't* have interfered

(133) (a)   He was ordered to *not* interfere
      (b)   *He was ordered *to n't* interfere

In the light of this assumption, let's look at how (104g) is derived. Consider first what will happen if we use a more economical auxiliariless structure like (134) below in which T contains only a past tense affix:

(134)   [$_{CP}$ Op$_{YNQ}$ [$_C$ ø] [$_{TP}$ he [$_T$ Af] [$_{NEGP}$ n't [$_{NEG}$ ø] [$_{VP}$ [$_V$ win] the race]]]]

If *n't* cliticises onto the affix in T in the syntax in (134), and if the resulting *Af+n't* string then undergoes T-to-C Movement in the syntax (and is suffixed to the null complementiser in C), this will give rise to the following structure:

(135)   [CP OpYNQ [C ø+*Af+n't*] [TP he [T ~~Af+n't~~] [NEGP ~~n't~~ [NEG ø] [VP [V win] the race]]]]

However, the resulting structure will violate both of the Attachment Conditions in (61), because the affix in C is not attached to an overt verb stem, and because the verb stem *win* has no inflectional affix attached to it. Accordingly, the structure in (135) crashes at the PF interface. (An interesting point to note in passing is that *n't* functions as a syntactic clitic rather than a phonological clitic in adult English: this means that it attaches to a T auxiliary like *should* in the syntax, forming the negative auxiliary *shouldn't*; if the auxiliary subsequently undergoes Inversion and moves to C in the syntax, the negative affix moves with it, so resulting in sentences like *Shouldn't he have interfered?* As noted in our earlier discussion of child sentences like 17a *Why could Snoopy couldn't fit in the boat?* children sometimes misanalyse *n't* as a phonological clitic.)

But now consider what happens if DO-support is used and a series of merge operations form the structure in (136) below:

(136)   [CP OpYNQ [C ø] [TP he [T do+Af] [NEGP **n't** [NEG ø] [VP [V win] the race]]]]

If T-to-C Movement applies to the structure in (136), it will result in all the material in T (i.e. *do+Af*) being adjoined to the null complementiser in C, so deriving the structure (137) below:

(137)   [CP OpYNQ [C *do+Af+ø*] [TP he [T ~~do+Af~~] [NEGP **n't** [NEG ø] [VP [V win] the race]]]]

However, the resulting structure would leave the bold-printed negative clitic stranded without a host to attach to. If we generalise the Attachment Condition (61i) in such a way as to require an affix to be attached to an appropriate overt host, the structure in (137) will violate this Generalised Attachment Condition. Let us therefore suppose that *n't* encliticises onto the T constituent in (136) in the *syntax*, so forming the structure in (138) below:

(138)   [CP OpYNQ [C ø] [TP he [T do+Af+**n't**] [NEGP ~~n't~~ [NEG ø] [VP [V win] the race]]]]

Let us further suppose that the null complementiser in C then attracts all the material in T to adjoin to the null complementiser in C, so forming the syntactic structure in (139) below:

(139)   [CP OpYNQ [C do+*Af*+**n't**+ø] [TP he [T ~~do+Af+n't~~] [NEGP ~~n't~~ [NEG ø] [VP [V win] the race]]]]

When the structure in (139) is handed over to the PF component, the *do+Af+n't+ø* string in C is spelled out as *didn't*, and the overall structure in (139) is spelled out as (104g) *Didn't he win the race?*

An interesting implication of the analysis in (139) is that it is in principle possible that the interrogative form of some auxiliaries may have a different spellout from their non-interrogative counterparts. This is because in their interrogative form they attach to a null affixal interrogative complementiser ø, whereas in their non-interrogative form they do not. A case in point is BE. When used with a first person singular subject (= *I*), this has the negative interrogative form *aren't* – a form which is not found with an *I* subject (in varieties of English like mine) in non-interrogative uses, as the following contrast shows:

(140) (a)   *Aren't* I entitled to claim Social Security benefits?
    (b)   *I *aren't* entitled to claim Social Security benefits (= *I'm not…*)

This can be accounted for by positing that the string $be+Af_{1SgPr}+n't+ø$ found in (140a) can be spelled out as *aren't* – but not the string $be+Af_{1SgPr}+n't$ in (140b) because this is not interrogative (by virtue of having no null interrogative affix attached to it).

The analysis outlined above assumes that contracted negative auxiliaries come about via a productive cliticisation operation whereby the contracted negative clitic *n't* attaches to the end of an immediately adjacent c-commanding finite T auxiliary in the syntax. However, this assumption is potentially problematic for several reasons. One is that contracted negative auxiliaries often show marked (and unpredictable) phonological differences from their positive counterparts – as can be seen by comparing pairs such as *am/aren't, can/can't, shall/shan't, will/won't* and *do/don't*. Furthermore, some auxiliaries have no contracted counterpart – and this holds in my variety of British English for *may* (which has no contracted negative *mayn't*) and *used* (which has no contracted negative *usedn't*). For reasons such as these, some linguists prefer to treat contracted negative forms like *can't* as inherently negative auxiliaries directly generated in T. This would mean that sentences such as (141a) and (142a) below have the respective structures indicated in (141b) and (142b):

(141) (a)   You can't go to her party
    (b)   [CP [C ø] [TP you [T *can't*] [VP [V go] to her party]]]

(142) (a)   You can't not go to her party
    (b)   [CP [C ø] [TP you [T *can't*] [NEGP not [NEG ø] [VP [V go] to her party]]]]

This assumption would account for double-negative sentences such as (142a).

A final detail which needs to be cleared up in relation to DO-support is the issue of why the verb following DO is in the infinitive form – e.g. why the verb *win* is in the infinitive form in a structure like (127) above, repeated in slightly simplified form in (143) below (where capitals mark emphatic stress):

(143)   [CP [C ø] [TP he [T DID] [VP [V win] it]]]

Given that the Attachment Condition (61ii) requires that 'Every verb stem must have an appropriate inflectional affix attached to it at PF', it follows that the verb *win* in (143) must carry a null infinitival inflection (an assumption made all the more plausible by the fact that the corresponding infinitive form *vincere*win in Italian carries the overt infinitival inflection *-re*). Thus, (143) has the fuller structure shown in (144) below, where *+Inf* denotes an infinitival suffix (albeit one with a silent spellout at PF):

(144)   [CP [C ø] [TP he [T DID] [VP [V win+Inf] it]]]

But why is the verb *win* required to be in the infinitive form in a DO-support structure like (144)? The traditional answer is that DO 'takes' an infinitive complement (as indeed do modal auxiliaries like *can/may/will*, etc.). It might seem as if we can account for this by supposing that DO selects a complement headed by a verb carrying an infinitive suffix: since VP is the complement/sister of T-*did* in (144) and *win* is the head V of VP, this would then account for why the verb WIN has to be in the infinitive form in (144).

However, a complication arises in relation to negative structures such as:

(145)

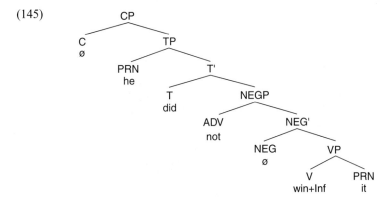

In a structure like (145), we can't simply say that DO 'takes an infinitive complement' (i.e. requires a complement whose head carries an infinitive inflection), since the complement (i.e. sister) of T-*did* is NEGP, and the head NEG of NEGP does not carry an infinitive inflection (nor does the verb *win* raise from V to NEG, as we see from VP-preposing structures like *Win it, he did not*). Rather, it seems that we need to say that an auxiliary like DO requires the closest verb which it c-commands to carry an infinitive inflection (and the same is true of modal auxiliaries like *may*, etc. and of the infinitive particle *to*). Since the closest verb c-commanded by T-*did* in (145) is *win*, it follows that *win* must be used in the infinitive form in (145) – i.e. it must have a null infinitive inflection attached to it.

This account of the morphological dependency between auxiliaries and verbs can be generalised from (145) to more complex cases such as the following structure:

(146)

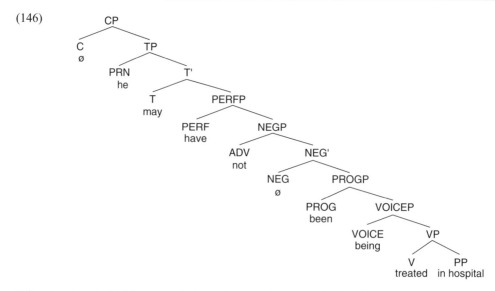

(The structure in 146 is somewhat cumbersome because the double-BE sequence *been being* is stylistically inelegant, but I will set this aside here.) Given the assumption that an auxiliary determines the morphological form of the closest verb which it c-commands, we can then account for the morphology of the non-finite verb forms *have/been/being/treated* as follows. The T auxiliary MAY (like DO) requires the closest verb which it c-commands (= the perfect auxiliary verb HAVE) to carry an infinitive inflection, and since this is null in English, HAVE is spelled out as *have*. The perfect auxiliary HAVE requires the closest verb which it c-commands (= the progressive auxiliary verb BE) to carry a perfect participle inflection, and this is ultimately spelled out as the affix -*en* on *been*. The progressive auxiliary BE requires the closest verb which it c-commands (= the passive voice auxiliary verb BE) to carry an -*ing* affix, and so the passive auxiliary is spelled out as *being*. Finally, the passive voice auxiliary BE requires the closest verb which it c-commands (= the verb TREAT) to carry a passive participle suffix, and this suffix is spelled out as the -*ed* ending on *treated*.

Having looked in some detail at the syntax of Head Movement in clauses in §§5.2–5.10, I now turn to look at cases of Head Movement internally within nominals.

5.11   Head Movement in nominals

Our discussion so far has focused entirely on Head Movement in clauses. To end this chapter, we look briefly at Head Movement in nominals (i.e. noun-containing structures). More particularly, we will look at **N-Movement** (i.e. the movement of a noun out of the head N position of NP into a higher head position within the nominal expression containing it). Although this kind of

movement operation is no longer productive in present-day English, it did occur
in earlier varieties of English. For example, in Chaucer's *Troilus and Criseyde* we
find nominals such as those in (147) below where the italicised noun precedes the
bold-printed adjective (and a literal word-for-word gloss is provided in
parentheses):

(147) (a)   a *thing* **immortal** (= a thing immortal)
    (b)   blosmy *bowes* **grene** (= blossomy branches green)
    (c)   hire *hornes* **pale** (= her horns pale)
    (a)   hire own *brother* **dere** (= her own brother dear)

In §4.11, it was suggested that attributive adjectives occupy the specifier position
within a modifier phrase (MODP) projection positioned above the noun they
modify. This being so, the present-day English counterpart of (147a) *an immortal
thing* will have the structure shown below:

(148)

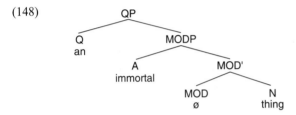

But if so, how could the noun *thing* come to be positioned above the adjective
immortal in the Chaucerian English structure (147a) *a thing immortal*? A plausible answer is that the noun *thing* moves out of its original position at the foot of
the structure to adjoin to a higher functional head of some kind which is positioned below the indefinite article/quantifier *an* but above the functional projection MODP containing the adjective *immortal*. What could be the nature of this
functional head? One influential suggestion which has been made in this regard is
that the relevant head is a **NUM**(ber) head which serves as the locus of the
number properties of nominals. Cross-linguistic support for the postulation of a
NUM head comes from languages like Hawaiian, which have a special morpheme (italicised below) marking plural number, as in:

(149) 'elua   a'u   *mau*   i'a
      two   my   PL   fish   (= 'my two fish'; Dryer 2005)

If languages like English contain a null counterpart of this head, we can
suppose that the italicised noun in structures like those in (147) moves to
adjoin to the head NUM/number constituent of a NUMP/number phrase
projection. And just as T was a strong head which carried a V-feature attracting
V to adjoin to it in auxiliariless finite clauses in earlier varieties of English, so
too we can assume that NUM was a strong head in earlier varieties of English
which carried an N-feature attracting N to adjoin to it. If so, a nominal
like (147a) *a thing immortal* would have the derivation shown in simplified
form in (150) below:

(150)

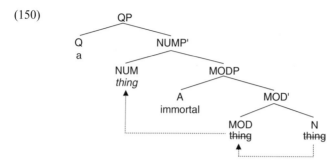

In consequence of the Head Movement Constraint (62) only allowing a head to move into the next highest head position above it, the noun *thing* would first have to move into the head MOD position of MODP before subsequently moving into the head NUM position of NUMP in the manner shown informally by the arrow above. More accurately, MOD would contain a null affix with an N-feature which attracts the noun *thing* to adjoin to it. Similarly, NUM would also contain a null affix with an N-feature attracting the noun *thing* in MOD to adjoin to it; but because the noun is adjoined to a null affix in MOD, the null affix in MOD will be pied-piped along with the noun *thing* when it adjoins to NUM. Consequently, NUM will end up containing not only the noun *thing* but also a null MOD affix and a null NUM affix (although this is not shown in the simplified tree diagram in 150).

But what are we to make of structures like (147b) *blosmy*blossomy *bowes*branches *grene*green in which the noun *bowes*branches ends up positioned between the higher adjective *blosmy*blossomy and the lower adjective *grene*green? If (as suggested in §4.11) each different adnominal adjective serves as the specifier of a different type of MOD head, (147b) will have a structure along the lines shown in (151) below (if we make the plausible assumption that the overall noun expression is a QP headed by a null quantifier):

(151)

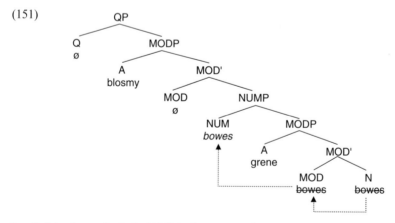

Implicit in the analysis in (151) is the assumption that different types of attributive adjective occupy different positions within the nominal expression containing them. For example, colour adjectives tend to be positioned closer to the nouns they modify than size adjectives (as we see from an expression like *a big red car*, where the colour adjective *red* is closer to the noun *car* than the size adjective *big*). Accordingly, the adjective *grene*green serves as the specifier of a MODP positioned below NUMP in (151), whereas the adjective *blosmy*blossomy serves as the specifier of a MODP positioned above NUMP, and the noun *bowes* moves to adjoin to the null head of the NUMP positioned between the two MODP projections.

A second context in which we find N-Movement in earlier varieties of English is in **vocative** nominals (i.e. expressions used to address someone). In this connection, contrast the two vocative expressions italicised below (from Chaucer's *Troilus and Criseyde*):

(152) (a)   'Iwis, *myn uncle*,' quod she
            'Certainly, my uncle,' said she
     (b)   'And whi so, *uncle myn*? whi so?' quod she
            'And why so, uncle mine, why so?' said she

As these examples show, the noun *uncle* can be positioned either before or after the possessive *myn* in vocative expressions. How can we account for this? One way is to suppose that possessive DPs in earlier varieties of English had a DP+POSSP structure, under which a possessor serves as the specifier of a POSSP (possessive phrase) projection which in turn serves as the complement of a null definite D constituent. If D in vocative DPs like *uncle myn* was strong (by virtue of containing a null affixal determiner with an N-feature which attracts a noun to adjoin to it), we can suppose that the noun *uncle* raised all the way out of the N position at the bottom of the structure into the D position at the top of the structure. If all nominals contain a NUMP projection (as suggested immediately above) and if N-Movement takes place in a successive-cyclic (one-head-at-a time) fashion in accordance with the Head Movement Constraint, the vocative nominal *uncle myn* will have the derivation shown in simplified form below:

(153)

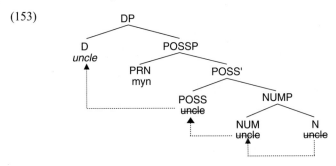

That is, the noun *uncle* will first move into NUM and then into POSS before finally moving into D and thereby ending up positioned above the possessive pronoun *myn*: we can suppose that each of the three functional heads in the structure (NUM, POSS and D) contains an affix with a strong N-feature which attracts a (head containing a) noun to adjoin to it.

   Although the idea that the nouns should move to adjoin to a null determiner in vocative structures like (153) might at first sight seem far-fetched, it should be pointed out that there are nominal structures such as the following in Norwegian in which a (bold-printed) noun seems to raise across a possessor to attach to the left of an (italicised) overt affixal determiner:

(154) **bøke***ne*   hans om   syntaks
        books+the his   about syntax   (= 'his books about syntax')   [Taraldsen 1990]

Structures like (154) make it plausible to posit that the noun is attracted to adjoin to a null affixal determiner in vocative structures such as (153).

   However, if D was strong in vocative DPs in Chaucer's day, how can we account for the POSSESSOR+NOUN order found in the vocative *myn uncle* in (152a)? One possibility is to suppose that vocatives like *myn uncle* are not full DP constituents, but rather project only as far as POSSP: after all, we saw in §4.11 that (predicative, exclamative and) vocative nominals do not have to project up to DP. If this is so, the topmost (DP) layer of structure in (153) can be omitted in vocatives: this in turn means that the noun *uncle* will be unable to raise to a position above the possessor *myn*, and may indeed only raise as far as NUM as in (155) below:

(155)

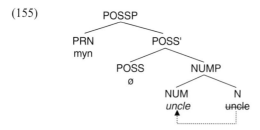

More specifically, if POSS is only a strong head in a vocative DP (i.e. when POSSP is selected as the complement of a strong vocative D), the noun *uncle* will only raise as far as NUM.

   The analysis outlined above of N-Movement in earlier varieties of English raises a number of questions about the structure of nominals in present-day English. Just as we find a last vestige of V-to-T raising in present-day English with BE, HAVE, NEED and DARE (in certain uses), we might wonder whether we find any last vestige of N-to-NUM raising in present-day English. One potential structure of this type occurs in NOUN+ADJECTIVE combinations like *battle royal, body politic, heir apparent, proof positive, time immemorial, governor general,* etc. However, these tend to be 'set phrases' rather than productive structures, and they are often archaic in flavour (albeit *Mission Impossible* is a contemporary film title, and *Amnesty International* a contemporary organisation): it is therefore probably better to treat them as 'fixed phrases' listed as such in the lexicon. A more promising potential source of N-to-NUM raising in contemporary

English can be found in expressions like that italicised in the following line from a duet sung by Frank and Nancy Sinatra:

(156)   And then I go and spoil it all by saying *something stupid* like 'I love you'

At first sight, it might seem tempting to analyse the italicised expression as derived from a structure like *some stupid thing* via the N-to-NUM raising operation arrowed in (157) below:

(157)

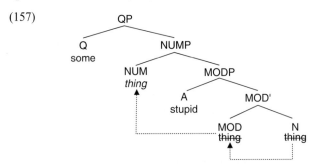

(with *thing* subsequently attaching to the end of the indefinite quantifier *some* to form the compound word *something*). The main problem with such an analysis is that this kind of N-Movement is not productive in present-day English, as illustrated by the ungrammaticality of the (b) examples below:

(158) (a)   a stupid idea
      (b)   *an idea stupid

(159) (a)   some sensible suggestions
      (b)   *some suggestions sensible

(160) (a)   several important people
      (b)   *several people important

So, if we wished to adopt the kind of N-Movement analysis in (157), we'd have to somehow restrict it to cases where it results in the formation of a compound word (like those italicised in '*somebody* nice', '*someplace* special', '*anything* suitable', etc.). One way of doing this is to suppose that items like *body/place/thing* in the relevant use are **light nouns** (i.e. nouns with little lexical semantic content), and that N-to-D Movement in present-day English is restricted to light nouns. We might then draw a parallel with the V-to-T raising operation discussed in §5.8, which allows only an auxiliary verb to raise to T: if auxiliaries are light verbs (i.e. verbs with little lexical semantic content), we could then say V-to-T Movement in present-day English is restricted to light verbs, in the same way as N-to-D Movement is restricted to light nouns.

But what of the N-to-D Movement found in vocatives like (153) above? At first sight, it might seem as if we can find an immediate counterpart of it in present-day English vocatives such as that italicised below:

(161)   *John dear*, would you mind closing the window?

That is to say, we might suppose that *John dear* in (161) is a vocative DP in which the noun *John* originates in the N position at the foot of the DP and subsequently raises (one head at a time) into the head D position of DP, and so comes to precede the modifying adjective *dear*. However, this seems unlikely, as such an analysis would wrongly predict that *John* should be able to cross a possessor like *mine* in a structure such as the following:

(162)   **John mine*, would you mind closing the window?

By contrast, present-day dialects which use possessors in vocatives show POSSESSOR+NOUN order (as in vocatives like *Come here, our John!* found in northern British English varieties). It seems more plausible to take (161) to involve a succession of two separate vocative nouns (*John* and *dear*) – and support for this suggestion comes from the fact that the two can be separated and positioned at opposite ends of the sentence, as in:

(163)   *John*, would you mind closing the window, *dear?*

Thus, the overall conclusion we reach is that N-Raising is no longer productive in present-day English (being permitted only with light nouns, if we adopt the analysis in 157).

This in turn raises interesting questions about whether we assume that nominals contain an internal NUMP projection in present-day English with a head which has become too weak to attract an N to adjoin to it, or whether the gradual erosion of (gender/number/case) inflections on nouns and adnominal adjectives over the past few hundred years has also led to the loss of the NUMP projection within nominals. The answer to a large extent depends on the theoretical assumptions we make, and this is too complex an issue to go into here.

The general conclusion to be drawn from this section is that we find evidence from earlier varieties of English that Head Movement may apply in nominal as well as clausal structures. In particular, we find evidence of two types of N-Movement operation: (i) movement of a noun to a NUM position intermediate between D and N; and (ii) movement of a noun to the head D position of DP (with the noun first moving to NUM before moving to D, in order for movement of the noun to be successive-cyclic and thereby satisfy the Head Movement Constraint). Neither movement seems to have survived into present-day English (except perhaps for a last vestige of N-to-NUM Movement with light nouns in structures like 157).

5.12   Summary

This chapter has been concerned with the syntax of Head Movement. We began by looking at Auxiliary Inversion in questions in English in §5.2, and I argued that this involves a T-to-C movement operation whereby an auxiliary moves from the head T position of TP to adjoin to a null complementiser occupying the head C position of CP. I argued that movement operations like Auxiliary Inversion involve separate copying and deletion operations: a copy of the auxiliary in T is adjoined to a null complementiser in C, and then the original occurrence of the auxiliary in T is deleted, in conformity with the Default Spellout Rule given in (164) below.

(164)   **Default Spellout Rule** (= 13)
          For a constituent whose spellout is not determined by some other rule or requirement, the highest copy of the constituent is pronounced at PF, and any lower copies are silent.

In §5.3, I suggested that Auxiliary Inversion is driven by a T-feature on C requiring a T auxiliary to be adjoined to C. I also noted that C is only licensed to carry an (Inversion-triggering) T-feature when C has an appropriate kind of specifier, in accordance with the Inversion Licensing Condition in (165) below.

(165)   **Inversion Licensing Condition** (= expanded version of 25)
          A null C is licensed to carry a T-feature triggering Auxiliary Inversion (i.e. adjunction of a T auxiliary to C) if

          (i) C has a negative or degree or conditional specifier

          or

          (ii) C has an interrogative specifier in a root clause.

In §5.4 we saw that Inversion can take place in *that*-clauses (like that bracketed in 'The kidnappers warned [that on no account *should she* contact the police]'), and I argued that such structures can be handled in terms of a CP recursion structure in which a CP headed by *that* takes as its complement another CP headed by the inverted auxiliary *should*. In §5.5 we looked at what triggers Auxiliary Inversion in main-clause yes–no questions. I argued that in such cases, there is a null yes–no question operator in spec-CP which licenses C to carry an (Inversion-triggering) T-feature in accordance with condition (165ii) above. I claimed that a parallel case can be made for C having a conditional operator as its specifier in inverted conditionals (like *Should anything happen to me* ...). I noted that the null operator in such cases would serve not only to licence Auxiliary Inversion but also to serve two further functions. One is to type the clause as conditional, in accordance with the Clause Typing Condition (166) below:

(166)   **Clause Typing Condition** (expanded version of 37)
          A CP is typed as interrogative (i.e. interpreted as interrogative in type in the semantic component) if it has an interrogative specifier, exclamative if it has an exclamative specifier, conditional if it has a conditional specifier, etc. Otherwise, a CP headed by an indicative complementiser is interpreted as declarative in type by default.

The other is to license polarity items, in accordance with the Polarity Licensing Condition (167) below:

(167)   **Polarity Licensing Condition** (= 39)
          A polarity expression must be c-commanded by an appropriate (e.g. nega-
          tive, interrogative or conditional) licenser.

In §5.6 we saw that finite main verbs in Elizabethan English could move from V
to T by an operation of V-to-T Movement (as is shown by word order in negative
sentences like *I care not for her*), but that this kind of movement is no longer
productive in present-day English. I suggested that a null finite T was strong in
Elizabethan English (containing a strong tense affix with a V-feature able to
trigger raising of a verb to T) but that its counterpart in present-day English is
weak (so that a tense affix in T is lowered onto a main verb by the morphological
operation of Affix Hopping/Affix Lowering). We saw that a tense affix needs to
be attached to an overt verb (and conversely an overt verb needs an affix attached
to it) in order to satisfy the conditions in (168) below:

(168)   **V-Attachment Conditions** (= 61)
          (i) Every verbal affix must be attached to an overt verb stem at PF.
          (ii) Every verb stem must have an appropriate inflectional affix attached to it
               at PF.

In §5.7 I argued that T-to-C Movement, V-to-T Movement and the morphological
operation of Affix Hopping (lowering an affix from T onto V) are different
reflexes of a more general Head Movement operation, and that Head
Movement is subject to a strict locality condition imposed by the Head
Movement Constraint (169) below:

(169)   **Head Movement Constraint/HMC** (= 62)
          Head Movement is only possible between a given head H and the head of the
          sister of H.

HMC means that Head Movement is only possible between a given head and the
next highest (or next lowest) head within the structure containing it.
Consequently, when a head undergoes long-distance Head Movement, it has to
do so in a successive-cyclic (stepwise) fashion. In §5.8 we saw that present-day
English has a last vestige of V-to-T raising in finite clauses whereby BE and HAVE
(when functioning as auxiliaries) and narrow-scope modals like NEED and DARE
raise from a lower head position into the head T position of TP. I suggested that a
finite T in present-day English contains a tense affix which is only strong enough
to attract an auxiliary verb (or light verb) to move to T, not a non-auxiliary verb:
and I noted that one implementation of this idea would be that a finite T in
present-day English can either be filled by a strong affix which requires an
auxiliary as its host (and so can trigger movement of an auxiliary into T), or by
a weak affix which requires a non-auxiliary verb as its host (with the affix being
lowered onto V in the PF component). In §5.9, we took another look at negation.
Revising the earlier analysis of *not* as a VP-specifier, I outlined an alternative
analysis under which *not* is the specifier of a NEGP constituent which was headed
by *ne* in Chaucerian English, but which is null in present-day English. On this

view, Shakespearean negatives like *He heard not that* involve movement of the verb from V through NEG into T, with both NEG and T carrying a V-feature attracting a verb to adjoin to them. Because NEG and T can no longer carry a V-feature in present-day English, they can no longer trigger movement of a lexical verb through NEG into T. The affix in T cannot lower from T through NEG onto V because lowering the affix from NEG onto V would be anticyclic by virtue of violating the following principle:

(170)   **Strict Cyclicity Principle/SCP** (= 103)
         At a stage of derivation where a given projection HP is being cycled/ processed, only operations involving the head H of HP and some other constituent c-commanded by H can apply.

In §5.10, I presented an *economy* account of Affix Lowering and DO-support, under which DO-support is used only as a last resort, where use of a more economical *do*-less structure would cause the derivation to crash. Conditions which played a key role in the account of DO-support presented in the main text include the following:

(171)   **Recoverability Condition** (= 111)
         Material can only be deleted if its content is recoverable.

(172)   **Duke of York Condition** (= 119)
         No constituent can move back into a position it has moved out of.

(173)   **Excorporation Constraint** (= 120)
         No head can excorporate (i.e. move) out of another head which it is adjoined to.

In §5.11, I presented evidence that Head Movement can also apply in nominal structures. I argued that nouns in Chaucerian English could raise to a head NUM(ber) position intermediate between D/Q and N in structures like *a thing immortal* (and perhaps also in present-day structures like *something stupid*) and that N could raise even further to D in Chaucerian vocatives like *uncle myn* 'uncle mine'.

5.13   Bibliographical background

The analysis of Auxiliary Inversion in §5.2 as involving a strong, affixal C constituent attracting a subordinate T auxiliary to adjoin to it is adapted from Chomsky (1993, 1995); for an alternative account of Auxiliary Inversion, see Ioannou (2011). On inversion in *so*-sentences like *John can speak French and so can Mary*, see Toda (2007). The idea that movement involves copying derives from Chomsky (1995); on why only the highest copy of a moved constituent is overtly spelled out, see Nunes (1995, 1999, 2001, 2004) for the theoretical basis of this choice. Children's auxiliary copying structures are discussed in Hiramatsu (2003). On the idea in §5.4 that certain types of structure involve CP recursion, see Escribano (1991), Iatridou and Kroch (1992), Fontana (1993) and Browning

(1996). On the split projection analysis of CP recursion structures, see Rizzi (1996, 1997, 2001, 2004, 2005, 2006, 2007, 2010, 2012, 2013, 2014, 2015), Rizzi and Shlonsky (2007), Shlonsky (2014), Haegeman (2000a, 2003, 2006a, 2006b, 2007, 2009, 2010, 2012), Cinque and Rizzi (2010): for a critique of the split CP analysis, see Newmeyer (2005b). The idea in §5.5 that yes–no questions contain a null operator echoes a similar claim made in Katz and Postal (1964), Bresnan (1970), Larson (1985a), Grimshaw (1993), Roberts (1993), den Dikken (2006) and Haegeman (2012). The Head Movement Constraint/HMC outlined in §5.7 has its origins in Travis (1984); a complication which arises with it is that some languages have a form of long-distance Head Movement operation which allows a verb to be moved out of one clause to the front of another in order to highlight the verb in some way, and which appears not to obey HMC: for relevant discussion, see Koopman (1984), van Riemsdijk (1989), Lema and Rivero (1990), Larson and Lefebvre (1991), Manzini (1994), Roberts (1994), Carnie (1995), Borsley, Rivero and Stephens (1996), Hoge (1998), Holmberg (1999), Toyoshima (2000), Fanselow (2002), and Landau (2006b). The idea that the relative strength or weakness of T in a language is correlated with the relative richness of the system of subject-agreement inflections on verbs has been put forward by a number of linguists, including Platzack and Holmberg (1989), Roberts (1993), Vikner (1995), Rohrbacher (1999), Koeneman (2000) and Tamburelli (2007) – though see Bobaljik (2000) for a dissenting view. The analysis of HAVE/BE raising in §5.8 dates back in spirit to Klima (1964); see Nomura (2006: 303–14) for discussion of HAVE/BE-raising in subjunctive clauses. On the syntax of modal and aspectual auxiliaries and HAVE/BE in English, see Chomsky (1957), Jackendoff (1972), Fiengo (1974), Akmajian and Wasow (1975), Akmajian, Steele and Wasow (1979), Bobaljik (1995), Lasnik (1995), Bobaljik and Thráinsson (1998), Adger (2003), Cormack and Smith (2012). The analysis of narrow-scope modal auxiliaries as originating in a lower position and subsequently raising to T is adapted from Roberts (1998) and Nomura (2006). On the defining characteristics of auxiliaries, see Pollock (1989), and Benincà and Poletto (2004). On the nature of historical change in syntax, see Kroch (2001). On the syntax of infinitival *to*, see Akmajian, Steele and Wasow (1979), Pullum (1982), Stowell (1982), van Gelderen (1996, 1997), Wurmbrandt (2003), Christensen (2007), Levine (2012). The NEGP analysis of negative clauses in §5.9 has its roots in earlier work by Pollock (1989), Laka (1990), Rizzi (1990), Ouhalla (1990), Iatridou (1990), Belletti (1990), Zanuttini (1991), Roberts (1993), Haegeman (1995), Chomsky (1995), Potsdam (1997a, 1998); on negation in earlier varieties of English, see Ingham (2000, 2002, 2007a,b); on contracted negative auxiliaries like *can't*, see Zwicky and Pullum (1983). On negative infinitives, see Fitzmaurice (2000) and Nomura (2006). On sentences like *Shouldn't you be at work?* see Cormack and Smith (2000, 2012). A range of alternative accounts of the DO-support phenomenon discussed in §5.10 can be found in Chomsky (1957), Halle and Marantz (1993), Bobaljik (1994, 1995), Lasnik (1995, 2000, 2003, 2006), Ochi (1999), Han (2000), Embick and Noyer

(2001), Bobaljik (2002), Freidin (2004), Schütze (2004), Radford (2009) and Escribano (2012). The analysis of N-Movement in §5.11 is loosely based on Cinque (1994) and Longobardi (1994); the assumption that nouns can move to an intermediate NUM(ber) head is defended in Picallo (1991) and Ritter (1991). See Kishimoto (2000) for arguments that present-day structures like *something nice* are a last vestige of a once-productive N-to-NUM Movement operation, deriving from *some nice thing* via movement of *thing* from N to NUM; but see also Larson and Marušič (2004) and Cardinaletti and Giusti (2006) for a critique of this analysis. See Cinque (1994) for a more extensive implementation of the idea that different kinds of adjective serve as the specifiers of different kinds of heads, but see Sadler and Arnold (1994) and Kennedy (1999) for alternative analyses; see also Giegerich (2005) for the claim that some ADJECTIVE+NOUN structures like *dental decay* are compounds formed in the lexicon; and see Cinque (1999) for an extension of the specifier analysis of modifiers to clausal adverbs. See also Longobardi (1994, 1996, 2001) and Bernstein (2001) for more general discussion of the syntax of nominals; and see Schwarzschild (2006) for discussion of the syntax of measure phrases like *lots of soap*. For a critique of the N-Movement analysis of postnominal adjectives, see Lamarche (1991), Alexiadou (2003), and Cinque (2010); for a defence of N-Movement, see Pereltsvaig (2006a, b).

Although I have taken Head Movement to be a syntactic operation here (following Baltin 2002; Roberts 2001; Donati 2006; Matushansky 2006; Nomura 2006), it should be noted that Chomsky (1999) takes it to be a morphological operation applying in the PF component, essentially designed to enable affixes to attach to appropriate heads: see Boeckx and Stjepanović (2001), Flagg (2002), Sauerland and Elbourne (2002), Lechner (2006, 2007) and Roberts (2011) for discussion of this idea. However, the picture is complicated by evidence from Zwart (2001) that Head Movement has some properties typical of syntactic operations, and others typical of PF operations. Chomsky (2013) goes back on his earlier analysis of Head Movement as a PF operation and instead treats it as a syntactic operation.

Workbook section

Exercise 5.1

Discuss the derivation of each of the following (declarative or interrogative) sentences, drawing a tree diagram to represent the structure of each sentence and saying why the relevant structure is (or is not) grammatical (in the case of 4, saying why it is ungrammatical as a main clause):

1. He helps her	2. *He d's help her	3. *Helps he her?
4. *If he helps her?	5. Does anyone help her?	6. I wonder if he helps her
7. *I wonder if does he help her	8. *I wonder if helps he her	9. *He helps not her
10. *He not helps her	11. He does not help her	12. He doesn't help her
13. Doesn't he help her?	14. He might not help her	15. He dare not help her

(Note that *d's* in 2 represents unstressed *does*, /dəz/.) In addition, discuss the derivation of each of the questions in 16–17 below, and say what is interesting about them:

16.   Have you any wool? (second line of the nursery rhyme *Baa Baa Black Sheep*)

17.   Does he be a bit more positive? (Roy Keane, ITV; asking whether the manager of Manchester United should change the team formation into a more attacking one)

Next, comment on the syntax of the following negative sentence produced by a boy called Abe at age 2;5.26 (2 years, 5 months, 26 days):

18.   I not can find it

and compare 18 with the corresponding adult structure

19.   I cannot find it.

Then discuss the use of unemphatic/unstressed DO in (20–27) below by various children aged 2–4 years (See e.g. Hollebrandse and Roeper 1999), and identify the nature of the child's error in each case, comparing the child's structure with its adult counterpart:

20.   Does it opens?
21.   Don't you don't want one?
22.   Does it doesn't move?
23.   I do have juice in my cup
24.   I did wear Bea's helmet
25.   I did fixed it
26.   Jenny did left with Daddy
27.   Do it be colored?

Consider, also, the derivation of the following questions reported (by Akmajian and Heny 1975: 17) to have been produced by an unnamed three-year-old girl:

28.   Is I can do that?
29.   Is you should eat the apple?
30.   Is the apple juice won't spill?
31.   Is the clock is working?

Next, say what is interesting about the sentences in 32, produced by a Dutch football manager:

32.   So much chances we don't have created today (Luis van Gaal, Sky Sports TV = 'We haven't created so many chances today').

And say what it unusual about the italicised tags in the following sentences (the first produced by a radio presenter who'd been working a five-hour night shift, and the second being internet-sourced):

33.   You've got to let people know, *don't you*? (Doton Adebayo, BBC Radio 5)
34.   'They ought to, *hadn't they*?' the girl replied, earnestly and confidently (github.com)
35.   They ought to be punished, them men, and Mrs Hedges and Mr Johnson, they ought to, *didn't they*, Mum? (Hilary Bailey, 2012, *Love, Money & Revenge*, books.google.co.uk)

Finally, say why although a sentence like (21b) in the main text is (repeated as 36 below) is ungrammatical as a statement, it is grammatical as a question like 37:

36. *Under some circumstances would the president accept a bribe

37. Under some circumstances, would the president accept a bribe?

Helpful hints

In 14, 15, 18 and 19, consider the scope relations between the auxiliary and *not*, and bear in mind the suggestion made in the main text that finite auxiliaries originate in a position below NEG if they fall within the scope of *not*. In 16, take *any wool* to be a QP headed by the partitive quantifier *any*, and say how use of the polarity item *any* is licensed; in 17 take *a bit more positive* to be an AP, but don't concern yourself with its internal structure. In relation to 20–27, bear in mind that some children may assume that the relation between DO and the verb heading its VP complement is not one of selection (whereby DO selects a complement headed by a verb in the infinitive form), but rather one of copying (whereby the tense/agreement features on DO are copied onto the head V of its VP complement). Consider also whether some children may mistakenly treat tense affixes as requiring an auxiliary as their host – or may simply assume that T can only be filled by an auxiliary, not by a tense affix. In 23, take *have juice in my cup* to be a VP, but don't concern yourself with its internal structure. In 28–31, consider the possibility that children may sometimes be confused as to whether a constituent positioned at the front of a clause gets there by Move or by Merge. In 32, take *so much chances* to be a QP which originates in comp-VP and moves to spec-CP, but don't concern yourself with its internal structure: instead, consider why he says *don't have* rather than *haven't*: bear in mind that considerations of lexical economy ('Never use two words if one will do') would normally lead to *haven't* being preferred over *don't have*, so could LvG have problems in handling the Auxiliary Raising operation discussed in §5.8? In relation to the contrast between 36 and 37, consider the possibility that the sentence in 36 contains only one CP layer, but sentence 37 involves two CP layers (as in the discussion of CP recursion in §5.4), and consider what might trigger Inversion in the inner CP.

Model answer for 1

Given the assumptions made in the text, 1 will have the simplified syntactic structure (i) below (where Af_{3SgPr} denotes a third person singular present tense affix):

(i)

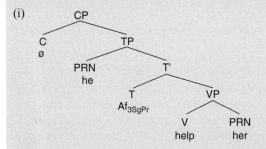

The overall clause is a CP headed by a null complementiser *ø* and is interpreted as declarative by default, in accordance with the Clause Typing Condition (166). CP has a TP complement headed by a T constituent which carries a present tense affix which is third person singular by agreement with the subject *he*. The structure (i) cannot survive as it is, since the affix stranded in T will violate the Attachment Condition (168i), and the uninflected/unaffixed verb *help* will violate condition (168ii). Since tense affixes are not strong enough to trigger raising of main/lexical verbs in present-day English (by virtue of not having a strong V-feature), the affix in T cannot attract the verb *help* to adjoin to it in the syntax. Instead, after the syntactic structure in (i) has been formed, it is handed over to the PF component, where it is processed in a bottom-up, cyclic fashion. On the T-cycle, the tense affix in T is lowered onto the end of the verb *help* by Affix Hopping: since the affix in T is lowered onto the head V of the VP which is the sister of T, the relevant lowering operation satisfies the Head Movement Constraint (169). Affix Hopping results in the formation of the compound V-head [*help*+Af_{3SgPr}], and this satisfies both of the Attachment Conditions in (168), because the affix is attached to an overt verb, and the verb stem has an affix attached to it. The resulting structure *help*+Af_{3SgPr} is ultimately spelled out as *helps*. The complement pronoun *her* is assigned accusative case in the syntax by the c-commanding transitive verb *help*, and the subject pronoun *he* is assigned nominative case by the c-commanding null intransitive finite complementiser *ø*.

Exercise 5.2

Discuss the derivation of the following Shakespearean sentences:

1. Thou marvell'st at my words (Macbeth, *Macbeth*, III.ii)
2. Macbeth doth come (Third Witch, *Macbeth*, I.iii)
3. He loves not you (Lysander, *Midsummer Night's Dream*, III.ii)
4. You do not look on me (Jessica, *Merchant of Venice*, II.vi)
5. Wilt thou use thy wit? (Claudio, *Much Ado About Nothing*, V.i)
6. Wrong I mine enemies? (Brutus, *Julius Caesar*, IV.ii)
7. Knows he not thy voice? (First Lord, *All's Well That Ends Well*, IV.i)
8. Didst thou not say he comes? (Baptista, *Taming of the Shrew*, III.ii)
9. Canst not rule her? (Leontes, *Winter's Tale*, II.iii)
10. Hath not a Jew eyes? (Shylock, *Merchant of Venice*, III.i)
11. Do not you love me? (Benedick, *Much Ado About Nothing*, V.iv)
12. Buy thou a rope! (Antipholus, *Comedy of Errors*, IV.i)
13. Fear you not him! (Tranio, *Taming of the Shrew*, Iv.iv)
14. Speak not you to him! (Escalus, *Measure for Measure*, V.i)
15. Do not you meddle! (Antonio, *Much Ado About Nothing*, V.i)
16. She not denies it (Leonato, *Much Ado About Nothing*, IV.i)

In addition, discuss the syntax of the vocative nominals italicised in the sentence extracts below, taken from Chaucer's *Troilus and Criseyde*:

17. 'Now, *uncle deere*$_{dear}$,' quod$_{said}$ she 'Telle$_{tell}$ it us for Goddes$_{God's}$ love'
18. 'O$_{oh}$, mercy, *dere*$_{dear}$ *nece*$_{niece}$,' anon$_{soon}$ quod$_{said}$ he
19. Now doth$_{it.does}$ hym$_{him}$ sitte$_{befit}$, *goode*$_{good}$ *nece*$_{niece}$ *deere*$_{dear}$, upon your beddes$_{bed's}$ syde$_{side}$…
20. 'That is wel seyde' quod$_{said}$ he '*my nece*$_{niece}$ *deere*$_{dear}$'
21. '*My dere*$_{dear}$ *nece*$_{niece}$' quod$_{said}$ he 'It am I' (= It's me)

Helpful hints

Assume that 9 has a null finite *pro* subject. Assume also that the sentences in 12–15 are **imperative** in force, and consider the possibility that V raises to C in imperatives in Elizabethan English (see Han 2001), with the movement being licensed by an abstract imperative operator (Op$_{IMP}$) in spec-CP. Assume too that C in Elizabethan imperatives and root interrogatives carries a strong T-feature enabling it to attract a tensed auxiliary or non-auxiliary verb in T to adjoin to C. Consider also the possibility that *not* had a dual status and could either function as an independent word (like present-day English *not*) or serve as an enclitic particle (like present-day English *n't*) which attached to the end of an immediately adjacent finite T constituent. Finally, say in what way(s) sentence 16 proves problematic in respect of the assumptions made in the main text (and in the model answer below), and see if you can think of possible solutions (e.g. what if the verb raised as far as NEG but not as far as T?). Assume that possessives like *my/mine/thy* are the specifiers of a DP headed by a null definite determiner.

Model answer for 1 and 2

Relevant aspects of the derivation of 1 (here presented in simplified form) are as follows. The verb *marvel* merges with its PP complement *at my words* to form the VP *marvel at my words*. This in turn is merged with a T constituent containing a strong present tense affix (= *Af*) to form the T-bar *Af marvel at my words*, which is in turn merged with its subject *thou* to form a TP. The tense affix agrees with *thou* and thus carries the features [second-person, singular-number, present-tense, indicative-mood], although these are not shown below. Being strong, the tense affix triggers raising of the verb *marvel* to adjoin to the affix in T. The resulting TP is merged with a null intransitive finite C which assigns nominative case to *thou*. 1 thus has the syntactic structure shown in simplified form in (i) below, with the dotted arrow indicating movement of the verb *marvel* from V to T:

(i)

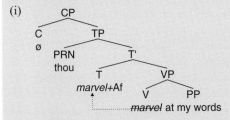

The string *marvel+Af*$_{2SgPr}$ is ultimately spelled out as *marvell'st* in the PF component. Since CP has no interrogative/exclamative/conditional, etc. specifier, it is interpreted as declarative by default, in accordance with the Clause Typing Condition (166).

Sentence 2 is derived as follows. Suppose that verb *come* merges with a tense affix in T, forming the T-bar *Af come*. This will in turn be merged with its subject *Macbeth*, which is a DP headed by a null determiner, in accordance with the **DP Hypothesis** of §4.11. Merging the resulting TP with a null complementiser will derive the syntactic structure shown in (ii) below:

(ii)

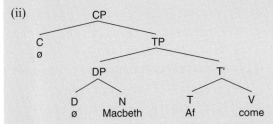

Since finite verbs can raise from V to T in Elizabethan English, what we'd expect to happen in (ii) is for the verb *come* to raise to adjoin to the tense affix in T, so forming the substructure *come+Af*, which would ultimately be spelled out as *cometh* (a dialectal variant of *comes*). However, although this is indeed one possible outcome, this is clearly not what happens in the case of 2 *Macbeth doth come*. Why not?

Let us suppose that the tense affix in a finite T in a structure like (ii) in Elizabethan English could be either strong or weak, and that Elizabethan English (perhaps because it had V-to-T raising) did not have any T-to-V lowering operation like the Affix Lowering operation found in present-day English. Where T is strong, the tense affix will trigger raising of the main verb from V to T; where it is weak, the verb will remain in situ, and the tense affix will remain unattached, and the stranded affix will violate the Attachment Condition (168i). The only way of 'rescuing' a structure containing a weak affix is to directly adjoin an auxiliary (like *do*) to the affix in T so that in place of the structure in (ii) above, we have that in (iii) below:

(iii)

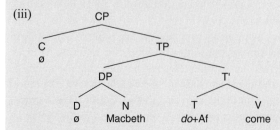

The resulting *do+Af* structure in T will then be spelled out as *doth* in the PF component, so deriving sentence 2 *Macbeth doth come*.

Such an analysis implies that there was considerably more morphosyntactic variation in Shakespearean English than we find in present-day varieties of Standard English – e.g. in respect of a finite tense affix being either strong or weak. Given that Shakespeare's writing contains a mixture of different dialect forms (as we see from the alternation between dialectal variants like *comes/cometh* and *does/doth*), this may not be implausible. However, as noted by Tieken-Boon van Ostade (1988), the origin of *do* is 'one of the great riddles of English linguistic history.'

However, an alternative possibility is that DO-support is used in (iii) for purely metrical reasons relating to poetic rhythm. This becomes clearer when we look at the context in which the sentence occurs, which is given below:

(iv)   THIRD WITCH: A drum, a drum!
                    Macbeth doth come

Since the first line spoken by the witch (A drum, a drum!) contains four syllables (the first and third being unstressed and the second and fourth stressed), the use of *doth* in the second sentence may be a last resort device intended to ensure that the following sentence has a parallel stress pattern.

6   Wh-Movement

6.1   Overview

In the previous chapter, we looked at the Head Movement operation by which a head can move into the next highest head position within the syntactic structure containing it. In this chapter, we look at a very different kind of movement operation traditionally termed Wh-Movement, by which a wh-word like *who* moves into the specifier position within CP, sometimes taking additional material along with it when it moves. This chapter focuses on Wh-Movement in questions, though in the next chapter we will turn to look at the syntax of other types of structure which also involve Wh-Movement (including exclamative and relative clauses).

6.2   Wh-Movement

In the previous chapter, we looked at the syntax of yes–no questions like *Is it raining?* I argued that these contain a null yes–no question operator in spec-CP, and that the inverted auxiliary moves from T to C. In this chapter, we turn to look at the syntax of wh-questions like those below:

(1) (a)   **Who** *have* they arrested?
    (b)   **What** *was* he doing?
    (c)   **Where** *have* you been?
    (d)   **Why** *would* anyone say anything?

Such sentences are termed wh-questions because they are typically introduced by a (bold-printed) interrogative **wh-word** – i.e. a question word beginning with *wh-*, like *what/which/who/where/when/why* (but note that *how* is treated as a wh-word because it has similar syntactic and semantic properties to other question words beginning with *wh-*). In the previous chapter, I suggested that the wh-word in sentences like (1d) occupies the specifier position within CP (with the inverted auxiliary moving into the head C position of CP), so that a sentence like (1d) above has the structure shown in simplified form below:

(2)

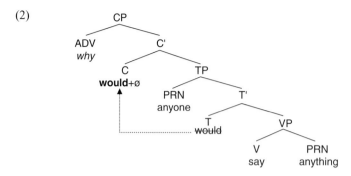

An analysis like (2) accounts for three key properties of a wh-question like (1a). The first is that the structure is typed/interpreted as a wh-question, in accordance with **Clause Typing Condition** of §4.7, repeated below:

(3)   **Clause Typing Condition**
A CP is typed (i.e. interpreted in the semantic component) as being interrogative/exclamative/conditional/imperative (etc.) in type if it has an interrogative/exclamative/conditional/imperative (etc.) specifier. Otherwise, an indicative CP is interpreted as declarative in type by default.

The second is that wh-questions trigger Inversion of an (italicised) auxiliary in main clauses like (1), in accordance with **Inversion Licensing Condition** of §5.3, repeated below:

(4)   **Inversion Licensing Condition**
A null C in a finite clause is licensed to carry a T-feature triggering Auxiliary Inversion if
(i) C has a negative or degree or conditional specifier
or
(ii) C has an interrogative specifier in a root/main clause.

Since C has the interrogative specifier *why* in (2) and the CP containing it is a root/main clause, it licenses Auxiliary Inversion in conformity with (4ii). The third is that a wh-question like (1d) licenses the occurrence of polarity items like (partitive) *anyone* and *anything*: this is because *anyone* and *anything* are c-commanded by the interrogative licenser *why*.

However, an important question overlooked in this discussion is how the wh-word comes to occupy spec-CP in wh-question structures like (2). Is it *merged* there or *moved* there? In other words, does the wh-word originate in spec-CP, or is it moved into spec-CP from some other position lower down in the structure? What I shall argue here is that question words originate in a position below C and move to spec-CP by an operation termed **Wh-Movement**.

An interesting piece of evidence in support of this claim comes from **echo questions** – i.e. wh-questions in which someone echoes a structure produced by someone else (often in an air of incredulity), but replaces part of the structure by a (phrase containing a) question word, and the question word is given emphatic stress (marking incredulity). Illustrative examples are given in (5–7) below, where the utterances produced by speaker B are echo questions, and capital letters mark emphatic stress:

(5)   SPEAKER A: They have arrested Lord Lancelotte Humpalotte
        SPEAKER B: They have arrested WHO?

(6)   SPEAKER A: He was oiling the flange sprocket
        SPEAKER B: He was oiling WHAT?

(7)   SPEAKER A: I went to
                   Llanfairpwllgwyngyllgogerychwyrndrobwllllantysiliogogogoch
        SPEAKER B: You went WHERE?

An interesting property of echo wh-questions like those in (5–7) is that the (capitalised) wh-word in the sentence produced by speaker B occupies the same (clause-internal) position as the corresponding (underlined) non-wh constituent produced by speaker A. For example, *who* is the complement of the verb *arrested* in (5B) and occupies the same position internally within VP as the non-wh complement *Lord Lancelotte Humpalotte* in (5A). Echo questions like (5B, 6B, 7B) suggest that wh-words like *who/what/where* originate internally within VP in the uses illustrated in (5–7). This suggests that in the corresponding non-echo questions where they appear at the beginning of the clause in (1b–d), *who/what/ where* undergo an operation like Wh-Movement repositioning them at the front of the overall clause, in spec-CP.

Further evidence in support of the same conclusion comes from multiple wh-questions – i.e. questions containing multiple wh-words. In such structures, one (bold-printed) wh-word is positioned at the beginning of the clause and other (italicised) wh-words are positioned internally within TP or VP – as illustrated by the multiple wh-questions below:

(8) (a)   **Who** hit *who* first?
    (b)   **Who** said *what* to *who*?
    (c)   **Who** went *where*?
    (d)   **Who** was arrested *when*?

In each case, the bold-printed wh-word *who* is positioned at the beginning of the clause, and the italicised wh-words are positioned internally within the clause. Sentences like (8) suggest that question words originate in a clause-internal position (italicised) and come to occupy clause-initial position in sentences like (1a–d) by moving from their original/initial position to their superficial/final position in spec-CP.

To take a specific example, *who* in (1a) *Who have they arrested?* originates as the complement of the verb *arrested* (as in the echo question *They have arrested* **who?**) and subsequently moves from its original position in comp-VP (i.e. the complement position within VP) to its superficial position in spec-CP (i.e. the specifier position within CP). This being so, (1b) will involve the movement operations arrowed in (10) below (where *who* has been assigned to the category PRN – albeit interrogative pronouns like *who* are pronominal quantifiers and hence Q-pronouns, and so *who* could alternatively be assigned to the category Q):

(9)

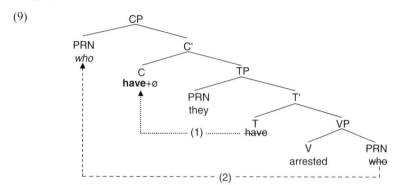

Two different kinds of movement operation (indicated by the two numbered arrows) are involved in (9): the movement arrowed in (1) involves the familiar operation of Head Movement by which the bold-printed auxiliary *have* moves from the head T position of TP to the head C position of CP (adjoining to a null complementiser ø); by contrast (2) involves movement of the italicised wh-word *who* from comp-VP into spec-CP, and this very different kind of movement operation is known as Wh-Movement. Whether each copy of the moved auxiliary *have* and the moved wh-pronoun *who* receives an overt or a null spellout at PF is determined by the Default Spellout Rule outlined in §5.2, repeated as (10) below:

(10)   **Default Spellout Rule**
         For a constituent whose spellout is not determined by some other rule or requirement, the highest copy of the constituent is pronounced at PF, and any lower copies are silent

In accordance with (10), the highest copy of the moved auxiliary *have* and the highest copy of the moved wh-pronoun *who* are given an overt spellout in the PF component, and the lower copies of each are given a silent spellout (marked by strikethrough in (9)).

6.3   Evidence for Wh-Movement

        In the previous section, I argued that a sentence like (1a) *Who have they arrested?* involves (in addition to Auxiliary Inversion) a Wh-Movement operation moving *who* from comp-VP to spec-CP. This assumption raises two important empirical questions. The first is what evidence there is that *who* originates in comp-VP as the complement of the verb *arrested*; and the second is what evidence there is that it ends up in spec-CP as the specifier of the inverted auxiliary *have*.

        One piece of evidence that *who* originates as the complement of *arrested* comes from selectional considerations. The verb *arrest* is a transitive verb which obligatorily selects (i.e. 'takes') a nominal complement like that italicised in (11a) below or a pronominal complement like that italicised in (11b). It cannot be used without such a complement as we see from the ungrammaticality of (11c):

(11) (a)   They arrested *Senator Slyme-Ball*
  (b)   They arrested *him*
  (c)   *They arrested

Under the Wh-Movement analysis in (9), the selectional requirements of the verb *arrest* are met at the stage of derivation when the verb *arrested* merges with its pronoun complement *who* to form the VP below:

(12)

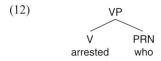

If *who* did not originate as the complement of the verb *arrested*, we would wrongly predict that sentences like (1a) *Who have they arrested?* are ungrammatical, because *arrested* would not have a complement at any stage of derivation. Subsequently, *who* moves from the comp-VP position in which it originates into the spec-CP position at the beginning of the sentence, as shown by the lower arrow in (9).

A second piece of evidence that *who* originates as the complement of *arrested* comes from case-marking. In formal styles of English, we find *whom* being used in place of *who* in sentences like (1a), so that in place of '*Who* have they arrested?' we find '*Whom* have they arrested?' How can we account for this? Let us suppose that the lexical/dictionary entry for the word WHO in English specifies that it is spelled out at PF as follows:

(13)   WHO is spelled out as *whose* if genitive, *whom* if accusative (in formal style) and *who* otherwise.

Thus, *whom* in a (formal-style) sentence like *Whom have they arrested?* is unambiguously accusative. But how does *whom* come to be assigned accusative case? The answer provided by the Wh-Movement analysis is the following. When it is first introduced into the derivation in (12), WHO is merged as the complement of the transitive verb *arrested*. In §3.9, we saw that case assignment (like other linguistic operations) obeys the following principle:

(14)   **Earliness Principle**
          Operations apply as early in a derivation as possible.

In consequence of (14), *who* will be assigned accusative case immediately it is merged with the verb *arrested* in (12), since *arrest* is a transitive verb and is the closest head c-commanding WHO. Accordingly, WHO will receive accusative case and will be spelled out as the form *whom* by (13) in a formal-style sentence like *Whom have they arrested?* and as the default ('otherwise') form *who* in a less formal style sentence like *Who have they arrested?* This is because it follows from (13) that the default form *who* is used not only to spell out nominative case but also to spell out accusative case in non-formal style.

Having looked at evidence that *who* originates as the complement of *arrested* in a structure like (9), let's now consider what evidence there is that *who* ends up in spec-CP when it moves to the front of the sentence. One such piece of evidence comes from the phenomenon of *have*-cliticisation discussed in §3.3, whereby in the PF component, *have* can cliticise onto an immediately preceding c-command-ing word ending in a vowel. In this connection, note that *have* can cliticise onto *they* in a statement like (15a) below, and onto *who* in a question like (15b):

(15) (a)   They've arrested him
    (b)   Who've they arrested?

How can we account for *have* being able to cliticise onto onto two different hosts in these two sentences, attaching to *they* in (15a) and *who* in (15b)? The auxiliary *have* in (15a) occupies the head T position of TP, and its subject *they* is its specifier and so occupies spec-TP – as shown in (16) below:

(16)

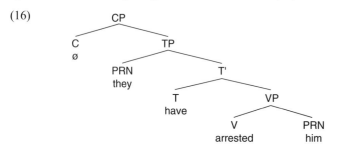

The grammaticality of (15a) suggests that *have* can cliticise onto the specifier of the closest phrase containing it (the phrase immediately containing *have* in 16 being TP, and its specifier being *they*). So, if *have* can cliticise onto its specifier, the analysis in (9) under which *have* moves to C and *who* moves to spec-CP provides us with a straightforward account of the grammaticality of (15b) *Who've they arrested?* since *have* in (9/15b) is in C and cliticises onto its own specifier *who* (*who* being in spec-CP). To phrase things rather differently, the possibility of *have* cliticising onto *who* in sentences like (15b) is consistent with the claim made in (9) that Wh-Movement involves a wh-word moving to spec-CP. More speci-fically, cliticisation is possible because *who* in (9) and *they* in (16) end in a vowel/diphthong, immediately precede the auxiliary *have* and also c-command *have*.

Additional evidence in support of the claim that Wh-Movement involves movement of a wh-word to spec-CP comes from Belfast English sentences such as those in (17a,b) below (from Henry 1995: 88):

(17) (a)   It depends [*who* **that** I see]
    (b)   I don't know [*when* **that** he's going]

The bracketed clauses in (17) are **embedded** questions (or **complement clause** questions) in which the bracketed interrogative clauses are embedded inside a verb phrase in which they function as the complement of the verb *depends/know*. But where is the italicised wh-word *who/when* positioned within the bracketed embedded interrogative clause? Since *who/when* immediately precedes *that*, and *that* is a complementiser occupying the head C position of CP, a reasonable assumption is that the wh-word occupies the specifier position within CP, so that the bracketed clauses in (17a,b) have the respective superficial structures shown in (18) below (simplified by showing only the structure of CP, and by omitting null constituents):

(18) (a)   [CP *who* [C **that**] I see]
     (b)   [CP *when* [C **that**] he is going]

On this view, clauses like those bracketed in (17) lend additional plausibility to the claim that a preposed interrogative wh-word moves into the specifier position within CP.

   An interesting question which arises in relation to the discussion in the previous paragraph is why *wh+that* clauses like those bracketed in (17) are ungrammatical in standard varieties of English. The answer given by Chomsky and Lasnik (1977) is that standard varieties of English impose a constraint on complementisers which they term the Doubly Filled COMP Filter, outlined informally below:

(19)   **Doubly Filled COMP Filter/DFCF**
            At PF, the edge of a CP headed by an overt complementiser (like *that/for/if/ whether*) cannot be doubly filled (i.e. cannot contain any other overt constituent)

(Note that the **edge** of a projection comprises its head and any constituent/s serving as an adjunct or specifier to the head. The relevant condition is termed a *filter* because it filters out PF structures which violate it: in more recent terms, it would be seen as a *PF interface condition*). It follows from (19) that wh-clauses like the CPs bracketed in (17/18) are ungrammatical in standard varieties of English because the overt complementiser *that* has the overt specifier *who/when* (resulting in two overt constituents being positioned on the edge of the bracketed CP). Instead of sentences like (17), standard varieties of English have sentences like (20a/b) below, where the bracketed embedded CPs have the respective structures shown in (21a/b):

(20) (a)   It depends [*who* I see]
     (b)   I don't know [*when* he's going]

(21) (a)   [CP *who* [C ø] I see]
     (b)   [CP *when* [C ø] he is going]

In other words, standard varieties of English use a null complementiser in place of *that*, and thereby avoid violating DFCF (19). This null complementiser does not trigger Auxiliary Inversion, because the Inversion Licensing Condition (4ii) specifies that a C with an interrogative specifier only triggers Inversion in a root/ main clause, and the bracketed clauses in (20/21) are embedded clauses.

To summarise the discussion so far: wh-questions have a superficial structure in which an interrogative wh-word occupies the specifier position in CP, so typing the clause as a wh-question in conformity with the Clause Typing Condition (3). Interrogative wh-words originate in a position below C and subsequently move to spec-CP by an operation known as Wh-Movement. Root/main-clause wh-questions trigger Auxiliary Inversion, in conformity with the Inversion Licensing Condition (4). The head C of CP in an embedded question cannot be occupied by an overt complementiser like *that* in standard varieties of English because of the Doubly Filled COMP Filter (19).

6.4   Driving Wh-Movement

Since the goal of linguistic theory is to explain why languages have the properties that they do, an important question to ask concerns the nature of the mechanism driving Wh-Movement in wh-questions like (1a) *Who have they arrested?* In the previous chapter, we saw that what drives Auxiliary Inversion in questions is a **T-feature** on C which attracts T to adjoin to C. Chomsky has suggested that Wh-Movement is likewise feature-driven, but in this case driven by an **edge feature** on C which requires C to project into a CP with an appropriate kind of specifier on the edge of CP. In order to satisfy the Clause Typing Condition (3), the specifier has to contain a question word in the case of a question, an exclamative word in the case of an exclamation, a relative pronoun in the case of a relative clause and so on. Since our concern for the time being is with questions, let us suppose that C in an interrogative clause carries a **Q-feature** requiring it to project into a CP with a **question operator** as its specifier. We saw in the previous chapter that in yes–no questions, this question operator is a null yes–no question operator which is directly merged in spec-CP. By contrast, in the case of wh-questions, it is an overt question word/question operator like *who/what/where/when/why/how* which originates in a position below C and subsequently *moves* into spec-CP by Wh-Movement. On this view, a yes–no question like *Are you going there?* will have a derivation like that in (22a) below, whereas a wh-question like *Where are you going?* will have a derivation like that in (22b):

(22)

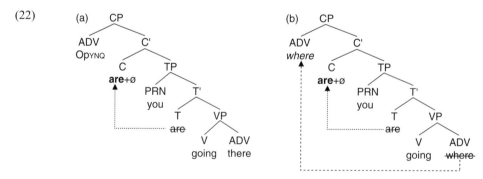

(Note that although *where/there* are given a traditional analysis as adverbs here, they would be analysed as PPs headed by a null counterpart of the preposition *to*, if we were to adopt the PP Hypothesis of §4.11.) By hypothesis, the C constituents in (22a) and (22b) will both carry a T-feature and a Q-feature (although these are not shown here). In both cases, the requirements of the T-feature on C are satisfied by T-*are* adjoining to C (so giving rise to Auxiliary Inversion). But now consider how the requirements of the Q-feature on C are satisfied. In the yes–no question (22a), they are satisfied by merging a null yes–no question operator in spec-CP. But in the wh-question (22b), they are satisfied by moving the question word *where* to become specifier of C.

A theoretical question arising from these assumptions is how come the Q-feature on C can be satisfied by two seemingly different kinds of operation (Merge and Move). The answer to this apparent conundrum is that movement involves merge, in the sense that when *where* moves to spec-CP in (22b), what happens is that a copy of *where* is created, and then this copy of *who* is merged with the root node in the structure, i.e. the C-bar *are you going where*. From this perspective, then, the Q-feature on C is an instruction to merge a Q-operator as the specifier of C. In a wh-question like (22b), the constituent merged with C-bar (= *where*) originates internally within the C-bar in (22b); for this reason, Chomsky refers to movement as **Internal Merge**. By contrast, in a yes–no question like (22a), the yes–no question operator merged with C-bar originates outside the relevant C-bar and so the relevant type of Merge operation is referred to as **External Merge**. Thus, Internal Merge involves merging a copy of a constituent positioned internally within a given structure with the root (i.e. highest node) of the structure, whereas External Merge involves introducing a new constituent into the structure and merging it with the root.

By way of further illustration, let's take another look at the derivation of (1a) *Who have they arrested?* As before, the verb *arrested* merges with the pronoun *who* to form the VP *arrested who* in (12). This VP is merged with T-*have* to form the T-bar *have arrested who*, and this T-bar is in turn merged with the pronoun *they* to form the TP *they have arrested who*. The resulting TP is merged with a null complementiser which carries both a Q-feature and a T-feature, so deriving the C-bar below:

(23)

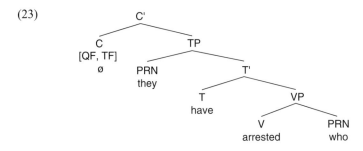

The T-feature on C attracts T-*have* to adjoin to C-ø, and the Q-feature on C requires C to have an interrogative specifier. The requirements of [QF] can be satisfied by C attracting *who* to move to spec-CP, so deriving (24) below, where arrows mark the two movements involved (the dotted arrow marking Head Movement, and the dashed arrow marking Wh-Movement):

(24)

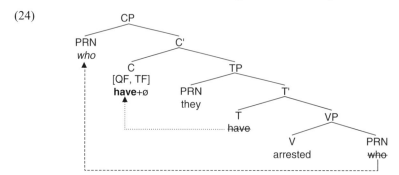

The resulting structure will ultimately be spelled out as the string (1a) *Who have they arrested?* at PF. In conformity with the Copy Theory of Movement (See §5.2), the moved wh-word leaves behind a copy of itself in its original position when it moves. Given the Default Spellout Rule (10), it follows that the higher copy of *who* in (24) will be pronounced, but the lower copy will be silent.

It is interesting to compare the structure of a **root** question (= main-clause question) like (1a) *Who have they arrested?* with that of the corresponding embedded question (= complement clause question) bracketed in (25) below:

(25)   I don't know [who they have arrested]

The difference between the two is that a root question like (1a) *Who have they arrested?* involves both Wh-Movement and Auxiliary Inversion, whereas an embedded question like that bracketed in (25) involves Wh-Movement without Auxiliary Inversion. In terms of the feature-driven account of movement presented here (under which Wh-Movement in questions is driven by a Q-feature on C, and Auxiliary Inversion by a T-feature on C), we can account for this by supposing that C carries the following features in operator questions:

(26)   **Feature Composition of C in operator questions**
         (i)   C carries an interrogative edge feature (= Q-feature/QF) in an operator question.
         (ii) In a finite root/main clause, if C has a Q-feature then C also has a T-feature.

The head C of CP in the embedded question bracketed in (25) will carry a Q-feature by (26i), but will not carry a T-feature because (26ii) specifies that C only carries a T-feature in finite root clauses. Accordingly, the italicised embedded question in (25) will have the structure in (27) below (with the Wh-Movement operation involved in its derivation being arrowed):

(27)

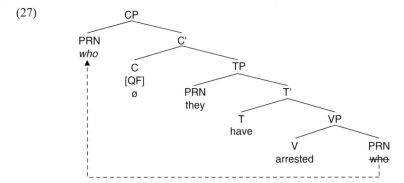

The resulting structure is spelled out at PF as the string bracketed in (25) 'I don't know [who they have arrested].'

An interesting property of wh-questions is that (in multiple wh-operator questions like those in 8 above) no more than one wh-word can be positioned in spec-CP. Moreover, there are constraints on which wh-word can be positioned there – as illustrated in (28) below:

(28) (a)   They might consider *who* to be responsible for **what**?
     (b)   *Who* might they consider to be responsible for **what**?
     (c)   *__What__ might they consider *who* to be responsible for?
     (d)   *__Who__ **what** might they consider to be responsible for?
     (e)   *__What__ *who* might they consider to be responsible for?

(28a) is an echo question (not an operator question), and hence does not involve Wh-Movement or Auxiliary Inversion. However, the remaining questions in (28b–e) are operator questions which involve movement of a question operator to the front of the sentence (i.e. to spec-CP). And yet the resulting structure is only grammatical if one question operator is fronted in this way (as in 28b), not if more than one is fronted (as in 28d,e). Moreover, the fronted operator has to be *who* (as in 28b) and not *what* (as in the ungrammatical 28c). How can we account for these restrictions?

In order to get to the bottom of what's going on, let's take a look at the derivation of (28b). Merging P *for* with PRN *what* forms the PP *for what*. Merging A *responsible* with this PP forms the AP *responsible for what*. Merging V *be* with this AP forms the VP *be responsible for what*. Merging T *to* with this VP forms the T-bar *to be responsible for what* and merging the pronoun *who* with this T-bar forms the TP *who to be responsible for what*. Merging V *consider* with this TP forms the VP *consider who to be responsible for what*. Merging T *might* with this VP forms the T-bar *might consider who to be responsible for what*. Merging the pronoun *they* with this T-bar forms the TP *they might consider who to be responsible for what.* Merging this TP with a null complementiser which (in accordance with 26) carries both a Q-feature and a T-feature forms the C-bar below:

(29)

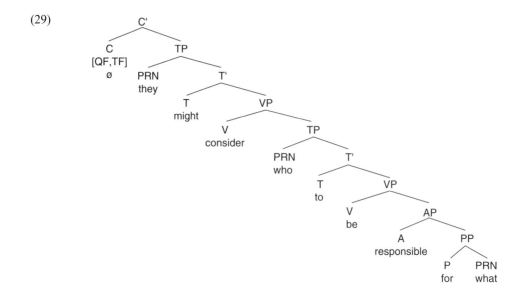

The Q-feature on C requires C to have a question operator as its specifier in order to type the relevant CP as a question in accordance with the Clause Typing Condition (3). There are two question operators in (29), namely *who* and *what*. Moving *who* and merging it with the C-bar constituent at the root of the tree in (29) leads to the grammatical outcome in (28b) *Who might they consider to be responsible for what?* However, moving *what* instead leads to the ungrammatical outcome in (28c) **What might they consider who to be responsible for?* So why should C be able to attract *who* but not *what*?

The answer lies in a principle of Universal Grammar which can be outlined informally as follows:

(30)   **Attract Closest Condition/ACC**
        A head which attracts a given kind of constituent attracts the *closest* constituent of the relevant kind

It follows from (30) that the Q-feature on C will attract the closest question operator to become its specifier. Since the closest question operator to C is *who*, this means that *who* will be attracted to become the specifier of C. At the same time, the T-feature on C will attract the T auxiliary *might* to adjoin to C. These two movements (arrowed below) will derive the following (simplified) structure:

(31)

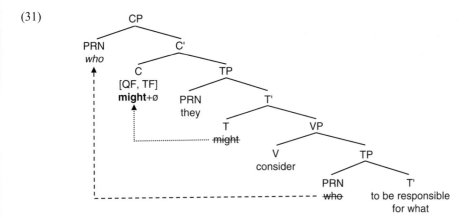

Positioning the wh-operator *who* in spec-CP results in the clause being typed as a wh-question. If (as claimed within Minimalism) movement only takes place in order to satisfy interface conditions, this means there is no possibility of a second wh-operator like *what* moving to the edge of CP as well as *who*, because this second movement would serve no function at the semantics interface (given that movement of *who* alone is sufficient to type the clause as a wh-operator question). These assumptions provide us with a principled account of the ungrammaticality of sentences like (28e) **What who might they consider to be responsible for?*

At a deeper level, the answer to the questions of why no more than one wh-word is preposed, and why the wh-word preposed is the closest one can be found in the Economy Principle discussed in §1.5, repeated below:

(32)   **Economy Principle**
         Structures and the operations used to form them should be as economical as possible.

After all, if the function of Wh-Movement in questions is to type a clause as interrogative by giving it an interrogative specifier, then moving only one wh-question word to the front of the overall sentence and ensuring that the wh-word moved is the closest one is the most economical way of achieving this. Although formulated in essentially linguistic terms in (32), the Economy Principle is at heart a more general efficiency principle governing natural systems in general – as noted in §1.5.

There is also another constraint which prevents *what* from being attracted to move to spec-CP in (29). The relevant constraint can be illustrated in terms of the following sentence:

(33)   **How **didn't** you fix the car?

Here, *how* is a VP adverb which modifies the verb phrase *fix the car*. We can see this from the fact that *how* is part of the echoic VP sentence fragment produced by speaker B in (34) below:

(34)   SPEAKER A: He said he was going to fix the car by hypnosis
         SPEAKER B: Fix the car HOW?

Thus, in order to get into its eventual spec-CP position at the beginning of the sentence in (33), *how* has to move out of its original position in the VP *fix the car how* where it originates and into the spec-CP position in which it ends up. In other words, *how* has to undergo the Wh-Movement operation shown by the arrow in the simplified structure in (35) below (where the negative auxiliary *didn't* is treated as a single word for the reasons outlined in §5.10, and moves from T to C as a result of Auxiliary Inversion):

(35)

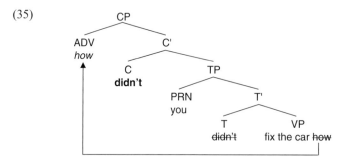

However, in moving out of VP into CP, the VP-adverb *how* crosses the intervening negative auxiliary *didn't*. This movement leads to violation of a constraint which can be outlined informally as follows:

(36)   **Intervention Condition**
          No constituent X can move from one position to another across an intervening constituent Y if X and Y are both sensitive to (the same kind of) intervention effects.

The constraint in (35) is violated because *how* moves across *didn't* (in the sense that *how* moves from a position c-commanded by *didn't* to a position c-commanding *didn't*) and both *how* and *didn't* are sensitive to the relevant kind of intervention effect (in that both *how* and *didn't* have **scope** properties). The resulting intervention violation accounts for the ungrammaticality of sentences like (33).

   In the light of our discussion of intervention effects, let's now return to ask why *what* can't undergo Wh-Movement to spec-CP in a sentences like (28c) above, in the manner shown by the arrow in (37) below:

(37)

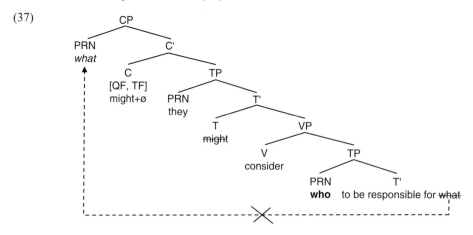

The answer is that any such movement would induce a violation of the Intervention Condition (36), because the interrogative operator *what* would end up moving across the intervening (bold-printed) interrogative operator *who* (in the sense that *what* originates in a position below *who* and moves to a position above *who*). Since interrogative operators have scope properties and are sensitive to intervention effects, this results in a violation of (36).

To summarise, Wh-Movement in operator questions is driven by a Q-feature on C which attracts an interrogative wh-operator to move to become the specifier of C, and thereby type the relevant clause as a wh-operator question. In consequence of the Attract Closest Condition and the Intervention Condition, the Q-feature on C attracts the closest question operator c-commanded by C to move to spec-CP.

6.5   Subject questions

Thus far, our discussion has mainly centred on complement questions – i.e. structures in which a the question word functions as the complement of a verb or preposition. In this section, we turn instead to look at subject questions – i.e. structures like (38) below in which the question word functions as the subject of the clause containing it:

(38) (a)   *Who* found it?
   (b)   *Who* has the keys?
   (c)   *What* happened to him?
   (d)   *What* upset you?

Two inter-related issues arise in relation to subject questions: one is where the wh-word is positioned; and the second is why subject questions like those in (38) don't require DO-support (except in emphatic contexts like *Who* DID *find it?* where use of DO is associated with emphasis rather than interrogativeness, as we see from the use of emphatic DO in non-interrogatives like *He* DID *find it*).

In relation to the position of the wh-word in subject questions, there are two conflicting perspectives found in the research literature. One is to suppose that the key requirement for a (non-echoic) wh-question is that it begin with an interrogative wh-constituent, and that this requirement can be met if the wh-subject occupies the same position as other subjects, namely spec-TP. On this (spec-TP) analysis, (38a) would have the syntactic structure in (39) below, where *Af* is a past tense affix:

(39)

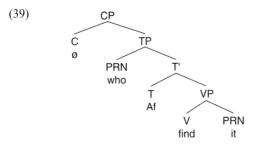

The key point to note here is that *who* (under the analysis in 39) is taken to be positioned in spec-TP, not in spec-CP. The past tense affix in T will lower onto the verb *find* in the PF component so that the verb is ultimately spelled out as the past tense form *found* in (38a) *Who found it?* If C triggers Auxiliary Inversion only when there is a question operator in spec-CP (in conformity with the Inversion Licensing Condition 4ii), the spec-TP analysis will correctly account for why there is no Auxiliary Inversion in subject questions. The reason is that the question word *who* in (39) is in spec-TP, and hence (if only operators in spec-CP trigger Inversion), it follows that there will be no Auxiliary Inversion in subject questions.

However, an alternative perspective on subject questions is the following. Since *who* in (38a) *Who found it?* is a question operator, it should behave like other operators which originate below C (e.g. *who* in 31) and move into the canonical spec-CP position occupied by question operators. Under this second (spec-CP) analysis, (38a) *Who found it?* will not have the structure (39) above but will instead have the structure (40) below. Under the analysis in (40), *who* originates in spec-TP and from there moves to spec-CP (via the arrowed Wh-Movement operation), leaving behind a copy of *who* in spec-TP which is subsequently given a silent spellout in the PF component by the Default Spellout Rule (10):

(40)

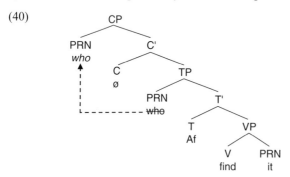

Subsequently the past tense affix in T will lower onto the verb in the PF component, with the result that the verb is spelled out as the past tense form *found* in (38a) *Who found it?* What then remains to be accounted for is why there is no DO-support and Auxiliary Inversion in a subject question structure like (40). Pending a more detailed discussion of this issue below, let's suppose that when C attracts an interrogative operator to move to spec-CP in a root/main clause, C only triggers Auxiliary Inversion if the attracted operator moves from a position below T: since *who* moves to spec-CP from a position above T (i.e. from spec-TP) in (40), it follows that there will be no Auxiliary Inversion.

As the discussion in the two previous paragraphs illustrates, there are two (seemingly equally plausible) competing analyses of subject questions: one supposes that the question word remains in spec-TP, the other that it moves to spec-CP. But which is the right analysis? As we will see, there are theoretical and empirical considerations favouring the spec-CP analysis in (40) over the spec-TP analysis in (39). For one thing, the spec-CP analysis is more consistent with our existing theoretical principles and assumptions. For example, the Clause Typing Condition (3) favours the spec-CP analysis, since it specifies that a clause will only be typed as an operator question if it contains an operator in spec-CP. Likewise, our account of the feature composition of C in questions in (26i) claims that C always has a Q-feature in operator questions, and if so an interrogative C will always require an interrogative specifier.

There is also empirical evidence which favours the spec-CP analysis. As we see from the examples in (41) below, a wh-word like *who* in a subject question like (38a) *Who found it?* can be substituted by *who on earth* or *who the hell*:

(41) (a)   *Who on earth* found it?
     (b)   *Who the hell* found it?

Examples like those in (42) below show that wh-expressions like *who on earth* and *who the hell* have the property that they cannot remain in situ in an echo question like (42b), but rather must move to spec-CP as in (42a):

(42) (a)   *Who on earth/Who the hell* is she going out with?
     (b)   *She is going out with *who on earth/who the hell*?

We find a similar restriction in multiple wh-questions like (43) below,

(43) (a)   I've no idea [*what the hell* she gave to **who** at Christmas]
     (b)   *I've no idea [**what** she gave to *who the hell* at Christmas]

If *wh-on-earth/wh-the-hell* constituents like those italicised in (42,43) always move to spec-CP, it follows that the italicised subjects in (41) must likewise have moved to spec-CP; by the same token, it is plausible to suppose that the same is true of the subject *who* in (38a) *Who found it?*

A second piece of empirical evidence favouring the spec-CP analysis comes from speakers of English who allow *wh+that* structures – i.e. CPs in which a wh-word or wh-phrase is positioned in front of the complementiser *that*. Such speakers allow a subject wh-constituent to be positioned before the complementiser *that* – as the bracketed clauses in the examples below (recorded from radio and TV programmes) illustrate:

(44) (a)   It'll probably be evident from the field [*which of the players* **that** are feeling the heat most] (Jimmy Hill, BBC1 TV; Radford 1988)
     (b)   Regardless of [*which version of the FEC bill* **that** is passed], . . . (Interviewee on NPR's *All Things Considered*, 31 August 1994; Zwicky 2002)
     (c)   . . . until late in the week, when we see [*how many people* **that** were arrested] (Interviewee on NPR's *All Things Considered*, 26 May 1998; Zwicky 2002)
     (d)   Yes, I fully understand [*what uproar* **that** would come about] (Public radio interview of Miami Chief of Police, 2 May 2000; Zwicky 2002)
     (e)   . . . and definitions vary as to [*which of these types of criteria* **that** are used] (Member of Göteborg University's English Department; Seppänen 1994)
     (f)   You're talking about [*what players* **that** might be coming into that huge football club] (Micky Gray, Talk Sport Radio)

(g)   I have to weigh up [*which of those promises* **that** are more important than others] (Stephen Williams, BBC Radio 5)

(h)   We'll have to see [*what* **that** happens] (Eddie Irvine, BBC1 TV)

(i)   They're not worried about [*what potential injuries* **that** might come] (Roy Keane, ITV)

The bracketed clauses in (44) are subject questions containing an italicized interrogative wh-subject followed by the complementiser *that*. If the wh-subject were in spec-TP, it would wrongly be predicted to follow the complementiser *that*. The fact that the wh-subject precedes *that* in sentences like (44) is consistent with the view that it moves from spec-TP to spec-CP. More generally, sentences like (44) lend empirical support to the spec-CP analysis.

Since theoretical and empirical considerations like those outlined above favour the spec-CP analysis of subject questions, this is the analysis which I will adopt from this point on. In the light of this assumption, let's take a closer look at the derivation of (38a) *Who found it?* The verb *find* merges with the pronoun *it* to form the VP *find it*. A past tense affix (*Af*) is merged with this VP to form the T-bar *Af find it*, and this T-bar is in turn merged with the pronoun *who* to form the TP *who Af find it*. The resulting TP is merged with a null interrogative C constituent which carries a Q-feature in accordance with (26i) and a T-feature in accordance with (26ii), so forming the structure below:

(45)

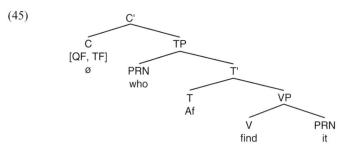

At this point, we might expect the derivation to continue as it did in (31), with the Q-feature on C attracting the question operator *who* to move to spec-CP, and the T-feature on C attracting the tense affix in T to adjoin to C (as shown by the two different arrows below), so deriving the following structure:

(46)

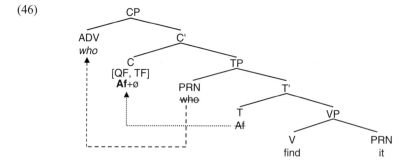

However, this would leave the inverted tense affix stranded in C without an overt host, so causing the derivation to crash.

The affix-stranding problem can be overcome if we make use of DO-support and merge the auxiliary *did* in T, and then raise it from T to C in the manner shown below (where *did* can be taken to comprise an irregular stem form of DO with the past tense affix *-d* adjoined to it):

(47)

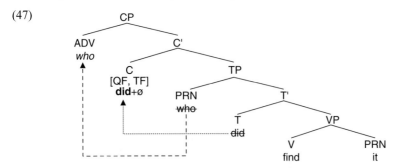

And yet the resulting sentence **Who did find it?* is ungrammatical if *did* is unstressed (as becomes clearer from a sentence like **Who'd find it yesterday?* where unstressed *did* is contracted to*'d*). Why should this be?

The likely answer is that a constraint of some kind rules out the dual movement in (47). But what kind of constraint? One possibility would be the following:

(48)   **Edge Constraint**
        No more than one constituent can be extracted from the edge of any given projection.

Such a constraint would prevent C from extracting both the T constituent *did* and its specifier *who* out of the edge of TP. The same constraint would also account for contrasts such as the following:

(49) (a)   The spare parts, how long *will* [~~it will~~ take to order ~~the spare parts~~]?
     (b)   **The spare parts*, how long *will* [~~the spare parts will~~ take to arrive]?

In (49a), only one constituent (= the auxiliary *will*) is moved out of the edge of the bracketed TP, and the resulting sentence is grammatical. By contrast in (49b) both the auxiliary *will* and the subject *the spare parts* are moved out of the edge of the bracketed TP (the latter perhaps moving to the specifier position in an outer CP, under a CP recursion analysis), and the resulting structure violates the Edge Constraint and so is ungrammatical.

An alternative way of accounting for the ungrammaticality of structures like (47) is to suppose that they violate a constraint against crossing movement paths which was formulated by Pesetsky (1982b: 309) in the following terms:

(50)   **Path Containment Condition**
        If two paths overlap, one must contain the other.

The effect of this constraint can be illustrated by comparing the movement paths for Wh-Movement and Auxiliary Inversion in the two structures below:

(51)   (a)   [CP *who* [C **did**] [TP ~~who~~ [T ~~did~~] [VP [V find] it]]]

(b)   [CP *who* [C **did**] [TP you [T ~~did~~] [VP [V find] ~~who~~]]]

In (51a), the movement path/chain for *did* and that for *who* cross each other, leading to ungrammaticality. By contrast, in the grammatical structure (51b), the *did*-chain is contained inside the *who*-chain, and this leads to a grammatical outcome (*Who did you find?*). (As you will no doubt have noted, the contrast in 51 could equally be handled in terms of the Edge Constraint, 48.)

So, the situation we face is the following. If both Wh-Movement and Auxiliary Inversion apply in root subject questions, the resulting structure will be ungrammatical by virtue of violating the Path Containment Condition and/or the Edge Constraint. But given the feature composition of C outlined in (26) above, root questions (whether subject questions or not) will always carry both a Q-feature and a T-feature. We would therefore expect the Q-feature to trigger Wh-Movement and the T-feature to trigger Auxiliary Inversion in all types of root question, including root subject questions. But (as we have seen), this will induce a constraint violation in root subject questions. How can we overcome this problem?

One way is as follows. Let us suppose that the T-feature on C (contrary to what we have assumed so far) does not necessarily require C to attract the head T of TP to adjoin to the head C of CP. Instead, let us suppose that the T-feature on C works in the manner specified by the generalisation below:

(52)   **T-Feature Generalisation**
A T-feature on C attracts a constituent on the edge of TP to move to the edge of CP.

Assuming (52), consider what happens when we reach the stage of derivation in (45) above, repeated as (53) below:

(53)

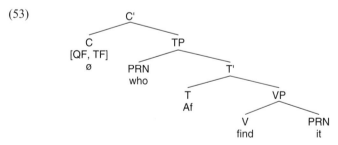

Let us suppose that a head can only move into another head position, and likewise a specifier can only move into another specifier position (below, we will see that this is the consequence of a constraint called the **Chain Uniformity Condition**). This being so, it follows from (52) that the T-feature on C in (53) can either attract the head T of TP to move to adjoin to the head C of CP or attract the specifier of T to move to become the specifier of C. In the light of this, let's return to consider what the Q-feature and the T-feature on C do in a structure like (53). As we have already seen, the Q-feature on C triggers Wh-Movement of the question operator *who* from spec-TP to spec-CP. But what of the T-feature on C? In accordance with the generalisation in (52), the requirements of the T-feature on C could in principle be satisfied by adjoining T to C (i.e. by T-to-C Movement/Auxiliary Inversion), since this results in movement of a head from the edge of TP to the edge of CP. However, the requirements of the T-feature on C could alternatively be satisfied by Wh-Movement of *who* from spec-TP to spec-CP, since this results in movement of a specifier from the edge of TP to the edge of CP – as shown by the arrow in (54) below:

(54)

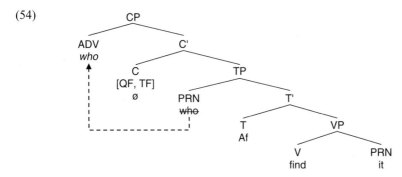

Under the analysis in (54), the requirements of two different features on the same head (the Q- and T-features on C) can both be satisfied by a single movement operation (Wh-Movement of *who* from spec-TP to spec-CP). Since the resulting structure in (54) contains an interrogative operator in spec-CP, it is typed as a wh-question in accordance with the Clause Typing Condition (3). The unattached past tense affix in T will then lower onto the verb FIND via Affix Lowering in the PF component, with the result that the verb is spelled out as the past tense form *found* in (38a) *Who found it?*

    Our discussion here shows that there are (in principle) two different ways of satisfying the requirements of the Q- and T-features on C in a subject question structure like (53). One is for the Q-feature on C to trigger Wh-Movement of *who* to spec-CP, and the T-feature on C to trigger Auxiliary Inversion (i.e. T-to-C Movement), as in the dual movement derivation in (47). However, an alternative possibility is for the Q- and T-features on C to work in tandem to trigger Wh-Movement of *who* to spec-CP, as in the single movement derivation in (54). Since a single movement derivation like (54) (involving only Wh-Movement) is more economical than a multiple movement derivation like (47) (involving both Wh-Movement and Auxiliary Inversion), the Economy Principle (32) requires us to use the former rather than the latter. Consequently, the single movement derivation in (54) yields a grammatical outcome, whereas the multiple movement derivation in (47) does not.

While the analysis in the preceding paragraph accounts for the absence of Auxiliary Inversion in subject questions, the issue arises of why (as claimed in 52) a T-feature on C should be able to attract either the head of TP or its specifier to move to the edge of CP. One conceptually attractive answer to this question is the following. Let us suppose that the T-feature on C actually attracts a tensed constituent (i.e. a constituent carrying a tense feature) to move to the edge of CP. Since T is the locus of tense in clauses, it is obvious why a T-feature on C should be able to attract T to move to the edge of CP and adjoin to C (in Auxiliary Inversion structures). But why should a T-feature on C alternatively be able to attract the subject/specifier of T? An intriguing answer is to suppose that the subject of T acquires a tense feature as a result of agreement between T and its subject/specifier. Reasoning along these lines, let us suppose that agreement between T and its subject works in the manner specified below:

(55)   **Subject agreement**
When T agrees with its subject/specifier
(i)   the person/number features of the subject are copied onto the auxiliary/ affix in T
(ii) the tense feature on T is copied onto the subject.

The idea that a nominal constituent could carry a tense feature might at first sight seem far-fetched, but it is plausible to suppose that certain nominals do have temporal properties (e.g. *my then wife, the future king, his past achievements*). Let's also assume that what is traditionally called 'nominative case' is actually a reflex of a subject being marked as *tensed*, thereby accounting for why only the subject of a *tensed* T receives nominative case, not the subject of an untensed infinitival T.

Given these assumptions, in a sentence like *He is lying*, agreement between the subject *he* and the T auxiliary *is* results in the third person singular features of *he* being copied onto *is* via (55i); and conversely, it results in the tense feature of *is* being copied onto *he* via (55ii). We can account for why the tensed subject is spelled out as *he* (rather than as *him* or *his*) if the dictionary entry for the pronoun HE specifies that it is spelled out at PF as follows:

(56)   HE is spelled out as *he* if tensed, *his* if genitive, and *him* otherwise.

In addition to making the assumptions in (55) and (56), let us also assume that derivations have to be as economical as possible, in consequence of the Economy Principle (32).

In the light of the assumptions in the previous paragraph, let's now reconsider how the requirements of the Q-feature and T-feature on C are satisfied in a subject question structure like (54) above. The arrowed Wh-Movement operation satisfies the Q-feature on C because it results in C having the question operator *who* as its specifier (so allowing the sentence to be typed as a wh-question); it also satisfies the T-feature on C because it results in the tensed subject *who* moving to the edge of CP (*who* being marked as tensed via agreement with the tense affix in

T in accordance with 55ii). Recall from (13) above that the dictionary entry for the pronoun WHO specifies that it is spelled out as follows:

(57)   WHO is spelled out as *whose* if genitive, *whom* if accusative (in formal style), *who* otherwise.

Via agreement with T, WHO in (54) is tensed (and not genitive or accusative), and so it is spelled out via (57) as the default ('otherwise') form *who* in (38a) *Who found it?* Since the Economy Principle (32) favours derivations involving fewer operations, it follows that the single-movement derivation in (54) will be preferred to the dual-movement derivation in (47), as we saw earlier.

The discussion in this section can be summarised as follows. Root subject questions (i.e. sentences in which the subject of a root clause is questioned) have the property that they do not trigger Auxiliary Inversion. One way of accounting for this is to suppose that subjects remain in spec-TP in subject questions, and there is no Auxiliary Inversion because only operators in spec-CP trigger Auxiliary Inversion. However, an alternative possibility (argued for here) is to suppose that C in all types of root operator questions has a Q-feature and a T-feature, and that these two can work together to trigger movement of a tensed interrogative subject from spec-TP to spec-CP. We have seen that there is some theoretical and empirical evidence favouring the spec-CP analysis.

6.6   Pied-piping

In most of the wh-questions that we have looked at so far, the head C of CP attracts a wh-word that originates below C to move to spec-CP on its own. However, as we see from a sentence like (58b) below, sometimes a (bold-printed) wh-word is unable to move on its own, and instead drags additional (italicised) material along with it when it moves, as in (58a):

(58) (a)   *Quite* **what** *kind of tax* are they proposing?
     (b)   *****What** are they proposing *quite kind of tax?*

To use a technical term introduced in §2.9, a wh-word sometimes **pied-pipes** (i.e. drags) additional material along with it when it moves. So, for example, the word *what* can't move on its own in (58) and instead has to pied-pipe the additional words *quite, kind, of* and *tax* along with it when it moves. This raises the following two questions: (i) Why should *what* be unable to move on its own? (ii) What determines the nature of the additional material that *what* pied-pipes along with it when it moves? In order to try and answer these questions, let's take a closer look at the derivation of (58a). If we make the plausible assumption that *quite* is an adverb that functions as the specifier of the wh-quantifier *what*, the sentences in (58) will have the structure shown below before Wh-Movement and Auxiliary Inversion take place:

(59)

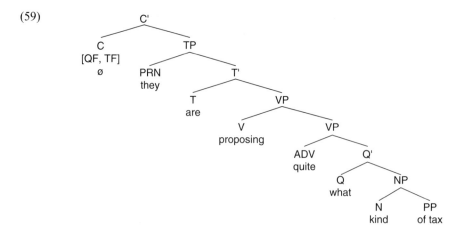

What we might expect to happen next is for the T-feature on C to attract the T auxiliary *are* to adjoin to C, and for the Q-feature on C to attract *what* to become the specifier of C, so resulting in the movements arrowed below:

(60)

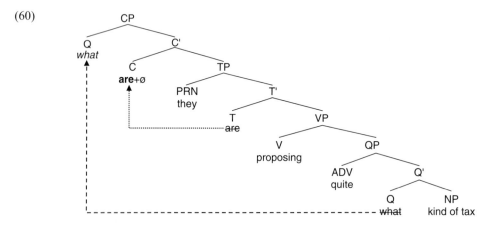

However, the resulting structure is ill-formed, as we see from the ungrammaticality of (58b) **What are they proposing quite kind of tax?* It would seem that movement of *what* on its own is barred by a constraint of some kind. But what kind of constraint could be involved?

Chomsky (1995) provides the following answer. As noted earlier, he argues that movement is a composite operation involving three separate suboperations of Copying, Merge and Deletion. Consequently, movement of *what* in (60) involves the three steps of (i) creating a copy of *what*, (ii) merging the newly created copy of *what* with the root of the structure in (59) (the root being the C-bar *are they proposing quite what kind of tax*) and (iii) giving a null spellout to the original occurrence of *what*. The two occurences/copies of *what* are linked by movement and so form a movement **chain**. Chomsky (1995: 253) maintains that movement chains must conform to the following UG principle:

(61)   **Chain Uniformity Condition**
         All links/copies in a chain must be uniform.

However, movement of *what* in (60) results in a wh-chain which is non-uniform in the following sense. The null copy ~~what~~ at the foot of the tree is the head Q of the QP *quite what kind of tax*, and so is a *minimal projection*; by contrast, the overt copy of *what* at the top of the tree is a solitary wh-word which has the status of a maximal projection by virtue of being the largest expression headed by the word *what* (since the constituent immediately above the higher copy of *what* is CP, and CP is not headed by *what*). The resulting wh-chain thus violates the Chain Uniformity Condition (61) because the higher copy of *what* is a maximal projection and the lower copy is a minimal projection.

Given that *what* cannot be moved on its own in (59), the only way of moving it is to move some larger constituent containing it. What if we try and move the Q-bar *what kind of tax* on its own (without *quite*), in the manner shown by the arrow below?

(62)

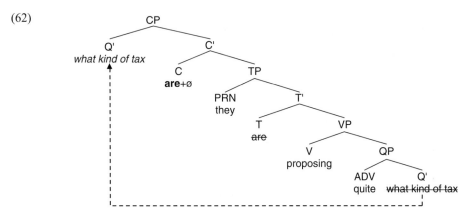

The answer is that the resulting structure (62) will once again violate the Chain Uniformity Condition (61), because it results in a non-uniform movement chain in which the italicised moved copy *what kind of tax* at the top of the tree is a maximal projection (because its mother is the CP node, and CP is not headed by *what*), but the null copy ~~what kind of tax~~ at the foot of the tree is an intermediate projection (because its mother is the QP *quite what kind of tax*, and this QP is headed by *what*): the resulting Chain Uniformity violation accounts for the ungrammaticality of **What kind of tax are they proposing quite?*

In addition, the movement arrowed in (62) will also violate a further constraint introduced in §3.6, and repeated below:

(63)   **Constituency Condition**
          Heads and maximal projections are the only types of constituent which can
          take part in linguistic operations like movement, agreement or ellipsis.

It follows from (63) that any operation moving an intermediate projection is illicit. Consequently, (63) rules out the possibility of moving the intermediate Q-bar projection *what kind of tax* in (62).

But now consider what happens if instead we move the whole QP *quite what kind of tax* to spec-CP, in the manner shown by the arrow below:

(64)

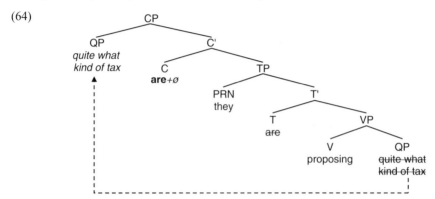

This results in the formation of a uniform wh-chain, because both the overt copy *quite what kind of tax* at the top of the tree and the null copy ~~quite what kind of tax~~ at the foot of the tree are maximal projections, since both are complete QPs which are the largest constituents headed by *what* (because both have mothers with a different head).

The conclusion which the foregoing discussion leads to is the following. It follows from the Chain Uniformity Condition that only a maximal projection can move into spec-CP. Since a solitary wh-word (i.e. a wh-word with no specifier or complement) is a maximal projection, this means that a solitary wh-word can move to spec-CP. However, when a wh-word is the head of a phrase, only a complete phrase containing the wh-word can be preposed.

Since C can attract a maximal projection containing a wh-word to become its specifier, the question arises of whether the Q-feature on C in (59) could alternatively attract the VP *proposing what kind of tax* to move to spec-CP. The answer is 'No', as we see from the ungrammaticality of the following:

(65)   *Proposing quite what kind of tax* are they?

Why should the VP *proposing quite what kind of tax* be unable to undergo Wh-Movement? After all, it is the maximal projection of the verb *proposing*, and it contains the wh-word *what*. So why can't it be preposed? The answer lies in a further principle of UG which can be formulated as follows:

(66)   **Attract Smallest Condition/ASC**
            A head which attracts a particular type of item attracts the smallest accessible constituent containing the relevant item.

(The term *smallest accessible constituent* means 'the smallest constituent which can move on its own without violating any principle/condition/constraint'. ASC is a specific instantiation of the more general Economy Principle, 32.) So, in a structure like (59) above, ASC tells us to try and satisfy the Q-feature on C by preposing the smallest constituent containing the question word *what* (the Q constituent *what* on its own), but movement of Q-*what* to spec-CP is not possible because this would violate the Chain Uniformity Condition (61) which only allows C to attract a maximal projection to become its specifier (either a solitary wh-word, or a complete wh-phrase). Because *what* can't be moved on its own, ASC forces us to try moving the next smallest constituent containing *what* – namely the Q-bar *what kind of proposal*. However, movement of Q-bar on its own will violate the Chain Uniformity Condition because Q-bar is an intermediate projection and not a maximal projection; in addition, movement of Q-bar will violate the Constituency Condition (63). Consequently, we try preposing the next smallest constituent containing *what*, and this is the QP *quite what kind of tax*: since this QP is a maximal projection, movement of QP to spec-CP will satisfy both the Chain Uniformity Condition and the Constituency Condition, so resulting in a structure (64) which is grammatical. Because QP is accessible to (i.e. can undergo) Wh-Movement in (59), there is no point in (or possibility of) preposing any larger maximal projection (such as the VP *proposing quite what kind of tax*) – thereby accounting for the ungrammaticality of (65) **Proposing quite what kind of tax are they?*

The combined effect of conditions like the Attract Closest Condition (30), the Chain Uniformity Condition (61), the Constituency Condition (63) and the Attract Smallest Condition (66) is that movement is subject to the following generalised condition (which is not a primitive condition but rather a generalisation extrapolated from other conditions already mentioned):

(67)   **Attraction Generalisation**
          When a head attracts a given type of item to become its specifier, it attracts
          the smallest accessible maximal projection containing the closest item of the
          relevant type.

In the case of a structure such as (59) above, the Q-feature on C attracts the closest question word. Since the only question word in the structure is *what* and the smallest accessible maximal projection containing *what* is the QP *quite what kind of tax*, it is this QP which moves to become the specifier of C, as in (64) above.

A further sentence type in which additional material is pied-piped along with a moved question word involves possessive structures such as the following:

(68) (a)   You have borrowed *whose* **book***?*
     (b)   **Whose* have you borrowed **book**?
     (c)   *Whose* **book** have you borrowed?

In the echo question (68a), the interrogative phrase *whose book* remains in situ in complement position within the verb phrase. In the corresponding operator questions in (68b,c) the genitive pronoun *whose* undergoes Wh-Movement on its own in (68b) but leads to an ungrammatical outcome, whereas the larger expression *whose book* undergoes Wh-Movement in (68c) and results in a grammatical sentence. The ungrammaticality of (68b) is all the more puzzling as the counterpart of structures like (68b) are grammatical in other languages – e.g. in Latin, as (69) below shows (where 2SgPr = second person, singular number, present tense):

(69)   *Cuius*   legis   **librum**?   (Ross 1986: 145)
        Whose   read$_{2SgPr}$ book
        'Whose book are you reading?'

This suggests that there is something special about the syntax of possessives in English which requires them to pied-pipe their complement along with them when they move. But what could it be?

Chomsky (1995: 263) provides an interesting answer to this question in the following terms. He suggests that *whose* should be decomposed into a possessor *who* and a possessive affix *'s* (in the same way as *John's* is decomposed into a possessor *John* and a possessive affix *'s*) and that it is simply an idiosyncratic quirk of the English spelling system that *who+'s* is written as *whose* rather than *who's*. Interesting evidence in support of decomposing *whose* into *who+'s* comes from the following (non-standard) relative clause structure which I heard produced by the presenter on the in-house radio station in a London superstore, in which *who* has been separated from the possessive affix *'s* by Wh-Movement:

(70)   He's the guy *who* I think*'s* sister is the lead singer in a new band (Radford 1988: 526)

The fact that Wh-Movement leads the possessor *who* to be separated from the possessive affix *'s* provides evidence in support of Chomsky's claim. More specifically, Chomsky maintains that the possessive affix *'s* is the head D of a DP constituent whose complement is the **possessum** (i.e. possessed object) *book* and whose specifier is the **possessor** *who/John*.

Further evidence in support of Chomsky's analysis comes from an observation credited to Jim McCloskey in Merchant (2002). McCloskey notes that *the hell* can be used to modify a preceding interrogative wh-word in sentences like (71) below, but not a preceding wh-phrase as in (72):

(71) (a)   *Who the hell* was he talking to?
     (b)   *What the hell* was he talking about?
     (c)   *When/where/why the hell* was he talking?
     (d)   *What the hell book* was he reading?!
     (d)   *What the hell kind of a doctor* is she, anyhow?!

(72) (a)   **What book the hell* was he reading!?
     (b)   **What kind the hell of a doctor* is she, anyhow?!
     (c)   **What kind of a doctor the hell* is she, anyhow!?

McCloskey also notes the following contrast:

(73) (a)   *Who the hell's car* is parked on the lawn?!
     (b)   **Whose the hell car* is parked on the lawn?!

Since sentences like (71,72) provide evidence that *the hell* can only modify a preceding wh-word and not preceding a wh-phrase, McCloskey concludes from (73) that *whose* is a wh-phrase rather than a wh-word. This is consistent with a *whose*-phrase being a DP headed by the possessive determiner *'s* (see 74 below).

Given these assumptions, let's return to consider how (68c) *Whose book have you borrowed?* is derived. The definite possessive determiner *'s* is merged with the possessum *book* to form the D-bar constituent *'s book*. This D-bar is merged with its possessor specifier *who* to form the DP *who 's book*, and this DP has an interpretation paraphraseable as 'the book belonging to who?' The resulting DP is merged with the verb *borrowed*, forming the VP *borrowed who 's book*. This VP is merged with T-*have*, forming the T-bar *have borrowed who 's book*, which in turn is merged with its subject *you* forming the TP *you have borrowed who 's ø book*. This TP is then merged with an interrogative C carrying a Q-feature in accordance with (26i) and a T-feature in accordance with (26ii), so forming the C-bar below:

(74)

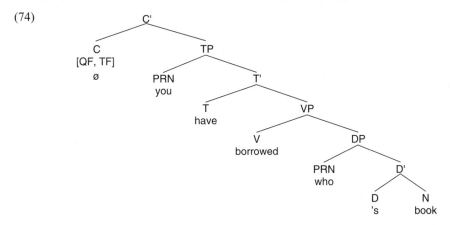

The T-feature on C triggers movement of the present tense auxiliary *have* from T to C, and the Q-feature on C attracts the smallest accessible maximal projection containing the closest question word to move to spec-CP. The closest (and only) question word in (74) is *who*, and this is a maximal projection by virtue of being the largest expression headed by the word *who* (because *who's book* is a DP headed by the possessive affix *'s*). So, we'd expect *who* to move to spec-CP on its own. However, *who* cannot be moved on its own in standard varieties of English, as we see from the ungrammaticality of:

(75)   **Who* have you borrowed *'s* book?

Why should (75) be ungrammatical? The answer is that the possessive affix *'s* in (75) ends up without an appropriate host (i.e. it ends up not attached to the possessor *who*), in violation of the following PF interface requirement (which is a generalised version of a condition on verbal affixes posited in §5.7):

(76)   **Affix Attachment Condition**
            An affix must be attached to an overt host of an appropriate kind at PF.

In standard varieties of English, possessive *'s* is a **selective** affix (i.e. one which is choosy about the kind of host that it can attach to) and only allows a possessor as its host: this means that *'s* cannot attach to the verb *borrowed* in (75). Consequently, *who* cannot move on its own in (74), because this would leave the possessive affix without a possessor host to attach to, in violation of the Affix Attachment Condition (76). Nor can *whose* be moved on its own either, because it is not a constituent: rather, *whose* comprises the head determiner *'s* and its specifier *who* (but without its complement *book*), and so is only an incomplete subpart of the whole DP *who's book*. Since *who* cannot move on its own, the Attraction Generalisation (67) tells us to move the next smallest maximal projection containing *who*, namely the DP *who+'s+book* (written as *whose book*), and this yields a successful outcome, as we see from the grammaticality of (68c) *Whose book have you borrowed?* (I note in passing that the radio presenter who produced sentence 70 appears to treat possessive *'s* as an **unselective** affix which is not restricted to attaching to a possessor, so can attach to the verb *think* in 70.)

The account of pied-piping outlined in this section is essentially Chomsky's (1995) **convergence** account, which posits that when an item moves, it 'carries along just enough material for convergence' (Chomsky 1995: 262, 26). A derivation is said to be *convergent* if it results in a well-formed structure which converges (i.e. satisfies all relevant requirements) at the semantic and phonetic interfaces (including satisfying the PF interface requirement in 76). In words of plain English, the essence of the convergence account is that we move the minimum amount of material needed to ensure that the resulting structure is well-formed.

However, a potential challenge to the convergence account comes from the phenomenon of *optional pied-piping*, whereby additional material is optionally pied-piped along with a moved constituent. One such case where additional material can optionally be pied-piped along with a fronted constituent is in structures such as the following:

(77) (a)   *Which hotel* is he staying **in**?
    (b)   **In** *which hotel* is he staying?

In both sentences, the interrogative wh-phrase *which hotel* originates as the object of the preposition *in*. In (77a), the wh-phrase is moved to spec-CP on its own, leaving the preposition *in* **stranded** at the end of the sentence. In (77b), however, the preposition *in* is pied-piped along with the wh-phrase when it is fronted, with the result that the whole PP *in which hotel* is moved to spec-CP. In such cases, it would appear that pied-piping of the preposition is optional. The convergence account (which requires us to move the minimum amount of material that will result in a grammatical outcome) would seem to wrongly predict that since preposing the wh-phrase *which hotel* leads to a grammatical outcome in (77a), it should not be possible to pied-pipe the preposition *in* along with it in (77b). How can we deal with the phenomenon of optional pied-piping in sentences like (77)?

One analysis which is compatible with the convergence-based view of pied-piping is to suppose that sentences like (77a) and (77b) belong to different varieties/styles/registers of English. Preposition stranding sentences like (77a) are characteristic of informal style, whereas preposition pied-piping sentences like (77b) are characteristic of formal style. Let us follow Chomsky (1995) in supposing that preposition pied-piping only takes place in languages (and language varieties) which have a constraint that 'bars preposition stranding' (Chomsky 1995: 264). This constraint can be characterised informally as follows:

(78)   **Preposition Stranding Constraint/PSC**
         In some languages (and in formal styles of English), no preposition can be stranded at PF.

(I will set aside here the question of whether PSC should be conflated with the Stranding Constraint of §2.6, which bars a functional category like D/determiner, Q/quantifier or C/complementiser from being stranded without its complement. An interesting possibility raised by the discussion in §2.4 of whether or not prepositions are functional categories is that they are functional categories in languages/varieties which don't allow them to be stranded, but are lexical categories in languages/varieties that do allow them to be stranded.) As is implicit in its formulation, (78) is a parameterised constraint: this is because it holds in some languages (e.g. in French, German, Italian, Russian, etc.) but not in others (e.g. not in Danish, Faroese, Norwegian or Vata). In English, the constraint is subject to stylistic parameterisation, in that it holds in formal (but not informal) styles. In formal styles, PSC operates, and so the wh-phrase *which hotel* cannot be fronted on its own in (77), since this would leave the preposition *in* stranded and induce a violation of PSC: consequently, the preposition has to be pied-piped along with the wh-phrase, as in (77b). In informal styles, PSC is inoperative and so nothing prevents the wh-phrase being fronted on its own, as in (77a).

To summarise: in this section, we have looked at the phenomenon of pied-piping, whereby additional material is sometimes pied-piped along with a question word when it undergoes Wh-Movement. We saw that (in consequence of the Attract Closest Condition), the Q-feature on C attracts the closest question word which it c-commands; that in consequence of the Chain Uniformity Condition, it attracts a maximal projection containing a question word to move to spec-CP; and that in consequence of the Attract Smallest Condition, it attracts the smallest accessible maximal projection containing the targeted question word. These assumptions lead to a convergence-based account under which the Q-feature on C attracts the smallest accessible maximal projection containing the closest question word to move to spec-CP.

6.7   Wh-Movement as copying

A tacit assumption underlying the analysis of Wh-Movement out-lined here (and made explicit in the discussion of the Chain Uniformity Condition in §6.6) is that just as a moved auxiliary leaves behind a null copy of itself in the position out of which it moves (as we saw in the previous chapter), so too a moved wh-constituent leaves behind a copy at its **extraction site** (i.e. in the position out of which it is **extracted**/moved). In earlier work in the 1970s and 1980s, moved constituents were said to leave behind a **trace** in the positions out of which they move (informally denoted as *t*), and traces were treated as being like pronouns in certain respects. Within the framework of Chomsky's more recent **Copy Theory of Movement**, a trace is taken to be an identical **copy** of a moved constituent. So, as we saw earlier, Wh-Movement in a sentence like (1a) *Who have they arrested?* involves making a copy of the wh-pronoun *who* (which originates as the complement of the verb *arrested*) and merging this copy with the C-bar constituent *have they arrested who* to form the CP *Who have they arrested ~~who~~* (with only the highest copy of a moved constituent being overtly spelled out in the PF component, in consequence of the Default Spellout Rule 10). On this view, movement involves three operations: (i) creating a copy of the constituent to be moved, (ii) merging the copy in a new position and (iii) giving a null spellout to the original copy. As noted earlier, Chomsky refers to movement as an internal merge operation, since it involves locating a constituent positioned internally within a given structure, making a copy of it and then merging the copy in a new position. By contrast, merge operations not involving movement are said to be instances of external merge, in that a constituent external to a structure (i.e. which is not already contained within the structure in question) is merged with the relevant structure. In this section, we look at evidence suggesting that Wh-Movement does indeed involve a copying operation.

This assumption can be defended on theoretical grounds, in terms of our desire to develop a unified theory of movement. Since it was argued in the previous chapter that auxiliaries leave behind a copy when they undergo Inversion (i.e. when they move from T to C), it is clear that we can achieve a unified account of movement if we suppose that all constituents leave behind a copy when they move – not only moved auxiliaries but also moved wh-constituents.

A further theoretical consideration leading to the same conclusion comes from a constraint devised by Chomsky which can be outlined informally as follows:

(79)   **No Tampering Condition/NTC**
        No syntactic operation can tamper with (i.e. change) any part of a structure other than the root.

The effect of this condition can be illustrated in relation to how movement applies to a structure such as (23) above, repeated as (80) below:

(80)

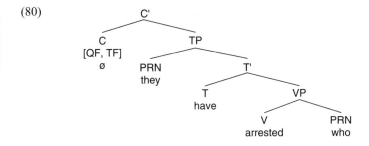

The T-feature on C attracts a copy of T *have* to adjoin to C; since C is the root head in the structure, this is permitted by the No Tampering Condition (79), if we take the condition to allow material to be added to the edge of a root projection (either to the root node in a tree, or to its head), and if we suppose that copying something does not constitute tampering with it. What is important from the perspective of Copy Theory, however, is that the No Tampering Condition will only be satisfied if the original copy of *have* remains in T. Likewise, the Q-feature on C attracts a copy of *who* to merge with the C-bar constituent at the root of the overall tree; once again, this will not violate NTC if the original copy of *who* remains in comp-VP. By contrast, if either *have* or *who* does not leave a trace copy behind when it moves, NTC will be violated. In accordance with the Default Spellout Rule (10), all but the highest copies of moved constituents will ultimately receive a null spellout in the PF component.

   In addition to theoretical considerations, there are also empirical considerations supporting the conclusion that Wh-Movement involves copying. One such piece of evidence comes from the familiar phenomenon of *have*-cliticisation in sentences like:

(81)   I have/I've been to Rome more often than I have/*I've to Paris

Although *have* can cliticise onto *I* in the string *I've been to Rome* in (81), cliticisation is not possible in the string *I've to Paris*. Why should this be? Let us make the reasonable assumption that *I've to Paris* in (81) is an elliptical variant of *I've been to Paris*, so that (81) has the fuller structure shown informally in (82) below, with strikethrough indicating that the ellipsed V receives a null spellout in the PF component:

(82)   I have been to Rome more often than I have ~~been~~ to Paris

The relevant type of cliticisation operation is subject to a constraint which can be characterised informally in the following terms:

(83)   **Cliticisation Constraint**
          Cliticisation is barred when a clitic is followed by a null constituent.

This accounts for the ungrammaticality of the string *I've to Paris* in (81), since *have* is immediately followed by a null copy of the verb *been* in (82) and so the constraint (83) blocks *have* from cliticising onto *I*.

In the light of the constraint in (83), consider why cliticisation is permitted (in British English varieties like my own) in (84) below, but not in (85):

(84) (a)   They have nothing in their bank account
     (b)   They've nothing in their bank account

(85) (a)   I wonder [what they have in their bank account]
     (b)   *I wonder [what they've in their bank account]

In (84b), there is no null constituent following (ha)ve, so cliticisation is permitted. But now consider what happens in the embedded interrogative complement clauses bracketed in (85), which show movement of the wh-word *what* to the front of the clause. If (as claimed here) Wh-Movement involves a copying operation, (85b) will have the fuller structure shown in (86) below:

(86)   I wonder [*what* they have ~~what~~ in their bank account]

That is, the wh-word *what* will originate as the complement of the verb *have*, and a copy of this wh-word will then be placed at the front of the bracketed interrogative complement clause, with the original occurrence of *what* receiving a null spellout (marked by strikethrough). But the null copy of *what* following the clitic *have* will then block *have* from contracting onto *they* in accordance with the Cliticisation Constraint in (83). Thus, the ungrammaticality of sentences like (85b) is consistent with the claim that Wh-Movement involves copying.

A different kind of evidence that preposed wh-constituents leave behind a copy when they move comes from a phenomenon which we can call **Preposition Copying**. In this connection, consider the following Shakespearean wh-questions:

(87) (a)   *In what enormity* is Marcius poor **in**? (Menenius, *Coriolanus*, II.i)
     (b)   *To what form but that he is* should wit larded with malice and malice forced with wit turn him **to**? (Thersites, *Troilus and Cressida*, V.i)

In these examples, the wh-phrase *what enormity/what form* has been moved to the front of the clause by Wh-Movement, and the preposition *in/to* has been pied-piped along with it. But a (bold-printed) copy of the preposition also appears at the end of the clause. In case you think that this is a Shakespearean quirk (or – Heaven forbid – a slip of the quill on the part of Will), the examples below show much the same thing happening in wh-questions in present-day English:

(88) (a)   *From which club* did the Arsenal sign him **from**? (Alan Brazil, Talk Sport Radio)
     (b)   *At what stage* are most athletes **at** now, preparing for the 2012 games? (Ian Danter, Talk Sport Radio)

How can we account for preposition copying in structures like (87) and (88)?

The Copy Theory of Movement enables us to provide a principled answer to this question, if (as suggested earlier) a movement operation like Wh-Movement is a composite of three suboperations of Copying, Merge and Deletion: the first stage of Wh-Movement is for a copy of the relevant wh-constituent to be created; the second stage is for the copy to be merged with the C-bar node at the root of the tree and thereby become the specifier of C; the third stage is for the original occurrence of the wh-constituent to be deleted (in the PF component, not in the syntax). From this perspective, preposition copying arises when the preposition at the original extraction site undergoes copying and merge but not PF deletion. To see what this means in more concrete terms, consider the syntax of (87a) *In what enormity is Marcius poor in?* This is derived as follows. The wh-quantifier *what* merges with the noun *enormity* to derive the quantifier phrase/QP *what enormity*. This in turn is merged with the preposition *in* to form the prepositional phrase/PP *in what enormity*. This PP is then merged with the adjective *poor* to form the adjectival phrase/AP *poor in what enormity*. This AP is merged with the copular verb *is* to form the verb phrase/VP *is poor in what enormity*. This VP is merged with a finite T constituent which triggers raising of the auxiliary/light verb *is* from V to T; the resulting T-bar constituent is merged with its subject *Marcius* (which is a DP headed by a null determiner, although I won't show the null determiner here) to form the tense phrase/TP *Marcius is ~~is~~ poor in what enormity*. Merging this TP with a C into which *is* moves (adjoining to a null complementiser not shown here) forms the C-bar *Is Marcius ~~is~~ ~~is~~ poor in what enormity?* Moving a copy of the PP *in what enormity* into spec-CP in turn derives (89) below (simplified by not showing null C, D and T heads), where lower copies of moved constituents are shown in italics:

(89)

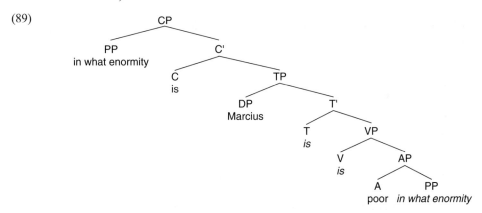

The two (italicised) lower copies of the moved copular verb *is* receive a null spellout in the PF component via **Copy Deletion**, and so are 'silent'. If we suppose that Copy Deletion in sentences like (87,88) deletes the smallest maximal projection containing the wh-word *what*, it will delete the italicised copy of the quantifier phrase *what enormity* in (89) rather than the italicised copy of the prepositional phrase *in what enormity*, so deriving (87a) *In what enormity is Marcius poor in?* Thus, preposition-copying structures like (87) and (88) provide evidence that Wh-Movement is a composite operation involving wh-copying and wh-deletion.

A related piece of evidence in support of Wh-Movement involving a copying operation comes from sentences such as the following:

(90) (a)   *What hope* **of finding any survivors** *could there be?*

　　(b)   *What hope could there be* **of finding any survivors?**

(91) (a)   *What proof* **that he was implicated** *have you found?*

　　(b)   *What proof have you found* **that he was implicated**?

The highlighted strings in (90b,91b) are **discontinuous constituents**, in the sense that (e.g.) *of finding any survivors* seems to be part of the larger constituent *what hope of finding any survivors* in (90b) and yet *what hope* is separated from *of finding any survivors* by the intervening string *could there be*. How do such discontinuous constituents come about?

In order to try and understand what's going on here, let's take a closer look at the derivation of (90). The expression *what hope of finding any survivors* in (90a) is a QP comprising the quantifier *what* and an NP complement which in turn comprises the noun *hope* and its PP complement *of finding any survivors* (with the polarity item *any* being licensed to occur because it is c-commanded by the interrogative quantifier *what*: see §3.7). The overall QP *what hope of finding any survivors* is initially merged as the complement of the verb *be*, but ultimately moves to the front of the overall sentence in (90a): this is unproblematic, since it involves Wh-Movement of the whole QP. But in (90b), it would seem as if only part of this QP (= the string *what hope*) undergoes Wh-Movement, leaving behind the remnant PP *of finding any survivors*. The problem with this is that the string *what hope* is not a constituent, only a subpart of the overall QP *what hope of finding any survivors*. Given the standard assumption that only complete constituents can undergo movement (in consequence of the Constituency Condition, 63), we clearly cannot maintain that the non-constituent string *what hope* gets moved on its own. So how can we account for sentences like (90b)?

Copy Theory provides us with an answer, if we suppose that Wh-Movement places a copy of the complete QP *what hope of finding any survivors* at the front of the overall sentence, so deriving the syntactic structure shown in skeletal form in (92a) below, which is subsequently spelled out as the PF structure in (92b), where strikethrough indicates constituents receiving a null spellout:

(92) (a)   **What hope of finding any survivors** could there be *what hope of finding any survivors*

　　(b)   **What hope** ~~**of finding any survivors**~~ could there be ~~*what hope*~~ *of finding any survivors*

On this view, the PP *of finding any survivors* is spelled out in its original position (i.e. in the italicised position it occupied before Wh-Movement applied), but the remaining constituents of the QP (the quantifier *what* and the noun *hope*) are spelled out in the superficial (bold-printed) position which they come to occupy after Wh-Movement. It should be clear that such an analysis relies crucially on the assumption that moved constituents leave behind full copies of themselves.

The analysis also assumes the possibility of **split/discontinuous spellout**, in the sense that (in sentences like 90b and 91b above) a PP or CP which is the complement of a particular type of moved constituent can be spelled out in one position (in the position where it originated), and the remainder of the constituent spelled out in another (in the position where it ends up). This means in turn that there must be a 'special' Low Spellout Rule allowing a PP or CP contained within a larger moved constituent to be spelled out in its initial position at the foot of the movement chain: the remaining parts of the moved constituent will then be spelled out in the final position which they end up in, via the Default Spellout Rule (10). More generally, our discussion here suggests that (in certain structures) there is a choice regarding which part of a movement chain gets deleted. A more radical possibility which this opens up is that wh-in-situ questions in languages like Chinese may involve Wh-Movement, but with the moved wh-constituent being spelled out in its initial position (at the foot of the movement chain) rather than in its final position (at the head of the movement chain).

A different source of evidence in support of positing that a moved wh-expression leaves behind a null copy comes from the semantics of wh-questions. Chomsky (1981: 324) argues that a wh-question like (93a) below has a semantic representation (more precisely, a **Logical Form/LF representation**) along the lines shown informally in (93b), with (93b) being paraphraseble as 'Of which x (such that x is a person) is it true that they have arrested x?'

(93) (a)   Who have they arrested?
     (b)   Which x (x a person), they have arrested x

In the LF representation (93b), the quantifier *which* functions as an interrogative **operator** which serves to **bind** the variable x. Since a grammar must compute a semantic representation for each syntactic structure which it generates/forms, important questions arise about how syntactic representations are to be mapped/converted into semantic representations. One such question is how a syntactic structure like (93a) can be mapped into an LF representation like (93b) containing an operator binding a variable. If a moved wh-expression leaves behind a copy, (93a) will have the superficial syntactic structure shown in simplified form in (94) below (repeated from 24 above, but omitting some irrelevant details):

(94)

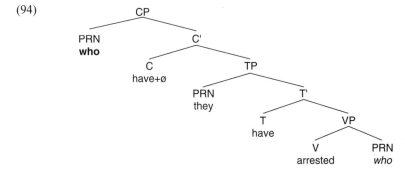

The LF representation for (93a) can be derived from the syntactic representation (94) in a straightforward fashion if we suppose that the lowest copy in a Wh-Movement chain (in this case, the italicised copy of *who* at the foot of the overall structure) is given an LF interpretation as a variable bound by the wh-operator in the highest link of the chain – i.e. by the bold-printed copy of *who*. (An incidental detail to note is that the lower copies of *who* and *have* will ultimately receive a null spellout by the Default Spellout Rule 10 when the syntactic structure in 94 is handed over to the PF component.)

The assumption that a wh-copy (i.e. a copy of a moved wh-constituent) has the semantic function of a variable which is bound by a wh-operator has interesting implications for the syntax of Wh-Movement. In Chapter 3, we saw that there is a c-command condition on binding to the effect that one constituent X can only bind another constituent Y if X c-commands Y. If we look at how Wh-Movement works, we find that it results in a structure in which the moved wh-constituent c-commands (by virtue of occuring higher up in the structure than) its original copy. For example, in the structure (94) above, the moved (bold-printed) wh-pronoun *who* c-commands its italicised copy *who* by virtue of the fact that the italicised copy is contained within (and hence is a constituent of) the C-bar [have they have arrested *who*] which is the sister of the PRN-node containing the bold-printed moved wh-pronoun **who**. It would therefore seem that a core syntactic property of Wh-Movement (namely that it always moves a wh-constituent into a *higher* position within the structure containing it) follows from a semantic requirement – namely that a wh-copy (by virtue of its semantic function as a variable) must be bound by a c-commanding wh-expression (which has the semantic function of an operator expression).

A further semantic argument in support of the Copy Theory of Movement is formulated by Chomsky (1995) in connection with the interpretation of reflexive anaphors in sentences such as the following:

(95)   Joe wonders which picture of himself Jim bought

In (95), the reflexive anaphor *himself* can refer either to *Joe* or to *Jim*. An obvious problem posed by the latter interpretation is that a reflexive has to be c-commanded by a local antecedent (one contained within the same TP, as we saw in §3.7), and yet *Jim* does not c-command *himself* in (95). How can we account for the dual interpretation of *himself*? The Copy Theory of Movement provides a principled answer to this question. The QP *which picture of himself* is initially merged as the complement of the verb *bought* but is subsequently moved to the front of the *bought* clause, leaving behind a copy in its original position, so deriving the structure shown in skeletal form in (96) below:

(96)   [CP [TP Joe wonders [CP **which picture of himself** [TP Jim bought *which picture of himself*]]]]

Although the italicised copy of the QP *which picture of himself* gets deleted in the PF component, Chomsky argues that copies of moved constituents remain visible in the semantic component, and that binding conditions apply to LF representations. If (96) is the LF representation of (95), the possibility of *himself* referring to *Jim* can be attributed to the fact that the italicised copy of *himself* is c-commanded by (and contained within the same TP as) *Jim* at LF. On the other hand, the possibility of *himself* referring to *Joe* can be attributed to the fact that the bold-printed copy of **himself** is c-commanded by (and occurs within the same TP as) *Joe*.

In this section, we have seen that there is a range of evidence which supports the claim that a constituent which undergoes Wh-Movement leaves behind a copy at its extraction site. This copy is normally given a null spellout in the PF component, although we have seen that copies may sometimes have an overt spellout, or indeed part of a moved phrase may be spelled out in one position and part in another. We have also seen that copies of moved wh-constituents are visible in the semantic component and play an important role (*inter alia*) in relation to the binding of anaphors and variables.

6.8   Long Wh-Movement

The account presented so far has led to the generalisation that (in Wh-Movement questions) C attracts the smallest accessible maximal projection containing the closest interrogative operator to move to become the specifier of C. But this assumption raises interesting questions about what happens in questions like (97) below where an interrogative operator originates in a lower clause (as the complement of the verb *hiding*) and subsequently moves to the spec-CP position in a higher clause:

(97)   *What* might he think [that she is hiding]?

Such structures (in which a wh-word originating in a lower clause moves to spec-CP in a higher clause) are said to involve **long (-distance) Wh-Movement** and hence are referred to as **long-distance questions**. In this section, we look at how long Wh-Movement works.

At first sight, the answer might seem obvious. That is, we might imagine that Wh-Movement in a sentence like (97) has the effect of moving the interrogative pronoun *what* directly from the position in which it originates (as the complement of the verb *hiding*) into the position where it ends up (as the specifier of the CP containing the inverted auxiliary *might*), in the manner shown by the arrow in the highly simplified structure below:

(98)   [CP *what* might [TP he think [CP that [TP she is hiding *what*]]]]

However, in research in the 1970s, Chomsky argued that movement is **bounded** (in the sense that there are bounds/limits on how far a constituent can move at any one go) in consequence of a constraint which he termed the **Subjacency Condition** which (for present purposes) we can formulate as follows:

(99)   **Subjacency Condition**
         No movement can cross more than one bounding node (where bounding
         nodes include S/TP).

A one-step long-distance movement operation such as that arrowed in (98) would violate the Subjacency Condition (99), in that *what* moves out of two different TP constituents in one go, by virtue of moving out of both the lower TP whose subject is *she* and the higher TP whose subject is *he*. Moreover, one-step Wh-Movement would also violate the following constraint introduced in §3.10:

(100)   **Impenetrability Condition**
         A constituent c-commanded by a complementiser C is impenetrable to (so cannot agree with, or be case-marked by, or be attracted by etc.) any constituent c-commanding the CP headed by C.

In §4.10, we saw that the Impenetrability Condition accounts for why the subject of the embedded clause cannot passivise in a structure like (101) below:

(101) (a)   We didn't intend [for *you* to hurt anyone]
      (b)   *_You_ weren't intended [for to hurt anyone]

In particular, we saw that the Impenetrability Condition prevents the main-clause T constituent *weren't* from attracting the pronoun *you* to become its subject/ specifier in the manner shown by the arrow below:

(102)   *[CP [C ø] [TP *you* [T weren't] intended [CP [C **for**] [TP ~~you~~ [T to] hurt anyone]]]]

The arrowed movement is ruled out because the passivised pronoun *you* originates in a position below the complementiser *for* and so can't be attracted by a higher head like T-*weren't* (positioned above the CP headed by *for*) to become its specifier. (It should be noted in passing that the Subjacency Condition offers no account of why the movement in 102 leads to ungrammaticality, so the Impenetrability Condition is descriptively superior to the Subjacency Condition in this respect.) Returning now to the one-step movement arrowed in (98), we can see that it violates the Impenetrability Condition (100) because *what* originates in a position below the complementiser *that* and is attracted by a higher head positioned above the CP headed by *that* (= by the main clause C constituent containing *might*) to become its specifier. Consequently, an analysis such as (98) would wrongly predict that sentences like (97) are ungrammatical by virtue of violating the Impenetrability Condition.

However, we can avoid violation of the Subjacency Condition and Impenetrability Condition if we suppose that Wh-Movement in sentences like (97) applies in two separate steps, moving the wh-pronoun *what* first to the spec-CP position in the complement clause and then into the spec-CP position at the front of the main clause – as shown by the two arrows numbered below:

(103)   [CP *what* [C might] [TP he [T ~~might~~] think [CP ~~*what*~~ [C that] [TP she [T is] hiding ~~*what*~~]]]]

Movement (1) in (103) involves the wh-word *what* being attracted by the lower C constituent (containing *that*) to become its specifier and thereby moving to the edge of the embedded CP; movement (2) involves *what* being attracted by the higher C constituent (containing a copy of the inverted auxiliary *might*) to move from the edge of the lower CP to the edge of the higher CP. Neither movement violates the Subjacency Condition (99), since (1) only involves movement across one TP (across the TP whose subject is *she*), and (2) likewise only involves movement across one TP (across the TP whose subject is *he*). In much the same way, neither movement leads to violation of the Impenetrability Condition (100), since neither involves movement out of the CP headed by the relevant complementiser: (1) involves C-*that* attracting *what* to move to a position *inside* the CP headed by *that*; and (2) involves C-*might* attracting *what* to move to a position *inside* the CP headed by C-*might*.

In consequence of the Subjacency Condition and the Impenetrability Condition, Wh-Movement is a **local/bounded** operation which applies in a **successive-cyclic** (one-clause-at-a-time) fashion, moving a wh-constituent in successive stages (or cycles) first to the front of the clause in which it originates, then to the front of the next highest clause ... and so on until the wh-constituent reaches its ultimate landing site at the front of the interrogative clause. (Note in passing that the string ~~*what*~~ *that* in the embedded clause in 103 does not violate the Doubly Filled COMP Filter 19 because the relevant copy of *what* is 'silent' at PF, and the filter bars an <u>overt</u> complementiser like *that* from having an <u>overt</u> specifier at PF; nor does the string *what might* in the main clause in 103 violate the filter, because *might* is an auxiliary and not a complementiser.)

The implication of the discussion above is that UG principles like the Subjacency Condition and the Impenetrability Condition require Wh-Movement to be a local operation moving wh-constituents one clause at a time. Moreover, there is a third UG principle (devised by Rizzi 1990: 7) which similarly requires long-distance movement to take place one clause at a time. Adapting this constraint from the framework used by Rizzi to that utilised here, we can formulate it as follows:

(104)   **Relativised Minimality Condition/RMC**
               A constituent can only be affected by (e.g. be attracted by, or agree with, or be case-marked by) the minimal (i.e. closest) constituent of the relevant type above it (i.e. c-commanding it).

The condition is relativized in the sense that (e.g.) where a constituent moves to is relative to the kind of movement operation involved: for example, a constituent undergoing Wh-Movement to spec-CP will move into the minimal/closest spec-CP position above it; whereas by contrast, a constituent undergoing Head Movement will adjoin to the minimal/closest head position above it (so that the Relativised Minimality Condition can be said to subsume – and thereby obviate the need for – the Head Movement Constraint outlined in §5.5). As should be clear, long-distance (single-step) Wh-Movement in the manner of (98) above would violate RMC because *what* moves directly to become the specifier of the main clause C constituent containing *might*, and yet this is not the closest C constituent above the original copy of *what*. Since the closest C constituent above the position in which *what* originates is the embedded clause complementiser *that*, RMC requires *what* to become the specifier of the embedded C constituent containing *that* before subsequently moving on to become the specifier of the next highest C constituent in the structure, namely the main clause C containing *might*: consequently, RMC requires Wh-Movement to apply one clause at a time, as in (103) above.

If (as assumed here) Wh-Movement of a question operator is driven by a Q-feature on C, and if Wh-Movement applies in a successive-cyclic (one-clause-at-a-time) fashion, it follows that the head C in each of the clauses through which a question operator moves must have a Q-feature of its own, enabling it to attract a (maximal projection containing a) question word to move to its specifier position. However, a complication which arises here is that certain types of embedded clause don't readily allow constituents to be extracted out of them, as we see from contrasts such as the following:

(105) (a)   *How* did Mike **say** [that he fixed the car - - -]?
      (b)   **How* did Mike **quip** [that he fixed the car - - -]?

Here, *how* originates in the gap position in the bracketed embedded clause as an adjunct to the VP headed by the verb *wearing* and moves first to become the specifier of the embedded clause C constituent *that* and then to become the specifier of the main-clause C constituent containing the inverted auxiliary *did*, in the manner shown for (105a) by the arrows below:

(106)   [CP *how* [C did] Mike say [CP how [C that] he fixed the car how]]

But how come long-distance Wh-Movement yields a grammatical outcome in (105a), but not in (105b)? An answer given in work dating back half a century is that a verb like *say* is a **bridge verb**, in the sense that it allows a fronted constituent to bridge (i.e. cross) the bracketed clause boundary separating the embedded clause from the main-clause verb, whereas a verb like *quip* is a **non-bridge verb** and doesn't allow any constituent to bridge/cross the boundary between the two clauses. In terms of the framework used here, this means that the head C of a CP used as the complement of a bridge verb like *say* can carry a Q-feature, but the head C of other types of embedded clause cannot. This suggests that we need to modify our earlier assumptions in (26) above about the (partial) feature composition of C by adding condition (107ii) below:

(107)   **Feature Composition of C in Operator Questions** (revised from 26 above)
  (i)   C carries an interrogative edge feature (= Q-feature/QF) in an operator-
        question clause
  (ii) C can also carry a Q-feature in a non-interrogative embedded clause
        which is the complement of a bridge verb
  (iii) In a finite root clause, if C has a Q-feature then C also has a T-feature

A useful rule of thumb for identifying a bridge verb is that any verb taking a *that*-clause complement which allows *that* to be substituted by a null complementiser is usually a bridge verb. In this respect, it is interesting to note the contrast below (where *ø* denotes a null complementiser):

(108) (a)   Mike **said/quipped** [*that* he fixed the car by kicking it]
      (b)   Mike **said/*quipped** [*ø* he fixed the car by kicking it]

Given the rule of thumb sketched above, it follows that *say* is a bridge verb because it allows a null complementiser to be used in (108b), whereas conversely *quip* is a non-bridge verb because it does not allow use of a null complementiser.
   In the light of these observations, let's return to consider the derivation of (97) *What might he think that she is hiding?* The verb *hiding* merges with the interrogative pronoun *what* to form the VP *hiding what*. This VP is merged with the T auxiliary *is* to form the T-bar *is hiding what*, which is then merged with the pronoun *she* to form the TP *she is hiding what*. The resulting TP is merged with the complementiser *that* to form the C-bar *that she is hiding what*. Since the *that*-clause in (97) is used as the complement of the verb *think* and *think* is a bridge verb (as we see from the possibility of replacing *that* by a null comple-mentiser in *He might think ø she is hiding something*), it follows that the complementiser *that* can carry a Q-feature in accordance with (107ii). The Q-feature on C *that* attracts *what* to move to spec-CP in the manner shown by the arrow below:

(109)

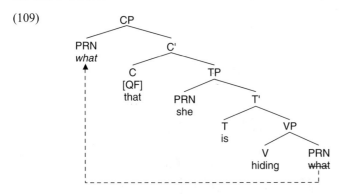

The lower copy of *what* subsequently receives a null spellout in the PF compo-nent. Note that a structure like (109) does not violate the Doubly Filled COMP Filter (19) which bars an overt complementiser from having an overt specifier, since (109) is an intermediate syntactic structure, and the Doubly Filled COMP Filter holds of PF structures.

The CP in (109) is then merged as the complement of the bridge verb *think*, forming the VP *think what that she is hiding ~~what~~*. The resulting VP is merged as the complement of the past tense modal T auxiliary *might*, forming the T-bar *might think what that she is hiding ~~what~~*. This T-bar is itself merged with the subject pronoun *he*, forming the TP *he might think what that she is hiding ~~what~~*. The TP thereby formed is merged with a null root interrogative C constituent *ø* which carries both a Q-feature (in accordance with 107i) and a T-feature (in accordance with 107iii), so forming the C-bar *ø he might think what that she is hiding ~~what~~*. The Q-feature of the complementiser attracts a copy of the interrogative pronoun *what* to move to become the specifier of C, and the T-feature of the null complementiser attracts a copy of the T auxiliary *might* to adjoin to C, so deriving the structure shown in simplified form in (110) below (with arrows indicating movements that take place in the course of the derivation, the dotted arrow representing Head Movement, and the dashed arrow representing Wh-Movement):

(110)

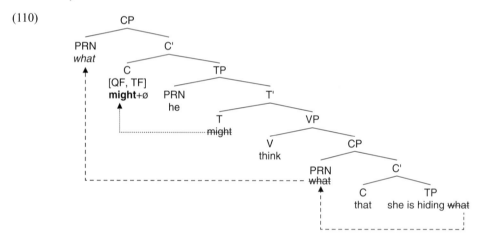

On this view, long Wh-Movement proceeds in a successive-cyclic fashion (i.e. in a succession of short steps, one clause at a time), with each individual step involving a local operation whereby an interrogative wh-constituent is attracted to become the specifier of the closest C constituent above it (thereby satisfying the Subjacency Condition 99, the Impenetrability Condition 100 and the Relativised Minimality Condition 104).

The key assumption made here is that putatively universal locality principles such as the Subjacency Condition, the Impenetrability Condition and the Relativised Minimality Condition require long-distance movement to take place in a series of short-distance steps. There is a considerable body of empirical evidence (both from English and from other languages) that Wh-Movement is indeed a local operation which moves a wh-constituent one clause at a time. Since our concern here is with English, in the remainder of this section, we'll look at evidence from a number of varieties of English.

An interesting piece of evidence that wh-expressions move one clause at a time comes from the phenomenon of stranding of material at intermediate landing sites under movement. In this connection, consider the following examples:

(111) (a)   You think they went *how far inside the tunnel*?
    (b)   *How far inside the tunnel* do you think they went
    (c)   *How far* do you think *inside the tunnel* they went?
    (d)   *How far* do you think they went *inside the tunnel*?

The prepositional phrase *how far inside the tunnel* originates as the complement of the verb *went* (as seems clear from its position in the echo question 111a) and can be taken to have the structure below:

(112)   [PP how far [P′ [P inside] the tunnel]]

That is to say, the preposition *inside* merges with its complement *the tunnel* to form the P-bar *inside the tunnel* and the resulting P-bar is in turn merged with the specifier *how far* to form the PP *how far inside the tunnel*. In (111b), the whole PP *how far inside the tunnel* moves to the front of the main clause. More puzzling is the structure (111c), in which *how far* is positioned at the front of the main clause, and *inside the tunnel* at the front of the complement clause. How can we account for this?

Given the assumption that wh-expressions move one clause at a time, we can account for sentences like (111c) in the following terms. Let us suppose that the whole (italicised) PP *how far inside the tunnel* first moves to the front of the complement clause CP (as shown by the lower arrow in 113 below), and then subsequently moves to the front of the main clause CP (as shown by the upper arrow in 113):

(113)

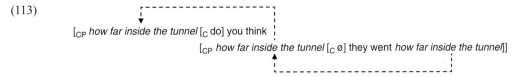

Let us further suppose that the string *how far* is spelled out overtly on the highest link of the movement chain (in order for the relevant clause to be identifiable as a wh-operator question), but that the string *inside the tunnel* can be spelled out on any one of the three links of the chain – hence. on the highest link as in (114a) below, on the intermediate link as in (114b) or on the lowest link as in (114c):

(114) (a)   [CP *How far inside the tunnel* [C do] you think [CP ~~how far inside the tunnel~~ [C ø] they went ~~how far inside the tunnel~~]]
    (b)   [CP *How far ~~inside the tunnel~~* [C do] you think [CP ~~how far~~ *inside the tunnel* [C ø] they went ~~how far inside the tunnel~~]]
    (c)   [CP *How far ~~inside the tunnel~~* [C do] you think [CP ~~how far inside the tunnel~~ [C ø] they went ~~how far~~ *inside the tunnel*]]

The fact that the prepositional expression *inside the tunnel* can be 'stranded' at the beginning of the complement clause in (114b) provides evidence that

Wh-Movement takes place one clause at a time. Structures like (114b,c) are further instances of the phenomenon of discontinuous spellout discussed in §5.7.

A related *stranding* argument that wh-expressions move one clause at a time is offered by McCloskey (2000, 2002), based on observations about **quantifier floating/stranding** in West Ulster English. In this variety, a wh-word can be modified by the universal quantifier *all*, giving rise to questions such as:

(115)   *What all* did you get for Christmas? (= 'What are all the things which you got for Christmas?')

McCloskey argues that in such sentences, the quantifier and the wh-word originate as a single constituent. He further maintains that under Wh-Movement, the wh-word *what* can either pied-pipe the quantifier *all* along with it as in (115) above, or can move on its own leaving the quantifier *all* stranded. In this connection, consider the sentences below:

(116) (a)   *What all* do you think that he'll say that we should buy?
      (b)   *What* do you think *all* that he'll say that we should buy?
      (c)   *What* do you think that he'll say *all* that we should buy?
      (d)   *What* do you think that he'll say that we should buy *all*?

McCloskey (2000: 63) claims that '*All* in wh-quantifier float constructions appears in positions for which there is considerable independent evidence that they are either positions in which Wh-Movement originates or positions through which Wh-Movement passes. We have in these observations a new kind of argument for the successive-cyclic character of long Wh-Movement.'

McCloskey argues that the derivation of (116a–d) proceeds along the following lines (simplified in a number of ways). The quantifier *all* merges with its complement *what* to form the structure [*all what*]. The wh-word *what* then raises to become the specifier of *all*, forming the overt QP [*what all* ~~what~~]. However, to simplify exposition, I will show only the overt constituents of QP, not the null copy of *what* following *all*. The resulting QP [*what all*] is merged as the object of *buy*, forming [*buy what all*]. If *what* undergoes Wh-Movement on its own in subsequent stages of derivation, we derive (116d) '*What* do you think that he'll say that we should buy *all*?' But suppose that the quantifier *all* is pied-piped along with *what* under Wh-Movement until we reach the stage shown in skeletal form below:

(117)   [$_{CP}$ *what all* [$_C$ that] we should buy]

If Wh-Movement then extracts *what* on its own, the quantifier *all* will be stranded in the most deeply embedded spec-CP position, so deriving (116c) '*What* do you think that he'll say *all* that we should buy?' By contrast, if *all* is pied-piped along with *what* until the end of the intermediate CP-cycle, we derive:

(118)   [$_{CP}$ *what all* [$_C$ that] he'll say that we should buy]

If Wh-Movement then extracts *what* on its own, the quantifier *all* will be stranded in the intermediate spec-CP position and we will ultimately derive (116b) '*What* do you think *all* that he'll say that we should buy?' But if *all* continues to be pied-piped along with *what* throughout the remaining stages of derivation, we ultimately derive (116a) '*What all* do you think that he'll say that we should buy?'

A further piece of evidence that wh-expressions move one clause at a time comes from Auxiliary Inversion in Belfast English. In her 1995 book on *Belfast English*, Alison Henry notes that in long-distance wh-questions in Belfast English, not only the main clause C but also intermediate C constituents show T-to-C Movement (i.e. Auxiliary Inversion), as illustrated below (1995: 108):

(119)   What *did* Mary claim [*did* they steal]?

We can account for Auxiliary Inversion in structures like (119) in the following terms. The main clause C constituent will carry a Q-feature by virtue of being interrogative, in accordance with (107i). Even though the embedded clause is declarative (as we see from the *that*-clause paraphrase in 'What did Mary claim *that* they stole?'), it can carry a Q-feature in accordance with the bridge condition in (107ii). If we suppose that in place of the Standard English condition (107iii) 'A root C with a Q-feature also has a T-feature' Belfast English has the slightly different condition '*Any* C with a Q-feature also has a T-feature', it follows that both the main clause C and the embedded clause C in (119) will carry a T-feature triggering Auxiliary Inversion and thereby attracting T to adjoin to C. More generally, the fact that the complement clause shows Auxiliary Inversion provides evidence that the preposed wh-word *what* moves through the spec-CP position in the bracketed complement clause in (119) before subsequently moving into the main-clause spec-CP position.

An additional piece of evidence that long Wh-Movement is successive-cyclic comes from the interpretation of reflexive anaphors like *himself* in standard varieties of English. As we saw in Exercise 2.2, these are subject to Principle A of Binding Theory which requires an anaphor to be locally bound and hence to have a c-commanding antecedent within the closest TP containing it. This requirement can be illustrated by the contrast below:

(120) (a)   *Jim was surprised that [$_{TP}$ Peter wasn't sure [$_{CP}$ that [$_{TP}$ Mary liked this picture of himself best]]]

      (b)   Jim was surprised that [$_{TP}$ Peter wasn't sure [$_{CP}$ which picture of himself [$_{TP}$ Mary liked best]]]

In (120a), the closest TP containing the reflexive anaphor *himself* is the bold-printed TP whose subject is *Mary*, and since there is no suitable (third person masculine singular) antecedent for *himself* within this TP, the resulting sentence violates Binding Principle A and so is ill-formed. However, in (120b) the wh-phrase *which picture of himself* has been moved to the specifier position within the bracketed CP, and the closest TP containing the reflexive anaphor is the italicised TP whose subject is *Peter*. Since this italicised TP does indeed contain a c-commanding antecedent for *himself* (namely its subject *Peter*), there is no violation of Principle A if *himself* is construed as bound by *Peter* – though Principle A prevents *Jim* from being the antecedent of *himself*.

In the light of the binding restriction on anaphors, consider the following sentence:

(121)   Which picture of himself does he think that she will like?

In (121), the antecedent of *himself* is *he* – and yet *himself* appears not to be c-commanded by *he*, as we see from (122) below (simplified in numerous ways, including by showing only overt constituents):

(122)

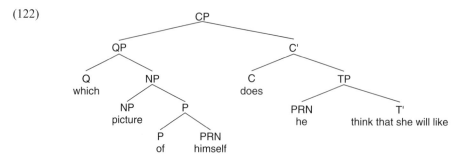

In fact, the only constituents c-commanded by the pronoun *he* in (122) are T-bar and the constituents it contains. But if *he* does not c-command *himself* in (122), how come *he* is interpreted as the antecedent of *himself* when we would have expected such a structure to violate Principle A of Binding Theory and hence to be ill-formed?

We can provide a principled answer to this question if we suppose that Wh-Movement operates in a successive-cyclic fashion, and that *which picture of himself* originates as the complement of *like* and then moves first to become the specifier of the CP headed by C-*that* (thereby coming to occupy the position italicised in 123 below) and then to become the specifier of the CP headed by the inverted auxiliary *does* (and thereby occupying the position bold-printed in 123). This being so, (121) will have the fuller syntactic structure shown in (123), with *which picture of himself* having the structure shown in (122):

(123)

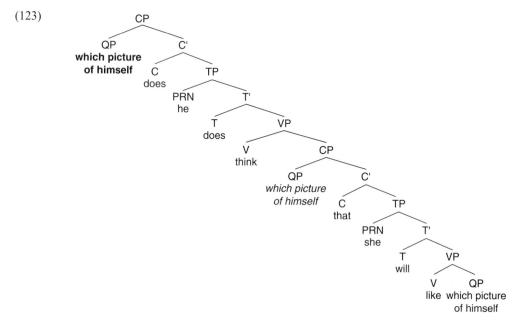

The syntactic structure in (123) will then be handed over to the phonological component (where lower copies of moved constituents will be given a null spellout), and to the semantic component. Given the assumption that the semantic component can 'see' all copies of moved constituents, it follows that all three copies of the anaphor *himself* will be visible for purposes of semantic interpretation. The intermediate (italicised) copy of *himself* is locally bound by *he* because *he* c-commands the italicised copy of *himself*, and because the closest TP containing *himself* is the TP headed by T-*does*, and this is also the closest TP containing *he*. Since there is a copy of *himself* which is locally bound by *he*, it follows that *himself* is interpreted as bound by *he* in (121/123).

A final piece of evidence that wh-expressions move one clause at a time comes from the phenomenon of **wh-copying** in Child English. Thornton (1995: 147) reports children producing long-distance wh-copy questions such as the following:

(124) (a)   **What** do you think [*what* Cookie Monster eats]?
      (b)   **How** do you think [*how* Superman fixed the car]?

In such cases, it would appear that the wh-word moves to the italicised spec-CP position within the bracketed complement clause before moving into its final landing site in the bold-printed spec-CP position in the main clause. While the children concerned 'know' that the original occurrence of the wh-word receives a null spellout, they wrongly assume that any wh-copy in any spec-CP position can be overtly spelled out (whereas only the highest such copy is overtly spelled out in adult English). Children's wh-copying structures thus provide evidence that wh-expressions move one clause at a time.

To summarise the discussion in this section: we have seen that long Wh-Movement proceeds in a successive-cyclic (one-clause-at-a-time) fashion so that a long-moved wh-constituent moves first to become the specifier of the closest CP containing it, then to become the specifier of the next closest CP containing it, and so on. Long-distance movement must take place in a succession of short-distance steps in order to avoid violating locality constraints such as the Subjacency Condition, the Impenetrability Condition and the Relativised Minimality Condition. Successive-cyclic movement is possible in structures where an embedded CP is the complement of a bridge verb, because the head C of CP in such cases can carry an edge feature (e.g. a Q-feature driving movement of a maximal projection containing a question operator to the edge of CP).

6.9   Constraints on movement

Our discussion in the previous section leads to the conclusion that (in consequence of locality constraints like the Subjacency Condition, the Impenetrability Condition and the Relativised Minimality Condition), long Wh-Movement takes place in a series of steps, one clause at a time. This reflects a more general phenomenon, whereby the question of how/whether movement operations can apply in a particular structure is regulated by a set of constraints – and indeed we have already encountered a number of other constraints on movement operations (or on the structures they give rise to) in this chapter (e.g. the Chain Uniformity Condition 61, the Constituency Condition 63, the Preposition Stranding Constraint 78 and the No Tampering Condition 79). In this section, we look briefly at a number of other constraints on movement operations like Wh-Movement.

The first monograph-length study of constraints on movement was a PhD dissertation (Ross 1967) which was subsequently published as a book (Ross 1986). Ross noted that certain structures are resistant to movement (in the sense that they don't allow anything to be extracted out of them), and he termed such constituents **islands** (the idea behind this colourful metaphor being that any constituent inside an island is marooned there and can't be got off the island by any movement operation). The spirit of Ross's work can be encapsulated in the following constraint (where a gap is a null copy of a moved constituent, and its antecedent is the moved constituent which left the null copy behind):

(125)   **Island Constraint**
          No gap inside an island can have an antecedent outside the island

Ross identified a number of different types of clause as islands, including subject clauses like that bracketed in (126a) below, adjunct clauses like that bracketed in (126b), interrogative clauses like that bracketed in (126c), noun complement clauses like that bracketed in (126d) and relative clauses like that bracketed in (126e):

(126) (a)   *What would [for me to do - - -] really upset him?
      (b)   *Which contract was he fired [after he lost - - -]?
      (c)   *What did he wonder [where John put - - -]? (Chomsky 1964: 44)
      (d)   *What did he deny the ridiculous allegation [that he had stolen - - -]?
      (e)   *Who did he do something [that upset - - -]?

Subsequent research refined or generalised these constraints, and identified additional constraints on movement. We'll take a brief look at some of these in this section.

We saw in the previous section that wh-constituents can in principle undergo long-distance movement. However, long movement can sometimes result in an ungrammatical structure – as illustrated in (127) below:

(127)   *Who were the police enquiring what had happened to?

In (127), *who* originates as the complement of the preposition *to*, and from there (via Wh-Movement) ultimately moves to the front of the main clause. And yet the resulting sentence (127) is ungrammatical? Why?

At first sight, the answer might appear to be straightforward. Consider what will happen if *what* moves to spec-CP in the embedded clause and we reach the stage of derivation shown in highly simplified form below:

(128)   [$_{CP}$ [$_C$ ø] the police were enquiring [$_{CP}$ what [$_C$ ø] ~~what~~ had happened to who]]

The bold-printed null C in the main/root clause will carry a Q-feature and a T-feature, as in all main-clause questions. The T-feature on the root C will attract T-*are* to adjoin to C, so triggering Auxiliary Inversion in the main clause. However, more interesting is the question of what the Q-feature/QF on the root C attracts. If QF attracts *what* to move from spec-CP in the lower clause into spec-CP in the main clause, this results in the structure shown in simplified form in (129a) below, spelled out at PF as the sentence in (129b).

(129) (a)   [CP *what* [C were] the police ~~were~~ enquiring [CP ~~what~~ [C ø] ~~what~~ had happened to who]]

    (b)   *What were the police enquiring had happened to who

What prevents movement of *what* to the front of the overall sentence in (129)? The answer is that *what* is positioned on the edge of the embedded clause in (128), and this embedded clause is interrogative in type because it serves as the complement of the verb ENQUIRE, and ENQUIRE selects an interrogative complement. Thus, *what* has to remain in place on the edge of the embedded clause in order for the embedded clause to be typed as interrogative by the Clause Typing Condition (3). Using the terminology of Rizzi and Shlonsky (2007), we can phrase things rather differently by saying that movement of *what* to the front of the main clause in (128/129) is barred by the following constraint:

(130)   **Criterial Freezing Condition**
    A constituent which occupies its criterial position is frozen in place.

(where the *criterial* position for a constituent is the position appropriate to its semantic interpretation). Let us suppose that the specifier position of an interrogative C is the criterial position for an interrogative operator, since the Clause Typing Condition 3 means that a clause is only interpreted as an operator question in the semantic component if it is a CP with an interrogative operator as its specifier. This means that since the embedded clause in (128) is interrogative in type, and since *what* is an interrogative operator which occupies its criterial spec-CP position within this interrogative clause, *what* is frozen in place.

So far, we have seen that in a structure like (128), *what* is prevented from moving by the Criterial Freezing Condition. But how about *who*? This can't move either, as we see from the ungrammaticality of (127) **Who were the police enquiring what had happened to?* How come? There are two ways in which *who* might move to the front of the main clause. One is for *who* to move directly from its underlying position as the complement of the preposition *to* into its superficial position as the specifier of *were* in the manner shown by the arrow in the (highly simplified) structure below:

(131)   [CP *who* [C were] the police ~~were~~ enquiring [CP ~~what~~ [C ø] what had happened to ~~who~~]]

The second is for *what* to move (in a successive-cyclic fashion) first to the edge of the embedded clause CP (becoming a second specifier for the null complementiser C-*ø* heading the embedded CP), and then from there to the edge of the main clause CP, in the manner shown by the two numbered arrows below:

(132)   [CP *who* [C were] the police ~~were~~ enquiring [CP ~~who~~ what [C ø] ~~what~~ had happened to ~~who~~]]

However, it is clear that both derivations must violate one or more constraints, since the resulting sentence (127) **Who were the police enquiring what had happened to?* is ungrammatical. But what constraints are violated by the derivations in (131) and (132)?

Consider first why the complementiser in the matrix clause cannot attract *who* to undergo single-step Wh-Movement in (131). One answer is that movement of *who* violates the Attract Closest Condition (30), because *what* is closer to the head C of the main clause CP than *who*. A second answer is that, by virtue of being positioned below the null complementiser in the embedded clause, *what* is prevented by the Impenetrability Condition (100) from being attracted by the main-clause complementiser to become its specifier. A third answer is that the arrowed movement in (131) violates the Intervention Condition (36), repeated as (133) below:

(133)   **Intervention Condition**
             No constituent X can move from one position to another across an intervening constituent Y if X and Y are both sensitive to (the same kind of) intervention effects.

Since question operators are intervention-sensitive (in the sense that they give rise to intervention effects), the constraint in (133) entails (*inter alia*) that no question operator can cross another question operator: consequently, (133) bars *who* from crossing *what* in (131). In addition, the relevant movement also violates the Island Constraint (125), since interrogative clauses are islands.

Now consider why successive-cyclic (two-step) movement of *who* is barred in (132). At first sight, the ungrammaticality of (132) might seem to be attributable to the embedded clause ending up with two specifiers (an inner specifier *what*, and an outer specifier ~~who~~). However, Chomsky (2013) argues that there is no constraint in principle against structures having multiple specifiers – and indeed the analysis of coordinate structures like *Peter, Paul and Mary* presented in §3.4 presupposed that a head can have more than one specifier. A more plausible answer is that the derivation in (132) violates the Intervention Condition (133), since (133) bars *who* from crossing *what* in the course of movement (1) in (132).

A wide range of other constraints have been proposed on movement operations in research dating back more than half a century: I will briefly mention only a few of these here. One such is a condition on movement posited by Wexler and Culicover (1980: 119) which they term the **Freezing Principle**, and which can be outlined informally as follows (It should be noted that this is a different constraint from the Criterial Freezing Condition 130):

(134)   **Freezing Principle**
          The constituents of a moved phrase are frozen internally within (and so cannot be extracted out of) the moved phrase.

The Freezing Principle can be illustrated by examples like those below:

(135) (a)   *Which hotel* do you think he is staying **in**?
      (b)   **In** *which hotel* do you think he is staying?
      (c)   **Which hotel* do you think **in** he is staying?

In (135), the wh-phrase *which hotel* originates as the complement of the preposition *in*. In (135a), *which hotel* undergoes Wh-Movement on its own, stranding the preposition *in* at the end of the sentence. In (135b), the preposition *in* is pied-piped along with *which hotel*, so that the whole PP *in which hotel* undergoes Wh-Movement. Given the arguments presented in the previous section that long Wh-Movement is successive cyclic, the PP *in which hotel* will move first to the edge of the CP in the embedded clause before moving to the edge of the CP in the main clause in (135b). But this assumption raises the question of what would prevent us from moving the PP *in which hotel* to the front of the embedded clause CP, and then moving the wh-phrase *which hotel* on its own to the front of the main clause CP, leaving the preposition *in* stranded at the beginning of the embedded CP, as shown below:

(136)

[cp *which hotel* [c do] you think [cp ~~in which hotel~~ [c ø] he is staying ~~in which hotel~~]]

Why does the derivation in (136) crash and lead to the ungrammatical outcome in (135c)? The answer is that the movement shown by the upper arrow violates the Freezing Principle (134), because *which hotel* has been extracted out of a larger phrase (= the PP *in which hotel*) which has itself undergone movement, in that the PP *in which hotel* undergoes the Wh-Movement operation indicated by the lower arrow. (The more eagle-eyed of you will have noted that we also need to block another possible derivation for 135c on which the whole PP *in which hotel* moves in a successive-cyclic fashion to the front of the overall clause, with the QP *which hotel* being spelled out on the highest link of the chain, and the P *in* being spelled out on the intermediate link. I will assume that this is blocked by some constraint on discontinuous spellout – though I will not speculate on what this might be.)

A further constraint on movement operations (dating back to work by Cattell 1976, Cinque 1978 and Huang 1982) can be characterised informally as follows:

(137)   **Constraint on Extraction Domains/CED**
          Extraction is only possible out of a complement, not out of a specifier or adjunct.

CED can be illustrated in terms of the following contrasts:

(138) (a)   They published [pictures of *which footballer*]?
      (b)   *Which footballer* did they publish [pictures of - - -]?

(139) (a)   Pictures of *which politician* upset the voters?

(b)   **Which politician* did [pictures of - - -] upset the voters? (Nunes & Uriagereka 2000: 21)

(140) (a)   John met a lot of girls [without going to *which club*]?

(b)   **Which club* did John meet a lot of girls [without going to - - -] (Cattell 1976: 38)

The (a) examples in (138–140) are echo questions in which the italicised interrogative *which*-phrase remains in situ, while the corresponding (b) examples are their Wh-Movement counterparts. In (138b), the wh-phrase *which footballer* is extracted out of a bracketed nominal expression which is the complement of the verb *published* and yields a grammatical outcome because there is no violation of CED (extraction out of complements being permitted by CED). In (139b), the wh-phrase *which politician* is extracted out of a bracketed expression which is the specifier of a TP headed by a null copy of the inverted auxiliary *did*, and since CED blocks extraction out of specifiers, the resulting sentence is ungrammatical. In (140b), the wh-phrase *which club* is extracted out of a bracketed adjunct introduced by *without*, and since CED blocks extraction out of adjuncts, the sentence is ungrammatical. (A point to note in passing is that some speakers are more tolerant of CED violations than others: e.g. some speakers find extraction out of indefinite subjects in sentences like 139b not too bad: see Haegeman, Jiménez-Fernández and Radford 2014 for discussion.)

At first sight, the robustness of CED might appear to be called into question by sentences such as the following:

(141)   Which reports did he file without reading?

Here, the wh-phrase *which reports* is the complement of the verb *reading*, and thus Wh-Movement appears to extract *which reports* out of an adjunct introduced by *without*, in apparent violation of CED. Note, however, that there is an additional complication posed by (141) – namely that *which reports* is also interpreted as the complement of the verb *file*. In other words, there are two gaps in (141) associated with *which reports*, as shown informally below:

(142)   Which reports did he file - - - without reading - - -?

If we make the reasonable assumption that any constituent which undergoes movement can only be initially merged in one position (not in more than one), then it follows that *which reports* can only originate in one of the two gap positions in (142), not in both of them. But which of the two gap positions does *which reports* originate in? Since we see from the ungrammaticality of sentences like (140b) that no extraction is possible out of an adjunct, it cannot be that *which reports* originates as the complement of the verb *reading* in (142), because it would then have to be extracted (illicitly) out of a PP adjunct introduced by the preposition *without*, so wrongly predicting that (142) is ungrammatical. It therefore seems that *which reports* must originate as the complement of the verb *file* – an assumption made all the more plausible by the grammaticality of *Which reports did he file?* In other words, Wh-Movement in (142) involves the operation arrowed in the informal representation below:

(143)   *which reports* did he file ~~which reports~~ without reading ---?

However, this raises questions about the nature of the gap (- - -) at the end of the sentence (serving as the complement of the verb *reading*). As we have just seen, this gap cannot arise via movement (i.e. it cannot be a null copy of a moved constituent), since the Constraint on Extraction Domains (137) bars extraction out of adjuncts. Rather, the gap must be an empty category of some kind. But of what kind?

   Interestingly, we can have a pronoun like *them* in place of the gap – as we see from (144):

(144)   Which reports did he file without reading *them*?

This suggests that the gap in (143) may be a null proform of some kind (e.g. a null counterpart of *them*), directly merged in situ. However, the gap in (143) seems to be parasitic (i.e. dependent) on the presence of a trace copy of a moved constituent, since without movement no gap is possible:

(145)   *He sometimes files reports without reading - - -

Because the type of gap found in structures like (143) is parasitic on movement, it is referred to as a **parasitic gap**. It is widely assumed in the research literature that a parasitic gap inside an island must be licensed by the presence of a trace which is not itself inside an island. On this view, the parasitic gap inside the adjunct island introduced by *without* in (143) is licensed by the trace copy of *which reports* that functions as the complement of the verb *reading*, since this trace is not itself inside an island. There is much more to be said about the factors which license parasitic gaps, but I will not attempt to delve into them here, since my main concern in this section has been to show how constraints can disrupt movement operations like Wh-Movement.

6.10   Summary

   This chapter has been concerned with the syntax of wh-operator questions. In §6.2 we saw that root (i.e. main-clause) wh-operator questions are CPs with an interrogative operator in spec-CP which serves to type the relevant structure as an operator question. The interrogative operator originates in a position below C and is moved into its superficial spec-CP position by an operation traditionally called Wh-Movement. The requirement for CP to have an interrogative specifier in questions is motivated by the need for CP to be typed as interrogative in accordance with the following condition:

(3)   **Clause Typing Condition**

A CP is typed (i.e. interpreted in the semantic component) as being inter-rogative/exclamative/conditional/imperative (etc.) in type if it has an inter-rogative/exclamative/conditional/imperative (etc.) specifier. Otherwise, an indicative CP is interpreted as declarative in type by default

In §6.3, we looked at evidence that in a root question like *Who have they arrested?* the wh-interrogative pronoun *who* originates in comp-VP (as the complement of the verb *arrested*) but ends up in spec-CP (as the specifier of the inverted auxiliary in C) as a result of Wh-Movement. We saw that C in a root/main-clause wh-question triggers Auxiliary Inversion (attracting an aux-iliary in T to adjoin to C), whereas C in an embedded question does not. In §6.4 we looked at the feature composition of C in wh-questions. We saw that in wh-operator questions, C carries a Q-feature requiring it to have a question operator as its specifier. The Q-feature on C is satisfied by moving a question operator from a position below C into spec-CP, leaving behind a copy which has a null spellout in the PF component, but is interpreted as a variable in the semantic component. In addition, in root questions, C also carries a T-feature triggering movement of T to adjoin to C (i.e. Auxiliary Inversion). We looked at the syntax of multiple wh-questions, asking why the Q-feature on the root C can attract *who* in *Who might they consider to be responsible for what?* but not *what* in **What might they consider who to be responsible for?* (nor both *who* and *what*). We saw that the function of Wh-Movement in questions is to type a clause as interrogative in accordance with (3) by giving it an interrogative specifier, and that the most economical way of achieving this via movement is by moving a single wh-question operator to the front of the overall sentence and ensuring that the operator moved is the closest one, in conformity with the following principle:

(32)   **Economy Principle**

Structures and the operations used to form them should be as economical as possible.

We also saw that movement of *what* would be barred by the following constraint (which prevents *what* from crossing the intervening wh-operator *who*):

(36)   **Intervention Condition**

No constituent X can move from one position to another across an interven-ing constituent Y if X and Y are both sensitive to (the same kind of) intervention effects.

In §6.5 we looked at the syntax of wh-subject questions, and at why root wh-subject questions like *Who found it?* don't show DO-support/Auxiliary Inversion. I argued that (as in the case of other root wh-questions), C in such questions carries both a Q-feature and a T-feature. I noted that if both Wh-Movement and Auxiliary Inversion were to apply in root subject questions, this would give rise to violation of the following constraints:

(48)   **Edge Constraint**
         No more than one constituent can be extracted from the edge of any given
         projection.

(50)   **Path Containment Condition**
         If two paths overlap, one must contain the other.

I suggested that this outcome can be avoided if the requirements of both the Q-
and T-features on C can be satisfied by moving a wh-interrogative subject from
spec-TP to spec-CP, and if the T-feature on C works as specified in the generalisation below:

(52)   **T-Feature Generalisation**
         A T-feature on C attracts a constituent on the edge of TP to move to the edge
         of CP.

I suggested that the reason why the T-feature on C is able to attract the subject of a
tensed TP to raise from spec-TP to spec-CP is that the subject of a tensed T is
marked as tensed via the agreement operation below:

(55)   **Subject Agreement**
         When T agrees with its subject/specifier
         (i) the person/number features of the subject are copied onto the auxiliary/
              affix in T
         (ii) the tense feature on T is copied onto the subject.

Given (55), the Q- and T-features on C can then both be satisfied by C attracting a
subject which is interrogative and tensed to move to spec-CP (with the tense
feature on the subject being spelled out at PF as nominative case). In §6.6 we saw
that a moved wh-word sometimes pied-pipes additional material along with it
when it moves, in accordance with the following generalisation:

(67)   **Attraction Generalisation**
         When a head attracts a given type of item to become its specifier, it attracts
         the smallest accessible maximal projection containing the closest item of the
         relevant type.

In consequence of (67), a C with a Q-feature attracts the smallest accessible
maximal projection containing the closest question word to move to spec-
CP. In the case of preposition pied-piping in formal style structures like '*To
whom* was he talking?', pied-piping of the preposition *to* along with the
fronted wh-word *whom* is forced by the need to avoid violating the following constraint:

(78)   **Preposition Stranding Constraint/PSC**
         In some languages (and in formal styles of English), no preposition can be
         stranded at PF.

In §6.7, we looked at evidence that Wh-Movement is a copying operation which
involves first creating a copy of the moved wh-constituent, then merging the
newly created copy with the root of the structure, and then giving a null spellout

to all but the highest copy of the moved constituent at PF, in conformity with the following spellout condition:

(10)   **Default Spellout Rule**
         For a constituent whose spellout is not determined by some other rule or requirement, the highest copy of the constituent is pronounced at PF, and any lower copies are silent.

We saw that both theoretical and empirical considerations lend support to the conclusion that Wh-Movement is a copying operation. In §6.8, we examined the phenomenon of long(-distance) Wh-Movement whereby a wh-constituent which originates in a lower clause can cross one or more clause boundaries and end up at the front of a higher clause. We saw that both theoretical and empirical considerations lead to the conclusion that long Wh-Movement takes place in a successive-cyclic fashion, whereby a fronted wh-constituent moves first to spec-CP in the clause containing it, then to spec-CP in the next highest clause, and so on. Successive-cyclic movement (one clause at a time) is forced by a number of different constraints proposed in work dating back several decades, including the following:

(99)   **Subjacency Condition**
         No movement can cross more than one bounding node (where bounding nodes include S/TP).

(100)   **Impenetrability Condition**
         A constituent c-commanded by a complementiser C is impenetrable to (so cannot agree with, or be case-marked by, or be attracted by, etc.) any constituent c-commanding the CP headed by C.

(104)   **Relativised Minimality Condition/RMC**
         A constituent can only be affected by (e.g. be attracted by, or agree with or be case-marked by) the minimal (i.e. closest) constituent of the relevant type above it (i.e. c-commanding it).

Given the twin assumptions that Wh-Movement of a question operator is driven by a Q-feature on C and that Wh-Movement applies in a successive-cyclic (one-clause-at-a-time) fashion, it follows that the head C in each of the clauses through which a question operator moves must have a Q-feature of its own, enabling it to attract a (maximal projection containing a) question word to move to its specifier position. Since only bridge verbs allow Wh-Movement out of their complement, I concluded that C in a non-interrogative embedded clause can only have a Q-feature if it is the complement of a bridge verb. I suggested that C has the following feature composition in clauses involving movement of an interrogative operator:

(107)   **Feature Composition of C in operator questions**
         (i)   C carries an interrogative edge feature (= Q-feature/QF) in an operator-question clause.
         (ii) C can also carry a Q-feature in a non-interrogative embedded clause which is the complement of a bridge verb.
         (iii) In a finite root clause, if C has a Q-feature then C also has a T-feature.

In §6.9 we saw how constraints limit the way in which movement operations like Wh-Movement apply, and the types of structure they can produce. In addition to constraints already mentioned, we have seen in this chapter that a wide range of other constraints limit the application of operations like Wh-Movement, including the following:

(30)   **Attract Closest Condition/ACC**
        A head which attracts a given kind of constituent attracts the *closest* constituent of the relevant kind.

(61)   **Chain Uniformity Condition**
        All links/copies in a chain must be uniform.

(63)   **Constituency Condition**
        Heads and maximal projections are the only types of constituent which can take part in linguistic operations like movement, agreement or ellipsis.

(66)   **Attract Smallest Condition/ASC**
        A head which attracts a particular type of word attracts the smallest accessible constituent containing the relevant word.

(79)   **No Tampering Condition/NTC**
        No syntactic operation can tamper with (i.e. change) any part of a structure other than the root.

(125)   **Island Constraint**
        No gap inside an island can have an antecedent outside the island.

(130)   **Criterial Freezing Condition**
        A constituent which occupies its criterial position is frozen in place.

(134)   **Freezing Principle**
        The constituents of a moved phrase are frozen internally within (and so cannot be extracted out of) the moved phrase.

(137)   **Constraint on Extraction Domains/CED**
        Extraction is only possible out of a complement, not out of a specifier or adjunct.

In addition, we saw that filters/PF conditions such as the following impose constraints on the types of PF structures which are well-formed:

(19)   **Doubly Filled COMP Filter**
        At PF, the edge of a CP headed by an overt complementiser (like *that/for/if/whether*) cannot be doubly filled (i.e. cannot contain any other overt constituent).

(76)   **Affix Attachment Condition**
        An affix must be attached to an overt host of an appropriate kind at PF.

As noted in the main text, (19) seems to be parameterised in that it holds in standard varieties of English but not in some other varieties (e.g. Belfast English).

6.11   Bibliographical background

On the idea of clause typing in §6.2, see Cheng (1997). For a survey of different types of question, see Huddleston (1994). On the Doubly Filled COMP Filter of §6.3, see Chomsky and Lasnik (1977), Seppänen and Trotta (2000), Koopman (2000a), Koopman and Szabolsci (2000), Zwicky (2002), Collins (2007), Baltin (2010), Collins and Radford (2015). On Wh-Movement in rhetorical questions, see Sprouse (2007). On the syntax of wh-questions in Belfast English, see Henry (1995). The Earliness Principle derives from Pesetsky (1995). The idea in §6.4 that Wh-Movement is driven by an edge feature on C derives from Chomsky (2008); on the idea that C in wh-questions carries a Q-feature, see Cable (2007, 2008, 2010a, 2010b). The claim that movement operations like Wh-Movement involve an Internal Merge operation derives from Chomsky (1998): Citko (2005) argues for a further type of merge operation which she calls Parallel Merge and claims that this is found in coordinate structures like *I wonder what Gretel recommended and Hansel read.* The Attract Closest Condition was formulated by Richards (1997, 2001) but has its historical antecedents in Chomsky's Superiority Condition (1973) and Minimal Link Condition (1995) and is related to Chomsky's Defective Intervention Constraint (1998): for an alternative account of locality effects, see Hornstein (1995); for an experimental study of these, see Clifton, Fanselow and Frazier (2006). The analysis of root subject wh-questions presented in §6.5 is loosely based on Pesetsky and Torrego (2001): for further evidence that wh-subjects move to spec-CP, see Maekawa (2007: 68–71); for potential pitfalls in Pesetsky and Torrego's analysis of subject questions, see Nordlinger and Sadler (2004) and Radford (2007). Alternative accounts of root wh-subject questions which assume that wh-subjects remain in spec-TP (and don't move to spec-CP) can be found in George (1980), Chomsky (1986b), Radford (1997a), Agbayani (2000, 2006) and Adger (2003). On the syntax of expressions like *who the hell*, see Pesetsky (1987), Pesetsky and Torrego (2001) and den Dikken and Giannakidou (2002). The Path Containment Condition of Pesetsky (1982b) has its origins in a Crossing Constraint devised by Kuno and Robinson (1972). The convergence account of pied-piping presented in §6.6 is loosely based on Chomsky (1995). The claim that sentences like *Which was he driving car?* involve violation of the Chain Uniformity Condition derives from Chomsky (1995: 91): it should be noted, however, that numerous languages permit similar structures – for discussion, see Uriagereka (1988), Borsley and Jaworska (1998), Corver (1990), Franks and Progovac (1994), Zlatić (1997), Merchant (2001), Fanselow and Ćavar (2002), Davies and Dubinsky (2004) and Bošković (2004, 2005). On the Attract Smallest Condition, see Akiyama (2004). The text analysis of possessive *whose* derives from Chomsky (1995: 263): see Bernstein and Tortora (2005) for an alternative account. The idea that preposition pied-piping correlates with a constraint barring preposition stranding derives from Chomsky (1995: 264). For alternative accounts of preposition pied-piping and preposition stranding, see Ross (1967, 1986), Sells (1985),

Cowper (1987), Webelhuth (1992), Kayne (1994), Ginzburg and Sag (2000), Grimshaw (2000), Koopman (2000b), Koopman and Szabolcsi (2000), Sternefeld (2001), Abels (2003), Watanabe (2006), Almeida and Yoshida (2007), Boeckx (2007), Horvath (2006), Heck (2004, 2008, 2009), Cable (2007, 2008, 2010a, 2010b) and Coon (2009). The claim made in §6.7 that movement involves copying derives from Chomsky (1995); the idea that there is parametric variation with respect to which copies in a movement chain are overtly spelled out and which are deleted is developed in Bobaljik (1995), Brody (1995), Groat and O'Neil (1996), Pesetsky (1997, 1998), Richards (1997), Roberts (1997), Franks (1999), Runner (1998), Cormack and Smith (1999), Nunes (1999, 2001, 2004), Bošković (2001), Fanselow and Ćavar (2002), Bobaljik (2002), Landau (2006b) and Polinsky and Potsdam (2006). On the nature of preposition copying, see Radford, Felser and Boxell (2012). The idea that wh-in-situ structures may involve a form of Wh-Movement in which the initial copy at the foot of the movement chain is overtly spelled out is developed in Pesetsky (2000) and Reintges, LeSourd and Chung (2002, 2006): see Watanabe (2001) for a more general discussion of wh-in-situ structures. For more detailed discussion of sentences like *Which picture of himself wasn't he sure that Mary liked best?* see Belletti and Rizzi (1988), Uriagereka (1988), Lebeaux (1991), Fox (2000) and Barss (2001). The No Tampering Condition derives from Chomsky (2005, 2007, 2008, 2013) and has its historical antecedents in the Inclusiveness Condition of Chomsky (1995). Additional evidence in support of the claim in §6.8 that long-distance Wh-Movement applies in a local (one-clause-at-a-time) fashion comes from a variety of other phenomena, including spellout of multiple copies of a moved wh-expression in Frisian (Hiemstra 1986), Romani (McDaniel 1989), German (Felser 2004), Afrikaans (Hong 2005) and Punjabi (Yang 2006); stranding of material on the edge of intermediate CPs, including prepositions in Afrikaans (du Plessis 1977), and *else* in Child English sentences like *What do you want else to eat?* (Boecks 2007); partial Wh-Movement in German and a variety of languages (see, e.g., Cole 1982; McDaniel 1986; Saddy 1991; Cole and Hermon 2000; Bruening 2006); postverbal subjects in French (Kayne and Pollock 1978), Spanish (Torrego 1984) and Basque (Ortiz de Urbina 1989); wh-marking of complementisers in Irish (McCloskey 2001, 2002) and of subject pronouns in Ewe (Collins 1993); and exceptional accusative case-marking by a higher transitive verb of the wh-subject of a lower finite clause (reported for English by Kayne 1983: 5 and for Hungarian by Bejar and Massam 1999: 66). On the semantic properties of multiple wh-questions, see Dayal (2002); on how they are parsed, see Sprouse et al. (2011). Although in languages like English, only one wh-constituent can be fronted in a wh-question, it should be pointed out that there are languages like Bulgarian which allow multiple wh-fronting question structures which can be paraphrased in English as 'Who what to whom said?', posing potential problems for the economy-based account of why only one wh-constituent is fronted under Wh-Movement in English: see Rudin (1988), Bošković (2002a) and Krapova and Cinque (2008). The Subjacency Condition derives from Chomsky (1973), the Relativised Minimality Condition from Rizzi (1990) and the Impenetrability Condition from the Phase Impenetrability Condition of Chomsky (1998). In relation to constraints on Wh-Movement discussed in §6.9, see Ross (1967, 1986) on island constraints. On the Criterial Freezing Condition, see Rizzi (2006, 2010) and Rizzi and Shlonsky (2007). On the Intervention Condition, see Starke (2001), Rizzi (2004), Endo (2007), Friedmann, Belletti and Rizzi (2009) and Haegeman (2012). The Freezing Principle dates back to work by Wexler and Culicover (1980) and has since been argued to be reducible to a primitive locality condition (Müller 2010) or to principles of linearisation and spellout (Uriagereka 1999; Nunes and Uriagereka 2000; Sheehan 2013a,b), or to labelling principles (Rizzi 2012), or to processing constraints (Hofmeister 2012). For a range of empirical, theoretical and experimental perspectives on the Constraint on Extraction Domains/CED, see Nunes and Uriagereka (2000), Sabel (2002), Rackowski and Richards (2005), Stepanov (2001, 2007), Jurka (2010), Jurka et al. (2011), Chaves (2012, 2013), Sheehan (2013a,b), Sprouse et al. (2013). It should be noted that CED has been claimed to be problematic because there are languages which allow extraction out of subjects (Stepanov 2001, 2007) or out of certain types of adjunct (Starke 2001: 40, fn.10; Truswell 2007, 2009, 2011; Chaves 2012). On parasitic gaps, see Ross (1967), Taraldsen (1980), Engdahl (1983, 1985), Postal (1993, 1994), Culicover and Postal (2001) and Chaves (2012, 2013).

Workbook section

Exercise 6.1

Discuss the derivation of the wh-questions below, drawing tree diagrams to show their superficial structure and saying why they are grammatical or ungrammatical in standard varieties of English.

1 a. Which film have you seen?
  b. *Which have you seen film?

2 a. Who dare contradict him?
  b. Do you know what she has done?

3 a. Who have they spoken to?
  b. Who've they spoken to?
  c. To whom/?To who have they spoken?
  d. *To who've they spoken?

4 a. Which picture of who have you chosen?
  b. *Which picture of who've you chosen?
  c. Which picture have you chosen of who?
  d. *Who've you chosen which picture of?

5 a. What excuse has he given?
  b. *What has he given excuse?
  c. *What excuse he has given?
  d. *What he has given excuse?

6 a. How many hotels has he stayed in?
   b. *How many has he stayed in hotels?
   c. In how many hotels has he stayed?
   d. *In how many has he stayed hotels?

7 a. I can't remember who she met
   b. *I can't remember who that she met
   b. *I can't remember who if she met
   d. *I can't remember who did she meet

8 a. Whose car did he think had crashed into what?
   b. *Whose did he think car had crashed into what?
   c. *Who did he think's car had crashed into what?
   d. *What did he think whose car had crashed into?

9 a. He is wondering who has done what
   b. *He is wondering what who has done
   c. *Who is he wondering has done what?
   d. *What is he wondering who has done?

10 a. Which of the two dresses do you think (that) she will prefer?
    b. %Which do you think of the two dresses (that) she will prefer?

11 a. How did he say that she had behaved?
    b. *How did he whisper that she had behaved?

12 a. Where did you think that she had gone?
    b. *Where did you ask whether she had gone?
    c. *Where did you ask who had gone?

13 a. *Which car did the driver of cause the accident?
    b. *Who did they ask which picture of you took?

Having analysed why the structures in 1–13 above are (un)grammatical in standard varieties of English, next consider how to analyse the non-standard wh-question structures in 14–20 below. Say what is interesting about the relevant sentences, and discuss the derivation of the wh-question clause that each contains. In sentences where an embedded wh-clause is bracketed, analyse only the structure of the bracketed clause, not that of the main clause. Begin by analysing the syntax of the wh-clause in (14a) below and of that bracketed in (14b), both taken from official tax forms issued in the town where I live, asking for information about ethnic origin:

14 a. To which of these groups do you consider that you belong to?
    b. May we ask you to indicate [which of these ethnic groups that you belong to]?

In addition, analyse the syntax of the questions in the sentences in 15 below, which I recorded from live, unscripted radio and TV broadcasts:

15 a. What would've Fergie done? (= 'What would Sir Alex Ferguson have done?'; Dominic Cork, Talk Sport Radio)
    b. The question's got to be asked [that who would you want to be manager?] (Lee Dixon, BBC2 TV)
    c. You simply do not know [what side that they will select] (Brian Moore, Talk Sport Radio)

    d. I'm just wondering [why, at the end of the season, that Lerner gave McLeish the job] (Listener, phone-in, BBC Radio 5)

    e. On Man United, Evra and Suarez, should they shake hands? (Adrian Durham, Talk Sport Radio)

Then, analyse the syntax of the Shakespearean wh-questions in 16:

16 a. What sayst thou? (Olivia, *Twelfth Night*, III.iv)
    b. What dost thou say? (Othello, *Othello*, III.iii)
    c. What didst not like? (Othello, *Othello*, III.iii)

After that, discuss the syntax of the African American English question in 17 (from Green 1998: 98):

17. How she's doing? (= 'How is she doing?')

Next, discuss the syntax of the bracketed interrogative complement clauses in Belfast English in the sentences in 18 and 19 below (adapted from Henry 1995):

18 a. They wondered [which one that he chose]
    b. They wondered [which one did he choose]
    c. *They wondered [which one that did he choose]

19 a. They wondered [if/whether (*that) we had gone]
    b. They wondered [*if/*whether had we gone]

Subsequently, discuss the syntax of the wh-question in 20 below (reported by Thornton 1995 to have been produced by a young child):

20. Who will he think who the cat was chasing? (= 'Who will he think the cat was chasing?')

Then, discuss the following wh-question structures reported by Brown and Radford (2006) to have been produced by Korean children 8–11 years of age who were acquiring English as a second language (their counterparts in Native English are given in parentheses):

21. What weapons does Andy think it's very dangerous ('Which weapons does Andy think are very dangerous?')
22. Who Miss Scarlett saw somebody? ('Who did Miss Scarlett see?')
23. Which Reverend Green open a door? ('Which door did Reverend Green open?')
24. Why did Detective Andy didn't find the revolver? ('Why didn't Detective Andy find the revolver?')
25. Why Professor Plum went to Egypt? ('Why did Professor Plum go to Egypt?')
26. Why does Miss Scarlett is going to billiard room? ('Why is Miss Scarlett going to the billiard room?')

Helpful hints

In (the somewhat archaic sentence) 2a, assume that *dare* (when used as an auxiliary) is a **polarity item** (see §2.6), and so must be c-commanded by an interrogative (or negative or conditional) licenser. In 3, a prefixed question mark (?) indicates that the use of *who* in the relevant sentence (for speakers like me) leads to stylistic incongruity (in that the accusative form *whom* and preposition pied-piping occur in more formal styles and the accusative form *who* and preposition stranding in less formal styles). In 3 and 4, assume (for the purposes of this exercise) that *have* can cliticise onto a preceding word W in the PF component if W ends in a vowel or diphthong, if W c-commands *have* and if W immediately precedes *have*. In 4, take *which picture of who* to be a QP formed by merging the quantifier *which* with the NP *picture of who*, which is in turn formed by merging the N *picture* with the PP *of who*; in relation to 4c, bear in mind the discussion of split spellout in §6.7. In 6, take *how many* to be a compound quantifier which has the status of a single word (so could be written as *howmany*), and treat it as the head of the QP *howmany hotels*. In 7, assume that *can't* is an inherently negative auxiliary positioned in T. In 10, treat *which of the two dresses* as a QP formed by merging the Q *two* (i.e. the numeral quantifier *two*) with N *dresses* to form the QP *two dresses*, then merging this QP with D *the* to form the DP *the two dresses*, then merging this DP with P *of* to form the PP *of the two dresses* and finally merging this PP with Q *which* to form the QP *which of the two dresses*; in relation to 10b, note that the percentage sign in front of the sentence means that this type of structure is only acceptable to some speakers, and bear in mind the discussion of split spellout in §6.7. In 11, assume that *how* is an adverb which originates as the complement of the verb *behave*, and bear in mind the discussion of bridge verbs in the main text. In 12, bear in mind the possibility (discussed in §5.5) that yes–no questions may contain a null operator in spec-CP, and that this operator may induce intervention effects; take *where* to originate as the complement of *gone*. In 13, bear in mind the discussion of constraints on extraction in §6.9, and in the light of these consider what constraint/s will bar *which car* from being extracted out of the DP *the driver of which car* in 13a, and likewise what constraint/s will bar *who* from being extracted out of the QP *which picture of who* in 13b. In 14b, analyse only the syntax of the bracketed complement clause, not that of the main clause; take *these ethnic groups* to be a DP, but don't concern yourself with its internal structure. In 15a, consider the possibility that *have* can cliticise onto an immediately adjacent c-commanding finite auxiliary (by a head-to-head adjunction operation similar to that by which T adjoins to C in Auxiliary Inversion structures) and that this is a PF operation for most speakers, but that some can treat it as a syntactic operation. In 15b–e, consider what structure the bracketed clauses would have if each separate constituent in the periphery of a clause (i.e. each constituent to the left of the clause subject) is contained within a separate CP projection, with *that* and inverted auxiliaries in C, and other constituents in spec-CP (see the discussion of CP recursion in §5.4); consider also the possibility of taking the complementiser *that* to mark finiteness and subordination in structures like 15b–d and not declarative clause type; and in 15d, take *give McLeish the job* to be a VP, but don't concern yourself with its internal structure. In relation to 16a–c, bear in mind the discussion of DO-support in the model answer for exercise 5.2; for 16c, assume that *didst* has a null (second person singular) *pro* subject. In 20, bear in mind that the same child also produced *How much do you think how much the bad guy stole?* In relation to the sentences produced by the Korean learners in 21–26, treat names as DPs (or alternatively as NPs, since Korean has no D constituents – e.g. no definite article), but don't concern yourself with their internal structure. Note that Korean is a wh-in-situ language with head-final word order – as we see from the following example from Brown and Radford (2006: 11), where TOP denotes a topic particle, ACC an accusative case particle and Q a question particle:

(i) Ne-num   nwuku-lul   sarangha-ni
     You-TOP   who-ACC   love-Q
     'Who do you love?'

What if (because their native language doesn't have Wh-Movement and wh-operators are generated in situ in Korean), the learners initially assume that question operators in English are likewise directly generated in situ (i.e. in their superficial position)? And what if (because Korean doesn't have Auxiliary Inversion), some Korean learners make a similar assumption about inverted auxiliaries? Bear in mind that each of the various examples in 21–26 was produced by a different speaker.

Model answer for 1a

1a is derived as follows. The interrogative quantifier *which* is merged with the noun *film* to form the QP *which film*. This is merged with the (perfect participle) verb *seen* to form the VP *seen which film*. This VP is in turn merged with the (present) tense auxiliary *have* to form the T-bar *have seen which film*. The resulting T-bar is merged with the pronoun *you* to form the TP *you have seen which film*. This TP is merged with a null C constituent carrying a Q-feature in accordance with (107i) and a T-feature in accordance with (107iii), so forming the C-bar in (i) below:

(i)

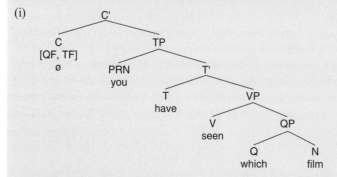

The T-feature on C attracts the present tense auxiliary *have* to move from T to C. In consequence of the Attraction Generalisation (67), the Q-feature on C attracts the smallest accessible maximal projection containing the closest question word to move to spec-CP. Since the closest question word to C (and indeed the only question word in the structure) is *which*, and the smallest maximal projection containing *which* is the QP *which film*, and since preposing this QP on its own does not violate any syntactic constraint, the QP *which film* moves to spec-CP. The structure which results after Head Movement and Wh-Movement have applied is that shown in simplified form below:

(ii)

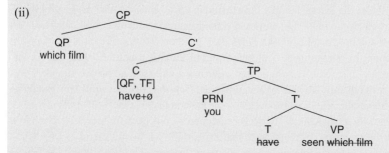

The resulting CP is typed as a wh-operator question by the Clause Typing Condition (3), by virtue of having the wh-interrogative operator phrase *which film* as its specifier. All but the highest copies of moved constituents are given a null spellout in the PF component in accordance with the Default Spellout Rule (10).

Exercise 6.2

Alongside the wh-operator questions discussed in the main text, in informal styles of English we find questions introduced by *how come*. Yoshio Endo and I administered an informal questionnaire to twenty university teachers from the UK, US, Canada, Australia and New Zealand, in which people were asked to rate sentences like those in 1 below on a 5-point acceptability scale (5/OK, 4/?, 3/??, 2/?* and 1/*):

1 a.   How come I fell in love with someone like you?
  b.   ?*How come that I fell in love with someone like you?
  c.   *How come did I fall in love with someone like you?

20/20 informants gave a high (4 or 5) acceptability rating to 1a, but only 1/20 gave a high rating to 1b, and likewise only 1/20 gave a high rating to 1c. The mean scores for each type of sentence were 4.9 for 1a, 2.0 for 1b and 1.3 for 1c (these scores being reflected in the star ratings in 1a–c). This suggests that most standard English speakers find sentences like 1a grammatical, but consider sentences like 1b and 1c ungrammatical. This exercise aims to get you to compare and evaluate different analyses of the syntax of *how come* questions for speakers who show the judgments in 1a–c. For the purpose of the exercise, consider the structure of the following sentence:

2.   How come the police have taken no action?

A number of analyses of such structures have been proposed in the research literature, but for present purposes I'll outline just three.

   One analysis (suggested by Zwicky and Zwicky 1971) is to take 2 to be an elliptical variant of a (biclausal) sentence like 3 below (where *come* has the archaic sense of 'happen'):

3.   How did it come that the police have taken no action?

In the PF component, the constituents marked by strikethrough in 4 below undergo deletion and thereby receive a null spellout:

4.   How ~~did it~~ come ~~that~~ the police have taken no action?

Let's call this the deletion analysis. The analysis gains potential plausibility from the observation that 3 is a reasonably close paraphrase of 1a.

   More recent analyses have treated *how come* sentences as monoclausal in present-day analysis. As we saw in §2.10, *how come* seems to function as a single word in present-day English (for many speakers, at least): hence I will write it as *howcome*. Collins (1991) argues that *howcome* functions as an interrogative complementiser, directly merged in the head C position of CP. Under Collins's *complementiser* analysis, 2 would have the structure shown in simplified form in 5 below:

5.

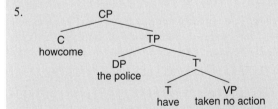

An alternative monoclausal analysis (proposed by Ochi 2004) is to treat *howcome* as directly merged in spec-CP, thereby typing the relevant clause as interrogative (by the Clause Typing Condition 3). Ochi does not say what kind of constituent *how come* is, but for the purpose of this exercise let's take it to be an adverb – as in 6 below:

6.

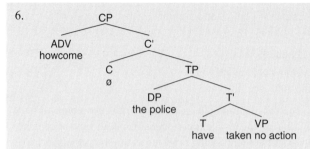

The sentences in 7–15 below illustrate a number of properties of *how come* questions which hold for most speakers of standard varieties of English. (N.B. They do not hold for all speakers in that you can Google examples of some of the structures treated as ungrammatical below: however, ignore this complication for the purposes of this exercise.) For each of the three analyses sketched above (the *deletion* analysis in 4, the *complementiser* analysis in 5 and the *adverb* analysis in 6), say whether or not it can account for the data below, and what problems if any arise.

7. How come/*comes/*came the police have taken no action?
8. How come you think the police have taken no action? (Can only mean 'What is the reason for your thinking the police have taken no action?' not 'What, in your view, is the reason for the police having taken no action')
9. ?*How come that the police have taken no action?
10. *How come have the police taken no action?
11. How/*However come the police have taken no action?
12. How (*the devil) come the police have taken no action?
13. *How, in your view, come the police have taken no action?
14. I have no idea [how come the police have taken no action]
15 a. I suspect the police have taken no action, and I want to know how come/why/for what reason
   b. *I suspect the police have taken no action, but I can't be sure whether/if

Overall, which of the three alternative analyses is best able to account for the full range of data?

Helpful hints

In relation to the possibility of treating *how come* as an interrogative adverb in 10, consider the suggestion made by Shlonsky and Soare (2011: 666) that '(English) subject-auxiliary inversion is triggered by interrogative operators linked to a syntactic variable (or trace)', and that *how come* is not an operator because it is directly merged in situ and so does not bind a trace/variable (i.e. it does not move from some position below C into spec-CP). In relation to a possible deletion analysis of sentences like 11–13, bear in mind that the following sentences are fine in English:

16 a. However did it come about that the police have taken no action?
   b. How the devil did it come about that the police have taken no action?
   c. How, in your view, did it come about that the police have taken no action?

In relation to a possible deletion analysis of 14, bear in mind that the following is ungrammatical:

17. *I have no idea [how did it come about that the police have taken no action]

In addition, treat the wh-clauses in 15 as involving a form of ellipsis referred to as Sluicing, and remind yourself of the conditions on Sluicing discussed in §2.9. For evalution purposes, you might want to bear in mind the Doubly Filled COMP Filter (19), and also the Root Complementiser Constraint of §4.7 which specifies that 'No overt complementiser can be the head of a root projection in a language like English.'

Model answer for 7 and 8

The data in 7 show that COME is invariable in *how come* questions and is always spelled out as *come*, not as, e.g., *comes* or *came*. This can be accounted for in a straightforward fashion under the deletion analysis in 4, since *come* is an infinitive form functioning as the head V of the VP complement of the auxiliary *did* (which takes an infinitival complement – as in 'He really **did** *come* back'). However, the same data can also be accounted for under the complementiser analysis in 5 or the adverb analysis in 6, if we suppose that *howcome* has been reanalysed as a single (invariable) word: because *howcome* is taken to be invariable, it follows that only the form *come* will occur. Consequently, all three of the suggested analyses can handle the data in 7.

The data in 8a show us that *howcome* can only be construed as modifying the *think* clause (i.e. as questioning the reason for the relevant thought), not as modifying the *taken* clause (i.e. not as questioning the reason for taking the relevant action): to use the relevant terminology, *howcome* can only have a *local* interpretation (as modifying the clause containing it), not a *long-distance* interpretation (as modifying a clause embedded in the one containing *how come*). The deletion analysis can account for this by positing that 8a derives from a structure like (i) below, where *how* originates in the position marked by the trace *t* and subsequently undergoes Wh-Movement and thereby comes to occupy the italicised spec-CP position at the front of the overall sentence

(i)   *How* ~~does it~~ come *t* ~~that~~ you think that the police have taken no action?

(A complication I will set aside is that such an analysis raises the question of why *how* could not originate lower in the relevant structure, e.g. in a position where it modifies the *taken* VP. A possible answer is that the clause following *howcome* is factive/presupposed to be true, and factive clauses are islands and hence block extraction, according to Oshima 2006.) The complementiser analysis accounts for the local interpretation of *how come* in a rather different way, namely by supposing that *howcome* is directly merged in situ in its criterial position as the head C of an interrogative CP, as in (ii) below:

(ii)   [$_{CP}$ [$_C$ *howcome*] you think that the police have taken no action]

Since it is directly merged in its criterial position, the Criterial Freezing Condition (130) means that *howcome* cannot undergo movement from a lower into a higher clause. Since *howcome* is contained (and, because of Criterial Freezing, must remain) in the *think*-clause, it follows that it will be interpreted as questioning the reason for the relevant thought. The adverb analysis offers a similar account, by supposing that *howcome* is directly merged in its criterial position in spec-CP, as in (iii) below:

(iii)   [$_{CP}$ *howcome* [$_C$ ø] you think that the police have taken no action]

As before, *howcome* is frozen in place by the Criterial Freezing Condition (123) and so can only be construed as modifying the clause containing it (i.e. the *think* clause).

7 A-bar Movement

7.1 Overview

The previous chapter focused on the syntax of Wh-Movement in interrogative clauses. In this chapter we will see that there are other types of clause which can be argued to involve Wh-Movement, including exclamative and relative clauses. In addition, we will look briefly at a number of other movement operations (including Neg-Movement, Deg-Movement, Top-Movement and Foc-Movement) which have in common with Wh-Movement that they move a constituent into spec-CP. We will see that these different kinds of movement operation are specific instances of a more general type of movement operation known as **A-bar Movement** (because it moves a constituent into an A-bar position like spec-CP – i.e. a position which is opaque/invisible to agreement and anaphor binding). This chapter also serves a second function of exposing you to alternative analyses that have been proposed for the syntax of relative clauses, and you'll become familiar with the ways in which analyses are refined in the light of new data, and with the kinds of argumentation which linguists use to evaluate alternative analyses. In the exercises, you'll have a chance to practise your analysis, argumentation and evaluation skills in relation to competing analyses of a range of types of relative clause.

7.2 Wh-exclamatives

In addition to wh-questions like those discussed in the previous chapter, English also has **wh-exclamatives** (i.e. wh-clauses used as exclamations). In the same way as wh-questions begin with an interrogative wh-word or wh-phrase, so too wh-exclamatives begin with an exclamative wh-word (like *how* in 1a below, or *what* in 1c) or an exclamative wh-phrase (like *how very strange* in 1b and *what big feet* in 1d):

(1) (a)   *How* he longed to see her again!
    (b)   *How very strange* her behaviour was!
    (c)   *What* I would give for a drink!
    (d)   *What big feet* you have!

Like their wh-question counterparts, wh-exclamatives can also serve as embedded clauses – as in the case of the clauses bracketed below:

(2) (a)   You wouldn't believe [*what a great time* we had]
    (b)   It's amazing [*how very fond of his grandmother* he is]

However, wh-exclamatives have a number of characteristic properties which differentiate them from wh-questions. Let's look at some of these.

One difference is that whereas a root/main-clause wh-question like (3a) below shows Auxiliary Inversion, a root wh-exclamative like (3b) does not:

(3) (a)   *How many dresses* does she have?
    (b)   *How many dresses* she has!

A further difference is that whereas a wh-constituent can remain in situ in a root wh-question like (4a) below, this is not possible in a root exclamative like (4b):

(4) (a)   He drives *what kind of car*?
    (b)   *He drives *what a fantastic car*!

A third difference is that exclamative words differ from their interrogative counterparts in respect of the range of expressions that they modify. For example, exclamative *what* can modify a nominal introduced by the indefinite article *a(n)* as in (5a) below, but interrogative *what* cannot be used in the same way (as we see from the ungrammaticality of 5b):

(5) (a)   *What a lovely dress* she was wearing!
    (b)   **What a lovely dress* was she wearing?

Similarly, exclamative *how* can be followed by a phrase in which an adverb modifies an adjective (as in 1b above/6a below, where *how* modifies the phrase *very strange*), but interrogative *how* cannot be used in the same way, as shown by the ungrammaticality of (6b):

(6) (a)   *How very strange* her behaviour was!
    (b)   **How very strange* was her behaviour?

A fourth difference is that an interrogative wh-constituent like that italicised in (7a) below can license the use of a polarity item like *ever*, whereas an exclamative wh-constituent cannot – as we see in (7b):

(7) (a)   *How many students* has he **ever** failed?
    (b)   **How many students* he has **ever** failed!

A fifth characteristic of wh-exclamative clauses is that (unlike wh-interrogatives) they are **factive** (i.e. their propositional content is presupposed to be factual/true). To see this, compare the question in (8a) below with the exclamation in (8b):

(8) (a)   *What stupid comments* (**if any**) did he make?
    (b)   *What stupid comments* (***if any**) he made!

The wh-interrogative (8a) leaves open the possibility that it may or may not be true that he made some stupid comments, and so *what stupid comments* can be qualified by *if any*. By contrast, the wh-exclamative in (8b) presupposes that he did indeed make some stupid comments, and hence adding *if any* (leaving open the possibility that he didn't) leads to semantic anomaly. Further evidence that exclamatives are indeed factive comes from the rather unusual structures in (9) (which I recorded from the radio), where the italicised exclamative clause is used as the complement of the noun *fact*:

(9) (a)   We all enjoy the **fact** *that how good a player he was* (Marcus Trescothick, Talk Sport Radio)

   (b)   You couldn't take away from the fact **that** *how important* this match is (John Murray, BBC Radio 5)

One consequence of this factivity property of exclamatives is that (when used as a complement clause), a wh-exclamative clause can only be used as the complement of a factive predicate (i.e. a predicate like KNOW whose complement is presupposed to be true), not as the complement of a non-factive predicate like THINK:

(10)   I know/*think [*what a huge struggle* he had with syntax]

Overall, then, there are significant syntactic, semantic and lexical differences between wh-exclamatives and wh-interrogatives.

   However, the issue that I will focus on here is the syntax of wh-exclamative clauses. In this connection, consider the derivation of the exclamative clauses below:

(11) (a)   *How many cakes* he ate!
   (b)   *What a mess* he has made!

Let's begin by looking at the constituent structure of the exclamative wh-phrase *how many cakes*. There are a number of possibilities to consider, but I'll discuss only three here. One is that *how* and *many* function as the heads of separate projections, with the degree adverb *how* heading an ADVP (or perhaps DEGP/ degree phrase) projection as in (12a) below, and the quantifier *many* heading a QP projection. Another possibility is that *how* serves as the specifier of a QP headed by the quantifier *many*, as in (12b). And a third possibility is that *how* is adjoined to *many* to form a compound quantifier which serves as the head Q of a QP projection as in (12c):

(12)

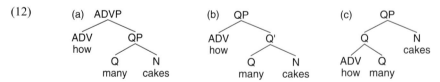

Of the three, the structure in (12a) seems the least likely, since it claims that the resulting phrase is adverbial in nature, when in actual fact it is a plural nominal – as we see from plural agreement with *were* in a sentence like *How many cakes there were on the table!* The analyses in (12b) and (12c) both account for its status as a plural nominal, since both claim that the ultimate head of the phrase is the plural nominal quantifier *many*. The compound quantifier analysis in (12c) is lent some cross-linguistic plausibility by the observation that some languages have a single word corresponding to English *how many* (e.g. French *combien* and Spanish *cuantos*). Furthermore, there is orthographic evidence (i.e. evidence based on writing) supporting a single-word analysis, since some people write *how many* as a single word, both in interrogative use (as in 13a,b below) and in exclamative use (as in 13c,d):

(13) (a) *Howmany* odin marks do you have? (forums.marvelheroes)

(b) In *howmany* possible ways can 4 customers lineup at the registers? (algebra .com)

(c) Boy, *howmany* situations in life that applies to! (ragan.com)

(d) *Howmany* times they would wonder what someone looked like by just listening to their voices (books.google.co.uk)

Moreover, phonological evidence supporting the putative single-word status of *how many* comes from the observation that it can be pronounced with a single stress on *how* and with the first vowel in *many* sometimes being truncated, as in [háumni]. Nevertheless, the relevant orthographic and phonological evidence is not overwhelming, since it could equally be that *how* and *many* function as separate words in the syntax, but can be fused together as a single word in the phonology when immediately adjacent.

Some evidence in support of the view that *how* and *many* do indeed function as separate words in the syntax comes from the fact that another word such as *very* can intrude between the two, as in the internet-sourced examples below:

(14) (a) Isn't is astonishing *how very many of us* (#Endosisters & #Hystersisters) are out there? (Aunt Jo on Twitter)

(b) But *how very many things* there are which we have forgotten! (John Wilkinson, Sermons,1835)

(c) *How very many layers* we operate on, and *how very many influences* we receive from our minds, our bodies, our histories, our families, our cities, our souls and our lunches! (Elizabeth Gilbert, *Eat, Pray, Love: One Woman's Search for Everything*, Google Books, 2007: 51)

Any suggestion that *how very many* could be a single word is further undermined by co-ordinate structures like:

(15)   How very many friends and very many contacts he has!

where *how* modifies both *very many friends* and *very many contacts*, suggesting that *how* is a separate constituent from *very many friends/contacts*. Nevertheless, things are by no means straightforward, since it is not obvious where *very* would be accommodated in an analysis like (12b). For this reason, I shall keep an open mind on whether (12b) or (12c) is a more appropriate analysis of *how many* (or indeed whether we need to propose a further alternative analysis).

Similar uncertainty surrounds the structure of the exclamative wh-phrase *what a mess* in (11b). One possibility is that *what* heads a QP projection and the indefinite article *a* heads a separate ARTP/article phrase projection, as in (16a) below; another is that *what* serves as the specifier of an ARTP projection headed by *a* as in (16b); and a third is that *what* and *a* form a single word, written as *whatta* in (16c):

(16)

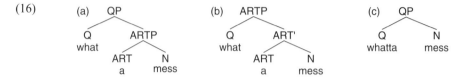

A property that needs to be accounted for is that *what a . . .* phrases are singular in number. Under the analysis in (16a), this can be accommodated by supposing that *what* agrees in number with its complement so that *what* is singular when it has an *a*-phrase complement (as in *what a mess*), but plural when it has a plural complement (as in *what fantasies*). Under the analysis in (16b), the singular number property of *what a . . .* phrases would follow from taking the singular article *a* to be the head of the overall ARTP structure. Likewise in (16c), we can account for the singular number property of the phrase if we suppose that *whatta* is a singular exclamative quantifier which (like the indefinite article *a*) requires a nominal complement containing a singular count noun (such as *mess* in 11b).

Some plausibility might appear to be lent to the single word analysis in (16c) by the fact that exclamative *what a* is written in colloquial English as *whatta* (as in the song *Whatta man!* made popular by Salt 'n' Pepa) or *whadda* (as in the restaurant *Whadda Pizza!* in Danville Pennsylvania). However, this could be accounted for equally well under the analysis in (16a) or (16b) by supposing that *a* can cliticise onto *what* in the PF component, resulting in a syntactic structure like (16a) or (16b) being mapped into a PF structure in which *what+a* functions as a compound head. Moreover, evidence that *what* and *a* can function as separate words in the syntax comes from coordinate structures like:

(17)   **What** *a fool* and *a loser* he is!

In (17), exclamative *what* seems to modify both *a fool* and *a loser*, and the single-word analysis in (16c) provides no straightforward way of accounting for this; by contrast, both the QP analysis in (16a) and the ARTP analysis in (16b) are compatible with data like (17). Once again, however, I shall remain open as to what the best analysis of structures like *what a mess* is. For the purpose of analysing the syntax of the wh-exclamatives in (11), I shall treat *how many cakes* and *what a mess* as QPs and set aside the issue of their precise internal structure (although this is an issue which I will touch on again shortly).

Having looked briefly at the internal structure of wh-exclamative phrases like *how many cakes* and *what a mess*, let's now turn to look at their external syntax (i.e. at the position which they occupy within the sentence containing them). Consider, for example, the syntax of the sentence (11b) *What a mess he has made!* It seems clear that the exclamative phrase *what a mess* originates as the complement of the verb *made*, since MAKE is a transitive verb which requires a nominal or pronominal complement (as we see from the ungrammaticality of **He has made*). Let us therefore suppose that *what a mess* originates in comp-VP, as the complement of the VP headed by the verb *made* – i.e. in the same position as is occupied by the italicised *such*-phrase in

(18)   He has made *such a mess*!

Let us further suppose that the exclamative phrase *what a mess* subsequently undergoes movement to some position to the left of the subject *he*. Since CP is the projection positioned above the TP containing the subject *he*, a plausible assumption is that *what a mess* undergoes Wh-Movement and thereby moves from comp-VP to spec-CP in the manner shown by the arrow below:

(19)

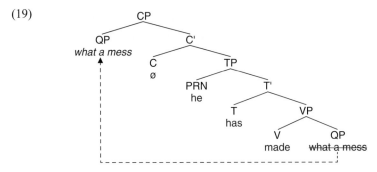

It follows from Copy Theory that the moved QP *what a mess* will leave behind a copy of itself when it moves, and this will be given a silent spellout in the PF component (marked by strikethrough in (19)). The assumption that the moved QP *what a mess* ends up in spec-CP will account for how the clause comes to be interpreted as exclamative, given the **Clause Typing Condition** introduced in §4.7 and repeated below:

(20)   **Clause Typing Condition**
          A CP is typed (i.e. interpreted in the semantic component) as being interrogative/exclamative/conditional/imperative (etc.) in type if it has an interrogative/exclamative/conditional/imperative (etc.) specifier. Otherwise, an indicative CP is interpreted as declarative in type by default.

It follows from (20) that the CP in (19) will be typed as an exclamative clause by virtue of having the exclamative phrase *what a mess* as its specifier. The factive nature of exclamative clauses can in turn be captured by supposing that the head C of an exclamative CP carries a factivity feature of some kind.

    The assumption that wh-exclamatives involve Wh-Movement raises the question of what triggers movement of the exclamative wh-constituent *what a mess* to the edge of CP in structures like (19). An answer consistent with the analysis of wh-questions presented in the previous chapter is to suppose that the head C of an exclamative CP carries an exclamative edge feature which requires C to be given an exclamative specifier – either via Merge, or via Movement. However, unlike root wh-questions, root wh-exclamatives do not trigger Auxiliary Inversion, as noted in relation to the contrast in (3) above. Why should this be? In the light of the discussion of Auxiliary Inversion in §5.3 and §6.8, the conditions licensing Inversion can be outlined informally as follows:

(21)   **Inversion Licensing Conditions**
        A null C in a finite clause is licensed to carry a T-feature triggering Auxiliary Inversion
        (i)   in any clause where C has an edge feature requiring it to have a negative or degree or conditional specifier
        or
        (ii) in a root clause where C has an edge feature requiring it to have an interrogative specifier.

It follows from (21) that neither root nor embedded exclamative clauses will carry a T-feature, and hence exclamatives won't trigger Auxiliary Inversion.
    In relation to (11b) *What a mess he has made!* this means that when C is introduced into the derivation, it will not carry a T-feature but will carry an exclamative edge feature (abbreviated to XF in tree diagrams, to save space), as in (22) below:

(22)

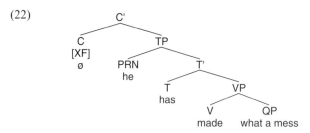

The exclamative feature [XF] on C requires C to have an exclamative specifier. Since the structure contains the exclamative word *what*, one way of satisfying the requirement for C to have an exclamative specifier would seemingly be to move exclamative *what* to spec-CP. However, as we see from (23) below, *what* cannot move on its own, but rather has to pied-pipe the string *a mess* along with it:

(23) (a)   *What a mess* he has made!
     (b)   **What* he has made a mess!

Why do we have to move the whole wh-phrase *what a mess* rather than just the wh-word *what*? Recall that in §6.6, it was suggested that movement to a specifier position obeys the following condition (extrapolated from other conditions):

(24)   **Attraction Generalisation**
        When a head attracts a given type of item to become its specifier, it attracts the smallest accessible maximal projection containing the closest item of the relevant type.

In the light of the generalisation in (24), consider which of the three alternative analyses of the phrase *what a mess* sketched in (16) above and repeated as (25) below will best account for the contrast in (23):

(25)

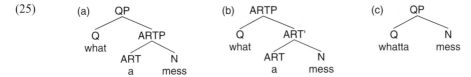

Under the analysis in (25a), *what* is the head Q of QP and thus is a head/ minimal projection, not a maximal projection; the smallest maximal projection containing *what* in (25a) is the QP *what a mess*, and thus the analysis in (25a) correctly predicts that only the whole phrase *what a mess* can be fronted. Much the same can be said about (25c), where *whatta* is a head/ minimal projection, and the smallest maximal projection containing *whatta* is the whole QP *whatta mess*. By contrast, the analysis in (25b) seems potentially problematic: here, *what* is a maximal projection by virtue of the fact that its mother is an ARTP constituent which is not a projection of *what* (since ARTP is a projection of the indefinite article *a*). Since *what* is a maximal projection in (25b), it follows from the generalisation in (24) that we would expect *what* to undergo Wh-Movement on its own; and yet the ungrammaticality of (23b) shows that this is not the case. Of course, we could reconcile the analysis in (25b) with the ungrammaticality of (23b) if there were some constraint which prevents the specifier of an indefinite article from being extracted on its own. However, the generality of any such constraint would seem to be called into question by sentences such as the following (sourced from from radio and TV broadcasts or the internet):

(26) (a)   Let's find out *how good* you are [- - - a driver]   (Jeremy Clarkson, BBC2 TV)

(b)   I'm surprised at *how hostile* she's had [- - - a reaction]   (Interviewee, BBC Radio 5)

(c)   *How big* is this [- - - an opportunity] for him?   (Mike Graham, Talk Sport Radio)

(d)   *How important* is this [- - - a consideration]?   (SpiderMonkeyTales.blogspot)

(e)   I can imagine *how sad* it was [- - - a nursing home]   (havealaughonme.com)

In these examples the italicised *how*-phrase originates in the gap (- - -) position as the specifier of the indefinite article *a*, and is subsequently extracted out of the bracketed nominal containing it, suggesting that there is no absolute constraint against extracting the specifier of an indefinite article. So, it's not clear that the analysis in (25b) provides a principled way of accounting for the ungrammaticality of (23b). Since we earlier saw that the analysis in (25c) is also problematic in that it can't handle sentences like (17), it would seem that (25a) is the most plausible analysis of an exclamative phrase like *what a mess*. (A complication to note in passing is that some speakers do not readily accept structures like 26, and indeed even for speakers like me who do, there are severe restrictions on the productivity of the type of structure in 26, as we see from the ungrammaticality of *'*How old* did you buy [- - - a house]'?).

Our discussion in this section has been designed to show that Wh-Movement is an operation which is found not only in wh-questions, but also in wh-exclamatives, albeit with the difference that (in consequence of the Inversion Licensing Conditions in 21) wh-questions trigger Auxiliary Inversion in root/main clauses, but wh-exclamatives do not. However, before closing I will note that there are a number of details concerning the syntax of wh-exclamatives which I have set aside here. These include why they are more resistant to preposition pied-piping than wh-questions, as observed by Emonds (1985) and discussed in Obenauer (1994): cf.

(27) (a)   With how many languages is she familiar?
      (b)   ?*With how many languages she is familiar!

Other issues not dealt with here include why wh-exclamatives are more resistant to long-distance Wh-Movement than wh-questions, what kinds of wh-word can occur in root and embedded exclamative clauses, how to deal with phrasal wh-exclamatives like *What a goal!*, how to deal with infinitival exclamatives like *What a lousy time to quit!* and how to deal with wh-less exclamatives like *Boy, is it hot!* Rather than delve into these questions (some of which you can examine in exercise 7.1), I will instead turn to look at the syntax of relative clauses in the next section, since these provide another potential source of Wh-Movement.

7.3   Relative clauses

There are traditionally said to be three types of relative clause – **restrictive relatives**, **appositive relatives** and **free relatives**. Typical restrictive relative clauses include those bracketed below:

(28) (a)   I only work with *people* [**who** I can trust]
      (b)   This is *something* [**which** you have to take seriously]
      (c)   There are *places* [**where** they sell counterfeit watches]
      (d)   They lived in *times* [**when** money was tight]
      (e)   There are *reasons* [**why** he kept quiet]

Restrictive relative clauses like those bracketed above typically serve to modify a nominal or pronominal antecedent (italicised in 28), and the relative clause usually immediately follows its antecedent. Such relatives are termed restrictive because they restrict the class of entities referred to by the antecedent to those which have the property described in the relative clause (e.g. the class of people referred to in 28a is restricted to those I can trust). As we see from the examples in (28), restrictive relatives can be introduced by a relative pronoun like *who/which/where/when/why*: for convenience, I'll use the term **wh-relatives** to denote relative clauses which contain an overt relative wh-pronoun.

Alongside wh-relatives like those in (28), we also find **wh-less relatives** like the restrictive relative clauses bracketed in (29) below, which are introduced by a complementiser but do not contain an overt relative wh-pronoun:

(29) (a)   He never listens to *things* [**that** I say]
(b)   I don't have *anyone* [**that** I can rely on]
(c)   There is *nothing* [**for** me to do]
(d)   There is *nobody* [**for** me to talk to]

There are several reasons to think that the items *that/for* are complementisers (and not relative pronouns) in relative clauses like those bracketed in (29). For one thing, they are homophonous with the complementisers *that* and *for* found in complement clauses like those bracketed below, and (unlike relative pronouns such as *who/which/where/when/why*) do not begin with *wh*:

(30) (a)   You know [**that** I love you]
(b)   He's anxious [**for** me to say nothing]

Moreover, the two sets of bold-printed items in (29,30) have the same grammatical properties: e.g. *that* requires a nominative subject like *I* in both relative and comple-ment clauses, and *for* requires an accusative subject like *me* in both types of clause. Furthermore, relative *that/for* differ from relative pronouns in that they are morpho-logically invariable: for example, they don't inflect for case (unlike the relative pronoun *who/whom/whose*), nor are they specified for animacy (in the sense that *that/for* can be used both with animate antecedents like *anyone/nobody* and with inanimates like *things/nothing*, whereas the relative pronoun *who* is used with human antecedents, and *which* with inanimate antecedents). In addition, the relative com-plementisers *that/for* are syntactically distinct from relative pronouns like *who/which* in that they don't allow preposition pied-piping – as we see from contrasts such as:

(31) (a)   There is nobody [*on* **whom** I can rely]
(b)   *There is nobody [*on* **that** I can rely]

(32) (a)   There's nothing [*about* **which** to complain]
(b)   *There's nothing [*about* **for** me to complain]

Instead, as we see from (29b,d) relative *that/for* requires preposition stranding in structures where the object of a preposition is relativized. Thus, the phonological, morphological and syntactic properties of relative *that/for* make it clear that they are complementisers, not relative pronouns.

So far, we have seen that there are some relative clauses introduced by a relative pronoun, and others introduced by a complementiser. However, there are also relative clauses like those bracketed below which contain neither an overt relative pronoun nor an overt complementiser:

(33) (a)   Mary is *someone* [he really cares about]
(b)   This is *something* [not to be taken lightly]

Relative clauses like those bracketed in (33a,b) are sometimes termed **zero relatives** because they contain no overt relative pronoun or overt complementiser in the clause periphery (i.e. on the edge of CP). Another term used for them is **contact relatives**, because there is direct contact between the antecedent and the first overt constituent below the head C of the relative clause CP, in the sense that *he* immediately follows the antecedent *someone* in (33a), and *not* immediately follows the antecedent *something* in (33b). In terms of the classification introduced earlier, contact/zero relatives are wh-less relatives, in the sense that they contain no overt relative wh-pronoun.

Although there is no overt evidence of any CP projection in contact/zero relatives, there are good reasons to take them to be CPs headed by a null complementiser. For one thing, this would allow us to attain a uniform analysis under which all relative clauses are CPs, in conformity with the following principle introduced in §4.7:

(34)   **Structural Uniformity Principle**
        All constituents of the same type belong to the same category.

Moreover, a CP analysis of relative clauses would be consistent with the account of case-marking given in §4.9, under which subjects are case-marked by complementisers. On this view, the bracketed relative clause in (33a) will be a CP headed by a null intransitive finite complementiser which assigns nominative case to the subject *he*; likewise, the bracketed relative clause in (33b) will be a CP headed by a null intransitive infinitival complementiser which assigns null case to the PRO subject of the relative clause.

Although I will not go into these here, I note in passing that there are puzzling restrictions on the use of contact relatives. For example, it it ungrammatical to omit *that* in a restrictive relative clause like the one bracketed in (35a) below or in the second (italicised) restrictive relative clause bracketed in (35b):

(35) (a)   The police stopped a car [that/*ø was speeding]
     (b)   The police stopped a car [that/ø they caught speeding] [*that/*ø they sus-*
            pected of being used in an armed robbery]

(35a) shows that a contact relative cannot generally be used to relativise a subject (although there are well-studied exceptions that I won't go into here); (35b) shows that when relative clauses are stacked (i.e. when more than one relative clause is used to modify an antecedent), only the one closest to the antecedent can be a contact clause.

Having briefly looked at restrictive relative clauses in English, let's now turn to look at appositive relative clauses like those italicised below:

(36) (a)   John (*who used to live in Cambridge*) is a very good friend of mine
     (b)   Yesterday I met my bank manager, *who was in an uncompromising mood*
     (c)   Mary has left home – *which is very upsetting for her parents*

Appositives generally serve as 'parenthetical comments' or 'afterthoughts' set off in a separate intonation group from the rest of the sentence in the spoken language (this being marked by parentheses in 36a, by a comma in 36b and by a hyphen in 36c). Unlike restrictives, appositives can be used to qualify unmodified proper nouns (i.e. proper nouns like *John* which are not modified by a determiner like *the*, as in 36a) and can also have a clausal antecedent (e.g. *which* has as its antecedent the clause *Mary has left home* in 36c). Moreover, only wh-relatives can function as appositives, as we see in relation to the parenthesised appositive relative clauses below:

(37) (a)   John (*who you met last week*) is a good friend of mine
     (b)   *John (*that you met last week*) is a good friend of mine
     (c)   *John (*you met last week*) is a good friend of mine

Thus, appositive relative clauses like those italicised in (37) must be wh-clauses introduced by a relative wh-word like *who* (as in 37a) and cannot be wh-less clauses introduced by an overt complementiser like *that* (as in 37b) or by a null complementiser (as in 37c).

A further difference between appositive and restrictive relatives is that only a restrictive relative clause can be used to modify a nominal quantified by a universal quantifier like *any/every* – as illustrated below:

(38) (a)   **Any/Every plane** *that has a problem* must be grounded
     (b)   ***Any/*Every plane**, *which has a problem*, must be grounded

Accordingly, use of a restrictive *that*-clause is fine in (38a), but use of an appositive *which*-clause leads to ungrammaticality in (38b).

Having looked at differences between restrictive and appositive relatives, let's now turn to look at a third type of relative clause, known as free relative clauses (but sometimes also termed **headless relative clauses** – where 'headless' means 'antecedentless'). Examples of free relative clauses include the structures bracketed below:

(39) (a)   [**What** he did] was amazing
     (b)   I don't like [**how** he treats her]
     (c)   You can have [**whatever** you want]
     (d)   [**Wherever** I lay my hat] that's my home (lyrics to a song by Marvin Gaye/ Paul Young)

At first sight, free relative structures like those bracketed in (39) might appear to be simple wh-clauses (i.e. CPs containing a wh-constituent in spec-CP). However, they function more like nominals than clauses: for example *what he did* in (39a) is paraphraseable as a NOMINAL+RELATIVE CLAUSE structure like 'the thing that he did', *how he treats her* in (39b) as 'the way that he treats her', *whatever you want* in (39c) as 'any thing that you want' and *wherever I lay my hat* in (39d) as 'any place where I lay my hat'. Thus, the challenge posed by free relatives is how to account for the observation that they are used in much the same way as relative clauses with nominal antecedents, even though they don't have any overt nominal antecedent. I note in passing that there are lexical differences between the set of wh-words found in free relatives and that found in restrictives or appositives: e.g. *what, how* and *wh+ever* words can occur in free relative clauses, but not in appositives or restrictives (in standard varieties of English); and conversely *which* can serve as a restrictive or appositive relative pronoun but not as a free relative pronoun.

Having looked briefly at the various types of relative clause found in English, in §§7.4–7.9 below, I'll explore the syntax of restrictive relative clauses (leaving you to evaluate alternative analyses of other types of relative clause in the exercises).

7.4   A Wh-Movement account of restrictive relatives

In this section, we'll take a closer look at wh-restrictives (i.e. restrictive relative clauses containing a relative pronoun like *who/which*). I'll begin by sketching a traditional analysis of these dating back to work in the 1960s. Transposing this into the framework used here, let us suppose that restrictive relativization involves adjoining a relative clause CP to an NP to form an even larger NP, and let's further suppose that the relative clause contains a relative operator/pronoun which undergoes Wh-Movement to spec-CP (in the same way as interrogative and exclamative wh-constituents move to spec-CP). For succinctness, let's call this the Wh-Movement analysis of restrictive relatives.

To see how the Wh-Movement analysis works, consider how it would handle relativisation in a DP like that italicised below:

(40)   *The photos of you which he has taken* are really nice

Let's suppose that the DP *the photos of you which he has taken* is derived as follows. The verb *taken* merges with the relative pronoun *which* to form the VP *taken which*. This VP is then merged with the T auxiliary *has* to form a T-bar constituent which in turn is merged with the pronoun *he* to form the TP *he has taken which*. The resulting TP is then merged with a null complementiser *ø* to form the C-bar *ø he has taken which*. The null complementiser attracts the wh-pronoun *which* to become its specifier, forming the CP *which ø he has taken which*. This CP is then adjoined to the noun phrase *photos of you* (formed independently by merging the noun *photos* with the PP *of you*) to form the even larger noun phrase *photos of you which ø he has taken ~~which~~*. This NP is in turn merged with the determiner *the* to form the DP below:

(41)

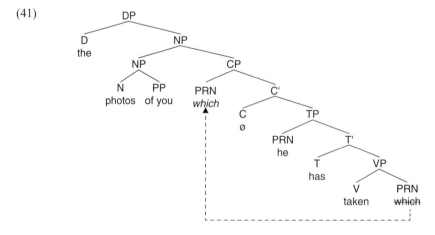

Let us suppose that the head C of the relative clause CP carries an edge feature (more specifically an R-feature/relative feature) which requires C to have a relative specifier, and so triggers movement of a relative pronoun to spec-CP. Given the Clause Typing Condition (20), the CP in (41) will be typed as a relative clause by virtue of having the relative pronoun *which* as its specifier.

An issue which arises from the assumption made in (41) that relative clauses are adjoined to their antecedents is how the PF component 'knows' that the relative clause has to be spelled out at PF as *following* rather than *preceding* its antecedent, since our brief discussion of word order in §3.8 discussed the relative ordering of heads, complements and specifiers but did not deal with adjuncts. It may be that the positioning of relative clauses *after* their antecedents is a reflex of a more general linearization rule to the effect the complex modifers follow the expressions they modify in English: thus, for example, we say 'a *proud* **woman**' in English, where the simple modifier *proud* precedes the noun *woman*, but 'a **woman** *proud of her son*' where the complex modifier *proud of her son* follows the noun *woman*. However, I will not attempt to explore the issue of the linearization of adjuncts any further here.

Interestingly, the head C position of CP must be null in a wh-relative structure like (41), since if C were filled by *that* the outcome would be ungrammatical – as we see from (42):

(42)   *The photos of you [*which that* he has taken] are really nice

Why should this be? The answer is that a *wh+that* string like that in (42) violates a constraint which was formulated in §6.3 in the following terms:

(43)   **Doubly Filled COMP Filter**
            At PF, the edge of a CP headed by an overt complementiser (like *that/for/if/ whether*) cannot be doubly filled (i.e. cannot contain any other overt constituent).

It follows that the head C position of the CP in (41) cannot be filled by *that* as this would mean that the edge of the relevant CP violates (43) because it would contain two overt constituents, namely the complementiser *that* and its specifier *which*.

The Wh-Movement analysis outlined in (41) can account for a number of characteristic properties of restrictive relatives. One of these is that restrictive relative clauses can be recursively **stacked** (in the sense that more than one restrictive clause can be used to modify a given nominal), as illustrated by the DP italicised in (44) below:

(44)   *The photos of you which I took which you liked* are on the mantlepiece

Here, the antecedent NP *photos of you* is modified by two different restrictive relative clauses (*which I took* and *which you liked*). This multiple modification can be accounted for in a straightforward fashion if relative clauses are adjoined to their antecedents, since adjunction can be recursive. Thus, the DP italicised in (44) involves first adjoining the relative clause *which I took* to the NP *photos of you* to form the larger NP *photos of you which I took*. Subsequently, the second relative clause *which you liked* is adjoined to the NP *photos of you which I took* to form the yet larger NP *photos of you which I took which you liked*. Merging the determiner *the* with this NP forms the structure shown in simplified form below (where subscripts are added purely for ease of identification):

(45)

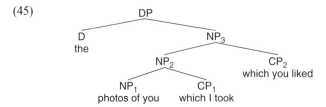

As (45) shows, NP$_1$ is projected into a larger nominal constituent (NP$_2$) by adjoining CP$_1$ to it, and NP$_2$ is in turn projected into an even larger nominal constituent (NP$_3$) by adjoining CP$_2$ to it. Each of the two relative clause CPs in (45) involves a Wh-Movement operation like that arrowed in (41) above, moving *which* to the front of the relative clause CP containing it.

A second property of relative clauses which can be accounted for under the Wh-Movement analysis is that the antecedent and the relative pronoun can differ in the morphological case that they carry – as can be illustrated by a structure such as the following (where ø is a null complementiser, and numeral subscripts are added to C and CP constituents purely for identification purposes):

(46)   [$_{CP1}$ [$_{C1}$ ø] the man [$_{CP2}$ whom [$_{C2}$ ø] they have arrested] is a suspected spy]

Under the account of case assignment given in §4.9, the determiner *the* and the antecedent noun *man* will be assigned (invisible) nominative case by the null main-clause complementiser C$_1$ which c-commands them. By contrast, the relative pronoun *whom* carries accusative case by virtue of originating as the direct object complement of the transitive verb *arrested*. Since the antecedent and relative pronoun are two entirely distinct constituents under the Wh-Movement analysis, it is only to be expected that they will differ in case if (as in 46) they occupy different kinds of position within the clauses containing them. In a language like Polish with a richer case morphology, the potentially distinct cases assigned to the relative pronoun and its antecedent are directly visible – as the following example from Borsley (1997: 635) illustrates (where the subscript 1SG denotes a first person singular form, and the subscripts ACC/NOM denote accusative/nominative forms):

(47)   Widziałem   tego   pana,   który   zbił   ci   szybę
          saw$_{1SG}$ the$_{ACC}$ man$_{ACC}$ who$_{NOM}$ broke   your   glass
          'I saw the man who broke your glass'

In (47), the antecedent noun *pana* is accusative (as is the determiner *tego*$_{the}$ modifying it), but the relative pronoun *który*$_{who}$ is nominative – precisely as would be expected under a Wh-Movement analysis in which the two are independent constituents.

A further piece of evidence in support of the Wh-Movement analysis of restrictive relatives sketched in (41) comes from so-called **reconstruction** effects (i.e. effects whereby a nominal is interpreted at the semantics interface in the position in which it originates rather than the position in which it ends up). The effects we are concerned with here relate to Principle C of Binding Theory (briefly touched on in exercise 3.2), which governs the interpretation of R-expressions (i.e. referential noun expressions like *John* or *the president*). In the light of assumptions made in the Copy Theory of Movement, this principle can be formulated as follows:

(48)   **Principle C of Binding Theory**
           No (copy of an) R-expression can be coreferential to any (copy of a) constituent c-commanding it.

We can illustrate how Principle C works in terms of the following example:

(49)   Which photo of John does he hate?

In (49), *John* and *he* cannot be corefererential; on the contrary, *he* must denote someone other than *John*. Why should this be? Under the Copy Theory of Movement, the interrogative phrase *which photo of John* originates as the complement of the verb *hate* and leaves a copy behind when it undergoes Wh-Movement so that (49) has the superficial syntactic structure shown in simplified form below:

(50)

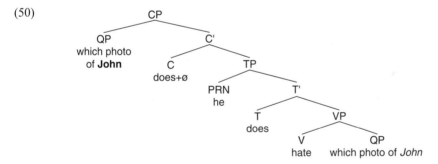

At the end of the syntactic derivation, the structure in (50) is handed over to the phonological and semantic components for further processing. The semantic component (*inter alia*) determines what can or can't refer to what and can 'see' all copies of moved constituents. Since the lower (italicised) copy of *John* is c-commanded by *he*, Principle C determines that *John* cannot be coreferential to *he*. (The lower copy of the wh-phrase *which photo of John* and the lower copy of the inverted auxiliary *does* are ultimately given a silent spellout in the phonological component.)

But now consider the relative clause structure below:

(51)   This is the photo of John which he hates

Given the assumptions made in this section, the DP *the photo of John which he hates* in (51) will have the superficial syntactic structure shown in (52) below (where *John* is taken to be a DP headed by a null D which is not shown here, and *Af* denotes a present tense affix which lowers onto the verb *hate* in the PF component, resulting in the verb ultimately being given the PF spellout *hates*):

(52)

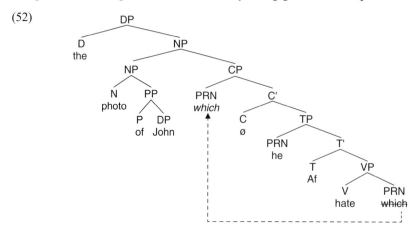

Since there is only one occurrence of *John* in this structure, and that occurrence of *John* is not c-commanded by *he*, it follows that Principle C (48) does not prevent *John* and *he* from being construed as coreferential. (Nor does Principle B either, which specifies that a non-anaphoric pronoun like *he* cannot be bound by any c-commanding clausemate constituent: the conditions for Principle B to apply are not met here because *John* and *he* are not clausemates and *John* does not c-command *he*.) Thus, the Wh-Movement analysis can account for the absence of Condition C reconstruction effects in wh-relatives.

Given the arguments presented here that wh-restrictives involve Wh-Movement, and given the evidence presented in Chapters 5 and 6 that movement is a copying operation, an important question to ask is whether there is any evidence for taking Wh-Movement in wh-restrictives to be a copying operation. The answer is that evidence in support of this view comes from the phenomenon of wh-copying found in relative clauses like those bracketed below:

(53) (a) It's a world record [**which** many of us thought *which* wasn't on the books at all] (Steve Cram, BBC2 TV)

(b) There are many others [**who** I am sure *who* can chip in] (c9v-forum.com)

(c) I will start with 8 reasons [**why** I think *why* William and Mary and the surrounding area is a wonderful place] (physicsgre.com)

(d) This is an area [**where** I think *where* shortsightedness could really come back and bite us in the ass, but it would happen in any society] (meta-rhetoric.com)

In the examples in (53), the bold-printed relative pronoun originates in the clause which is the complement of *think/thought/sure* and then (via Wh-Movement) moves first to the italicised spec-CP position in the complement clause, and then to the bold-printed spec-CP position in the relative clause. Both copies of the wh-pronoun in spec-CP are spelled out overtly (one at the beginning of the relative clause, another at the beginning of the complement clause), providing evidence that Wh-Movement applies in a successive-cyclic fashion. (Of course, a question which this assumption raises in its wake is why two copies of the wh-pronoun are spelled out overtly when economy and efficiency considerations dictate that only the highest copy should normally be spelled out overtly. The answer may well be that sentences like 53 are the result of a processing error, perhaps arising when speakers forget that the CP containing the italicised relative pronoun isn't the beginning of the relative clause.)

The general conclusion which our discussion in this section leads us to is that a Wh-Movement analysis of wh-restrictives can provide a principled account of a number of properties of wh-restrictives. However, this raises the question of how to deal with wh-less restrictives (i.e. restrictive relatives which do not contain an overt relative pronoun). One answer is to treat wh-less restrictives as covert wh-relatives. What this means is that in the same way as wh-restrictives involve movement of an overt wh-operator to spec-CP, so too wh-less restrictives are treated as involving movement of a covert/null/silent/unpronounced wh-operator to spec-CP. To see how such an analysis might work, consider the derivation of a sentence like (54) below:

(54)   The guests that she has invited have turned up

This will have the derivation shown in simplified form in (55) below under the null operator analysis (if we use Op_{REL} to denote a null relative operator, and if we categorise *guests* as an NP on the grounds that it is a maximal projection – as we see from the fact that it is replaceable by an NP like *friends of yours*):

(55)

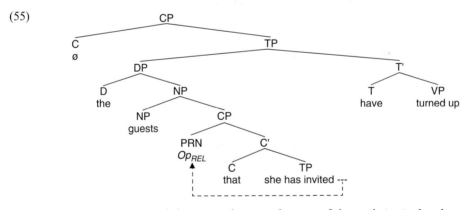

The null relative operator originates as the complement of the verb *invited* and subsequently moves (via the arrowed Wh-Movement operation) to become the specifier of the relative clause CP, with movement of the operator being driven by an R-feature on C. If the operator is a pronoun specified for case (in the same way as an overt relative pronoun like *who*), it will be assigned accusative case in its initial (gap) position by the transitive verb *invited*. By contrast, the determiner *the* and the noun *guests* will be assigned nominative case by the null finite complementiser which c-commands them (at the top of the tree), under the account of nominative case assignment in §4.9.

One implementation of the null operator analysis is to suppose that some overt relative pronouns (including *who, which, where, when* and *why*) have null variants that are used in the same contexts as their overt counterparts, whereas others have no null counterpart. The dictionary entry for individual relative pronouns will specify whether or not they have an overt and/or silent spellout in a given use. For example, the dictionary entry for the relative pronoun WHO might specify that it is spelled out as *whose* if genitive, *whom* if accusative (in formal styles) and *who/ø* otherwise. This assumption would mean that the null operator in a structure like (55) is a silent counterpart of the default form *who*.

An interesting piece of potential evidence in support of analysing wh-less relatives as involving movement of a silent wh-operator comes from non-standard varieties of English which use *what* in place of *that* in relative clauses, as illustrated by the examples in (56) below (from Berizzi and Rossi 2010; see their paper for sources):

(56) (a)   He is the man **what** looks after the cows

(b)   I think at one time we used to get eh thirty shillings for every baby **what** we had

(c)   And they used to move that belt every day in that track **what** you'd took the coal from, yeah

Berizzi and Rossi argue that *what* in this use is a complementiser and that it is only used in finite relative clauses. But why should the complementiser be spelled out as *what* when the normal spellout for a complementiser in a finite indicative clause is *that*? Under the null wh-operator movement analysis in (55), the complementiser *that* will carry an R-feature attracting a relative wh-pronoun to become its specifier. A plausible assumption, therefore, is that the complementiser *that* (in the relevant dialects) is spelled out as its wh-marked counterpart *what* when it carries an R-feature (i.e. in a relative clause). Wh-marking of the complementiser *that* (resulting in it being spelled out as *what*) thus provides further evidence in support of analysing *that*-relatives as involving movement of a relative wh-pronoun driven by an edge feature on C: this edge feature has a silent spellout in standard varieties of English, but can have an overt spellout (allowing *that* to be spelled out as *what*) in some non-standard varieties.

A very different kind of evidence in support of a Wh-Movement analysis of wh-less restrictives comes from (internet-sourced) sentences such as the following:

(57) (a)   Here are some pics of some sisters [**that** I am sure *who* have been rocking them for years] (supahwomanadayinthelifeof.blogspot.com)

(b)   And this is something [**that** I think *which* exists in various parts of the world] (pbs.org)

Here, the null relative operator originates in the clause which is the complement of *sure/think*, then moves to the spec-CP position at the front of the complement clause and subsequently moves to the spec-CP position at the front of the bracketed relative clause. The fact that the operator is overtly spelled out as *who/which* at the beginning of the complement clause provides evidence that the clause does indeed involve movement of a relative operator. (Indeed, it could further be said to provide evidence that the moved operator is actually the item *who/which* itself and that this item can receive a null spellout at PF.)

As should be obvious, the null operator analysis of *that*-restrictives can be extended to zero/contact restrictives (i.e. restrictives which contain neither an overt relative pronoun nor an overt complementiser) in a straightforward fashion. On this view, a sentence like the following would have the same derivation as in (55) above, save that the head C constituent of CP would be null rather than filled by *that*:

(58)   The guests she has invited have turned up

If wh-less restrictives do indeed involve Wh-Movement of a null operator, we can arrive at a unitary analysis of restrictive relatives under which both wh-restrictives and wh-less restrictives involve Wh-Movement of an (overt or null) wh-operator. However, this does not mean that null and overt operator relatives can always be used interchangeably. Sometimes there are differences between the two, as illustrated by the DPs italicised below:

(59) (a)   *The man whose car they have seized* is walking home
     (b)   **The man that's car they have seized* is walking home

In order to try and understand what's going on here, consider the derivation of the DP in (59a,b). Prior to Wh-Movement, these DPs will have the structure below, if we adopt Chomsky's (1995: 263) analysis of possessive DPs sketched in §6.6:

(60)

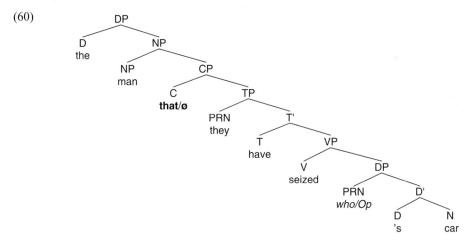

The bold-printed complementiser will carry an R-feature which attracts an (italicised) overt/null relative pronoun to move to spec-CP. As we saw in §6.6, *who* cannot move on its own, because this will leave possessive *'s* stranded without an overt possessor host, in violation of the following condition posited in §6.6:

(61)   **Affix Attachment Condition/AAC**
An affix must be attached to an overt host of an appropriate kind at PF.

However, if the whole DP *who's car* moves to spec-CP, the possessive affix can attach to the possessor *who* and so will not be stranded, and the resulting DP *the man whose car they have seized* is well-formed. By contrast, use of a null operator in place of *who* cannot yield a grammatical outcome. Movement of the null operator on its own will leave possessive *'s* stranded, in violation of AAC; but movement of the whole DP *Op + 's + car* (where *Op* is a null relative operator) will also leave possessive *'s* without the overt possessor host that it requires, again violating AAC. Thus, although overt and null operator relatives have parallel derivations, this does not mean that both of them always yield a convergent/grammatical outcome.

In this section, I have argued that restrictive relative clauses can be analysed as CPs adjoined to the NPs that they modify, with the relative clause CP showing movement of an overt or null relative operator to spec-CP. However, as we will see in the next section, the Wh-Movement analysis is not without posing problems.

7.5   Problems with the Wh-Movement analysis

Although (as we saw in the previous section) a Wh-Movement analysis can provide a unitary account of the syntax of both wh-restrictives and their wh-less counterparts, there are certain types of restrictive relative structure which it seems unable to handle. In this section, we'll look at three of these.

One type of structure which poses problems for the Wh-Movement analysis of wh-restrictives concerns relativisation of **idiom chunk** nouns – i.e. nouns which are part of an idiom chunk like '**make** *headway*', '**keep** *track*' and '**pay** *heed*'. In such idiom chunks, the italicised noun (in its idiomatic use) must originate as the complement of the bold-printed verb. Interestingly, however, these idiom chunk nouns can be relativized in structures like those below:

(62) (a)   The *headway* [which they have made] is impressive
(b)   The careful *track* [that she's keeping of her expenses] is commendable
(c)   The scant *heed* [he paid to my proposal] was scandalous

The problem posed by sentences like (62) for the Wh-Movement analysis of wh-restrictives is the following. If *which* is a relative pronoun that originates as the complement of the verb *made* and from there moves to the edge of the relative clause CP, the DP *the headway which they have made* in (62a) will have the structure shown in simplified form below:

(63)   [DP [D the] [NP [N headway] [CP *which* [C ø] they have made ~~which~~]]] is impressive

However, (63) does not satisfy the constraint that the idiomatic noun *headway* must initially be merged as the complement of the verb MAKE, since the noun

headway in (63) originates outside the relative clause CP, and the initial complement of the verb MAKE is the relative pronoun *which*. How can we deal with the
problem posed for the Wh-Movement analysis by the relativisation of idiom
chunk nouns in sentences like (62)?

One answer is to adopt a **matching** account and suppose that a matching copy
of the antecedent noun *headway* serves as the complement of *which*. On this view,
which is a relative determiner which merges with the noun *headway* in (62a) to
form the DP *which headway*. This DP subsequently moves to the edge of a
relative clause CP, and this CP is adjoined to another copy of the noun *headway*,
so deriving the structure shown below (with items marked by strikethrough
subsequently being deleted in the PF component):

(64)   [DP [D the] [NP [N **headway**] [CP *which* ~~headway~~ [C ø] they have made ~~which~~
            ~~headway~~]]]

It will then be the case that the lowest copy of the noun *headway* originates as the
complement of the verb *made*, as required.

However, the matching analysis is potentially problematic, for five reasons.
Firstly, the highest (bold-printed) copy of the noun *headway* (in the antecedent
position) does not function as the complement of the verb *made*, but rather as the
subject of *is impressive* in (62a), so violating the requirement that the noun *headway*
must originate as the complement of the verb MAKE. Secondly, it requires us to posit
an ad hoc deletion operation to ensure that the occurrence of the noun *headway*
inside the relative clause is obligatorily deleted. If we suppose that the copy of
headway following *which* is deleted because it matches (i.e. is identical to) its
antecedent and so is redundant, we face a third problem – namely that the two
don't match in case: the bold-printed antecedent is nominative in (62a) because it is
(part of) the subject of the finite *is*-clause, whereas the null copy of *headway*
following *which* is accusative because it originated as the complement of the
transitive verb *made*.

Furthermore, if the matching analysis were generalised to all relative clauses,
we'd face a fourth problem, which can be illustrated in relation to a DP like:

(65)   The portrait of Diana whose frame was damaged

If (as the matching analysis claims) the relative clause contains a copy of the
antecedent NP *portrait of Diana*, and if possessive DPs have the structure outlined in §6.6, the relative DP *whose frame* will have a structure like that below
(with the NP *portrait of Diana* given a null spellout at PF):

(66)

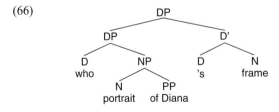

However, such an analysis requires us to assume that *who* is a determiner which allows an inanimate NP like *portrait of Diana* as its complement – even though *who* is an animate pronoun which never normally allows any NP complement (cf. *'You can choose **who** portrait you like best').

A fifth problem is that it is hard to see how the matching analysis could be made to work for sentences like those below (after Alexiadou et al. 2000) in which a relative pronoun like *who* has more than one antecedent:

(67) (a)   The police eventually released the *man* and the **woman** [who were arrested]
   (b)   John saw a *man* and Mary saw a **woman** [who were wanted by the police]

It's simply not obvious what the complement of *who* would be under the matching analysis in such multiple antecedent cases.

Having seen that relativised idiom chunk nouns pose problems for the Wh-Movement analysis (and that the matching analysis designed to patch it up is also problematic), let's now look at another type of structure which is equally problematic for a Wh-Movement account. In this connection, consider relativisation of the noun *way* in the following (internet-sourced) examples:

(68) (a)   And of course you can see this impacting on the **way** *which* people behave (hitchensdebates.blogspot.com)
   (b)   How can I alter the **way** *which* the Digi TS16 assembles serial data . . .? (digi .com)
   (c)   I would certainly agree that the **way** *which* she behaved and escalated it was plain wrong . . .(cyclechat.net)
   (d)   The inquest is normally the **way** *which* the state carries this out . . . (inquest .org.uk)
   (e)   But there were several angry calls from the public gallery about the cuts and the **way** *which* the late changes were proposed (bbc.co.uk)
   (f)   But Abassi also criticised the **way** *which* the media had focused on the local Muslim community in its reporting of the Rigby killing (aljazeera.com)

In this use, the noun *way* describes the manner in which something happens. What is puzzling, however, is that if we replace the noun *way* by the noun *manner*, it becomes obligatory for the relative pronoun *which* to be used with the preposition *in*: cf.

(69)   The **manner** *(in)* *which* she behaved was appalling

So why can the preposition *in* be omitted if we use the noun *way*, but not if we use the noun *manner*?

The answer lies in the PP Hypothesis outlined in §4.11, under which certain nouns can be used adverbially, and in this adverbial use they are PPs headed by a preposition which can be given a null spellout. The noun *way* is one such noun which can be used adverbially (as we see from the Comunards' song *Don't leave me this way*) but the noun *manner* is not (cf. *Don't leave me this manner*). In the light of this observation, consider how we handle the contrast between *the*

way which people behave in (68a) and **the manner which people behave.*
Under the Wh-Movement analysis, the pronoun *which* would serve as the object
of the manner preposition *in* (cf. *the way/manner in which people behave*). The
PP *in which* would originate as the complement of *behave* and from there move
to the front of the relative clause, so deriving the structure shown in simplified
form below:

(70)   [DP the way/manner [CP *in which* people behave - - -]]

But now the problem we face is determining whether or not the preposition *in* can
be given a null spellout. As we saw in our earlier discussion of *Don't leave me this*
*way/*manner*, the preposition can have a null spellout if its complement includes
the noun *way*, but not if it includes the noun *manner*. Under the Wh-Movement
analysis in (70), however, the object of the preposition is simply the relative
pronoun *which*, and since the preposition can only 'see' constituents inside its
own PP, it has no way of knowing whether the antecedent of *which* is *way* or
manner. How can we overcome this problem?

    The matching analysis provides us with a possible solution, if we suppose that
the fronted wh-PP contains a copy of the relativized noun. This will mean that in
place of the structure in (70) above, we will have the syntactic structures in (71a,
b) below:

(71) (a)   [DP the way [CP *in which way* people behave - - -]]
      (b)   [DP the manner [CP *in which manner* people behave - - -]]

We can then say that *in* can be deleted in (71a) because the fronted PP contains the
noun *way*, but not in (71b) because the fronted PP contains the noun *manner*. In
addition, the italicised occurrence of the noun *way/manner* inside the relative
clause will also be deleted at PF. But although a matching analysis can be made to
work mechanically, it poses numerous problems. For one thing it is uneconomical
in requiring us to posit that the underlying structure contains two occurrences of
the antecedent, when the superficial structure of the sentence contains only one.
Moreover, the operation deleting the copy of the antecedent inside the relative
clause is essentially ad hoc (i.e. unprincipled and unprecedented). In addition, the
matching analysis faces other problems alluded to in our earlier discussion of
relativizing idiom chunk nouns.

    Let's now move on to look at a third type of structure which poses
problems for the Wh-Movement analysis of restrictive relatives, arising
from sentences like:

(72)   The *photos of himself* [which Jim has taken - - -] are really nice

Under the Wh-Movement analysis outlined here, the DP *the photos of himself*
which Jim has taken would have the derivation in (73) below (where *Jim* is taken
to be a DP headed by a null determiner, in accordance with the DP Hypothesis of
§4.11):

(73)

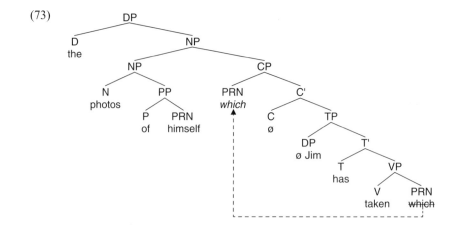

However, the problem posed by such a derivation is that it fails to provide us with a principled account of how the reflexive anaphor *himself* comes to be interpreted as bound by the DP containing *Jim*. Let us suppose that anaphors are subject to the following binding requirement:

(74)   **Principle A of Binding Theory (Anaphor Binding Principle)**
        An anaphor can only be bound by a given antecedent if (some copy of) the
        anaphor is locally c-commanded by (some copy of) the antecedent.

The problem posed by the structure in (73) is that the *Jim*-DP does not c-command (and is not contained in the closest TP containing) the anaphor *himself*. So, it would seem that Wh-Movement analysis can't handle sentences like (72) in any straight-forward fashion.

Having argued that there are a number of types of restrictive relative clause structure which the Wh-Movement analysis doesn't provide a straightforward account of, in the next section I turn to consider an alternative analysis of restrictive relatives which overcomes these problems.

7.6   An Antecedent Raising account of restrictive relatives

In this section, I'll present an alternative account of the syntax of restrictive relative clauses, loosely based on an **Antecedent Raising** analysis developed by Donati and Cecchetto (2011). I'll simplify the account in this section in certain ways for expository purposes, before refining and revising it in subsequent sections. I'll begin by looking at wh-less restrictives, before going on to consider how the analysis can be extended to wh-restrictives.

As a starting point for discussion, consider the structure of the wh-less restrictive relative clause bracketed below:

(75)   The cuts [(that) we are facing] are severe

Here, the noun *cuts* is relativized (i.e. modified by a relative clause) and serves a dual role – one *internal* to the bracketed relative clause and the other *external* to it. Its internal role is to serve as the complement of the verb *facing*, as in 'We are facing *cuts*.' Its external role is to serve as (part of) the subject of the matrix clause (i.e. of the clause containing the relative clause), as in 'The *cuts* are severe.' Any account of the syntax of restrictive relative clauses needs to be able to account for the dual role played by the relativized constituent in restrictive relatives. But how?

Closer inspection of the internal structure of the bracketed relative clause in (75) reveals that there is a **gap** (i.e. null/empty constituent) in the relative clause after the verb *facing*, marked by - - - below:

(76)   The cuts [(*that*) we are facing - - -] are severe

It is interesting to note that the gap (- - -) in (76) occurs precisely where the relativised noun *cuts* would have occurred in the corresponding non-relative clause 'We are facing *cuts*.' This raises the possibility that the noun *cuts* originates as the complement of the verb *facing* and from there moves to the superficial position which it occupies in front of the complementiser *that*.

A specific implementation of this idea (to be revised in the next section) is the following. Let us suppose that the noun *cuts* is initially merged as the complement of the verb *facing*, forming the VP *facing cuts*. This VP is then merged with the T auxiliary *are* to form a T-bar constituent *are facing cuts* which in turn is merged with the pronoun *we* to form the TP *we are facing cuts*. The resulting TP is then merged with the complementiser *that* to form the CP *that we are facing cuts*. The noun *cuts* is subsequently moved out of the *that*-clause, and **remerged** with the *that*-clause as the head N of the NP *cuts that we are facing* ~~cuts~~. This NP is then merged with the determiner *the* to form the DP shown below:

(77)

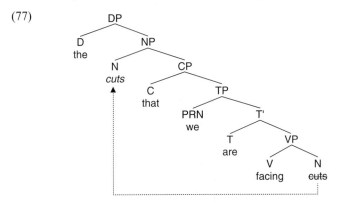

Since (77) supposes that the antecedent of the relative clause originates inside the relative clause and subsequently moves to a position outside it, we can refer to this kind of analysis in general terms as involving Antecedent Raising. Given that the raised antecedent in (77) is a noun (= *cuts*) which raises to become the head N of a new NP, the specific kind of movement operation arrowed in (77) can be termed **Head Raising**. It should be noted that Head Raising represents a different kind of movement operation from the Head Movement operation outlined in Chapter 5. This is because Head Raising in relative clauses involves the raised noun remerging with the CP out of which it is raised to form an NP (whereas the Head Movement operation described in Chapter 5 involves a lower head adjoining to a higher head, e.g. T adjoining to C in questions with Auxiliary Inversion to form a complex C constituent). A DP like *the cuts [we are facing]* would have the same derivation as (77), except that the head C position of CP is filled by a null counterpart of the complementiser *that*.

A specific claim embodied in the derivation in (77) is that the determiner *the* c-commands the relative clause and all its constituents. Empirical support for this claim comes from sentences such as the following:

(78)   No cuts [that anyone has proposed] are going to be acceptable to the unions

Under the Head Raising analysis, the phrase *no cuts that anyone has proposed* in (78) will be a QP headed by the negative quantifier *no*, and will have the derivation shown below:

(79)

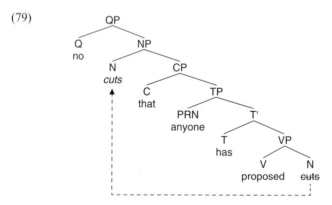

Note that the relative clause CP in (79) contains the polarity item *anyone*. In §3.7, we saw that the Polarity Licensing Condition requires a polarity item to be c-commanded by an appropriate (e.g. negative, interrogative or conditional) licenser. This condition is satisfied in (79), because the pronoun *anyone* falls within the c-command domain of the negative quantifier *no* (in that the mother of Q *no* is QP, and QP contains *anyone*).

A further claim embodied in the analysis in (79) is that the relative *that*-clause CP forms a separate constituent from its antecedent *cuts* in the superficial structure of the sentence. Evidence that this is so comes from the observation that a relative clause CP can undergo Ellipsis in a sentence such as (80a) below (adapted from Collins 2015: 1), where the italicised constituent *one girl* can be interpreted as synonymous with the italicised phrase *one girl that I know* in (80b):

(80) (a)   At the party, I saw three boys that I know, and *one girl*
     (b)   At the party, I saw three boys that I know, and *one girl that I know*

On the interpretation italicised in (80b), the string *one girl* in (80a) has the structure shown in simplified form in (81) below, if we take *one* to be a (numeral) quantifier:

(81)

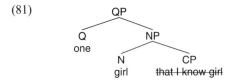

The CP marked by strikethrough undergoes Ellipsis in the PF component. The observation that it is possible for the relative clause CP in (81) to undergo Ellipsis in turn provides evidence that the relative clause CP forms an independent constituent from its antecedent – precisely as claimed by the Head Raising analysis in (79). (I note in passing that *one girl* in 80a can also have a second interpretation on which it is not modified by a deleted relative clause, but this is irrelevant for present purposes.)

A further argument in support of the Head Raising analysis of wh-less restrictives is that it provides us with a way of dealing with structures which proved problematic for the Wh-Movement analysis. One such structure involves the relativisation of idiom chunk nouns in sentences like the following:

(82)   The **headway** *that they have made* is impressive

As we saw in the previous section, what is puzzling about structures like (82) is that the bold-printed noun ends up in a position where it does not function as the complement of its associated verb (e.g. the noun *headway* in 82 is superficially not the complement of *made* but rather part of the subject of *is impressive*). Thus, we should expect sentences like (82) to be ungrammatical, and yet they are fully grammatical. The Head Raising analysis provides a principled answer to this conundrum, because it posits that the noun *headway* is originally merged as the complement of the verb *made* and then raises out of the CP headed by *that* to remerge with the same CP. It thereby comes to be the head N of a new NP which in turn merges with the determiner *the* to form the DP structure shown in simplified form below:

(83)   [DP [D the] [NP [N *headway*] [CP [C that] they have made headway]]]

By positing that the noun *headway* originates as the complement of the verb *made* in (83), the Head Raising analysis allows us to maintain the generalisation that *headway* must be initially merged in a position where it is the complement of the verb *made*. The reason it ends up in front of *that* in a relative clause structure like (82) is that it undergoes the Head Raising operation arrowed in (83). Thus, the Head Raising analysis provides a plausible account of how idiom chunk nouns can be relativized.

Moreover, it also provides us with an account of how adverbial nouns are relativized in DPs like that italicised below:

(84)   *The way that she behaved* was appalling

Under the Head Raising analysis, the adverbial noun *way* originates as the complement of a null counterpart of the preposition *in* and subsequently raises up to remerge with the relative clause CP, in the manner shown below:

(85)   [$_{DP}$ [$_D$ the] [$_{NP}$ [$_N$ *way*] [$_{CP}$ [$_C$ that] she behaved ~~in way~~]]]

This type of structure is only possible where the relativized constituent is a noun like *way* which can be used adverbially, not when it is a noun like *manner*.

Finally, I note that a more unusual source of potential evidence for the Head Raising analysis comes from a type of speech production error which I will term Antecedent Copying. It is exemplified by the structure in (86) below, produced by golfer Tiger Woods during a radio interview when asked a rather pointed question about his strategy for coping with having lost his form:

(86)   I hit **shots** [that I know I can hit *shots*] (Tiger Woods, BBC Radio 5)

(Woods seemingly means that he only attempts shots which he feels confident that he can execute satisfactorily.) In (86), a (bold-printed) copy of the relativized noun appears outside the relative clause, as expected. However, what is unexpected is that another (italicised) copy of the relativized noun appears inside the relative clause, in a position where we would normally expect a gap to appear (as in *I hit shots that I know I can hit - - -*). How can we account for the occurrence of a second copy of the relativized noun? The Head Raising analysis provides a straightforward answer to this question, if we suppose that the noun *shots* originates as the complement of the verb *hit* and is subsequently remerged with the *that*-clause containing it to serve as the head N of the NP *shots that I know I can hit shots*. In the pressure of doing a live interview after posting a disappointing (over-par) score in the relevant round, Tiger Woods forgets to erase the original copy of the noun *shots* at PF, so giving rise to the Antecedent Copying error in (86).

Although the type of copying error produced by Tiger Woods in (86) is as rare in English as a hole in one in golf, there are other languages which make productive use of copy relatives like (86) – as we see from the example below (from the Kombai language spoken in Papua, Indonesia; de Vries 1993: 78):

(87)   [[doü   adiyanono]   doü]   deyalukhe
          sago   they.ate   sago   finished
          'The sago they ate is finished' (literally 'The sago they ate *sago* is finished')

Cinque (2011) terms structures like (86,87) **double-headed relatives** and provides additional examples from other languages.

Thus far in this section, we have seen that the Head Raising analysis provides a plausible account of the syntax of wh-less restrictive relative clauses. Donati and Cecchetto (2011: 528) maintain that the Head Raising analysis can be extended in a straightforward fashion to account for the syntax of wh-restrictive relatives like that bracketed below:

(88)   The cuts [*which* we are facing] are severe

They argue that these involve Head Raising working in conjunction with Wh-Movement. They posit that the relative pronoun *which* is a determiner that merges with the relativized noun *cuts* to form the DP *which cuts*. This DP then merges with the verb *facing* to form the VP *facing which cuts*. Merging this VP with the T auxiliary *are* then forms a T-bar which in turn is merged with the pronoun *we* to form the TP *we are facing which cuts*. This is then merged with a null C to form a C-bar, and the null complementiser attracts the wh-DP *which cuts* to move to the edge of CP, as shown by the arrow below:

(89)

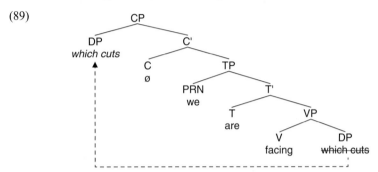

Subsequently, the noun *cuts* raises out of the CP in (89) and remerges with it, forming the NP *cuts which ~~cuts~~ we are facing ~~which cuts~~*. Merging this NP with the determiner *the* then forms the DP shown in simplified form below (with the arrow showing Head Raising of the noun *cuts*):

(90)

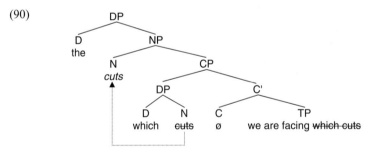

The resulting structure (90) is spelled out at PF as the string *the cuts which we are facing*. On this view, restrictive wh-relatives involve the same Remerge operation (involving Head Raising) as wh-less relatives.

The analysis outlined in this section (which is a slightly simplified version of the analysis presented in Donati and Cecchetto 2011) enables us to arrive at a unitary characterisation of the syntax of restrictive relative clauses. On the account presented here, restrictive relatives can be formed through a Head Raising operation by which a nominal head is raised out of the relative clause CP in which it originates and remerges with the relevant CP to become the head N of a higher NP projection. The difference between wh-less restrictives and their wh-counterparts is that wh-less relatives involve Head Raising alone, whereas wh-restrictives involve Wh-Movement followed by Head Raising.

However, in the next section, I will highlight a number of potential problems that arise with the Head Raising analysis of restrictive relative clauses and refine it in ways designed to overcome these problems.

7.7   Refining the Antecedent Raising analysis

Under the analysis of the syntax of relative clauses sketched in the previous section, restrictive relative clauses can be derived by Head Raising (i.e. raising a noun out of a relative clause to become the head N of a new NP and thereby serve as the antecedent of the relative clause), and this is preceded by Wh-Movement in the case of wh-restrictives. However, the Head Raising account is not without posing problems. In this section, we look at some problems that arise and at possible ways of refining the analysis in such a way as to overcome them.

Consider first the syntax of a wh-less restrictive relative clause structure like that bracketed in (91a) below, which, under the Head Raising analysis outlined in §7.6, will have the derivation shown in simplified form in (91b):

(91)   (a) [the man that they have arrested] will be charged

         (b) [DP [D the] [NP [N *man*] [CP [C that] [TP they [T have] [VP [V arrested] man]]]]]

The relativized noun *man* originates as the complement of the verb *arrested* and then (via Head Raising) remerges with the relative clause CP as the head N of a higher NP. However, as we shall see, there are numerous problems with an analysis like that in (91b).

One is that under the DP Hypothesis outlined in §4.11, definite nominal arguments are DPs, not simply bare nouns. Accordingly, the analysis in (91b) is problematic because it assumes that the noun *man* originates in a position where it is an argument of the verb *arrested* and yet has the status of an N (not a DP). Donati and Cecchetto (2011: 12) address this problem by positing that there is 'a null determiner . . . in the base position of the noun head'. On their view, a DP like that bracketed in (91a) has the derivation in (92) below rather than that in (91b):

(92)

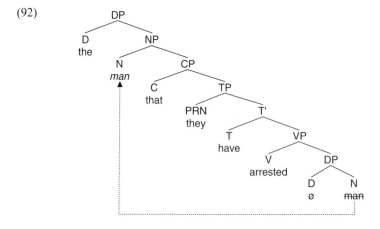

More specifically, the noun *man* originates inside the relative as the complement of a null determiner: this means that the complement of the verb *arrested* is a DP, so satisfying the requirement of the DP Hypothesis that definite nominal arguments are DPs.

However, the assumption that there is a null determiner modifying the noun *man* in (90) is problematic because English does not allow a singular count noun like *man* to be modified by a null determiner in other types of clause (i.e. in clauses which are not relative clauses) – as we see from the ungrammaticality of the following:

(93)   They have arrested [D the/*ø] man

This raises the question of how we restrict the relevant null determiner to use in relative clauses.

A second problem is that the Head Raising operation arrowed in (90) violates locality conditions on movement such as the Impenetrability Condition of §4.11, which prevents any constituent moving directly from a position below C to a position above CP. The Impenetrability violation arises because the noun *man* in (92) moves from an initial position below (more precisely, where it is c-commanded by) the complementiser *that* to a superficial position above (more precisely, where it c-commands) the CP headed by *that*. The locality problem is exacerbated in structures like (94a) below, where the antecedent seemingly undergoes the long-distance movement operation arrowed in (94b):

(94) (a)   the man that they say that they have arrested
     (b)   the man that they say that they have arrested

[DP [D the] [NP [N *man*] [CP [C that] they say [CP [C that] they have arrested *man*]]]]

If the antecedent undergoes the movement arrowed in (94b), this will lead to a double Impenetrabililty violation, by virtue of extracting *man* out of two containing CPs.

The discussion in the previous paragraph highlights two potential problems posed by the analysis of wh-less restrictive relatives outlined in §7.6. However, both of these can be overcome if we take wh-less relatives to have essentially the same syntax as wh-relatives, except that they involve the use of a null relative determiner/operator (below denoted as *Op*) in place of an overt relative determiner/operator like *which*. On this view, the bracketed DP *the man that they have arrested* in (91a) will have the following derivation. The noun *man* is merged as the complement of a null relative determiner/operator (*Op*), forming the DP *Op man*. This DP undergoes Wh-Movement to the edge of the relative clause CP. Subsequently, the relativized noun *man* undergoes the Head Raising operation arrowed below and is thereby remerged with CP to form an NP which in turn is merged with the determiner *the* to form the DP below (where --- marks the gap left behind by movement of the DP *Op man* to spec-CP):

(95)

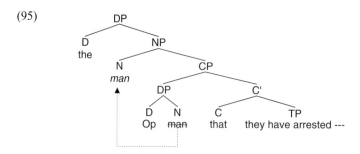

Since the noun *man* originates as the complement of a null relative determiner/operator, the analysis in (95) is consistent with the DP Hypothesis in §4.11, under which definite nominal arguments are DPs. Since (by its very nature) the null relative determiner/operator only occurs in relative clauses, it follows that it will not occur in main clauses like (93). Moreover, since the relativized DP undergoes Wh-Movement to the edge of CP before undergoing Head Raising, there is no violation of the Impenetrability Condition: this is because Wh-Movement moves the wh-DP to a position *inside* CP, and Head Raising moves the noun *man* from a position inside a wh-DP which is *above* C to a position above CP (so that in neither case is movement from a position below C to a position above CP). Similarly, long-distance movement of the antecedent in structures like (94a) can be taken to involve successive-cyclic Wh-Movement of the operator phrase *Op man* (as shown by the lower arrows in 96 below) followed by Head Raising of the noun *man* (shown by the upper arrow):

(96)

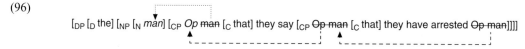

Under the analysis in (95,96), wh-less relatives have the same derivation as their wh-counterparts, and differ only in that they contain a null rather than an overt relative operator. This results in a more unitary account of the syntax of the two types of restrictive clause, under which both wh-restrictives and their wh-less counterparts involve Wh-Movement followed by N-Raising.

   However, the assumption that restrictive relative clauses always involve raising a *noun* out of the relative clause to be remerged with the relative clause to form an NP runs into problems in respect of structures like those below in which the (italicised) relativised constituent comprises a phrase containing a noun rather than a noun on its own:

(97) (a)   The *short shrift* [which he gave --- to my proposal] was disgraceful
     (b)   The *cold water* [which they poured --- on my suggestion] was demoralising
     (c)   The *lip service* [which the government pays --- to civil liberties] is scandalous
     (d)   The *clean breast* [which he made --- of things] will be favourably viewed by the judge

(e)   The *dim view* [which society takes - - - of such behaviour] will mean that he is ostracised

(f)   The *hard line* [which the government took - - - on drugs] has been welcomed in the press

(98) (a)   The *portrait of himself* [which John has painted - - -] is extremely flattering

(b)   The *faith in each other* [which they have shown - - -] is touching

In (97a) it is not simply the noun *shrift* which must raise out of the gap (together with the fronted wh-determiner *which*), but rather the whole phrase *short shrift*, since the relevant idiom is not **give shrift to* but rather *give short shrift to*. Likewise in (97b) it is the whole phrase *cold water* which raises out of the gap, since the idiom is *pour cold water on* ... Similarly in (97c) it is the phrase *lip service* which raises out of the gap, since the idiom is *pay lip service to*. In (98a) what is raised from the gap position into the italicised position is not simply the head noun *portrait* but rather the whole NP *portrait of himself*, because the reciprocal anaphor *himself* needs to originate in a position inside the relative clause where it can be bound by the relative clause subject (*John*). Likewise, what raises in (98b) is the whole NP *faith in each other*, since the reflexive anaphor *each other* needs to originate in a position inside the relative clause where it can be bound by the relative clause subject *they*. Thus, in each of the sentences in (97–98) the raised constituent is a phrase containing a noun rather than a noun alone. There is no straightforward way of accommodating phrasal relativisation structures like (97–98) in the Wh-Movement+Head Raising analysis, for the obvious reason that a *phrase* cannot move to become the head *word* of another phrase.

However, one way of modifying the Head Raising analysis in order to accommodate phrasal relativisation is the following. Let us suppose that phrasal relativisation in a structure like (98a) involves not raising the noun *portrait* to become the head of a higher projection, but rather raising the NP *portrait of himself* to become the specifier of a higher projection. This is the analysis proposed by Bhatt (2002: 81), who suggests that the relativized nominal moves to become the specifier of a higher functional projection.

Bhatt doesn't say what kind of functional projection it is (simply labelling it as an unidentified XP), but since it serves as the complement of a determiner, let's take it to be an NP headed by a null N which attracts the relativized nominal to move into its specifier position. In the light of this assumption, let's take a closer look at the derivation of the DP *the portrait of himself which John has painted* in (98a).

The relative determiner *which* merges with the NP *portrait of himself* to form the DP *which portrait of himself*. This DP undergoes Wh-Movement and thereby moves to the edge of the CP containing it. The resulting CP is merged with a null N which attracts the relativized NP *portrait of himself* to undergo Antecedent Raising and thereby move to become the specifier of the relevant NP, as shown by the arrow below. The resulting NP is then merged with the determiner *the* to form the DP shown below (where the argument *John* is analysed as a DP headed by a null D, in accordance with the DP Hypothesis of §4.11):

(99)

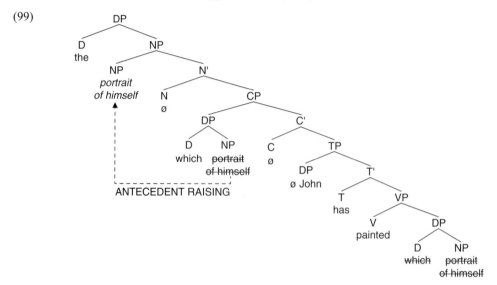

The analysis in (99) retains Donati and Cecchetto's intuition that wh-restrictives involve Wh-Movement followed by Antecedent Raising, with the difference that the raised antecedent is a maximal projection which moves to the specifier position in a higher NP projection (rather than a minimal projection moving to become the head of a higher NP projection).

The Wh-Movement+NP-Raising account in (99) provides us with a principled account of how the anaphor *himself* comes to be interpreted as bound by the DP *ø John*, even though in the superficial structure of the sentence *himself* is neither c-commanded by nor contained within the same TP as *John*. This is because the lowest copy of the anaphor *himself* in (99) can be interpreted as locally bound by the DP *ø John*: the reason is that the lowest copy of *himself* is c-commanded by the DP *ø John*, and the closest TP containing *himself* (namely the TP node headed by T-*has*) is also the closest TP containing the DP *ø John*. Thus, this new account can deal with a type of structure which proved problematic for the Wh-Movement analysis.

The Wh-Movement+NP-Raising analysis in (99) can be extended from the wh-clause in (98a) to its wh-less counterpart in (100) below:

(100)   The *portrait of himself* [(that) John has painted - - -] is extremely flattering

Given the assumptions made here, (100) will have the same Wh-Movement+NP-Raising derivation as in (99) above, with the difference that (100) involves the use of a null relative determiner/operator in place of the overt relative determiner/operator *which*. An important difference between overt and null operator relatives is that (in consequence of the Doubly Filled COMP Filter 43), only null operators can be used in a relative clause headed by the overt complementiser *that* (cf. 'the portrait *Op/*which* **that** he painted').

The Wh-Movement+NP-Raising analysis outlined in (99) can further be extended to cases where the relativised constituent is a simple noun like that italicised in:

(101)   The *portrait* [which John has painted - - -] is extremely flattering

This is because the noun *portrait* (by virtue of being the largest constituent headed by the noun *portrait*) is a maximal projection, and thus is an NP (albeit one comprising simply the noun *portrait*). On this view, Antecedent Raising in (101) involves raising a nominal phrase/maximal projection into a higher specifier position (and not raising a head/minimal projection into a higher head position). As should be apparent from sentences like (97), other types of nominal can also be relativized in this way (e.g. the idiomatic nominal *short shrift* in 97a).

7.8   Problems with the Antecedent Raising analysis

In the previous section, I presented a revised version of the Antecedent Raising analysis under which a wh-DP headed by an (overt or null) relative wh-determiner which has the antecedent NP as its complement is moved into the specifier position of the relative clause CP by Wh-Movement, and then the antecedent is moved into the specifier position in a higher NP by an Antecedent Movement operation. In this section, I will show that this analysis gives rise to a number of potential problems, and I will explore ways of overcoming these problems.

As a starting point for our discussion, consider the derivation of the following sentence:

(102)   [The man who they have arrested] will be charged

Under the Wh-Movement+Antecedent Raising analysis outlined in the previous section, *who* will be a relative determiner which merges with the relativized noun *man* to form the DP *who man*: in order to mark the status of *man* as a maximal projection (by virtue of being the largest constituent headed by the noun *man*), I shall label *man* as an NP below. The DP *who man* is initially merged as the complement of the transitive verb *arrested*, forming the VP *arrested who man*. This VP is in turn merged as the complement of a T auxiliary *have*, forming a T-bar which is then merged with the pronoun *they* to form the TP below:

(103)

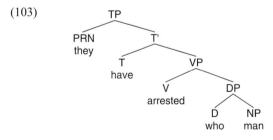

The resulting TP is then merged with a null C with an edge feature that attracts the DP *who man* to move to the edge of CP via Wh-Movement. Subsequently, the NP *man* undergoes an Antecedent Raising operation which raises it out of the CP containing it to become the specifier of a higher NP with a null head. This higher NP in turn merges with the determiner *the* to form a DP which is subsequently merged as the specifier of the T-bar *will be charged*. Merging the resulting TP with a null C forms the CP shown in simplified form below (where subscripts on nodes are added purely for ease of identification, and the arrow indicates the Antecedent Raising component of the analysis).

(104)

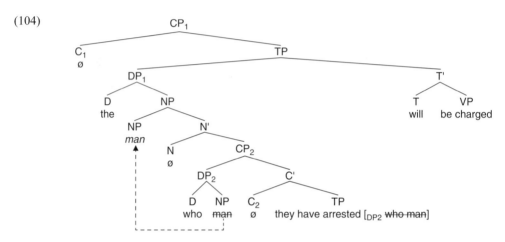

(104) will be spelled out at PF as the string *The man who they have arrested will be charged*.

Although the derivation in (104) seems straightforward enough at first sight, closer inspection reveals a number of potential problems. One such concerns the claim embodied in the analysis that relative pronouns (like *which/who*, etc.) are determiners which take a nominal complement. This claim is by no means implausible for *which*, since we find *which* used as a determiner with a (bold-printed) noun complement both in relative clauses like that bracketed in (105a) below and in interrogative clauses like that bracketed in (105b):

(105) (a)   There was a loud explosion, [at *which* **point** everyone dived for cover]
      (b)   I have no idea [*which* **suspect** they are going to charge]

However, the claim is less plausible for other relative pronouns. For example, the claim that relative *who* is a determiner poses the problem that *who* is never used with a nominal complement – neither in a relative clause like that bracketed in (106a) below nor in an interrogative clause like that bracketed in (106b):

(106) (a)   *The police arrested a suspect [*who* **suspect** they subsequently charged]
      (b)   *I have no idea [*who* **suspect** they are going to charge]

Moreover, when used as an interrogative determiner, *which* can modify both human nouns (like *suspect* in 105b) and inanimate nouns (like *film* in '*Which* **film** is your favourite?'), whereas when used as a relative determiner, it can only have an inanimate antecedent (cf. 'the **film**/***boy** *which* you were watching'). In addition, although relative *which* can modify an idiom chunk noun (as in 62a 'The **headway** [*which* they have made] is impressive'), interrogative *which* cannot do so (cf. '*What*/*Which **headway** have they made?').

Similarly, a wh-determiner analysis is also potentially problematic for relative pronouns like *when, where* and *why* in structures such as:

(107) (a)   the time [*when* I left]
      (b)   the place [*where* I live]
      (c)   the reason [*why* I left]

Under the Antecedent Raising analysis, *when*/*where*/*why* will originate as relative determiners which take the nouns *time*/*place*/*reason* as their complement. The problem this poses is that DPs like *when time, *where place and *why reason never occur in English relatives or interrogatives. Such considerations call into question the plausibility of a determiner analysis of relative pronouns.

However, it may be that there are ways of getting round this kind of problem. For example, in the case of *who*/*which*, we could take interrogative determiners and their relative counterparts to be separate (but related) lexical items which share some (but not all) of their properties in common. For instance, we could suppose that the lexical entry for interrogative *which* specifies that it can be a determiner for any type of nominal (whether human or inanimate), can only introduce a referring expression (hence cannot modify an idiom chunk) and can occur with or without a nominal complement at PF (as in *Which dress/Which do you like best?*). By contrast, the entry for relative *which* specifies that it can be a determiner for any kind of inanimate nominal (including an idiom chunk noun) and cannot have an overt complement at PF (except in structures like 105). In much the same way, we could suppose that the lexical entry for relative *who* specifies that it can only serve as a determiner for a human nominal, but cannot have an overt complement at PF. Similarly, we could suppose that *when*/*where*/*why* have the property that they cannot have an overt nominal complement at PF. In relative clauses, this *no-overt-complement* condition is satisfied by Antecedent Raising; in interrogative clauses, it is claimed by some (e.g. Collins 2007) to arise by deletion of a light noun like PLACE (so that *where* derives from a DP *where* PLACE, with the noun *place* undergoing deletion at PF). Questions of implementation arise, but it seems reasonable to conjecture that these involve matters of detail rather than issues of principle.

Let's therefore move on to consider a second potential problem raised by the analysis in (104), concerning the case-marking of the relative pronoun and its antecedent. By virtue of originating as part of a DP (*who man*) which was initially merged as the object of the transitive verb *arrested* (as shown in 103 above) we should expect both *who* and *man* to receive accusative case. And indeed evidence in support of this comes from the observation that the relative pronoun WHO can be spelled out as the overtly accusative form *whom* in formal styles of English, as we see from the following:

(108)   The man *whom* they have arrested will be charged

However, the NP *man* subsequently raises into an (italicised) position in (104) in which it is c-commanded by the finite intransitive (null) complementiser in the main clause (C_1). Accordingly the NP *man* would be expected to be assigned nominative case by this complementiser, in accordance with the following case condition posited in §4.9:

(109)   **Nominative Case Assignment**
             An intransitive finite complementiser assigns nominative case to a noun or pronoun constituent which it c-commands.

But this results in a situation in which the NP *man* receives accusative case from the transitive verb *arrested* in the embedded clause, and nominative case from the complementiser (C_1) heading the main clause (CP_1). But while there are languages in which nouns can inflect for two different cases (e.g. Australian Aboriginal languages – see Blake 2001 and Sadler and Nordlinger 2006), this is not so in English. Accordingly, if the noun *man* is assigned both nominative and accusative case features, this conflicting feature specification will arguably lead to violation of the following constraint:

(110)   **Feature Conflict Constraint**
             No constituent can carry conflicting specifications for any feature/s.

(110) is a condition which holds at the PF interface (and arguably also at the LF interface) because the PF component is unable to spell out items which carry conflicting feature specifications (e.g. the PF component has no means of spelling out a word as both masculine and feminine, or both singular and plural, or both nominative and accusative). The resulting case conflict causes the derivation to crash at the PF interface, so wrongly predicting that sentences such as (102/108) are ungrammatical.

   A possible solution to the case conflict problem is to make use of the **case over-ride** mechanism posited in work on other structures by Kayne (1983), Bejar and Massam (1999) and Brattico (2010). The core assumption underlying this mechanism is that a case assigned by a lower case-assigner can be over-ridden (i.e. deleted and replaced) by a case subsequently assigned by a higher case-assigner. This would mean that the lower copy of the noun *man* in (104) is assigned accusative case by the verb *arrested*, but that this case feature on the higher copy is over-ridden by the nominative case feature assigned by the main-clause complementiser. This would result in a situation in which the relative pronoun *whom* and the lower copy of the noun *man* have accusative case, but the higher copy has nominative case – and indeed this is what is claimed by Donati and Cecchetto (2011: 531).

However, the case over-ride solution is incompatible with the following constraint posited in §6.7:

(111)   **No Tampering Condition/NTC**
          No syntactic operation can tamper with (i.e. change) any part of a structure other than the root.

Since case over-ride in a structure like (104) involves deleting an accusative case feature assigned to the noun *man* and replacing it by a nominative feature, it can be argued to give rise to a clear-cut NTC violation. (Note that an implicit assumption being made here is that assigning a case feature to a constituent which does not yet have one and needs one does not involve 'tampering', but assigning a new case to a constituent which already has a case feature does indeed involve tampering.) Let's therefore explore an alternative way of resolving the case conflict problem.

One possibility is to treat case assignment as (in principle) optional, and to suppose that at the stage of derivation in (103) the verb *arrested* assigns accusative case to the relative determiner *who* but not to the NP *man*. This would leave the NP *man* active for movement into a higher case position (i.e. a higher position in which it can receive case), so enabling it to undergo the Antecedent Raising operation arrowed in (104) and thereby move into a position where (like the determiner *the*) it can be assigned nominative case by the main clause complementiser. There would be no violation of the No Tampering Condition (111) under this analysis, since no case reassignment takes place. Nor is there is any case conflict, since *man* carries only one case (nominative). On this view the relativized NP and any determiner modifying it are assigned case in the matrix clause but the relative pronoun is assigned case in the relative clause; and empirical support for this claim comes in Polish sentences like (47) above, repeated as (112) below:

(112)   Widziałem   tego   *pana*,   **który**   zbił   ci   szybę
          saw$_{1SG}$ the$_{ACC}$ man$_{ACC}$ who$_{NOM}$ broke   your   glass
          'I saw the man who broke your glass'

In (112), the relativised NP *pana*$_{man}$ originates as the subject of the relative clause and (under the Antecedent Raising analysis) is raised out of the relative clause into a position in the main clause where (like the determiner *tego*$_{the}$) it falls within the case domain of (and so is assigned accusative case by) the transitive verb *widziałem*$_{saw}$. By contrast, the relative pronoun *który*$_{who}$ is nominative by virtue of being the initial subject of the relative clause and remaining within the relative clause.

However, even if we can resolve the problems posed by treating relative *who* as a determiner, and the further problems relating to the case-marking of the relative pronoun and its antecedent, there remains a further problem with analysis in (104), under which restrictive relatives involve Wh-Movement followed by Antecedent Raising. The problem is that the Antecedent Raising operation gives rise to violation of several constraints. To see how, let's take a closer look at how

Antecedent Raising works in the DP *the man who they have arrested*, which (under the analysis in 104 above) has the derivation shown in simplified form below:

(113)

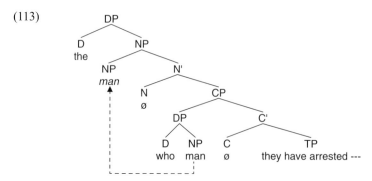

One constraint violated by the arrowed Antecedent Raising operation arrowed in (113) is the following (introduced in §3.6):

(114)   **Stranding Constraint**
No D/determiner, Q/quantifier or C/complementiser can be stranded without its complement.

The reason why the constraint is violated is that Antecedent Raising results in the determiner *who* being stranded without its complement *man*. Still, it may be that we can somehow get round this problem by supposing that the constraint only holds for prenominal determiners like *the*, not for pronominal determiners like *who*.

However, a second constraint violated by Antecedent Movement in (113) is the following (from §6.9):

(115)   **Freezing Principle/FP**
The constituents of a moved phrase are frozen internally within (and so cannot be extracted out of) the moved phrase.

The reason why the arrowed movement in (113) violates FP is that *man* is extracted out of a moved wh-phrase (i.e. out of the phrase *who man* which underwent Wh-Movement to get to the edge of CP in 113). However, it may be that we can get round this problem by supposing that freezing effects should not be handled in terms of the Freezing Principle in (115) above, but rather in terms of the Criterial Freezing Condition, which was given the following formulation in §6.9:

(116)   **Criterial Freezing Condition**
A constituent which occupies its criterial position is frozen in place.

We could then say that the arrowed movement in (113) does not violate the Criterial Freezing Condition (116) for the following reason. When the wh-phrase *who man* moves to the edge of the relative clause, the relativiser *who* is in its criterial position (on the edge of a relative clause) and so is frozen in place. By contrast, the antecedent *man* is not yet in its criterial position, and so is free to move to its own criterial position on the edge of the NP above the CP. (See Rizzi 2014: 21–2 for cases in Italian where a constituent contained within a wh-phrase which has moved to its criterial position can be extracted out of the wh-phrase.)

However, there is yet a further constraint (discussed in §6.9) which is violated by the arrowed Antecedent Raising operation in (113), namely:

(117)   **Constraint on Extraction Domains/CED**
           Material can only be extracted out of complement, not out of a specifier or adjunct,

Since CED bars extraction out of a specifier, Antecedent Raising induces a CED violation in (113), because *man* is extracted out of a DP (*who man*) which is the specifier of the relative clause CP.

More generally, every restrictive relative clause will induce CED violations under the Wh-Movement+Antecedent Raising analysis in (113). And yet, the corresponding relative clauses are fully grammatical. How come? The answer is far from clear. However, I note that there are precedents for the type of analysis in (113) in which material extracted from the specifier of a lower CP becomes the specifier of a higher constituent. One such can be found in an analysis of a type of elliptical structure termed **Swiping** by Ross (1969). The phenomenon of Swiping can be illustrated by the elliptical structure italicised in (118a) below (from Hartman and Ai 2009), where the bracketed clause is said to have undergone Swiping (an operation which involves fronting of a head-last wh-PP containing a preposition positioned after its wh-complement, and deletion of other material in the clause):

(118)   He fought in the civil war, but I don't know [*which side for* ~~he fought~~]

Under an analysis of Swiping proposed by van Craenenbroek (2004, 2010), the italicised elliptical clause is a CP recursion structure. The DP *which side* originates as the complement of the preposition *for*, and the whole PP moves to become the specifier of an inner CP, so resulting in the structure shown in simplified form below:

(119)

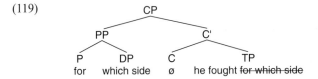

The CP in (119) is embedded as the complement of a null complementiser which then attracts the wh-DP *which side* to become its specifier, in the manner shown by the arrow in (120) below. In the PF component, the TP complement of the lower CP subsequently undergoes a form of ellipsis known as **Sluicing**, ensuring that the constituents of TP receive a silent spellout (marked by strikethrough below). The italicised string in (118) thus has the superficial structure shown below (where subscripts are added purely for ease of identification):

(120)

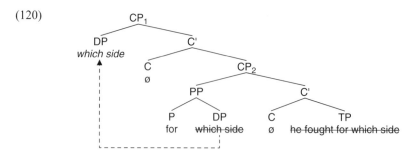

Note that a crucial assumption embodied in the analysis in (120) is that the DP *which side* is extracted out of a *for*-PP which is the specifer of CP$_2$ and raised into a position where it becomes the specifier of CP$_1$, in apparent violation of CED and FP. And yet, the resulting structure is grammatical, casting doubt on the robustness of these constraints.

Further doubt is cast on the inviolability of CED/FP by sentences such as the following (sourced from the Internet unless otherwise specified; italics, square brackets and gaps are added by me):

(121) (a)   The horror food was pumpkin pie, *which* [the very thought of - - -] makes me shudder (hands-on-illustrations-co.uk)

(b)   So I understand and totally respect you trying to give advice (*which* I think [most of - - -] is great) (board.crossfit.com)

(c)   There is discussion in the book about the motivation for serial killers, *which* I don't know [how much of - - -] I agree with (agathaslifelessons.blogspot.com)

(d)   This is the handout *which* I can't remember [how many copies of - - -] we have to print (adapted from Chaves 2013: 6, 6a)

In (121a,b), the relative pronoun *which* is extracted out of a bracketed subject in spec-TP, while in (121c,d) it is extracted out of a bracketed moved wh-phrase in spec-CP. This gives rise to a CED violation in all the examples in (121); and yet structures like those in (121) are commonplace in everyday language.

The overall conclusion to be drawn from our discussion of CED effects is the following. Although Antecedent Raising in structures like (113) induces CED and Freezing violations, it should be noted that such violations appear to be tolerated in Swiping structures like (118/120), and also in sentences like those in (121). Thus, the issue of whether the CED/Freezing violations it induces undermine the Antecedent Raising analysis of restrictive relative clauses is a moot one.

An interesting consequence of the Wh-Movement+Antecedent Raising analysis is that it supposes that relativisation is a process by which an NP is expanded into a larger NP by modifying it by a restrictive relative clause: for instance, relativisation of the NP *man* in (113) leads to the formation of the larger NP *man who they have arrested*. An interesting prediction of this analysis is that restrictive relativisation should be potentially recursive (i.e. an NP should be able to be modified by multiple restrictive relative clauses). And indeed this prediction is correct, as we see from sentences like (122) below, where the underlined NP is modified by two separate relative clauses (the bold-printed one being a wh-restrictive, and the italicised one being a wh-less restrictive):

(122)   This is the only <u>photo of Jim</u> *that I took* **which you liked**

Under the Wh-Movement+Antecedent Raising analysis outlined above, the DP *the only photo of Jim that I took which you liked* in (122) will be derived as follows. A null relative operator/determiner will merge with the NP *photo of Jim* to form the DP *Op photo of Jim* (where *Op* is a null counterpart of relative *which*). This DP will be initially merged as the complement of the verb *took*, but will subsequently be wh-moved out of the gap position in (123) below to become the specifier of the complementiser *that*. The NP *photo of Jim* will then be raised into the specifier position of an NP immediately above the CP headed by *that* in the manner shown by the arrow below, so deriving:

(123)

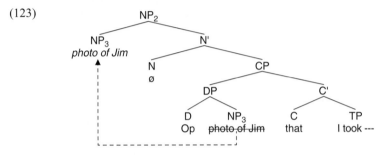

The resulting NP (NP$_2$) *photo of Jim that I took* will then be merged as the complement of the relative determiner/operator *which*, forming the DP *which photo of Jim that I took*. This wh-DP is then merged as the complement of the verb *liked*, and subsequently wh-moved out of the gap position in (124) below to become the specifier of the null complementiser heading the CP in the *liked*-clause. After that, the NP *photo of Jim that I took* is moved to become the specifier of an NP immediately above this CP (in the manner shown by the arrow below). The resulting NP is then merged with the quantifier *only* to form a QP, and the resulting QP is merged with the determiner *the* to form the DP below (where NP$_2$ has the structure shown in 123 above):

(124)

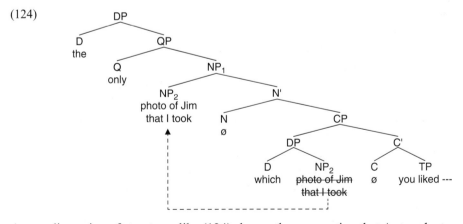

As our discussion of structures like (124) shows, the assumption that Antecedent Raising involves raising an antecedent to become the specifier of a superordinate/

higher NP makes the correct prediction that restrictive relative clauses (whether wh- or wh-less clauses) can be recursively stacked.

To summarise: in this section, I have discussed potential problems arising from the analysis of restrictive relatives outlined in §7.7, under which restrictive relatives involve Wh-Movement followed by Antecedent Raising. I noted, for example, that treating relative pronouns as determiners which take the antecedent as their initial complement gives rise to a number of complications, though I concluded that these could reasonably be considered to be questions of detail rather than issues of principle. I went on to discuss the case conflict problem which arises if the antecedent NP is assigned one case in the relative clause and another case in the matrix clause; however, I noted that this problem could be circumvented if case assignment is treated as optional (and you will have the chance to evaluate other potential solutions to the case conflict problem in the exercises). In addition, I noted that Antecedent Raising gives rise to violation of the Constraint on Extraction Domains; however, I noted that (for reasons which are unclear) this kind of violation also seems to be permitted in other structures (including Swiping).

7.9   Two sources for restrictive relative clauses

In §7.4, I sketched an analysis of relative clauses whereby a CP containing an overt or null relative operator which undergoes Wh-Movement is adjoined to an NP, thereby projecting it into an even larger NP. In §7.5, I showed that such a Wh-Movement analysis faces problems in accounting for certain types of restrictive relative clause – e.g. those which involve relativisation of an idiom chunk noun (as in *The headway which/that we made was impressive*), or relativisation of an adverbial noun (as in *The way which/that she behaved was appalling*), or relativisation of an NP containing an anaphor whose antecedent lies inside the relative clause (in sentences like *The portrait of himself which/that John has painted is impressive*). In §§7.6–7.8, I presented an alternative Antecedent Raising analysis under which the antecedent NP originates as part of a wh-phrase headed by a relative determiner like *who/which*, the wh-phrase moves via Wh-Movement to the edge of CP, and then the antecedent NP is extracted out of the wh-phrase and raised to become the specifier of a higher NP. I showed how this Antecedent Raising analysis could provide a relatively straightforward account of the relativisation of NPs containing idiom chunk nouns or anaphors.

At this point, it might seem as if the most plausible conclusion to draw is that we should abandon the Wh-Movement analysis in favour of the Antecedent Raising analysis. However, the problem this poses is that there are certain types of restrictive relative clause structure which are not amenable to an Antecedent Raising derivation, and which seem to require a Wh-Movement derivation. A case in point are structures where additional material is pied-piped along with a relative operator. By way of examples, consider possessive structures like the following (after Bhatt 2002: 76, 62):

(125)   He was *the king of Egypt whose brother's wife they executed*

Under the version of Antecedent Raising outlined in §7.8 and given the assumptions about the syntax of possessives made in §6.6, the DP italicised in (125) will be derived as follows

(126)

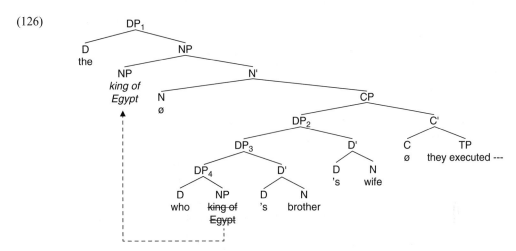

That is to say, the wh-DP *who king of Egypt's brother's wife* will originate in the gap (- - -) position in (126) as the complement of the verb *executed* and will then be wh-moved to the edge of CP. Subsequently, the NP *king of Egypt* will undergo the arrowed Antecedent Raising operation and thereby move to become the specifier of a higher NP.

   However, although the resulting DP italicised in (125) is grammatical, the Antecedent Raising operation arrowed in (126) is hugely problematic. The reason is that it leads to a triple violation of the Constraint on Extraction Domains/CED (117). This is because the NP *King of Egypt* is extracted out of the specifier of a specifier of a specifier: more precisely, it is extracted out of DP$_4$ (which is the specifier of DP$_3$), and out of DP$_3$ (which is the specifier of DP$_2$), and out of DP$_2$ (which is the specifier of the relative clause CP). And the ungrammaticality of a sentences like (127) below shows that extraction out of a possessor is not exempt from CED:

(127)   **Which country* did they execute [the king of - - -'s brother]?

Thus, the Antecedent Raising analysis wrongly predicts that a DP like that italicised in (125) should incur a triple CED violation and hence be severely ungrammatical. But since the resulting sentence (125) is perfectly grammatical, the conclusion we reach is that there must be some other source for such relative clauses. And the Wh-Movement analysis sketched in §7.4 provides an appropriate alternative source. Let's see how.

Given the analysis sketched in §7.4 and the assumptions about the syntax of possessives made in §6.6, the DP italicised in (125) will have the derivation shown below (where the material undergoing Wh-Movement is enclosed in a box, for clarity of exposition):

(128)

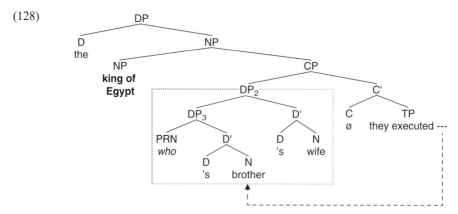

The bold-printed antecedent NP *king of Egypt* will originate outside the relative clause CP, but the relative pronoun *who* (which refers back to the antecedent) will originate inside the relative clause. An edge feature (R-feature) on the head C of the relative clause will attract the relative pronoun/operator *who* to move to spec-CP. However, because the possessive *'s* suffix must have an immediately adjacent possessor to attach to at PF, this means that *who* cannot move on its own, since this would result in a structure (**the king of Egypt who they executed --- 's brother's wife*) in which the bold-printed occurrence of possessive *'s* is illicitly stranded without an immediately adjacent overt possessor host to attach to. Nor, for the same reason, can DP₃ *who's brother* be wh-moved on its own (**the king of Egypt whose brother they executed --- 's wife*) because once again this would result in a possessive affix being stranded without an immediately adjacent overt possessor to attach to. Consequently, the whole of DP₂ (*whose brother's wife*) has to undergo the Wh-Movement operation arrowed in (128). The resulting derivation converges (i.e. produces a successful outcome), as we see from the grammaticality of (125).

What the above discussion illustrates is that there are some restrictive relative clauses which cannot be given an Antecedent Raising derivation (in which the antecedent NP originates in a position inside the relative clause and from there moves to a position immediately above the relative clause), but rather require a derivation in which the antecedent originates in a position outside the relative clause and is associated with a wh-moved relative pronoun/operator inside the relative clause that refers back to the antecedent. Let's briefly look at a few more instances of this kind.

Other types of relative clause which require a Wh-Movement derivation include structures like those in (129) below (repeated from 67 above) in which a relative clause has more than one antecedent:

(129) (a)   The police eventually released the *man* and the **woman** [who were arrested]
     (b)   John saw a *man* and Mary saw a **woman** [who were wanted by the police]

In (129a), the relative pronoun *who* has a **coordinate antecedent**, whereas in (129b) it has a **split antecedent** (i.e. an antecedent comprising two separate constituents). Clearly, it would be implausible to propose an Antecedent Raising analysis for such structures under which both *man* and *woman* originate as the complement of *who*, and somehow they subsequently raise into two entirely distinct positions (*man* raising into the italicised position and *woman* into the bold-printed position). It is simply not obvious how such a derivation could be made to work, especially as coordinate structures (e.g. like *the man and the woman*) are islands (i.e. structures which don't allow anything to be moved into or out of them). It might seem as if we can solve the problem by positing that each of the two nouns is modified by a separate relative clause, with the first relative clause undergoing deletion in the PF component so that the string *the man and the woman who were arrested* in (129a) has the fuller structure shown below:

(130)   the man [~~who was arrested~~] and the woman [who was arrested]

However, such an analysis fails to account for the auxiliary *were* being plural in (129a) when the analysis in (130) wrongly predicts that the singular form *was* should be required.

  Although I will not go into details here, it should be apparent that a Wh-Movement analysis of restrictive relatives can handle structures like those in (129). This is because the relative pronoun *who* will originate inside the relative clause and its multiple antecedents outside. As the examples in (131) below show, even in non-relative structures, a plural pronoun (like *they*) can have split or coordinate antecedents:

(131) (a)   The police initially released the *man* and the **woman**, but <u>they</u> were subse-
             quently re-arrested
     (b)   I saw a *man* and you saw a **woman**, but <u>they</u> weren't people we knew

Consequently, the use of a plural relative pronoun with two singular antecedents in structures like (129a,b) seems to be attributable to a more general phenomenon.

  Other relative clauses which likewise require a Wh-Movement derivation include those in which a pronominal (like *he*) inside a relative clause can be coreferential to a nominal contained within the antecedent of the relative clause – e.g. in sentences like (132) below (repeated from 51 above) in which *he* can refer to *John*:

(132)   This is the photo of John [which he hates]

An Antecedent Raising derivation for the relative clause in a sentence like (132) wrongly rules out the possibility of *he* referring to *John*, for the following reason. Under the Antecedent Raising derivation, the relative determiner *which* will merge with the NP *photo of John* to form the wh-DP *which photo of John*. This wh-DP will undergo Wh-Movement and thereby move to the spec-CP position at the beginning of the relative clause. Subsequently, the NP *photo of John* will undergo Antecedent Raising and thereby raise up to become the specifier of a higher NP, which in turn merges with the determiner *the* to derive the DP shown in (133) below:

(133)

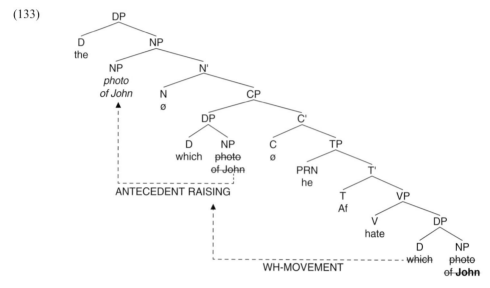

However, the lowest (bold-printed) copy of *John* at the foot of the tree is c-commanded by *he*, since the mother of *he* is TP, and TP contains *John*. But this means that any possibility of *John* and *he* being coreferential will be ruled out by Principle C of Binding Theory, which was given the following formulation in (48) above:

(134)   **Principle C of Binding Theory**
        No (copy of an) R-expression can be coreferential to any (copy of a) con-
        stituent c-commanding it.

So, because the lowest (bold-printed) copy of *John* is c-commanded by *he*, Principle C specifies that *John* cannot be coreferential to *he*. And yet, this is an incorrect outcome, because *John* can indeed be coreferential to *he*. So, the problem we face is that an Antecedent Raising derivation for a sentence like (132) wrongly predicts that it should give rise to a Principle C violation if *he* refers to *John*. By contrast (although I will not repeat the relevant discussion here), the Wh-Movement derivation sketched in (52) above makes precisely the right prediction that nothing prevents *he* from referring to *John*. Or, to put things another way, sentences like (132) represent another kind of relative clause which requires a Wh-Movement derivation.

The overall conclusion to be drawn from our discussion here is that we need to posit two distinct types of derivation for restrictive relative clauses: (i) a Wh-Movement analysis like that sketched in §7.4; and (ii) an Antecedent Raising analysis like that sketched in §7.7. An interesting structural difference between the two types of derivation is the following. Under the Antecedent Raising derivation, an NP originating inside the relative clause moves to a position outside it: but given the requirement that a trace (i.e. a copy left behind by movement) must be c-commanded by its antecedent, it follows that the relative clause cannot be separated from its antecedent. For example, when the NP *photo of John* undergoes Antecedent Raising in (133), this results in a structure in which the raised NP c-commands its trace. As should be obvious, this c-command relation between the antecedent and its trace will not hold if the relative clause containing the trace of the antecedent is not the complement of the NP containing the antecedent (e.g. if the relative clause is detached/separated from its antecedent in some way). This leads to the prediction that a relative clause must always be immediately adjacent to its antecedent in cases where relativisation involves Antecedent Raising.

By contrast, no such restriction would be expected to hold in cases where relativisation involves Wh-Movement alone. This is because under a pure Wh-Movement analysis, all movement takes place inside the relative clause CP itself (i.e. a relative pronoun moves into spec-CP within the relative clause), and nothing moves out of the relative clause. Given this assumption, there would appear to be no necessity for the relative clause to be immediately adjacent to (i.e. adjoined to) its antecedent. On the contrary, nothing would preclude the possibility of a restrictive relative clause being separated from its antecedent by one or more intervening constituents. In this connection, it is interesting to note that Hulsey and Sauerland (2006) make the claim that restrictive relative clauses involving Antecedent Raising cannot be **extraposed** (i.e. separated from their antecedents by other material and positioned at the end of the relevant clause), and they illustrate this claim with examples including the following (where the italicised adverb separates the bold-printed antecedent from the bracketed relative clause:

(135) (a)   *Mary praised the **headway** *last year* [that John made]
      (b)   *I saw the **picture of himself** *yesterday* [that John liked]

By contrast (they note) no such strict adjacency requirement holds for relative clauses like those bracketed below, which can freely be extraposed:

(136) (a)   Mary praised the **pot roast** *yesterday* [that John made]
      (b)   I saw the **picture of myself** *yesterday* [that John liked]

The reason is that relative clauses like those in (136) can have a Wh-Movement derivation, and such a derivation allows **Extraposition** of the relative clause.

The overall conclusion to be drawn from our discussion in this section is the following. Relative clauses are structurally ambiguous and can involve either Wh-Movement alone or Wh-Movement with subsequent Antecedent Raising. Interesting support for this structural ambiguity claim comes from minimal pairs (i.e. pairs of sentences which differ minimally from each other in only one key respect) where one member of the pair requires a Wh-Movement derivation, and the other requires an Antecedent Raising derivation. As a case in point, consider the bracketed restrictive relative clauses in the minimal pair below (adapted from Nunberg, Sag and Wasow 1994: 510, 33):

(137) (a)   The strings [which Pat pulled] got Chris the job
      (b)   Pat pulled the strings [which got Chris the job]

Here, the relevant idiom is *pull strings*, so we can suppose that *strings* must be initially merged as (part of) the complement of the verb *pull*. Consider first the derivation of (137a). If this had a Wh-Movement derivation, the relative pronoun *which* would originate as the complement of *pulled* and from there move to the front of the relative clause by Wh-Movement, as shown by the arrow in the partial structure below:

(138)   [DP [D the] [NP [NP strings] [CP *which* [C ø] Pat pulled ~~which~~]]] got Chris the job

However, since at no point would the NP *strings* occur as the complement of the verb *pulled*, the Wh-Movement derivation in (138) would wrongly predict that (137a) is ungrammatical. However, this problem can be overcome if we suppose that an alternative Antecedent Raising derivation is available for (137a). On this alternative derivation, the relative determiner *which* merges with the noun *strings* to form the DP *which strings*, and this DP is then merged as the complement of the verb *pull*. Via Wh-Movement, *which strings* moves to the edge of the relative clause CP (as shown by the lower arrow in 139 below), and subsequently *strings* moves to the edge of a higher NP (as shown by the upper arrow):

(139)

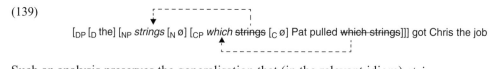

[DP [D the] [NP *strings* [N ø] [CP *which* ~~strings~~ [C ø] Pat pulled ~~which strings~~]]] got Chris the job

Such an analysis preserves the generalisation that (in the relevant idiom) *strings* must originate within a nominal which is the complement of the verb *pull*. Thus, the assumption that relative clauses can have an Antecedent Raising derivation provides us with a way of handling (137a).

But now consider what would happen under an Antecedent Raising analysis of (137b). As before, the noun *strings* would be merged with the determiner *which* to form the DP *which strings*, and this DP would originate as the subject of the *got*-clause (in spec-TP), and from there move to spec-CP by Wh-Movement, as shown by the lower arrow in (140) below. Subsequent Antecedent Raising would raise *strings* to the edge of a superordinate NP (as shown by the upper arrow):

(140)

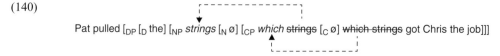

Pat pulled [DP [D the] [NP *strings* [N ø] [CP *which* ~~strings~~ [C ø] ~~which strings~~ got Chris the job]]]

However, the problem posed by the derivation in (140) is that *which strings* is not initially merged as the object of *pull*, but rather as the subject of the *got*-clause. Thus, a grammar which assumes that all restrictive relative clauses involve Antecedent Raising wrongly predicts that sentences like (137b) should be ungrammatical, because the items *pull* and *strings* originate in separate clauses.

By contrast, if (as here) we suppose that relative clauses are structurally ambiguous, it follows that restrictives like (137b) could alternatively have the kind of Wh-Movement derivation sketched in §7.4. If so, the relative pronoun *which* will originate as the subject of the relative clause in spec-TP, and from there move to the edge of CP by Wh-Movement. The relativized noun *strings* originates in situ within the main clause (as part of the complement of the verb *pulled*) and is construed as the antecedent of the relative pronoun *which*. The relative clause CP adjoins to the NP *strings* to form the even larger NP *strings which got Chris the job* so that (137b) has the derivation below (simplified by not showing the internal structure of the TP in the relative clause, in order to save space):

(141)

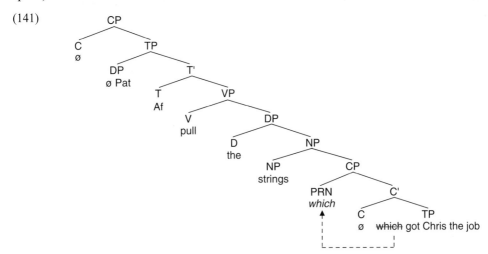

Here, the NP *strings* is initially merged as one of the constituents of the DP complement of the verb *pull*, so allowing the relevant string to have an idiomatic interpretation.

The overall conclusion to be drawn from our discussion in this section is the following. Restrictive relative clauses are in principle structurally ambiguous and can have either a derivation involving Wh-Movement alone or a derivation involving Wh-Movement followed by Antecedent Raising. This leads us to a conclusion which (in a way) is not surprising – namely that the antecedent of a restrictive relative clause can either be directly merged in situ outside the relative clause, or originate inside the relative clause and come to occupy its superficial position ouside the relative clause by movement. Most types of relative clause can have either derivation; however, some yield a convergent outcome under only one of the two derivations. Thus, as we have seen, a Wh-Movement analysis is the only one which can handle structures where a relativised idiom chunk noun is the complement of a predicate in the main clause (as in 'Pat **pulled** the *strings* which got Chris the job'), or where additional material is pied-piped along with the relative pronoun, or where the relative pronoun has split antecedents, or where the relative clause contains a pronominal which refers to a constituent contained within the antecedent of the relative clause (as in 'This is the photo of **John** which *he* hates'), or where the relative clause is extraposed. By contrast, an Antecedent Raising analysis is required to handle relativisation of idiom chunk nouns which function as the complement of a predicate in the relative clause (as in 'The *headway* which/that we **made** was impressive'), or relativisation of an adverbial noun (as in 'The *way* which/that she behaved was appalling'), or relativisation of an NP containing an anaphor whose antecedent lies inside the relative clause (in sentences like 'The portrait of *himself* which/that **John** has painted is impressive').

An important implication of the assumption that there are two ways of forming restrictive relative clauses is the following. A given restrictive relative clause structure will be grammatical if there is at least one way of deriving it which is convergent (i.e. which satisfies all relevant constraints and interface conditions, and which can be mapped into a pronounceable PF representation and an interpretable LF representation). By contrast, a restrictive relative clause structure will be ungrammatical if neither of the two derivations yields a convergent outcome.

7.10   A-bar Movement

In the previous chapter, we saw that Wh-Movement plays a central role in the syntax of wh-questions. In this chapter, we have seen that it also plays a central role in the syntax of exclamative and relative clauses. It has been argued by a number of linguists that Wh-Movement is an even more pervasive operation which is found in a much wider range of clauses, including unconditional clauses like that italicised in (142a), comparative clauses like that italicised in (142b), *as*-clauses like that italicised in (142c) and *tough*-clauses like that italicised in (142d):

(142) (a)   *Whatever you decide to do*, I will support you
      (b)   It is bigger than *I expected it to be*
      (c)   Ames was a spy, *as the FBI eventually discovered*
      (d)   Syntax is tough *to understand*

The italicised clause in (142a) involves Wh-Movement of the overt wh-word *whatever*, but the italicised clauses in (142c–d) have been argued to involve movement of a **null wh-operator**. In this respect, it is interesting to note that (142b) has a variant form containing the overt wh-word *what* in varieties of

English where we find *It is bigger than* **what** *I expected it to be*. I shall have no more to say about structures like those in (142), however. Instead, I will go on to show that there are also movement operations which move other types of constituent to the edge of CP, and these cannot be treated as cases of Wh-Movement because they do not involve the movement of an (overt or null) wh-constituent.

By way of illustration, consider movement of the two constituents italicised below, discussed in §5.2:

(143) (a)   *No fear* **did** they show - - -
      (b)   The soldiers were all awarded medals, *such gallantry* **did** they show - - -

In (143a), the negative phrase *no fear* originates in the gap position (as the complement of the verb *show*) and from there moves into the italicised position in front of the inverted auxiliary *did*. Given the arguments presented in §5.2 that inverted auxiliaries are in C and that Auxiliary Inversion is triggered by a C which has a specific kind of specifier (e.g. an interrogative, negative or degree expression), it is plausible to suppose that the fronted negative phrase in (143a) is in spec-CP. Since the fronted constituent is negative, the relevant movement operation might be termed **Neg-Movement**. In much the same way, the degree phrase *such gallantry* in (143b) can be argued to originate in the gap position (as the complement of *show*), and from there move to become the specifier of a CP headed by a C containing an inverted auxiliary. The relevant type of movement could be called **Deg-Movement**.

However, although they have been given different names here, Neg-Movement and Deg-Movement in (143) seem to involve essentially the same movement operation whereby a QP (in one case the QP *no fear* headed by the negative quantifier *no*, and in the other case the QP *such gallantry* headed by the degree quantifier *such*) moves from comp-VP to spec-CP (i.e. from being the complement of VP to becoming the specifier of CP). Moreover, Wh-Movement in a question such as:

(144)   *What qualities* **did** they show - - -?

involves a parallel movement operation in which the wh-phrase *what qualities* (which is a QP headed by the interrogative quantifier *what*) moves from comp-VP to spec-CP. The similarities between these three types of movement operation are shown in graphic form below:

(145)

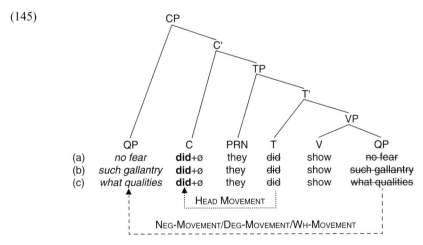

If we look closely at the movement represented by the lower (dashed) arrow in (145), we see that Neg-Movement, Deg-Movement and Wh-Movement all involve essentially the same type of movement operation whereby a negative, degree or interrogative QP moves from its original position internally within the clause to its derived position on the edge of the clause (in spec-CP). Given the apparent parallels between the three types of movement operation, economy considerations suggest that we should treat all three as involving the same type of movement operation; and the standard term used to denote this movement operation in work over more than half a century has been A-bar Movement. On this view, Neg-Movement, Deg-Movement and Wh-Movement are three specific instances of a more general A-bar Movement operation.

But why is the term A-bar Movement used? It is important to note here that the suffix *-bar* has a very different meaning from that found in category labels like T-bar (where it denotes an intermediate constituent larger than T but smaller than TP). By contrast, in the phrase *A-bar Movement*, the *-bar* suffix marks negation, so that A-bar Movement denotes 'movement to a non-A position' (i.e. to a position which is not an A-position). This of course raises the question of what an A-position is. The answer is that an A-position is an Argument/Agreement/Anaphor-binding position. To put things less cryptically, an A-position is an argument position, or a position which can contain the **controller** of agreement with some head (in a sense to be made precise below), or a position which can contain the **antecedent** of an anaphor.

We can illustrate the difference between A-positions and A-bar positions in terms of the following examples:

(146) (a)   **Jim** has hurt *himself*
    (b)   *__Who__ do few photos of *himself* flatter?

(147) (a)   There **have** recently been discovered *many previously unknown tombs*
    (b)   *There **have** recently been discovered *how many tombs* the robbers plundered

Given the assumptions made here, (146a,b) will have the respective superficial structures shown in simplified form below:

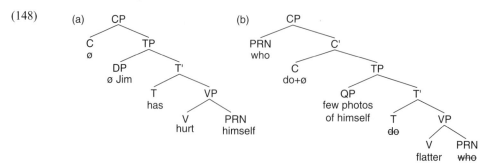

In (148a) the reflexive anaphor *himself* is interpreted as bound by the c-commanding clausemate constituent *Jim* (or, more precisely, by the DP containing *Jim*). Since the *Jim*-DP in (148a) serves as the specifier of the TP headed by the T auxiliary *has*, this tells us that spec-TP is an A-position (by virtue of being a position that can contain the antecedent of an anaphor). By contrast, in (148b), *himself* cannot be interpreted as bound by *who*, even though *who* c-commands *himself* and is a clausemate of *himself* (in the sense that both of them are contained in the same CP). So why can't *who* bind *himself* in (148b)? The answer is that *who* is in spec-CP, and spec-CP is an A-bar position (by virtue of being a position that cannot house the antecedent of an anaphor).

Now consider the sentences in (147). In expletive *there* sentences, T generally agrees with the **associate** of the expletive. In (147a), the associate of *there* is the italicised QP *many previously unknown tombs*, and this occupies an argument position (by virtue of being an argument of the passive verb *discovered*); more importantly for our purposes, it serves as the controller of agreement with T *have* (i.e. it is the constituent which *have* agrees in person and number with). Since an argument position is an A-position, this QP can serve as the controller of agreement with the T auxiliary *have*. By contrast in (147b), the QP *how many tombs* is intended to be used as the associate of *there*, and yet T *are* cannot agree with this QP. Why not? The answer is that the interrogative QP *how many tombs* undergoes Wh-Movement and thereby becomes the specifier of the interrogative CP containing the verb *plundered*. But since spec-CP is an A-bar position, no agreement can take place between T *are* and a wh-QP in spec-CP. (I note in passing that there are a number of West Germanic languages and language varieties which have a phenomenon termed **Complementiser Agreement**: in typical cases, this involves a complementiser inflecting for agreement with the clause subject in spec-TP. However, note that the controller of the agreement is in spec-TP, and spec-TP is an A-position, so this is not a counterexample to the claim that only a constituent in an A-position can be the controller of agreement with a head. See the entry for Complementiser Agreement in the Glossary for examples and references.)

From the criteria given above, it follows that spec-CP is not an A-position, but rather is an A-bar position. Hence, any operation which involves moving some constituent into spec-CP can be said to be an instance of A-bar Movement. In the case of operations like Neg-Movement and Deg-Movement (and Wh-Movement in root clause questions), A-bar Movement to spec-CP is accompanied by concomitant Auxiliary Inversion (i.e. Head Movement of an auxiliary from T to C). However this is not always the case, as we see from the absence of Auxiliary Inversion in exclamatives, relatives and embedded interrogatives. Similarly, there is no Auxiliary Inversion in the kind of **Top(ic)-Movement** operation by which the italicised DP moves from the gap position to the italicised position in a sentence like that produced by speaker B in (149) below, in order to topicalise it (i.e. mark it as a topic):

(149)   SPEAKER A: The demonstrators have been looting shops and setting fire to cars
           SPEAKER B: They must realise that *this kind of behaviour*, we will simply not put
                      up with - - -

Here, the italicised phrase *this kind of behaviour* is the topic of the bracketed embedded clause in (149B) in the sense that it refers back to the activity of looting shops and setting fire to cars which is old/familiar information by virtue of having been mentioned earlier by speaker A. There is a gap in (149B) in that the transitive preposition *with* has no object immediately following it; in fact, it is the topic *this kind of behaviour* which is interpreted as the object of *with*. Since gaps can arise via movement, a plausible analysis of (149B) is to suppose that the DP *this kind of behaviour* originates as the complement of *with* and then (in order to mark it as a topic) undergoes a Top-Movement operation which moves it to the front of the relevant clause. But where does the preposed topic move to? A plausible assumption is that it moves to the edge of an inner CP which serves as the complement of an outer CP headed by *that*, so the embedded clause involves the kind of CP recursion structure discussed in §5.4. On this view, Topicalisation in the embedded clause in (149B) involves the movement operation arrowed below:

(150)

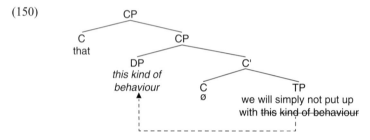

The arrowed Top-Movement (or Topicalisation) operation is yet a further instance of A-bar Movement, since the italicised topicalised DP is moved into spec-CP, and this is an A-bar position. Note that Topicalisation does not trigger concomitant Auxiliary Inversion, with the result that C cannot attract the auxiliary *will* to adjoin to it (cf. **They must realise that this kind of behaviour will we simply not put up with*).

A further type of A-bar Movement operation which does not trigger concomitant Auxiliary Inversion is **Focus-Movement** – i.e. movement of a focused/focalised constituent. From a discourse perspective, a focused constituent represents *new* information (i.e. information not previously mentioned in the discourse and assumed to be unfamiliar to the hearer). Because focusing introduces new information and wh-questions typically ask for new information (e.g. *Who did you see?* asks for the identity of the person you saw), focusing can be used in a reply to a wh-question. By way of illustration, consider the following dialogue:

(151)   SPEAKER A: How many goals did Alfredo di Stéfano score for Real Madrid?
          SPEAKER B: *308 goals* he scored - - - in 396 games. Amazing!

Here, the italicised phrase produced by speaker B originates in the gap position as the complement of the verb *scored* and is then moved to the periphery of the bracketed clause in order to focus it (i.e. mark it as conveying new information). If Foc-Movement is another instance of A-bar Movement under which a focused constituent is moved to spec-CP in order to mark it out as focused, Focusing in (151B) will involve the movement operation arrowed below:

(152)

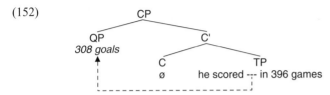

As in the case of the Topicalisation structure in (150), the head C constituent of the inner CP does not trigger Auxiliary Inversion. (A complication I note in passing is that some linguists take Neg-Movement to involve focusing of a negative constituent – although Maekawa 2007 argues that fronted negative constituents are not always focused.)

Our discussion in this section has been aimed at showing that Wh-Movement is not the only operation which moves constituents to spec-CP. On the contrary, there are numerous other movement operations (like Neg-Movement, Deg-Movement, Top-Movement and Foc-Movement) which move a range of different types of constituent to spec-CP. Since spec-CP is an A-bar position (i.e. one which is opaque/invisible to agreement and anaphor binding), all these various movement operations can be seen as specific instances of a more general A-bar Movement operation by which a maximal projection is moved into an A-bar position. Whether or not A-bar Movement is associated with concomitant Auxiliary Inversion will depend on the type of specifier which C has (e.g. a fronted topic does not trigger Inversion, but a fronted negative constituent does) and will be determined by the Inversion Licensing Conditions in (21).

7.11   Summary

This chapter began with an outline of the syntax of wh-exclamatives in §7.2. We saw that there are a number of syntactic, semantic and lexical differences between wh-exclamatives and wh-interrogatives – e.g. exclamatives differ from interrogatives in allowing *what* to modify an *a*-phrase (as in *What a great goal!*), in being factive, in not showing Auxiliary Inversion and in not licensing polarity items. I argued that wh-exclamatives involve a C constituent which carries an exclamative edge feature [XF] attracting an exclamative wh-constituent to move to spec-CP. In §7.3, I described differences between appositive, restrictive and free relative clauses in English, and drew a distinction between wh-relatives (i.e. relative clauses containing a wh-pronoun like *who/which*, etc.) and wh-less relatives. In §7.4, I outlined an account of restrictive relative clauses in which the relative clause CP is adjoined to the constituent that it modifies, and a relative wh-pronoun inside the relative clause undergoes Wh-Movement to the edge of the relative clause. I argued that the Wh-Movement analysis can be extended to wh-less restrictives, if these are analysed as involving movement of a null wh-operator. However in §7.5, I acknowledged that the Wh-Movement analysis faces potential problems in handling relativisation of (i) idiomatic nominals associated with a verb inside the relative clause in sentences like *The headway which they have made is impressive*, (ii) adverbial nouns in sentences like *The way (which) she behaved was appalling* and (iii) anaphor binding in structures like *The photos of himself which Jim has taken*. In §7.6, I presented an alternative Antecedent Raising analysis of wh-less restrictive relative DPs like *the cuts that we are facing*, under which the antecedent noun *cuts* originates as the complement of the verb *facing* and (via a Head Raising operation) is subsequently raised out of the relative *that*-clause to become its antecedent by being remerged as the head N of the NP *cuts that we are facing*. I noted that this analysis can be extended to wh-restrictives like *the cuts which we are facing* if the antecedent noun *cuts* originates as the complement of *which*, and if *which cuts* moves to the edge of CP and then *cuts* remerges with CP to become the head N of an NP. However in §7.7, I noted that this type of structure will not handle DPs like *the photo of himself which Jim took*, where the raised antecedent is the NP *photo of himself*. I suggested an alternative analysis under which the antecedent *photo of himself* originates as the complement of *which*, then the wh-phrase *which photo of himself* moves to the edge of CP and finally the NP *photo of himself* raises to become the specifier of a higher NP. In §7.8, I identified a number of potential problems with the Antecedent Raising analysis of wh-restrictives (e.g. it induces Stranding/Freezing/CED violations), but conjectured that these can probably be overcome. In §7.9, I concluded that we need to assume that restrictive relative clauses have two alternative derivations, one involving Wh-Movement alone, and the other involving Wh-Movement with subsequent Antecedent Raising. In §7.10, I took a brief look at a number of other movement operations (including Neg-Movement, Deg-Movement, Top-Movement and Foc-Movement) and noted that these have in common with Wh-Movement that they move a constituent into spec-CP. I argued that these different kinds of movement operation are specific instances of a more general type of movement operation known as A-bar Movement, because it moves a constituent into an A-bar position like spec-CP – i.e. a position which is opaque/ invisible to agreement and anaphor binding.

Conditions/Constraints/Principles/Rules which have played an important role in the discussion in this chapter include the following:

(20)   **Clause Typing Condition**
         A CP is typed (i.e. interpreted in the semantic component) as being interrogative/exclamative/conditional/imperative (etc.) in type if it has an interrogative/exclamative/conditional/imperative (etc.) specifier. Otherwise, an indicative CP is interpreted as declarative in type by default.

(21)   **Inversion Licensing Conditions**
A null C in a finite clause is licensed to carry a T-feature triggering Auxiliary Inversion
(i)   in any clause where C has an edge feature requiring it to have a negative or degree or conditional specifier
or
(ii)   in a root clause where C has an edge feature requiring it to have an interrogative specifier.

(24)   **Attraction Generalisation**
When a head attracts a given type of item to become its specifier, it attracts the smallest accessible maximal projection containing the closest item of the relevant type.

(34)   **Structural Uniformity Principle**
All constituents of the same type belong to the same category.

(43)   **Doubly Filled COMP Filter**
At PF, the edge of a CP headed by an overt complementiser (like *that/for/if/ whether*) cannot be doubly filled (i.e. cannot contain any other overt constituent).

(48)   **Principle C of Binding Theory**
No (copy of an) R-expression can be coreferential to any (copy of a) constituent c-commanding it.

(61)   **Affix Attachment Condition/AAC**
An affix must be attached to an overt host of an appropriate kind at PF.

(74)   **Principle A of Binding Theory (Anaphor Binding Principle)**
An anaphor can only be bound by a given antecedent if (some copy of) the anaphor is locally c-commanded by (some copy of) the antecedent.

(110)   **Feature Conflict Constraint**
No constituent can carry conflicting specifications for any feature/s.

(111)   **No Tampering Condition/NTC**
No syntactic operation can tamper with (i.e. change) any part of a structure other than the root.

(114)   **Stranding Constraint**
No D/determiner, Q/quantifier or C/complementiser can be stranded without its complement.

(115)   **Freezing Principle/FP**
The constituents of a moved phrase are frozen internally within (and so cannot be extracted out of) the moved phrase.

(116)   **Criterial Freezing Condition**
A constituent which occupies its criterial position is frozen in place.

(117)   **Constraint on Extraction Domains/CED**
Material can only be extracted out of complement, not out of a specifier or adjunct.

7.12   Bibliographical background

On the syntax and semantics of wh-exclamatives (discussed in §7.2), see Elliot (1974), Gérard (1980), Radford (1982, 1989b, 1997c), Obenauer (1994), Benincà (1995, 1996), Graffi (1996), Michaelis and Lambrecht (1996), Portner and Zanuttini (2000), Zanuttini and Portner (2000, 2003), Villalba (2001), d'Avis (2002), Castroviejo (2006) and Abels (2007, 2010). On the factive nature of exclamatives, see Grimshaw (1979) and Abels (2010). On the possibility that factive clauses contain a null factivity operator, see Watanabe (1993a,b), Zubizaretta (2001), Starke (2004) and Haegeman (2012). On the differences between the various types of relative clause discussed in §7.3, see Huddleston and Pullum (2002: 1058–68). On the nature of appositive relative clauses, see Borsley (1997), De Vries (2002: 181–231 and 2006), Cinque (2008), and Citko (2008). On free relatives, see Hirschbühler (1976, 1978), Bresnan and Grimshaw (1978), Groos and van Riemsdijk (1981), Harbert (1983), Larson (1987), Battye (1989), Grosu (1989, 1994), Kayne (1994), Rooryck (1994), Jacobson (1995), Izvorski (2000), Munaro (2001), Vogel (2001), Caponigro (2002, 2004), M. de Vries (2002), Grosu (2003), Citko (2004), Cable (2005), Donati (2006), van Riemsdijk (2006), Caponigro and Pearl (2009), Donati and Cecchetto (2011), Ott (2011), Benincà (2012) and Caponigro, Torrence and Cisneros (2013). On restrictive relatives, see Fabb (1990), Borsley (1992, 1997, 2001), L. de Vries (1993), Sag (1997), Wiltschko (1998), Safir (1999), Alexiadou, Law, Meinunger and Wilder (2000), M. de Vries (2002, 2006), Aoun and Li (2003), del Gobbo (2003), Authier and Reed (2005), Adger and Ramchand (2005), Donati (2006), Kayne (2007), Sportiche (2008), Caponigro and Pearl (2008, 2009), Cecchetto and Donati (2010), Cinque (2011, 2013), Donati and Cecchetto (2011), Collins (2015) and Collins and Radford (2015). On the idea that restrictive relatives are structurally ambiguous (in respect of whether the antecedent originates in a position internal or external to the relative clause), see Carlson (1977), Heim (1987), Sauerland (1998, 2000, 2002) and Hulsey and Sauerland (2006). On the syntax of contact relative clauses, see Erdmann (1980), Harris and Vincent (1980), Weisler (1980), Napoli (1982), Lambrecht (1988), Rizzi (1990), Doherty (1993, 1994) and Haegeman et al. (2015a). On the nature of resumptive relatives (like those discussed in ex. 7.3) see Ross (1967, 1986), Morgan (1972), Perlmutter (1972), McCloskey (1979, 1990, 2002, 2006a), Kroch (1981), Chao and Sells (1983), Sells (1984, 1987), Prince (1990), Contreras (1991), Demirdache (1991), Erteschik-Shir (1992), Shlonsky (1992), Pérez-Leroux (1995), Suñer (1998), Varlokosta and Armon-Lotem (1998), Sharvit (1999), Aoun (2000), Aoun, Choueiri and Hornstein (2001), McKee and McDaniel (2001), Cresswell (2002), Rouveret (2002, 2011), Boeckx (2003, 2007, 2012), Merchant (2003), Asudeh (2004), Ferreira and Swets (2005), Grolla (2005), Alexopoulou and Keller (2007), Hornstein (2007), Bianchi (2008), Friedmann, Novogrodsky, Szterman and Preminger (2008), Herdan (2008), Alexopoulou

(2010), Omaki and Nakao (2010), Heestand, Xiang and Polinsky (2011) and Hofmeister and Norcliffe (2013). On dialects which use *that's* as a genitive in relative clauses, see Seppänen and Kjellmer (1994). On dialects which use *what* in restrictive and appositive relative clauses, see Berizzi and Rossi (2010). For discussion of structures which potentially involve a hidden wh-operator, see Rawlins (2008) on unconditional clauses; Kennedy and Merchant (2000), Lechner (2001), Kennedy (2002), Bhatt and Pancheva (2004) and Grosu and Horvath (2006) on comparative clauses; Potts (2002) on *as*-clauses; and Chomsky (1977) on *tough* structures.

Workbook section

Exercise 7.1

Discuss the syntax of the wh-exclamative structures below in present-day English (in the case of examples containing italicised material, analysing only the italicised material):

1. *What a great save*, wasn't it?! (Gary Lineker, BBC1 TV)
2. *What a lot of people*, aren't there?! (J. Krishnamurti, public talk, Ojai)
3. What an awful day I've had!
4. *What I've had an awful day!
5. *What an awful I've had day!
6. *What an awful day have I had!
7. What a mistake for him to make!
8. *What an awful mistake to make*, wasn't it?!
9. What a place it was to live in!

In addition, analyse the syntax of the Shakespearean English exclamatives in 10 and 11 below, and say how they differ from their counterparts in present-day English.

10. What visions have I seen! (Titania, *Midsummer Night's Dream*, 5.i)
11. What a head have I! (Nurse, *Romeo and Juliet*, II.v)

Consider whether the position of the auxiliary/verb in examples like 10 and 11 may reflect a more general word-order pattern which is also found in non-exclamative sentences such as the following:

12. That letter hath she delivered (Speed, *Two Gentlemen of Verona*, II.i)
13. One only daughter have I (Old Athenian, *Timon of Athens*, I.i)

Finally, consider the nature of the errors made by the (Amsterdam-born) manager of Manchester United when he produced the following exclamative in the course of a TV interview:

14. What a spirit showed my team! (Luis van Gaal, Sky Sports TV = 'What spirit my team showed!')

Helpful hints

In relation to 10–13, consider the possibility that Shakespearean English was a V2/Verb-Second language in which finite (auxiliary or main) verbs in root clauses occupy second position in the sentence (i.e they move into the head C position of CP whenever CP has a specifier). In 13, take *one only daughter* to be a QP, but don't concern yourself with its internal structure. In relation to 14, consider the possibility of interference from Dutch (which is also a V2 language).

Model Answer for 1

At first sight, the expression *What a great save!* would appear to be a phrasal exclamative – i.e. one which is not a clause, but rather simply comprises a wh-QP, perhaps with a structure along the lines shown below (if we treat attributive adjectives as specifiers of a modifier phrase/MODP projection as in §4.11)

(i)

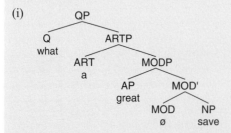

(On analysing *great* and *save* as maximal projections, see §3.5.) However, what undermines a phrasal analysis like (i) is the fact that the example in 1 carries the tag *wasn't it*? Such a tag is typically attached to a clause which contains an inanimate nominal or pronominal subject and the T auxiliary *was*, as in:

(ii)   *The weather/it* **was** changing, wasn't it?

Thus, considerations relating to tag formation suggest that *What a great save!* is in fact a concealed clausal exclamative which has the fuller form shown in highly simplified form in (iii) below, where strikethrough marks words which are present in the syntax, but given a null spellout at PF:

(iii)   What a great save ~~it was~~!

A clausal analysis like (iii) would provide a straightforward account of why the tag *wasn't it?* occurs in 1. On this view, *What a great save!* would be a clausal exclamative derived as follows.

    The verb *be* merges with the exclamative QP *what a great save* to form the VP *be what a great save*, where the QP has the structure shown in (i). The resulting VP then merges with an abstract T constituent containing a past tense affix (*Af*) to form a T-bar which in turn merges with the subject *it* to form the TP *It Af be what a great save*. Under the Auxiliary Raising account of the copula *be* in §5.8, the affix in T will attract the auxiliary *be* to raise from V to T, in the manner shown by the arrow below:

(iv)

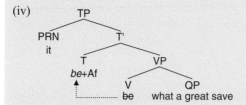

The string *be+Af* will ultimately be spelled out as the past tense form *was* in the PF component.

The TP in (iv) is then merged with a null exclamative C which carries an exclamative edge feature which attracts an exclamative wh-constituent to move to the edge of CP. The question of what moves to the edge of CP is determined by the following condition:

(v)   **Attraction Generalisation**

When a head attracts a given type of item to become its specifier, it attracts the smallest accessible maximal projection containing the closest item of the relevant type.

Since the smallest maximal projection containing exclamative *what* in (i) is the whole QP *what a great save*, this moves to the edge of CP, via the Wh-Movement operation arrowed below:

(vi)

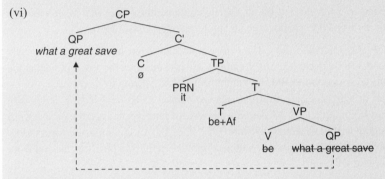

The string *be+Af* would be expected to be spelled out in the PF component as *was*, so deriving *What a great save it was!* Tag formation would then result in *What a great save it was, wasn't it?!* However, it would seem that English allows the subject and auxiliary in this type of exclamative clause to be given a null spellout in the PF component, so resulting in *What a great save ~~it was~~, wasn't it?!*

Model Answer for 7

At first sight, infinitival exclamatives like 7 *What a mistake for him to make!* might seem to be straightforward to deal with. Thus, we might suppose that the overall structure is a root infinitive clause (headed by the complementiser *for*) in which the wh-phrase *what a mistake* originates as the complement of the verb *make* and then raises up into spec-CP, via the Wh-Movement operation arrowed below:

(vii)

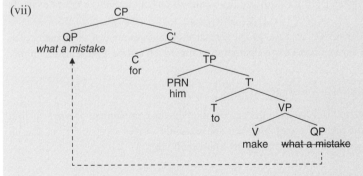

The resulting structure (vii) would be typed as exclamative by the Clause Typing Condition in virtue of having an exclamative specifier.

However, the analysis in (vii) is problematic in at least two respects. Firstly, it violates the following constraint outlined informally in §4.7:

(viii)   **Root Complementiser Constraint/RCC**

No overt complementiser can be the head of a root projection in a language like English.

RCC is violated because the CP in (vii) is a root clause which contains (more accurately, *is headed by*) the overt complementiser *for*. Furthermore, the analysis in (vii) also violates the following constraint posited in §6.3:

(ix)   **Doubly Filled COMP Filter/DFCF**

At PF, the edge of a CP headed by an overt complementiser (like *that/for/if/whether*) cannot be doubly filled (i.e. cannot contain any other overt constituent).

The violation of DFCF arises because the CP in (vii) has both an overt head (*for*) and an overt specifier (*what a mistake*). These two constraint violations call into question the assumption that the infinitive clause in (vii) is a root clause. But if it isn't a root clause, what is it?

A plausible answer is that it is an infinitival relative clause. If so, and if (for expository purposes) we adopt the Adjunction+Wh-Movement analysis of relative clauses, the phrase *what a mistake for him to make* will have a structure along the lines shown in simplified form below (where Op_{REL} denotes a null relative operator which originates in the gap position - - - and from there moves to the edge of CP):

(x)

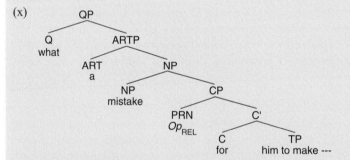

The infinitival CP in (x) does not violate RCC because it is not a root clause and does not violate DFCF because it has a null (rather than overt) specifier. The infinitival clause is typed as relative in accordance with the Clause Typing Condition, by virtue of having a relative operator as its specifier.

However, if (as the model answer for 1 suggests) phrasal exclamatives are clausal in nature, the exclamative QP in (x) will derive from a more abstract structure which can be represented in highly simplified form as follows:

(xi)   *What a mistake for him to make* it was - - - !

That is, the italicised wh-phrase originates in the gap position (as the complement of *was* – as in *It was such a big mistake for him to make*) and then subsequently moves to spec-CP. In the PF component, the string *it was* can optionally be given a null spellout.

Exercise 7.2

The purpose of this exercise is to get you to compare two competing analyses of restrictive relative clauses outlined in the main text, namely (i) the Wh-Movement analysis outlined in §7.4, and (ii) the Wh-Movement+Antecedent Raising analysis outlined in §7.7. Say whether/how each of these analyses can provide a principled account of the (un)grammaticality of the italicised relative structures in the examples below, discussing (and attempting to resolve) any issues that arise:

1 a.   There are *some points of detail which (*that) we must clarify*
  b.   There are *some points of detail (that) we must clarify*
  c.   There are *some points of detail (for us) to clarify*
  d.   *There are *some points of detail which (for us) to clarify*

2 a.   There's *no hotel in which (*that) I can stay*
  b.   There's *no hotel which (*that) I can stay in*
  c.   There's *no hotel (that) I can stay in*
  d.   *There's *no hotel in (that) I can stay*

3 a.   There's *no hotel in which (*for me) to stay*
  b.   *There's *no hotel which (for me) to stay in*
  c.   There's *no hotel (for me) to stay in*
  d.   *There's *no hotel in (for me) to stay*

4 a.   I'm looking for *an expert on computers who (*that) can fix the glitch*
  b.   *I'm looking for *an expert on computers who to fix the glitch*
  c.   I'm looking for *an expert on computers that can fix the glitch*
  d.   I'm looking for *an expert on computers to fix the glitch*

5 a.   There is *no reason why (*that) he should resign from the board*
  b.   *There is *no reason (for him) to resign from the board*
  c.   There is *no reason (that) he should resign from the board*
  d.   There is *no reason (for him) to resign from the board*

In addition, discuss how to account for the quantifier scope ambiguity in the italicised structure in the following sentence:

6.   *The two cars which each of them drove* were Ferraris

Sentence 6 has one interpretation (6i) on which *two cars* has scope over *each of them* and the sentence can be paraphrased as 'There were two cars that each of them drove and they were both Ferraris' (i.e. they each drove the same two Ferraris); however, it also has another reading (6ii) on which *each of them* has scope over *two cars* and the sentence is paraphraseable as 'Each of them drove two cars and all the cars they drove were Ferraris', and on this reading it is possible that each individual drove two Ferraris that were different from the two driven by any other individual (e.g. if there were two drivers, between them they may have driven four different Ferraris).

Helpful hints

Look carefully at the model answers before tackling this exercise, since they will give you a number of ideas for analysing the examples. Assume that relativized nominals are grammatical if at least one of the two alternative derivations yields a convergent outcome (i.e. an outcome satisfying all relevant constraints and interface conditions), and ungrammatical if neither derivation leads to a convergent outcome. In 1–5, take the expressions *points of detail, hotel, expert on computers* and *reason* to be NPs, but don't concern yourself with their internal structure. In relation to 4b, bear in mind that interrogative clauses like that bracketed in *I have no idea* [**who** *can/*to fix the glitch*] are ungrammatical if infinitival: look closely at what case would be assigned to the subject of the infinitive in such structures, bearing in mind the discussion of case in the model answer for 4d given below. In relation to 5, bear in mind that under the PP Hypothesis outlined in §4.11, 'Adverbial (pro)nominals are PPs headed by a null preposition': see the brief discussion of this in the model answer for 3b. Recall too that in §4.11 it was suggested that *why* serves as the complement of a null counterpart of the preposition *for* (which appears overtly in structures like 'He doesn't like me, and I'll tell you **for** *why*'). For the purposes of this exercise, assume that the PP *for why* originates as a VP adjunct which adjoins to the VP *resign from the board* to form the larger VP *resign from the board for why*. In 6, take *two cars* to be a QP headed by the numeral quantifier *two*, and take *each of them* to be a QP headed by the quantifier *each*: assume that a given quantifier phrase QP_1 can have scope over another quantifier phrase QP_2 if (some copy of) QP_1 c-commands (some copy of) QP_2. Consider the possibility (not discussed in the text) that Antecedent Raising can raise a QP constituent out of the relative clause containing it to become the specifier of a higher QP which has a null Q head that in turn has the relative clause CP as its complement.

Model answer for 3b

Consider how to account for the ungrammaticality of **There's no hotel which for me to stay in*. Under the Wh-Movement analysis, the NP *hotel* is directly merged in situ outside the relative clause CP, and the relative clause is adjoined to it. The relative pronoun *which* originates as the complement of the preposition *in* and is moved to spec-CP by the Wh-Movement operation arrowed in (i) below:

(i)
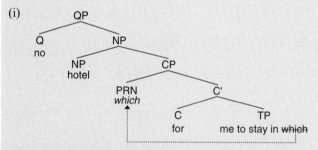

By contrast, under the Antecedent Raising derivation, the NP *hotel* will originate as the complement of the determiner *which*, and the DP *which hotel* will in turn originate as the complement of the preposition *in*. The DP *which hotel* undergoes Wh-Movement into the specifier position of the CP headed by infinitival *for*. Subsequently, the NP *hotel* undergoes the Antecedent Raising operation arrowed in (ii) below, giving rise to the formation of an NP which in turn is merged with the negative quantifier *no* to form the QP shown below:

(ii)
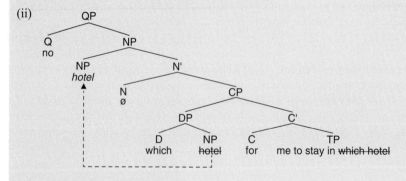

(In the discussion of Antecedent Raising in this and similar structures, I will ignore the observation made in the main text that Antecedent Raising violates constraints like the Freezing Principle and the Constraint on Extraction Domains, since this is an inherent characteristic of the Antecedent Raising analysis.) Both structures (i and ii) violate the Doubly Filled COMP Filter, because both result in a PF structure in which an overt complementiser (*for*) has an overt specifier (*which*, or a DP containing *which*). Thus, since both derivations induce a violation of the Doubly Filled COMP Filter, the resulting sentence *There's no hotel which for me to stay in* is correctly specified to be ungrammatical.

Now consider how we account for the ungrammaticality of *There's no hotel which to stay in*. Under the Wh-Movement analysis, this will have a similar derivation to (i), except that the head C position of CP will be occupied by a null infinitival complementiser and the infinitive subject will be PRO – as below:

(iii)

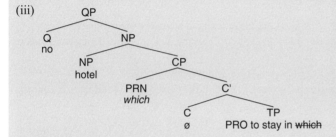

Under the alternative Antecedent Raising analysis, the relevant QP will have the same structure as in (ii), save that the head C position of CP is occupied by a null infinitival complementiser (rather than *for*), and the infinitive subject will be PRO (rather than *me*) – as below:

(iv)

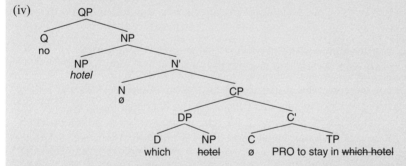

However, the resulting structures (iii, iv) are both ungrammatical, and it is far from obvious why. Since neither (iii) nor (iv) violates the Doubly Filled COMP Filter, the source of the ungrammaticality must lie elsewhere. One way of ruling out such structures would be in terms of a PF constraint such as:

(v) **Infinitival Relative Constraint**
   No (DP headed by an) overt relative operator can be the specifier/daughter of an infinitival CP at PF.

The constraint (v) will be violated by the Wh-Movement structure in (iii) because the relative pronoun *which* is the daughter of an infinitival CP. The constraint will also be violated by the Antecedent Raising structure (iv), since a DP headed by the overt relative D *which* serves as the specifier of an infinitival CP. Given that both ways of deriving the structure violate the constraint (v), we can account for the ungrammaticality of sentences like *There's no hotel which to stay in*.

However, the downside of this analysis is that the condition in (v) appears to be arbitrary, stipulative and non-explanatory. Indeed, the condition doesn't even extend to interrogative clauses, since an infinitival CP like that bracketed in (vi) below can have an (italicised) interrogative specifier:

(vi)   I wasn't sure [*which (dress)* to choose]

Thus, invoking the condition in (v) seems to provide us with a less than fully satisfactory answer to the question of why an infinitival relative clause can't begin with an overt wh-pronoun.

Interestingly, for some speakers, the constraint (v) seems to apply only to simple pronouns like *which/who*, not to adverbial pronouns like *why/where/how/when*. Thus, there are speakers who produce infinitival relatives like those bracketed below (sourced from the Internet):

(vii) a.   The best place [*where* to exchange your currency is in a bank] (www.tripadvisor.com)
     b.   Can you give one good reason [*why* to support Palestine and not Israel]? (answers.yahoo.com)
     c.   Best way [*how* to hard boil eggs perfectly] (eggtutor.com)
     d.   The best time [*when* to prune a fig tree] will be in the (dormant) winter season (uk.ask.com)

Why should relative clauses like those in (vii) not fall foul of the constraint in (v)? One possible answer is the following. Under the PP Hypothesis outlined in §4.11, adverbial (pro)nominals are PPs headed by a null preposition. If (in the spirit of this proposal) we take the italicised adverbial relative pronouns in (vii) to be PPs headed by a null preposition, the specifier of the bracketed CPs in (vii) will not be a simple wh-word but rather a PP headed by a null preposition. And as we see from structures like (viii) below, an infinitival relative clause can indeed have a PP as its specifier:

(viii) a.   It's not an easy angle [*from which* to create] (Peter Drury, Sky Sports TV)
      b.   It's been an easy pitch [*on which* to bowl] (Michael Holding, Sky Sports TV)

This is precisely what the constraint in (v) would lead us to expect, because the relative pronoun *which* in (viii) is not the daughter of a CP constituent, but rather the daughter of a PP constituent. Likewise, under the PP Hypothesis, the relative pronoun *where* in (vii.a) will be the daughter of a PP headed by a null counterpart of *in*, so that (vii.a) will not violate the constraint in (v) either.

Model answer for 3d

Consider first how to account for the ungrammaticality of *There's no hotel in for me to stay*. Let's suppose that there are (in principle) two alternative ways of deriving restrictive relative clauses – namely (i) via Wh-Movement alone, or (ii) via Wh-Movement followed by Antecedent Raising. Under a pure Wh-Movement analysis, the NP *hotel* (which is an NP by virtue of being the largest constituent headed by the noun *hotel*) is directly merged in situ, and an infinitival relative clause CP is adjoined to it. Inside the relative CP, a null relative operator (*Op*) originates as the complement of the preposition *in*, and the PP *in Op* moves from the gap position (- - -) shown below to spec-CP by the arrowed Wh-Movement operation:

(ix)

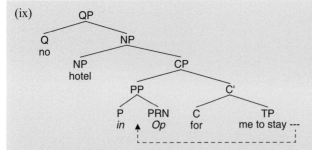

By contrast, under the Antecedent Raising analysis, the NP *hotel* would be merged with a null D constituent containing a relative operator (*Op*) to form the DP *Op hotel*. This DP is merged with the preposition *in* to form the PP *in Op hotel*. The resulting PP then undergoes A-bar Movement from the gap position in (x) below to the edge of the CP headed by the infinitival complementiser *for*. Subsequently, the NP *hotel* undergoes the Antecedent Raising operation arrowed below and thereby becomes the specifier of a larger NP which in turn is merged with the negative quantifier *no* to form the QP shown below:

(x)

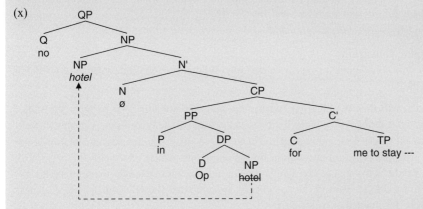

Both of the derivations in (ix) and (x) violate the Doubly Filled COMP Filter, since both result in a CP with an overt complementiser (= *for*) and an overt specifier (namely a PP headed by the overt preposition *in*). Thus, we can account for the ungrammaticality of *There's no hotel in for me to stay* because each of the two possible derivations induces a violation of the Doubly Filled COMP Filter.

However, this can't be the whole story, because *There's no hotel in to stay* is also ungrammatical. This can be derived in essentially the same ways as in (ix) and (x), except that the infinitival CP has a null complementiser as its head, and a null PRO as its subject. Under a pure Wh-Movement derivation, the QP containing the relative clause will have the following structure:

(xi)

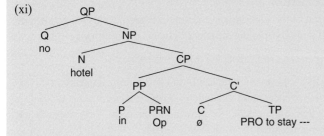

By contrast, under the alternative Wh-Movement+Antecedent derivation, the QP will instead have the structure below:

(xii)

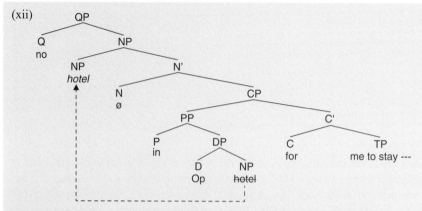

Neither (xi) nor (xii) violates the Doubly Filled COMP Filter, and yet the corresponding sentence *There's no hotel in to stay* is clearly ungrammatical. So why are the resulting structures ungrammatical?

One possibility is that such structures violate a constraint on pied-piping suggested by Chomsky (1999: 19), which for present purposes can be formulated as follows (where a *superordinate* constituent is one asymmetrically c-commanding the null constituent that moves):

(xiii)   **Pied-Piping Constraint**
When a null constituent moves, it cannot pied-pipe any overt superordinate constituent along with it.

Both (xi) and (xii) will then be ruled out because the null operator illicitly pied-pipes the super-ordinate preposition *in* along with it when it moves, in violation of the Pied-Piping Constraint (xiii).

However, (xiii) seems to be somewhat ad hoc in nature, so an obvious question to ask is whether there are more principled ways of accounting for the ungrammaticality of structures like (xi, xii). One possibility would be to suppose that a null operator must be 'close enough' to its antecedent for the antecedent to be able to identify the contents of the operator. The relevant locality/closeness condition might be formulated as follows:

(xiv)   **Relative Identification Condition**
The antecedent of a null relative operator must be identifiable, and can only be identified if the null operator is c-commanded by and immediately adjacent to (i.e. not separated by any overt constituent/s from) its antecedent.

(xiv) can plausibly be taken to be PF interface condition designed to make sentences easier to parse (by making it easier to locate the antecedent of a null operator). The condition (xiv) rules out the structures in (xi,xii) because the antecedent is not immediately adjacent to the operator (the two being separated by the intervening preposition *in*).

However, the particular formulation of the Identification Condition given in (xiv) appears to be too restrictive/strong, since it would wrongly rule out structures such as the following:

(xv)   An *incident* took place yesterday [CP **Op** [C that] the police are aware of]

Here, the bracketed restrictive relative clause is extraposed, and the bold-printed relative Op/ operator is separated from its italicised antecedent by the underlined material *took place yesterday*: consequently, (xiv) wrongly predicts that sentences like (xv) are ungrammatical. This suggests that we need some alternative formulation of the Identification Condition which will rule out structures like (xi/xii) but not rule out structures like (xv). One possibility would be to revise (xiv) along the following lines:

(xvi)   **Relative Identification Condition** (revised)

A null relative operator must be identifiable as a relative operator either by being (the head of a DP which is) the specifier of an overt relative complementiser, or by being c-commanded by and immediately adjacent to (i.e. not separated by any overt constituent/s from) its antecedent.

The revised formulation in (xvi) will allow a structure like (xv) because the null relative operator is the specifier of the overt relative complementiser *that*. However, it will rule out structures like (xi) and (xii) because in both cases the overt preposition *in* intervenes between operator and antecedent, and this means that the immediate adjacency condition in (xvi) is not met. Interestingly, (xvi) will also correctly rule out structures like the following:

(xvii) *An *incident* <u>took place yesterday</u> [$_{CP}$ **Op** [$_C$ ø] the police are aware of]

This is because the operator is neither the specifier of an *overt* relative complementiser in (xvii), nor immediately adjacent to its italicised antecedent. The condition in (xvi) is arguably part of a more general constraint requiring empty categories to be identifiable, but I will not pursue this issue further here.

Yet a further alternative would be to suppose that structures like (xi, xii) involve some kind of case violation. Reasoning along these lines, let us suppose that a null operator cannot in principle be assigned nominative/accusative/genitive case, because it has no means of spelling out this case (e.g. we can't add the accusative *-m* affix of *whom* or the genitive *-s* affix of *whose* to a null operator, since the Affix Attachment Condition of §6.6 requires that 'An affix must be attached to an *overt* host of an appropriate kind at PF'). Because it is **case-resistant**, an operator must move to a position where it is outside the domain of any case-assigner and so can avoid being assigned case. We can embody this condition in terms of the following constraint:

(xviii) **Case Resistance Constraint**

No case-resistant constituent can occupy a case position (i.e. a position within the domain of a case assigner) at PF.

If the operator moves on its own into spec-CP (stranding the preposition at the end of the clause), it will be in a caseless position where it is not within the case domain of the transitive preposition *in*. However, if the operator pied-pipes the preposition *in* along with it (as in xi and xii), the operator will be in a case position (by virtue of being within the domain of the transitive preposition *in*) and the relevant structures will violate (xviii).

Some empirical support for the constraint in (xviii) comes from contrasts such as the following:

(xix) a   I am now sure (***of**) *that he is innocent*
     b   **Of* that he is innocent*, I am now sure - - -
     c   *That he is innocent*, I am now sure **of** - - -

Safir (1986) argues that the complementiser *that* is case-resistant, and for this reason a *that*-clause cannot serve as the complement of a transitive preposition like *of*, since this would violate the constraint in (xviii). Fronting the *of*-PP in (xix.b) does not improve matters, since it still leaves *that* within the case domain of the preposition *of*, in violation of (xviii). However, fronting the *that*-clause in (xix.c) leaves the preposition at the end of the sentence and the *that*-clause at the beginning, with the result that (xix.c) does not violate the constraint (xviii).

Model answer for 4d

How consider the derivation of the italicised nominal in 4d 'I'm looking for *an expert on computers to fix the glitch.*' If (as claimed here) relative clauses are structurally ambiguous, this can be derived either via Wh-Movement alone or via Wh-Movement and subsequent Antecedent Raising. Under the Wh-Movement-only analysis, the NP *expert on computers* will be directly merged in situ, and the relative clause CP will be adjoined to it. A null relative operator will originate as the subject/specifier of the TP *to fix the glitch* and will move to spec-CP by the Wh-Movement operation arrowed below:

(xx)

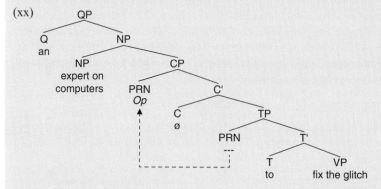

If (as suggested in the model answer for 3d) the null operator is case-resistant, we can suppose that movement of the operator to spec-CP in (xx) takes it out of the case domain of the (null-case-assigning) complementiser, thereby avoiding any violation of the Case Resistance Constraint (xviii). However, an alternative possibility would be to suppose that the null operator is only resistant to being assigned the kind of case that overt constituents carry (nominative, accusative or genitive) and that nothing prevents a null operator from being assigned null case (in the same way as the null PRO subject of control infinitives is assigned null case). If so, the null complementiser could assign null case to the null operator in (xx) at the point where the operator is in its initial (- - -) position in spec-TP. This would mean that the operator in (xx) carries null case rather than no case.

Now consider what would happen under the alternative Antecedent Raising analysis. The NP *expert on computers* would be merged with a D constituent containing a null relative operator (*Op*), so forming the DP *Op expert on computers*, which originates as the subject of *to fix the glitch*. The resulting DP will then be moved to the edge of the relative clause CP. Subsequently, the NP *expert on computers* will raise up (in the manner shown by the arrow below) to become the specifier of a higher NP, which in turn merges with the indefinite article/quantifier *a* to form the structure below:

(xxi)

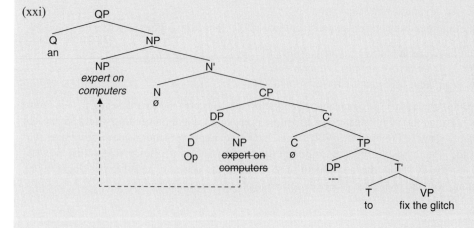

An interesting issue that then arises concerns the case-marking of the null operator on the one hand, and the noun *expert* on the other. One possibility is that the relative clause complementiser does not assign case to either, and the caseless operator moves to a caseless position on the edge of CP, while the NP *expert on computers* moves into a case position within the domain of the transitive preposition *for*, so allowing the noun *expert* to be assigned accusative case by *for*. Another is that the complementiser assigns null case to the operator (in its initial position as the head D of the DP subject of *to fix the glitch*) but not to the NP *expert on computers*, and that the NP *expert on computers* only receives case (from *for*) after it has raised out of the relative clause CP into spec-NP. Under either account, there would be a mismatch between the operator (which would have either null case or no case) and the NP *expert on computers* (which would receive accusative case from *for*). However, even if this case conflict causes the derivation to crash, there is an alternative Wh-Movement derivation available in (xx) on which the operator and antecedent remain distinct constituents throughout the derivation, and hence can have different case properties. Given that there is at least one convergent way of deriving the sentence (4d) 'I'm looking for *an expert on computers to fix the glitch*', we correctly predict that the sentence is grammatical.

Exercise 7.3

This exercise asks you to evaluate a number of alternative analyses of a type of wh-clause not discussed in the main text of this chapter or the last, namely WH+COMP clauses whose periphery contains a wh-constituent followed by an overt complementiser. Such clauses occur frequently in spoken English (and indeed I have collected hundreds of authentic examples from live broadcasts and from the Internet). For instance, many speakers produce embedded exclamative clauses like those bracketed in 1 below (sourced from the Internet unless otherwise specified), containing an italicised exclamative wh-phrase followed by a bold complementiser:

1 a.   It shows [*what a fantastic squad* **that** they have] (Gordon Strachan, ITV)
  b.   That proved [*how big a race* **that** it is] (Jonjo O'Neill, Talk Sport Radio)
  c.   You will be amazed [*how quickly* **that** people you care about come round to the idea]
  d.   It just shows you [*how invincible* **that** they have been at the Etihad] (Dominic McGinnis, Talk Sport Radio)

Similar WH+COMP exclamative structures are also found in root clauses like those in 2 below (sourced from the Internet unless otherwise specified):

2 a.   *What a run* **that** they're having! (Mark Pougatch, BBC Radio 5)
  b.   *What a legend* **that** Frank Lampard is! (John Cross, Talk Sport Radio: NB *that* = [ðət])
  c.   *How quickly* **that** people forget!
  d.   *How pretty* **that** she looks in this photo!

One possible analysis of structures like those in 1 and 2 is to take *that* to be a factive complementiser heading a CP which contains a fronted wh-phrase as its specifier. On this view, 2a would have the derivation shown in simplified form below, with the arrow marking Wh-Movement of the exclamative QP *what a run*:

3.   [$_{CP}$ *what a run* [$_{C}$ **that**$_{FACT}$] [$_{TP}$ they [$_{T}$ are] [$_{VP}$ [$_{V}$ having] ~~what a run~~]]]

The FACT subscript on the complementiser *that* in 3 serves to indicate that it marks factivity.

However, a question arising from the analysis in 3 is whether it will satisfy PF interface conditions, like the following (which impose constraints on the type of structures which are admissible at PF):

4. **Root Complementiser Constraint**

    At PF, no overt complementiser can be the head of a root projection (in a language like English).

5. **Doubly Filled COMP Filter**

    At PF, the edge of a CP headed by an overt complementiser (like *that/for/if/whether*) cannot be doubly filled (i.e. cannot contain any other overt constituent).

Consider whether, under the analysis in 3, a sentence like 1a violates either or both of the constraints in 4 and 5, and likewise whether a sentence like 2a violates either or both of the constraints in 4 and 5.

Now consider an alternative analysis of *wh+that* exclamatives proposed by Zwicky (2002: 227), under which *wh+that* exclamatives are reduced clefts, so that, e.g., 2a is a reduced variant of the cleft sentence structure shown below (simplified by showing only CP projections):

6.   [$_{CP}$ what a run [$_C$ ø] *it is* [$_{CP}$ [$_C$ that] they're having - - -]]

The cleft sentence structure comprises a main clause CP containing the string *it is* and an embedded clause CP introduced by *that*. The *it is* string is ultimately given a null spellout in the phonological component by a Cleft Reduction operation of some kind. Say whether or not the kind of structure in 6 would violate either or both of the constraints in 4 and 5. In addition, say whether the single CP analysis of exclamatives in 3 or the cleft analysis in 6 would account for the kind of tag found in sentences like those below:

7 a.   *What a run that they're having, *isn't it?*

   b.   What a run that they're having, *aren't they?*

Bear in mind that in tag sentences like *The rich think that the president should reduce taxes, don't they?* the tag comprises a negated copy of the main-clause auxiliary followed by a pronominal copy of the main-clause subject.

Now consider a third analysis for WH+COMP exclamatives, modelled on an analysis of similar structures in Paduan (a variety of Italian spoken in Padua) in Zanuttini and Portner (2003). They propose a CP recursion analysis under which there is an outer CP with a null head and an exclamative specifier, and an inner CP headed by *that* which has a null factivity operator as its specifier. If we extend this type of analysis to English, 2a *What a run that they're having!* would have the structure shown in simplified form below, where Op_{FACT} denotes a null factivity operator, and the exclamative QP *what a run* originates in the position marked by the gap (as the complement of the verb *having*) and ultimately ends up (via Wh-Movement) in the italicized spec-CP position in the main clause:

8.   [$_{CP}$ *what a run* [$_C$ ø] [$_{CP}$ Op_{FACT} [$_C$ that] [$_{TP}$ they [$_T$ are] [$_{VP}$ [$_V$ having] - - -]]]]

Would the analysis in 8 violate either or both of the constraints in 4 and 5? And would it violate the condition in 9 below (from §4.10) and/or that in 10 below (from §6.4)?

9. **Impenetrability Condition**

    A constituent c-commanded by a complementiser C is impenetrable to (so cannot agree with, or be case-marked by, or be attracted by, etc.) any constituent c-commanding the CP headed by C.

10. **Intervention Condition**

No intervention-sensitive constituent can move across an intervening intervention-sensitive constituent of the same type.

You might find it helpful to know that Haegeman (2012: 264) argues that factive clauses contain a null factive operator in spec-CP, and the Intervention Condition blocks movement of the interrogative operator *how* from the gap position (- - -) to the italicized position across an intervening factive operator in a structure such as:

11. *$[_{CP}$ *How* $[_{C}$ does] John know $[_{CP}$ Op$_{FACT}$ $[_{C}$ that] Fred behaved - - -]]?

What (if any) would be the implication/s for the single CP analysis in 3 above on the one hand (and for the CP recursion analysis in 8 on the other) if the Root Complementiser Constraint in 4 were reformulated as in 12 below?

12. **Root Complementiser Constraint** (*revised*)

At PF, a complementiser cannot be the first overt word in a root projection.

And what difference (if any) would it make if the Doubly Filled COMP Filter in 5 were reformulated as in 13 below:

13. **Doubly Filled COMP Filter**

At PF, no more than one overt constituent can be positioned on the edge of CP.

Would there still remain problems with the analysis in 3 (and/or with that in 8) if 12 were adopted in place of 4, and if 13 were adopted in place of 5?

Now discuss the syntax of other types of WH+COMP clauses found in spoken English, including embedded interrogatives like those bracketed in 14 below, and relative clauses like those bracketed in 15:

14 a.   You simply do not know [*what side* **that** they will select] (Brian Moore, Talk Sport Radio)
   b.   It just shows you [*how invincible* **that** they have been at the Etihad] (Dominic McGinnis, Talk Sport Radio)
   c.   It will be interesting to see [*how seriously* **that** they will take these issues] (Andy Jacobs, Talk Sport Radio]
   d.   I just don't know [*whether* **that** they will have the same attitude] (Mark Saggers, Talk Sport Radio)

15 a.   I'm aware of the speed [*with which* **that** they work] (Tim Vickery, BBC Radio 5)
   b.   The reason [*why* **that** there is a buzz in here] is because Mark Webber is in pole position (Jake Humphreys, BBC1 TV)
   c.   As Liverpool chase the game, there may be more room [*in which* **for** Manchester United to manoeuvre] (Commentator, Sky Sports TV)

For the purposes of this exercise, analyse only the syntax of the (highlighted) periphery of the embedded clauses bracketed in 14 and 15. To what extent (if at all) does the analysis of these clauses depend on whether the Root Complementiser Constraint is given the formulation in 4 or that in 12?

Next, consider how the issue of whether the Doubly Filled COMP Filter is given the formulation in 5 or that in 13 will affect how we analyse root/main clauses like those in 16 below:

16 a. *Which hotel* **are** you staying in?

   b. *No effort* **did** they spare

In addition, say how the formulation of the Doubly Filled COMP Filter will affect the analysis of the (CP) periphery of root clauses such as those in 17a/b below and embedded clauses like those bracketed in 17c in which the periphery of the clause comprises an italicised wh-constituent, a bold-printed complementiser or inverted auxiliary in C and an additional (underlined) constituent positioned between the two:

17 a. *Under what circumstances* <u>during the holidays</u> **would** you go into the office? (Sobin 2003: 193)

   b. *At no point*, <u>in spite of being provoked</u>, **did** I hit him

   c. I'm just wondering [*why*, <u>at the end of the season</u>, **that** Lerner gave McLeish the job] (Listener, phone-in, BBC Radio 5)

Finally, consider how the alternative formulations of the Doubly Filled COMP Filter in (5) and (13) will affect the way we analyse clauses like those bracketed below:

18 a. I swear [**that** *on no account* <u>during the holidays</u> **will** I write a paper] (Haegeman 2012: 23, fn.19)

   b. There's some unclarity as to [*whether*, <u>if they go into administration</u>, **that** they will get a 9-point penalty] (Simon Jordan, BBC Radio 5)

In your discussion, concentrate on the structure of the clause periphery, and don't concern yourself with the internal structure of TP. Overall, show how the question of what is the optimal analysis of any given structure may depend on the assumptions we make (e.g. on the precise formulation that we give to specific constraints).

Helpful hints

For the purposes of this exercise, assume that *what a fantastic squad* in 1a and *what a run* in 2a are exclamative QPs, but don't concern yourself with their internal structure. In 14d, take *the same attitude* to be a DP, but don't concern yourself with its internal structure. In 17 and 18, take the italicised and underlined constituents to be clausal adjuncts directly merged in situ, and take the phrases introduced by *during/in/at* to be PPs, but don't concern yourself with their structure; take the *if*-clause in 18b to be a projection of the SUB (i.e. subordinating conjunction) *if* and hence to be a SUBP, but don't concern yourself with its internal structure. In 14–18, consider the implications of making two different sets of assumptions about the structure of the periphery in such sentences: <u>either</u> (i) the Doubly Filled COMP Filter doesn't hold for speakers who produce *wh+that/for* structures, and such speakers allow an overt complementiser to have one or more overt specifiers; <u>or</u> (ii) the version of the Doubly Filled COMP Filter in (13) holds universally, including in *wh+that/for* varieties of English.

Model Answer for 18a

By hypothesis, *that* in 18a is a complementiser which is directly merged in the head C position of CP. Likewise, under the analysis of Auxiliary Inversion in §5.2, *will* is an inverted auxiliary which moves from T to C. Consequently, there must be at least two different CPs in 18a – an outer one headed by *that* and an inner one headed by *will*. If these are the only two CPs in the structure, then the PP *on no account* and the PP *during the holidays* which each serve as a separate specifier of the

C constituent containing the inverted auxiliary *will*, and the periphery of the bracketed clause in 18a will have the structure shown below (simplified by showing only overt constituents):

(i)

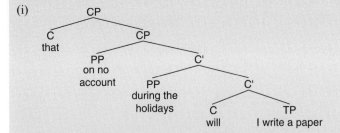

On this view, the lower C constituent containing *will* has two specifiers, the inner one being the PP *during the holidays* and the outer one being the PP *on no account*.

   The structure in (i) does not violate the Root Complementiser Condition (irrespective of whether this is formulated as in 4 or as in 12) because the outer CP headed by *that* in (i) is not a *root* projection, by virtue of the fact that – although this is not shown in (i) – it is embedded within a VP headed by the verb *swear*. The structure in (i) does not violate the version of the Doubly Filled COMP Filter in 5 either, because the inner CP is headed by the auxiliary *will* (and not by an overt complementiser), and hence the filter is not applicable to it. By contrast, however, the structure in (i) violates the alternative version of the filter given in 13, because there are three overt constituents on the edge of the inner CP in (i), namely the auxilary *will*, the PP *during the holidays*, and the additional PP *on no account*. However, we can avoid any violation of 13 if we suppose that each of these three constituents is contained in a separate CP, so that the *that*-clause has the structure shown in simplified form in (ii) below rather than that in 19 above (where numeral subscripts on CPs are added purely for identification purposes):

(ii)

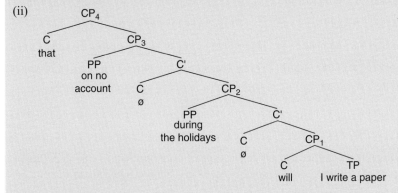

This results in a CP recursion structure in which there are four different CPs, each containing only one overt constituent on its edge (either an overt head and no specifier, or an overt specifier and a null head).

   An issue arising from a multiple CP analysis like that in (ii) is how to capture the insight that Inversion of *will* is contingent on the presence of the negative PP *on no account*. Under the Inversion Licensing Condition in (21i), C triggers Auxiliary Inversion when it has a negative specifier. Under the analysis in (i), we can maintain the claim in (21i) that a C with a negative specifier has a T-feature which attracts a T auxiliary like *will* to move to C, but in order to maintain the analysis in (i), we have to adopt the version of the Doubly Filled COMP Filter in 5. However, the analysis in (ii) is seemingly irreconciliable with the account of Inversion in (21i) because the negative PP and the inverted auxiliary are not positioned on the edge of the same CP (nor even in immediately adjacent CPs). One way of getting round the problem, however, would be to posit that the negative PP *on no account* originates within TP and from there moves to become the specifier of CP$_1$ before moving on to occupy its criterial position as the specifier of CP$_3$. This would mean that the negative PP can trigger Auxiliary Inversion at the stage of derivation where it is the specifier of CP$_1$.

Exercise 7.4

This exercise asks you to critically evaluate four alternative analyses of free relative clauses, like that bracketed in 1:

1. [What we are facing] is a severe economic downturn

The challenge posed by such structures is to account for how what appears to be a clause/CP can function as a nominal/DP. Donati and Cecchetto (2011) propose a Head Raising account of pronominal free relatives (i.e. free relatives in which the wh-constituent is a pronoun like *what*) under which the structure bracketed in 1 would be derived as follows. The verb *facing* merges with the pronominal D constituent *what* to form the VP *facing what*. This VP is then merged with the T auxiliary *are* to form a T-bar which in turn merges with the pronoun *we* to form the TP *we are facing what*. This TP then merges with a null complementiser to form the CP *ø we are facing what*. The D-pronoun *what* then moves out of – and remerges with – this CP, coming to serve as the head D of the DP shown below (with the arrow showing movement of *what*):

2.

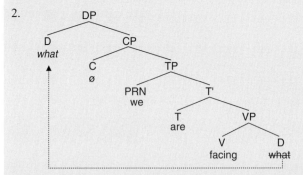

Since the resulting structure is a DP, it can occur in the same range of positions as other DPs (hence, e.g., as the complement of a transitive preposition like *about* in 'I am concerned **about** *what we are facing*').

However, Donati and Cecchetto note that a Head Raising analysis won't handle phrasal free relative structures like that bracketed below, in which the italicised wh-constituent is a phrase:

3. I will visit [*whatever part of town* you will visit]

They suggest (2011: 554) that phrasal free relative structures like 3 have a different derivation, under which *whatever* is 'an external determiner' and the bracketed relative structure in 3 is a DP+CP structure in which the relativized nominal (= the NP *part of town*) moves to the edge of CP in the manner shown by the arrow below, and the resulting CP is then merged with the wh-determiner *whatever* to form the structure shown in simplified form below:

4.

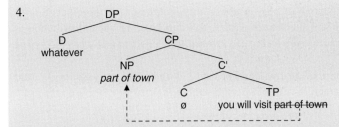

An alternative way of dealing with structures like 3 is to treat the antecedent NP as originating outside the relative clause CP as well, and to treat the CP as involving Wh-Movement of a null relative operator (below denoted as Op_{REL}) to spec-CP. On this view, the bracketed free relative structure in 3 would have the derivation shown in simplified form below:

5.

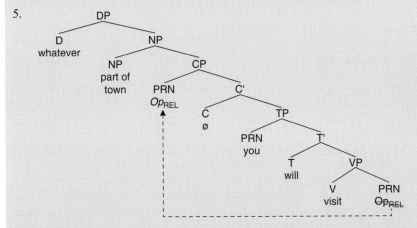

The null relative operator can be thought of as a null counterpart of a relative pronoun like *which*. It may be that the use of an overt relative pronoun like *which* in place of the null operator is barred (cf *I will visit whatever part of town **which** you will visit*) because the head D of the overall DP is a wh-marked constituent (*whatever*), and there is some constraint which filters out relative clause structures in which both the antecedent and the operator are wh-marked (although it should be noted that WH+WH strings are OK where a wh-interrogative antecedent is modified by a wh-relative operator, as in *Which film which you saw did you like best?*).

Caponigro and Pearl (2009) and Ott (2011) propose a different analysis which can handle both phrasal free relatives like that bracketed in 3 and non-phrasal free relatives like that bracketed in 1 in a unitary fashion. They propose a simple Wh-Movement analysis, under which the free relative clause is simply a CP, and the wh-constituent is a maximal projection which undergoes Wh-Movement to spec-CP, in the manner arrowed below:

6
    a. [$_{CP}$ *what* [$_C$ ø] [$_{TP}$ we [$_T$ are] [$_{VP}$ [$_V$ facing] ~~what~~]]]

    b. [$_{CP}$ *whatever part of town* [$_C$ ø] [$_{TP}$ you [$_T$ will] [$_{VP}$ [$_V$ visit] ~~whatever part of town~~]]]

They posit that the categorial properties of a free relative CP are determined by those of its specifier rather than by those of its head, with the result that the free relative clause 'assumes the category of whatever element is moved to its edge' (Ott 2011: 186, fn.3). It will then follow from the analysis in

6 that if C has a D/DP constituent (like *what/whatever part of town*) as its specifier, the CP containing the relevant specifier will function like a DP, and thus have the same distribution as any other DP (and hence, e.g., *what we are facing* can serve as the subject of *is a severe economic downturn* in 1).

Discuss which (if any) of the four analyses outlined in 2, 4 and 5 can account for the (un) grammaticality of free relative structures like those italicised below:

7. *What (*that) we are facing* is a severe economic downturn
8. The Court have said that she's well within her rights to choose *whichever provider that she wants* (Doton Adebayo, BBC Radio 5)
9. A basic principle of football management is that *whatever that goes on inside the dressing-room* stays inside the dressing-room (Sir Geoff Hurst, BBC Radio 5)
10. I'll go *to whatever gigs (that) you go to*
11. *I'll go *to whatever gigs (that) you go*
12. *What few friends (that) he had* have deserted him
13. I will go *where (*that) he goes to*
14. I will go *where (*that) he goes*
15. I don't like *how (*that) he treats her*
16. I'll treat him *how (*that) he treats me*

Helpful hints

In 9, treat *goes on inside the dressing room* as a VP, but do not concern yourself with its internal structure. In 13–16, suppose that *where* is a free relative pronoun meaning 'what(ever) place', and *how* is a free relative pronoun meaning 'what(ever) way'; bear in mind that under the PP Hypothesis of §4.11, such pronouns serve as the complement of a null preposition when used adverbially (but not when used nominally). Consider whether each analysis you evaluate is (or is not) consistent with relevant constraints (e.g. the Impenetrability Condition, the Conflict Constraint, the Doubly Filled COMP Filter, etc.). Consider also whether your analyses lead you to the conclusion that pronominal and phrasal relatives have different derivations, or can be given a unitary derivation.

Model answer for 7

Under Donati and Cecchetto's Head Raising analysis of pronominal free relatives outlined in 2, the free relative structure *what we are facing* will be a DP with the derivation shown in 2 above, repeated as (i) below:

(i)

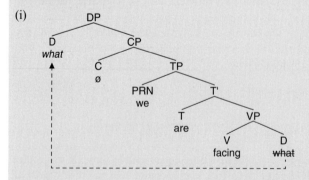

However, the analysis in (i) violates a number of well-established constraints. For example, the movement arrowed in (i) violates the Impenetrability Condition, since *what* moves directly from a position below the null C in (i) to a position above the CP headed by the same C. Moreover, the arrowed movement also violates the Head Movement Constraint, since *what* moves out of VP but does not move to become the head of the closest phrase above VP (= TP). Furthermore, the analysis in (i) does not account for why the head C position of CP in (i) cannot be filled by *that*, as in (ii) below:

(ii)   [DP [D *what*] [CP [C **that**] [TP we [T are] [VP [V facing] ~~what~~]]]]

(ii) does not violate the Doubly Filled COMP Filter (which specifies that an overt complementiser cannot have an overt specifier), because *what* is not the specifier of CP but rather the head of DP: consequently, the Head Raising analysis in (i) wrongly predicts that sentences like 7 **What that we are facing is a severe economic downturn* are grammatical.

It might seem as if we can get round these problems by proposing a dual movement analysis for free relatives, under which *what* first undergoes Wh-Movement to spec-CP, and then undergoes Head Raising and remerges with CP to form a DP, in the manner shown in (iii) below:

(iii)

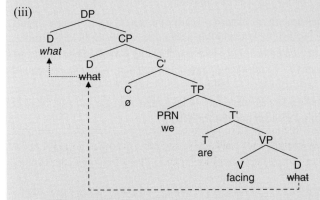

Under the analysis in (iii), the first step of the movement (from comp-VP to spec-CP) involves a Wh-Movement operation which does not incur an Impenetrability violation (since *what* moves to a position inside CP), and the second step (from spec-CP to head-DP) involves a Head Raising operation which does not violate the Head Movement Constraint because *what* moves out of CP to become the head of the projection immediately above CP. Unfortunately, however, the Head Raising operation in (iii) leads to a violation of the constraint in (iv) below (from §6.6):

(iv)   **Chain Uniformity Condition/CUC**
       All links/copies in a chain must be uniform.

The CUC violation arises because movement of *what* from spec-CP to head-DP shown by the upper arrow in (iii) results in a non-uniform chain in which the highest link of the chain in head-DP is a minimal projection, but the intermediate link in spec-CP is a maximal projection. Thus, the derivation in (iii) wrongly predicts the string *what we are facing* to be ungrammatical. Furthermore, the derivation in (iii) doesn't explain why it is ungrammatical for the complementiser to be spelled out as *that* in 7, since (for the reason already noted) this would not violate the Doubly Filled COMP Filter.

We can avoid Impenetrability and Uniformity violations if we treat free relatives as involving a wh-marked antecedent modified by a relative clause containing a null operator in spec-CP – as in 5 above. One implementation of this analysis would be to suppose that the free relative *what we are facing* has the derivation shown below:

(v)

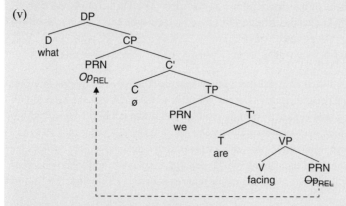

While (v) would not induce an Impenetrability violation (because the null operator moves from a position below C to a higher position inside CP), it would fail to account for why the head C position of CP cannot be filled by the overt complementiser *that*, since use of *that* in (v) would not violate the Doubly Filled COMP Filter, and hence (v) would wrongly predict **what that we are facing* should be grammatical.

But now consider the alternative Wh-Movement analysis in 6, under which the free relative string *what we are facing* is a CP with the derivation shown below:

(vi)

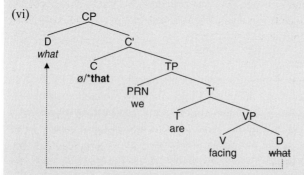

The analysis in (vi) does not induce any violation of the Impenetrability Condition because *what* moves from a position below C to a higher position inside CP (and not to an illicit position outside CP). There is no violation of the Head Movement Constraint either, since the movement operation is Wh-Movement, and this moves a maximal projection into spec-CP (*what* being a maximal projection here because its mother is the VP node, and VP is not a projection of *what*). Moreover, use of *that* in (vi) will induce a Doubly Filled COMP violation, since it results in a structure in which an overt C (= *that*) has an overt specifier (= *what*): consequently, the analysis in (vi) can account for the ungrammaticality of free relative structures like **what that we are facing*.

However, a problem that faces the Wh-Movement account of free relatives in (vi) is that it gives rise to case conflict (i.e. to a situation in which the wh-word carries conflicting case specifications) – as we see from sentences like 1 *What we are facing is a severe economic crisis*. This is because *what* is assigned accusative case by virtue of originating as the object of *facing*, and nominative case by virtue of ending up as the subject of *is a severe economic downturn*. How can this conflict issue be addressed – an issue which also arises under the analyses in (i) and (iii)?

One possibility would be to suppose that an item can be assigned two different cases, and this will not cause a crash at PF if the relevant item has a phonetic form which can spell out both of the cases. We could then say that *what* in 1 is assigned both nominative and accusative case, but that this is unproblematic because *what* is a case-ambiguous item which can spell out both nominative case (as in *What has happened?*) and accusative case (as in *What are you doing?*).

An alternative possibility would be to suppose that an item is assigned case as early as possible in a derivation (in accordance with the Earliness Principle of §4.9) and thereafter retains the case it was originally assigned. This would mean that *what* in 7 is accusative, since it was initially the complement of the transitive verb *facing*. This analysis would account for the use of the accusative form *whomever* in the following example from an online blog about the use of *whoever/whomever* by Jane Strauss:

(vii)   [*Whomever* you elect] will serve a four-year term (www.whitesmoke.com/janestrauss_6):

Here, the free relative pronoun *whomever* originates as the complement of (and so is assigned accusative case by) the verb *elect*, even though it ends up as the subject of *will*.

However, the *earliness* account of case-marking is called into question by the use of *whom* in relative clause structures such as the following (discussed by Kayne 1983: 7):

(viii)   a man *whom* I don't think has any friends

Kayne posits that the italicised relative pronoun undergoes successive-cyclic Wh-Movement, and thereby moves from spec-TP to spec-CP in the *has*-clause, and from there into spec-CP in the *think*-clause, in the manner shown by the arrows below:

(ix)   [CP *whom* [C ø] [TP I [T don't] [VP [V think] [CP ~~whom~~ [C ø] [TP ~~whom~~ [T ø] [VP [V has] any friends]]]]]]

Kayne argues that the pronoun *whom* in such structures receives two cases: it gets nominative case in its original position in spec-TP, by virtue of being the subject of a finite clause (and hence being in the domain of an intransitive finite complementiser); however, it subsequently gets accusative case from the transitive verb *think* at the point where it moves into the specifier position of the lower CP, and hence is immediately adjacent to *think*. It might be expected that this would lead to case conflict (because *whom* is marked as both nominative and accusative), and that this conflict will cause the derivation to crash. However, the relevant sentence in (viii) is grammatical. How come? Kayne (1983: 7) suggests that 'The application of case marking to an NP previously marked for case deletes the prior marking, replacing it with the new one.' This means that the nominative case initially assigned to *whom* in spec-TP is **overwritten** by the accusative case assigned to it in spec-CP – so accounting for the use of *whom* in (viii).

However, Kayne's overwrite analysis won't account for the use of *whomever* in (vii). To see why, let's take a closer look at the derivation of (vii), shown in (x) below (where numerical subscripts are added purely for ease of identification):

(x)

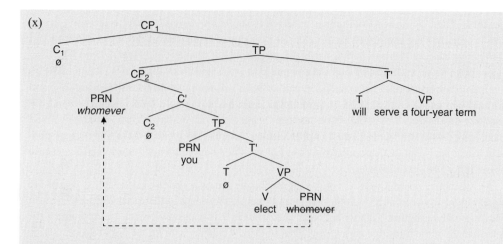

The pronoun *whomever* originates as the complement of the transitive verb *elect*, and so will initially be assigned accusative case by *elect*. It then moves to become the specifier of the free relative clause (CP₂), and in this position it can be assigned nominative case by the finite complementiser (C₁) in the main clause, under the account of nominative case assignment in §4.9. Given Kayne's assumptions, we would expect this second (nominative) case to overwrite (and hence replace) the initial (accusative) case assigned to *whomever*: but this would predict that the nominative form *whoever* is required, so leaving us with no account of how *whomever* comes to appear in (vii). So, Kayne's analysis makes the incorrect prediction that (vii) should be ungrammatical. Moreover, Kayne's analysis is equally undesirable from a theoretical perspective, since we arguably want to avoid feature values being changed in the course of a derivation, in violation of the NoTampering Condition.

One way of avoiding this dilemma is to suppose that case-marking can take place at any stage of derivation, with the proviso that a nominal or pronominal constituent must be assigned case at some point in the course of the derivation. In the case of (x), this means that the wh-pronoun can be assigned either accusative case at the point where it is in comp-VP (and so be spelled out as *whomever* in formal styles), or nominative case at the point where it is in spec-CP (and so be spelled out as *whoever*). Such an analysis would also (correctly) predict that nominative *who* can be used as an alternative to accusative *whom* in (viii).

However, two words of caution need to be emphasised at this point. Firstly, the forms *who/whoever* can be used to spell out accusative case in informal styles, so we can't always be sure whether *who/whoever* in a given sentence carries nominative or accusative case. Secondly, the forms *whom/whomever* have dropped out of use in colloquial English and survive only in arcane styles of written English; moreover, they have been argued by Sobin (1997) to be artificial forms which are not part of the mental grammar internalised by native speakers but rather are the result of a grammatical virus which has wormed its way into the written language through the norms imposed by prescriptive grammarians (inculcated into students in secondary school). Hence, it may be that we should not attach too much weight to data relating to the *who/whom* and *whoever/whomever* distinction.

Exercise 7.5

In spoken English, we find a type of restrictive relative clause which is illustrated by the bracketed structures in the examples below (which I recorded from live, unscripted radio broadcasts):

1 a.   He's one *player* [that I'm really pleased for **him**] (Martin Keown, BBC Radio 5)
  b.   It's a *situation* [that **it**'s not crept up on us] (Alan Pardew, BBC Radio 5)
  c.   He's a *player* [I've played against **him** many times] (Lee Dixon, BBC Radio 5)
  d.   You need *someone* [you can trust **him** implicitly] (Chris Coleman, BBC Radio 5)

These can be termed **resumptive relatives**, since they involve the use of a (bold-printed) **resumptive pronoun** like *him/it* which 'resumes' (i.e. refers back to) the (italicised) antecedent. Donati and Cecchetto (2011: 530) propose a Head Raising analysis of resumptive relatives, under which the resumptive pronoun functions as the head D constituent of a DP, and the relativized noun originates as its complement. If we extend this analysis to 1a and treat *one* as a (numeral) quantifier, the nominal *one player that I'm really pleased for him* will be a QP which has the derivation shown in simplified form below:

2. $[_{QP} [_Q \text{ one}] [_{NP} [_N \text{ } player] [_{CP} [_C \text{ that}] \text{ I'm really pleased for } [_{DP} [_D \text{ him}] [_N \text{ } \text{player}]]]]]$

On this view, the noun *player* originates as a constituent of the DP *him player*, with *him* functioning as a determiner modifying *player*: this is consistent with the suggestion made in §2.6 that personal pronouns like *him* can be analysed as D constituents. Subsequently, the noun *player* undergoes the arrowed Head Raising operation and is thereby raised out of the relative clause CP to become the head N of a new NP. The head D of DP is thereby left stranded without an overt complement, since the lower copy of the noun *player* is given a null spellout at PF. If the relevant determiner is spelled out at PF in the prenominal form *the* when it has an overt complement (as in *the player*) but in a pronominal form like *him* when it has a null complement, it follows that the determiner in 2 will be spelled out in the pronominal form *him* at PF because it has a null complement (its complement being a null copy of the moved noun *player*). Donati and Cecchetto note (2011: 530) that their analysis of resumptive relatives predicts that 'the distribution of resumptive pronouns of this kind is restricted to *that*-relatives'. More accurately, their analysis predicts that resumptive pronouns are only found in wh-less relatives (i.e. *that*-relatives or zero/contact relatives).

But now consider an alternative Merge account under which resumptive relatives involve a structure in which the antecedent is directly merged in situ, and in which the relative clause contains an (overt or null) relativiser (below denoted as REL) directly merged in situ in spec-CP, and an associated in situ resumptive pronoun (italicised below):

3. $[_{QP} [_Q \text{ one}] [_{NP} [_N \text{ player}] [_{CP} \text{ REL } [_C \text{ that}] \text{ I'm really pleased for } him]]]]$

The relativiser can be either an overt relative pronoun like *who*, or a null relative pronoun (as in the case of 1). On this account, resumptive relatives involve no movement of any kind, since the antecedent, operator and resumptive are all directly merged in situ: this means (*inter alia*) that resumptive relatives cannot in principle give rise to violation of constraints on movement. Moreover, no case conflict arises either, since the antecedent, relativiser and resumptive each carry one and only one case: e.g. in 1, the resumptive *him* is assigned accusative case by the transitive preposition *for*; the relativiser (if this is a null relative pronoun carrying a case feature) is assigned default case by virtue of not falling within the domain of any case-assigner; and the antecedent *(one) player* is assigned accusative case by whatever mechanism assigns accusative case to *me* in 'I know you wouldn't have done that, but then you're not *me*' (perhaps an instance of default case assignment).

Evaluate these two competing analyses (the Raising analysis and the Merge analysis) by considering whether either or both of them can account for wh-less resumptive relative structures like those italicised in 4 and wh-resumptive structures like those italicised in 5 (all the relevant examples being recorded by me from a variety of live radio and TV programmes):

4 a. They're *a team that they play high on confidence* (Ally McCoist, Sky Sports TV)
  b. We're *the only club in England that we're in all four competitions* (Listener, Talk Sport Radio)
  c. Chelsea have *a group of players that some of them are world-class players* (Graeme Souness, Sky Sports TV)
  d. They've got *a manager that they don't know what is happening with him* (Sam Matterface, Talk Sport Radio)
  e. There were *certain players I didn't know if they were gonna be that good* (Pat Nevin, BBC Radio 5)
  f. He's *a guy that I really appreciate his opinion* (Paul McGinley, BBC Radio 5)
  g. Newcastle and Spurs in particular are *the two clubs that he knows the club* (Jason Cundy, Talk Sport Radio)
  h. 'Punch Drunk' is *the one that I will stand by that film* (Mark Kermode, BBC Radio 5 = '*Punch Drunk* is the one film that I will stand by')

5 a. This is *a group of players who I would imagine they've never played together before* (Football official, BBC Radio 5)
  b. We're one of *seven teams who any one of them could get automatic promotion* (David Connelly, Talk Sport Radio)
  c. Martin was *a manager who, everything on the football side, he was responsible for* (Graham Taylor, BBC Radio 5)
  d. This includes *children who their performance at school is suffering* (Social worker, BBC Radio 5)
  e. That implies *a cost which, if you had a healthier life style, we could reduce that cost* (Doctor, BBC Radio 5)

Helpful hints

Look at the model answer for 5a before attempting to analyse any of the examples in 4 or 5. In 4a, take *play high on confidence* to be a VP, but ignore its internal structure. In 4b, take *only* to be a quantifier; take *club in England* to be an NP but ignore its internal structure; take *(a)re* to be a copular verb that originates in V and raises to T; and take *in all four competitions* to be a PP, but ignore its internal structure. In 4c, take *(a)re* to be a copular verb that originates in V and raises to T; and take *world-class players* to be an NP, but ignore its internal structure. In 4d, take *don't* to be a negative auxiliary directly merged in T. In 4e, take *certain* to be a quantifier; take *didn't* to be a negative auxiliary directly merged in T; and take *gonna be that good* to be a VP but ignore its internal structure. In 4f, take *really* to be an adverb which adjoins to the VP *appreciate his opinion* to form the even larger VP *really appreciate his opinion*; take *his opinion* to be a DP headed by a genitive affix *Af* whose complement is the noun *opinion* and whose specifier is the pronoun *he*, with the affix attaching to *he* at PF and *he+Af* being spelled out as *his*. In 4g, take *two* to be a NUM/ numeral quantifier. Likewise in 4h, take *one* to be a NUM head as well. In 5a, take *never played together before* to be a VP, but ignore its internal structure. In 5b, take *any* to be a Q/quantifier; take *one/seven* to be NUM/numeral constituents; and take *get automatic promotion* to be a VP but ignore its internal structure. In 5c, treat *everything on the football side* to be a QP which originates as the complement of the preposition *for* and is moved to spec-CP in order to focus it, but ignore its internal structure; take *was* to be a copular verb which originates in V and raises to T. In 5d, take *their performance at school* to be a DP whose head is a genitive affix *Af*, whose specifier is the pronoun *they* and whose complement is the NP *performance at school* (ignore the internal structure of this NP), with *Af* attaching to *they* at PF and *they+Af* being spelled out as *their*. In 5e, take the *if*-clause to be a SUBP which is a projection of the SUB/subordinating conjunction *if*, and assume that SUBP is a clausal adjunct directly merged in situ as the specifier of the CP containing it, but ignore the internal structure of the *if*-clause/SUBP. In all the examples, consider whether a movement analysis will induce violation of (Stranding, Impenetrability, Intervention, Extraction Domain, etc.) constraints.

Model answer for 5a

In 5a, the antecedent of the pronoun *who* is the collective NP *group of players*, and the resumptive pronoun is *they*. Under Donati and Cecchetto's account of resumptive relatives sketched in 2 above, the relativized noun originates as the complement of the resumptive pronoun, and then (via Head Raising) remerges with the relative clause CP to become the head N of an NP. However, a Head Raising analysis seems unworkable for a resumptive relative structure like that in 5a for several reasons. Firstly, such an analysis assumes that the NP *group of players* originates as the complement of (what Donati and Cecchetto take to be) the determiner *they*; however, this is problematic because *they* is plural and an NP like *group of players* can only serve as the complement of a singular determiner (cf. '*this* group of players'/*'these* group of players'). Secondly, the relativized constituent is a phrase (= the NP *group of players*), and a phrase would be prevented by the Chain Uniformity Condition from raising to become the head N of an NP projection. Thirdly, the Head Raising analysis fails to account for the presence of *who* in the relative clause – indeed, Donati and Cecchetto (2011: 530) explicitly claim that their analysis predicts that resumptive pronouns only occur in wh-less relatives. However, data I have collected on resumptive relatives in spoken English from live radio and TV broadcasts call this claim into question. I have recorded 206 relative clauses involving the use of a resumptive personal pronoun: 105 of these are wh-less relatives and 101 are wh-relatives, suggesting that resumptive pronouns occur in both wh-relatives and wh-less relatives in English, with more or less equal frequency. Overall, then, it would seem that the Head Raising analysis fails to account for wh-resumptives like that in 5a.

However, one way of exploiting Donati and Cecchetto's intuition that resumptive pronouns are determiners which are stranded by movement of their complement would be to propose an alternative analysis under which wh-resumptives involve Wh-Movement of a relative pronoun out of a DP headed by a resumptive pronoun like *they*. On one implementation of this analysis, the relativized NP *group of players* would be generated in situ, and the relative clause CP would be adjoined to it to form a larger NP, which in turn merges with the indefinite article to form the structure below:

(i)

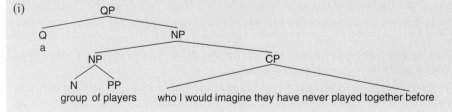

The relative pronoun *who* in (i) would initially be merged with D *they* to form the DP *they who*. The pronoun *who* would subsequently undergo successive-cyclic Wh-Movement, moving first to the edge of the CP in the *have* clause, and then to the edge of the CP in the *would* clause so that the CP in (i) above would have the derivation in (ii) below:

(ii)

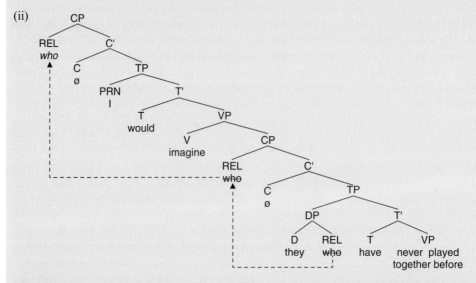

The idea that a relative pronoun can serve as the complement of a determiner is by no means implausible, since in earlier varieties of English we find DETERMINER+RELATIVE PRONOUN strings like those highlighted in the internet-sourced examples below (from the King James version of the Bible):

(iii) a. Take heed therefore unto yourselves, and to all the flock, over **the** *which* the Holy Ghost hath made you overseers, to feed the church of God . . . (biblehub.com)

   b. Noah . . . prepared an ark to the saving of his house, by **the** *which* he condemned the world . . . (biblegateway.com)

   c. Because he hath appointed a day, in **the** *which* he will judge the world . . . (forums.carm.org)

There would be no number mismatch between the determiner *they* and the relative pronoun *who* if both are plural. Nor is it a problem accounting for how plural *who/they* can be used to refer to the singular collective nominal *group of* players, since we see from the examples below that a plural relative or non-relative pronoun can be used to refer back to a singular collective nominal which denotes a set of individuals (a phenomenon loosely termed 'semantic agreement'):

(iv) a. 'I want to play for *a team* **who** <u>are</u> going to match my skills and ambitions' said Fabius Fabb

   b. 'When I play for *a team*, I give **them** one hundred and ten percent', said Rufus Ruff

Furthermore, under the Wh-Movement analysis in (i–ii), no case conflict arises (i.e. no item is assigned more than one case), because the antecedent, the relative pronoun and the resumptive are each assigned one and only one case: e.g. the antecedent noun *group* is assigned default accusative case (in the same way as *me* in *This is me*), and *who* and *they* are each assigned nominative case by virtue of originating as the subject of a finite clause.

The Wh-Movement analysis of resumptive wh-relatives could be generalised to resumptive wh-less relatives, if the latter involve the fronting of a null relative operator, which can be thought of as a null counterpart of relative pronouns like *which/who*. On this view, the bracketed wh-less relative clause in a sentence like *This is a group of players* [**that** *I would imagine they've never played together before*] would have the same derivation as in (i–ii), except that the head C of the higher CP would be filled by *that*, and in place of *who* we have a null relative operator. This would allow us to develop a unitary Wh-Movement analysis of resumptive relatives, under which wh-resumptives and wh-less resumptives alike involve Wh-Movement of an (overt or null) relative pronoun/operator.

Unfortunately, however, the Wh-Movement analysis of resumptive relative clauses sketched in (ii) turns out to be problematic from both an empirical and a theoretical perspective. The empirical problem relates to accounting for *have* being able to cliticise onto *they* in 5a. In §4.3, we saw that *have*-cliticisation is a PF operation which applies under the conditions specified below:

(v)   ***Have*-cliticisation**
        The word *have* can encliticise to (i.e. attach to the end of) another word W in the phonological component, provided that
        (i)   W ends in a vowel/diphthong
        (ii)   W immediately precedes *have*
        (iii)   W c-commands *have*.

Given the derivation in (ii), the edge of the TP headed by *have* will have the superficial structure below:

(vi)

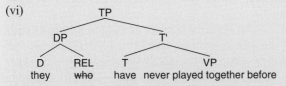

However, such a structure wrongly predicts that *have* cannot cliticise onto *they* here, because *they* does not c-command *have* (*they* only c-commands ~~who~~), and *they* does not immediately precede *have* (the two are separated by a null copy of *who*). Nor can *have* cliticise onto the DP headed by *they*, since (as v claims) *have*-cliticisation allows *have* to cliticise onto a *head* ending in a vowel, not onto a DP ending in a vowel – as we see from the ungrammaticality of sentence like **The Masai've been driven out of their traditional homelands*).

Moreover, the Wh-Movement operation by which *who* moves out of its initial position in (ii) into spec-CP in the *have*-clause is also problematic, because it violates at least two constraints. Thus, the Stranding Constraint is violated because movement of *who* leaves the determiner *they* stranded without its complement. Furthermore, the Constraint on Extraction Domains is also violated, because *who* is extracted out of a specifier (more precisely, out of the DP *they who* which occupies the specifier position in the TP headed by *have*). Overall, then, the Wh-Movement analysis of resumptive relatives sketched in (ii) is potentially problematic in certain respects.

Let's therefore consider how the alternative Merge analysis sketched in 3 would deal with a sentence like 5a. Under the Merge analysis, the antecedent NP *group of players* would be directly merged in situ and have the relative clause CP adjoined to it, as in (i) above. The relative pronoun *who* would be directly merged in situ on the edge of the overall relative clause (as the specifier of the CP in the *would*-clause), and the resumptive pronoun *they* would be directly merged in situ as the specifier of the TP headed by T-*have*, so that the relevant nominal has the structure in (vii) below:

(vii)

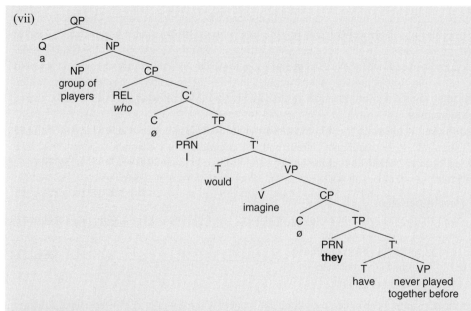

The resumptive pronoun *they* c-commands and is immediately adjacent to the auxiliary *have*, and so the analysis in (vii) correctly predicts that *have* can cliticise onto *they* in accordance with the conditions imposed in (v), so accounting for the occurrence of *they've* in 5a. No case conflict arises (i.e. no constituent ends up carrying more than one case), since each of the relevant constituents carries only one case. More specifically, the relative pronoun *who* is assigned default case (or perhaps no case at all) by virtue of not falling within the domain of any case-assigner. In either eventuality, the relative pronoun will be spelled out as the default/otherwise form *who* if we suppose that WHO has the following spellout forms:

(viii)   WHO > *whose* if genitive, *whom* if accusative in formal styles and *who* otherwise

By contrast, the resumptive pronoun *they* is assigned nominative case by the (null, intransitive) finite complementiser adjacent to it; and the article *a* and the noun *group* are assigned default accusative case (in the same way as *me* in 'This is *me*'). As for the use of the plural pronoun *they* to refer back to the singular NP *group of players*, this can be attributed to the possibility of using a plural pronoun to refer back to a singular collective nominal denoting a set of individuals, as illustrated earlier in (iv).

Under the Merge analysis sketched in (vii), parallels can be drawn between resumptive relative clauses and resumptive 'dislocated topic' structures like those in (ix) below:

(ix) a. *Some of the circuits*, he has never driven **them** before (Graham Courtney, Talk Sport Radio)
   b. *Smalling and Jones*, neither of **them** have made it for this match (John Murray, BBC Radio 5)
   c. And *the throw*, if **it** had hit, he was out (Jonathan Agnew, BBC Radio 5 Sports Extra)
   d. *Me*, **I**'m confident that, somewhere down the line, that will happen (Steven Gerrard, BBC Radio 5).
   e. *Lee*, I've been following **his** progress very much over the last month (Colin Montgomerie, BBC Radio 5)

In dislocated topic structures like (ix), the italicised dislocated topic is reprised by a bold-printed resumptive pronoun. The topic seems to be merged in situ on the edge of the relevant CP and is reprised by a resumptive pronoun directly merged in some position within TP. On this view, a sentence like (ix.a) has the structure shown in simplified form in (x) below:

(x)   [$_{CP}$ *some of the circuits* [$_C$ ø] [$_{TP}$ he [$_T$ has] never driven **them** before]]

It is unlikely that such dislocated topic structures involve movement of the topic from the bold-printed to the italicised position, for several reasons – though I will give only two here. For one thing, the relevant movement operation would violate the Condition on Extraction Domains in sentence (ix.b) (by extracting the topic out of a *neither*-phrase which is the specifier of the T auxiliary *have*) and in sentence (ix.c) (by extracting the topic out of an adjunct clause which is the specifier of a CP). For another thing, there is a mismatch between the case of the topic and that of the resumptive, and movement preserves case: e.g. the topic *me* has default accusative case in (ix.d) by virtue of not falling within the domain of any case-assigner, but the resumptive pronoun *I* has nominative case; likewise, the topic *Lee* has default acusative case in (ix.e), but the resumptive pronoun *his* has genitive case. Such considerations suggest that the topic and the resumptive are directly merged in situ.

An interesting feature of dislocated topic structures is that the topic can be reprised not only by a pronominal resumptive, but also by a nominal – as with the bold-printed expressions below:

(xi) a.   *The truth*, we're not quite sure who is telling **the truth** in this situation (Jason Burt, Talk Sport Radio)

   b.   *The pressure that you were under today*, your players are going to have to face **that kind of pressure** throughout the season (Connor MacNamara, BBC Radio 5)

   c.   *Gareth Bale*, I wouldn't be surprised if Man City were in for **Bale** (Robbie Savage, BBC Radio 5)

   d.   *The Championship*, one of the greatest things about **that league** is that it's the most unpredictable league around (Listener, BBC Radio 5)

In a sentence like (xi.a), the resumptive is an exact copy of the topic. However, in sentences like (xi.b–c), the resumptive is only a partial copy of the topic. And in a sentence like (xi.d), the resumptive is a nominal completely distinct from the topic. Given the lack of required identity between topic and resumptive nominal, it is implausible to posit that the relevant structures involve movement of the topic from the bold-printed to the italicised position. If resumptive relatives have essentially the same merge derivation as dislocated topics, we would expect to find that the relative pronoun can be reprised not only by a resumptive pronoun but also by a resumptive nominal. This expectation seems to be borne out by relative clauses such as that bracketed below:

(xii)   This information is asked for on <u>the census-form</u>, [**which** they threaten to fine you up to a thousand pounds if you don't fill *the thing* in] (Civil Liberty spokesman, BBC Radio 5)

In (xii), the resumptive noun *thing* (sometimes termed an **epithet** in this kind of use) clearly cannot be analysed as a copy of the antecedent noun *census-form*, suggesting that relative clauses like that bracketed in (xii) must involve Merge rather that Head Raising. (It should be noted, however, that the bracketed relative clause in xii is appositive, not restrictive.)

Glossary and list of abbreviations

Bold print is used to indicate technical terms and to cross-refer to entries elsewhere in the Glossary. Abbreviations used here are: ch. 2 = Chapter 2; §6.8 = Chapter 6, section 8; ex. 7.2. = exercise 2 in Chapter 7.

&: Coordinating conjunction, see **Conjunction**.

A: See **Adjective**, **A-head**, **A-position**, **Binding**.

A-bar: An A-bar position is a position which is not an Argument/Agreement/ Anaphor-binding position. In other words, it is not a position in which an argument is directly merged, nor a position from which a constituent can agree with an auxiliary, nor a position from which an antecedent can bind an anaphor.

A-bar Movement This is a movement operation (like **Wh-Movement**) which moves a constituent to an A-bar position like spec-CP. See §7.10.

ACC: Attract Closest Condition. See **Attract**.

Acc(usative): See **Case**.

Acquisition: The process by which people acquire their first language (= L1 acquisition) or a second language which is not their mother tongue (= L2 acquisition).

Active: A contrast is traditionally drawn between sentence pairs such as (i) and (ii) below:

 (i) The thieves stole the jewels
 (ii) The jewels were stolen by the thieves

(i) is said to be an **active** clause (or sentence), and (ii) to be its **passive** counterpart; similarly, the verb *stole* is said to be an active verb (or a verb in the active **voice**) in (i), whereas the verb *stolen* is said to be a passive verb (or a verb in the passive voice – more specifically, a passive **participle**) in (ii); likewise, the auxiliary *were* in (ii) is said to be a passive **auxiliary**.

Adjacency condition: A condition requiring that two expressions must be immediately adjacent (i.e. there must be no constituent intervening between the two) in order for some operation to apply. For example, *have* must be immediately adjacent to *they* in order to **cliticise** onto it in structures such as *They've gone home*.

Adjective: This is a category of word (abbreviated to A) which often denotes states (e.g. *happy, sad*), which typically has an adverb counterpart in *-ly* (cf. *sad/sadly*), which typically has comparative/superlative forms in *-er/-est* (cf. *sadder/saddest*), which can often take the prefix *un-* (cf. *unhappy*), and which can often form a noun by the addition of the suffix *-ness* (cf. *sadness*), etc.

Adjoin: See **Adjunction**.

Adjunct: One way in which this term is used is to denote an optional constituent typically used to specify, e.g., the time, place or manner in which an event takes place. Another way in which it is used is to denote a constituent which has been attached to another to form a larger constituent of the same type. (See **Adjunction**.)

Adjunction: This is a process by which one constituent is adjoined (= attached) to another to form a larger constituent of the same type. For example, we could say that in a sentence like *He should not go*, the negative particle *not* (in the guise of its contracted form *n't*) can be adjoined to the auxiliary *should* to form the negative auxiliary *shouldn't*.

Adposition: A cover term subsuming **preposition** and **postposition**. For example, the English word *in* is a preposition since it is positioned before its complement (cf. *in Tokyo*), whereas its Japanese counterpart is a postposition because it is positioned after its complement *Tokyo*. Both words are **adpositions**.

ADV(erb)/ADVP: An ADV/adverb is a category of word which typically indicates manner (e.g. 'wait *patiently*') or degree (e.g. '*exceedingly* patient'). In English, most (but not all) adverbs end in *-ly* (cf. *quickly* – but also *almost*). An **ADVP** is an adverbial phrase, like that italicised in 'She made up her mind *independently of me*', where the head of the italicised phrase is the adverb *independently*.

Af: See **Affix**.

Affective: An affective constituent is an (e.g. negative, interrogative or conditional) expression which licenses (i.e. allows a structure to contain) a **polarity expression** like (partitive) *any*. So, for example, interrogative *if* is an affective constituent as we see from the fact that an interrogative *if*-clause can contain partitive *any* in a sentence such as 'I wonder *if* he has *any* news about Jim.' See §3.7.

Affix/Affixal: The term **affix** (abbreviated to *Af*) is typically used to describe a grammatical morpheme which cannot stand on its own as an independent word, but which must be attached to a **host** word of an appropriate kind. An affix which attaches to the beginning of a word (e.g. *un-* in *unhappy*) is called a **prefix**; an affix which attaches to the end of a word (e.g. *-s* in *chases*) is called a **suffix**. An **affixal** head is one which behaves like an affix in needing to attach to a particular kind of host word. See also **Clitic**. **Affix Hopping** (or **Affix Lowering**) is an operation by which an unattached affix in T is lowered onto the closest V below T (i.e. c-commanded by T) in the PF component: see §4.4. On the **Affix Attachment Condition/AAC**, see **Attachment**.

Agreement: An operation by which (e.g. in a sentence like *They are lying*) the person/number features of the auxiliary *are* get assigned the same values as those of its subject *they*, so that *are* is third person plural because it agrees in

person and **number** with its third person plural subject *they*. On the idea that **subject agreement** may involve copying the tense feature from T onto its subject, see §6.5. On Complementiser Agreement, see **Complementiser**. A language has **rich agreement** if it uses a wide range of distinctive person/number inflections on verbs, and **poor agreement** if it does not: see §5.7.

Anaphor: This is an expression (like *himself*) which cannot have independent reference, but which must take its reference from an appropriate **antecedent** (i.e. expression which it refers to) within the same phrase or sentence. Hence, while we can say *John is deluding himself* (where *himself* refers back to *John*), we cannot say **For himself to have to wait would be unthinkable*, since the anaphor *himself* here has no antecedent. A traditional distinction is drawn between **reflexive anaphors** (i.e. *self* forms like *myself/ourselves/yourself/yourselves/himself/herself/itself/themselves*) and the **reciprocal anaphors** *each other/one another* (cf. 'They help *each other/one another*'). See §3.6. On **anaphor binding**, see **Bind**.

Animate: The term **animate** is used to denote (the gender of) an expression which denotes a living being (e.g. a human being or animal), while the term **inanimate** is used in relation to an expression which denotes lifeless entities. For example, the **relative pronoun** *who* could be said to be animate in gender and the relative pronoun *which* inanimate – hence we say *someone who upsets people* and *something which upsets people*.

Antecedent: An expression which is referred to by a pronoun or anaphor of some kind. For example, in *John cut himself shaving*, *John* is the antecedent of the anaphor *himself*, since *himself* refers back to *John*. In a sentence such as *He is someone who we respect*, the antecedent of the **relative pronoun** *who* is *someone*. By extension, in cases of **ellipsis** like 'I can *speak French* better than you can ~~speak French~~', the italicised constituent is said to be the antecedent of the deleted constituent. **Antecedent Raising** is an operation whereby the antecedent of a **relative clause** originates inside the relative clause and then raises to a position outside it: see §§7.6–7.9.

Anticyclic: See **Cycle**.

Antonym: One word is an antonym of another if it has an opposite meaning (e.g. *tall* and *short* are antonyms because they represent opposite points on a scale of height).

AP: Adjectival phrase – i.e. a phrase headed by an adjective, such as *fond of chocolate, keen on sport, good at syntax*, etc.

Appositive relative clause: See **Relative clause**.

A-position: An Argument/Agreement/Anaphor-binding position – i.e. a position which an argument occupies if it doesn't undergo movement, or a position which can trigger agreement (e.g. with an auxiliary in T), or a position from which an antecedent can bind an anaphor: see §7.9.

Arbitrary: When (in criticising some proposal) we say that it is arbitrary, we mean that it is unprincipled and/or not supported by independent evidence. When we say that an expression has **arbitrary reference**, we mean that it can denote an unspecified set of individuals, and hence have much the same meaning as English *one/people* or French *on*. In a sentence such as *It is difficult* [PRO *to learn Japanese*], the bracketed clause is said to have an abstract pronoun subject PRO which can have arbitrary reference, in which case the sentence is paraphraseable as *It's difficult for people to learn Japanese.* See §3.2.

Argument: This is a term borrowed by linguists from philosophy (more specifically, from predicate calculus) to describe the role played by particular types of expression in the semantic structure of sentences. In a sentence such as *John hit Fred*, the overall sentence is said to be a **proposition** (a term used to describe the semantic content of a clause), and to consist of the predicate *hit* and its two arguments *John* and *Fred*. The two arguments represent the two participants in the act of hitting, and the predicate is the expression (in this case the verb *hit*) which describes the activity in which they are engaged. By extension, in a sentence such as *John says he hates syntax* the predicate in the main clause is the verb *says*, and its two arguments are *John* and the clause *he hates syntax*; the argument *he hates syntax* is in turn a proposition whose predicate is *hates*, and whose two arguments are *he* and *syntax*. An **argument position** is a position in which an argument which has not undergone movement is merged. For example, in *John is enjoying syntax, syntax* occupies an argument position in comp-VP, and *John* occupies an argument position in spec-TP. But if we move *syntax* to the front of the sentence to highlight it (as in *Syntax, John is enjoying*) it no longer occupies an argument position (but rather has been moved out of its original argument position into a new spec-CP position at the front of the clause).

Array: The **lexical array** for a given expression denotes the set of lexical items out of which the expression is formed: see §5.2.

ART/Article/ARTP: The term **article** is used in traditional grammar to describe a particular subclass of determiner/quantifier: the word *the* is traditionally called the **definite article**, and the word *a* is termed the **indefinite article**. Some linguists take a phrase like *a book* to be an **ARTP/article phrase** which is headed by the indefinite article (although for the most part the indefinite article is treated as subtype of **Q/quantifier** in this book).

ASP/Aspect/ASPP: Aspect is a term typically used to denote the duration of the activity described by a verb (e.g. whether the activity is ongoing or completed). In sentences such as:

(i) He has taken the medicine
(ii) He is taking the medicine

the auxiliary *has* is said to be an auxiliary which marks **perfect aspect** (and hence to be a **perfect auxiliary**) in that it marks the perfection (in the sense of 'completion' or 'termination') of the activity of taking the medicine; for analogous reasons, *taken* is said to be a **perfect participle** verb form in (i) (though is sometimes referred to in traditional grammars as a 'past participle').

Similarly, *is* functions as an auxiliary which marks **progressive aspect** in (ii), because it relates to an activity which is ongoing or in progress (for this reason, *is* in (ii) is also referred to as a **progressive auxiliary**); in the same way, the verb *taking* in (ii) is said to be the **progressive participle** form of the verb (though is sometimes known in traditional grammars as a 'present participle'). An auxiliary which marks aspect (like *have* and *be* in the above examples) is referred to as an **aspectual auxiliary**. An **aspect phrase/ASPP** is a phrase with an ASP/aspect head which marks (e.g. perfect or progressive) aspect.

Associate: An expression with which the auxiliary/verb agrees in an expletive *there* clause, and which is associated with the expletive subject *there*. For example, *many previously unknown tombs* is the associate of expletive *there* (and agrees with *have*) in a sentence like 'There **have** recently been discovered *many previously unknown tombs*.'

Asymmetric c-command: See **C-command**.

Attachment: The **V-Attachment Conditions** of §5.7 specify that (i) every verbal affix must be attached to an overt verb stem at PF, and (ii) every verb stem must have an appropriate inflectional affix attached to it at PF. The **Affix Attachment Condition/AAC** of §6.6 requires that an affix must be attached to an overt host of an appropriate kind at PF.

Attract/Attraction: To say that a head H attracts a constituent C is to say that H triggers movement of C to some position on the **edge** of HP (so that C may move to adjoin to H, or to become the specifier of H). The **Attract Closest Condition/ACC** requires that a head which attracts a particular type of constituent X attracts the **closest** X which it c-commands: see §6.4. The **Attract Smallest Condition/ASC** requires that a head which attracts a particular type of item attracts the smallest constituent containing such an item which will not lead to violation of any UG principle: see §6.6. The **Attraction Generalisation** specifies that 'When a head attracts a given type of item to become its specifier, it attracts the smallest accessible maximal projection containing the closest item of the relevant type'; see §6.6. The **T-Feature Generalisation** of §6.5 specifies that a T-feature on C attracts a constituent on the edge of TP to move to the edge of CP.

Attribute: See **Value**.

Attributive: An adjective (or adjectival phrase) which modifies a noun is said to be attributive if it precedes the noun (as in 'a *proud* mother'), and **predicative** in other uses (e.g. 'She is *proud of her son*', or 'a mother *proud of her son*').

AUX/Auxiliary: A term used to **categorise** items such as *will/would/can/could/shall/should/may/might/must/ought* and some uses of *have/be/do/need/dare*. Such items have a number of idiosyncratic properties, including the fact that they can undergo **Inversion** (e.g. in questions like '*Can* you speak French?'). By contrast, **main verbs** (i.e. verbs which are not auxiliaries) cannot undergo Inversion – as we see from the ungrammaticality of *'*Speak* you French?' See §2.7.

Auxiliary copying/doubling: A phenomenon whereby a moved auxiliary leaves behind an overt copy of itself when it moves – as with *can* in a Child English question like *What can I can have for dinner?*

Auxiliary Inversion: See **Inversion**.

Auxiliary Raising: An operation by which (in present-day English) an auxiliary verb occupying a position below T moves into the head T position of TP if T contains an unattached tense affix. See §5.8.

B: On **Principle B** of Binding Theory, see **Bind**.

bar: When used as a suffix attached to a category label such as N, V, P, etc. (as in N-bar, V-bar, P-bar, T-bar, etc.), it denotes an **intermediate projection** which is larger than a word but smaller than a phrase. Hence, in a phrase such as *university policy on drugs*, we might say that the string *policy on drugs* is an N-bar, since it is a projection of the head noun *policy*, but is an intermediate projection in that it has a larger projection into the NP *university policy on drugs*. The term **bar notation** used in the theory known as **X-bar Syntax** refers to a system of representing projection levels which posits that (first-) merge of a head H with its complement forms an H-bar constituent, and (second-) merge of a head with a specifier forms an H-double-bar constituent (with the **maximal projection** of H being labelled HP). On **A-bar position**, see **A-bar**.

Bare: A **bare form** (of a word) is one which is uninflected. A **bare infinitive** structure is one which contains a verb in the infinitive form, but does not contain the infinitive particle *to* (e.g. the italicised clause in 'He won't let *you help him*'). A **bare noun/nominal** is a noun/noun phrase used without any overt quantifier or determiner to modify it (e.g. *fish* in *Fish is expensive*). A **bare clause** is one not introduced by an overt complementiser (e.g. *he was tired* in *John said he was tired*.

Base form: The base form (or **stem form**) of a word is the simplest, uninflected form of the word (the form under which the relevant word would be listed in an English dictionary) – hence forms like *go/be/have/see/want/love* are the base forms of the relevant verbs. The base form of a verb can typically function either as an **infinitive** (cf. 'Try to *stay*'), an **imperative** (cf. '*Stay* with me tonight!'), a present tense **indicative** form ('They sometimes *stay* with me') or a **subjunctive** form (cf. 'I demand that he *stay* with me').

Binarity/Binary: The word **binary** is a term relating to a two-way contrast. For example, **number** is a binary property in English, in that we have a two-way contrast between **singular** forms like *cat* and **plural** forms like *cats*. It is widely assumed that **parameters** have binary settings, that features have binary values and that all branching in syntactic structure is binary. A **binary-branching** tree diagram is one in which every non-terminal node has two daughters; a category/node which has two daughters is also binary-branching. The **Binarity Principle** is a principle of Universal Grammar specifying that all non-terminal nodes in syntactic structures (i.e. tree-diagrams) are binary-branching. See §3.2.

Biolinguistics: The search for aspects of language which are genetically determined.

Bind/Binding: To say that one constituent X binds another constituent Y (and conversely that Y is bound by X) is to say that X determines properties (usually, referential properties) of Y. For example, in a sentence such as *John blamed himself*, the reflexive anaphor *himself* is bound by *John* in the sense that the referential properties of *himself* are determined by *John* (so that the two refer to the same individual). **Principle A of Binding Theory** (the **Anaphor Binding Principle**) specifies that an anaphor (e.g. *himself*) must be locally bound (i.e. the closest TP containing the anaphor must contain an appropriate antecedent which c-commands the anaphor). **Principle B** specifies that a pronominal (i.e. a non-anaphoric pronoun like *him*) cannot be coreferential to any constituent which c-commands it within the closest TP containing the pronominal. **Principle C** specifies that an R-expression (i.e. a referential noun expression like *the president*) cannot be coreferential to any constituent c-commanding it. On the principles of **Binding Theory**, see §3.7, ex. 3.2, §7.4 and §7.5.

Blend: A **blend** is a structure formed by combining aspects/parts of one structure with those of another. For example, I recorded the following sentence on the radio: 'We look at Arsenal and we see *what the squad they have*' (Steve Claridge, BBC Radio 5). The italicised clause appears to be a blend between two structures – namely *the squad they have* and *what squad they have*.

Bottom-up: To say that a syntactic structure is derived in a **bottom-up** fashion is to say that the structure is built up from bottom to top, with lower parts of the structure being formed before higher parts.

Bound: In a traditional use of this term, a bound form is one which cannot stand alone and be used as an independent word, but rather must be attached to some other morpheme (e.g. negative *n't*, which has to attach to some auxiliary such as *could*). In a completely different use of the term, a bound constituent is one which has an antecedent within the structure containing it (see **Bind**).

Bracketing: A technique for representing the categorial status of an expression, whereby the expression is enclosed within a pair of square brackets, and the left-hand bracket is labelled with an appropriate category symbol – e.g. [D the].

Branch: A term used to represent a solid line linking a pair of nodes in a tree diagram, marking a mother/daughter (i.e. containment) relation between them.

Bridge: A **bridge verb** is one which allows extraction out of its complement (like *think* in *How do you think that she behaved - - -?*); a **non-bridge verb** is one which bars extraction out of its complement (like *quip* in **How did he quip that she behaved - - -?*).

C: See **Complementiser**.

Canonical: A term used to mean 'usual', 'typical' or 'normal', as in *The canonical word order in English is specifier+head+complement.*

Case: The different case forms of a pronoun are the different forms which the pronoun has in different sentence positions. It is traditionally said that English has three cases – **nominative** (abbreviated to **NOM**), **accusative** (= **ACC**, sometimes also referred to as **objective**) and **genitive** (= **GEN**). Personal pronouns typically inflect overtly for all three cases, whereas noun expressions inflect only for genitive case. The different case forms of typical pronouns and noun expressions are given below:

nominative	I	we	you	he	she	it	they	who	the king
accusative	me	us	you	him	her	it	them	who(m)	the king
genitive	my	our	your	his	her	its	their	whose	the king's
	mine	ours	yours		hers		theirs		

As is apparent, some pronouns have two distinct genitive forms: a **weak** (shorter) form used when they are immediately followed by a noun (as in 'This is *my* car'), and a **strong** (longer) form used when they are not immediately followed by a noun (as in 'This car is *mine*'). The null subject PRO found in **control** constructions is treated in this book as carrying null case. In languages like English where certain types of expression are assigned case by virtue of the structural position they occupy in a given clause (e.g. accusative if c-commanded by a transitive head, nominative if c-commanded by finite intransitive head), the relevant expressions are said to receive **structural case**, and the phenomenon is referred to as **structural case-marking**. The **Structural Case Assignment Conditions** outlined in §4.9 specify that:

> A noun or pronoun expression is assigned:
>
> (i) accusative case if the closest case-assigner c-commanding it is a transitive head (e.g a transitive verb like *meet*, or a transitive preposition like *with*, or a transitive complementiser like *for/~~for~~*)
>
> (ii) nominative case if the closest case-assigner c-commanding it is an intransitive finite complementiser (like *that*, or *if*, or *whether* in finite clauses, or the null complementiser ø introducing bare indicative clauses)
>
> (iii) null case if the closest case-assigner c-commanding it is an intransitive non-finite complementiser (like ø in control clauses, or *whether* in infinitival clauses)

The **Default Case Assignment** Condition of §4.9 specifies that:

> A noun or pronoun expression which does not fall within the domain of (i.e. which is not c-commanded by) any case-assigner receives default case.

The default case in English is accusative.

Case-assigner: A constituent which case-marks (i.e. assigns case to) some other constituent: e.g. the verb *stop* assigns accusative case to *him* in *Stop him!*

Caseless: A constituent is caseless if it is not assigned any case. A caseless position is a position to which no case can be assigned.

Case over-ride/overwrite: A mechanism by which a case assigned to a constituent at an earlier stage of derivation is over-ridden/overwritten (i.e. replaced) by one assigned at a later stage. See §7.8.

Case particle: Some linguists take *of* in structures like *destruction of the city* or *fond of pasta* to be a particle marking **genitive** case and belonging to the category K of 'case particle'. On this analysis, the *of*-phrase (*of the city/of pasta*) is taken to have genitive case, and *of* is said to be the morpheme which marks genitive case. Likewise, some linguists take *to* in a sentence like *John gave it to Mary* to be a case particle marking **dative** case. See §2.4.

Case position: A case position is a position in which case is assigned to some constituent (i.e. a position which falls within the domain of a case-assigner). See §2.10, §7.8, and ex. 7.2.

Case-resistant/Case resistance: A constituent is case-resistant if it cannot occur in a **case position** (i.e. a position within the domain of a case-assigner). For example, *that*-clauses are case-resistant, and hence cannot be used as the complement of an accusative-case-assigning preposition like *about* (as in **'I am worried **about** that she is not eating properly'*). The **Case Resistance Constraint** of ex. 7.2 specifies that 'No case-resistant constituent can occupy a case position (i.e. a position within the domain of a case assigner) at PF.'

Caseless: A constituent is caseless if it is not assigned any case. A caseless position is a position to which no case can be assigned.

Categorial: Categorial information is information about the grammatical category that an item belongs to. A categorial property is one associated with members of a particular grammatical category.

Categorise/Categorisation: Assign(ing) an expression to a (grammatical) **category**.

Category: A term used to denote a set of expressions which share a common set of linguistic properties. In syntax, the term is used for expressions which share a common set of grammatical properties. For example, *boy* and *girl* belong to the (grammatical) category **noun** because they both inflect for plural number (cf. *boys/girls*) and can both be used to end a sentence such as *The police haven't yet found the missing* - - -. In traditional grammar, the term **parts of speech** was used in place of **categories**. On the nature of categories, see ch. 2.

Causative verb: A verb which has much the same sense as 'cause'. For example, the verb *have* in sentences such as *He had them expelled* or *He had them review the case* might be said to be causative in sense (hence to be a causative verb).

C-command: A structural relation between two constituents. To say that one constituent X c-commands another constituent Y is (informally) to say that X is no lower than Y in the structure (i.e. either X is higher up in the structure than Y, or the two are at the same height). More formally, in a structure containing two different constituents X and Y, X c-commands Y if X is independent of Y (i.e. if neither contains the other), and if the mother of X contains Y. If we think of a tree diagram as a network of train stations, we can say that one constituent X c-commands another constituent Y if you can get from X to Y by taking a northbound train, getting off at the first station, changing trains there and then travelling one or more stops south on a different line. A constituent X **asymmetrically c-commands** another constituent Y if X c-commands Y but Y does not c-command X; or, to use the train metaphor, X asymmetrically c-commands Y if you can get from X to Y by taking a northbound train, getting off at the first station, changing trains there and then travelling more than one stop south on a different line. See §3.7 and ex. 3.2.

C-command condition on binding: A condition to the effect that a bound constituent (e.g. a **reflexive anaphor** like *himself* or the trace of a moved constituent) must be **c-commanded** by its **antecedent** (i.e. by the expression which binds it). See §3.7 and ex. 3.2; see also **Bind**.

CED: Abbreviation for **Condition on Extraction Domains**: see **Extract/Extraction**.

Chain: A set of constituents comprising an expression and any trace copies associated with it. Where a constituent does not undergo movement, it forms a single-membered chain/trivial chain.

Chain Uniformity Condition: A condition which specifies that all the links in a movement chain must have the same structural status (e.g. all the links must be heads, or all the links must be maximal projections): see §6.6.

Clause: A clause is defined in traditional grammar as an expression which contains (at least) a **subject** and a **predicate**, and which may contain other types of expression as well (e.g. one or more **complements** and/or **adjuncts**). In most cases, the predicate in a clause is a lexical (= main) verb, so that there will be as many different clauses in a sentence as there are different lexical verbs. For example, in a sentence such as *She may think that you are cheating on her*, there are two lexical verbs (*think* and *cheating*), and hence two clauses. The *cheating* clause is *that you are cheating on her*, and the *think* clause is *She may think that you are cheating on her*, so that the *cheating* clause is one of the constituents of the *think* clause. More specifically, the *cheating* clause is the **complement** of the *think* clause, and so is said to function as a **complement clause** in this type of sentence. Clauses whose predicate is not a verb (i.e. verbless clauses) are known as **small clauses**: hence, in *John considers [Mary intelligent]*, the bracketed expression is sometimes referred to as a **small clause**: see §4.6 for one account of the structure of small clauses.

Clausemate: One constituent is a clausemate of another if the two are immediately contained within the same clause.

Clause type/Clause Typing Condition: A clause is said to be declarative in type if used to make a statement, interrogative in type if used to ask a question, imperative in type if used to issue an order, etc. The **Clause Typing Condition** (posited in §4.7) specifies that a clause/CP is typed as interrogative if it has an interrogative specifier, exclamative if it has an exclamative specifier, relative if it has a relative specifier, etc. – but as declarative by default if it is an indicative clause with no clause-typing specifier.

Cleft sentence: A structure such as 'It was *syntax* that he hated most', where *syntax* is said to occupy **focus position** within the cleft sentence.

Clitic(isation): The term **clitic** denotes an item which is (generally) a reduced form of another word, and which has the property that (in its reduced form) it must cliticise (i.e. attach itself to) an appropriate kind of **host** (i.e. to another word). For example, we could say that the contracted negative particle *n't* is a clitic form of the negative particle *not* which attaches itself to a finite auxiliary verb, so giving rise to forms like *isn't, shouldn't, mightn't*, etc. Likewise, we could say that *'ve* is a clitic form of *have* which attaches itself to a pronoun ending in a vowel, so giving rise to forms like *we've, you've, they've*, etc. When a clitic attaches to the end of another word, it is said to be an **enclitic** (and hence to **encliticise** onto the relevant word). Clitics differ from **affixes** in that a clitic is generally a reduced form of a full word and has a corresponding full form (so that *'ll* is the clitic form of *will*, for example), whereas an affix (like noun plural *-s* in *cats*) has no full-word counterpart. **Clitic Movement** is an operation by which a clitic moves to a position where it is immediately adjacent to an appropriate **host**. The **Cliticisation Constraint** of §6.7 posits that cliticisation is barred when a clitic is followed by a null constituent.

Closest: In structures in which a head X attracts a particular kind of constituent Y to move to the **edge** of XP, X is said to attract the **closest** constituent of type Y, in accordance with the **Attract Closest Condition/ACC**. See also **Local**.

Cognition/Cognitive: (Relating to) the study of human knowledge.

Common noun: See **Noun**.

COMP/comp: The label 'COMP' is an abbreviation for **Complementiser**. By contrast, 'comp' is an abbreviation for **complement**, so comp-VP denotes 'the complement position in VP'.

Comparative: The comparative form of an adjective or adverb is the form (typically ending in *-er*) used when comparing two individuals or properties: cf. 'John is *taller* than Mary', where *taller* is the comparative form of the adjective *tall*.

Competence: A term used to represent native speakers' tacit/subconscious knowledge of the grammar of their native language(s).

Complement: This is a term used to denote a specific grammatical function (in the same way that the term **subject** denotes a specific grammatical function). A complement is an expression which is directly **merged** with (and hence is the **sister** of) a head word, thereby projecting the head into a larger structure of essentially the same kind. In *close the door, the door* is the complement of the verb *close*; in *after dinner, dinner* is the complement of the preposition *after*; in *good at physics, at physics* is the complement of the adjective *good*; in *loss of face, of face* is the complement of the noun *loss*. As these examples illustrate, complements typically follow their heads in English. The choice of complement (and the morphological form of the complement) is determined by properties of the head: for example, an auxiliary such as *will* requires as its complement an expression headed by a verb in the infinitive form (cf. 'He will *go/*going/*gone*'). Moreover, complements bear a close semantic relation to their heads (e.g. in *Kill him, him* is the complement of the verb *kill* and is an argument of the verb *kill*, representing the victim. Thus, a complement has a close morphological, syntactic and semantic relation to its head. A **complement clause** is a clause which is used as the complement of some other word (typically as the complement of a verb, adjective or noun). Thus, in a sentence such as *He never expected that she would come*, the clause *that she would come* serves as the complement of the verb *expected* and so is a complement clause.

Complementiser: This term is used in two ways. On the one hand, it denotes a particular category of clause-introducing word such as *that/if/whether/for*, as used in sentences such as 'I think *that* you should apologize', 'I don't know *if/whether* she realises', 'They're keen *for* you to show up.' On the other hand, it is used to denote the pre-subject position in clauses ('the complementiser position') which is typically occupied by a complementiser like *that/if/whether/for*, but which can also be occupied by an inverted auxiliary in sentences such as *Can you help?*, where *can* is said to occupy the complementiser position in the clause. A **complementiser phrase/projection (CP)** is a phrase/clause/expression headed by a complementiser (or by an auxiliary or verb occupying the complementiser position). The term **complementiser** is abbreviated to **COMP** in earlier work and to **C** in later work. **Complementiser Agreement** is a phenomenon (found in some West Germanic languages and language varieties) whereby a complementiser inflects for agreement, typically with the subject of its own clause – as in the following Katwijk Dutch example from van Koppen (2005):

(i)   ... datt-**e**   *we* naar Leie   gaan
         that-PL we to   Leiden go   ('... that we are going to Leiden')

Here, the plural ending *-e* on the complementiser marks agreement with the plural subject *we*. On the nature of Complementiser Agreement, see Bayer (1984), Law (1971), Haegeman (1992), Zwart (1993, 1997, 2006), Shlonsky (1994), Carstens (2003), Fuβ (2004), van Koppen (2005), Weiβ (2005), Gruber (2008) and Haegeman and van Koppen (2012).

Complex sentence: A sentence which contains more than one **clause**.

Component: A grammar is said to have three main components: a **syntactic/computational component** which generates syntactic structures, a **semantic component** which assigns each such syntactic structure an appropriate **semantic interpretation** and a **PF component** which assigns each syntactic structure generated by the computational component an appropriate **phonetic form**. See §1.5.

Compound: A compound head is one formed by combining two other heads together. For example, by combining the noun *can* with the noun *opener* we can form the compound *can-opener*. Similarly, by combining the adjective *black* with the noun *board* we form the compound *blackboard*.

COMP-Trace Filter: A condition specifying that any structure in which an overt complementiser is immediately adjacent to and c-commands a **trace** (i.e. a gap left behind by a moved constituent) is filtered out as ill-formed at PF: see §4.7.

Computational component: See **Component**.

Concord: A traditional term to describe an operation whereby a noun and any adjectives or determiners modifying it are assigned the same values for features such as number, gender and case.

Condition: See **Constraint**.

Conditional: A term used to represent a type of clause (typically introduced by *if* or *unless*) which lays down conditions – e.g. '*If you don't behave*, I'll bar you', or '*Unless you behave*, I'll bar you.' In these examples, the italicised are **conditional clauses**.

Conflict: On the **Feature Conflict Constraint**, see **Feature**.

CONJ: See **Conjunction**.

Conjoin: To join together two or more expressions by a **coordinating conjunction** such as *and/or/but*. For example, in *naughty but nice, naughty* has been conjoined with *nice* (and conversely *nice* has been conjoined with *naughty*).

Conjunct: One of a set of expressions which have been **conjoined**. For example, in *rather tired but otherwise alright*, the two conjuncts (i.e. expressions which have been conjoined) are *rather tired* and *otherwise alright*.

Conjunction/CONJ: A word which is used to join two or more expressions together. For example, in a sentence such as *John was tired but happy*, the word *but* serves the function of being a **coordinating conjunction** (abbreviated to **&**) because it coordinates (i.e. joins together) the adjectives *tired* and *happy*; and in *John felt angry and Mary felt bitter*, the co-ordinating conjunction *and* is used to coordinate the two clauses *John felt angry* and *Mary felt bitter*. In a sentence like *Although I was tired, I stayed up to watch the film, although* is a conjunction which links the subordinate clause *I was tired* to the main clause *I stayed up to watch the film* and so is termed a **subordinating conjunction** (**SUB**). In traditional grammar, **complementisers** like *that/for/if/whether* are categorised as (one particular type of) subordinating conjunction.

Constituency/Constituent: A constituent is a structural unit – i.e. an expression which is one of the components out of which a phrase or sentence is built up. For example, the two constituents of a **prepositional phrase** (= PP) such as *into touch* (e.g. as a reply to *Where did the ball go?*) are the preposition *into* and the noun *touch*. The **immediate constituents** of a constituent are its **daughters**. The **constituent structure** (or **phrase structure**, or **syntactic structure**) of an expression is (a representation of) the set of constituents which the expression contains. Syntactic structure is usually represented in terms of a **labelled bracketing** or a **tree diagram**. The **Constituency Condition** of §3.6 specifies that heads and maximal projections are the only types of constituent which can take part in linguistic operations like Movement, Agreement or Ellipsis.

Constraint: A structural restriction which blocks the application of some process to a particular type of structure. The term tends to be used with the rather more specific meaning of 'A grammatical principle which prevents certain types of grammatical operation from applying to certain types of structure.' The terms **condition** and **principle** are used in much the same way.

Contact relative: See **Relative clause**.

Contain/Containment: To say that one constituent X **contains** another constituent Y is to say that Y is one of the constituents out of which X is formed by a Merge operation of some kind. In terms of tree diagrams, we can say that X contains Y if X occurs higher up in the tree than Y, and X is connected to Y by a continuous (unbroken) set of downward branches (the branches being represented by the solid lines connecting pairs of nodes in a tree diagram). If we think of a tree diagram as a network of train stations, we can say that X **contains** Y if it is possible to get from X to Y by travelling one or more stations south. To say that one constituent X **immediately contains** another constituent Y is to say that Y occurs immediately below X in a tree and is connected to X via a branch (or, that X contains Y and there is no intervening constituent Z which contains Y and which is contained by X). To say that a tree diagram represents **containment** relations is to say that it shows which constituents are contained within which other constituents. See §3.7.

Content: This term is generally used to refer to the semantic content (i.e. meaning) of an expression (typically, of a word). However, it can also be used as a more general way to refer to the linguistic properties of an expression: e.g. the expression **phonetic content** is sometimes used to refer to the phonetic form of (e.g.) a word: hence, we might say that PRO is a pronoun which has no phonetic content (meaning that it is a 'silent' pronoun with no audible form).

Contentives/content words: Words which have intrinsic descriptive content (as opposed to **functors**, i.e. words which serve essentially to mark particular grammatical functions). Nouns, verbs, adjectives and (most) prepositions are traditionally classified as contentives, while pronouns, auxiliaries, determiners, complementisers and particles of various kinds (e.g. infinitival *to*, genitive *of*) are classified as functors.

Contraction: A process by which two different words are combined into a single word, with either or both words being reduced in form. For example, by contraction, *want to* can be reduced to *wanna, going to* to *gonna, he is* to *he's, they have* to *they've, did not* to *didn't*, etc. See also **Cliticisation**.

Contrastive: In a sentence like '*Syntax,* I hate but *phonology* I enjoy', the expressions *syntax* and *phonology* are contrasted, and each is said to be **contrastive** in use.

Control/Controller: In non-finite clauses with a PRO subject which has an antecedent, the antecedent is said to be the **controller** of PRO (or to **control** PRO), and conversely PRO is said to be controlled by its antecedent; and the relevant kind of structure is called a **control clause/structure**. So, in a structure like *John tried PRO to quit, John* is the controller of PRO, and conversely PRO is controlled by

John. The term **control predicate/verb** denotes a word like *try* which takes an infinitive complement with a (controlled) PRO subject. In a structure like *John promised* PRO *to go to see the film together,* PRO is said to be **partially controlled** by *John,* in the sense that PRO refers to *John* and one or more other people: see §4.2. In a somewhat different use of the word, the **controller** of agreement (e.g. with an auxiliary) is the constituent which determines the (person/number) agreement properties of the auxiliary. For example, in a sentence like *I am feeling hungry,* the subject *I* is the controller of agreement with the auxiliary *am,* in the sense that *am* is first person singular here because it agrees in person and number with its controller (i.e. with its first person singular subject *I*).

Converge(nce): A **derivation** converges/is convergent (and hence results in a well-formed sentence) if the relevant derivation does not violate any constraint and results in a structure which satisfies interface conditions, and is pronounceable and meaningful (i.e. it can be mapped into well-formed phonetic and semantic representations).

Coordinate/Coordination: A **coordinate structure** is a structure containing two or more expressions joined together by a coordinating **conjunction** such as *and/but/or/nor* (e.g. *John and Mary* is a coordinate structure.). A pronoun is said to have a **coordinate antecedent** if its antecedent is a coordinate structure (as in '*John and Mary* agreed that <u>they</u> would compromise'). **Coordination** is an operation by which two or more expressions are joined together by a coordinating conjunction. The **Coordination Condition** of §3.6 specifies that only constituents of the same type can be coordinated.

Copula/Copular verb: A 'linking verb', used to link a subject with a non-verbal predicate. The main copular verb in English is *be* (though verbs like *become, remain, stay,* etc. have much the same linking function). In sentences such as *They are lazy, They are fools* and *They are outside,* the verb *are* is said to be a **copula** (or **copular verb**) in that it links the subject *they* to the adjectival predicate *lazy,* or the nominal predicate *fools,* or the prepositional predicate *outside.*

Copy/Copying: The **Copy Theory of Movement** is a theory developed by Chomsky which maintains that a moved constituent leaves behind a (**trace**) copy of itself when it moves, with the copy generally having its phonetic features deleted, via a **Copy Deletion** operation, and so being **null**: see §5.3 and §6.7.

Coreferential: Two expressions are coreferential if they refer to the same entity. For example, in *John cut himself while shaving, himself* and *John* are coreferential in the sense that they refer to the same individual.

Count/Countability: A **count(able) noun** is a noun which can be counted. Hence, a noun such as *chair* is a count noun since we can say 'One chair, two chairs, three chairs, etc.'; but a noun such as *furniture* is a **non-count/ uncountable/mass noun** since we cannot say '*one furniture, *two furnitures, etc.' The **countability** properties of a noun determine whether the relevant item is a **count noun** or not.

CP: Complementiser phrase (see **Complementiser**). The **CP Hypothesis** of §4.11 specifies that all non-defective clauses are CPs, but defective clauses (e.g. bare non-finite complement clauses with passivisable subjects) lack the CP projection found in non-defective clauses. A **CP recursion** structure is one in which one CP is contained inside another within the periphery of the same clause: see §5.4.

Crash: A derivation is said to **crash** if it violates some constraint/s or interface condition/s, or results in a structure which can't be assigned a phonetic form and/or a semantic interpretation.

Criterial Freezing Condition: A constraint specifying that a constituent which occupies its criterial position is frozen in place. See §6.9.

Cycle/Cyclic: An operation (like movement) is said to apply in a cyclic fashion if it first applies to the lowest constituent of the relevant kind in the structure, then to the next lowest, and then to the next lowest but one (and so on). An operation is **anticyclic** if it does not apply in a cyclic fashion

D: see **DET/Determiner**.

Dative: Some linguists claim that English has a dative case typically used to mark an indirect object (see **Object**). On this view, in a sentence like *Give me them!* the indirect object *me* is dative. It is sometimes also claimed that when the preposition *to* is used to introduce an indirect object (as in *Give them to me!*), it functions as a dative case particle.

Daughter: A node X is the daughter of another node Y if Y is the next highest node up in the tree from X, and the two are connected by a **branch** (solid line).

Declarative: A term used as a classification of the **force** (i.e. semantic type) of a clause which is used to make a statement (as opposed to an **interrogative**, **exclamative** or **imperative** clause).

Default: A default value or property is one which obtains if all else fails (i.e. if other conditions are not satisfied). For example, if we say that *-ø* is the default verbal inflection for regular verbs in English, we mean that regular verbs carry the inflection *-s* if third person singular present tense forms, *-d* if past, perfect or passive forms, *-ing* if progressive or gerund forms and *-ø* otherwise (by default). Likewise, default case is a case assigned by default to a constituent which does not fall within the domain of any case-assigner (e.g. *Me* when used to reply to a question like *Who wants an ice cream?*): see Schütze (2001). The **Default Spellout Rule** of §5.2 specifies that where the spellout of a constituent is not determined by some other rule or requirement, the highest copy of the constituent is pronounced at PF, and any lower copies are silent.

Defective: A defective item is one which lacks certain properties (e.g. *beware* is a defective verb in that it lacks the *ing*-form **bewaring*). A **defective clause** is one which lacks the CP layer of structure found in most clauses: see §4.10.

Definite: Expressions containing determiners like *the, this, that*, etc. are said to have **definite reference** in that they refer to an entity which is assumed to be known to the addressee(s): e.g. in a sentence such as *I hated the course*, the DP *the course* refers to a specific course whose identity is assumed to be known to the hearer/reader. In much the same way, personal pronouns like *he/she/it/they*, etc. are said to have definite reference. By contrast, expressions containing the article *a* are **indefinite**, in that (e.g.) if you say *I'm taking a course*, you don't assume that the hearer/reader knows what course you are taking. The **Definiteness Constraint** is a constraint which bars a constituent from being moved/extracted out of a definite nominal – e.g. it bars *what* from being extracted out of the bracketed DP in **'What* did they arrest [the owner of ---]'.

DEG: A degree word like *so/such*. **DEGP** is a degree phrase – i.e. a phrase headed by a degree word. **Deg-Movement** is the movement operation which fronts the italicised degree phrase in sentences like '*Such gallantry* did they show that they were all awarded medals', or '*So tired* were they that they went straight to bed.'

Degree adverb: See **ADV(erb)**.

Deletion: A type of operation by which a constituent present in the syntactic structure of a sentence is given a silent spellout (i.e. is unpronounced) in the PF component.

Demonstrative: This is a term used to refer to words like *this/that, these/those* and *here/there* which indicate a location relatively nearer to or further from the speaker (e.g. *this book* means 'the book relatively close to me', and *that book* means 'the book somewhat further away from me').

Derivation: The derivation of a phrase or clause is the set of syntactic (e.g. merge, movement, agreement, case-marking, etc.) operations used to form the relevant structure. The derivation of a word is the set of morphological operations used to form the word.

Derivational morphology: The study of the processes by which a word can be used to form a different kind of word by the addition of an **affix** of some kind (e.g. by adding *-ness* to the adjective *ill* we can form the noun *illness*).

Derive: To **derive** a structure is to say how it is formed (i.e. specify the operations by which it is formed).

Descriptive: The descriptive approach to grammar sees the task of grammar as being that of describing the way people speak (and write) in contemporary society. A grammar of a language is said to be **descriptively adequate** (or achieve **descriptive adequacy**) if it provides a comprehensive description of the full range of structures found in the language. See §1.2.

DET/Determiner: A word like *the/this/that* used to modify a noun or noun phrase is a **determiner** in the sense that it determines the referential properties of the noun (phrase). For example, *the* in a sentence like *Shall we take the car?* serves to indicate that the phrase *the car* is a definite referring expression, in the sense that it refers to a definite (specific) car which is assumed to be familiar to the hearer/addressee.

Determiner phrase/DP: A phrase like *the king (of Utopia)* which comprises a determiner *the*, and a noun complement like *king* or a noun phrase complement like *king of Utopia*. In work before the mid 1980s, a structure like *the king of Utopia* would have been analysed as a noun phrase (= NP), comprising the head noun *king*, its complement *of Utopia* and its specifier *the*. Since Abney

(1987), such expressions have been taken to have the status of DP/determiner phrase.

Direct object: See **Object**.

Direct speech: Direct (**free**) speech is a stretch of speech enclosed in inverted commas which is a direct representation of the exact words used by the person speaking. For instance, in a sentence like (i) below the italicised material is an instance of direct speech: it involves the use of inverted commas, the first word starts with a capital letter, and the clause ends with a question mark.

(i) Jim asked Mary: '*Are you leaving?*'

By contrast, the clause italicised in (ii) is an instance of **indirect speech** (or **reported speech**):

(ii) Jim asked Mary *if she was leaving*

Note that there are no inverted commas, no capital letter at the beginning of the clause, no question mark and no Auxiliary Inversion, and in addition there is tense transposition (present tense *are* changes to past tense *was*) and person transposition (second person *you* changes to third person *she*). Now compare the clauses italicised in (i) and (ii) with the italicised clause in (iii), which is an instance of **free indirect speech**:

(iii) Jim asked Mary *was she leaving*

The free indirect speech italicised in (iii) shows the Auxiliary Inversion typical of direct speech, but resembles indirect speech in that it lacks inverted commas, an initial capital letter and a final question mark, and also shows tense and person transposition. See §2.9.

Discontinuous spellout: This phenomenon (also termed **split spellout**) arises when part of a moved phrase is spelled out in the position in which it originates, and the remainder in the position in which it ends up – as in '*How much* do you believe *of what he tells you?*', where the wh-phrase *how much of what he tells you* moves to the front of the sentence, with *how much* being spelled out in the position it moves to, and *of what he tells you* being spelled out in the position in which it originates. This gives rise to the formation of a **discontinuous constituent**. See §6.7.

Discourse: Discourse factors are factors relating to the extrasentential setting in which an expression occurs (where extrasentential means 'outside the immediate sentence containing the relevant expression'). For example, to say that PRO has a **discourse controller** in a sentence such as *It would be wise* PRO *to prepare yourself for the worst* means that PRO has no antecedent within the sentence immediately containing it, but rather refers to some individual(s) outside the sentence (in this case, the person being spoken to).

Distribution: The distribution of a word/phrase is the range of positions it can occupy within sentences.

Domain: The **domain** (or, more fully, **c-command domain**) of a head H is the set of constituents c-commanded by H – namely its sister and all the constituents contained within its sister. For example, the domain of C includes its TP complement and all constituents of the relevant TP.

DO-support: This refers to the use of the 'dummy' (i.e. meaningless) auxiliary DO to form questions, negatives or tags in sentences which would otherwise contain no auxiliary. Hence, because a non-auxiliary verb like *want* requires DO-support in questions/negatives/tags, we have sentences such as '*Does* he want some?', 'He *doesn't* want any' and 'He wants some, *does* he?' See §5.10.

Double-headed relatives: Relative clauses in which one copy of the relativized constituent appears inside the relative clause, and another appears outside it – as in the following example discussed in §7.6: 'I hit **shots** [that I know I can hit *shots*]' (Tiger Woods, BBC Radio 5).

Double object construction: See **Object**.

Doubly Filled Comp Filter/DFCF: A PF constraint specifying that the edge of a CP headed by an overt complementiser (like *that/for/if/whether*) cannot be doubly filled (i.e. cannot contain any other overt constituent). See §6.3.

DP: See **Determiner phrase**.

DP Hypothesis: The hypothesis that all definite nominal **arguments** have the status of DPs – not just nominals like *the president* which contain an overt determiner, but also proper names like *John*. See §4.11.

D-pronoun: A pronoun like *that* in *I don't like that* which seems to be a pronominal determiner. Personal pronouns like *he/him* are also taken to be D-pronouns by some linguists. See §2.6

Duke of York Condition: A constraint which bars operations in which a constituent moves into some new position and subsequently moves back into its old position. See §5.10.

Dummy: A word with little or no intrinsic lexical semantic content (e.g. the expletive pronoun *there* and the auxiliary *do*).

Earliness Principle: A principle which says that linguistic operations must apply as early in a derivation as possible.

Early Modern English/EME: The type of English found in the early seventeenth century (i.e. at around the time Shakespeare wrote most of his plays, between 1590 and 1620).

Echo question: A type of sentence used to question something which someone else has just said (often in an air of incredulity), repeating all or most of what they have just said. For example, if I say 'I once met Nim Chimpsky' and you don't believe me (or don't know who I'm talking about), you could reply with an echo question such as 'You once met who?'

ECM: See **Exceptional case-marking**.

Economy Principle: A principle which specifies that 'Structures and the operations used to form them should be as economical as possible': see §1.4.

ECP: See **Empty (Category Principle)**.

Edge: The edge of a given projection HP is that part of HP which excludes the complement of H (hence, that part of the structure which includes the head H and any specifier/s or adjunct/s which it has). An **edge feature** is a feature on a head (like C) which requires it to have an appropriate kind of specifier (by Merge or Move). The **Edge Constraint** suggested in §6.5 specifies that 'No more than one constituent can be extracted from the edge of any given projection.'

Elizabethan English: The type of English found in the early seventeenth century, during the reign of Queen Elizabeth I (i.e. at around the time Shakespeare wrote most of his plays, between 1590 and 1620).

Ellipsis/Elliptical: Ellipsis is an operation by which an expression is omitted in order to avoid repetition. An ellipsed constituent is generally taken to be present in the syntax, but given a silent pronunciation in the PF component. For example, in a sentence such as *I will do it if you will do it*, we can ellipse (i.e. give a silent pronunciation to) the second occurrence of the verb phrase *do it* to avoid repetition, and hence say *I will do it if you will*: this type of ellipsis is referred to as **VP ellipsis**. An **elliptical** structure is one containing an 'understood' constituent which has undergone ellipsis (i.e. been omitted).

Embedded: An embedded clause is one which is positioned internally within another constituent. For example, in a sentence such as *He may suspect that I hid them*, the *hid*-clause (= *that I hid them*) is embedded within (and is the complement of) the verb phrase headed by the verb *suspect*. Likewise, in *The fact that he didn't apologise is significant*, the *that*-clause (*that he didn't apologise*) is an embedded clause in the sense that it is embedded within a noun phrase headed by the noun *fact*. A clause which is not embedded within any other expression is a **root clause** (see **Root clause**) or **main clause**.

EME: See **Early Modern English**.

Empirical evidence: Evidence based on observed linguistic phenomena. In syntax, the term generally means 'evidence based on grammaticality judgments by native speakers.' For example, the fact that sentences like **For himself to apologise would be unthinkable* are judged ungrammatical by native speakers of Standard English provides us with empirical evidence that anaphors like *himself* can't be used without an appropriate antecedent (i.e. an expression which they refer back to).

Empty: A constituent is empty/null if it is 'silent' and hence has no overt phonetic form. Empty categories include null subject pronouns like **PRO** and **pro**, null relative operators (like that in 'someone *Op* I know well'), null determiners (like that in 'I know *ø John*'), and null trace copies of moved constituents. See ch. 4. The **Empty Category Principle** of §4.7 specifies that an empty category must be licensed.

Enclitic/Encliticise: See **Clitic**.

Entry: A **lexical entry** is an entry for a particular word in a dictionary (and hence by extension refers to the set of information about the word given in the relevant dictionary entry).

Epithet: An epithet is a descriptive word or phrase used in place of a referring expression. An example would be the epithet *the poor fool* used in order to avoid repeating *John* in 'Mary flashed her big brown beautiful eyes at John, and *the poor fool* was immediately besotted.'

EPP: This was originally an abbreviation for the **Extended Projection Principle**, which posited that every T constituent must be extended into a TP projection which has a **specifier**. In more recent work, the requirement for a T constituent like *will* to have a specifier is said to be a consequence of T carrying an [**EPP**] feature requiring it to project a specifier.

Exceptional case-marking/ECM: Accusative subjects of infinitive clauses (e.g. *him* in 'I believe *him to be innocent*') are said to carry exceptional case (in that the case of the accusative subject is assigned by the main-clause verb *believe*, and it is exceptional for the case of the subject of one clause to be assigned by the verb in a higher clause). Verbs (like *believe*) which take an infinitive complement with an accusative subject are said to be **ECM verbs**. The infinitive clause in such cases is said to be an **exceptional clause** or **ECM clause**. See §4.10.

Exclamative: A type of structure used to exclaim surprise, delight, annoyance, etc. In English syntax, the term is restricted largely to clauses beginning with wh-exclamative words like *What*! or *How*! – e.g. 'What a fool I was!' or 'How blind I was!' See §7.2.

Excorporation Constraint: A constraint which bars one head from being excorporated out of (i.e. detached from) another head which it is adjoined to. See §5.10.

Existential: An existential sentence is one which is about the existence of some entity. For example, a sentence such as *Is there any coffee?* questions the existence of coffee. Consequently, the word *any* here is sometimes said to be an **existential quantifier** (as is *some* in a sentence like *There is some coffee in the pot*).

Experience: Children's experience is the speech input which they receive (or, more generally, the speech activity which they observe) in the course of acquiring their native language.

Expletive: A 'dummy' constituent with little or no inherent semantic content, such as the pronoun *there* in existential sentences like *There is no truth in the rumour*, or the impersonal pronoun *it* in sentences such as *It is unclear why he resigned*.

Explicit: Explicit knowledge is conscious knowledge.

Expression: This word is used in the text as an informal term meaning a string (i.e. continuous sequence) of one or more words which form a **constituent**.

Extended Projection Principle: See **EPP**.

External Merge: See **Merge**.

Extract/Extraction: Extract(ion) is another term for **move(ment)**, and so denotes an operation by which one constituent is moved out of another. E.g. in a structure such as *Who do you think [he saw - - -]*, the pronoun *who* has been extracted out of the bracketed clause (i.e. it is been moved out of the gap position marked `---`) and moved to the front of the overall sentence. The **extraction site** for a moved constituent is the position which it occupied before undergoing movement (i.e. the gap position in the above sentence). The **Constraint on Extraction Domains/CED** specifies that extraction is only possible out of a complement, not out of a specifier or adjunct.

Extraposed/Extraposition: In structures where a relative clause is separated from (and follows) its antecedent, the relative clause is said to have been extraposed or to have undergone Extraposition. So, for example, in:

(i) *Someone* rang me yesterday [who claimed to be from the bank]

the bracketed relative clause is separated from its antecedent *someone* and positioned at the end of the sentence (and so is said to have been extraposed).

F: This symbol is used as a convenient notational device to denote an abstract functional head (or an abstract feature) of some kind.

Factive: A clause is factive if it is presupposed to be factual/true. For example, in a sentence such as 'I had never believed *that she was pregnant*', the italicised complement clause is non-factive, and hence the speaker can subsequently go on and deny that it is true (e.g. *I had never believed that she was pregnant, and sure enough it subsequently turned out that she wasn't*). By contrast, the italicised complement clause in 'I hadn't known *that she was pregnant*' is indeed factive, and so it is anomalous/contradictory to say *I hadn't known that she was pregnant, and indeed it subsequently turned out that she wasn't*. A verb like *know* which selects a factive clause as its complement is termed a **factive predicate**. Factive clauses are **islands** for extraction (in the sense that they are resistant to allowing constituents to be extracted out of them).

Faculty of Language: See **Language Faculty**.

Feature: A device used to describe a particular grammatical property. For example, the distinction between count and non-count nouns might be described in terms of a feature such as [±COUNT]. See §3.2. The **Feature Conflict Constraint** of §7.5 specifies that no constituent can carry conflicting specifications for any feature/s. In §6.8, C was said to have the following **Feature Composition** in operator questions:

(i) C carries an interrogative edge feature (= Q-feature/QF) in an operator-question clause.

(ii) C can also carry a Q-feature in a non-interrogative embedded clause which is the complement of a bridge verb.

(iii) In a finite root clause, if C has a Q-feature then C also has a T-feature.

Feminine: This term is used in discussion of grammatical **gender** to denote pronouns like *she/her/hers* which refer to female entities.

Filled: To say that a given position in a structure must be filled is to say that it cannot remain empty but rather must be occupied (usually by an overt constituent of an appropriate kind).

Finite: The term **finite verb/finite clause** denotes (a clause containing) an auxiliary or non-auxiliary verb which can have a nominative subject like *I/we/he/she/they*. For example, compare the two bracketed clauses in:

(i) What if [people annoy her]?
(ii) Don't let [people annoy her]

The bracketed clause and the verb *annoy* in (i) are finite because in place of the subject *people* we can have a nominative pronoun like *they*; by contrast, the bracketed clause and the verb *annoy* are non-finite in (ii) because *people* cannot be replaced by a nominative pronoun like *they* (only by an accusative pronoun like *them*): cf.

(iii) What if [*they* annoy her]?
(iv) Don't let [*them/*they* annoy her]

By contrast, a verb or clause which has a subject with accusative or null case in English is non-finite; hence the bracketed clauses and italicised verbs are non-finite in the examples below:

(v) Don't let [them *annoy* her]
(vi) You should try [PRO to *help*]

Non-finite forms include **infinitive** forms like *be*, and **participle** forms like *being/been*. A **finite null subject** is the kind of null (**pro**) subject found in finite clauses in languages like Italian; a **non-finite null subject** is the kind of null (**PRO**) subject found in seemingly subjectless nonfinite clauses: see §4.2.

First Person: See **Person**.

FL: Faculty of Language: see **Language Faculty**.

Floating quantifier: A quantifier which is separated from the expression which it quantifies. For example, in a sentence such as 'The students have *all* passed their exams', *all* quantifies (but is not positioned next to) *the students*, so that *all* is a floating/stranded quantifier here.

FOC/Focalise/Focus/FOCP: Focus position in a sentence is a position occupied by a constituent which is emphasised in some way (usually in order to mark it as containing 'new' or 'unfamiliar' information). For example, in a **cleft sentence** such as 'It's *syntax* that they hate most' or a **pseudo-cleft** sentence such as 'What they hate most is *syntax*', the expression *syntax* is said to occupy focus position within the relevant sentence, and to be focused/focalised. **Foc(us)-Movement** is an operation (discussed in §7.10) by which a focused constituent is moved to the beginning of a clause in order to mark it as introducing new information. Thus, in the dialogue below, the two italicised constituents have undergone Foc(us)-Movement:

SPEAKER A: What are the subjects you enjoy most and least?
SPEAKER B: *Syntax* I enjoy most. *Phonetics* I enjoy least

In work on split CP projections by Luigi Rizzi (briefly mentioned in §5.4), preposed focused expressions are said to occupy the specifier position within a **FOCP**/focus phrase projection which is headed by an abstract **FOC**/focus head. The **Focus Condition** of §3.6 specifies that only a maximal projection can be focused.

Foot: The foot of a (movement) chain is the constituent which occupies the lowest position in the chain.

FORCE/FORCEP: The complementisers *that/if* in a sentence such as *I didn't know* [*that/if he was lying*] are said to indicate that the bracketed clauses are declarative/interrogative in force (in the sense that they have the force of a question/a statement). In work on split CP projections by Luigi Rizzi (briefly touched on in §5.4), complementisers are said to constitute a **FORCE** head which can project into a **FORCEP** 'force phrase'.

Formal: A formal speech style denotes a very careful and stylised form of speech (as opposed to the kind of informal colloquial speech style used in a casual conversation in a bar).

Fragment: An utterance which is not a complete sentence (in the sense that it does not constitute a clause). So, a phrase such as *A new dress* used in reply to a question such as *What did you buy?* would be a sentence fragment. (By contrast, a sentence such as *I bought a new dress* would not be a sentence fragment, since it contains a complete clause.) The **Fragment Condition** of §3.6 specifies that only a maximal projection can serve as a sentence fragment.

Free: See **Direct speech**. On **free (indirect) speech**, see **Direct speech**. In terms of **binding** theory, a constituent is free in a given domain if it is unbound within that domain (i.e. if there is no antecedent for it within the relevant domain): see ex. 3.2. On **free relative pronoun/clause**, see **Relative clause**.

Freezing Principle: A constraint specifying that the constituents of a moved phrase are frozen internally within (and so cannot be extracted out of) the moved phrase. See §6.9.

Front/Fronting: Fronting is an informal term to denote a movement operation by which a given expression is fronted – i.e. moved to the front of some phrase or sentence.

Function: Expressions such as **subject, specifier, complement, object, head** and **adjunct** are said to denote the grammatical function which a particular expression fulfils in a particular structure (which in turn relates to the position which it occupies and certain of its grammatical properties – e.g. case and agreement properties).

Functional category/Functional head/Function word/Functor: A word which has no **descriptive content** and which serves an essentially grammatical function is said to be a function word or functor. (By contrast, a word which has descriptive content is a **content word** or **contentive**.) A functional category is a category whose members are function words: hence, categories such as complementiser, auxiliary, infinitive particle, case particle or determiner are all functional categories – as well as the expressions they head (e.g. C-bar/CP, T-bar/TP, D-bar/DP, etc.).

Gap: A 'hole' in a given position in a structure which results from a constituent undergoing **ellipsis** (as with the second occurrence of *ate* in *John ate an apple and Mary ~~ate~~ a pear*) or movement (as with *where* in *Where has he gone ~~where?~~*). On the notion **parasitic gap**, see the discussion of examples 141–5 in §6.9.

Gapping: A form of **ellipsis** in which the head word is omitted from one (or more) of the conjuncts in a coordinate structure in order to avoid repetition. For example, the italicised second occurrence of *bought* can be gapped (i.e. omitted) in a sentence such as 'John bought an apple and Mary *bought* a pear', giving 'John bought an apple, and Mary a pear.'

Gen: In one use, an abbreviation for **genitive case**; in another, an abbreviation for **gender**.

Gender: A grammatical property whereby words are divided into different grammatical classes which play a role in **agreement/concord** relationships. In French, for example, nouns are intrinsically masculine or feminine in gender (e.g. *pommier* 'apple tree' is masculine, but *pomme* 'apple' is feminine), and articles inflect for gender, so that *un* 'a' is the masculine form of the indefinite article, and *une* is its feminine form. Articles in French have to agree in gender with the nouns they modify, hence we say *un pommier* 'an apple tree', but *une pomme* 'an apple'. In English, nouns no longer have inherent gender properties, and their modifiers don't inflect for gender either. Only personal pronouns like *he/she/it* carry gender properties in modern English, and these are traditionally said to carry **masculine/feminine/neuter** gender respectively (though the term **inanimate** is sometimes used in place of **neuter**).

Generate/Generative: The syntactic component of a grammar is said to **generate** (i.e. specify how to form) a set of syntactic structures. A grammar which does so is said to be a **generative grammar**.

Generic: To say that an expression like *eggs* in a sentence such as *Eggs are fattening* has a generic interpretation is to say that it is interpreted as meaning 'eggs in general'.

Genitive: See **Case**.

Gerund: When used in conjunction with the progressive aspect auxiliary *be*, verb forms ending in *-ing* are **progressive participles**; in other uses they generally function as **gerunds** (traditionally considered to be verbal nouns, by which is meant 'nouns derived from verbs'). In particular, *-ing* verb forms are gerunds when they can be used as subjects, or as complements of verbs or prepositions, and when (in literary styles) they can have a genitive subject like *my*. Thus *writing* is a gerund (verb form) in a sentence such as 'She was annoyed at [my *writing* to her mother]', since the bracketed gerund structure is used as the complement of the preposition *at* and has a genitive subject *my*.

Gradable: A gradable adjective (like *happy*) is one which denotes a property that can exist in varying degrees, and can be modified by an adverb like *very* (as in 'She is *very happy*').

Grammar: In traditional terms, the word grammar relates to the study of morphology and syntax. In a broader Chomskyan sense, grammar includes the study of phonology and semantics: i.e. a grammar of a language is a computational system which derives the phonetic form and semantic representation of expressions.

Grammatical: An expression is **grammatical** if it contains no morphological or syntactic error, and **ungrammatical** if it contains one or more morphological or syntactic errors. **Grammatical features** are (e.g. person, number, gender, case, etc.) features which play a role in grammatical operations (e.g. in determining case or agreement properties). On **grammatical function**, see **Function**.

***Have*-cliticisation:** An operation by which *have* (in the guise of its contracted clitic variant /v/) attaches to an immediately preceding c-commanding word ending in a vowel or diphthong, resulting in forms such as *I've, we've, they've*, etc. See §4.3.

Head: This term has two main uses. The head (constituent) of a compound noun or a phrase is the key word which determines the syntactic and semantic properties of the compound or phrase. So, in a compound noun such as *coat hooks*, the head of the compound is *hooks* since the compound describes types of hook, not types of coat. Likewise, in a phrase such as *fond of fast food*, the head of the phrase is the adjective *fond*, and consequently the phrase is an adjectival phrase (and hence can occupy typical positions associated with adjectival expressions – e.g. as the complement of *is* in 'He is *fond of fast food*'). In many cases, the term **head** is paraphraseable as 'word' (e.g. in sentences such as 'An accusative pronoun can be used as the complement of a transitive head'). In a different use of the same word, the head of a movement chain is the highest constituent in the chain.

Headed/Headedness Principle: An expression is **headed** if it has a **head**. The **Headedness Principle** specifies that every constituent must be headed by a lexical item (e.g. have a word or affix as its head). So, for example, an expression like *fond of fast food* is headed by the adjective *fond* and so is an adjectival phrase. See **Head**, and §3.2.

Head-first/-last: A head-first structure is one in which the head of the structure is positioned before its complement(s); a head-last structure is one in which the head of the structure is positioned after its complement(s). See §1.7.

Headless relative: See **Relative clause/pronoun**.

Head Movement: Movement of a word from one head position to another (e.g. movement of an auxiliary from T to C, or of a verb from V to T, or of a noun from N to D). See ch. 5.

Head Movement Constraint/HMC: A principle of Universal Grammar which specifies that movement between one head position and another is only possible between the head of a given structure and the head of its complement in a given type of structure. See §5.7.

Head Position Parameter: The parameter which determines whether a language positions heads before or after their complements in a given type of structure. See §1.7.

Head Raising. An operation by which an antecedent noun which originates inside a relative clause is raised to a position outside it where it becomes the antecedent of the relative clause. See §7.6.

Head Strength Parameter: A parameter whose setting determines whether a given kind of head is **strong** and can trigger movement of a lower head to attach to it, or **weak** and so cannot attract a lower head to move to attach to it. See §5.7.

HMC: See **Head Movement Constraint**.

Homophonous: Two different expressions are homophonous if they have the same phonetic form (e.g. *we've* and *weave*).

Host: An expression to which a **clitic** or **affix** attaches. For example, when *n't* cliticises onto *could* in expressions like *couldn't*, we can say that *could* is the host onto which *n't* cliticises.

I: See **INFL**.

Idiom chunk: A string of words which has an idiosyncratic, idiomatic meaning (e.g. *hit the roof* in the sense of 'get angry').

I-language: I-language is a linguistic system internalised (i.e. internally represented) within the brain. See §1.2.

Immediate constituent: See **Constituent**.

Immediately contain: See **Contain**.

Impenetrable/Impenetrability Condition. The **Impenetrability Condition** says that a constituent c-commanded by a complementiser cannot be affected by (e.g. agree with, or be case-marked by, or be attracted by) any constituent c-commanding the CP headed by the complementiser. See §4.10.

Imperative: A term employed to classify a type of sentence used to issue an order (e.g. *Be quiet!*, *Don't say anything!*), and also to classify the type of verb form used in an imperative sentence (e.g. *be* is a verb in the imperative **mood** in *Be quiet!*). Imperatives can generally contain *please* (e.g. *Please be quiet!*). An **imperative null subject** is a null counterpart of *you* which can be used as the subject of an imperative: see §4.2.

Inanimate: See **Animate**.

Indefinite: See **Definite**.

Independent clause: See **Root clause**.

Indicative: Indicative (auxiliary and main) verb forms are finite forms which are used (*inter alia*) in declarative and interrogative clauses (i.e. statements and questions). Thus, the italicised items are said to be indicative in **mood** in the following sentences: 'He *is* teasing you', '*Can* he speak French?', 'He *had* been smoking', 'He *loves* chocolate', 'He *hated* syntax'. An **indicative clause** is a clause which contains an indicative (auxiliary or non-auxiliary) verb. See **Mood**.

Indirect speech. See **Direct speech**.

Infinitive/infinitival: The infinitive (or **infinitival**) form of a verb is the (uninflected) form which is used (*inter alia*) when the verb is the complement of a modal auxiliary like *can*, or of the infinitive particle *to*. Accordingly, the italicised verbs are infinitive/infinitival forms in sentences like 'He can *speak* French', and 'He's trying to *learn* French.' An **infinitive/infinitival clause** is a clause which contains a verb in the infinitive form. Hence, the bracketed clauses are infinitive clauses in: *He is trying* [*to help her*], and *Why not let* [*him help her*]? (In both examples, *help* is an infinitive verb form, and *to* when used with an infinitive complement is said to be an **infinitive particle**.) Since clauses are analysed as phrases within the framework used here, the term **infinitive phrase** can be used interchangeably with **infinitive clause**, to denote a TP projection headed by the infinitive particle *to* (or by a null counterpart of the infinitive particle *to*). The **Infinitival Relative Constraint** proposed in ex. 7.2 specifies that 'No (DP headed by an) overt relative operator can be the specifier/daughter of an infinitival CP at PF.'

INFL: A category devised by Chomsky (1981) whose members include finite auxiliaries (which are INFLected for tense/agreement), and the INFinitivaL particle *to*. INFL was abbreviated to **I** in Chomsky (1986), and replaced by **T** (= tense marker) in later work.

Inflection/Inflectional: An inflection is an **affix** which marks grammatical properties such as number, person, tense, case. For example, a plural noun such as *dogs* in English comprises the stem form *dog* and the plural number inflection *-s*. **Inflectional morphology** is the study of the grammar of inflections.

Innateness Hypothesis: The hypothesis that children have a biologically endowed innate Language Faculty. See §1.6.

In situ: A constituent is said to remain in situ (i.e. 'in place') if it doesn't undergo movement.

Interface levels: Levels at which the grammar interfaces (i.e. connects) with speech and thought systems which lie outside the domain of grammar. **Phonetic form** is the level at which the grammar interfaces with articulatory-perceptual (speech) systems, and **semantic representation** is the level at which it interfaces with conceptual-intentional (thought) systems. **Interface conditions** are conditions which structures must meet in order to be processable by thought or speech systems. See §1.5.

Intermediate projection: See **Project(ion)**.

Internalised grammar: A grammar which is internally represented within the mind/brain.

Internal Merge: See **Merge**.

Interpretation: To say that an expression has a particular (semantic) interpretation is to say that it expresses a particular meaning. So, for example, we might say that a sentence such as *He loves you more than Sam* has two different interpretations – one on which *Sam* has a subject interpretation and is implicitly understood as the subject of *loves you*, and a second on which *Sam* has an object interpretation and is implicitly understood as the object of *he loves*. The first interpretation can be paraphrased as 'He loves you more than Sam loves you', and the second as 'He loves you more than he loves Sam.'

Interrogative: An interrogative clause or sentence is one which asks a question. See **Question**.

Intervention Condition: A principle of grammar specifying that no constituent X can move from one position to another across an intervening constituent Y if X and Y are both sensitive to (the same kind of) intervention effects. See §6.4.

Intransitive: see **Transitive**.

Intuitions: Judgments given by native speakers about the grammaticality, interpretation and structure of expressions in their language.

Inversion/Inverted: A term used to denote a movement process by which the relative order of two expressions is reversed. It is most frequently used in relation to the more specific operation by which an auxiliary (and, in earlier stages of English, non-auxiliary) verb comes to be positioned before its subject, e.g. in questions such as '*Can* **you** speak Swahili?', where *can* is positioned in front of its subject *you*. See ch. 5. An **inverted auxiliary/verb** is one which is positioned in front of its subject (e.g. *will* in '*Will* I pass the syntax exam?'). The **Inversion Licensing Condition** specifies that a null C is licensed to carry a T-feature triggering Auxiliary Inversion (i.e. adjunction of a T auxiliary to C) *either* if C has a negative or degree or conditional specifier *or* if C has an interrogative specifier in a root clause. See §5.3 and §5.12.

Irrealis: An infinitive complement like that italicised in 'They would prefer (*for*) *you to abstain*' is said to denote an *irrealis* (a Latin word meaning 'unreal') event in the sense that the act of abstention is a hypothetical event which has not yet happened and may never happen.

Island: A structure out of which no subpart can be extracted by any movement operation. The **Island Constraint** is a constraint devised by Ross (1967, 1986) specifying that no constituent inside an island can be extracted out of the island. For example, co-ordinate structures like *William and Harry* are **islands**. Hence, in a sentence like *I admire William and Harry*, we can topicalise the whole coordinate structure *William and Harry* by moving it to the front of the overall sentence (as in '*William and Harry*, I admire'), but we cannot topicalise *Harry* alone (as we see from the ungrammaticality of *'*Harry* I admire William and').

K: See **Case particle**.

Label: A notational device used to represent linguistic (particularly categorial) properties of constituents. For example, if we say that the word *man* belongs to the category N of noun, we are using N as a label to indicate the categorial properties of the word *man* (i.e. to tell us what grammatical category *man* belongs to).

Labelled bracketing: See **Bracketing**.

Landing site: The landing site for a moved constituent is the position it ends up in after it has been moved (e.g. the specifier position within CP is the landing site for a moved wh-constituent).

Language Faculty: Chomsky argues that humans beings have an innate Language Faculty (or Faculty of Language, FL) which provides them with an algorithm (i.e. set of procedures or program) for acquiring a grammar of their native language(s). See §1.6.

Learnability: A criterion of adequacy for linguistic theory. An adequate theory must explain how children come to learn the grammar of their native languages in such a short period of time, and hence must provide for grammars of languages which are easily learnable by children. See §1.8.

Level: In the sense in which this term is used in this book, constituents like T, T-bar and TP represent different projection levels – i.e. successively larger types of category (T being a **minimal projection**, T-bar an **intermediate projection** and TP a **maximal projection**). See **Projection**.

Lexical (item)/Lexicon: The word **lexical** is used in a number of different ways. Since a **lexicon** is a dictionary (i.e. a list of all the words in a language and their idiosyncratic linguistic properties), the expression **lexical item** in effect means 'word', the expression **lexical entry** means 'the entry in the dictionary for a particular word', the term **lexical property** means 'property of some individual word', the term **lexical learning** means 'learning words and their idiosyncratic properties' and the term **lexical array** means 'the set of words out of which a given expression is formed'. However, the word lexical is also used in a second sense, in which it is contrasted with **functional** (and hence means 'non-functional'). In this second sense, a **lexical category** is a category whose members are **contentives** (i.e. items with idiosyncratic descriptive content): hence, categories such as noun, verb, adjective or preposition are lexical categories in this sense. So, for example, the term **lexical verb** means 'main verb' (i.e. a non-auxiliary verb like *go, find, hate, want,* etc.).

LF(-representation): (A representation of the) logical form (of an expression). See **Representation**. The **LF-component** of a grammar is the (semantic) component which converts syntactic structures into LF-representations.

License(r): To say that *not* licenses (or is the licenser for) *any* in a sentence like *He has not made any comment* is to say that the presence of *not* allows *any* to be used – i.e. *any* can only occur if *not* is present (cf. **He has made any comment*).

Light noun/verb: An item which is a noun/verb but has relatively little semantic content. So, for example, the verbs *take/make* in expressions like *make fun of* and *take heed of* are sometimes said to be light verbs. Likewise, the noun *thing* in expressions like *something/nothing/everything* is sometimes said to be a light noun.

Linear/Linearisation: Linear ordering is the left-to-right ordering of words in a sentence. **Linearisation** is an operation by which unordered syntactic structures are assigned a linear ordering by Linearisation Conditions in the PF component. The **Head-Complement Linearisation Condition** of §3.7 says that heads precede their complements in English. The **Specifier-Head Linearisation Condition** of §3.7 says that specifiers precede their heads.

Link: A constituent (or position) which is part of a movement **chain**.

Local/locality: A number of linguistic operations (e.g. agreement, case-marking, movement, anaphor binding, etc.) are said to be local in the sense that they can only apply when one constituent is sufficiently close to another. For example, Auxiliary Inversion involves adjoining a T auxiliary to the closest head above it (i.e. to C), and Wh-Movement involves a wh-phrase being attracted to become the specifier of the closest C constituent above it. This kind of locality requirement is imposed by constraints like the **Head Movement Constraint**, the **Impenetrability Condition** and the **Relativised Minimality Condition**.

locative: A locative expression is one which denotes place. So, for example, *there/where* are locative pronouns in sentences such as *Are you going there?* or *Where are you going?*

Locus: To say that T is the **locus** of tense is to say that T is the constituent which normally carries the tense properties of (present or past tense) clauses.

Logical Form/LF: A structure which represents the logical relations (e.g. **scope** relations) between constituents in a phrase or sentence.

Long (distance) movement: A long-distance movement operation is one which moves a constituent out of one clause (TP/CP) into another.

M: Mood.

Main clause: See **Root clause**.

Main verb: A non-auxiliary verb. See **Auxiliary**.

Major categories: Categories which have a very large membership, such as noun, verb, adjective, adverb and (less obviously so) preposition. See §1.3.

Marginal: A marginal sentence is one which is of somewhat questionable grammaticality, marked by a preposed question mark (e.g. ?'I ought to have apologised, shouldn't I?')

Masc(uline): This term is used in discussions of grammatical **gender** to denote pronouns like *he/him/his* which refer to male entities. See **Gender**.

Mass noun: See **Count noun**.

Matching: The **matching** analysis of restrictive relative clauses is one which supposes that there is a matching (but null) copy of the antecedent after the relative pronoun so that a structure like *the book which you wrote* has the fuller structure *the book which ~~book~~ you wrote*.

Matrix: In a sentence such as 'I think *he lied*', the (italicised) *lied* clause is an **embedded/complement clause** (by virtue of being embedded as the complement of the verb *think*), and the *think* clause is the **matrix clause**, in the sense that it is the clause immediately containing the *lied* clause.

Maximal projection: See **Projection**.

Merge: An operation by which two constituents are combined together to form a single larger constituent: see ch. 3. **Internal Merge** involves merging a copy of a constituent positioned internally within a given structure with the root (i.e.

highest node) of the structure. **External Merge** involves introducing a new constituent into the structure and merging it with the root.

Minimalism/Minimalist program: A theory of grammar developed by Chomsky which seeks to minimise (and in the best case scenario eliminate) recourse to constructs or principles which are not conceptually necessary (i.e. which are not imposed by interface requirements, or by biological or natural principles). See §1.5.

Minimal projection: See **Projection**.

Minor categories: Categories which have a very small membership, such as determiner, quantifier, pronoun, conjunction, complementiser, auxiliary, etc. See §1.3.

MOD/MODP: A MODP/modifier phrase is a constituent which contains a word or phrase used to modify some other constituent. For example, in a sentence like *It was a better than average piece of work*, the adjectival phrase/AP *better than average* is a modifier of the noun phrase/NP *piece of work*, and under the analysis outlined in §4.11 this AP would be the specifier of a MODP projection with a null MOD/modifier constituent as its head, and the NP as its complement.

Modal/Modality: A modal item is one which expresses modality (i.e. notions such as possibility, futurity or necessity). The set of modal auxiliaries found in English is usually assumed to include *will/would/can/could/shall/should/may/might/must/ought*, and *need/dare* when followed by a 'bare' (*to*-less) infinitive complement. The set of modal adverbs found in English includes words like *possibly, perhaps, maybe, probably, conceivably, definitely* and *certainly*.

Modification/Modifier/Modify: In an expression such as *tall men*, it is traditionally said that the adjective *tall* modifies (i.e. attributes some property to) or is a modifier of the noun *men*. Likewise, in a sentence such as *Eat slowly!*, the adverb *slowly* is said to modify the verb *eat* (in the sense that it describes the manner in which the speaker is being told to eat). The **Modification Condition** of §3.6 specifies that only a (string of words which forms) a constituent can be modified by an appropriate type of modifier.

Mood: This is a term describing inflectional properties of finite verbs. (Auxiliary and non-auxiliary) verbs in English can be in the **indicative mood, subjunctive mood** or **imperative mood**. Examples of each type of mood are given by the italicised verb forms in the following: 'He *hates* [= indicative] spaghetti'; 'The court ordered that he *be* [= subjunctive] detained indefinitely'; '*Keep* [= imperative] quiet!' The mood of the verb determines aspects of the interpretation of the relevant clause, so that, e.g., subjunctive verbs occur in **irrealis** clauses.

Morpheme: The smallest unit of grammatical structure. Thus, a plural noun such as *cats* comprises two morphemes, namely the stem *cat* and the plural suffix -*s*.

Morphology/morphological: Morphology studies how **morphemes** are combined together to form words. Morphological properties are properties relating to the form of words (i.e. relating to the inflections or affixes they carry). For example, it is a morphological property of regular count nouns that they have a plural form ending in -*s*.

Morphosyntactic: A morphosyntactic property is a grammatical property, i.e. a property which affects (or is affected by) relevant aspects of morphology and syntax. For instance, **case** is a morphosyntactic property in that (e.g.) pronouns have different morphological forms and occupy different syntactic positions according to their case: e.g. the nominative form of the first person plural pronoun is *we* and its accusative form is *us*; the two occupy different syntactic positions in that the nominative form occurs as the subject of a finite verb, whereas the accusative form occurs as the complement of a transitive verb or preposition: cf. '*We* disagree', 'Join *us*'.

Mother: A constituent X is the mother of another constituent Y if X is the next highest node up in the tree from Y, and the two are connected by a branch (solid line). See §3.7.

Move/Movement: An operation by which (a copy of) a constituent is displaced from one position in a given structure and comes to occupy another position in the structure.

MP: A modal phrase/projection – i.e. a phrase headed by a **modal** auxiliary: see §5.8.

Multiple wh-questions: Questions containing more than one wh-word. See §6.2.

N: See **Noun**.

Native: A native speaker of English is someone who has acquired and used English as a first language in an English-speaking environment from birth (or early childhood), and who speaks the language fluently. **Native English** is the kind of English spoken by a fluent adult native speaker of English.

Natural language: A language acquired in a natural setting by human beings (hence, excluding, e.g., computer languages, animal communication systems, etc.).

NEG: The head constituent of a **NEGP** (i.e. of a negation phrase constituent which contains *not* as its specifier). See §5.9.

Negation: A process or construction in which some proposition is said to be false. Negation involves the use of some negative item such as *not, n't, nobody, nothing, never*, etc. – though most discussions of negation in English tend to be about the negative adverbs *not/n't*. See §5.9.

Negative evidence: In the context of discussions about the nature of the evidence which children make use of in acquiring their native language(s), this term relates to evidence based on the non-occurrence of certain structures in the child's speech input, or on correction of children by others (e.g. adults). See §1.8.

Negative particle: This term typically denotes the negative adverbs *not/n't*.

Neg-Movement: A movement operation by which a negative expression is moved to the front of a clause (like that italicised in '*Not a single word* did he utter'): see §7.10.

NEGP: See **NEG**.

Neuter: See **Gender**.

Neutralise: To say that a distinction between (e.g.) a singular noun like *dog* and a plural noun like *dogs* is neutralised or syncretised in a noun like *sheep* is to say that there is no visible marking of the singular–plural distinction on a noun like *sheep* (hence: *one/two sheep*).

N-Movement: Movement of a noun to a higher position within a nominal expression. See §5.11.

Node: A term used to denote each point in a tree diagram which carries a category label. Each node represents a separate constituent in the relevant structure.

Nom: An abbreviation for **nominative**. See **Case**.

Nominal: This is the adjective associated with the word *noun*, so that a **nominal (expression)** is an expression containing or comprising a noun. However, the term is sometimes extended to mean 'expression containing or comprising a noun *or pronoun*'.

Nominative: See **Case**.

Non-argument: A (pro)nominal expression which is not an **argument** but instead has a vocative, predicative or exclamative function: see 4.11.

Non-auxiliary verb: A lexical verb or main verb (like *want, try, hate, smell, buy,* etc.) which requires **do-support** to form questions, negatives and tags.

Non-bridge: See **Bridge**.

Non-constituent: A non-constituent string is a sequence of words which do not together form a constituent.

Non-count noun: See **Count noun**.

Non-echo(ic) question: A question which can be used in any context, not just to echo something previously said.

No-Negative-Evidence Hypothesis: The hypothesis that children acquire their native language(s) on the basis of positive evidence alone and do not make use of negative evidence. See §1.8.

Non-finite: See **Finite**.

Non-terminal: See **Terminal**.

No Tampering Condition/NTC: A constraint specifying that no syntactic operation can tamper with (i.e. change) any part of a structure other than the root. See §6.7.

Noun/N: A category of word (whose members include items such as *boy/friend/ thought/sadness/computer*) which typically denotes an entity of some kind. In traditional grammar, a distinction is drawn between **common nouns** and **proper nouns**. Proper nouns are names of individual people (e.g. *Chomsky*), places (e.g. *Colchester, Essex, England*), dates (e.g. *Tuesday, February, Easter*), magazines (e.g. *Cosmopolitan*), etc., whereas common nouns (e.g. *boy, table, syntax,* etc.) are nouns denoting general (non-individual) entities. Proper nouns have the semantic property of having unique reference, and the syntactic property that (unless themselves modified) they generally can't be modified by a determiner (cf. **the London*).

Noun phrase/NP: A phrase whose head is a noun. In work prior to the mid 1980s, a structure such as *the king of Utopia* was taken to be a noun phrase/NP comprising the head noun *king*, its complement *of Utopia* and its specifier *the*. In more recent work, such expressions are taken to be **determiner phrases/ DPs** comprising the head determiner *the* and a noun phrase/NP complement *king of Utopia*, with the NP in turn comprising the head noun *king* and its complement *of Utopia*. See §3.5.

NP: See **Noun phrase**.

N-pronoun: A pronoun like *one* in *Mary bought a green one* which has the morphological and syntactic properties of a (count) noun.

NTC: See **No Tampering Condition**.

Null: A null constituent is one which is 'silent' or 'unpronounced' and so has no overt phonetic form. Such a constituent is said to receive a **null spellout** in the phonological component. See ch. 4.

Null case: The case carried by **PRO** (See **Case**).

Null operator: See **Operator**.

Null subject: A subject which has grammatical and semantic properties but no overt phonetic form. There are a variety of different types of null subject, including the null **pro** subject which can be used in any finite clause in a language like Italian, the null counterpart of *you* found in English imperative clauses like *Shut the door!*, the null **PRO** subject found in non-finite control clauses like that bracketed in *The prisoners tried* [PRO *to escape*], and the null truncated subject found in sentences like *Can't find my pen. Must be on my desk at home.* See §4.2.

Null subject language: This term is used to denote a language which allows any finite clause of any kind to have a null **pro** subject. For example, Italian is a null subject language and so allows us to say *Sei simpatico* (literally *Are nice*, meaning 'You are nice'); by contrast, English is a **non-null subject language** in the sense that it doesn't allow the subject to be omitted in this type of structure (Hence **Are nice* is ungrammatical in English).

Null Subject Parameter: A parameter whose setting determines whether a language is a **null subject language** or not. See §1.7.

NUM: An abbreviation for **Number**. In work in syntax, it is sometimes used as a category label denoting a particular head which is claimed by some to be the **locus** of number properties in noun expressions. It may correspond to the position which a noun like *invasione* 'invasion' moves to in an Italian nominal such as *la grande invasione italiana dell'Albania* (literally 'The great invasion Italian of.the Albania', and more idiomatically 'the great Italian invasion of Albania'). A phrase headed by a **NUM** constituent is labelled **NUMP**/number phrase. See §5.11.

Number: A term used to denote the contrast between singular and plural forms. In English, we find number contrasts in nouns (cf. 'one *dog*', 'two *dogs*'), in some determiners (cf. '*this* book', '*these* books'), in pronouns (cf. *it/they*) and in finite (auxiliary or main) verbs (cf. 'It *smells*', 'They *smell*').

Object: The complement of a transitive item (e.g. in *help me, me* is the object of the transitive verb *help*; and in *for me, me* is the object of the transitive preposition *for*). The term **object** is generally restricted to complements which carry accusative case – i.e. to nominal or pronominal complements: hence, *nothing* would be the object (and complement) of *said* in *He said nothing*, but the *that*-clause would be the **complement** (but not the object) of *said* in *He said that he was tired* – though some traditional grammars extend the term object to cover clausal complements as well as (pro)nominal complements. In sentences such as *She gave him them* the verb *give* is traditionally said to have two objects, namely *him* and *them*: the first object (representing the recipient) is termed the **indirect object**, and the second object (representing the gift) is termed the **direct object**; the relevant construction is known as the **double object construction**. Where a verb has a single object (e.g. *nothing* in *He said nothing*), this is the direct object of the relevant verb.

Objective: Another term for **accusative**. See **Case**.

One-place predicate: A predicate which has only one argument. See **Argument**.

Op/Operator: This term is used in syntax to denote a (e.g. negative, interrogative, conditional, or imperative or relative) constituent whose semantic function is to convert a proposition into, e.g., a negative or interrogative or conditional or imperative or relative clause. A **question operator** is a constituent which types a clause as a question. So, for example, a yes–no question like *Have you eaten anything?* can be analysed as containing a null/silent **yes–no question operator** which types the clause as a yes–no question, which triggers Auxiliary Inversion, and which **licenses** the **polarity item** *anything*. Likewise, an interrogative word like *what* in a sentence like *What has anyone ever done to you?* is a **wh-question operator**, since it types the relevant clause as a wh-question. And a relative clause like that bracketed in *the film* [*we watched*] can be argued to contain a **null wh-operator** (i.e. a null counterpart of the relative operator *which*) that types the bracketed clause as relative. See §5.5.

Over-ride: See **Case over-ride**.

Overt: An expression is overt if it has a non-null phonetic form, but **null** if it has no phonetic content. Thus, *him* is an overt pronoun, but **PRO** is a null pronoun.

Overwrite: See **Case over-ride**.

P: See **Preposition**.

Paraphrase: A paraphrase is an expression which has roughly the same meaning as the expression which it is being used to paraphrase, but which brings out the relevant meaning more clearly. For example, we can bring out the ambiguity of a sentence like *He loves you more than me* by saying that it has two different **interpretations**, one of which can be paraphrased as 'He loves you more than he loves me', and the other of which can be paraphrased as 'He loves you more than I love you.'

Parameter/Parameterised/Parametric: A parameter is a dimension of grammatical variation between different languages or different language varieties (e.g. the **Null Subject Parameter, Head Position Parameter, Wh-**

Parameter). Parametric variation relates to differences between languages which reflect differences in the setting of one or more parameters. A property is parameterised if it varies from one language to another. On parameters, see §1.7. **Parameter setting** is the process by which children determine which setting of a parameter is appropriate for the native language they are acquiring. See §1.8. **Parameter resetting** is an operation by which children reset the initial setting of a parameter given by the Language Faculty if this is inappropriate to the language they are acquiring. See §1.8.

Partial: A **labelled bracketing** is partial if it shows only part of the structure of a given sentence or expression (other parts being omitted to simplify exposition). On **partial control**, see **Control**.

Participle: A non-finite verb form which encodes **aspect** or **voice**. English has three types of participle: **progressive participles** (ending in *-ing*) used in conjunction with the progressive aspect auxiliary *be* in sentences like 'It is *raining*'; **perfect participles** (generally ending in *-d* or *-n*) used in conjunction with the perfect aspect auxiliary *have* in sentences like 'He has *gone* home'; and **passive participles** (also generally ending in *-d* or *-n*) used in conjunction with the passive voice auxiliary *be* in sentences like 'He was *arrested* by Percy Plodd'.

Particle/PRT: This is an informal term used to describe a range of (typically monosyllabic) items which are invariable in form, and which don't fit easily into traditional systems of grammatical categories. For example, infinitival *to* (cf. *Try to be nice*) is said to be an **infinitive particle**; *of* as used in expressions like *loss of face* is sometimes said to be a **genitive case particle**; *not* and *n't* are said to be **negative particles**. The term is sometimes extended to include prepositions used without a complement (e.g. *down* in *He fell down*). See §1.3.

Partitive: A partitive quantifier is a word like *some/any* which quantifies over part of the members of a given set (as in '*Some* students enjoy syntax').

Part of speech: See **Category**.

Passive: See **Active**, **Passivisation**.

Passive participle: See **Active**, **Participle**.

Passivisation: A movement operation whereby an expression which is the complement of a verb becomes the subject of the same clause (as in '*The jewels* were stolen') or the subject of another clause (as in '*The minister* was said to have lied to Parliament').

Past tense: See **Tense**.

Path Containment Condition: A condition proposed by Pesetsky (1982b: 309) to the effect that 'If two paths overlap, one must contain the other' (where a *path* is a set of links in a movement chain).

PERF/PERFP: PERF denotes an auxiliary marking **perfect aspect**. **PERFP** denotes a phrase headed by a perfect auxiliary (e.g. *have lied to her* in 'He may *have lied to her*').

Perfect: In a sentence like *He has gone home, has* is an auxiliary marking **perfect aspect**, and *gone* is a **perfect participle**: see **Aspect**, **Participle**.

Performance: A term which denotes observed language behaviour – e.g. the kind of things people actually say when they speak a language, and what meanings they assign to sentences produced by themselves or other people. Performance can be impaired by factors such as tiredness or drunkenness, giving rise to **performance errors**. Performance is contrasted with **competence** (which denotes fluent native speakers' knowledge of the grammar of their native language). See §1.2.

Periphery: The periphery of a clause is that part of the clause structure which is positioned above TP. So, in a sentence like '*Syntax, why do* students struggle to understand it?', the italicised constituents are positioned in the clause periphery.

Pers: An abbreviation of **Person**.

Person/Pers: In traditional grammar, English is said to have three grammatical persons. A first person expression (e.g. *I/we*) is one whose reference includes the speaker(s); a second person expression (e.g. *you*) is one which excludes the speaker(s) but includes the addressee(s) (i.e. the person or people being spoken to); a third person expression (e.g. *he/she/it/they*) is one whose reference excludes both the speaker(s) and the addressee(s) – i.e. an expression which refers to someone or something other than the speaker(s) or addressee(s).

Personal pronouns: These are pronouns which carry inherent **person** properties – i.e. first person pronouns such as *I/we*, second person pronouns such as *you*, and third person pronouns such as *he/she/it/they*. See **Person**.

PF: An abbreviation for phonetic form. A **PF representation** is a representation of the phonetic form (of an expression): see **Representation**. The **PF component** of a grammar is the component which converts the syntactic structures generated by the computational/syntactic component of the grammar into PF representations, via a series of morphological and phonological operations.

Phonetic form: See **Interface levels**.

Phonetic representation: See **Representation**.

Phrase: The term **phrase** is used to denote an expression larger than a word which is a **maximal projection**: see **Projection**. In traditional grammar, the term refers strictly to non-clausal expressions (Hence, *reading a book* is a phrase, but *He is reading a book* is a clause, not a phrase). However, in more recent work, **clauses** are analysed as types of phrases: e.g. *He will resign* is a tense phrase (TP), and *that he will resign* is a complementiser phrase (CP). See §3.3.

Phrase-marker/P-marker: A tree diagram used to represent the syntactic structure of a phrase or sentence. See §3.7.

Phrase structure: See **constituent structure**.

Pied-piping: A process by which a moved constituent drags one or more other constituents along with it when it moves. For example, if we compare a sentence like *Who were you talking to?* with *To whom were you talking?*, we can say that in both cases the pronoun *who(m)* is moved to the front of the sentence, but that in the second sentence the preposition *to* is **pied-piped** along with the pronoun *who(m)*. See §6.6. The **Pied-Piping Constraint** of ex. 7.2 specifies that 'When a null constituent moves, it cannot pied-pipe any overt superordinate constituent along with it.'

Pl: See **Plural**.

Plural/Pl: A plural expression is one which denotes more than one entity (e.g. *these cars* is a plural expression, whereas *this car* is a **singular** expression).

P-marker: See **Phrase-marker**.

Polarity: A **polarity item/expression** is a word/phrase (e.g. a word like *ever* or a phrase like *at all* or *care a damn*) which has an inherent **affective** polarity and hence is restricted to occurring within the scope of an affective (e.g. negative, interrogative or conditional) constituent (See **Affective**). The **Polarity Licensing Condition** of §3.7 specifies that a polarity expression must be c-commanded by an appropriate (e.g. negative, interrogative or conditional) licenser.

Positive evidence: In discussions of child language acquisition, this expression denotes evidence based on the actual occurrence of certain types of structure in the child's speech input. For example, hearing an adult say *Open it!* gives a child **positive evidence** that verbs are canonically positioned before their complements in English. See §1.8.

POSS/Possessive/Possessor/Possessum: A possessive structure is one which indicates possession: the term is most commonly used in relation to expressions like *John's book*. In such structures, the person possessing the item in question (here *John*) is termed the **possessor** (and is assigned genitive **case**), and the possessed object (here *book*) is termed the **possessum**. POSS is the head of a POSSP 'possessive phrase' projection which has the possessor as its specifier and the possessum as its complement.

Postposition: A type of word which is the counterpart of a **preposition** in languages which position prepositions after their complements. See **Adposition**.

Postulate: A postulate is a theoretical assumption or hypothesis; to postulate is to hypothesise.

PP: See **Prepositional phrase**. The **PP Hypothesis** of §4.11 specifies that adverbial (pro)nominals are PPs headed by a null preposition.

PPT: See **Principles and Parameters Theory**.

Pragmatics: The study of how non-linguistic knowledge is integrated with linguistic knowledge in our use of language.

Pr: An abbreviation for the feature [present-tense]. See **Tense**.

Precede(nce): To say that one constituent precedes another is to say that it is positioned to its left (on the printed page) and that neither constituent contains the other. Precedence is left-to-right linear ordering.

Predicate/predication: The term **predicate** is used in two rather different ways: in traditional grammar on the one hand, and in logic on the other. In traditional grammar, a predicate is an expression that combines with a **subject** to form a

clause in which the predicate says something about the subject: the process by which a subject is combined with the predicate is termed **predication**. For example, in a sentence such as *John smokes*, the subject is the noun *John* and the predicate is the verb *smokes*. In logic, by contrast, the term predicate indicates a word/expression denoting an action, event or state involving one or more participants (said to be the **arguments** of the predicate). The difference between these two uses of the term predicate can be illustrated in relation to a sentence like *John smokes cigars*. In traditional grammar, this is a sentence comprising the subject *John* and the predicate *smokes cigars*. In logic, by, contrast, the proposition expressed by the sentence contains the predicate *smokes* and two arguments – namely the subject *John* and the complement *cigars*. Some earlier work (e.g. Chomsky 1955) attempted to reconcile these two different uses of the term predicate by positing that an expression like *smokes cigars* is a predicate phrase/PredP constituent, where a PredP can be formed by combining a predicate like *smokes* with a complement like *cigars*, and perhaps also with an **adjunct** like *occasionally*, giving rise to the formation of a complex predicate: on this view, the sentence *John smokes cigars occasionally* is formed by combining the subject *John* with the predicate phrase *smokes cigars occasionally*. On **predicate nominal**, see **Predicative**.

Predicative: In a clause such as 'John is *out of control/very silly/a liar*' or in a **small clause** like that bracketed in 'I consider [John *out of control/very silly/a liar*]', the italicised expressions are said to be **predicative** in that they predicate the property of being out of control/very silly/a liar of John (i.e. they attribute the relevant property to John): a nominal like a *liar* when used predicatively is also referred to as a **predicate nominal**; on the difference between predicative and attributive adjectives, see **Attributive**.

Prefix: See **Affix**.

Prenominal: A prenominal expression is one which is positioned in front of a noun expression. For example, both *a* and *red* are prenominal in an expression such as *a red car*.

Prepose/Preposing: See **Front/Fronting**. The **Preposing Condition** of §3.6 specifies that when material is preposed in order to highlight it, what is preposed is the smallest possible maximal projection containing the highlighted material: the Preposing Condition is reformulated as the **Attraction Generalisation** in §6.6.

Preposition/P: A preposition is a word generally used to express location, manner, etc. – e.g. *at/in/on/under/by/with/from/against/down*, etc. In English, it is a characteristic property of prepositions that they are invariable, and that they can generally be modified by *straight/right*. Where a preposition has a nominal or pronominal complement, it is said to be **transitive**; where it has no complement, it is said to be **intransitive**. Hence *down* is a transitive preposition in *He fell down the stairs*, but an intransitive preposition in *He fell down*. See §2.4. **Preposition copying** is a phenomenon found in spoken English whereby two copies of a preposition are found in sentences like '**From** *which club* did the Arsenal sign him **from**?' (Alan Brazil, Talk Sport Radio): see §6.7.

Prepositional phrase/PP: A phrase whose head is a preposition – e.g. *in town, on Sunday, to the market, for someone else*, etc.

Preposition stranding: See **Stranding**.

Pres/Present tense: See **Tense**.

Prescriptive: The prescriptive approach to grammar sees the aim of grammar as being to prescribe norms for grammatical correctness, linguistic purity and literary excellence. See §1.2.

Principal clause: See **Root clause**.

Principles: Principles of Universal Grammar/UG principles describe potentially universal properties of natural language grammars: the terms **condition** and **constraint** are also used with much the same meaning as the term **principle**. Potential principles of Universal Grammar include the **Headedness Principle, Binarity Principle, Attract Closest Principle** and **Impenetrability Condition**. On Principles A, B, and C of Binding Theory, see **Bind**.

Principles-and-Parameters Theory/PPT: This theory, developed in Chomsky (1981) and much subsequent work, claims that natural language grammars incorporate not only a set of innate universal **principles** which account for those aspects of grammar which are common to all languages, but also a set of **parameters** which account for those aspects of grammar which vary from one language to another. See **Principles** and **Parameters**.

PRN: An abbreviation for **pronoun**.

PRO: A null case pronoun (known informally as 'big PRO', because it is written in capital letters) which represents the understood subject of an infinitive complement of a **control** predicate, e.g. in a structure such as *John decided PRO to leave*. See §4.2.

pro: A null nominative pronoun (known informally as 'little pro', because it is written in lower-case letters) which represents the understood null subject of a finite clause in a **null subject language**. A Shakespearean sentence such as *Wilt come?* (= 'Will you come?', Stephano, *The Tempest*, III.ii) could be argued to have a null **pro** subject, and hence to have the structure *Wilt* pro *come?*, with *pro* here having essentially the same interpretation as the second person singular pronoun *thou*. See §4.2.

Pro-Drop Parameter: Another name for the **Null Subject Parameter**.

Proform: A proform is an expression (typically a word) which has no specific content of its own, but which derives its content from an **antecedent**. For example, in a sentence such as *Mary may have been tired, but she didn't seem so*, the antecedent of the word *so* is the adjective *tired*: hence *so* (in the use illustrated here) can be said to be an adjectival proform.

PROG/PROGP: PROG denotes an auxiliary marking progressive aspect: see **Aspect**. PROGP denotes a progressive phrase (like *be lying* in *He may be lying*). See §4.3.

Progressive: See **Aspect**.

Project(ion): A **projection** is a constituent containing a head word. For example, a noun phrase such as *students of Linguistics* is a **projection** of its head noun *students* (equivalently, we can say that the noun *students* here **projects** into the noun phrase *students of linguistics*). A **minimal projection** is a constituent which is not a projection of some other constituent: hence, heads (i.e. words) are minimal projections. An **intermediate projection** is a constituent which is larger than a word, but smaller than a phrase (e.g. *is working* in *He is working*). A **maximal projection** is a constituent which is not contained within any larger constituent with the same head: for a more precise definition of these terms, see (17) in §3.3. So, for example, in a sentence like 'I've heard several *accounts of what happened*', the italicised noun phrase *accounts of what happened* is a maximal projection, since it is a projection of the noun *accounts* but is not contained within any larger projection of the noun *accounts* (if we assume that *several accounts of what happened* is a quantifier phrase headed by the quantifier *several*). By contrast, in a sentence such as 'I've heard several *accounts*', the italicised noun *accounts* is both a minimal projection (by virtue of the fact that it is not a projection of some other head) and a maximal projection (by virtue of the fact that it is not contained within any larger structure which has the same head noun). See §3.3.

Pronominal: A pronominal (expression) is a non-anaphoric pronoun like *him* which obeys **Principle B** of **Binding Theory** (and hence must not refer to any c-commanding constituent within the closest TP containing the pronominal). See Ex. 2.2.

Pronoun/PRN: The word *pronoun* is composed of the two morphemes – namely *pro* (meaning 'on behalf of') and *noun*: hence, a pronoun is traditionally said to be a word used in place of a noun expression. Pronouns differ from nouns in that they have no intrinsic descriptive content, and so are functors. There are a range of different types of pronoun found in English, including the pronominal noun *one(s)* used in sentences like *I'll take the red one(s)*, pronominal quantifiers like *any* in *I couldn't find any* and pronominal determiners like *this* in *This is hard*. The term *pronoun* is most frequently used to indicate a class of items (like *he/him/his*) traditionally referred to as **personal pronouns** (though analysed in some work as pronominal determiners). See §2.6.

Proper noun: See **Noun**.

Proposition: This is a term used to describe the semantic content (i.e. meaning) of a sentence. For example, we might say that the sentence *Does John smoke?* questions the truth of the proposition that *John smokes*.

PRT: See **Particle**.

Pseudo-cleft sentence: A sentence such as 'What he hated most was *syntax*', where *syntax* is said to occupy **focus position** within the overall sentence.

Q: In one use, an abbreviation for **quantifier**; in another use, an abbreviation for **question particle**.

Q-feature: A Q-feature on C is a feature which requires C to have an interrogative operator as its specifier. See §6.4.

QP/Quantifier phrase: A phrase whose head is a quantifier – e.g. an expression
such as *many people*, or *few of the students*. The **QP Hypothesis** specifies that
all indefinite nominal arguments are QPs (headed by an overt or null Q): see
§4.11.

Q-pronoun: A pronoun like *many* in 'I don't eat *many*' which seems to be a
pronominal quantifier.

Quantifier/Q: A quantifier is a special type of word used to denote quantity.
Typical quantifiers include the universal quantifiers *all/both*, the free choice
quantifiers *any/whatever* (as in *You can choose any/whatever book you like*),
the distributive quantifiers *each/every*, the existential/partitive quantifiers
some/any, etc. See §2.5.

Quantifier floating/stranding: See **Floating quantifier**.

Question: This refers to a type of sentence which is used to ask whether something is true, or to ask about the identity of some entity. See **Yes–no question**
and **Wh-question**.

Question particle/Q: The analysis of yes–no questions presented in §4.7 suggests that they contain a null question particle (or question **operator**).

Raising: The term **raising** denotes a movement operation which involves moving some constituent from a 'lower' to a 'higher' position in a structure.

RCC: Root Complementiser Constraint: See **Root**.

Realis: A realis verb form is one which can be used to describe a real state of
affairs and is typically **indicative** in **mood** – e.g. the italicised verbs in 'He
cheats/cheated at cards.'

Reciprocal: See **Anaphor**.

Reconstruction. This phenomenon arises in a sentence like *Which picture of
himself do you think Harry prefers?* where the phrase *which picture of himself*
originates as the complement of the verb *prefers* and then moves to the front of
the *think* clause. In order for the semantic component to account for the
anaphor *himself* being bound by (i.e. interpreted as referring to) *Harry*, the
phrase *which picture of himself* has to be reconstructed back into the position in
which it originates, where it is c-commanded by (and contained within) the
same TP as *Harry*.

Recoverability Condition: A constraint on deletion specifying that a constituent
can only be deleted if its content is recoverable. See §5.10.

Recursion/Recursive: A structure is recursive (or involves recursion) if it contains more than one instance of a particular category. For example, CP recursion structures are clauses which contain more than one CP projection (like the
clause italicised in 'He said *that, unless she does as he says, that he will tell her
father*'). See §5.9.

Reduced: A reduced form is a form of a word which has lost one or more of its
phonological segments (i.e. vowel/consonants), and/or which contains a vowel
which loses its defining characteristics and is realised as a neutral vowel like

schwa /ə/. For example, the auxiliary *have* has the full (unreduced) form /hæv/ when stressed, but has the various reduced forms /həv/, /əv/ and /v/ when unstressed.

Reference/Referential/Referring: The reference of an expression is the entity (e.g. object, concept, state of affairs) in the external world to which it refers. A **referential/referring expression** is one which refers to such an entity; conversely, a **non-referential expression** is one which does not refer to any such entity. For example, the second *there* in a sentence such as '*There* was nobody *there*' is referential (it can be paraphrased as 'in that place'), whereas the first *there* is non-referential and so cannot have its reference questioned by *where*? (cf. **'Where* was nobody there?').

Reflexive: See **Anaphor**.

Relative clause/pronoun: In a sentence such as 'He's someone [*who* you can trust]', the bracketed clause is said to be a **relative clause** because it 'relates to' (i.e. modifies) the pronoun *someone*. The pronoun *who* which introduces the clause is said to be a **relative pronoun**, since it 'relates to' the expression *someone* (in the sense that *someone* is the **antecedent** of *who*). **Restrictive relative clauses** serve the function of restricting the class of entities referred to by the antecedent to those which have the property described in the relative clause: e.g. in a sentence like 'I need to work with people *who I can trust*', the italicised restrictive relative clause restricts the class of people referred to in the sentence to those such that I can trust them). **Free/headless relative clauses** are so-called because they contain a **free/headless relative pronoun** (i.e. one which doesn't have any overt antecedent), like *what* in '*What* you say is true'. **Appositive relative clauses** generally serve as 'parenthetical comments' or 'afterthoughts' set off in a separate intonation group from the rest of the sentence, as with the italicised clause in 'I spoke to my bank manager yesterday, *who was in a filthy mood*.' **Contact/Zero relative clauses** are structures in which the edge of the relative clause CP contains no overt material (e.g. no relative pronoun or complementiser), as with the italicised relative clause in 'There's a farmer *I buy vegetables from in the village*.' **Resumptive relative clauses** are relative clauses which contain a **resumptive pronoun** (or nominal), as with the italicised clause in 'He's someone *that I don't know anyone who trusts* **him**.' On the differences between various types of relative clause, see §7.3. On the syntax of restrictive relatives, see §§7.4–7.9; on the analysis of other types of relative clauses, see ex. 7.2–7.5. The **Relative Identification Condition** is a condition proposed in ex. 7.2 specifying that 'A null relative operator must be identifiable as a relative operator either by being (the head of a DP which is) the specifier of an overt relative complementiser, or by being c-commanded by and immediately adjacent to (i.e. not separated by any overt constituent/s from) its antecedent.'

Relativised Minimality Condition/RMC: A principle of grammar which specifies that a constituent X can only be affected (e.g. attracted) by the minimal (i.e. closest) constituent of the relevant type above it (i.e. c-commanding X). See §6.8.

Remerge: An operation by which a copy of an item merged in one position is merged in a new position at the root of the structure: see §7.6.

Reported speech: See **Direct speech**.

Representation: A **syntactic representation** (or **structural representation**) is a notation/device (typically, a tree diagram or labelled bracketing) used to represent the **syntactic structure** of an expression (i.e. the way in which it is structured out of words and phrases): a **semantic representation** is a representation of linguistic aspects of the meaning of an expression; a **PF-representation** or **phonetic representation** is a representation of the phonetic form of an expression.

Reset(ting): See **Parameter**.

Restrictive relative clause: See **Relative clause**.

Resumptive relative clause: See **Relative clause**.

R-expression: A referring expression comprising or containing a noun, like *John* or *the man next door*. See **Bind** and ex. 3.2.

Root: The root of a tree is the topmost node in the tree. Hence, a **root clause** is a free-standing clause, i.e. a clause which is not contained within any other expression. In traditional grammar, a root clause is termed a **principal clause, independent clause** or **main clause**. By contrast, an **embedded clause** is a clause which is contained within some larger expression; and a **complement clause** is an (embedded) clause which is used as the complement of some item. So, in a sentence such as *I think he loves you*, the *think* clause (i.e. the expression *I think he loves you*) is a root clause, whereas the *loves* clause (i.e. the expression *he loves you*) is an embedded clause. Moreover, the *loves* clause is also a complement clause, since it serves as the complement of the verb *think*. The **Root Complementiser Constraint** of §4.7 specifies that no overt complementiser can occur in a root projection in a language like English.

S/S′/S-bar: Category labels used in work in the 1960s and 1970s to designate a **sentence** or **clause**. See §3.3.

Scope: The scope of an expression is the set of constituents which it modifies or which fall within (what we might informally call) its 'sphere of influence'. For example, a sentence like *He cannot be telling the truth* has a meaning paraphraseable as 'It is not possible that he is telling the truth', and in such a sentence the negative *not* is said to have scope over the modal auxiliary *can* (and conversely *can* is said to fall within the scope of *not*, or to have **narrow scope** with respect to *not*). By contrast, a sentence such as *You mustn't tell lies* has a meaning paraphraseable as 'It is necessary that you not tell lies', and in such a sentence, the auxiliary *must* is said to have scope over (or to have **wide scope** with respect to) the negative particle *n't*.

SCP: See **Strict Cyclicity Principle**.

Second person: See **Person**.

Select(ion)/Selectional/Selector: When a word has a particular type of complement, it is said to **select** (i.e. 'take' or 'allow') the relevant type of complement (and the relevant phenomenon is referred to as **complement selection**). For example, we can say that the word *expect* has the **selectional property** that it can select an infinitive complement (e.g. in structures like 'They expect *to win*'). In this structure, the verb *expect* is the **selector** for the infinitive complement *to win*, in the sense that it is the item which selects *to win* as its complement.

Selective: A selective affix/clitic can only attach to a certain type of **host** word; an unselective one can attach to any kind of word. For example, possessive *'s* can only attach to a possessor like *John* in (i), and not, e.g., to the verb *think* in (ii):

(i) **John**'s idea I think doesn't work
(ii) *John I **think**'s idea doesn't work

By contrast, the contracted form *'s* of the auxiliary *is* can be said to be **unselective** in the sense that it can attach to any kind of preceding word, including the adverb *why* in (iii) and the verb *think* in (iv):

(iii) **Why**'s he lying?
(iv) John I **think**'s lying

Semantics/Semantic component: Semantics is the study of linguistic aspects of meaning. The **semantic component** of a grammar is the component which maps syntactic structures into semantic representations. See **Representation**.

Sentence: This term is usually used to denote a **root clause** – i.e. a free-standing clause which is not contained within some larger expression. See **Root**.

Sentence fragment: See **Fragment**.

Sg: An abbreviation for **singular**.

Shakespeare: Shakespeare's plays were written between (around) 1590 and 1620, and are examples of **Early Modern English/Elizabethan English** (though some have suggested that Shakespeare's English is rather conservative, and hence is more representative of a slightly earlier stage of English).

Silent: See **Null**.

Simple sentence: One which contains a single **clause**.

Singular: A singular expression is one which denotes a single entity (e.g. *this car* is a **singular/Sg** expression, whereas *these cars* is a **plural/Pl** expression).

Sister: Two nodes are sisters if they have the same mother (i.e. if they are directly merged with each other at some stage of derivation). See §3.7.

Sluicing: A form of **ellipsis** in which the material following an interrogative constituent is given a silent pronunciation – as with the material following *when* (marked by strikethrough) in 'I knew he was leaving, but forgot to ask *when* ~~he was leaving~~.'

Small clause: See **Clause**, and the discussion in §4.6.

SMT: Strong Minimalist Thesis: See **Strong**.

Spec: See **Specifier**. Terms like **spec-C(P)/spec-T(P)** (etc.) denote the specifier position within CP/TP.

Specification: The specification of an item is the set of features which it carries.

Specifier/Spec: The grammatical function fulfilled by certain types of constituent which precede the head of their containing phrase. For example, in a sentence such as *John is working*, *John* is superficially the specifier (and subject) of *is working*. In a sentence such as *What did John do?*, *what* is superficially the specifier of the CP headed by a C constituent containing the inverted auxiliary *did*. In a phrase such as *straight through the window*, *straight* is the specifier of the PP headed by the preposition *through*. In structures in which a head has two different specifiers, the lower one is said to be the **inner** specifier, and the higher one the **outer** specifier. See §3.4.

Spellout: The pronunciation of an expression: e.g. to say that an item has a **null spellout** is to say that it is 'silent' and so has a null phonetic form.

Split antecedents: A pronoun is said to have split antecedents if it has two or more separate antecedents (i.e. constituents it refers to). For example, in a sentence like '*John* spoke to *Mary*, and **they** agreed on what to do', the pronoun *they* can refer to *John* and *Mary*, and in such a use, *they* is said to have split antecedents (i.e. more than one antecedent).

Split (CP) projection: Work briefly touched on in §5.4 suggests that CP can be split into a number of separate projections/phrases, e.g. a focus phrase/FOCP, topic phrase/TOPP, etc.

Split spellout: See **Discontinuous spellout**.

Stack/Stacking: Stacking is a process by which more than one constituent of the same type can be used to modify some other constituent. For example, a noun like *stranger* can be modified by numerous different adjectives in a phrase like 'a *sensitive, tall, dark, handsome* **stranger**'. In this particular example, four different (italicised) adjectives are said to have been stacked to the left of the noun *stranger*.

Star: An asterisk (*) used in front of an expression to indicate that the expression is ungrammatical.

Stem: The stem (or **base form**) of a word is the form to which inflectional affixes are added. So, a verb form like *going* comprises the stem *go* and the inflectional suffix *-ing*.

Strand/Stranding: A stranded preposition is one which has been separated from its complement (by movement of the complement). For example, in an echo question like *You're waiting for who?*, the preposition *for* has not been stranded, since it is immediately followed by its complement *who*. But in *Who are you waiting for?*, the preposition *for* has been **stranded**, in that it has been separated from its complement *who*: the relevant phenomenon is termed **preposition stranding**. The **Stranding Constraint** of §3.6 specifies that no D/determiner, Q/quantifier or C/complementiser can be stranded without its complement. The **Preposition Stranding Constraint/PSC** of §6.6 specifies that no preposition can be stranded without its complement at PF, in formal styles of English (and in many other languages).

Strict Cyclicity Principle/SCP: A UG principle which specifies that a **cyclic** operation can only affect the overall head H of a structure and some other constituent c-commanded by H. See §5.9.

String: A continuous sequence of words contained within the same phrase or sentence. For example, in the sentence *They hate syntax*, the sequences *They hate, hate syntax* and *They hate syntax* are all strings – but *They syntax* is not. Note that a string need not be a **constituent**.

Strong: A strong head is one which can attract (i.e. trigger movement of) another head; a **weak** head is one which cannot attract another head. For example, C in an interrogative main clause is strong in present-day English, and so attracts an auxiliary to move from T to C – e.g. in sentences like *Can you speak French?* On an entirely different use of these terms in the expressions **weak/strong genitive pronoun**, see **Case**. In a third use of the term, the phrase **Strong Minimalist Thesis** refers to the hypothesis put forward by Chomsky that all properties of natural language grammars reflect 'properties of language that are logically or conceptually necessary, properties such that if a system failed to have them we would simply not call it a language' (Chomsky 1980: 28–9): see §1.5.

Structural: See **Case, Representation**.

Structural Uniformity Principle: A principle to the effect that all expressions of the same type have the same structure (e.g. all declarative clauses are CPs, both main clauses and complement clauses). See §4.7.

Structure: See **Constituent Structure**. The **Structure Dependence Principle** of §3.8 specifies that all syntactic operations are structure-dependent (in the sense that they are sensitive only to hierarchical containment relations between constituents, not left-to-right linear ordering).

Stylistic variation: Variation correlated with stylistic factors. For example, *whom* is used in formal styles and *who* in other styles in sentences like 'He is someone *whom/who* I admire greatly.'

Subjacency Condition: A constraint on movement operations specifying that 'No movement can cross more than one bounding node' (where bounding nodes include S/TP).

Subject: The (superficial structural) subject of a clause is a noun or pronoun expression which is normally positioned between a complementiser and an (auxiliary or non-auxiliary) verb. Syntactic characteristics of subjects include the fact that they can trigger agreement with auxiliaries (as in *The president is lying*, where the auxiliary *is* agrees with the subject *the president*), and they can be inverted with auxiliaries in main clause questions (as in *Is the president lying?*, where the auxiliary *is* has been inverted with the subject *the president*).

Subjunctive: In a (formal style) sentence such as 'The judge ordered that he *be* detained indefinitely', the passive auxiliary verb *be* is traditionally said to be in the **subjunctive mood**, since although it has exactly the same form as the infinitive form *be* (e.g. in infinitive structures such as 'To *be* or not to *be* – that is the question'), it has a nominative subject *he*, and hence is a **finite** verb form.

In present-day spoken English, constructions containing subjunctive verbs are generally avoided, as they are felt to be archaic or excessively formal in style by many speakers. See **Mood**. On the structure of subjunctive clauses, see §4.5.

Substantive category: This is a category (like noun, verb, adjective, adverb, preposition) whose members are **contentives** (i.e. items with idiosyncratic descriptive content).

Substitution: A technique used to determine the category which a given expression belongs to. An expression belongs to a given type of category if it can be substituted (i.e. replaced) in phrases or sentences like that in which it occurs by another expression which clearly belongs to the category in question. For example, we might say that *clearer* is an adverb in 'John speaks *clearer* than you' because it can be replaced by the adverbial expression *more clearly*.

Successive-cyclic movement: Movement in a succession of short steps. See §5.7 and §6.8.

Suffix: See **Affix**.

Superlative: The superlative is a form of an adjective/adverb (typically carrying the suffix *-est*) used to mark the highest value for a particular property in comparison with others. For example, *hardest* is the superlative form of *hard* in 'John is the *hardest* worker because he works *hardest*'.

Swiping: A form of ellipsis found in an interrogative clause like that italicised in 'He went to the cinema, but I'm not sure *who with he went to the cinema*.' In this type of structure, a prepositional phrase comprising a preposition (here, *with*) and an interrogative complement (here, *who*) is moved to the front of the italicised clause, the remaining material in the clause is deleted (marked by strikethrough), and preposition is positioned after its complement *who*. The deletion operation involved is **Sluicing**.

Syncretise/Syncretism: To say that two heads (or projections) are syncretised means they are conflated/collapsed into one. See §5.8; see also **Neutralise**.

Syntactic representation/structure: See **Representation**.

Syntax: The component of a grammar which determines how words are combined together to form phrases and sentences.

T: A tense-marking constituent containing either a tensed auxiliary, or an abstract tense affix or a non-finite tense particle like infinitival *to*. **T-to-C Movement** is movement of an auxiliary or non-auxiliary verb from the head T position of TP into the head C position of CP – as with the italicised inverted auxiliary in '*Is* it raining?' A **T-feature** on C is a feature which attracts an auxiliary in T to move to C. The **T-Feature Generalisation** specifies that a T-feature on C attracts a constituent on the edge of TP to move to the edge of CP.

Tacit: Tacit knowledge (e.g. of a language) is subconscious knowledge.

Tag: A string usually consisting of an auxiliary and a subject pronoun which is 'tagged' onto the end of a sentence. Thus, the italicised string is the tag in the following: 'The president isn't underestimating his opponents, *is he*?', and the overall sentence is known as a **tag question/tag sentence**. The tag usually contains a copy of the auxiliary in the main clause, and a pronominal copy of the subject.

Taxonomy: A **taxonomy** is a classificatory system. A **taxonomic** theory of language is one which classifies constituents into different types.

Tense: Finite auxiliary and main verbs in English show a binary (two-way) tense contrast, traditionally said to be between **present (Pres/Pr) tense** forms and **past tense** forms. Thus, in 'John *hates* syntax', *hates* is a present tense verb form, whereas in 'John *hated* syntax', *hated* is a past tense verb form (An alternative classification which many linguists prefer is into [±PAST] verb forms, so that *hated* is [+PAST], and *hates* [–PAST]). This present/past tense distinction correlates (to some extent) with time reference, so that (e.g.) past tense verbs typically describe an event taking place in the past, whereas present tense verbs typically describe an event taking place in the present (or future). However, the correlation is an imperfect one, since, e.g., in a sentence such as 'I *might* go there tomorrow', the auxiliary *might* carries the past tense inflection *-t* (found on past tense main verbs like *left*) but does not denote past time. Infinitival *to* is sometimes said to carry **non-finite** tense (i.e. to have tense properties which are not spelled out overtly), in contrast to present/past tense verbs which carry **finite** tense.

Tensed: A tensed (auxiliary or non-auxiliary) verb form is one which carries (present/past) **tense** – e.g. *is, will, could, hates, went*, etc. By extension, a tensed clause is one containing a tensed auxiliary or main verb. See **Tense**.

Terminal: A terminal node in a tree diagram is one at the bottom of the tree; a non-terminal node is one which is not at the bottom of the tree.

Ternary: Three-way. For example, person properties might be described in terms of a ternary (three-valued) feature such as [1/2/3-Pers], with first person pronouns like *we* being [1-Pers], second person pronouns like *you* being [2-Pers] and third person pronouns like they being [3-Pers]. A ternary-branching constituent is one which has three daughters.

Third Person: See **Person**.

Three-place predicate: A predicate (typically a verb) which takes three arguments – e.g. the verb *give* in *John gave Mary something* (where the three arguments of *give* are *John, Mary* and *something*). See **Argument**.

TOP/Topic/Topicalisation/TOPP: In a dialogue such as the following:

SPEAKER A: I've been having problems with the Fantasy Syntax seminar

SPEAKER B: *That kind of course*, very few students seem to be able to get their heads round

the italicised expression *that kind of course* can be said to be the **topic** of the sentence produced by speaker B, in the sense that it refers back to *the Fantasy Syntax seminar* mentioned by the previous speaker: more generally an expression which represents 'old' or 'familiar' information in this way is said to be a topic. The movement operation by which the italicised expression moves from being the complement of the preposition *round* to the front of the overall sentence is traditionally termed **Topicalisation** (though is referred to as **Top-Movement** in

§7.10). In work by Luigi Rizzi on split CP projections briefly touched on in §5.4, topic expressions which occur at the beginning of clauses are said to be contained within a **TOPP/topic phrase** projection, headed by an abstract **TOP/topic** constituent.

TP: Tense projection/tense phrase – i.e. phrase headed by a tense-marked auxiliary or an abstract tense affix *Af.* See §§3.2–3.3. The **TP Hypothesis** of §4.4 specifies that all clauses contain a TP headed by an (overt or null) T constituent.

Trace (theory): A **trace** of a moved constituent is a null copy left behind (as a result of movement) in each position out of which a constituent moves. **Trace theory** is a theory which posits that moved constituents leave behind a trace **copy** in each position out of which they move. See §5.3 and §6.7.

Traditional grammar: The study of grammar in traditional reference grammars, or in practical grammars used as an aid to second language learning.

Transitive: A word is traditionally said to be transitive (in a given use) if it assigns **accusative** case to a noun or pronoun expression which it **c-commands**. So, *likes* in 'John *likes* him' is a transitive verb, since it assigns accusative case to its complement *him*. Likewise, infinitival *for* is a transitive complementiser, since it assigns accusative case to the subject of its infinitive complement (cf. 'I'm keen [for *him* to participate more actively]'). A verb or complementiser is **intransitive** (in a particular structure) if it does not assign accusative case to any constituent in the relevant structure.

Tree (diagram): A form of graph used to represent the syntactic structure of a phrase or sentence.

Truncate(d)/Truncation: Truncation is an operation by which a sentence is shortened by not pronouncing one or more unstressed words at the beginning. For example, we can truncate a question like *Are you going anywhere nice on holiday?* by not pronouncing *are* and say *You going anywhere nice on holiday?* and can further truncate the sentence by not pronouncing *you* to give *Going anywhere nice on holiday?* A **truncated null subject** is a null subject which arises via Truncation: see §4.2.

T-to-C Movement: See **T**.

Two-place predicate: A predicate which has two arguments – e.g. *tease* in *William teased Harry* where the two arguments of the predicate *tease* are *William* and *Harry*. See **Argument**.

UG: See **Universal Grammar**.

Unary-branching. A unary-branching node is one which has a single daughter. See §3.5.

Unbound: A constituent is unbound if it has no appropriate antecedent in an appropriate position within a given structure. For example, *himself* is unbound in a sentence such as **For himself to lie to her would be unthinkable*, since *her* is not an appropriate antecedent for *himself*, and there is no other appropriate antecedent for *himself* anywhere within the sentence.

Uncountable: See **Count**.

Ungradable: An ungradable adjective is one (like *absent*) which denotes an absolute property (in the sense that it denotes a property which cannot exist in varying degrees) and so cannot be modified by adverbs like *fairly/very* (cf. **He was very absent from the class*).

Ungrammatical: See **Grammatical**.

Universal Grammar/UG: Those aspects of grammar which are universal, and which are assumed by Chomsky to be part of a child's innate knowledge.

Unreduced: See **Reduced**.

Unselective: See **Selective**.

V: See **Verb**.

Value: In relation to a feature such as [Singular-Number], **number** is said to be an **attribute** (and represents the property being described) and **singular** its value.

Variety: A particular (e.g. geographical or social) form of a language.

V-Attachment Conditions: See **Attachment**.

Verb/V: A category of word which has the morphological property that it can carry a specific range of inflections (e.g. the verb *show* can carry past tense *-d*, third person singular present tense *-s*, perfect *-n* and progressive *-ing*, giving rise to *shows/showed/shown/showing*), and the syntactic property that it can head the complement of infinitival *to* (cf. 'Do you want to *show* me?') On **V/Verb Movement**, see **V-to-T Movement**.

Verb phrase/VP: A phrase which is headed by a verb – e.g. the italicised phrase in 'They will *help you*.' See ch. 3.

V-to-T Movement: Movement of a verb out of the head V position in VP into the head T position in TP (also known as **Verb Movement**). See §5.6.

Vocative: A vocative expression is one which is used to address one or more individuals, and which is set off in a separate tone-group usually at the beginning or end of the sentence (marked in the spelling by the use of a comma). So, for example, *Fred* is a vocative expression in *Fred, can you give me a hand?* and similarly, *you two* is a vocative expression in *Come here, you two!*

Voice: See **Active**. A **VOICEP** constituent is a voice phrase headed by a VOICE constituent like the passive auxiliary *be*: see 5.8.

VP: On VP, see **Verb phrase**. A **VP-adverb** is an adverb which adjoins to a VP to form an even larger VP (e.g. in *He may have completely forgotten what you asked* the adverb *completely* is adjoined to the VP *forgotten what you asked*). On **VP Ellipsis**, see **Ellipsis**.

Weak: See **Strong**.

Wh: This is widely used as a feature carried by constituents which undergo Wh-Movement (hence e.g. the relative pronoun *who* in *someone who I think is lying* can be described as a wh-pronoun, as can the interrogative pronoun *who* in *Who are you waiting for?* and the exclamative quantifier *what* in *What fun we had!*

Wh-copying: A phenomenon whereby a moved wh-expression leaves behind an overt copy of itself when it moves – as with movement of *who* in a Child English question such as *Who do you think who chased the cat?*

Wh-exclamative: An **exclamative** clause beginning with a wh-expression, like that italicised in '*What a great time* we had!'

Wh-expression: An expression containing or comprising a **wh-word**.

Wh-Movement: A type of movement operation whereby a **wh-expression** is moved to the front of a particular type of structure (e.g. to the front of the overall sentence in '*Where* has he gone?'). See chs. 6–7.

Wh-operator: See **Operator**.

Wh-parameter: A parameter whose setting determines whether wh-expressions are (or are not) moved to the front of an appropriate type of clause (e.g. in wh-questions). See §1.7.

Wh-phrase: A phrase containing a **wh-word**.

Wh-question: A question which contains an interrogative **wh-word**, e.g. '*What* are you doing?' On **wh-question operator**, see **Operator**.

Wh-relative: A relative clause which contains a wh-word, like that bracketed in *the car* [*which I bought*]. A **wh-less relative** is a relative clause which does not contain a wh-word, like that in *the car* [*I bought*].

Wh-word: A word which begins with *wh* (e.g. *who/what/which/where/when/why*), or which has a similar syntax to *wh*-words (e.g. *how*).

Word order: The linear sequencing (left-to-right ordering) of words within a phrase or sentence.

X-bar Syntax: A theory of syntactic structure which makes use of the **bar notation**: see **Bar**.

Yes–no question: A question to which 'Yes' or 'No' would be an appropriate answer - e.g. *Is it raining?* On **yes–no question operator**, see **Operator**.

Zero relative: See **Relative clause**.

References

Aarts, B. (1992) *Small Clauses in English: The Nonverbal Types*, Mouton De Gruyter, Berlin.

Abeillé, A. & Borsley, R. D. (2006) 'Comparative correlatives and parameters', ms. University of Essex.

Abels, K. (2003) 'Successive-cyclicity, anti-locality and adposition stranding', PhD diss. University of Connecticut.

(2007) 'Deriving selectional properties of "exclamative" predicates', in A. Späth (ed.), *Interfaces and Interface Conditions*, Mouton De Gruyter, Berlin, pp. 115–40.

(2010) 'Factivity in exclamatives is a presupposition', *Studia Linguistica* 64: 141–57.

Abels, K. & Neeleman, A. (2012) 'Linear asymmetries and the LCA', *Syntax* 15: 25–74.

Abney, S. P. (1987) 'The English noun phrase in its sentential aspect', PhD diss. MIT.

Acquaviva, P. (2002) 'The morphological dimension of polarity licensing', *Linguistics* 40: 925–59.

Adger, D. (2003) *Core Syntax: A Minimalist Approach*, Oxford University Press.

Adger, D. & Ramchand, G. (2005) 'Merge and move: wh-dependencies revisited', *Linguistic Inquiry* 36: 161–93.

Aelbrecht, L. (2009) 'You have the right to remain silent: the syntactic licensing of ellipsis', PhD diss. Catholic University of Brussels.

(2010) *The Syntactic Licensing of Ellipsis*, Benjamins, Amsterdam.

Agbayani, B. (2000) 'Wh-subjects in English and the Vacuous Movement Hypothesis', *Linguistic Inquiry* 31: 703–13.

(2006) 'Pied-piping, feature movement and *wh*-subjects', in Cheng & Corver (eds.), pp. 71–93.

Agüero-Bautista, C. (2007) 'Diagnosing cyclicity in Sluicing', *Linguistic Inquiry* 38: 413–43.

Akiyama, M. (2004) 'Multiple nominative constructions in Japanese and economy', *Linguistic Inquiry* 35: 671–83.

Akmajian, A. & Heny, F. (1975) *An Introduction to the Principles of Transformational Syntax*, MIT Press, Cambridge, MA.

Akmajian, A. & Wasow, T. (1975) 'The constituent structure of VP and AUX and the position of the verb *be*', *Linguistic Analysis* 1: 205–45.

Akmajian, A., Steele, S. & Wasow, T. (1979) 'The category AUX in universal grammar', *Linguistic Inquiry* 10: 1–64.

Alexiadou, A. (2003) 'Adjective syntax and (the absence of) noun raising in the DP', *UCLA Working Papers in Linguistics* 10: 1–39.

Alexiadou, A. E. & Anagnostopoulou, E. (1998) 'Parameterizing AGR: word order, V-Movement and EPP checking', *Natural Language and Linguistic Theory* 16: 491–539.

Alexiadou, A. & Wilder, C. (eds.) (1998) *Possessors, Predicates and Movement in the Determiner Phrase*, Benjamins, Amsterdam.

Alexiadou, A., Law, P., Meinunger, A. & Wilder, C. (2000) 'Introduction', in Alexiadou et al. (eds.), pp. 1–51.

Alexiadou, A., Law, P., Meinunger, A. & Wilder, C. (eds.) (2000) *The Syntax of Relative Clauses*, John Benjamins, Amsterdam.

Alexopoulou, D. (2010) 'Truly intrusive: resumptive pronominals in questions and relative clauses', *Lingua* 120: 485–505.

Alexopoulou, T. & F. Keller (2007) 'Locality, cyclicity, and resumption: at the interface between the grammar and the human sentence processor', *Language* 83: 110–60.

Alhorais, N. (2007) 'The categorial status of the small clause node: a Minimalist approach', ms. University of Newcastle.

Almeida, D. A. de A. & Yoshida. M. (2007) 'A problem for the preposition stranding generalization', *Linguistic Inquiry* 38: 349–62.

Al-Mutairi, F. (2011) 'The Strong Minimalist Thesis: its nature and plausibility', PhD diss. University of Essex.

(2014) *The Minimalist Program: The Nature and Plausibility of Chomsky's Biolinguistics*, Cambridge University Press.

Anderson, S. R. & Lightfoot, D. W. (2002) *The Language Organ: Linguistics as Cognitive Physiology*, Cambridge University Press.

Antony, L. M. & Hornstein, N. (2003) *Chomsky and His Critics*, Blackwell, Oxford.

Aoun, J. (2000) 'Resumption and last resort', *Documentação de Estudos em Lingüística Teórica e Aplicada* 16: 13–43.

Aoun, J. & Benmamoun, E. (1999) 'Further remarks on first conjunct agreement', *Linguistic Inquiry* 30: 669–81.

Aoun, J., Choueiri, L. & Hornstein, N. (2001) 'Resumption, movement and derivational economy', *Linguistic Inquiry* 32: 371–403.

Aoun, J. L. & Li, Y.-H. A. (2003) *Essays on the Representational and Derivational Nature of Grammar: The Diversity of Wh-Constructions*, MIT Press, Cambridge, MA.

Aronoff, M. & Fuhrhop, N. (2002) 'Restricting suffix combinations in German and English: closing suffixes and the Monosuffix Constraint', *Natural Language & Linguistic Theory* 20: 451–90.

Asudeh, A. (2004) 'Resumption as resource management', Ph.D. diss. Stanford University.

Atkinson, M. & Al-Mutairi, F. (2012) 'UG or not UG: where is recursion?', *Iberia* 4: 35–60.

Authier, J.-M. (1989) 'Arbitrary null objects and unselective binding', in O. Jaeggli & K. Safir (eds.), *The Null Subject Parameter*, Reidel, Dordrecht, pp. 45–67.

Authier, J.-M. & Reed, L. (2005) 'The diverse nature of non-interrogative Wh', *Linguistic Inquiry* 36: 635–47.

Baltin, M. (2002) 'Movement to the higher V is remnant movement', *Linguistic Inquiry* 33: 653–9.

(2010) 'The nonreality of doubly filled Comps', *Linguistic Inquiry* 41: 331–5.

Baltin, M. & Collins, C. (eds.) (2001) *The Handbook of Contemporary Syntactic Theory*, Blackwell, Oxford.

Banfield, A. (1982) *Unspeakable Sentences: Narration and Representation in the Language of Fiction*, Routledge and Paul, Boston.

Barbosa, P. (1995) 'Null subjects', PhD diss. MIT.

(2000) 'Clitics: a window into the null subject property', in J. Costa (ed.), *Portuguese Syntax: Comparative Studies*, Oxford University Press, pp. 31–93.

(2007) 'Two kinds of subject *pro*', ms. Universidade do Minho.

Barbosa, P., Duarte M. E. L. & Kato M. A. (2005) 'Null subjects in European and Brasilian Portuguese', *Journal of Portuguese Linguistics* 4: 11–52.

Barss, A. (2001) 'Syntactic reconstruction effects', in Baltin & Collins (eds.), pp. 670–96.

Basilico, D. (2003) 'The topic of small clauses', *Linguistic Inquiry* 34: 1–35.

Battye, A. C. (1989) 'Free relatives, pseudo-free relatives and the syntax of CP in Italian', *Rivista di Linguistica* 1: 219–46.

Bauer, L., Lieber, R. & Plag, I. (2013) *The Oxford Reference Guide to English Morphology*, Oxford University Press.

Bayer, J. (1984) 'COMP in Bavarian syntax', *The Linguistic Review* 3: 209–74.

Bayer, S. (1996) 'The coordination of unlike categories', *Language* 72: 579–616.

Bejar, S. & Massam, D. (1999) 'Multiple case checking', *Syntax* 2: 65–79.

Belletti, A. (1990) *Generalized Verb Movement: Aspects of Verb Syntax*, Rosenberg and Sellier, Turin.

Belletti, A. & Rizzi, L. (1988) 'Psych-verbs and θ-theory', *Natural Language and Linguistic Theory*, 6: 291–352.

Benincà, P. (1995) 'Il tipo esclamativo', in L. Renzi, G. Salvi & A. Cardinaletti (eds.), *Grande Grammatica Italiana di Consultazione,* vol. III, Il Mulino, Bologna, pp. 127–52.

(1996) 'La struttura della frase esclamativa alla luce del dialetto padovano', in Benincà et al. (eds.), pp. 23–43.

(2012) 'Lexical complementisers and headless relatives', in L. Brugè, A. Cardinaletti, G. Giusti, N. Munaro & C. Poletto (eds.), *Functional Heads: The Cartography of Syntactic Structures,* vol. VII, Oxford University Press, pp. 29–41.

Benincà, P. & Poletto C. (2004) 'Topic, Focus and V2: defining the CP sublayers', in L. Rizzi (ed.), *The Structure of IP and CP: The Cartography of Syntactic Structures*, vol. II, Oxford University Press, pp. 52–75.

Benincà, P., Cinque, G., De Mauro, T. & Vincent, N. (eds.) (1996) *Italiano e dialetti nel tempo: Saggi di grammatica per Giulio C. Lepschy*, Bulzoni, Roma.

Benmamoun, E. (2006) 'Licensing configurations: the puzzle of head negative polarity items', *Linguistic Inquiry* 37: 141–9.

Berizzi, M. & Rossi, S. (2010) '"Something here what made me think." Some new views on relative *what* in the dialects of English', *Language at the University of Essex (LangUE) Proceedings 2009*, 14–26.

Bernstein, J. B. (1993) 'Topics in the syntax of nominal structures across Romance', PhD diss. City University of New York.

(2001) 'The DP hypothesis: identifying clausal properties in the nominal domain', in Baltin & Collins (eds.), pp. 536–61.

Bernstein, J. B. & Tortora, C. (2005) 'Two types of possessive forms in English', *Lingua* 115: 1221–42.

Berwick, R. C., Pietroski, P., Yankama, B. & Chomsky, N. (2011) 'Poverty of the stimulus revisited', *Cognitive Science* 35: 1207–42.

Bhatt, R. (2002) 'The raising analysis of relative clauses', *Natural Language Semantics* 10: 43–90.

Bhatt, R. & Pancheva, R. (2004) 'Late Merge of degree clauses', *Linguistic Inquiry* 35: 1–45.

Bianchi, V. (2008) 'Resumptives and LF chains', ms. University of Siena.

Biberauer, T., Holmberg, A. & Roberts, I. (2007) 'Disharmonic word-order systems and the Final-over-Final-Constraint (FOFC)', in A. Bisetto and F. E. Barbieri (eds.), *Proceedings of the* XXXIII *Incontro di Grammatica Generativa*, Dipartimento di Lingue e Letterature Straniere Moderne, Università di Bologna, pp. 86–105 (http://amsacta.cib.unibo.it/archive/00002397/01/PROCEEDINGS_IGG33.pdf).

Blake, B. J. (2001) *Case* (2nd edn), Cambridge University Press.

Bloomfield, L. (1935) *Language*, George Allen and Unwin, London.

Bobaljik, J. (1994) 'What does adjacency do?', *MIT Working Papers in Linguistics* 22: 1–32.

(1995) 'Morphosyntax: the syntax of verbal inflection', PhD diss. MIT.

(2000) 'The rich agreement hypothesis in review', ms. McGill University (www .mcgill.ca/Linguistics/Faculty/Bobaljik)

(2002) 'A-chains at the PF-interface: copies and "covert" movement', *Natural Language and Linguistic Theory* 20: 197–267.

Bobaljik, J. & Thráinsson, H. (1998) 'Two heads aren't always better than one', *Syntax* 1: 37–71.

Boeckx, C. (2003) *Islands and Chains: Resumption as Stranding*, Benjamins, Amsterdam.

(2007) *Understanding Minimalist Syntax*, Blackwell, Oxford.

(2010) 'What principles and parameters got wrong', ms. Autonomous University of Barcelona.

(2012) *Syntactic Islands*, Cambridge University Press.

Boeckx, C. & Stjepanović, S. (2001) 'Head-ing towards PF', *Linguistic Inquiry* 32: 345–55.

Borroff, M. L. (2006) 'Degree phrase inversion in the scope of negation', *Linguistic Inquiry* 37: 514–21.

Borsley, R. D. (1992) 'More on the difference between English restrictive and non-restrictive relative clauses', *Journal of Linguistics* 28: 139–48.

(1994) 'In defence of co-ordinate structures', *Linguistic Analysis* 24: 218–46.

(1997) 'Relative clauses and the theory of phrase structure', *Linguistic Inquiry* 28: 629–47.

(2001). 'More on the raising analysis of relative clauses', ms. University of Essex (http://privatewww.essex.ac.uk/~rborsley/relatives.pdf).

(2005) 'Against ConjP', *Lingua* 115: 461–82.

Borsley, R. & Jaworska, E. (1998) 'A note on prepositions and case-marking in Polish', *Linguistic Inquiry* 19: 685–91.

Borsley, R., Rivero, M. L. & Stephens, J. (1996) 'Long head movement in Breton', in R. Borsley & I. Roberts (eds.), *The Syntax of the Celtic Languages: A Comparative Perspective*, Cambridge University Press, pp. 53–74.

Bošković, Ž. (1996) 'Selection and the categorial status of infinitival complements', *Natural Language and Linguistic Theory* 14: 269–304.

(1997) *The Syntax of Nonfinite Complementation: An Economy Approach*, MIT Press, Cambridge, MA.

(2001) *On the Nature of the Syntax–Phonology Interface: Cliticization and Related Phenomena*, Elsevier, Amsterdam.

(2002a) 'On multiple *wh*-fronting', *Linguistic Inquiry* 33: 351–83.

(2002b) 'A-Movement and the EPP', *Syntax* 5: 167–218.

(2004) 'Topicalization, focalization, lexical insertion and scrambling', *Linguistic Inquiry* 35: 613–38.

(2005) 'On the locality of left branch extraction and the structure of NP', *Studia Linguistica* 59: 1–45 (http://web2.uconn.edu/boskovic/papers/leftbranch.pdf).

(2008) 'What will you have, DP or NP?', *Proceedings of the North East Linguistic Society* 37: 101–14.

(2009) 'More on the no-DP analysis of article-less languages', *Studia Linguistica* 63: 187–203.

Bošković, Z. & Lasnik, H. (2003) 'On the distribution of null complementisers', *Linguistic Inquiry* 34: 527–46.

Bowerman, M. (1988) 'The "no negative evidence" problem: how do children avoid an overly general grammar?', in J. Hawkins (ed.), *Explaining Language Universals*, Blackwell, Oxford, pp. 73–101.

Bowers, J. (2001) 'Predication', in Baltin & Collins (eds.), pp. 299–333.

Braine, M. D. S. (1971) 'Three suggestions regarding grammatical analyses of children's language', in C. A. Ferguson & D. I. Slobin (eds.), *Studies of Child Language Development*, Holt Rinehart and Winston, New York, pp. 421–9.

Brattico, P. (2010) 'The one-part and two-part models of nominal case: evidence from case distribution', *Journal of Linguistics* 45: 1–35.

Bresnan, J. (1970) 'On complementizers: toward a syntactic theory of complement types', *Foundations of Language* 6: 297–321.

(1972) *Theory of Complementation in English Syntax*, PhD diss. MIT (published as Bresnan 1979).

(1979) *Theory of Complementation in English Syntax*, Garland, New York.

Bresnan, J. & Grimshaw, J. (1978) 'The syntax of free relatives in English', *Linguistic Inquiry* 9: 331–91.

Brody, M. (1995) *A Radically Minimalist Theory*, MIT Press, Cambridge, MA.

Brown, E. & Radford, A. (2006) 'The role of UG constraints and input in classroom-based child L2: evidence from the acquisition of Wh-Movement and Auxiliary Inversion by Korean learners of English', *Chomskyan Studies* 1: 1–57.

Brown, R., Cazden, C. & Bellugi, U. (1968) 'The child's grammar from I to III', in J. P. Hill (ed.), *Minnesota Symposium on Child Development*, vol. II, pp. 28–73.

Brown, R. & Hanlon, C. (1970) 'Derivational complexity and order of acquisition in child speech', in J. R. Hayes (ed.), *Cognition and the Development of Language*, Wiley, New York, pp. 11–53.

Browning, M. A. (1996) 'CP recursion and *that-t* effects', *Linguistic Inquiry* 27: 237–55.

Bruening, B. (2006) 'Differences between the wh-scope-marking and wh-copy constructions in Passamaquoddy', *Linguistic Inquiry* 37: 25–49.

(2007) 'Wh-in-situ does not correlate with *wh*-indefinites or question particles', *Linguistic Inquiry* 38: 139–66.

Büring, D. (2005) *Binding Theory*, Cambridge University Press.

Cable, S. (2005) 'Free relatives in Lingít and Haida: evidence that the mover projects', ms. (http://people.umass.edu/scable).

(2007) 'The grammar of Q: Q-particles and the nature of wh-fronting, as revealed by the wh-questions of Tlingit', PhD diss. MIT.

(2008) 'Question particles and the nature of *wh*-fronting', in L. Matthewson (ed.), *Quantification: A Cross-Linguistic Perspective*, Emerald, Bingley, UK, pp. 105–78.

(2010a) *The Grammar of Q: Q-particles, Wh-Movement, and Pied-Piping*, Oxford University Press.

(2010b) 'Against the existence of pied-piping: evidence from Tlingit', *Linguistic Inquiry* 41: 563–94.

Caponigro, I. (2002) 'Free relatives as DPs with a silent D and a CP complement', in V. Samiian (ed.), *Proceedings of WECOL 2000*, California State University Fresno, Department of Linguistics, pp. 140–50.

(2004) 'The semantic contribution of *wh*-words and type shifts: evidence from free relatives crosslinguistically', in R. B. Young (ed.), *Proceedings from Semantics and Linguistic Theory (SALT) XIV*, CLC Publications, Cornell University, Ithaca, NY, pp. 38–55.

Caponigro, I. & Pearl, L. (2008) 'Silent prepositions: evidence from free relatives', in A. Asbury, J. Dotlačil, B. Gehrke & R. Nouwen (eds.), *The Syntax and Semantics of Spatial P*, Benjamins, Amsterdam, pp. 365–85.

(2009) The nominal nature of *when, where*, and *how*: evidence from free relatives. *Linguistic Inquiry* 40: 155–75.

Caponigro, I., Torrence, H. & Cisneros, C. (2013). 'Free relative clauses in two Mixtec languages', *International Journal of American Linguistics* 79(1): 61–96.

Cardinaletti, A. & Giusti, G. (2006) 'The syntax of quantified phrases and quantitative clitics', in Everaert & van Riemsdijk (eds.), pp. 23–93.

Cardinaletti, A. & Guasti, M. T. (eds.) (1995) *Syntax and Semantics,* vol. 28: *Small Clauses*, Academic Press, New York.

Cardinaletti, A. & Starke, M. (1999) 'The typology of structural deficiency: a case study of the three classes of pronouns', in H. van Riemsdijk (ed.), *Clitics in the Languages of Europe*, Mouton de Gruyter, Berlin, pp. 145–233.

Carlson, G. (1977) 'Amount relatives', *Language* 53: 520–42.

Carlson, K., Dickey, M. W. & Kennedy, C. (2005) 'Structural economy in the processing and representation of gapping sentences', *Syntax* 8: 208–28.

Carnie, A. (1995) 'Nonverbal predication and Head Movement', PhD diss. MIT.

Carnie, A. & Medeiros, D. (2005) 'Tree maximization and the Extended Projection Principle', *Coyote Working Papers in Linguistics* 14: 51–5.

Carstairs-McCarthy, A. (2002) *An Introduction to English Morphology: Words and their Structure*, Edinburgh University Press.

Carstens, V. (2003) 'Rethinking complementiser agreement: agree with a case-checked goal', *Linguistic Inquiry* 4: 275–343.

Castroviejo Miró, E. (2006) 'Wh-exclamatives in Catalan', PhD diss. Universitat de Barcelona.

Cattell, R. (1976) 'Constraints on movement rules', *Language* 52: 18–50.

Cecchetto, C. & Donati, C. (2010) 'On labelling: Principle C and head movement', *Syntax* 13: 241–78.

Cecchetto, C. & Oniga, R. (2004) 'A challenge to null case theory', *Linguistic Inquiry* 35: 141–9.

Chao, W. & Sells, P. (1983) 'On the interpretation of resumptive pronouns', *Proceedings of the North East Linguistic Society* 13: 47–61.

Chaves, R. (2012) 'On the grammar of extraction and coordination', *Natural Language and Linguistic Theory* 30: 465–512.

(2013) 'An expectation-based account of subject islands and parasitism', *Journal of Linguistics* 49: 285–327.

Cheng, L. (1997) *On the Typology of Wh-Questions*, Garland, New York.

Cheng, L. & Corver, N. (eds.) (2006) *Wh-Movement: Moving On*, MIT Press, Cambridge, MA.

(2013) *Diagnosing Syntax*, Oxford University Press.

Cheng, L. & Rooryck, J. (2000) 'Licensing *wh*-in-situ', *Syntax* 3: 1–19.

Cherniak, C. (2005) 'Innateness and brain-wiring optimization: non-genomic nativism', in A. Zhilao (ed.), *Evolution, Rationality and Cognition*, Routledge, New York, pp. 103–12.

(2009) 'Brain wiring optimization and non-genomic nativism', in M. Piattelli-Palmarini, J. Uriagareka & P. Salaburu (eds.), *Of Minds and Language: The Basque Country Encounter with Noam Chomsky*, Oxford University Press, pp. 108–19.

Chiba, S. (1987) *Present Subjunctives in Present-Day English*, Shinozaki Shorin, Tokyo.

Chierchia, G. (2006) 'Broaden your views: implicatures of domain widening and the "logicality" of language', *Linguistic Inquiry* 37: 535–90.

Chomsky, N. (1955) *The Logical Structure of Linguistic Theory*, mimeo, MIT (subsequently published as Chomsky 1975).

(1957) *Syntactic Structures*, Mouton, The Hague.

(1964) *Current Issues in Linguistic Theory*, Mouton, The Hague.

(1965) *Aspects of the Theory of Syntax*, MIT Press, Cambridge, MA.

(1968) 'Interview with S. Hampshire', *The Listener*, May 1968.

(1970) 'Remarks on nominalization', in R. A. Jacobs & P. S. Rosenbaum (eds.), *Readings in English Transformational Grammar*, Ginn, Waltham, MA, pp. 184–221.

(1972) *Language and Mind* (enlarged edn), Harcourt Brace Jovanovich, New York.

(1973) 'Conditions on transformations', in S. R. Anderson & P. Kiparsky (eds.), *A Festschrift for Morris Halle*, Holt, Rinehart and Winston, New York, pp. 232–86.

(1975) *The Logical Structure of Linguistic Theory*, Plenum Press, New York.

(1977) 'On Wh-movement', in P. W. Culicover, T. Wasow & A. Akmajian (eds.), *Formal Syntax*, Academic Press, New York, pp. 71–132.

(1980) 'On binding', *Linguistic Inquiry* 11: 1–46.

(1981) *Lectures on Government and Binding*, Foris, Dordrecht.

(1982) *Some Concepts and Consequences of the Theory of Government and Binding*, MIT Press, Cambridge, MA.

(1986a) *Knowledge of Language: Its Nature, Origin and Use*, Praeger, New York.

(1986b) *Barriers*, MIT Press, Cambridge, MA.

(1989) 'Some notes on economy of derivation and representation', *MIT Working Papers in Linguistics* 10: 43–74 (reprinted as ch. 2 of Chomsky 1995).

(1993) 'A minimalist program for linguistic theory', in Hale & Keyser (eds.), pp. 1–52 (reprinted as ch. 3 of Chomsky 1995).

(1995) *The Minimalist Program*, MIT Press, Cambridge, MA.

(1998) Minimalist inquiries: the framework, *MIT Occasional Papers in Linguistics*, no 15; also published in R. Martin, D. Michaels & J. Uriagereka (eds.) (2000), *Step by Step: Essays on Minimalism in Honor of Howard Lasnik*, MIT Press, Cambridge, MA, pp. 89–155.

(1999) Derivation by Phase, *MIT Occasional Papers in Linguistics*, no. 18; also published in Kenstowicz (ed.) (2001), pp. 1–52.

(2001) 'Beyond explanatory adequacy', ms. MIT; a published version appeared in A. Belletti (ed.) (2004), *Structures and Beyond: The Cartography of Syntactic Structures*, vol. III, Oxford University Press, pp. 104–31.

(2002) *On Nature and Language*, Cambridge University Press.

(2005) 'Three factors in language design', *Linguistic Inquiry* 36: 1–22.

(2007) 'Approaching UG from Below', in Sauerland & Gärtner (eds.), pp. 1–29.

(2008) 'On phases', in R. Freidin, C. Otero & M. L. Zubizarreta (eds.), *Foundational Issues in Linguistic Theory: Essays in Honor of Jean-Roger Vergnaud*, MIT Press, Cambridge, MA, pp. 133–65.

(2010) 'Some evo devo theses: how true might they be for language?', in R. K. Larson, V. Déprez & H. Yamakido (eds.), *The Evolution of Human Language*, Cambridge University Press, pp. 45–62.

(2013) 'Problems of projection', *Lingua* 130: 33–49.

(2014) 'Minimal recursion: exploring the prospects', *Studies in Theoretical Psycholinguistics* 43: 1–15.

Chomsky, N. & Lasnik, H. (1977) 'Filters and Control', *Linguistic Inquiry* 8: 425–504.

(1993) 'The theory of principles and parameters', in J. Jacobs, A. von Stechow, W. Sternefeld & T. Venneman (eds.), *Syntax: An International Handbook of Contemporary Research*, Mouton de Gruyter, Berlin, pp. 506–69 (reprinted in Chomsky 1995, pp. 13–127).

Christensen, K. R. (2007) 'The infinitival marker across Scandinavian', *Nordlyd* 34: 147–65.

Cinque, G. (1978) 'Towards a unified treatment of island constraints', in W. U. Dressler & W. Meid (eds.), *Proceedings of the Twelfth International Congress of Linguists*, Innsbrücker Beiträge zur Sprachwissenschaft, pp. 344–8.

(1994) 'Evidence for partial N-movement in the Romance DP', in G. Cinque, J. Koster, J.-Y. Pollock, L. Rizzi & R. Zanuttini (eds.), *Paths Towards Universal Grammar: Studies in Honor of Richard Kayne*, Georgetown University Press, Washington, DC, pp. 85–110.

(1999) *Adverbs and Functional Heads*, Oxford University Press.

(2008) 'Two types of non-restrictive relatives', *Empirical Issues in Syntax and Semantics* 7: 99–137 (http://www.cssp.cnrs.fr/eiss6).

(2010) *The Syntax of Adjectives: A Comparative Study*, MIT Press, Cambridge, MA.

(2011) 'On double-headed relative clauses', *Revista de Estudos Linguisticos da Universidade do Porto* 1: 67–91.

(2013) *Typological Studies: Word Order and Relative Clauses*, Routledge, New York.

Cinque, G. & Kayne, R. S. (eds.) (2005) *Handbook of Comparative Syntax*, Oxford University Press.

Cinque, G. & Rizzi. L. (2010) 'The cartography of syntactic structures', in B. Heine & H. Narrog (eds.), *The Oxford Handbook of Grammatical Analysis*, Oxford University Press, pp. 51–65.

Citko, B. (2004) 'On headed, headless, and light-headed relatives', *Natural Language and Linguistic Theory* 22: 95–126.

(2005) 'On the nature of merge: external merge, internal merge and parallel merge', *Linguistic Inquiry* 36: 475–96.

(2006) 'The interaction between across-the-board *wh*-movement and left branch extraction', *Syntax* 9: 225–47.

(2008) 'An argument against assimilating appositive relatives to coordinate structures', *Linguistic Inquiry* 39: 633–55.

Clahsen, H. (2008) 'Chomskyan syntactic theory and language disorders', in M. J. Ball, M. Perkins, N. Mueller & S. Howard (eds.), *The Handbook of Clinical Linguistics*, Blackwell, Oxford, pp. 165–83.

Clifton, C., Fanselow, G. & Frazier, L. (2006) 'Amnestying superiority violations: processing multiple questions', *Linguistic Inquiry* 37: 51–68.

Cole, P. (1982) *Imbabura Quechua*, North-Holland, The Hague.

Cole, P. & Hermon, G. (1998) 'The typology of wh-movement: *wh*-questions in Malay', *Syntax* 1: 221–58.

(2000) 'Partial wh-movement: evidence from Malay', in Lutz, Müller & van Stechow (eds.), pp. 101–30.

Collins, C. (1991) '*Why* and *how come*', *MIT Working Papers in Linguistics* 15: 1–45.

(1993) 'Topics in Ewe syntax', PhD diss. MIT.

(2005) 'A smuggling approach to the passive in English', *Syntax* 8: 81–120.

(2007) 'Home sweet home', *NYU Working Papers in Linguistics* 1: 1–34.

(2014) 'Merge (X,Y) = {X,Y}', ms. New York University.

(2015) 'Relative clause deletion', *MIT Working Papers in Linguistics* 77: 57–70.

Collins, C. & Radford, A. (2015) 'Gaps, ghosts and gapless relatives in spoken English', *Studia Linguistica* 69: 191–235.

Comrie, B. (1984) 'Russian', in W. S. Chisholm, L. T. Milic & J. A. C. Greppin (eds.), *Interrogativity*, Benjamins, Amsterdam, pp. 7–46.

Conroy, A. (2006) 'The semantics of *how come*: a look at how factivity does it all', *University of Maryland Working Papers in Linguistics* 14: 1–24.

Contreras, H. (1987) 'Small clauses in Spanish and English', *Natural Language and Linguistic Theory*, 5: 225–44.

(1991) 'On resumptive pronouns', in H. Campos & F. Martinez-Gil (eds.), *Current Studies in Spanish Linguistics*, Georgetown University Press, Washington, DC, pp. 143–63.

Coon, J. (2009) 'Interrogative possessors and the problem with pied-piping in Chol', *Linguistic Inquiry* 40: 165–75.

Coppock, L. (2002) 'Gapping: in defense of deletion', *Chicago Linguistic Society Papers* 37: 133–48.

Cormack, A. & Smith, N. (1999) 'Where is a sign merged?', *Glot International* 4, 6: 21.

(2000) 'Head movement and negation in English', *Transactions of the Philological Society* 98: 49–85.

(2012) 'The English extended verbal projection', ms. (ling.auf.new/lingbuzz/001615).

Corver, N. (1990) 'The syntax of left branch extractions', PhD diss. Tilburg University.

Cowart, W. (1997) *Experimental Syntax: Applying Objective Methods to Sentence Judgments*, Sage Publications, Thousand Oaks, CA.

Cowper, E. (1987) 'Pied-piping, feature percolation and the structure of the noun phrase', *Canadian Journal of Linguistics* 32: 321–38.

Craenenbroeck, J. van (2004) 'Ellipsis in Dutch dialects', PhD diss. Leiden University.

(2010) *The Syntax of Ellipsis: Evidence from Dutch Dialects*, Oxford University Press.

Craenenbroeck, J. van & Dikken, M. van (2006) 'Ellipsis and EPP repair', *Linguistic Inquiry* 37: 653–64.

Craenenbroeck, J. van & Merchant, J. (2013) 'Ellipsis phenomena', in M. den Dikken (ed.) *The Cambridge Handbook of Generative Syntax*, Cambridge University Press, pp. 701–45.

Crain, S. & Pietroski, P. (2002) 'Why language acquisition is a snap', *The Linguistic Review* 19: 163–83.

Cresswell, C. (2002) 'Resumptive pronouns, Wh-island violations, and sentence production', in *Proceedings of the Sixth International Workshop on Tree Adjoining Grammar and Related Frameworks (TAG+ 6)*, Università di Venezia, pp. 101–9.

Cuervo, M. C. (1999) 'Quirky but not eccentric: dative subjects in Spanish', *MIT Working Papers in Linguistics* 34: 213–27.

Culicover, P. W. & Nowak, A. (2003) *Dynamical Grammar: Minimalism, Acquisition and Change*, Oxford University Press.

Culicover, P. W. & Postal, P. M. (eds.) (2001) *Parasitic Gaps*. MIT Press, Cambridge, MA.

Cummins, S. & Roberge, Y. (2004) 'Null objects in French and English', in J. Auger, C. Clements & B. Vance (eds.), *Contemporary Approaches to Romance Linguistics*, John Benjamins, Amsterdam, pp. 121–38.

 (2005) 'A modular account of null objects in French', *Syntax* 8: 44–64.

Curtiss, S. (1977) *Genie: A Psycholinguistic Study of a Modern Day 'Wild Child'*, Academic Press, London.

Danon, G. (2011) 'Agreement and DP-internal feature distribution', *Syntax* 14: 297–317.

Davies, W. D. & Dubinsky, S. (2004) *The Grammar of Raising and Control: A Course in Syntactic Argumentation*, Blackwell, Oxford.

d'Avis, F.-J. (2002) 'On the interpretation of wh-clauses in exclamative environments', *Theoretical Linguistics* 28: 5–31.

Dayal, V. (2002) 'Single-pair versus multiple-pair answers: Wh-in-situ and scope', *Linguistic Inquiry* 33: 512–20.

Déchaine, R.-M. & Wiltschko, M. (2002) 'Decomposing pronouns', *Linguistic Inquiry* 33: 409–42.

del Gobbo, F. (2003) 'Appositives at the interface', PhD diss. University of California, Irvine.

den. Names like *den Dikken* are listed under the name following *den* (e.g. *Dikken*).

Demirdache, H. (1991) 'Resumptive chains in restrictive relatives, appositives, and dislocation structures', PhD diss. MIT, Cambridge, MA.

Denham, K. (2000) 'Optional *wh*-movement in Babine-Witsuwit'en', *Natural Language and Linguistic Theory* 18: 199–251.

Déprez, V. (2000) 'Parallel (a)symmetries and the internal structure of negative expressions', *Natural Language and Linguistic Theory* 18: 253–342.

de Vries, L. (1993) *Forms and Functions in Kombai, an Awyu language of Irian Jaya*, Pacific Linguistics series B-108, Australian National University, Canberra.

de Vries, M. (2002) *The Syntax of Relativization*, LOT, Utrecht.

 (2006) 'The syntax of appositive relativization: on specifying co-ordination, false free relatives and promotion', *Linguistic Inquiry* 37: 229–70.

Dikken, M. den (2006) '*Either* float and the syntax of co-*or*-dination', *Natural Language and Linguistic Theory* 24: 689–749.

Dikken, M. den & Giannakidou, A. (2002) 'From *hell* to polarity: "aggressively non-D-linked wh-phrases" as polarity items', *Linguistic Inquiry* 33: 31–61.

Doherty, C. (1993) 'Clauses without *that*: the case for bare sentential complementation in English', PhD diss. University of California, Santa Cruz.

(1994) 'The syntax of subject contact relatives', *Chicago Linguistic Society Papers* 29: 55–65.

(1997) 'Clauses without complementizers: finite IP-complementation in English', *The Linguistic Review* 14: 197–220.

Donati, C. (2006) 'On *wh*-head movement', in Cheng & Corver (eds.) pp. 21–46.

Donati C. & Cecchetto C. (2011) 'Relabeling heads: a unified account for relativization structures', *Linguistic Inquiry* 42: 519–60.

Dryer, M. S. (2005) 'Coding of nominal plurality', in M. Haspelmath, M. S. Dryer, D. Gil & B. Comrie (eds.), *The World Atlas of Language Structures*, Oxford University Press, pp. 138–41.

du Plessis, H. (1977) 'Wh-movement in Afrikaans', *Linguistic Inquiry* 8: 211–22.

Elliot, D. E. (1974) 'Toward a grammar of exclamations', *Foundations of Language* 11: 231–46.

Embick, D. & Noyer, R. (2001) 'Movement operations after syntax', *Linguistic Inquiry* 32: 555–95.

Emonds, J. E. (1976) *A Transformational Approach to English Syntax*, Academic Press, New York.

(1985) *A Unified Theory of Syntactic Categories*. Dordrecht: Foris.

(1987) 'The Invisible Category Principle', *Linguistic Inquiry* 18: 613–32.

Endo, Y. (2007) *Locality and Information Structure: A Cartographic Approach to Japanese*, Benjamins, Amsterdam.

Engdahl, E. (1983) 'Parasitic gaps', *Linguistics and Philosophy* 6: 3–34.

(1985) 'Parasitic gaps, resumptive pronouns, and subject extraction', *Linguistics* 23: 3–44.

Epstein, S. D. & Hornstein, N. (eds.) (1999) *Working Minimalism*, MIT Press, Cambridge, MA.

Epstein, S. D. & Seely, D. T. (eds.) (2002) *Derivation and Explanation in the Minimalist Program*, Blackwell, Oxford.

Epstein, S. D., Pires A., and Seely, T. D. (2005) 'EPP in T: More controversial subjects', *Syntax* 8: 65–80.

Erdmann, P. (1980) 'On the history of subject contact relatives in English', *Folia Linguistica Historica* 1: 139–70.

Erteschik-Shir, N. (1992) 'Resumptive Pronouns in Islands', in H. Goodluck & M. Rochemont (eds.), *Island Constraints: Theory, Acquisition, and Processing*, Kluwer, Dordrecht, pp. 89–108.

Escribano, J. L. G. (1991) *Una teoría de la Oración*, University of Oviedo Publications Service, Oviedo.

(2004) 'Head-final effects and the nature of modification', *Journal of Linguistics* 40: 1–43.

(2012) 'Against dummy *do*: the low *do*-aux hypothesis', *Transactions of the Philological Society* 110: 1–33.

Everaert, M. & Riemsdijk, H. van (eds.) (2006) *The Blackwell Companion to Syntax,* vol. V, Oxford University Press.

Everett, D. (2005a) 'Biology and language: a consideration of alternatives', *Journal of Linguistics* 41: 157–75.

(2005b) 'Cultural constraints on grammar and cognition in Pirahã', *Current Anthropology* 46: 621–46.

(2006) Biology and language: response to Anderson & Lightfoot. *Journal of Linguistics* 42: 385–93.

(2009) 'Pirahã culture and grammar: a response to some criticisms', *Language* 85: 405–42.

Eynde, F. van (2006) 'NP-internal agreement and the structure of the noun phrase', *Journal of Linguistics* 42: 139–86.

Fabb, N. (1990) 'The difference between English restrictive and non-restrictive clauses', *Journal of Linguistics* 26: 57–78.

Fanselow, G. (2002) 'Against remnant VP-movement', in A. Alexiadou, E. Anagnostopoulou, S. Barbiers & H.-M. Gaertner (eds.), *Dimensions of Movement: From Features to Remnants*, Benjamins, Amsterdam, pp. 91–125.

Fanselow, G. & Ćavar, D. (2002) 'Distributed deletion', in A. Alexiadou (ed.), *Theoretical Approaches to Universals*, Benjamins, Amsterdam, pp. 65–107.

Farrell, P. (1990) 'Null objects in Brazilian Portuguese', *Natural Language and Linguistic Theory* 8: 325–46.

Fasold, R. (1980) 'The relation between black and white speech in the south', ms. School of Languages and Linguistics, Georgetown University, Washington, DC.

Fauconnier, G. (1975) 'Polarity and the scale principle', *Chicago Linguistic Society Papers* 11: 188–99.

(1978) 'Implication reversal in a natural language', in F. Guenthner & S. J. Schmidt (eds.), *Formal Semantics and Pragmatics for Natural Languages*, Reidel, Dordrecht, pp. 289–302.

Feist, J. M. (2008) 'The order of premodifiers in English nominal phrases', PhD diss. University of Auckland (http://researchspace.auckland.ac.nz/bitstream/2292/3301/7/02whole.pdf).

Felser, C. (1999a) *Verbal Complement Clauses: A Minimalist Study of Direct Perception Constructions*, Benjamins, Amsterdam.

(1999b) 'Perception and control: a Minimalist analysis of English direct perception complements', *Journal of Linguistics* 34: 351–85.

(2004) 'Wh-copying, phases and successive cyclicity', *Lingua* 114: 543–74.

Ferreira, F. & Swets, B. (2005) 'The production and comprehension of resumptive pronouns in relative clause "island" contexts', in A. Cutler (ed.), *Twenty-First Century Psycholinguistics: Four Cornerstones*, Lawrence Erlbaum Associates, Mahway, NJ, pp. 263–78.

Fiengo, R. (1974) 'Semantic conditions on surface structures', PhD diss. MIT.

Fintel, K. von (1999) 'NPI licensing, Strawson entailment and context dependency', *Journal of Semantics* 16: 97–148.

Fitch, W. T., Hauser, M. D. & Chomsky, N. (2005) 'The evolution of the Language Faculty: clarification and implications', *Cognition* 97: 179–210.

Fitzmaurice, S. (2000) 'Remarks on the de-grammaticalization of infinitival *to* in present-day American English', in O. Fischer, A. Rosenberg & D. Stein (eds.), *Pathways of Change: Grammaticalization in English*, Benjamins, Amsterdam, pp. 171–86.

Fitzpatrick, J. (2005) 'The whys and how comes of presupposition and NPI licensing in questions', *Proceedings of the West Coast Conference on Formal Linguistics* 24: 138–45.

Flagg, E. (2002) 'Interface issues in the English imperative', PhD diss. MIT, Cambridge, MA.

Fodor, J. D. (2001) 'Setting syntactic parameters', in Baltin & Collins (eds.), pp. 730–67.

Fodor, J. D. & Crowther, C. (2002) 'Understanding stimulus poverty arguments', *The Linguistic Review* 19: 105–45.

Fodor, J. D. & Sakas, W. G. (2005) 'The subset principle in syntax: costs of compliance', *Journal of Linguistics* 41: 513–69.

Fontana, J. M. (1993) 'Phrase structure and the syntax of clitics in the history of Spanish', PhD diss. University of Pennsylvania.

Fox, D. (2000) *Economy and Semantic Interpretation*, MIT Press, Cambridge, MA.

Fox, D. & Lasnik, H. (2003) 'Successive-cyclic movement and island repair: the difference between sluicing and VP ellipsis', *Linguistic Inquiry* 34: 143–54.

Frank, R. & Vijay-Shanker, K. (2001) 'Primitive c-command', *Syntax* 4: 164–204.

Franks, S. (1999) 'Optimality theory and clitics at PF', *Formal Approaches to Slavic Linguistics* 7: 101–16.

(2005) 'What is *that*?' *Indiana University Working Papers in Linguistics* 5: 33–62.

Franks, S. & Progovac L. (1994) 'On the placement of Serbo-Croatian clitics', *Indiana Linguistic Studies* 7: 69–78.

Frazier, L. & Clifton, C. (2005) 'The syntax-discourse divide: processing ellipsis', *Syntax* 8: 121–74.

Freidin, R. (2004) '*Syntactic Structures* redux', *Syntax* 7: 101–27.

Freidin, R. & Vergnaud, J. R. (2001) 'Exquisite connections: some remarks on the evolution of linguistic theory', *Lingua* 111: 639–66.

Friedmann, N., Belletti, A. & Rizzi, L. (2009) 'Relativized minimality: types of intervention in the acquisition of A-bar dependencies', *Lingua* 119: 67–88.

Friedmann, N., Novogrodsky, R., Szterman, R. & Preminger, O. (2008) 'Resumptive pronouns as a last resort when movement is impaired: relative clauses in hearing impairment', in A.-L. Sharon, G. Danon & S. D. Rothstein (eds.), *Current Issues in Generative Hebrew Linguistics*, vol. VII, pp. 267–90.

Fuß, E. (2004) 'Diachronic clues to pro-drop and complementiser agreement in Bavarian', in E. Fuß & C. Trips (eds.), *Diachronic Clues to Synchronic Grammar*, Benjamins, Amsterdam, pp. 59–100.

Gelderen, E. van (1996) 'The reanalysis of grammaticalised prepositions', *Studia Linguistica* 50: 106–24.

(1997) *Verbal Agreement and the Grammar behind its Breakdown*, Niemeyer, Tübingen.

George, L. (1980) 'Analogical generalization in natural language syntax', PhD diss. MIT.

Gérard, J. (1980) *L'exclamation en français*, Tübingen: Niemeyer.

Giannakidou, A. (1997) 'The landscape of polarity items', PhD diss. University of Groningen.

(1998) *Polarity Sensitivity as (Non)veridical Dependency*, Benjamins, Amsterdam.

(1999) 'Affective dependencies', *Linguistics and Philosophy* 22: 367–421.

Giegerich, H. J. (2005) 'Associative adjectives in English and the lexicon–syntax interface', *Journal of Linguistics* 41: 571–91.

Ginzburg, J. & Sag, I. (2000) *Interrogative Investigations: The Form, Meaning, and Use of English Interrogatives*, CSLI Publications, Stanford, CA.

Giorgi, A. (2007) 'On the nature of long-distance anaphors', *Linguistic Inquiry* 38: 321–42.

Giorgi, A. & Longobardi, G. (1991) *The Syntax of Noun Phrases*, Cambridge University Press, Cambridge.

Giusti, G. (1991) 'The categorial status of quantifier nominals', *Linguistische Berichte* 136: 438–52.

(1997) 'The categorial status of determiners', in L. Haegeman (ed.), *The New Comparative Syntax*, Cambridge University Press, pp. 94–113.

Givón, T. (2002) *Biolinguistics: The Santa Barbara Lectures*, Benjamins, Amsterdam.

Goodall, G. (1987) *Parallel Structures in Syntax: Co-ordination, Causatives and Restructuring*, Cambridge University Press.

Graffi, G. (1996) 'Alcune riflessioni sugli imperativi italiani', in Benincà et al. (eds.), pp. 143–8.

Green, L. (1998) 'Semantic and syntactic patterns in African American English', ms. University of Massachusetts.

Greenberg, J. H. (1963) 'Some universals of grammar with particular reference to the order of meaningful elements', in J. H. Greenberg (ed.), *Universals of Language*, MIT Press, Cambridge, MA, pp. 73–113.

Grice, H. P. (1975) 'Logic and conversation', in P. Cole & J. Morgan (eds.), *Syntax and Semantics,* vol. II: *Speech Acts*, Academic Press, New York, pp. 41–58.

Grimshaw, J. (1979) 'Complement selection and the lexicon', *Linguistic Inquiry* 10: 279–326.

(1993) 'Minimal projection, heads, and optimality', ms. Rutgers University.

(2000) 'Locality and extended projections', in P. Coopmans, M. Everaert & J. Grimshaw (eds.), *Lexical Specification and Insertion*, Benjamins, Amsterdam, pp. 115–34.

(2005) *Words and Structure*, CLSI Publications, Stanford, CA.

Groat, E. & O'Neil, J. (1996) 'Spell-out at the LF interface', in W. Abraham, S. D. Epstein, H. Thráinsson & C. J.-W. Zwart (eds.), *Minimal Ideas*, Benjamins, Amsterdam, pp. 113–39.

Groefsema, M. (1995) 'Understood arguments: a semantic/pragmatic approach', *Lingua* 96: 139–61.

Grohmann, K. K. (2003) *Prolific Domains*, Benjamins, Amsterdam.

(2006) 'Top issues in questions: topics – topicalization – topicalizability', in Cheng & Corver (eds.), pp. 249–88.

Grohmann, K. K. & Haegeman, L. (2002) 'Resuming reflexives' (ling.auf.net/lingbuzz000140).

Grohmann, K. K., Drury J. & Castillo, J. C. (2000) 'No more EPP', *Proceedings of the West Coast Conference on Formal Linguistics* 19: 153–66.

Grolla, E. (2005) 'Resumptive pronouns as last resort: implications for language acquisition', in S. Arunachalam, T. Scheffler, S. Sundaresan & J. Tauberer (eds.), *Penn Working Papers in Linguistics* 11: 71–84.

Groos, A. & Riemsdijk, H. C. van (1981) 'Matching effects with free relatives: a parameter of core grammar', in A. Belletti, L. Brandi & L. Rizzi (eds.), *Theory of Markedness in Generative Grammar: Proceedings of the 1979 GLOW Conference*, Scuola Normale Superiore, Pisa, pp. 171–216.

Grosu, A. (1989) 'Pied-piping and the matching parameter', *The Linguistic Review* 6: 41–58.

(1994) *Three Studies in Locality and Case*, Routledge, London.

(2003) 'A unified theory of "standard" and "transparent" free relatives', *Natural Language and Linguistic Theory* 21: 247–331.

Grosu, A. & Horvath, J. (2006) 'Reply to Bhatt and Pancheva's "late merge of degree clauses": the irrelevance of (non)conservativity', *Linguistic Inquiry* 37: 457–83.

Gruber, B. (2008) 'Complementiser agreement in Bavarian: new evidence from the Upper Austrian variant of Gmunden', MA diss. University of Vienna.

Gualmini, A. & Crain, S. (2005) 'The structure of children's linguistic knowledge', *Linguistic Inquiry* 36: 463–74.

Guasti, M. T. (2002) *Language Acquisition: The Growth of Grammar*, Bradford books, MIT Press, Cambridge, MA.

Guasti, M. T., Thornton, R. & Wexler, K. (1995) 'Negation in children's questions: the case of English', *Proceedings of the Boston University Conference on Language Development* 19: 228–39.

Haeberli, E. (2003) 'Categorial features as the source of EPP and abstract Case phenomena', in E. Brandner & H. Zinsmeister (eds.), *New Perspectives on Case Theory*, CSLI publications, Stanford, CA, pp. 89–126.

Haegeman, L. (1986) 'The present subjunctive in contemporary British English', *Studia Anglica Posnaniensa* 19: 61–74.

(1990) 'Non-overt subjects in diary contexts', in J. Mascaró & M. Nespor (eds.), *Grammar in Progress*, Foris, Dordrecht, pp. 167–74.

(1992) *Theory and Description in Generative Syntax: A Case Study in West Flemish*, Cambridge University Press.

(1995) *The Syntax of Negation*, Cambridge University Press.

(1997) 'Register variation, truncation and subject omission in English and in French', *English Language and Linguistics* 1: 233–70.

(2000a) 'Adult null subjects in non *pro*-drop languages', in M.-A. Friedemann & L. Rizzi (eds.), *The Acquisition of Syntax*, Addison, Wesley and Longman, London, pp. 129–69.

(2000b) 'Inversion, non-adjacent inversion and adjuncts in CP', *Transactions of the Philological Society* 98: 121–60.

(2003) 'Notes on long adverbial fronting in English and the left periphery', *Linguistic Inquiry* 34: 640–9.

(2006a) 'Argument Fronting in English, Romance CLLD and the Left Periphery', in R. Zanuttini, H. Campos, E. Herburger & P. Portner (eds.), *Negation, Tense and Clausal Architecture: Cross-Linguistic Investigations*, Georgetown University Press, Washington, DC, pp. 27–52.

(2006b) 'Conditionals, factives and the left periphery', *Lingua* 116: 1651–69.

(2007) 'Operator movement and topicalization in adverbial clauses', *Folia Linguistica* 18: 485–502.

(2008) 'Subject omission in present-day written English: on the theoretical relevance of peripheral data', *Rivista di Grammatica Generativa* 32: 91–124.

(2009) 'The movement analysis of temporal adverbial clauses', *English Language and Linguistics* 13: 385–408.

(2010) 'The internal syntax of adverbial clauses', *Lingua* 120: 628–48.

(2012) *Adverbial Clauses, Main Clause Phenomena, and Composition of the Left Periphery*, Oxford University Press.

Haegeman, L. & Ihsane, T. (1999) 'Subject ellipsis in embedded clauses in English', *Journal of English Language and Linguistics* 3: 117–45.

(2002) 'Adult null subjects in the non-pro drop languages: two diary dialects', *Language Acquisition* 9: 329–46.

Haegeman, L. & Koppen, M. van (2012) 'Complementizer agreement and the relation between C^0 and T^0', *Linguistic Inquiry* 43: 441–54.

Haegeman, L., Jiménez-Fernández, Á. & Radford, A. (2014) 'Deconstructing the Subject Condition in terms of cumulative constraint violation', *The Linguistic Review* 31: 73–150.

Haegeman, L., Weir, A., Danckaert, L., D'Hulster, T. and Buelens, L. (2015) 'Against the root analysis of subject contact relatives in English', *Lingua* 163: 61–74.

Hale, K. & Keyser, S. J. (eds.) (1993) *The View from Building 20*, MIT Press, Cambridge, Mass.

Halle, M. & Marantz, A. (1993) 'Distributed morphology and the pieces of inflection', in Hale & Keyser (eds.), pp.111–76.

Han, C.-H. (2000) 'The evolution of *do*-support in English imperatives', in S. Pintzuk, G. Tsoulas & A. Warner (eds.), *Diachronic Syntax: Models and Mechanisms*, Oxford University Press, pp. 275–95.

(2001) 'Force, negation and imperatives', *The Linguistic Review* 18: 289–325.

Hankamer, J. (1971) 'Constraints on deletion in syntax', PhD diss. Yale University.

Hankamer, J. & Sag, I. (1976) 'Deep and surface anaphora', *Linguistic Inquiry* 7: 391–428.

Harbert, W. (1983) 'On the nature of the matching parameter', *The Linguistic Review* 2: 237–84.

Hardt, D. (1993) 'Verb phrase ellipsis: form, meaning and processing', PhD diss. University of Pennsylvania

Harley, H. (2006) *English Words: A Linguistic Introduction*. Blackwell, Oxford.

Harris, M. & Vincent, N. (1980) 'On zero relatives', *Linguistic Inquiry* 11: 805–7.

Hartman, J. & Ai, R. R. (2009) 'A Focus account of Swiping', in K. K. Grohmann and P. Panagiotidis (eds.), *Selected Papers from the 2006 Cyprus Syntaxfest*, pp. 92–122 (http://web.mit.edu/hartmanj/www/swiping.pdf).

Hartmann, J. M. (2005) '*Wh*-movement and the small clause analyses of the English *there*-construction', *Leiden Papers in Linguistics* 2: 93–106.

Haspelmath, M. (2007) 'Pre-established categories don't exist: consequences for language description and typology', *Linguistic Typology* 11: 119–32.

(2010) 'Comparative concepts and descriptive categories in crosslinguistic studies', *Language* 86: 663–87.

Hawkins, J. A. (2001) 'Why are categories adjacent?', *Journal of Linguistics* 37: 1–34.

Hauser, M. D., Chomsky, N. & Fitch, W. T. (2002) 'The faculty of language: what is it, who has it, and how did it evolve?', *Science* 298: 1569–79.

Heck, F. (2004) 'A theory of pied-piping', PhD diss. Universität Tübingen.

(2008) *On Pied-Piping: wh-movement and Beyond*, Mouton de Gruyter, Berlin.

(2009) 'On certain properties of pied-piping', *Linguistic Inquiry* 40: 75–111.

Heestand, D., Xiang, M. & Polinsky, M. (2011) 'Resumption still does not rescue islands', *Linguistic Inquiry* 42: 138–52.

Heim, I. (1987) 'Where does the definiteness restriction apply? Evidence from the definiteness of variables', in Reuland & ter Meulen (eds.) pp. 21–42.

Henry, A. (1995) *Belfast English and Standard English: Dialect Variation and Parameter-Setting*, Oxford University Press.

Herdan, S. (2008) *Degrees and Amounts in Relative Clauses*, Proquest, Google Books.

Herdan, S. & Sharvit, Y. (2006) 'Definite and non-definite superlatives and NPI licensing', *Syntax* 9: 1–31.

Hiemstra, I. (1986) 'Some aspects of wh-questions in Frisian', *North-Western European Language Evolution (NOWELE)* 8: 97–110.

Hill, J. A. C. (1983) *A Computational Model of Language Acquisition in the Two-Year-Old*, Indiana University Linguistics Club, Bloomington, IN.

Hiramatsu, K. (2003) 'Children's judgments on negative questions', *Language Acquisition* 11: 99–126.

Hirschbühler, P. (1976) 'Two analyses of free relatives in French', *Le Langage et l'homme* 31: 71–81.

(1978) *The Syntax and Semantics of Wh-constructions*, Indiana University Linguistics Club, Bloomington, IN.

Hofmeister, P. (2012) 'Effects of processing on the acceptability of "frozen" extraposed constituents', ms. University of Essex.

Hofmeister, P. & Norcliffe, E. (2013) 'Does resumption facilitate sentence comprehension', in P. Hofmeister & E. Norcliffe (eds.), *The Core and the Periphery: Data-driven Perspectives on Syntax Inspired by Ivan A. Sag*, CSLI publications, Stanford, CA, pp. 225–46.

Hoge, K. (1998) 'The Yiddish double verb construction', *Oxford University Working Papers in Linguistics, Philology and Phonetics* 2: 85–97.

Hojo, K. (1971) 'The present subjunctive in English NP complements', *Ronshuu* 17: 93–112.

Hollebrandse, B. & Roeper, T. (1999) 'The concept of *do*-insertion and the theory of INFL in acquisition', in C. Koster & F. Wijnen (eds.), *Proceedings of GALA*, Centre for Language and Cognition, Groningen, pp. 1–57.

Holmberg, A. (1999) 'Remarks on Holmberg's generalization', *Studia Linguistica* 53: 1–39.

(2000) 'Scandinavian stylistic fronting: how any category can become an expletive', *Linguistic Inquiry* 31: 445–83.

(2005) 'Is there a little pro? Evidence from Finnish', *Linguistic Inquiry* 36: 533–64.

Hong, S.-H. (2005) 'Aspects of the syntax of questions in English and Korean', PhD diss. University of Essex.

Hornstein, N. (1995) *Logical Form: From GB to Minimalism*, Blackwell, Oxford.

(2001) *Move: A Minimalist Theory of Construal*, Blackwell, Oxford.

(2007) 'Pronouns in a Minimalist Setting', in N. Corver & J. Nunes (eds.), *The Copy Theory of Movement*, Benjamins, Amsterdam, pp: 351–85.

Hornstein, N. & Pietroski, P. (2009) 'Basic operations: minimal syntax-semantics', *Catalan Journal of Linguistics* 8: 113–39.

Horvath, J. (2006) 'Pied-piping', in Everaert & van Riemsdijk (eds.), pp. 569–630.

Huang, C.-T. J. (1982) 'Logical relations in Chinese and the theory of grammar', PhD diss. MIT.

(1984) 'On the distribution and reference of empty pronouns', *Linguistic Inquiry* 15: 531–74.

(1991) 'Remarks on the status of the null object', in R. Freidin (ed.), *Principles and Parameters in Comparative Grammar*, MIT Press, Cambridge, MA, pp. 56–76.

Huddleston, R. (1994) 'The Contrast between interrogatives and questions', *Journal of Linguistics* 30: 411–39.

Huddleston, R. & Pullum, G. K. (2002) *The Cambridge Grammar of English Language*, Cambridge University Press.

Hulsey, S. & Sauerland, U. (2006) 'Sorting out relative clauses', *Natural Language Semantics* 14: 111–37.

Hurford, J. (1991) 'The evolution of the critical period for language acquisition', *Cognition* 40: 159–201.

Hyams, N. (1986) *Language Acquisition and the Theory of Parameters*, Reidel, Dordrecht.

(1992) 'A reanalysis of null subjects in child language', in J. Weissenborn, H. Goodluck & T. Roeper (eds.), *Theoretical Issues in Language Acquisition*, Lawrence Erlbaum Associates, London, pp. 249–67.

Iatridou, S. (1990) 'About Agr(P)', *Linguistic Inquiry* 21: 766–72.

Iatridou, S. & Kroch, A. (1992) 'The licensing of CP-recursion and its relevance to the Germanic verb-second phenomenon', *Working Papers in Scandinavian Syntax* 50: 1–24.

Ingham, R. (1992) 'The optional subject phenomenon in young children's English: a case study', *Journal of Child Language* 19: 133–51.

(2000) 'Negation and OV order in Late Middle English', *Journal of Linguistics* 36: 13–38.

(2002) 'Negated subjects and objects in 15th century non-literary English', *Language Variation and Change* 14: 291–322.

(2007a) 'A structural constraint on negation in Late Middle and Early Modern English', *Medieval English Mirror* 3: 55–67.

(2007b) 'NegP and negated constituent movement in the history of English', *Transactions of the Philological Society* 105: 365–97.

Ioannou, G. (2011) 'On the nature of T-to-C Movement in English wh-interrogatives', PhD diss. University of Essex.

Isac, D. (2006) 'In defense of a quantificational account of definite DPs', *Linguistic Inquiry* 37: 275–88.

Ishii, T. (2006) 'On the relaxation of intervention effects', in Cheng & Corver (eds.), pp. 217–46.

Izvorski, R. (2000) 'Free adjunct free relatives', *Proceedings of the West Coast Conference in Formal Linguistics* 19: 232–45.

Jackendoff, R. S. (1972) *Semantic Interpretation in Generative Grammar*, MIT Press, Cambridge, MA.

(1974) *Introduction to the X-bar Convention*, Indiana University Linguistics Club.

(1977a) *X-bar Syntax: A Study of Phrase Structure*, MIT Press, Cambridge MA.

(1977b) 'Constraints on phrase structure rules', in P. W. Culicover, T. Wasow & A. Akmajian (eds.), *Formal* Syntax, Academic Press, New York, pp. 249–83.

Jacobson, P. (1995) 'On the quantificational force of English free relatives', in E. Bach, E. Jelinek, A. Kratzer & B. H. Partee (eds.), *Quantification in Natural Languages*, Kluwer, Dordrecht, pp. 451–86.

Jaeggli, O. (1982) *Topics in Romance Syntax*, Foris, Dordrecht.

(1984) 'Subject extraction and the null subject parameter', *Proceedings of the North East Linguistic Society* 14: 132–53.

Jaeggli, O. & Safir, K. (1989) *The Null Subject Parameter*, Kluwer, Dordrecht.

Jiménez, Á. (2000a) 'The interpretation of tense and aspect in argument small clauses', *Revista Canaria de Estudios Ingleses* 40: 279–98.

(2000b) 'The aspectual morpheme *as* and feature movement in argument small clauses', *Generative Linguistics in Poland* 1: 59–69.

Johanessen, J. B. (1993) 'Co-ordination: a Minimalist approach', PhD diss. University of Oslo.

(1996) 'Partial agreement and co-ordination', *Linguistic Inquiry* 27: 661–76.

(1998) *The Syntax of Co-ordination*, Oxford University Press.

Johnson, K. (2000) 'Few dogs like Whiskas or cats Alpo', *University of Massachusetts Occasional Papers* 23: 59–82.

(2001) 'What VP-ellipsis can do, and what it can't, but not why', in Baltin & Collins (eds.), pp. 439–79.

(2002) 'Restoring exotic co-ordinations to normalcy', *Linguistic Inquiry* 33: 97–156.

Julien, M. (2001) 'The syntax of complex tenses', *The Linguistic Review* 18: 125–67.

Jurka, J. (2010) 'The importance of being a complement: CED effects revisited', PhD diss. University of Maryland.

Jurka, J., Nakao, C. & Omaki, A. (2011) 'It's not the end of the CED as we know it: revisiting German and Japanese Subject Islands', *Proceedings of the West Coast Conference on Formal Linguistics* 28: 124–32.

Kaplan, J. P. (1988) 'Small clauses and the projection principle', *Proceedings of the Berkeley Linguistics Society*, 14: 78–87.

Kato, M. A. (1999) 'Strong pronouns and weak pronominals in the null subject parameter', *Probus* 11: 1–37.

(2000) 'The partial *pro-drop* nature and the restricted VS order in Brazilian Portuguese', in M. A. Kato & E. V. Negrão (eds.), *The Null Subject Parameter in Brazilian Portuguese*, Vervuert-IberoAmericana, Madrid, pp. 223–58.

Katz, J. J. & Postal, P. M. (1964) *An Integrated Theory of Linguistic Descriptions*, MIT Press, Cambridge, MA.

Kayne, R. S. (1983) *Connectedness and Binary Branching*, Foris, Dordrect.

(1994) *The Antisymmetry of Syntax*, MIT Press, Cambridge, MA.

(2002) 'Pronouns and their antecedents', in Epstein & Seely (eds.), pp. 133–66.

(2007) 'Some thoughts on grammaticalization: the case of *that*', talk delivered at XVIII *Conférence internationale de linguistique historique*, UQAM, Montreal.

Kayne, R. S. & Pollock, J.-Y. (1978) 'Stylistic inversion, successive cyclicity, and Move NP in French', *Linguistic Inquiry* 9: 595–621.

(2002) 'Comparative deletion and optimality in syntax', *Natural Language and Linguistic Theory* 20: 553–621.

(2003) 'Ellipsis and syntactic representation', in K. Schwabe & S. Winkler (eds.), *The Syntax–Semantics Interface: Interpreting (Omitted) Structure*, Benjamins, Amsterdam, pp. 29–53.

Kennedy, C. & Merchant, J. (2000), 'Attributive comparative deletion', *Natural Language and Linguistic Theory* 18: 89–146.

Kenstowicz, M. (ed.) (2001) *Ken Hale: A Life in Language*, MIT Press, Cambridge, MA.

Kim, C. S, Kobele, G. M., Runner, J. T. & Hale, J. T. (2011) 'The acceptability cline in VP Ellipsis', *Syntax* 14: 318–54.

Kim, J.-B. & Kim, O. (2011) 'English *how come* construction: a double life', paper presented to *Arizona Linguistics Circle 5*, 28–30 October 2011.

Kiparsky, P. & Kiparsky, C. (1970) 'Fact', in D. D. Steinberg & L. A. Jakobovits (eds.), *Semantics: An Interdisciplinary Reader in Philosophy, Linguistics and Psychology*, Cambridge University Press, London, pp. 345–69.

Kishimoto, H. (2000) 'Indefinite pronouns and overt N-raising', *Linguistic Inquiry* 31: 557–66.

(2006) 'On the existence of null complementisers in syntax', *Linguistic Inquiry* 37: 339–45.

Kiss, É. K. (2001) 'The EPP in a topic-prominent language', in P. Svenonius (ed.), *Subjects, Expletives and the EPP*, Oxford University Press, pp. 107–24.

Kitagawa, Y. (1985) 'Small but clausal', *Chicago Linguistic Society Papers* 21: 210–20.

Klima, E. S. (1964) 'Negation in English', in J. A. Fodor & J. J. Katz (eds.), *The Structure of Language*, Prentice-Hall, Englewood Cliffs, NJ, pp. 246–323.

Ko, H. (2005) 'Syntactic edges and linearization', PhD diss, MIT.

Koeneman, O. (2000) 'The flexible nature of verb movement', PhD diss. University of Utrecht.

Koopman, H. (1984) *The Syntax of Verbs: From Verb Movement Rules in the Kru Languages to Universal Grammar*, Foris, Dordrecht.

(2000a) *The Syntax of Specifiers and Heads*, Routledge, London.

(2000b) 'Prepositions, postpositions, circumpositions and particles: The structure of Dutch PPs', in *The Syntax of Specifiers and Heads: Collected Essays of Hilda J. Koopman*, Routledge, London, pp. 204–60.

Koopman, H. & Szabolsci, A. (2000) *Verbal Complexes*. MIT Press, Cambridge, MA.

Koppen, M. van. (2005) 'One probe – two goals: aspects of agreement in Dutch dialects', PhD diss. University of Leiden.

Koster, J. (1975) 'Dutch as an SOV language', *Linguistic Analysis* 1: 111–36.

Krapova, I. & Cinque, G. (2008) 'On the order of *wh*-phrases in Bulgarian multiple *wh*-fronting', in. G. Zybatow, L. Szucsich, U. Junghanns & R. Meyer (eds.), *Formal Description of Slavic Languages*, Peter Lang, Frankfurt am Main, pp. 318–36.

Kroch, A. (1981) 'On the role of resumptive pronouns in amnestying Island Constraint violations', *Chicago Linguistic Society Papers* 17: 125–35.

(2001) 'Syntactic change', in Baltin & Collins (eds.), pp. 699–729.

Kuno, S. (1981) 'Functional syntax', *Syntax and Semantics* 13: 117–35.

Kuno, S. & Robinson, J. (1972) 'Multiple *wh*-questions', *Linguistic Inquiry* 3: 463–87.

Kural, M. (2005) 'Tree traversal and word order', *Linguistic Inquiry* 36: 367–87.

Labov, W. (1969) 'Contraction, deletion and the inherent variability of the English copula', *Language* 45: 715–62.

Ladusaw, W. (1979) 'Polarity sensitivity as inherent scope relations', PhD diss. University of Texas, Austin.

Lahiri, U. (1998) 'Focus and negative polarity in Hindi', *Natural Language Semantics* 6: 57–123.

Laka, M. I. (1990) 'Negation in syntax: on the nature of functional categories and projections', PhD diss. MIT.

Lamarche, J. (1991) 'Problems for N°-movement to NumP', *Probus* 3: 215–36.

Lambrecht, K. (1988) 'There was a farmer had a dog: syntactic amalgams revisited', *Proceedings of the Berkeley Linguistics Society* 14: 319–39.

Landau, I. (1999) 'Elements of control', PhD diss. MIT.

(2001) 'Control and extraposition: the case of Super-Equi', *Natural Language and Linguistic Theory* 19: 109–52.

(2003) 'Movement out of control', *Linguistic Inquiry* 34: 471–98.

(2004) 'The scale of finiteness and the calculus of control', *Natural Language and Linguistic Theory* 22: 811–77.

(2006a) 'Severing the distribution of PRO from case', *Syntax* 9: 153–70.

(2006b) 'Chain resolution in Hebrew V(P) fronting', *Syntax* 9: 32–66.

(2007) 'EPP extensions', *Linguistic Inquiry* 38: 485–523.

Langendonck, W. van (1994) 'Determiners as heads?' *Cognitive Linguistics* 5: 243–59.

Lappin, S. & Shieber, S. (2007), 'Machine learning theory and practice as a source of insight into universal grammar', *Journal of Linguistics* 43: 393–427.

Larson, R. K. (1985a) 'On the syntax of disjunction scope', *Natural Language and Linguistic Theory* 3: 217–64.

(1985b) 'Bare-NP adverbs', *Linguistic Inquiry* 16: 595–621.

(1987) '"Missing prepositions" and the analysis of English free relative clauses', *Linguistic Inquiry* 18: 239–66.

Larson, R. K. & Lefebvre, C. (1991) 'Predicate cleft in Haitian Creole', *Proceedings of the North East Linguistic Society* 21: 247–61.

Larson, R. K. & Marušič, F. (2004) 'On indefinite pronoun structures with APs: reply to Kishimoto', *Linguistic Inquiry* 35: 268–87.

Lasnik, H. (1981) 'Restricting the theory of transformations', in N. Hornstein & D. Lightfoot (eds.), *Explanation in Linguistics*, Longman, London, pp. 152–73.

(1995) 'Verbal Morphology: *Syntactic Structures* meets the Minimalist Program', in H. Campos & P. Kempchinksky (eds.), *Evolution and Revolution in Linguistic Theory*, Georgetown University Press, Washington, DC, pp. 251–75.

(2000) *Syntactic Structures Revisited: Contemporary Lectures on Classic Transformational Theory*, MIT Press, Cambridge, MA (with M. Depiante & A. Stepanov).

(2003) *Minimalist Investigations in Linguistic Theory*, Routledge, London.

(2006) 'Conceptions of the cycle', in Cheng & Corver (eds.), pp. 197–216.

Lasnik, H. & Uriagereka, J. (2002) 'On the poverty of the challenge', *The Linguistic Review* 19: 147–50.

Law, P. (1971) 'Effects of head-movement on theories of subjacency and proper government', PhD diss. MIT.

Lebeaux, D. (1991) 'Relative clauses, licensing and the nature of derivation', in S. Rothstein (ed.), *Syntax and Semantics 25: Perspectives on Phrase Structure*, Academic Press, New York, pp. 209–39.

Lechner, W. (2001) 'Reduced and phrasal comparatives', *Natural Language and Linguistic Theory* 19: 683–735.

(2006) 'An interpretive effect of head movement', in M. Frascarelli (ed.), *Phases of Interpretation*, Mouton de Gruyter, Berlin, pp. 45–71.

(2007) 'Interpretive effects of head movement' (ling.auf.net/lingbuzz/000178).

Legate, J. A. (2010) 'On how *how* is used instead of *that*', *Natural Language and Linguistic Theory* 28: 121–34.

Legate, J. A. & Yang, C. D (2002) 'Empirical re-assessment of stimulus poverty arguments', *The Linguistic Review* 19: 151–62.

Lema, J. & Rivero, M. L. (1990) 'Long head movement: ECP vs. HMC', *Proceedings of the North East Linguistic Society* 28: 219–45.

Lenneberg, E. (1967) *Biological Foundations of Language*, Wiley, New York.

Levine, R. (2012) 'Auxiliaries: *To*'s company', *Journal of Linguistics* 48: 187–203.

Lewis, J. & Elman, J. (2002) 'Learnability and the statistical study of language: poverty of stimulus arguments revisited', *Proceedings of the Boston University Conference on Language Development*, 26: 359–70.

Lightfoot, D. (1999) *The Development of Language: Acquisition, Change and Evolution*, Blackwell, Oxford.

Lightfoot, D. & Hornstein, N. (eds.) (1994) *Verb Movement*, Cambridge University Press.

Lin, T.-H. J. (2011) 'Finiteness of clauses and raising of arguments in Mandarin Chinese', *Syntax* 14: 48–73.

Linebarger, M. (1987) 'Negative polarity and grammatical representation', *Linguistics and Philosophy* 10: 325–87.

Lobeck, A. (1995) *Ellipsis: Functional Heads, Licensing and Identification*, Oxford University Press.

Löbel, E. (1989) 'Q as a functional category', in C. Bhatt, E. Löbel & C. Schmidt (eds.), *Syntactic Phrase Structure Phenomena*, Benjamins, Amsterdam, pp. 133–58.

Longobardi, G. (1994) 'Reference and proper names', *Linguistic Inquiry* 25: 609–66.

(1996) 'The syntax of N-raising: a minimalist theory', *OTS Working Papers no. 5*, Research Institute for Language and Speech, Utrecht.

(2001) 'The Structure of DPs: some principles, parameters and problems', in Baltin & Collins (eds.), pp. 562–603.

Los, B. (2005) *The Rise of the To-Infinitive*, Oxford University Press.

Lundin, K. (2003) *Small Clauses in Swedish: Towards a Unified Account*, Studentlitteratur, Lund.

Lust, B. (2006) *Child Language: Acquisition and Growth*, Cambridge University Press.

Lutz, U., Müller, G. & von Stechow A. (eds.) (2000) *Wh-Scope Marking*, Benjamins, Amsterdam.

Lyons, C. (1999) *Definiteness*, Cambridge University Press.

McCawley, J. D. (1988) Adverbial NPs: bare or clad in see-through garb? *Language* 64: 583–90.

(1993) 'Gapping with shared operators', *Proceedings of the Berkeley Linguistics Society* 19: 245–54.

McCloskey, J. (1979) *Transformational Syntax and Model Theoretic Semantics*, Reidel, Dordrecht.

(1990) 'Resumptive pronouns, A'-binding, and levels of representation in Irish', in R. Hendrik (ed.), *Syntax and Semantics*, vol. 23: *The Syntax of Modern Celtic Languages*, Academic Press, New York, pp. 199–248.

(2000) 'Quantifier float and *wh*-movement in an Irish English', *Linguistic Inquiry* 31: 57–84.

(2001) 'The morphosyntax of WH-extraction in Irish', *Journal of Linguistics* 37: 67–100.

(2002) 'Resumption, successive cyclicity, and the locality of operations', in Epstein & Seely (eds.), pp. 184–226.

(2006a) 'Resumption', in Everaert & van Riemsdijk (eds.), pp. 94–117.

(2006b) 'Questions and questioning in a local English', in R. Zanuttini, H. Campos, E. Herburger & P. Portner (eds.), *Negation, Tense and Clausal Architecture:*

Cross-linguistic Investigations, Georgetown University Press, Washington, DC, pp. 86–126.

McDaniel, D. (1986) 'Conditions on Wh-chains', PhD diss. City University of New York.
   (1989) 'Partial and multiple wh-movement', *Natural Language and Linguistic Theory* 7: 565–604.

McKee, C. & McDaniel, D. (2001) 'Resumptive pronouns in English relative clauses', *Language Acquisition*, 9: 113–56.

McNeill, D. (1966) 'Developmental psycholinguistics', in F. Smith & G. A. Miller (eds.), *The Genesis of Language*, MIT Press, Cambridge, MA, pp. 15–84.

Maekawa, T. (2007) 'The English left periphery in linearisation-based HPSG', PhD diss. University of Essex.

Manzini, M. R. (1994) 'Locality, minimalism and parasitic gaps', *Linguistic Inquiry* 25: 481–508.

Manzini, M. R. & Wexler, K. (1987) 'Parameters, binding theory and learnability', *Linguistic Inquiry* 18: 413–44.

Marelj, M. (2011) 'Bound-variable anaphora and Left Branch Condition', *Syntax* 14: 205–29.

Marcus, G. F. (1993) 'Negative evidence in language acquisition', *Cognition* 46: 53–85.

Martin, R. (1996) 'A Minimalist theory of PRO and control', PhD diss. University of Connecticut, Storrs.
   (2001) 'Null case and the distribution of PRO', *Linguistic Inquiry* 32: 141–66.

Masullo, P. (1993) 'Two types of quirky subjects: Spanish versus Icelandic', *Proceedings of the North East Linguistic Society* 23: 303–17.

Matsui, C. (1981) 'The present subjunctive in embedded *that* clauses', *Insight* 13: 45–59.

Matushansky, O. (2006) 'Head movement in linguistic theory', *Linguistic Inquiry* 37: 69–109.

Merchant, J. (1999) 'The syntax of silence: sluicing, islands, and identity of ellipsis', PhD diss, UCSC.
   (2001) *The Syntax of Silence: Sluicing, Islands and Identity in Ellipsis*, Oxford University Press.
   (2002) 'Swiping in Germanic', in W. Abraham & J.-W. Zwart (eds.), *Studies in Comparative Germanic Syntax*, Benjamins, Amsterdam, pp. 295–321.
   (2003) 'Subject-Auxiliary Inversion in comparatives and PF output constraints', in K. Schwabe & S. Winkler (eds.), *The Interfaces: Deriving and Interpreting Omitted Structures*, Benjamins, Amsterdam, pp. 55–77.
   (2004) 'Fragments and ellipsis', *Linguistics and Philosophy* 27: 661–738.
   (2006) 'Sluicing', in Everaert & van Riemsdijk (eds.), pp. 269–89.
   (2008a) 'Variable island repair under ellipsis', in K. Johnson (ed.), *Topics in Ellipsis*, Cambridge University Press, pp. 132–53.
   (2008b) 'An asymmetry in voice mismatches in VP ellipsis and pseudogapping', *Linguistic Inquiry* 39: 169–79.
   (2013a) 'Diagnosing ellipsis', in Cheng & Corver (eds.), pp. 537–42.
   (2013b) 'Polarity items under ellipsis', in Cheng & Corver (eds.), pp. 441–62.

Michaelis, L. and Lambrecht, K. (1996) 'The exclamative sentence type in English', in A. Goldberg (ed.), *Conceptual Structure, Discourse and Language*, CSLI Publications, Stanford, CA, pp. 375–89.

Miyagawa, S. (2005) 'On the EPP', *MIT Working Papers in Linguistics* 49: 201–36.

(2006) 'Moving to the edge', in *Proceedings of the 2006 KALS-KASELL International Conference on English and Linguistics*, Pusan National University, Busan, Korea, pp. 3–18.

(2010) *Why Agree? Why Move?* MIT Press, Cambridge MA.

Montalbetti, M. (1984) 'After Binding', PhD diss. MIT.

Moore, J. & Perlmutter, D. M. (2000). 'What does it take to be a dative subject?', *Natural Language and Linguistic Theory* 18: 373–416.

Morgan, J. (1972) 'Some aspects of relative clauses in English and Albanian', in Peranteau et al. (eds.), pp. 63–72.

Morgan, J. L. & Travis, L. (1989) 'Limits on negative information in language input', *Journal of Child Language* 16: 531–52.

Moro, A. (1997) *The Raising of Predicates*, Cambridge University Press.

Müller, Gereon (2010) 'On deriving CED effects from the PIC', *Linguistic Inquiry* 41: 35–82.

Munaro, N. (2001), 'Free relatives as defective *wh* elements: evidence from the NorthWestern Italian dialects', in Y. D'Hulst, J. Rooryk & J. Schroten (eds.), *Romance Languages and Linguistic Theory 1999*, Benjamins, Amsterdam, pp. 281–306.

Munn, A. (1993) 'Topics in the syntax and semantics of co-ordinate structures', PhD diss. University of Maryland.

(1999) 'First conjunct agreement: against a clausal analysis', *Linguistic Inquiry* 30: 643–68.

Nakao, C. (2009) 'Island repair and non-repair by PF strategies', PhD diss. University of Maryland.

Namai, K. (2000) 'Gender features in English', *Linguistics* 38: 771–9.

Napoli, D. J. (1982) 'Initial material deletion in English', *Glossa* 16: 85–111.

(1993) *Syntax: Theory and Problems*, Oxford University Press.

Neeleman, A. & Szendrői, K. (2005) 'Pro drop and pronouns', *Proceedings of the West Coast Conference on Formal Linguistics* 24: 299–307.

Nevins, A., Pesetsky, D. & Rodrigues, C. (2009a) 'Pirahã exceptionality: a reassessment', *Language* 85: 355–404.

(2009b) 'Evidence and argumentation: a reply to Everett (2009)', *Language* 85: 671–81.

Newmeyer, F. J. (2003) 'Grammar is grammar and usage is usage', *Language* 79: 682–707.

(2004) 'Against a parameter-setting approach to language variation', *Linguistic Variation Yearbook* 4: 181–234.

(2005a) 'A reply to the critiques of "grammar is grammar and usage is usage"', *Language* 81: 229–36.

(2005b) 'On split CPs, uninterpretable features and the "perfectness" of language', *Zentrum für allgemeine Sprachwissentshaft Papers in Linguistics* 35: 399–422.

(2006a) 'On Gahl and Garnsey on grammar and usage', *Language* 82: 399–404.

(2006b) 'Grammar and usage: a response to Gregory R. Guy', *Language* 82: 705–6.

(2006c) 'A rejoinder to "On the role of parameters in Universal Grammar: a reply to Newmeyer" by Ian Roberts and Anders Holmberg', ms. University of Washington.

(2007) 'Linguistic typology requires crosslinguistic formal categories', *Linguistic Typology* 11: 133–57.

Nomura, T. (2006) *ModalP and Subjunctive Present*, Hituzi Syobo, Tokyo.

Nordlinger, R. & Sadler, L. (2004) 'Tense beyond the verb: encoding clausal tense/aspect/ mood on nominal dependents', *Natural Language and Linguistic Theory* 22: 597–641.

Nunberg, G., Sag, I. A. & Wasow, T. (1994) 'Idioms', *Language* 70: 491–538.

Nunes, J. (1995) 'The Copy Theory of Movement and linearization of chains in the Minimalist Program', PhD diss, University of Maryland at College Park.

(1999) 'Linearization of chains and phonetic realisation of chain links', in Epstein & Hornstein (eds.), pp. 217–49.

(2001) 'Sideward movement', *Linguistic Inquiry* 32: 303–44.

(2004) *Linearization of Chains and Sideward Movement*, MIT Press, Cambridge, MA.

Nunes, J. & Uriagereka, J. (2000) 'Cyclicity and extraction domains', *Syntax* 3: 20–43.

Nye, R. (2013) 'How complement clauses distribute: Complementiser-*how* and the case against clause-type', PhD diss, University of Ghent.

Obenauer, H.-G. (1994) 'Aspects de la syntaxe A-barre: effets d'intervention et mouvement des quantifieurs', PhD diss. University of Paris VIII.

Ochi, M. (1999) 'Multiple spell-out and PF-adjacency', *Proceedings of the North East Linguistic Society* 29: 293–306.

(2004) '*How come* and other adjunct *wh*-phrases: a cross-linguistic perspective', *Language and Linguistics* 5: 29–57.

Omaki, A. & Nakao, C. (2010) 'Does English resumption really help to repair island violations?', *Snippets* 21: 11–12.

Ormazabal, J. (1995) 'The syntax of complementation', PhD diss. University of Connecticut.

Ortiz de Urbina, J. (1989) *Parameters in the Grammar of Basque*, Foris, Dordrecht.

Oshima, D.Y. (2006) 'On Factive Islands: pragmatic anomaly vs. pragmatic infelicity', in T. Washio, K. Satoh, H. Terada & A. Inokuchi (eds.), *New Frontiers in Artificial Intelligence: Joint JSAI 2006 Workshop Post-Proceedings*, Springer, Heidelberg, pp. 147–61.

Ott, D. (2011) 'A note on free relative clauses in the theory of phases', *Linguistic Inquiry* 42: 183–92.

Ouhalla, J. (1990) 'Sentential negation, relativized minimality and the aspectual status of auxiliaries', *The Linguistic Review* 7: 183–231.

Palmer, F. R. (1983) *Modality and the English Modals*, Longman, London.

(1986) *Mood and Modality*, Cambridge University Press.

(1990) *Modality and the English Modals*, Longman, London.

(2001) *Mood and Modality* (2nd edn), Cambridge University Press.

Peranteau, P. M., Levi, J. N. & Phares, G. C. (eds.) (1972) *The Chicago Which Hunt: Papers from the Relative Clause Festival*, Chicago Linguistic Society.

Pereltsvaig, A. (2006a) 'Passing by cardinals: in support of Head Movement in nominals', *Formal Approaches to Slavic Linguistics* 14: 277–92.

(2006b) 'Head movement in Hebrew nominals: A reply to Shlonsky', *Lingua* 116: 1–40.

Pérez-Leroux, A. T. (1995) 'Resumptives in the acquisition of relative clauses', *Language Acquisition* 4: 105–38.

Perlmutter, D. (1972) 'Evidence for shadow pronouns in French relativization', in Peranteau et al. (eds.), pp. 73–105.

Pesetsky, D. (1982a) 'Complementiser-trace phenomena and the Nominative Island Condition', *Linguistic Review* 1: 297–343.

(1982b) 'Paths and categories', PhD diss. MIT.

(1987) '*Wh*-in-situ: movement and unselective binding' in Reuland & ter Meulen (eds.), pp. 98–129.

(1989) 'Language-particular processes and the earliness principle', ms. MIT (http://web.mit.edu/linguistics/www/pesetsky.home.html).

(1995) *Zero Syntax: Experiencers and Cascades*, MIT Press, Cambridge, MA.

(1997) 'Optimality theory and syntax: movement and pronunciation', in D. Archangeli & D. T. Langendoen (eds.), *Optimality Theory: An Overview*, Blackwell, Oxford, pp. 134–70.

(1998) 'Some optimality principles of sentence pronunciation' in P. Barbosa, D. Fox, P. Hagstrom, M. McGinnis & D. Pesetsky (eds.), *Is the Best Good Enough?* MIT Press, Cambridge, MA, pp. 337–83.

(2000) *Phrasal Movement and Its Kin*, MIT Press, Cambridge, MA.

Pesetsky, D. & Torrego, E. (2001) 'T-to-C movement: causes and consequences', in Kenstowicz (ed.), pp. 355–426.

Phillips, C. (2003) 'Linear order and constituency', *Linguistic Inquiry* 34: 37–90.

Picallo, M. C. (1991) 'Nominals and nominalization in Catalan', *Probus* 3: 279–316.

Plag, I. (2003) *Word Formation in English*, Cambridge University Press.

Platzack, C. & Holmberg, A. (1989) 'The role of AGR and finiteness', *Working Papers in Scandinavian Syntax* 44: 101–17.

Polinksky, M. & Potsdam, E. (2006) 'Expanding the scope of control and raising', *Syntax* 9: 171–92.

Pollard, C. & Sag, I. A. (1994) *Head-Driven Phrase Structure Grammar*, CSLI Publications, Chicago.

Pollock, J.-Y. (1989) 'Verb movement, Universal Grammar, and the structure of IP', *Linguistic Inquiry* 20: 365–424.

Portner, P. & Zanuttini, R. (2000) 'The force of negation in Wh exclamatives and interrogatives', in L. R. Horn & Y. Kato (eds.), *Studies in Negation and Polarity: Syntactic and Semantic Perspectives*, Oxford University Press, pp. 201–39.

Postal, P. M. (1966) 'On so-called pronouns in English', in F. Dinneen (ed.), *Report on the Seventeenth Annual Round Table Meeting on Linguistics and Language Studies*, Georgetown University Press, Washington, DC, pp. 177–206.

(1993) 'Parasitic gaps and the across-the-board phenomenon', *Linguistic Inquiry* 24: 735–54.

(1994) 'Parasitic and pseudoparasitic gaps', *Linguistic Inquiry* 25: 63–117.

(2003) '(Virtually) conceptually necessary', *Journal of Linguistics* 39: 599–620.

Potsdam, E. (1997a) 'NegP and subjunctive', *Linguistic Inquiry* 28: 533–41.

(1997b) 'English verbal morphology and VP ellipsis', *Proceedings of the North East Linguistic Society* 27: 353–68.

(1998) *Syntactic Issues in the English Imperative*, Garland, New York.

Potts, C. (2002) 'The syntax and semantics of *as*-parentheticals', *Natural Language and Linguistic Theory* 20: 623–89.

Prince, E. (1990) 'Syntax and discourse: a look at resumptive pronouns', *Proceedings of the Berkeley Linguistics Society* 16: 482–97.

Progovac, L. (2004) 'Small utterances and small clauses: the syntax', ms. Wayne State University, Detroit, MI.

Pullum, G. K. (1976) 'The Duke of York gambit', *Journal of Linguistics* 12: 83–102.

(1982) 'Syncategorematicity and English infinitival *to*', *Glossa* 16: 181–215.

Pullum, G. K. & Scholz, B. C. (2002) 'Empirical assessment of stimulus poverty arguments', *The Linguistic Review* 19: 9–50.

Rackowski, A. & Richards, N. (2005) 'Phase edge and extraction: a Tagalog case study', *Linguistic Inquiry* 36: 565–99.

Radford, A. (1981) *Transformational Syntax*, Cambridge University Press.

(1982) 'The syntax of verbal wh-exclamatives in Italian', in N. Vincent & M. Harris (eds.), *Studies in the Romance Verb*, Croom Helm, London, pp. 185–204.

(1988) *Transformational Grammar: A First Course*, Cambridge University Press.

(1989a) 'The syntax of attributive adjectives in English and the problems of inheritance', written version of a paper entitled 'The syntax of attributive adjectives in English: abnegating Abney', presented at the Colloquium on Noun Phrase Structure, University of Manchester, 1989 (http://privatewww.essex.ac.uk/~radford/PapersPublications/adjectives.htm).

(1989b) 'The status of exclamative particles in French', in D. J. Arnold, M. Atkinson, J. Durand, C. Grover & L. Sadler (eds.), *Essays on Grammatical Theory and Universal Grammar*, Oxford University Press, pp. 223–84.

(1993) 'Head-hunting: on the trail of the nominal Janus', in G. Corbett, N. M. Fraser & S. McGlashan (eds.), *Heads in Grammatical Theory*, Cambridge University Press, pp. 73–111.

(1997a) *Syntactic Theory and the Structure of English*, Cambridge University Press.

(1997b) *Syntax: A Minimalist Introduction*, Cambridge University Press.

(1997c) 'Verso un'analisi delle frasi esclamative in italiano' (= 'Towards an analysis of clausal exclamatives in Italian'), in L. Renzi & M. Cortelazzo (eds.), *La Linguistica Italiana Fuori d'Italia*, Bulzoni, Società Linguistica Italiana, Rome, pp. 93–123.

(2004) *Minimalist Syntax: Exploring the Structure of English*, Cambridge University Press.

(2007) 'Split projections, percolation, syncretism and interrogative auxiliary inversion', *Research Reports in Linguistics* 53: 157–91.

(2009) *Analysing English Sentences*, Cambridge University Press.

(2015) 'How come?', ms. University of Essex.

Radford, A. & Iwasaki, E. (2015) 'On Swiping in English', *Natural Language and Linguistic Theory* 33: 703–44.

Radford, A., Atkinson M., Britain D., Clahsen H. & Spencer A. (2009) *Linguistics: An Introduction* (2nd edn), Cambridge University Press.

Radford, A., Felser, C. & Boxell, O. (2012) 'Preposition copying and pruning in present-day English', *English Language and Linguistics* 16: 403–26.

Ramat, P. (2014) 'Categories, features and values in the definition of a word class', *Italian Linguistic Studies* 52, 2.

Raposo, E. (1986) 'On the null object in European Portuguese', in O. Jaeggli & C. Silva-Corvalan (eds.), *Studies in Romance Linguistics*, Foris, Dordrecht, pp. 373–90.

Rawlins, K. (2008) '(Un)conditionals: an investigation in the syntax and semantics of conditional structures', PhD diss. UCSC.

Reinhart, T. (1998) '*Wh*-in-situ in the framework of the Minimalist Program', *Natural Language Semantics* 6: 29–56.

Reintges, C. H., LeSourd, P. & Chung, S. (2002) 'Movement, wh-agreement and apparent wh-in-situ', paper presented to Workshop on Wh-Movement, University of Leiden, December 2002.

   (2006) 'Movement, *wh*-agreement and apparent *wh*-in-situ', in Cheng & Corver (eds.), pp. 165–94.

Reuland, E. J. (2001) 'Primitives of binding', *Linguistic Inquiry* 32: 439–92.

Reuland, E. J. & Everaert, M. (2001) 'Deconstructing binding' in Baltin & Collins (eds.), pp. 634–70.

Reuland, E. J. and ter Meulen, A. G. B. (eds.) (1987) *The Representation of (In)definiteness*, MIT Press, Cambridge, MA.

Rezac, M. (2003) 'The fine structure of cyclic Agree', *Syntax* 6: 156–82.

Richards, N. (1997) 'What moves where when in which language?' PhD diss. MIT.

   (2001) *Movement in Language: Interactions and Architectures*, Oxford University Press.

Riemsdijk, H. van (1989) 'Movement and regeneration', in P. Benincà (ed.), *Dialectal Variation and the Theory of Grammar*, Foris, Dordrecht, pp. 105–36.

   (2006) 'Free relatives', in Everaert & van Riemsdijk (eds.), pp. 338–82.

Ritter, E. (1991) 'Two functional categories in noun phrases: evidence from Modern Hebrew', in S. Rothstein (ed.), *Perspectives on Phrase Structure: Heads and Licensing*, Academic Press, New York, pp. 37–62.

Rivero, M. L. (2004) 'Spanish quirky subjects, person restrictions, and the Person-Case Constraint', *Linguistic Inquiry* 35: 494–502.

Rizzi, L. (1982) *Issues in Italian Syntax*, Foris, Dordrecht.

   (1986) 'Null objects in Italian and the theory of *pro*', *Linguistic Inquiry* 17: 501–57.

   (1990) *Relativised Minimality*, MIT Press, Cambridge, MA.

   (1994) 'Early null subjects and root null subjects', in T. Hoekstra & B. Schwartz (eds.), *Language Acquisition Studies in Generative Grammar*, Benjamins, Amsterdam, pp. 151–76.

   (1996) 'Residual verb-second and the *wh*-criterion', in A. Belletti & L. Rizzi (eds.), *Parameters and Functional Heads*, Oxford University Press, pp. 63–90.

   (1997) 'The fine structure of the left periphery', in L. Haegeman (ed.), *Elements of Grammar*, Kluwer, Dordrecht, pp. 281–337.

   (2000) 'Remarks on early null subjects', in M.-A. Freidemann & L. Rizzi (eds.), *The Acquisition of Syntax*, Longman, London, pp. 269–92.

   (2001) 'On the position "Int(errogative)" in the left periphery of the clause', in G. Cinque & G. Salvi (eds.), *Current Issues in Italian Syntax*, Elsevier, Amsterdam, pp. 287–96.

   (2004) 'Locality and left periphery', in A. Belletti (ed.), *Structures and Beyond: The Cartography of Syntactic Structures*, vol. III, Oxford University Press, pp. 223–51.

   (2005) 'On some properties of subjects and topics', in L. Brugé, G. Giusti, N. Munaro, W. Schweikert & G. Turano (eds.), *Proceedings of the XXX Incontro di Grammatica Generativa*, Cafoscarina, Venezia, pp. 203–24.

   (2006) 'On the form of chains: Criterial positions and ECP effects', in Cheng & Corver (eds.), pp. 97–133.

   (2007) 'On some properties of criterial freezing', *CISCL Working Papers on Language and Cognition* 1: 145–58.

(2010) 'On some properties of criterial freezing', in E. P. Panagiotidis (ed.), *The Complementizer Phase: Subjects and Operators*, Oxford University Press, pp. 17–32.

(2012) 'Cartography, criteria and labelling', Blaise Pascal lectures, Ealing, Paris, 11–13 September.

(2013) 'Notes on cartography and further explanation', *Probus* 25: 197–226.

(2014) 'Some consequences of criterial freezing', in P. Svenonius (ed.), *Functional Structure from Top to Toe*, Oxford Univerity Press, pp. 19–45.

(2015) 'The cartography of syntactic structures: locality and freezing effects on movement', ms. University of Siena; to appear in A. Cardinaletti, G. Cinque & Y. Endo (eds.), *On Peripheries*, Hituzi Publishing, Tokyo.

Rizzi, L. & Shlonsky, U. (2007) 'Strategies of subject extraction', in Sauerland & Gärtner (eds.), pp. 115–60.

Roberts, I. (1985) 'Agreement parameters and the development of English modal auxiliaries', *Natural Language and Linguistic Theory*, 3: 21–58.

(1993) *Verbs and Diachronic Syntax*, Kluwer, Dordrecht.

(1994) 'Two types of head movement in Romance', in Lightfoot & Hornstein (eds.), pp. 207–42.

(1997) 'Restructuring, head movement and locality', *Linguistic Inquiry* 28: 423–60.

(1998) '*Have/Be* raising, move F and procrastinate', *Linguistic Inquiry* 29: 113–25.

(2001) 'Head movement', in Baltin & Collins (eds.), pp. 113–47.

(2011) 'Head movement and the Minimalist Program', in C. Boeckx (ed.), *Oxford Handbook of Minimalism*, Oxford University Press, pp. 195–219.

Roberts, I. & Holmberg, A. (2006) 'On the role of parameters in Universal Grammar: a reply to Newmeyer', ms. University of Cambridge.

Roberts, I. & Roussou, A. (2002) 'The Extended Projection Principle as a condition on the tense dependency', in. P Svenonius (ed.), *Subjects, Expletives and the EPP*, Oxford University Press, pp. 125–55.

Roeper, T. & Rohrbacher, B. (2000) 'True pro-drop in child English and the principle of economy of projection', in C. Hamann & S. Powers (eds.), *The Acquisition of Scrambling and Cliticisation*, Kluwer, Dordrecht, pp. 349–96.

Rohrbacher, B. (1999) *Morphology-Driven Syntax: A Theory of V-to-I Raising and Pro-Drop*, Benjamins, Amsterdam.

Rooryck, J. (1994) 'Generalized transformations and the *wh*-cycle: free relatives as bare *wh*-CPs', *Groninger Arbeiten zur germanistischen Linguistik* 37: 195–208.

Rosenbaum, P. S. (1965) 'The grammar of English predicate complement constructions', PhD diss. MIT.

(1967) *The Grammar of English Predicate Complement Constructions*, MIT Press, Cambridge, MA.

Rosengren, I. (2002) 'A syntactic device in the service of semantics', *Studia Linguistica* 56: 145–90.

Ross, J. R. (1967) 'Constraints on variables in syntax', PhD diss. MIT (published as Ross 1986).

(1969) 'Guess who', *Chicago Linguistic Society Papers* 5: 252–86.

(1970) 'On declarative sentences', in R. A. Jacobs & P. S. Rosenbaum (eds.), *Readings in English Transformational Grammar*, Ginn, Waltham, MA, pp. 222–72.

(1986) *Infinite Syntax!* Ablex Publishing Corporation, Norwood, NJ.

Rothstein, S. D. (1983) 'The syntactic form of predication', PhD diss. MIT.

Rouveret, A. (2002) 'How are resumptive pronouns linked to the periphery?', *Linguistic Variation Yearbook* 2: 123–84.

  (ed.) (2011) *Resumptive Pronouns at the Interfaces*, Benjamins, Amsterdam.

  (2012) 'VP ellipsis, phases and the syntax of morphology', *Natural Language and Linguistic Theory* 30: 897–963.

Rudin, C. (1988) 'On multiple questions and multiple *wh*-fronting', *Natural Language and Linguistic Theory* 6: 445–501.

Runner, J. (1998) *Noun Phrase Licensing and Interpretation*, Garland, New York.

Rupp, L. (2003) *The Syntax of Imperatives in English and Germanic: Word Order Variation in the Minimalist Framework*, Palgrave Macmillan, New York.

Rymer, R. (1993) *Genie: A Scientific Tragedy*, Harper Perennial, New York.

Sabel, J. (2002) 'A minimalist analysis of syntactic islands', *The Linguistic Review* 19: 271–315.

Saddy, D. (1991) 'Wh scope mechanisms in Bahasa Indonesia', *MIT Working Papers in Linguistics* 15: 183–218.

Sadiqi, Fatima (1986) 'The notion of COMP in Berber', ms. University of Fès.

Sadler, L. & Arnold, D. J. (1994) 'Prenominal adjectives and the phrasal/lexical distinction', *Journal of Linguistics* 30: 187–226.

Sadler, L. & Nordlinger, R. (2006) 'Case stacking in realizational morphology', *Linguistics* 44: 459–87.

Safir, K. (1983) 'On small clauses as constituents', *Linguistic Inquiry* 14: 730–5.

  (1984) 'Missing subjects in German', in I. Toman (ed.), *Studies in German Grammar*, Foris, Dordrecht, pp. 193–230.

  (1986) *Syntactic Chains*, Cambridge University Press.

  (1993) 'Perception, selection and structural economy', *Natural Language Semantics* 2: 47–70.

  (1999) 'Vehicle change and reconstruction in A-bar chains', *Linguistic Inquiry* 30: 587–620.

Sag, I. (1980) *Deletion and Logical Form*, Garland, New York.

  (1997) 'English relative clause constructions', *Journal of Linguistics* 33: 431–83.

Sag, I., Gazdar, G., Wasow, T. & Weisler, S. (1985) 'Co-ordination and how to distinguish categories', *Natural Language and Linguistic Theory* 3: 117–71.

Sampson, G. (2002) 'Exploring the richness of the stimulus', *The Linguistic Review* 19: 73–104.

  (2005) *The Language Instinct Debate*, Continuum International Publishing Group, London.

Sauerland, Uli (1998) 'The meaning of chains', PhD diss. MIT.

  (2000) 'Two structures for English restrictive relative clauses', in M. Saito, Y. Abe, H. Aoyagi, J. Arimoto, K. Murasugi, & T. Suzuki. (eds.), *Proceedings of the Nanzan GLOW*, Nanzan University, Nagoya, Japan, pp. 351–66.

  (2002) 'Unpronounced heads in relative clauses', in K. Schwabe & S. Winkler (eds.), *The Interfaces: Deriving and Interpreting Omitted Structures*, Benjamins, Amsterdam, pp. 205–26.

Sauerland, U. & Elbourne, P. (2002) 'Total reconstruction, PF movement and derivational order', *Linguistic Inquiry* 33: 283–319.

Sauerland, U. & Gärtner, H.-M. (eds.) (2007) *Interfaces + Recursion = Language?* Mouton de Gruyter, Berlin.

Sawada, H. (1995) *Studies in English and Japanese Auxiliaries: A Multi-Stratal Approach*, Hituzi Syobo, Tokyo.

Scholz, B. C. & Pullum, G. K. (2002) 'Searching for arguments to support linguistic nativism', *The Linguistic Review* 19: 185–223.

Schütze, C. (1996) *The Empirical Basis of Linguistics: Grammaticality Judgments and Linguistic Methodology*, University of Chicago Press.

(2001) 'On the nature of default case', *Syntax* 4: 205–38

(2004) 'Synchronic and diachronic microvariation in English *do*', *Lingua* 114: 495–516.

(2009) 'Web searches should supplement judgements, not supplant them', *Zeitschrift für Sprachwissenschaft* 28: 151–6.

Schütze, C. & Sprouse, J. (2012) 'Judgment data', ms. University of California, Los Angeles and University of California, Irvine.

Schwarz, B. (1999) 'On the syntax of *either . . . or*', *Natural Language and Linguistic Theory* 17: 339–70.

(2000) *Topics in Ellipsis*, GLSA, Amherst, MA.

Schwarzschild, R. (2006) 'The role of dimensions in the syntax of Noun Phrases', *Syntax* 9: 67–110.

Sells, P. (1984) *Syntax and Semantics of Resumptive Pronouns*, GLSA, Amherst, MA.

(1985) 'Pied-piping and the feature [WH]', ms. Stanford University, CA.

(1987) 'Binding resumptive pronouns', *Linguistics and Philosophy* 10: 261–98.

Seppänen, A. (1994) 'Subject gap phenomena in English and Swedish', in C. Hedlund & A. Holmberg (eds.), *Proceedings of the XIVth Conference of Linguistics and the VIIIth Conference of Nordic and General Linguistics*, Department of Linguistics, University of Göteborg, pp. 127–44.

Seppänen, A. & Kjellmer, G. (1994) 'The dog that's leg was run over: on the genitive of the relative pronoun', ms, English Department, University of Göteborg.

Seppänen, A. & Trotta, J. (2000) 'The *wh+that* pattern in present-day English', in J. M. Kirk (ed.), *Corpora Galore: Analyses and Techniques in Describing English*, Rodopi, Amsterdam, pp. 161–75.

Sharvit, Y. (1999) 'Resumptive pronouns in relative clauses', *Natural Language and Linguistic Theory* 17: 587–612.

Sheehan, M. (2013a) 'The resuscitation of CED', *Proceedings of the North East Linguistic Society* 40: 135–50.

(2013b) 'Some implications of a copy theory of labelling', *Syntax* 16: 362–96.

Shlonsky, U. (1991) 'Quantifiers as functional heads: A study of quantifier float in Hebrew', *Lingua* 84: 159–80.

(1992) 'Resumptive pronouns as a last resort', *Linguistic Inquiry* 23: 443–68.

(1994) 'Agreement in Comp', *The Linguistic Review* 11: 351–75.

(2014) 'Subject positions, subject extraction, EPP, and the Subject Criterion', in E. Aboh, M. T. Guasti & I. Roberts (eds.), *Locality*, Oxford University Press, pp. 58–85.

Shlonsky, U. & Soare, G. (2011) 'Where's "why"'? *Linguistic Inquiry* 42: 651–69.

Sigurðsson, H. Á. (2002) 'To be an oblique subject: Russian vs Icelandic', *Natural Language and Linguistic Theory* 20: 691–724.

Smith, N. (1998) 'Jackdaws, sex and language acquisition', *Glot International* 3, 7: 7.

(2004) *Chomsky: Ideas and Ideals* (2nd edn), Cambridge University Press.

Smith, N. & Allott, N. E. (forthcoming) *Chomsky: Ideas and Ideals* (3rd edn), Cambridge University Press.

Sobin, N. (1997) 'Agreement, default rules and grammatical viruses', *Linguistic Inquiry* 28: 318–43.

(2003) 'Negative inversion as non-movement', *Syntax* 6: 183–212.

Spencer, A. (2004) 'English (Indo-European: Germanic)', in G. Booij, C. Lehmann, J. Mugdan & S. Skopeteas (eds.), *Morphology: An International Handbook on Inflection and Word-Formation*, vol. II, Mouton de Gruyter, Berlin, pp. 1255–67.

Spinillo, M. G (2004) 'Reconceptualising the English determiner class', PhD diss. University College London.

Sportiche, D. (2008) 'Inward bound: splitting the wh-paradigm and French Relative *qui*' (ling.auf.net/lingbuzz/000623).

Sproat, R. & Shih, C. (1988) 'Prenominal adjectival ordering in English and Mandarin', *Proceedings of the North East Linguistic Society* 18: 465–89.

(1990) 'The cross-linguistic distribution of adjectival ordering restrictions', in C. Georgopoulos & R. Ishihara (eds.), *Interdisciplinary Approaches to Language: Essays in Honor of S-Y. Kuroda*, Kluwer, Dordrecht, pp. 565–93.

Sprouse, J. (2007) 'Rhetorical questions and wh-movement', *Linguistic Inquiry* 38: 572–80.

(2011) 'A test of the cognitive assumptions of magnitude estimation: commutativity does not hold for acceptability judgments', *Language* 87: 274–88.

Sprouse, J., Caponigro, I., Greco, C. & Cecchetto, C. (2013) 'Experimental syntax and the crosslinguistic variation of island effects in English and Italian', ms. Universities of California (Irvine and San Diego), and Milan-Bicocca.

Sprouse, J. & Almeida, D. (2011) 'Power in acceptability judgment experiments and the reliability of data in syntax', ms. University of California, Irvine and Michigan State University.

(2012a) 'Assessing the reliability of textbook data in syntax: *Adger's Core Syntax*', *Journal of Linguistics* 48: 609–52.

(2012b) 'The empirical status of data in syntax: a reply to Gibson and Fedorenko', *Language and Cognitive Processes*. iFirst: 1–7

Sprouse, J., Fukuda, S., Ono, H. & Kluender, R. (2011) 'Reverse island effects and the backward search for a licensor in multiple wh-questions', *Syntax* 14: 179–203.

Sprouse, J. Schütze, C. & Almeida, D. (2011) 'A comparison of informal and formal acceptability judgments using a random sample from *Linguistic Inquiry* 2001–2010', ms. University of California (Irvine and Los Angeles) and Michigan State University.

Starke, M. (2001) 'Move dissolves into Merge: a theory of locality', PhD diss. University of Geneva.

(2004) 'On the inexistence of specifiers and the nature of heads', in A. Belletti (ed.), *Structures and Beyond*, Oxford University Press, pp. 225–67.

Stepanov, A. (2001) 'Late adjunction and minimalist phrase structure', *Syntax* 4: 94–125.

(2007) 'The end of CED? Minimalism and extraction domains', *Linguistic Inquiry* 10: 80–126.

Sternefeld, W. (2001) 'Partial movement constructions, pied-piping and higher order choice functions', in C. Féry & W. Sternefeld (eds.), *Audiatur vox sapientiae: A festschrift for Arnim von Stechow*, Akademie Verlag, Berlin, pp. 473–86.

Stockwell, R., Schachter, P. & Partee, B. (1973) *The Major Syntactic Structures of English*, Holt Rinehart and Winston, New York.

Stowell, T. (1981) 'Origins of phrase structure', PhD diss. MIT.

(1982) 'The tense of infinitives', *Linguistic Inquiry* 13: 561–70.

(1983) 'Subjects across categories', *The Linguistic Review* 2: 285–312.

(1991) 'Small clause restructuring', in R. Freidin (ed.), *Principles and Parameters in Comparative Grammar*, MIT Press, Cambridge, MA, pp. 182–218.

Suñer, M. (1984) 'Controlled *pro*', in P. Baldi (ed.), *Papers from the XIIth Linguistic Symposium on Romance Languages*, University Park Press, Baltimore, pp. 254–73.

(1998) 'Resumptive restrictive relatives: a crosslinguistic perspective', *Language* 74: 335–64.

Surányi, B. (2006) 'Mechanisms of wh-saturation and interpretation in multiple wh-movement', in Cheng & Corver (eds.), pp. 288–318.

Tamburelli, M. (2006) 'Remarks on richness', *UCL Working Papers in Linguistics* 18: 1–17.

(2007) 'The role of lexical acquisition in simultaneous bilingualism', PhD diss. University College London.

Taraldsen, K. T. (1980) 'The theoretical interpretation of a class of marked extractions', in A. Belleti, L. Brandi & L. Rizzi (eds.), *The Third GLOW Conference*, Annali della Scuola Normale Superiore, Pisa, pp. 475–516.

(1990) 'D-projections and N-projections in Norwegian', in M. Nespor & J. Mascarò (eds.), *Grammar in Progress*, Foris, Dordrecht, pp. 419–31.

Thomas, M. (2002) 'Development of the concept of "the poverty of stimulus"', *The Linguistic Review* 19: 51–71.

Thornton, R. (1995) 'Referentiality and *wh*-movement in Child English: juvenile D-Linkuency', *Language Acquisition* 4: 139–75.

Thrasher, R. (1977) *One Way to Say More by Saying Less: A Study of So-Called Subjectless Sentences*. Kwansei Gakuin University Monograph Series, vol. 11, Eihosha Ltd, Tokyo.

Ticio, M. E. (2003) 'On the structure of DPs', PhD diss. University of Connecticut.

(2005) 'Locality and anti-locality in Spanish DPs', *Syntax* 8: 229–86.

Tieken-Boon van Ostade, I. (1988) 'The origins and development of periphrastic auxiliary *do*: a case of destigmatisation', *Dutch Working Papers in English Language and Linguistics* 3: 1–30.

Toda, T. (2007) '*So*-inversion revisited', *Linguistic Inquiry* 38: 188–95.

Torrego, E. (1984) 'On inversion in Spanish and some of its effects', *Linguistic Inquiry* 15: 103–29.

Toyoshima, T. (2000) 'Heading for their own places', *MIT Working Papers in Linguistics* 36: 93–108.

Traugott, E. C. (1972) *A History of English Syntax: A Transformational Approach to the History of English Sentence Structure*, Holt, Rinehart and Winston, New York.

Travis, L. (1984) 'Parameters and effects of word order variation', PhD diss. MIT.

Truswell, R. (2007) 'Extraction from adjuncts and the structure of events', *Lingua* 117: 1355–77.

(2009) 'Preposition stranding, passivisation, and extraction from adjuncts in Germanic', *Linguistic Variation Yearbook* 8: 131–77.

(2011) *Events, Phrases, and Questions*, Oxford University Press.

Uriagereka, J. (1988) 'On government', PhD diss. University of Connecticut.

(1999) 'Multiple spell-out', in Epstein & Hornstein (eds.), pp. 251–82.

(2000) 'On the emptiness of "design" polemics', *Natural Language and Linguistic Theory* 18: 863–71.

Vainikka, A. & Levy, Y. (1999) 'Empty subjects in Finnish and Hebrew', *Natural Language and Linguistic Theory* 17: 613–71.

Valian, V. (1991) 'Syntactic subjects in the early speech of American and Italian children', *Cognition* 40: 21–81.

Valois, D. (1991a) 'The Internal syntax of DP and adjectival placement in French and English', *Proceedings of the North East Linguistic Society* 21: 367–82.

(1991b) 'The internal syntax of DP', PhD diss. UCLA.

(1996) 'On the structure of the French DP', *Canadian Journal of Linguistics* 41: 349–75.

(2011) 'Adjective order within DP', ms. University of Montreal.

van. Names like *van Gelderen* are listed under the name following *van* (e.g. Gelderen)

Varlokosta, S. & Armon-Lotem, S. (1998) 'Resumptives and wh-movement in the acquisition of relative clauses in modern Greek and Hebrew', *Proceedings of the Boston University Conference on Language Development* 22: 737–46.

Vikner, S. (1995) *Verb Movement and Expletive Subjects in Germanic Languages*, Oxford University Press.

Villalba, X. (2001) 'The right edge of exclamative sentences in Catalan', *Catalan Working Papers in Linguistics* 9: 119–35.

Visser, F. T. (1966) *A Historical Syntax of the English Language*, Part II, Brill, Leiden.

Vogel, R. (2001) 'Case conflict in German free-relative constructions: an optimality-theoretic treatment', in G. Müller & W. Sternefeld (eds.), *Competition in Syntax*, Mouton de Gruyter, Berlin, pp. 341–75.

Watanabe, A. (1993a) 'Agr-based case theory and its interaction with the A-bar system', PhD diss. MIT.

(1993b) 'Larsonian CP recursion, factive complements and selection', *Proceedings of the North East Linguistic Society* 23: 523–37.

(2001) '*Wh*-in-situ languages', in Baltin & Collins (eds.), pp. 203–25.

(2004) 'The genesis of negative concord: syntax and morphology of negative doubling', *Linguistic Inquiry* 35: 559–612.

(2006) 'The pied-piper feature', in Cheng & Corver (eds.), pp. 47–70.

Webelhuth, G. (1992) *Principles and Parameters of Syntactic Saturation*, Oxford University Press.

Weir, A. (2008) 'Subject pronoun drop in informal English', MA thesis, University of Edinburgh.

(2012) 'Left-edge deletion in English and subject omission in diaries', *English Language and Linguistics* 16: 105–29.

Weisler, S. (1980) 'The syntax of *that*-less relatives', *Linguistic Inquiry* 11: 624–31.

Weiß, H. (2005) 'Inflected complementizers in continental West Germanic dialects', *Zeitschrift für Dialektologie und Linguistik* 72: 148–66.

Weskott, T. & Fanselow, G. (2011) 'On the informativity of different measures of linguistic acceptability', *Language* 87: 249–73.

Wexler, K. (1994) 'Optional infinitives, head movement and the economy of derivations', in Lightfoot & Hornstein (eds.), pp. 305–50.

(1998) 'Very early parameter-setting and the unique checking constraint: a new explanation of the optional infinitive stage', *Lingua* 106: 23–79.

Wexler, K. & Culicover, P. W. (1980) *Formal Principles of Language Acquisition*, MIT Press, Cambridge, MA.

Williams, E. (1981) 'On the notions "lexically related" and "head of a word"', *Linguistic Inquiry* 12: 245–74.

(1982) 'Another argument that passive is transformational' *Linguistic Inquiry* 13: 160–3.

(1983) 'Against small clauses', *Linguistic Inquiry* 14: 287–308.

(2006) 'The subject-predicate theory of *there*', *Linguistic Inquiry* 36: 648–51.

Wiltschko, M. (1998) 'On the syntax and semantics of (relative) pronouns and determiners', *Journal of Comparative Germanic Linguistics* 2: 143–81.

(2001) 'The syntax of pronouns: evidence from Halkomelem Salish', *Natural Language and Linguistic Theory* 20: 157–95.

Wolfram, W. (1971) 'Black–white speech differences revisited', in W. Wolfram & N. H. Clark (eds.), *Black–White Speech Relationships*, Center for Applied Linguistics, Washington, DC, pp. 139–60.

Wurmbrandt, S. (2003) *Infinitives: Restructuring and Clause Structure*, Mouton de Gruyter, Berlin.

Xu, L. (2003) 'Choice between the overt and the covert', *Transactions of the Philological Society* 101: 81–107.

Yang, C. D. (1999) 'Unordered merge and its linearization', *Syntax* 1: 38–64.

Yang, H. (2006) 'On overt and covert wh- and relative movement in Hindi and Punjabi', in Cheng & Corver (eds.), pp. 135–64.

Zamparelli, R. (2000) *Layers in the Determiner Phrase*, Garland, New York.

Zanuttini, R. (1991) 'Syntactic properties of sentential negation: a comparative study of Romance languages', PhD diss. University of Pennsylvania.

Zanuttini, R. & Portner, P. (2000) 'The characterization of exclamative clauses in Paduan', *Language* 76: 123–32.

(2003) 'Exclamative clauses: at the syntax–semantics interface', *Language* 79: 39–81.

Zlatić, L. (1997) 'The structure of the Serbian noun phrase', PhD diss. University of Texas, Austin.

Zoerner, E. C. (1995) 'Co-ordination: the syntax of &P', PhD diss. University of California, Irvine.

Zribi-Hertz, A. (1997) 'On the dual nature of the "possessive" marker in Modern English', *Journal of Linguistics* 33: 511–37.

Zubizaretta, M.-L. (2001) 'The constraint on preverbal subjects in Romance interrogatives', in A. Hulk and J.-Y. Pollock (eds.), *Subject Inversion in Romance and the Theory of Universal Grammar*, Oxford University Press, pp. 183–204.

Zwart, C. J.-W. (1993) 'Dutch syntax: a minimalist approach', PhD diss. University of Groningen.

(1997) *Morphosyntax of verb movement*, Kluwer, Dordrecht.

(2006) 'Complementizer agreement and dependency marking typology', *Leiden Working Papers in Linguistics* 3: 53–72.

(2001) 'Syntactic and phonological verb movement', *Syntax* 4: 34–62.

Zwicky, A. (2002) 'I wonder what kind of construction that this kind of example illustrates', in D. Beaver, L. D. Casillas Martínez, B. Z. Clark & S. Kaufmann (eds.), *The Construction of Meaning*, CSLI Publications, Stanford, CA, pp. 219–48.

Zwicky, A. & Pullum, G. K. (1983) 'Cliticization vs. inflection: English *n't*', *Language* 59: 502–13.

Zwicky, A. M. & Zwicky, A. D. (1971) 'How come and what for', *Ohio State University Working Papers in Linguistics* 8: 173–85.

Index